Brothers ★ Rivals ★ Victors

ALSO BY JONATHAN W. JORDAN

*Lone Star Navy: Texas, the Fight for the Gulf of Mexico,
and the Shaping of the American West*

AS EDITOR

*To the People of Texas: An Appeal in Vindication of His Conduct of
the Navy* by Commodore Edwin Ward Moore

Brothers ★ Rivals ★ Victors

EISENHOWER, PATTON, BRADLEY, AND THE PARTNERSHIP THAT DROVE THE ALLIED CONQUEST IN EUROPE

★

Jonathan W. Jordan

NAL
CALIBER

NAL CALIBER
Published by New American Library, a division of
Penguin Group (USA) Inc., 375 Hudson Street,
New York, New York 10014, USA
Penguin Group (Canada), 90 Eglinton Avenue East, Suite 700, Toronto,
Ontario M4P 2Y3, Canada (a division of Pearson Penguin Canada Inc.)
Penguin Books Ltd., 80 Strand, London WC2R 0RL, England
Penguin Ireland, 25 St. Stephen's Green, Dublin 2,
Ireland (a division of Penguin Books Ltd.)
Penguin Group (Australia), 250 Camberwell Road, Camberwell, Victoria 3124,
Australia (a division of Pearson Australia Group Pty. Ltd.)
Penguin Books India Pvt. Ltd., 11 Community Centre, Panchsheel Park,
New Delhi – 110 017, India
Penguin Group (NZ), 67 Apollo Drive, Rosedale, North Shore 0632,
New Zealand (a division of Pearson New Zealand Ltd.)
Penguin Books (South Africa) (Pty.) Ltd., 24 Sturdee Avenue,
Rosebank, Johannesburg 2196, South Africa

Penguin Books Ltd., Registered Offices: 80 Strand, London WC2R 0RL, England

First published by NAL Caliber, an imprint of New American Library, a division of Penguin Group (USA) Inc.

First Printing, April 2011
10 9 8 7 6 5 4 3 2 1

Copyright © Jonathan W. Jordan, 2011
Maps by Chris Erichsen
Photo credits and permissions appear on pages 637–38.
All rights reserved

NAL CALIBER and the "C" logo are trademarks of Penguin Group (USA) Inc.

LIBRARY OF CONGRESS CATALOGING-IN-PUBLICATION DATA:

Jordan, Jonathan W., 1967–
    Brothers, rivals, victors: Eisenhower, Patton, Bradley, and the partnership that drove the Allied conquest in Europe/Jonathan W. Jordan.
        p. cm.
    ISBN 978-0-451-23212-0
    1. World War, 1939–1945—Campaigns—Europe.   2. United States Army—History—World War,
1939–1945.   3. Eisenhower, Dwight D. (Dwight David), 1890–1969.   4. Patton, George S. (George Smith),
1885–1945.   5. Bradley, Omar Nelson, 1893–1981.   6. Generals—United States—Biography.   I. Title.
    D756.J67 2011
    940.54'12730922—dc22   2010034841

Set in Adobe Garamond
Designed by Ginger Legato

Printed in the United States of America

To Austin, Emily, and Rachel

INTRODUCTION

THIS IS THE STORY OF THREE MEN sent to tear down an empire.

It is a story of war and politics told through the eyes of three extraordinary soldiers, eyes tinted with biases, strengths, foibles, and wisdom collected over a half century of American life. It is a story of a rich man from southern California, a poor man from the Missouri backwoods, and a middle-class man from middle-class Kansas. It is the tale of three conflicting personalities that blended together to form one of the greatest command teams ever fielded, and it is the story of a decades-old friendship that would be tragically scorched by the fires of war.

This account of the campaign to liberate Europe is drawn from the words, observations, and writings of Generals Eisenhower, Bradley, and Patton, as well as those of the many aides, staffers, superiors, secretaries, stenographers, celebrities, chauffeurs, and orderlies who walked with them through their great struggle. Because it is told through the prisms of three individuals—rather than the omniscient perspective of a twenty-first-century narrator perched atop a mountain of history books—this is in no way a complete story of that great conflict, nor is it an altogether objective one. The documented thoughts of Patton and Bradley are riddled with contradictions, as the esteem in which the trio of soldiers held one another ebbed and flowed with the conflicting tides of politics, war, and personality.

* * *

Popular images of the three protagonists—a scowling "Blood and Guts" Patton, the unassuming "GI's General," Omar Bradley, and the endearing, grinning photograph affixed to the slogan "I LIKE IKE"—are comfortably accurate in some ways. Yet they are astonishingly untrue in others. For example, Eisenhower's explosive profanity was, word for word, at times nearly a match for Patton's (though much less given to studied eloquence), while Bradley's legendary calm demeanor, his associates would find, clothed a thin, troubled skin. Patton's capacity for erudition and groveling before his superiors, meanwhile, was as pronounced as Bradley's penchant for backbiting and ruthlessness.

Patton was fond of saying, "Wars may be fought with weapons, but they are won by men." The Allied struggle against fascism bears out Patton's theorum. The Second World War's tumultuous events—TORCH and OVERLORD, Kasserine and the Bulge, Sicily and the Rhineland—are but reflections of the many warriors who planned and fought on those fields; warriors who brought to the battlefield their own talents, fears, flaws, and desires. The "secret" to the Allied victory was the patriotic and well-intentioned interplay of a cadre of talented, headstrong men who fought, deceived, schemed, bullied, and accommodated one another. It is thus the personal, sometimes dark story of three of the war's great battle captains, recounted in their trailers, offices, and private conversations, that this book lures into the sunlight.

Because the men depicted here were, by any honest measure, a mixture of the good and the bad America offered the world in the mid–twentieth century, readers looking for an unyielding march toward greatness, or the validation or destruction of cherished public icons, will find little consistent support among the words and deeds of the three generals. They could be brilliant and selfless, and they could be shortsighted and petty. What follows, for better and worse, is a story more ambiguous, yet more resonant to the modern soul vexed with genuine troubles, insecurities, strengths, and contradictions. It is a story of the ancient struggles between friendship and duty, between ambition and sacrifice. Of brotherhood, of rivalry, and, in the end, of victory.

ACKNOWLEDGMENTS

NEARLY EVERY PERSON INTIMATELY ASSOCIATED with Generals Eisenhower, Bradley, and Patton during the Second World War has passed away, and the wartime record of those three legendary men has effectively become a closed, if sometimes elusive, set. This narrative draws from thousands of pages of diaries, letters to family and friends, reports, cables, oral histories, memoirs, transcripts, maps, photographs, sound recordings, and film footage of players in this drama. Those sources could not have been accessed and blended without the generous help of many scholars, historians, and specialists. In researching this book, I have become deeply indebted to the generous staffs of the Eisenhower Library, the Library of Congress, the U.S. Army Heritage and Education Center, the George C. Marshall Foundation Library, the National Archives and Records Administration, the Patton Museum, the United States Military Academy Library, the Ohio University Library, the Cobb County Public Library, and Emory University's Woodruff Library. To those I express my heartfelt thanks. Additionally, to Brent Howard, Jerry Morelock, John S. D. Eisenhower, Kate Jordan, Dan Crosswell, Allegra Jordan, Hal Elrod, Jim Hornfischer, Sally Jordan, Cindy Pope-Koch, Thad Wilson, LTC Andrew Ring, John Tent, and dozens of bloggers and history forum participants, I must express my deep gratitude for their generous editorial, scholarly, logistical, and commonsense help.

"The only thing worse than fighting a war with allies
is fighting a war without them."

—Winston Churchill

CONTENTS

MAPS

Brothers ★ Rivals ★ Victors

PROLOGUE

DECEMBER 1944

AS THE INCISORS OF THE NAZI JAWS bit deep into the American front, a bleary-eyed Dwight Eisenhower stared at the tangle of red grease-pencil lines snaking across his smudged maps. He winced. The tall, bald general whom every man in uniform saluted was painfully aware of what those advancing red lines represented: regiments cracking, support units overrun, supplies captured, men cut down along a fifty-mile swath.

His men. Americans.

He had pored over situation maps and casualty reports for two days, and "Ike" Eisenhower saw in bright, vivid colors the truth he feared his lieutenants failed to grasp: that Hitler's latest surge through the Ardennes Forest was no feint, no spoiling attack, no prelude to something else, somewhere else. It was the real show, and damned if his generals were ready for it.[1]

The great German offensive, the one no one thought possible, rolled out the day Eisenhower received his fifth star. The violent surge now threatened the lives of some eighty thousand GIs who stood in the steamroller's path. American lines began to crumble, troops scurried west, and for the first moment in a very long time, the conclusion of the war seemed in doubt. And in the midst of this growing rout, one beleaguered general from Abilene, Kansas, felt the anxious gaze of four governments reaching all the way to his headquarters outside Paris.[2]

The vise that gripped Ike's stomach was nothing new. Over the past

★ 1 ★

two and a half years his smooth, genial face had tightened into a pale mask, a mask etched by fatigue, depression, and anxiety. The drifting cigarette smoke parted whenever he paced, which was often. His famous grin—that resilient, human feature that had charmed politicians, journalists, and generals across three continents—looked more like a stretched facade as each hour brought fresh tidings of disaster in the Ardennes.

As he studied his maps, Ike knew the problem lay, at least in part, with his field commanders. The men were fighting like wildcats, but his field generals were stunned, reeling, almost punch-drunk from the force of Hitler's armored thrust. If something were to be done, Ike thought, he would have to shake his lieutenants out of their stupor, regroup their forces, and get them moving east again. So on the night of December 18, he summoned his senior commanders to a conference at Twelfth Army Group headquarters at the French city of Verdun.[3]

The Supreme Commander left his headquarters on the morning of December 19, brown mud and gray slush spewing behind the tires of his armored Cadillac as he mulled the god-awful mess in which his army found itself. Preceded by jeeps crammed with stony-faced MPs, Eisenhower's entourage motored down the ancient road to Verdun, the main headquarters of his senior American army group commander. The convoy passed under the old stone arch that guarded the city's entrance and wound its way through Verdun's narrow streets. Soon the Caddy's wheels splashed to a muddy stop alongside an old stone barracks on the northeast edge of town.[4]

Ushered in by the commander's orderlies, Eisenhower climbed the creaking steps into a cold, dilapidated meeting room that was as colorless as his frozen cheeks. Inside the room, amid the worn wooden table, the maps, the chairs, the papers and briefcases, he surveyed his generals.

Waiting in this collision of boardroom and crypt was Lieutenant General Omar Nelson Bradley. The tall, dark-eyed Missourian wore a grimace atop his plain but neatly pressed uniform, a dense shell jacket buttoned against the elements as he waited quietly near the center of the room.

Three years younger than his West Point classmate, General Bradley stood stiffly, his tight jaw clenched, his round, steel-rimmed glasses clouding in the frosty air. His expression gave more the appearance of a senior cadet on inspection than the general who commanded the largest army ever fielded by his nation. This hadn't been a meeting Bradley had wanted to host; as commander of the pivotal Twelfth Army Group, it was his front being riddled by Hitler's panzers. "We had been caught flat-footed," he later admitted, and he was looking for a way out of the yawning disaster.[5]

Until recently, Bradley had been remarkably successful. He had methodically, often deftly, led the Americans from Normandy's beaches to the German frontier with few checks and no outright defeats. His armies were almost to the Rhine River, and his superiors—both the military species and the political, pie-in-the-sky type—had been bandying talk of winning the war by Christmas, or at the very least by the early weeks of 1945. Pressure was mounting on Bradley to punch his way into the Fatherland, but with Hitler's sword jabbing into his side, Bradley found himself groping for a way to parry the blow and resume his advance.

While Eisenhower and Bradley hovered near the room's sole source of heat—a lukewarm potbellied stove—the impromptu headquarters began filling with drab-looking gentlemen in trench coats and field jackets. In addition to Bradley and his staff, Ike had summoned his air marshal, his senior intelligence officer, the commander of the adjoining Sixth Army Group, the commander of British ground forces, and several subordinate commanders. Around this small galaxy swirled the usual supporting cast—anonymous aides, deputies, senior staffers, all shuffling across the planked floors at the beck of their masters, rifling paper, studies, and maps, quietly conferring with one another before the meeting began.

Shortly before eleven o'clock, into the hum of discussion strode the commander of Bradley's Third Army, Lieutenant General George S. Patton Jr., his tall brown cavalryman's boots thudding on the floor as he entered the room. He removed his trademark steel-pot helmet to reveal a shock of fine white hair and a leathery face sagging around prominent cheekbones as his breath escaped in small white puffs.

Patton's long stride and slight, cocky smile set him apart from the tired, cynical men who lined the table. He fished out a fat cigar from his coat pocket, elbows bent wide as he cupped smoke and match before his face. He puffed away, oblivious to the cold, his blue-gray eyes shooting across the room with the defiant confidence of a man who holds a simple, violent solution to a delicate problem that has perplexed delicate men.

With all players in attendance, Eisenhower stood up and took the floor. "The present situation," he began in his sharp Midwestern twang, "is to be regarded as one of opportunity for us and not of disaster. There will only be cheerful faces at this conference table."[6]

Nobody budged until a high, nasal voice broke the silence.

"Hell, let's have the guts to let the sons of bitches go all the way to Paris. Then we'll really cut 'em up and chew 'em up!"

It was vintage Patton. Muted laughter rumbled around the room. Forced, nervous laughter, but laughter nonetheless. It was a start, at least, for a meeting that was in bad need of a start.

"That's fine, George," Eisenhower answered, a bit testily, "but the enemy must never be allowed to cross the Meuse."

His basic point established, Ike turned to the question of how they would push back two huge panzer armies. The generals already had tentative proposals to plug the bleeding ulcer in the Allied line. Once the attackers were contained at the tip of the "bulge," they decided, three divisions from Patton's Third Army, plus another three on loan from Bradley, would hit the enemy hard from the south, smashing the Nazi columns in the flank and, God willing, their rear.

Supreme Allied Headquarters was full of smart planners, and they had come up with a smart plan. But for their smart plan to work, they needed someone to bring striking power—hard, deliberate, violent striking power—onto the battlefield. And they needed someone who believed the plan would work. So they had sent for Patton.

Turning to his old friend, Eisenhower announced his decision. "George, I want you to command this move—under Brad's supervision, of course—making a strong counterattack with at least six divisions. When can you start?"

"As soon as you're finished with me."

"When can you attack?"

"On December twenty-second, with three divisions."[7]

December 22. Three days.

A few deputies chuckled. Generals leaned back in their chairs, arms folded, eyes narrowed. Boots shuffled under the table. Bradley said nothing.

No army could do that, as everyone knew. Patton would have to pull thousands of soldiers out of a hostile line, turn every man ninety degrees, secure their flanks against attack, then find roads, transfer stockpiles, designate jump-off points, print new maps, and move thousands of frozen, grumbling GIs and their vehicles, guns, pots, pans, food, and telephone wires over a hundred miles of ice and slush. Patton's blunt promise, they knew, was more showboating from a man whose showboating had already alienated most of Eisenhower's better generals—not least of all Patton's former understudy, General Bradley.[8]

Ike snapped back in a tone Patton had heard many times before. "Don't be fatuous, George," he said. "If you try to go that early, you won't have all three divisions ready and you'll go piecemeal." Ike told Patton he wanted a one-day delay in the attack, to make sure his men were ready to launch a coordinated offensive.[9]

Patton said nothing. Through painful experience, he had learned to keep his mouth shut at times like this—times when that sharp, preemptive Eisenhower voice told him there would be no discussion.

But inside, Patton knew he was right. He had spent days studying the enemy's position along the northern frontier, and before leaving his headquarters at Nancy, he had instructed his staff to prepare three plans, one of which included an all-out drive through Luxembourg. One call to headquarters—one code word—would send three divisions and a cavalry regiment up the snow-choked roads and into the exposed German flank.[10]

Having set Patton on a proper timetable, Ike brightened visibly. For the rest of the conference, Patton's restless confidence slowly buoyed the American high command from its bog of pessimism. The room began to warm as the feisty old tanker leaned across Bradley's map, plucking the cigar from his mouth and jabbing it toward the vulnerable German bulge as he outlined his plan of attack.

"The Kraut's stuck his head in a meat grinder," he said with a wicked grin, twisting his fist in the air. "And this time I've got hold of the handle."[11]

After fleshing out the plan, the three old soldiers left the ancient barracks, not thinking at that moment about how their partnership, forged in war and peace, had carried them to the U.S. Army's finest hour. They didn't dwell on the old arguments, the plans, ambitions, and fears of Africa, Sicily, England, and France. They were fighting a desperate battle that they aimed to turn into an American victory. The rejuvenated five-star general and two of his oldest friends were about to climb into the engineer's cockpit and drive a huge, roaring freight train through the front door of the Third Reich.

But as they stepped toward the frosty December air, Eisenhower, a twinkle in his eye, turned to Patton and remarked, "Funny thing, George, every time I get a new star I get attacked."

The old cavalryman shot back a toothy smile.

"And every time you get attacked, Ike, I pull you out."[12]

ONE

A HANGOVER OF WAR

Ike, this war may happen just about twenty years from now. This is what we'll do. I'll be Jackson, you'll be Lee. I don't want to do the heavy thinking; you do that and I'll get loose among our #%&%$# enemies.

—George to Ike, 1920

THE BALDING LIEUTENANT COLONEL IN THE RUMPLED SHIRT saw little enough to smile about. As the oak leaves began to turn and the lazy autumn wind stirred, he shuffled along the dusty lanes and rambling wooden barracks that framed Camp Meade, Maryland, home to the once-mighty U.S. Tank Corps. A corps going through the slow, deliberate motions of peacetime army routine.

The year before, Camp Meade had been a beehive of activity: doughboys marching in columns, belching tanks churning up mud on the driving courses, staccato cracks from the rifle range, the din of a thousand conversations in the crowded chow halls. Even the warm, if all too elusive, presence of the "Hello Girls" working the Army's tangled telephone lines.

But now, he thought, the place looked empty. Forgotten. Just like his career.

Eighteen months earlier, an enthusiastic twenty-seven-year-old named Dwight David Eisenhower had been running a bustling enterprise christened Camp Colt, a Pennsylvania proving ground for American tankers training to fight the Kaiser in Europe. Back then, "Ike" Eisenhower had been fired up, desperate to get into combat before war's end. He had even offered to take a demotion to major if that would get him a ticket overseas.

But the Army wasn't interested. It liked Ike, like most everyone else did, but it wanted Ike training men, not leading them. The Army kept him stateside, and when the shooting stopped in France, Ike and his big Liberty

★ 7 ★

tanks sat on the shelf at Camp Meade, riding out the anticlimax of the War to End All Wars.

Sitting in his nondescript wooden office in the fall of 1919, Eisenhower could calculate with precision the day his fortunes sank: November 11, 1918. The day everything about the Army changed. Salutes went limp, informality crept into enlisted men's greetings, and everyone, it seemed, just wanted to get home. The men had done their duty, the war was over, and they were savoring thoughts of lives free of salutes, reveille, drill instructors, and pointless marches.

But not Eisenhower. He was a career officer in a sour time to be a career officer—a time when his biggest job was to send his men back to their homes.

"No human enterprise goes flat so instantly as an Army training camp when war ends," Ike dolefully remarked long after the last train of bright-faced draftees pulled away. "As for my professional career," he added, "the prospects were none too bright. I saw myself in the years ahead putting on weight in a meaningless chair-bound assignment, shuffling papers and filling out forms. If not depressed, I was mad, disappointed, and resented the fact that the war had passed me by."[1]

The only break in the monotony of that lackluster fall was the arrival of a hard-charging Californian named George Patton, a colonel who had been assigned command of a light tank outfit temporarily in Ike's care. Tall and spotless in his tailored jacket, riding breeches, and mirror-polished boots, Colonel Patton looked like he had stepped off the cover of an officer's field manual. He carried his six-foot, one-inch frame as if the world were one great parade square. He dressed with the precision of an honor guardsman, and his blue-gray eyes squinted over a practiced scowl as he barked out commands in a high-tenored, almost feminine voice.[2]

The two officers could hardly have been more different. George Smith Patton Jr. was an eclectic mix of socialite patrician and profane horse soldier, a field officer whose family wealth allowed him to maintain a lifestyle even a general's pay couldn't support. Ike, two inches shorter and five years Patton's junior, was an instinctively likable infantryman whose meager salary made it hard for his family to make ends meet. Patton, who had descended from Confederate and Revolutionary War heroes, believed that greatness could be bred, much like speed in racehorses or strength in bulls. Ike, whose Kansas and Pennsylvania forebears, as far as he knew, had never been more than modestly successful, could point to nothing in his lineage that would mark him for the history books.

Both men had quick, powerful tempers and cursed violently, but Eisenhower's rough edges were softened by an easygoing charm and an infectious grin—the wide, full smile toothpaste companies pay big money to put on advertisements—while the strutting, cursing Colonel Patton remained "onstage" to anyone outside his inner circle of friends. Even their marriage partners were a study in contrasts; Beatrice Ayer Patton, the fiery, athletic, cultured Boston heiress, grew up in a world of New England privilege that Ike's wife, the shrewd, plain Mamie Doud Eisenhower, could never understand or, for that matter, care much about.[3]

One personal connection they shared, a source of pride to both officers, was their alma mater. Patton had graduated from the United States Military Academy at West Point, New York, in 1909, and a lanky Cadet Eisenhower had come through those same hallowed halls a half dozen years later.

But after graduation, the two men's careers were night and day. Working his way onto the Army's fast track, Colonel Patton had chased Pancho Villa with Pershing, carried the Army's torch in the 1912 Stockholm Olympics, redesigned the cavalry's saber, established the Tank Corps, fought in France, and returned from Europe with a bullet wound, four battle stars, a Distinguished Service Cross, a Distinguished Service Medal, and the Croix de Guerre. Eisenhower, whose athletic career had been cut short by a knee injury, had little to show for his fifteen years in uniform beyond a fine record as a small-time football coach and a local reputation as a solid administrator. During the war, his service was all stateside and all humble, most of it near the Gettysburg battlefield where one of George's Confederate ancestors had been killed by a Union bullet. Instead of leading men into combat, Eisenhower had spent the Great War teaching others to fight under battle captains. Men like Colonel Patton.[4]

For all his accomplishments, George Patton arrived at Camp Meade in the midst of a blue funk. Beneath his woolen tunic and flint-hard skin, George struggled with a depression that had slugged him on his thirty-third birthday, November 11, 1918. The day the guns, to his dismay, fell silent.

Months of tactical training, and years of sharpening his mind and body—everything he had worked for—had come together in just two precious days of fighting. Then Colonel Patton's war ended, courtesy of a single, damnable Mauser bullet on the opening day of the Meuse-Argonne offensive. By the time Patton had recovered from Fate's kick in the ass (or, more precisely, a shot through his upper thigh, which emerged from his buttocks), the thing had ended. The Great War. The war everyone had been waiting for. The adventure George had pursued all his young life.

Amidst a peace that brought broad smiles to those around him, George Patton found himself adrift in a frustrating, empty existence where the things he held dear didn't seem to matter to anyone. War had expanded his horizons, shaped his spirit, shown him her power and majesty. But after a brief, delicious taste of smoke and fury, he was rudely dumped back into a petty world of small men. Men of peace. The men of Camp Meade, 1919.

Patton's youngest daughter later described the land into which this disciple of Mars had returned:

> [H]e was in considerable pain at the time; worried about the future in the tank corps of his creation; and having a hangover from the war, which is a very real thing. A man goes from the command of thousands of men where his judgement means victory or defeat, life or death, to the shrinking command of a handful of men, and the narrowing horizons of peacetime duty with not enough money and not enough troops, and the tender trap of home and family— and, it is a let-down. I guess things didn't come up to Georgie's expectations. . . .[5]

As flavorless as life had become for the two young officers, within weeks of their first meeting they managed to rekindle a fire in each other, a fire based on evolving military theory. What bound the two unlikely friends together, they discovered, was a veneration of the tank, the steel horse they conceived to be the saber's slicing edge on the modern battlefield. As Ike summed up their early relationship, "From the beginning [George] and I got along famously. . . . Both of us were students of current military doctrine. Part of our passion was our belief in tanks—a belief derided at the time by others."[6]

Army doctrine, based on the prevailing practice in Europe, held that a tank's job was to support the infantry by providing cover, smashing through barbed wire and directing close fire support. A tank need not go much faster than five miles per hour, since its function was tied to the foot soldier who crouched, ducked and stumbled through No-Man's-Land. The two young officers envisioned a new, independent role for tanks in which they would be free to drive deep into the enemy's rear areas.

It was only a theoretical pursuit, and the two men's fervor would remain academic until the next big war erupted—if it ever did. But in a peacetime army, the two tankers relished their role as the young, up-and-coming intellectuals. Unpersuaded by the Wilsonian crowd that war was a relic of man's unenlightened past, they spent their evenings on porches and around heating stoves debating how tanks might create breakthroughs in imaginary battles, spinning hypotheticals and arguing solutions late into the night.[7]

Their passion for the armored breakthrough—a confluence of imagination and optimism many of their superiors lacked—forged a friendship between George and Ike that would shape their lives in ways they couldn't begin to imagine in the fall of 1919. But the one thing they both saw clearly was the coming of another war, someday, somewhere. As Ike remembered it, "George was not only a believer, he was a flaming apostle. In idle conversations and in the studies we jointly undertook, he never said 'if' war might break out, it always was 'when.' As we worked, talked and studied together we became close friends."[8]

As they drew close, the two friends discovered other interests that stoked their kinship. Though Ike could never dream of joining Patton in polo, a wealthy man's sport (and one that required healthy knees), he and George, both hitting their early thirties, loved casual riding and shooting, and they craved any small-time adventure they could gin up in the pastoral Camp Meade setting.[9]

Sometimes their itch for a little excitement produced odd larks for two otherwise responsible officers. Learning that unarmed travelers on the road leading to camp were being preyed upon by highwaymen, the two officers climbed into Patton's touring car and drove up and down the darkened road at night, hoping to draw out banditos on whom they would turn the tables with a half dozen pistols.[10]

Another sunny afternoon found the two officers on the machine gun range, happily blazing away with a .30-caliber Browning to determine how long they could fire the weapon before its barrel overheated and its accuracy dropped off. Patton, delighted to be the trigger man, obligingly fired several long bursts while Ike, field glasses pressed to his squinting eyes, watched the bullets arc downrange.

After George ran through part of a long ammunition belt, Ike suggested they take a break and check their targets. But they had not stepped far downrange when they heard the old Browning behind them bark. Then again. And again. The steaming gun was cooking, sending bullets flying past them with insistent pops, each of which reheated the gun.

"George, that gun's so hot it's just going to keep on shooting!" Ike yelled as both men dashed for cover. Sprinting clear of the buzzing .30-caliber rounds, Ike and George scampered back to the gun like two lanky characters scurrying across a Norman Rockwell canvas. Patton grabbed the ammunition belt and gave it a hard twist, and the jammed weapon fell silent.

The two officers, looking sheepishly at each other, decided not to push their luck any more that day.[11]

Another time, the two self-appointed tank technicians conducted an experiment to learn whether a heavy Liberty tank could tow three light Renault tanks using steel cables. As the grunting Liberty strained forward, the cable stretched, twisted, and finally snapped, sending the frayed end slashing like a rapier just inches from both men's heads. Realizing that "we were certainly not more than five or six inches from sudden death," Ike later recalled, "We were too startled at the moment to realize what had happened, but then we looked at each other. I'm sure I was just as pale as George."

That night over dinner a reflective George compared their close encounter with the cable to his near-death experience in the Meuse-Argonne.

"Ike, were you as scared as I was?" he asked.

Ike nodded. "I was afraid to bring the subject up."[12]

The "bandit patrol," the cooked Browning, and the tank cable incidents, though quixotic, were honest parts of Ike and George as the 1920s opened. Ike had grown up a Kansas schoolyard scrapper, while George, in a more studied way, had sought out danger, especially where "civilized" weapons were employed. As the two men goaded each other into odd little adventures—mental and physical tests in a game of "us against the world"—each impressed the other as a man's man: tough, disciplined, ready to fight. In the bucolic days of the peacetime Army, these whimsical adventures provided a taste of the excitement George and Ike had missed during the war. They also tempered the iron in their friendship.

At Camp Meade, the Patton and Eisenhower families lived next door to each other in two abandoned barracks that the Army had permitted them to convert into officer quarters. It took a lot of work to turn an oversize wooden bunkhouse into something approaching a decent family home, but the Patton-Eisenhower barracks renovation project became another brick in their relationship. They hired off-duty enlisted men to knock out walls, rerouted plumbing, and sectioned off each building for three bedrooms, allowing the two families to accommodate the two Patton daughters, Ike's baby boy, and guests. They repainted walls, they hung curtains, and before long, the old, rambling shacks took on a comfortable, even inviting appearance. As a homey touch, Ike and Mamie planted flowers and vegetables outside their quarters; as Ike recalled, "I had put in too many years coaxing corn and tomatoes and green grass out of the Kansas soil ever to give it up." As their homes took shape, the two families grew close; Ike's two-year-old son, Doud Dwight, nicknamed "Icky," spent many hours at the Patton household playing with George's daughters, Bea and Ruth Ellen, who idolized the charming Mamie and doted on her little boy.[13]

As was the custom among Old Army officers, George and Ike kept active social lives. Patton's high standing within the War Department occasionally drew visitors from Washington and other parts, and George and Beatrice frequently entertained guests over lavish dinners at which Ike and Mamie were regular faces. Ike and George also played poker with their brother officers. Ike, a cardsharp, usually took the lion's share of the pot at George's expense, but George never complained. Patton could afford to lose, and as a gambler, he never tried very hard when the stakes were merely money. He was hoarding his luck for bigger stakes.[14]

While Ike and George were becoming fast friends, their robust personalities occasionally threw off sparks. Ike remembered that the two had "heated, sometimes almost screaming, arguments over matters that more often than not were doctrinal and academic rather than personal or material." One rocking-chair topic on which they would never agree, for instance, was the unanswerable question of the most vital condition to military victory. George, a romantic at heart, argued vehemently that battlefield leadership trumped all other factors. His heroes—Hannibal, Caesar, Napoleon, Stonewall Jackson—had triumphed over incredible odds through audacity, boldness, and conspicuous leadership, the kind of showmanship that puts fire into the ranks and keeps rational men advancing into steel and fire. From his childhood study of history to his battlefield experience in France, everything Patton knew *insisted* that leadership wins battles. And battles decide wars.[15]

Ike, a Midwesterner who hailed from a land of interdependent farming and mercantile communities, felt that personal leadership was just one of several ingredients that influence a battle's outcome. While personal leadership was important, he thought George too willing to denigrate the mundane—logistics and alliances, for instance—in favor of the warrior-king's more picturesque role of plunging into battle, broadsword swinging. Men-at-arms had to be organized, fed, and supplied with effective weapons to be useful on the battlefield, he argued. Ike agreed with Voltaire that God is on the side of bigger battalions, but he believed a general at the head of a starving mob would lose his war, no matter how inspiring his personal deportment might be. This philosophy was an integral part of Ike Eisenhower, the product of his upbringing in turn-of-the-century Kansas as much as his formal studies.

In late 1920, the Patton-Eisenhower collaboration reached its peak as each wrote scholarly articles predicting that tanks would play an independent role in future conflicts. In May 1920, Colonel Patton published an article in the highly respected *Infantry Journal* entitled "Tanks in Future Wars," in which he debunked the Army's prevailing doctrine that the sole place of the tank was to support the infantry. "The tank corps grafted onto infantry, cavalry, artillery, or engineers will be like a third leg to a duck," he wrote, "worthless for control, for combat impotent."

Later that year Ike, also writing for the *Infantry Journal*, proposed that American tanks be fitted with heavier guns. He predicted that in future wars, tanks would use their mobility and firepower to crush the enemy from the flanks. As Ike would recall late in life, their theories were "the beginnings of a comprehensive tank doctrine that in George Patton's case would make him a legend. Naturally, as enthusiasts, we tried to win converts. This wasn't easy but George and I had the enthusiasm of zealots."[16]

In arguing for the supremacy of armor over infantry, Eisenhower and Patton were not indulging in mere refinement. Their ideas, if put into practice, would take the tank out of its supporting role and place it on center stage in the next war, giving the snorting, ornery beasts the shock role once held by the armored knights of the Middle Ages. They were advocating revolution, pure and simple, and they were proselytizing in the infantry, the most conservative branch of the nation's most conservative institution.

This sort of talk was anathema to the infantry overlord, Major General Charles Farnsworth, who could not believe any responsible officer would willingly advocate an armored force as something other than fire support for the foot soldier. Farnsworth abruptly summoned Eisenhower to Washington, and in a short but icy interview, the Chief of Infantry threatened to break Ike's career if he wrote any further on the subject.[17]

A chastened Ike conceded the point—outwardly, at least. He recanted his heresy and penned an unpublished essay that concluded, "tanks can never take over the mission of the infantry, no matter to what degree developed." But inside, this military Galileo was still a believer. Whatever hidebound old generals like Farnsworth might say, Ike *knew* tanks would change the way nations fought wars.[18]

Patton, for his part, never lacked for shrill enthusiasm, but in the rigid confines of a shrinking army, shrill enthusiasm didn't count for much, and at this stage in his life, he knew enough to stop bucking the system. He and Ike might hack with all their might at the roots and branches of the "infantry first" doctrine, but in the end the tree stood: tall, solid, and unbent.[19]

The injunction from Washington's khaki cardinals was a blow to the Patton-Eisenhower crusade, but as with most persecutions, the disciples simply circled their wagons and stuck quietly to their beliefs. They cursed and joked about brain atrophy among the top brass, and they filled their days riding, studying, and debating wars of the future, without openly trying to convert the unsaved.[20]

Months of debate, practice, drill, and theory—as well as poker, persecution, and the occasional odd adventure—cemented a friendship that would last nearly a lifetime. Life was stimulating and enjoyable, and the two talented officers had many a good year ahead of them in the Tank Corps, so they thought. But in 1920 the War Department folded the Tank Corps into the infantry branch under a law reorganizing the peacetime Army. George's heart led him back to the cavalry, his first love, while Ike, an infantryman by training, remained with the tanks. Separated into different branches, the two friends, both reduced to their permanent ranks, would see little of each other over the next two decades. But, as is common in Army life, they kept the fire of their friendship stoked with infrequent but heartfelt correspondence.[21]

By the time George and Ike parted ways in October of 1920, each man had developed a vague understanding of his place in the next big war, which they saw as the inevitable result of the Treaty of Versailles. George, the senior man, did not want to run the whole show; that involved too much staff work, too much paperwork, not enough battlefield leadership. No, he would let Ike handle the planning. In the next war, Patton would lead flesh-and-blood men to victory on horseback—or, perhaps, in a tank. As Ike recalled:

In all his speculative ramblings George always saw himself as commander of highly mobile troops. Initially he likened himself to

Ashby, the brilliant cavalry leader under Stonewall Jackson. But he soon raised his sights. "Ike," he'd say, "This war may happen just about twenty years from now. This is what we'll do. I'll be Jackson, you'll be Lee. I don't want to do the heavy thinking; you do that and I'll get loose among our #%&%$# enemies." This thought was repeated time and time again.[22]

George's brash words may have been the bemused ramblings of two buddies drinking beer on the front porch. But a small yet supremely convinced voice told George and Ike they would do something together, something big. As Ike summed up those heady days, "In our outlook on the future we were always partners; in those days it never occurred to either that we might, in war, become separated from each other."[23]

Separation, and her ugly handmaiden, disappointment, were facts of Army life. Major Bradley had learned that lesson the hard way.

The dark-eyed Missourian had left West Point in July 1915 with the accoutrements of a newly minted officer: a .45 Colt pistol, a broad-brimmed campaign hat, a marginally useful sword, and a pair of six-power field glasses. For the succeeding two years, Omar Nelson Bradley had criss-crossed the country from New York to Washington State, leading one company of infantrymen after another, never firing a shot in anger.[24]

The major with the taut grimace and lean athletic frame should have been commanding a battalion in Europe. There certainly was enough fighting to go around, and he had enough training and field experience under his belt to rightfully expect a combat command. But things never seemed to work out for Omar. War with Mexico came and went, and "Brad" was stranded on the sidelines. War in Europe spilled across the Atlantic, and the Army, in its unbounded wisdom, shunted Brad off to the 14th Infantry Regiment, a luckless outfit scattered across dull garrison posts from Alaska to Montana.[25]

The 14th was a dead-end assignment, and Brad's efforts to transfer to a fighting command came to nothing. The only battlefield he would see during the World War was near the Anaconda copper mines of central Montana, where the enemy consisted of strikers and labor agitators instead of spike-helmeted Germans. On St. Patrick's Day, 1918, union men of the Industrial Workers of the World attempted a riot in nearby Butte. Hundreds of roughnecks armed with brass knuckles and knives marched down Main Street, and Brad ordered his ninety-one-man company out, bayonets fixed, ready to cut down anyone foolish enough to charge their lines. The look of determination on Bradley's doughboys cooled the passions of the strikers, and the IWW left the town alone.[26]

That was it. Four American divisions were fighting German storm troopers in France, and Brad was playing small-town sheriff in Montana. He might as well have remained in the poverty-stricken backwoods of southern Missouri he had left as a teenager.

It was an anxious time for the square-jawed left fielder, for like Ike Eisenhower, his old Academy classmate, the thing Brad feared most was to be left behind. The Great War was fast becoming what he feared most. To add to his misery, the childhood sweetheart who became his bride, Mary Quayle Bradley, delivered their first child, a son, on the day he faced the rioting miners. Stillborn. The loss of what would be his only son was a bitter blow to a man whose family had seen hard times. This particular wound would sting for the rest of Brad's days.[27]

The melancholy major endured six more dreary months of administrative duty before the first serious rumor of action reached his company, and in late 1918 the 14th Regiment was ordered to assemble at Camp Dodge, near Des Moines, Iowa. The order was just the news Brad longed to hear— splendid news, for it portended a quick trip to Europe. It meant fighting in France, leading men into battle. Finally, Brad thought, after years of drilling dull-witted enlisted men, processing Army paperwork, and maintaining order in one godforsaken outpost after the next, Bradley's stoicism would be rewarded, and perhaps soon.[28]

But the world changed again as Brad and Mary strolled down the streets of Des Moines one afternoon. Whistles began to blow. Church bells rang. A seismic wave rolled over the city. Streets began filling with people smiling, waving, spreading the good news.

Armistice! The Kaiser had abdicated. The war was over![29]

The war was over.

The phrase had an oddly hollow ring to a fighting man left at home. To a crack shot with a rifle who never got to pull a trigger in battle.

Over.

While Brad could never admit that he wished the war had lasted six months longer—he was, like everyone else, relieved to see the casualty lists come to an end—he was miserable about missing his big chance at success. "I was glad the war had stopped," he wrote later, "but I was now absolutely convinced that, having missed the war, I was professionally ruined. I could only look forward to a career lifetime of dull routine assignments and would be lucky to retire after thirty years as a lieutenant colonel."[30]

Facing down club-wielding strikers and busting drunken enlisted men wasn't much to call a wartime experience, and Brad had the bittersweet pleasure of welcoming home classmates returning from France with medals, high rank, and riveting tales of fighting under the legendary "Black Jack" Pershing.

He could not hope to compete with peers who had seen the face of battle, friends whose places in the Army's grand history were secure. Apart from a meager salary and a temporary major's rank that would probably tumble to lieutenant once Congress demobilized the Army, the country boy from Moberly, Missouri, had nothing to show for the last five years of his life. Staring at an empty horizon, Brad shelved his hopes for adventure.

But even in peacetime, the Army still offered a regular paycheck—something his family never saw when he was a child—and Bradley had invested nine years of his life into a military career. So he considered trying his hand at military academics. Teaching was in his blood, after all—his father had been a rural schoolmaster—and in his late twenties, Brad was warming up to classroom instruction, the kind of pedagogy he and Cadet Eisenhower had blithely ignored when they roamed the yards of West Point, focusing on their athletic careers. Perhaps, Brad thought, he could make his mark as an instructor in infantry theory, or maybe even teach at his alma mater. Almost anything, he decided, was better than sweating out another hot summer in Arizona or Texas, marking a long, plodding march to retirement.

So as the 1920s opened to a nation grateful to be at peace, Omar Bradley readjusted his sights and scrounged around for new, less ambitious opportunities. With few attractive options and a young family to support, he was quietly determined to make the best of whatever the Army would give him.

Two decades later, Brad, Ike, and George would be running toward the same endless horizon, wondering how it would all end.

TWO

DIFFERENT PATHS

It slowly dawned on me that my failure to get to France had not ruined me professionally after all.

—Bradley

THE LONG SEASON THAT SPANNED between demobilization and the war's outbreak hardened George Patton. He dropped from his wartime rank of colonel down to his permanent rank, captain, and as he climbed the wobbly rungs of the peacetime army from 1920 to 1939, he whiled away the decades as a gentleman soldier—sailing, playing polo, socializing, writing, speaking, and pondering the shape of future wars. He did exceptionally well at the cavalry's Advanced Officer's School at Fort Riley, Kansas, and he graduated with honors from the Command and General Staff School at Fort Leavenworth.[1]

After Patton was transferred to overseas duty with the Hawaiian Division in 1925, he was appointed the division's G-3, or chief operations officer. There, his martinet instincts, never dormant for long, returned with a vengeance. In his official reports, he criticized junior officers like Major Henry "Hap" Arnold. He also committed harsh opinions of his superiors to writing—a questionable practice in any profession, and one doubly hazardous in a peacetime army. The ill wind Patton stirred blew back upon him, earning George what amounted to a demotion by his division commander for being "too outspoken."[2]

Too outspoken. It was a chronic problem that had plagued George since his West Point days. As a lowly second corporal during his second year, he had so enthusiastically bawled out plebes with his high-pitched voice that his antics earned him the nickname "Quill"—a disparaging term for an upperclassman who delights in reporting lower classmen for demerits. Smarting from the reaction, George complained to his father,

> *[I] am not very popular not because there is any thing the matter except that I am "Too damed military." That is I am better than they are. Now no one is more unjust than he who feels himself an inferior but dam them and let them keep on some day I will show and make them feel how infernally inferior they are.*[3]

But Patton's "too damed military" approach at West Point had backfired when he was ingloriously demoted to sixth corporal, and the reputation as a martinet dogged him through the years. He alienated his colleagues in Hawaii, and in 1928 his commanding officer summed up the emerging consensus on George Patton: "This man would be invaluable in time of war but is a disturbing element in time of peace."[4]

The only action Patton saw during the interwar years was as President Hoover's cavalry commander during the Bonus March, in the summer of 1932. The marchers, homeless Great War veterans and a smattering of left-wing agitators, had set up shantytowns in the nation's capital, where they demanded early payment of bonuses Congress had approved at the war's end. On July 28, as the demonstrators sweated out their sixth week in their sprawling camp, Secretary of War Patrick J. Hurley ordered his swaggering Army Chief of Staff, General Douglas MacArthur, to ensure the security of the capital. MacArthur summoned local troops to repel the "insurrection," and one of the first units to arrive was Patton's 3rd Cavalry Regiment from nearby Fort Myer. Brandishing drawn sabers and equipped with gas masks and carbines, the horsemen galloped off to clean out an offending "Hooverville" just across the Anacostia River.[5]

MacArthur's combined-arms attack easily drove off the unarmed demonstrators. But Patton's cavalry horses, so nimble on Fort Myer's parade grounds, found cantering difficult among Washington's littered sidewalks and stairwells. The jumbled horse soldiers drew catcalls, curses, and projectiles from bitter demonstrators. Although the regiment drove back the protestors, Patton's lone combat victory seems to have been roughing up a veteran who was badgering MacArthur.[6]

In riding to the rescue of the Hoover Administration, George saw himself as the republic's hussar in a modern-day reenactment of Napoleon's famed "whiff of grapeshot" foray against the Paris mob. George later denounced the Bonus March assault as "a most distasteful form of service," but he insisted, as did MacArthur, that the ranks of protestors were filled with disgruntled vagrants and Bolshevik agitators.[7]

As the thirties dragged on and middle age claimed him, George watched in desperation as his career stagnated. His stomach began to protrude over his jodhpurs, his thinning blond hair faded to white, and his ruddy skin began to sag under his high cheekbones. His profanity and patrician manner stirred up bad blood among his subordinates, and he had at least one public run-in with his division commander. As he shuffled from one dull peacetime post to the next, George sank into a debilitating mix of depression and erratic behavior, his melancholy dulled only momentarily by dinners, costume parties, polo matches, and society balls. He saw himself fading into irrelevance, a late-summer firefly whose nearly invisible existence was punctuated by sporadic glimmers of light—followed by long pauses in an impenetrable darkness.[8]

In 1935, George turned fifty, and he began showing advanced signs of a midlife crisis. While he had always consumed liquor in moderation—he admitted during his West Point years, "I can't 'hit the booze' in the way a future second Lieut of Cavalry should"—in his life's autumn he began drinking recklessly at social functions. His inebriation, a symptom rather than a cause, inflicted pain on his devoted wife, Beatrice, and their family. To hasten his downward spiral, he commenced an affair with Jean Gordon, a twenty-one-year-old friend of his daughter's and a half-niece by marriage. Not surprisingly, the tryst nearly undid his marriage, and it inflicted lasting pain upon Beatrice and his children.[9]

The dominant theme of George's tailspin was his abiding fear that his life would end before he had fulfilled his destiny—a destiny, he believed, to command legions in a great, climactic battle. He began to panic as he realized the greater part of his life had passed without the Ragnarok he craved. As George once recalled, one of his personal heroes, Britain's Sir Edmund Allenby, had remarked, "for every Napoleon, Alexander, and Jesus Christ that made roles of history, there were several born. Only the lucky ones made it to the summit." Allenby, George said, "felt that in every age and time, men were born ready to serve their country and their god, but sometimes were not needed; you had to be in the right place at the right time—you had to be lucky."[10]

George lived in dread of becoming one of those unlucky souls.

For Dwight Eisenhower, the long spell following the Great War was punctuated by deep, piercing pain. A few months after George left Camp Meade in October 1920, scarlet fever carried away Ike's firstborn, Icky. Ike sought shelter from the cloud of grief by immersing himself in work, and he struggled to shut out the picture of a smiling, laughing toddler who had brightened his world. His withdrawal into an office cocoon only strained his relationship with Mamie, and the long hours he spent wrestling with black, oppressive thoughts drove him to the edge of a nervous breakdown.[11]

The sting of Icky's death would never abate, could never be blunted, but an opportunity to leave Camp Meade masked some of Ike's heartache. Over dinner with the Pattons earlier in the year, George had introduced Ike to Brigadier General Fox Conner, an old friend of Patton's who was close to General Pershing.

Conner had graduated from West Point two decades ahead of Eisenhower, and the Mississippi native had emerged as one of the Army's leading thinkers. In a relaxed front-porch conversation with the two young officers, Conner asked George and Ike to tell him about their tank theories. For the rest of the day, the eager young officers showed Conner around their post, and the general was impressed with the efficiency of the tank brigades and the men who ran them. Ike and General Connor, taking an instant liking to each other, parted as friends.[12]

In early 1921, Ike received a call from General Conner, who asked him to come to the Panama Canal Zone as the executive officer of the 20th Infantry Brigade, an overseas field command of mostly Puerto Rican recruits. Ike was thrilled to hold a position of real responsibility among fighting men, and from the day he arrived at Camp Gaillard, he commenced a two-year apprenticeship that would change his life.[13]

Mosquitoes and tropical diseases presented the chief enemies, so the former Marine post in the middle of the Panamanian isthmus was hardly a taxing one. Ike and Conner spent their free hours together riding horses, sitting around campfires, and discussing strategy and tactics. Conner introduced Ike to Plato, Tacitus, Nietzsche, the memoirs of Grant and Sherman, and Clausewitz's philosophical *On War*, the dense nineteenth-century text that a youthful Patton had once described as "hard reading as any thing can well be and is as full of notes of equal abstruceness as a dog is of flees." Conner was a brilliant teacher, and he fired up in his pupil an intellectual spark that had been slow to emerge—the spark of a serious, enthusiastic interest in the profession of arms. The transformation was short and remarkable: Ike became less superficial, less parochial, and more focused on the military's relationship to society's economic, political, and industrial pursuits.[14]

Ike's newfound passion swept him out of a deep depression and changed the way he viewed his profession. Under Conner's tutelage, Ike began learning grand strategy, not just tactics. The big picture, not just maneuver. War, not just the sum of its battles. He soaked up Conner's teachings, and when the Army transferred him home, he left Panama convinced that America would one day integrate its armies into a larger allied command structure.[15]

It should have been predictable to the Army's battalions of psychologists that Ike Eisenhower would develop into a three-dimensional thinker more easily than most of his uniformed peers. Growing up a middle-class family of six boys in Abilene, Kansas, a classic small American town, Ike was comfortable jostling his way around loud, unruly crowds. On the streets, in backyard lots, and on the playing fields of his youth, Ike had learned the value of allies—allies like his older brothers, Arthur and Edgar—yet he cultivated the kind of self-reliance that enables a scrawny, tow-headed boy to stand up to a big brother or the neighborhood bully. Ike's Midwestern roots and his passion for social pursuits, such as poker, golf, and dinners, primed him for jobs that blended the personal with the technical, assignments where an animating human touch was needed to bring the machine to life. A soldier's duties where the political carries almost as much weight as the martial.[16]

From afar, Fox Conner helped Ike pick his way through the bureaucratic and political minefield that was the peacetime Army. In 1925 Eisenhower, a major again, was accepted into the Command and General Staff School. A delighted George Patton sent Ike a hundred pages of his notes covering all aspects of the course. Ike graduated first in his class; George, learning of his friend's class standing through the Army grapevine, wrote Ike, *"It shows that Leavenworth is a good school if a HE man can come out one."* George also graciously assured the young major that he would have done just as well without his extensive notes—though George probably believed his notes were Ike's ace in the hole for reaching the top of his class.[17]

If so, he would have been off the mark. Both men had mastered the field officer's technique, but while Patton often butted his head against the military establishment, Ike had learned to play the game. It was a strange role reversal for the West Point martinet and the West Point maverick, and it would one day pay dividends to Eisenhower and extract a price from Patton. As their mutual friend Brad Chynoweth once remarked, Patton dismissed the Army's "approved solutions" to tactical problems as implausible dogma, while to Ike, "[s]chool doctrine was his religion." Chynoweth added, "Ike had been 100 percent conformist, never deviated, and stood first in his class."[18]

During the early twenties Ike and George, stationed hundreds of miles apart, kept in touch from time to time by letter, and their personal correspondence reveals two diverging outlooks on military operations—part of their running debate over leadership and logistics. *We talk a hell of a lot about tactics and such and we never get to brass tacks,"* George wrote Ike in 1926. *"Namely what it is that makes the Poor S.O.B. who constitutes the casualtie lists fight and in what formation he is going to fight. The answer to the first is Leadership that to the second—I don't know."* Ike, George advised, should *"stop thinking about drafting orders and moving supplies and start thinking about 'some means of making the infantry move under fire,'"* because *"victory in the next war will depend on EXECUTION not PLANS."*[19]

That may have been true in Patton's world. But it would be *PLANS*, as well as their much-derided sisters, *LOGISTICS* and *STRATEGY*, that would loom large as Eisenhower worked his way through the Army's officer corps.

In December 1926, Major Eisenhower received orders to report to the War Department in Washington. Unlike Patton, whose time at Fort Myer was spent mixing with brother officers and the occasional high-society guest, Ike's stint in the marble capital gave him a pigeon's-eye view of Washington's political establishment. His younger brother Milton, now a rising star at the Department of Agriculture, was a frequent guest in the Coolidge White House, and during many a late-night talk with Milton over bridge and gin, Ike gained an appreciation for the challenges of civil governance that many colleagues in the Army, such as Patton, sorely lacked.[20]

While living in Washington, Ike delighted in renewing his friendship with George Patton, who had been reposted to Fort Myer. The Eisenhowers were frequent lunch or dinner guests at the Patton home, and from time to time Ike would unfurl the sails with George as they floated along the Chesapeake's waters in George's schooner. Ike's second son, John, recalled a young boy's impressions of the imposing George Patton:

> I always held the Pattons in considerable awe, because of their obvious wealth and the fact that Patton was a lieutenant colonel while Dad was a major. . . . Patton was a good-humored man who loved to joke. His language was full of purple expressions for which he later became famous. I was astonished that he not only swore profusely around ladies but also encouraged all three of his children to do the same. When young George, a fine boy slightly younger than I, would come out with an appropriate piece of blasphemy, Patton would roar with pleasure.[21]

While the Eisenhowers enjoyed Washington life, Ike's long days at the War Department began taking their toll on his health. He paid a heavy price for long hours spent reading thick position papers, chain smoking, eating poorly, and working from dawn till dusk. Gastrointestinal ailments and bursitis plagued him, and the social responsibilities of a young General Staff officer nearly broke the Eisenhower family's tenuous finances. Looking like a bald, middle-aged banker in the civilian suit he wore to the office, Ike compensated for the stress of work under General Douglas MacArthur, the Army's chief of staff, by reaching out to old friends—Patton, Leonard T. "Gee" Gerow, a classmate from Leavenworth, and Everett S. Hughes, among others. Ike tapped into a network of civilian and military friends, both old and new, to keep his spirits up; rounds of golf and riding, and evenings of dinner, bridge, drinks, and conversation became a tonic for this extrovert.[22]

As the months passed, Ike grew disenchanted with the egotistical MacArthur, and he began calling his boss's judgment into serious question during the Bonus March. While MacArthur condemned the protest as a left-wing threat to the Republic, the capital city's journalists, as Ike had feared, saw things differently. They saw shabby, ill-fed veterans beaten by reactionaries on horseback. They saw shacks burned and children blinded by tear gas. They saw the common man, the salt of the earth who had served his country, roughed up by a callous, self-serving government.[23]

The strident response of influential columnists like the *Washington Post*'s Drew Pearson to MacArthur's crowing to the press about saving the capital from "communist insurrectionists" underscored to Ike the importance of not picking on the downtrodden or lowly when the press was around. It was a lesson that would involve George, Ike, and Pearson in the distant future.

In 1935, Roosevelt sent MacArthur to the Philippine Islands as the American military representative, and Ike spent the late 1930s as MacArthur's chief of staff, a vague job that ran the gamut from speechwriting and diplomacy to bean counting and paper pushing. As the months dragged by, Ike's relationship with the general soured. He second-guessed the general's opinions, and he committed the cardinal sin of letting on when he disagreed with MacArthur. As the touchy general reciprocated Ike's feelings, Ike's sense of imprisonment on the hot, sticky island hardened. The final blow fell in 1938, while Ike was on leave to the United States; MacArthur abruptly demoted Eisenhower from chief of staff to senior planner, replacing the opinionated Kansan with more pliable sycophants.[24]

Ike, now perilously close to fifty, grew desperate to escape Manila's starspangled prima donna, and in his desperation he turned to an old West Point schoolmate, Colonel Mark W. Clark. Wayne, as Clark's friends called him, was luckier than Ike; during the Great War he had been shipped overseas, and he had served as an acting battalion commander in France. After the war, the lanky colonel had made a name for himself as a training officer, and by 1938 Clark was one of the Army's rising stars. Tall, intelligent, and extremely ambitious, Wayne Clark was confident or conceited, efficient or arrogant, depending on who was asked.[25]

At a meeting at Fort Lewis, Washington, in 1938, Eisenhower and Clark rekindled their old friendship, and a forlorn Ike poured out his frustrations to Clark. Clark promised to do his best to secure him a stateside command, and Ike left, Clark said later, looking "like a boy who has been promised an electric train for Christmas."[26]

Clark was as good as his word, and in May 1939 Ike received a message from the War Department ordering him to report to Fort Lewis as an infantry battalion commander. His assumption of command in the fall of 1939 was a breath of fresh air, and it coincided with two events that would change his life forever—General George C. Marshall's appointment as Army Chief of Staff, and Hitler's invasion of Poland.[27]

The demobilization of 1920 hit Major Bradley hard. He dropped a pay grade, to captain, and he spent the next year helping the Army dismantle surplus training camps. Scrounging for opportunity in the humdrum peacetime world, Brad applied for a position as an ROTC instructor, and the War Department assigned him to a tiny college in a cold, bleak corner of South Dakota. There, he and his pretty wife, Mary, struggled to get by on a bone-sliced captain's salary of $350 per month. Isolated and dreary, the outpost was a fitting backdrop for Bradley's stagnant career: a place so far removed from anything that folks barely noticed Congress was slashing the Regular Army down to almost nothing. Which, by extension, left Bradley near the bottom of almost nothing.[28]

Throughout the 1920s, Brad renewed old friendships, took up golf, and played poker and bridge with his fellow officers. He stayed in touch with some classmates, but drifted away from others, including his West Point football teammate Ike Eisenhower, the affable plunging back whom Bradley had outranked at the Academy when they were officers in Company F.[29]

Like Eisenhower, Bradley used his card winnings to supplement his feeble income. The extra money he scraped together made little difference in his social life, however. Mary's strong opinions about distilled spirits put a crimp in Bradley's evenings with the bootlegged whiskey crowd. As a result, Brad wrote, "we led a rather quiet life compared to most of our friends."

He socialized as much as possible for an Army officer living through Prohibition, but he had never been much of a lion in that regard anyway. He had come from a poor, rural family, and his father had died when he was thirteen, so he grew up lacking the social confidence many of his middle- and upper-class friends enjoyed.[30]

In most company, Brad didn't smile much; he just gave a sort of tight-lipped, almost noncommittal grin to express pleasure or jocularity. His sense of humor was as threadbare as his salary—he could easily wrap his mind around complex mathematical formulae, but he could never remember jokes—and a childhood skating accident had smashed his teeth and jaw, leaving him with a broad, almost comically pronounced chin. As a self-conscious teenager, he had learned to suppress any facial expression that exposed his jumbled incisors to the world, and this deformity added to the insecurity he felt as a young adult. His black hair had flecks of gray before he graduated from the Academy, and he was plagued with a diverse palette of awkward food allergies. The combination of these physical deficiencies drew Bradley to the periphery of any gathering, never the center. Whether in a crowd or a small circle of friends, Omar Bradley would be the tall, quiet man no one would think to take notice of.[31]

But the men who knew and worked with Major Bradley liked him. He was bright, he was likable, he worked hard, and he was a natural at outdoor and field sports. It did not take long before the dark-eyed officer from the Missouri backwoods became a steady fixture among the Army's academicians. He kept himself in excellent physical shape, he was an outstanding shot with clay pigeons or on a hunt, and he was a fine partner on the golf course. During his best baseball season at West Point, he had swung his slugger to a .383 average, and he held the West Point record for longest baseball throw. Since those days on the diamond, only the appearance of steel-rimmed spectacles, frosted hair, and the inevitable facial lines hinted at the passage of time.[32]

After four years of teaching mathematics at West Point, Bradley, now a major again, was admitted to the advanced officer course at the Army's infantry school in Fort Benning, Georgia. Benning awakened him to the realities of modern warfare—realities that, to Brad's surprise, shrugged off Brad's lack of experience in the Great War walking trenches and parapets. Looking back on his Benning years, he reflected, "[I]t slowly dawned on me that my failure to get to France had not ruined me professionally after all. The emphasis at Benning was on open warfare or 'war of maneuver. . . .' My classmates who had served in France had great difficulty adjusting to these concepts. They had fixed, inflexible ideas whereas I, who had been denied that experience, still had an open mind and I grasped the theories under discussion more easily."[33]

Bradley graduated second in his Benning class in May 1925, and the War Department sent him to Hawaii as a battalion commander with the 27th Infantry Regiment. It was, by Army standards, a great job. "Peacetime garrison life in Hawaii for a major and his family was pleasant indeed," Brad wrote afterward. "We worked only half-days and seldom on weekends." The regiment's colonel let Brad do his job with a minimum of interference, and Brad did likewise with his four company commanders. He played golf four or five days a week, and he recalled, "[a]fter one match on a newly opened course near Honolulu, I stopped in at the 'nineteenth hole' and, at age thirty-three, had the first drink of whiskey in my life—some kind of Hawaiian rotgut. I found it pleasantly relaxing and thereafter made a habit of having a bourbon and water or two (but never more) before dinner."[34]

One officer stationed in Hawaii at the same time was, he later wrote, "one of the most extraordinary men—military or civilian—I ever met. He was

George S. Patton, Jr." Patton, the division's G-2 officer, ran in entirely different circles from the financially strapped Bradley clan. "In Hawaii," Brad recalled, "we hardly knew the Pattons at all. We were not inclined toward the heavy social life they led. Besides that, Patton was a dedicated horseman. . . . Since I had little use for horses, we had not much in common."[35]

Brad's first encounter with the imperious colonel was inauspicious. Patton was organizing a local trap shooting team, and, having heard that Major Bradley was a "fair shot," he gave Brad a chance to try out. Brad missed his first two clays, but he nailed the next twenty-three in a row, a ninety-two percent kill rate. To this impressive feat, George sniffed, "You'll do." After that introduction, Brad wasn't certain he wanted to join Patton's team. "Patton's style," he wrote, "did not at all appeal to me."[36]

Of course it didn't. George Patton was a wealthy prima donna, part of the high-and-mighty polo set. A cavalryman. Omar Bradley had grown up in a dirt-poor family in a dirt-poor county of lower Missouri, a region populated by hardscrabble farmers and backwoods hunters like himself. Apart from their mutual assignment to the Hawaiian Division and their indoctrination from West Point onward, Brad and George had almost nothing in common.

Still, the Army was full of men with whom Brad had little in common. Brad loved shooting, and he signed on to Patton's team and enjoyed the trap competition, as he did all sports.

After his four years in the tropical paradise, the Army assigned Bradley to the Command and General Staff School at Leavenworth. He finished the course, graduating with a "satisfactory" rating. Not bad, but not great, either. Although he enjoyed teaching, his intellectual curiosity was still limited, and once he uncovered the textbook answer, he showed little interest in applying himself to wider applications with the fanatical vigor of a Patton or an Eisenhower.[37]

It was possible, Bradley mused in his later years, to be too smart in school. The top West Point students, he recalled, invariably went into the Engineer Corps, the Army's exalted branch in which promotions came faster than in other branches. It was an accelerator for a young officer's career, but the work to which the Engineers were detailed—building bridges, surveying rivers, constructing forts—was not well suited to fostering leadership among the Army's rank-and-file doughboys, the men doing the fighting in a war of "fire and maneuver." That was why, quite often, the best students became the Army's most valuable staff officers, and the middle files became the Army's top field commanders.[38]

Bradley had little interest in becoming a valued staff officer—and little in staff work, until he met one of the most extraordinary men of his life.

Because he was a veteran of the Benning and Leavenworth schools, in 1929 Bradley was offered teaching positions at both West Point and Fort Benning. He chose the informality of West Georgia over the regimented comforts of the Academy. It turned out to be "the most fortunate decision of my life," he said afterward, because it brought him into contact with "the most impressive man I ever knew, one of the greatest military minds the world has produced: George Catlett Marshall."[39]

Born to upper-middle-class parents in Uniontown, Pennsylvania, George C. Marshall graduated from Virginia Military Institute. After a year's duty in the Philippines, he was accepted to the Army Command and General Staff College in Leavenworth, Kansas. In June 1917, the Army shipped him off to Europe, where he rose to become chief of staff for the 1st Infantry Division, the famed "Big Red One." General Pershing soon acquired Marshall for himself, assigning him to AEF headquarters in July 1918. At Pershing's side, Marshall planned the American drive in September 1918 to reduce the St-Mihiel salient. Moving from strength to strength, the same month he engineered the massive troop movements that led to the great American victory at Meuse-Argonne.[40]

After the Armistice, Marshall settled into the role of General Pershing's top aide. He served a three-year tour in China, then returned to Fort Benning as assistant commandant of the infantry school. At Benning, the stern, unflappable officer overhauled the school's curriculum to emphasize mobility, air cover, and firepower. In doing so, he engineered an unseen intellectual revolution in the infantry branch.[41]

By the end of Omar Bradley's first year at Fort Benning, Marshall had marked the plainspoken weapons instructor as a man on the rise. When he left Benning, Marshall rated the Missourian a "superior" officer and wrote in Bradley's efficiency report: "Quiet, unassuming, capable, sound common sense. Absolute dependability. Give him a job and forget about it. Recommended command: regiment in peace, division in war."[42]

After attending the War College and serving another tour as a West Point instructor, Bradley, a lieutenant colonel by 1938, reported for duty in

Washington. This time his assignment was with the personnel section of the War Department's General Staff.

As part of the Washington politico-military hub, Brad and his fellow staffers labored for hours on end preparing draft legislation for mobilization plans with a bewildering number of permutations, schedules, appendices, and projections. It was tedious work, but it taught Bradley about the synapses that governed the seemingly random distribution of men throughout the Army. He also learned a great deal about the Byzantine world of Army politics; whenever he was invited, he made it a point to accompany General Marshall, the Deputy Chief of Staff, on bird hunts and other non-equine pursuits, which cemented the relationship between Marshall and Bradley, one of Marshall's "Benning men."[43]

The lieutenant colonel from Moberly, Missouri, had come a long way since the bells of peace rang out in Des Moines that far-off day in 1918. He had absorbed the Army's teachings and had passed them on to cadets and younger officers. He felt he was ready for bigger assignments—or at least he hoped he was—on September 1, 1939, the day Marshall was given his temporary rank of four-star general and sworn in as the Army's Chief of Staff.[44]

By coincidence, the very day Hitler's tanks set a continent on fire.

THREE

MARSHALL'S MEN

If you want to take a chance, I will ask for you now.... Hoping we are together in a long and BLOODY war.

—George to Ike, October 1, 1940

MARSHALL'S APPOINTMENT was a godsend to Eisenhower, Patton, Bradley, Clark, and dozens of other talented but junior commanders. The new chief reorganized the Army's structure, broke the backs of the branch chiefs, emancipated the Air Corps, and established an independent armored force. He quietly won congressional authority to grant temporary promotions, just as he could in wartime, and he created a board of retired generals—the "plucking committee"—to make recommendations on older officers who could be forced into retirement. Before the war's end, the plucking committee would put nearly seven hundred senior officers out to pasture, leaving room for Marshall to restock his upper ranks with men of talent, vigor, and ability. Men like George, Ike, and Brad.[1]

The first to benefit from Marshall's appointment was the cavalry commandant of Fort Myer, which was the chief of staff's official residence. In a "pretty snappy move," as he put it, Patton hosted General Marshall at his personal quarters while Marshall's Fort Myer quarters were being refurbished. *"He and I are batching it,"* George gloated to Beatrice. *"I think that once I can get my natural charm working, I won't need any letters [of reference] from John J.P. or any one else."* George, obsequious in the presence of superiors, procured a set of eight silver stars from a New York jeweler as a gift for the incoming chief, and he entertained Marshall on the Chesapeake aboard the Patton yacht, the beautifully appointed Maine schooner *When and If.*[2]

George's bootlicking campaign with Marshall was unnecessary, given Marshall's favorable opinion of George. Marshall considered Colonel Patton an outstanding combat commander—notwithstanding his age (fifty-four in the summer of 1940) and his well-known eccentricities. As Marshall summed up his view of Patton in a letter to one of Ike's old friends, Gee Gerow, *"Patton is by far the best tank man in the Army. I know this from the First World War. . . . I realize he is a difficult man but I know how to handle him."*[3]

So did Marshall's wife, Katherine, who occasionally accompanied her husband and his senior men on morning horseback rides. Her presence naturally inhibited the rougher language most officers tossed about, but George took no pains to restrain his adroit and vulgar tongue. During one morning ride, after a typically profane Patton tirade, Mrs. Marshall looked at Patton and said, in a tone only women can get away with, "George, you mustn't talk like that. You say these outrageous things and then you look at me to see if I'm going to smile. Now you could do that as a captain or a major, but you aspire to be a general, and a general cannot talk in any such wild way."[4]

Katherine Marshall's advice fell on largely deaf ears, for George felt that bluntness, even to the point of obscenity, was part of his job as a motivator, a trainer, a leader of fighting men. Eisenhower felt it was a conscious, studied part of his friend's personality: "George Patton loved to shock people," he wrote years later. "Anything that popped into his mind came promptly out his mouth, especially if it was bizarre. This may have seemed inadvertent but in my opinion he had, throughout his life, cultivated this habit. He loved to shake members of a social gathering by exploding a few rounds of outrageous profanity. If he created any effect, he would indulge in more of the same. If no one paid any attention, he would quiet down."[5]

Here Ike hit pretty close to the mark. Back in 1919, George's father, a gentleman lawyer and politician, warned his son:

> *Among other things, I have been worrying for fear that the "gift of gab" you have developed may get you into trouble. . . . You are now 34—and a Col and the dignity going with your rank invests what you say with more importance so I hope in your speeches you will be very careful & self restrained—for your own good & for your future. Another gift you have developed I really regret—and that is the ability to write verse upon vulgar &*

smutty subjects. . . . All my life I have known such instances—and never has it failed in my experience—that the Club wit—who indulges in smutty stuff hurts himself.[6]

As with Katherine Marshall, none of the senior Patton's advice stuck. George didn't give a damn what polite society, even society wearing stars, thought of his approach. Military men were in the business of killing, a violent, crude, obscene enterprise that called for violent, crude, obscene language. The men needed motivation, and motivation sometimes required profanity. As far as Patton was concerned, after his company grades had licked the Japs or the Boche or the Reds in the next war, they could go back to Miss Flossy's Finishing School and forget everything he had taught them. Until then, they reported to Colonel George S. Patton Jr., and as long as they did, they took the message exactly as he gave it to them.

As the summer of 1941 approached, George Patton, the man who redesigned the cavalry's saber and chased Pancho Villa with Pershing, looked for new ways to improve his division's effectiveness. Some of his brainstorms were highly successful; he concluded, for instance, that an armored division needed a light scouting plane that could land on unimproved fields and provide up-to-date reconnaissance. Eventually he adopted the Piper Cub, which became a standard tool throughout the Army.[7]

Others did not work out so well. One project, which could only have been inspired by his cavalry hero, Napoleon's colorful marshal Joachim Murat, was a uniform George designed for the tank corps. The outfit, which he personally modeled for the press, consisted of green padded trousers, a green jacket with a row of brass buttons running down one side, a shoulder holster, and a football-style helmet painted gold and capped with large round riding goggles.

Although he pronounced the new uniform "better than the abortion the Ordnance invented," it looked ridiculous. The press dubbed it the "Green Hornet Suit," and even George's son-in-law John Waters, a tank officer with the 2nd Armored Division, admitted, "[N]obody was ready to accept it. He had enough sense to put it away and not try to force the issue." The Green Hornet Suit would spend the next war in George's closet.[8]

Having returned from his indentured servitude with MacArthur, a khaki-clad Ike Eisenhower reported to Fort Lewis, Washington, the home of the

15th Infantry Regiment. He was delighted to get back to field duty, running combat drills, camping under the stars, and—seeing war clouds on two horizons—preparing fighting men for combat. As he wrote to his old classmate Omar Bradley, *"I . . . am having the time of my life. Like everyone else in the army, we are up to our necks in work and in problems, big and little. But this work is fun!"*[9]

Before long, though, the not-so-fun staff work, that dull office practice of logistics and charts and unending memoranda, called him back again. By the autumn of 1941, Ike's superiors pulled him out of combat command and moved him into a series of top-level staff positions. In rapid succession he was appointed chief of staff of the 3rd Infantry Division, then of the IX Corps, then finally, of the Third Army under Lieutenant General Walter Krueger. The move up the staff chain bumped him up in rank as well, and by March 1941 Ike had made "full bird" colonel. He was becoming one of the Army's most sought-after staff chiefs, and the increase in responsibility, rank, status, and pay was, of course, a source of pride to Colonel and Mamie Eisenhower.

But Ike had signed on to lead troops in battle, not manage their logistical tail. It was hard for him to warm to the notion that what he *wanted* to do and what he was *good at* might be two very different things.[10]

As the forties opened, George and Ike resumed their on-again, off-again correspondence, each man looking for a way to work with the other—Ike seeking a combat command, George wanting Ike's talents in any capacity. In September, Patton, a brigadier general, invited Colonel Eisenhower to join the 2nd Armored Division, which he was slated to take over at the end of the month. Ike, elated at the prospect of working for George, wrote back:

Dear George:

Thanks a lot for your recent note; I am flattered by your suggestion that I come to your outfit. It would be great to be in the tanks once more, and even better to be associated with you again. . . . I suppose it's too much to hope that I could have a regiment in your division, because I'm still almost three years away from my colonelcy. But I think I could do a damn good job of commanding a regiment. . . . Anyway, if there's a chance of that kind of an assignment, I'd be for it 100%. Will you write to me again about it, so that I may know what you had in mind?[11]

George to Ike:

> It seems highly probable that I will get one of the next two armored divisions which we firmly believe will be created in January or February, depending on production. If I do, I shall ask for you either as Chief of Staff, which I should prefer, or as a regimental commander. You can tell me which you want, for no matter how we get together we will go PLACES. If you get a better offer in the meantime, take it, as I can't be sure, but I hope we can get together. At the moment there is nothing in the brigade good enough for you. However, if you want to take a chance, I will ask for you now. . . . Hoping we are together in a long and BLOODY war.[12]

George to Ike (later):

> If I were you, I would apply for a transfer to the Armored Corps NOW. There will be at least one vacancy shortly. . . . If you apply for a transfer . . . say that you are an old tanker. If you have any pull, use it for there will be 10 new generals in this corps pretty damn soon.[13]

Ike to George (later):

> I am probably to be allowed to stay with the troops. So I ought to be available and eligible for transfer when the time comes. . . . Good luck—and maybe I'll be seeing you in the spring.[14]

Ike, now hooked, began pulling strings like a harp player to get an Armored Corps command. At the end of October, he wrote to Clark for help getting the assignment approved by the higher-ups:

> As you know, George Patton rather expects to get one of the new divisions that are to be organized next year. . . . In any event, that is exactly the thing I would like to do and I am sure that George Patton intends to ask for me in that capacity. . . . Actually, I will be delighted to serve in the Armored Corps in almost any

capacity, but I do hope to avoid Staff and stay on troop duty for some time to come.[15]

He also wrote to T. J. Davis, an old friend from his Philippines days, now in the Adjutant General's office: *"My ambition is to go, eventually, to the armored outfit . . . as one of [Patton's] regimental commanders. That would be a swell job, and I only hope the War Department won't consider me too junior in rank to get a regiment."*[16]

Ike felt he had a position with the 2nd Armored locked in, and he was able to tell George in mid-November, *"I ought to be available and eligible for transfer when the time comes."*[17]

Events moved quickly for Patton in the summer of 1940. As Marshall's reforms shook up the old order, George sensed an opportunity to leave the cavalry and reunite with his secret love, the Tank Corps. He penned a letter, pleading for an appointment, to Brigadier General Adna Chaffee, head of the newly formed Armored Force, and before long Chaffee tapped Patton to lead one of the two tank brigades of the 2nd Armored Division. At the end of September 1940, Patton was thrilled to learn that he would receive his first star, finally rising above the rank he held in 1919, and before long the War Department appointed Patton acting commander of the 2nd Armored Division, which adopted the Pattonesque nickname "Hell on Wheels."[18]

Soon afterward, Chaffee's health began to decline. The Department reached into the field artillery ranks and appointed George's classmate and polo-playing friend Major General Jacob L. Devers to head up the Armored Force. Devers tapped Patton to lead the newly formed I Armored Corps, and ordered him to Indio, California, to establish the Army's Desert Training Center.[19]

Secretary of War Henry Stimson, Patton's old friend and longtime patron in Washington, pressed President Roosevelt to nominate Patton for promotion from brigadier to major general. Patton's star collection doubled on April 10, 1941, and George busied himself writing letters of appreciation to Stimson, Marshall, and several other officers in his evaluation chain, crediting each man for promotion. He even directed a lobbying campaign to a higher authority, writing his aunt Susie in San Marino: *"Knowing that you have a great drag with the Lord, I trust that you will bring all your efforts to prayerful intercession that I may soon get another star and be a Lieutenant General."* From any other man, it would have seemed insincere or even blasphemous. For George, it was just covering his bases.[20]

* * *

From the day General Marshall was sworn in as Chief of Staff, Lieutenant Colonel Omar Bradley had spent long hours in the personnel department at the Army's nerve center, the old, dilapidated Munitions Building on Constitution Avenue. Like dozens of other nondescript officers, Brad spent his days, and many nights, in a plain office, attending interminable conferences and staring through his round glasses at piles of studies, papers, and memoranda to determine what his boss would review. As he recalled those mind-numbing days manning personnel desks: "Perhaps never in the history of the U.S. Army had so many officers labored so long with typewriters and charts. Each day an Everest of paper rose on our desks. We worked deep into the nights, digesting and analyzing, preparing our presentations for Marshall."[21]

He may have been burning barrels of midnight oil, and it may have been drudgery, but it was a heady time for Omar Bradley. His position as the senior gatekeeper allowed him to make recommendations and, occasionally, decisions on matters of Army policy. It also gave him a bird's-eye view of the Army's position on the Washington stage, and he worked with a small, influential group of up-and-comers all handpicked by the Chief. In time, he even became privy to the nation's most carefully guarded secret, the decryption of Japan's supposedly impregnable "Purple" diplomatic code.[22]

Although the work put him at the center of the Army's power structure, Brad, as he later put it, got a case of "itchy feet." Marshall had treated him well, but he wanted to be a commander in the field, not some chairborne commando growing fat behind a government-issue desk. So when the Department's personnel section gave Brad a chance to transfer to West Point as commandant of cadets—technically a command position—he volunteered immediately and Marshall approved the transfer.[23]

Bradley was ready to pack his bags for the Hudson once again, but Marshall, uncharacteristically, had second thoughts. The lieutenant colonel had performed brilliantly under demanding circumstances. With the Army ballooning to a half million men, Marshall knew Bradley's talents would be needed to train fighting men, not teenage cadets. So a few days later, Marshall paid a visit to his assistant and casually asked him, "Bradley, are you sure you want to go to West Point?"

Brad responded, "Yes, sir. It's a command job and it will give me a chance to help develop the officers there. I've had twelve years at West Point, including four as a cadet, and I believe I know their problems."

"How'd you like to have Hodges's job?"

Brad's heart leaped into his throat. General Courtney Hodges was Fort Benning's Infantry School commandant. It was a plumb job. *A brigadier general's job.*

Without a second's hesitation, Brad revised his answer. "Sir, that's a new situation. I would much prefer Hodges's job."

"All right," Marshall said. "We'll fix it up."[24]

Brad arrived at Benning in February, and within a few weeks a telegram from the War Department delivered tidings he could not have hoped for in Washington: The United States Senate had approved his promotion to brigadier general.

Brigadier general. Brad was elated. He had skipped an entire grade, and had become the first man in the Class of 1915 to wear a general's stars! And for the icing on a very sweet cake, Brad was taking the place of one man he respected nearly as much as Marshall—Courtney Hicks Hodges, a Georgia-born hero from World War I whose Distinguished Service Cross, Silver Star, and Bronze Star were accented with three hard-won battle stars. Hodges, as distinguished for his modesty as for his bravery, would be a tough act to follow, but it was a challenge that would thrill anyone in Brad's shoes.[25]

At Fort Benning, the new brigadier set to work with a vengeance. He revamped training programs, toughened fitness requirements, and worked with the fort's resident unit commanders, an elite group that included the boisterous commander of the Hell on Wheels Division. Brad hadn't seen George Patton since Hawaii, but the doughboy and the horseman got along fine in the backwoods confines of Benning's campus. As he saw more of Patton's persona in action, however, Brad began to sense things in George that didn't seem to be quite right.[26]

The maneuvers of 1941 were General Marshall's largest and most public effort to mold the Army's regular and National Guard forces into a modern fighting force. At Marshall's direction, the greatest clash of troops in North American history would take place in Louisiana and Texas during September 1941. The congregation would involve over 400,000 soldiers, more than twice the number that clashed at Gettysburg eighty years before. Marshall billed it as a "combat college for troop leading," knowing that the maneuvers would expose flaws in Army doctrine as well as weakness in his senior officers—weaknesses he wanted fixed by design in America, rather than by necessity in Europe.[27]

To write the scenario for the exercise, Lieutenant General Lesley McNair, Chief of Army Ground Forces, tapped his number one planner, Brigadier General Mark Wayne Clark. Clark's scenario, which encompassed 30,000 square miles of western Louisiana between the Red and Sabine rivers, was a model of simplicity: Lieutenant General Ben Lear's 160,000-man Second Army would cross the Red River into "Blue" territory, defended by General Krueger's 240,000-man Third Army. Simulating the makeup of Hitler's panzer armies, General Lear was allocated the bulk of the Armored Force, including Patton's 2nd Armored Division, while Krueger's Blue Force got the bulk of the infantry and antitank units. During the second phase, the roles would be reversed, although the armor would change sides so that it would, again, play the role of the attacker.[28]

Patton would have the pleasure of attacking his old friend Ike, who worked for Krueger, and with a devilish grin he offered his men a $50 reward for the capture of "a certain s.o.b. called Eisenhower." But when Lear's attacking army jumped off the morning of September 15 in a miserable rainstorm, his advance units were spotted by Krueger's reconnaissance pilots as they crossed the Red River. In no time Krueger and Ike were funneling antitank, infantry, and cavalry forces down U.S. Highway 171 to bog down the invaders, surround them, and crush them. When it was obvious that Third Army had won the "war," General McNair pulled the plug on the first phase of the exercise.[29]

The second phase opened on September 24 with a Third Army counterattack against Lear's army. Patton's armored division, now teamed with Ike's Third Army, fared much better this time. Krueger and Ike sent their infantry north toward Shreveport to overrun General Lear's defense lines. When Lear pulled back, "destroying" bridges along the way, Krueger sent the Hell on Wheels Division on a tough, dirty, two-hundred-mile flanking march into Texas and back to Louisiana behind the enemy capital of Shreveport.[30]

Seeing a once-in-a-lifetime chance to prove himself to his superiors, Patton drove his men all night on a "lights low" ride. The weather was terrible, even for road movement, and Patton's tanks were outnumbered. But George's division crashed into Lear's rear echelons with a vengeance. Working from the top of a light tank, his face blackened with exhaust soot except for two white goggle-circles around his eyes, Patton forced his way into Shreveport four days after the exercise began. McNair called off the exercise the next day.[31]

Bradley, escorting two senators to the maneuvers at Marshall's request, recalled, "Patton broke all the old-fashioned rules, smashing his mechanized forces ever onward with dazzling speed and surprise. He was criticized by the umpire-generals for his unorthodoxy, for leaving his command post and prowling the 'front line,' for running his division 'roughshod' over the enemy. But it was clear to anybody in the U.S. Army with the eyes to see that we had on our hands one of the most extraordinary fighting generals the Army had ever produced."[32]

George's ruthless drive put his tanks and men exactly where they needed to be to win the battle, and with the eyes of the country upon him, Patton pulled off his greatest peacetime coup. As his reward, Patton was promoted to command of I Armored Corps.[33]

While George reveled in the role of the dashing cavalryman, the popular hero of the Louisiana maneuvers turned out to be the congenial, unassuming chief of staff of the victorious Third Army. As make-believe battles raged in the woods, reporters like CBS's Eric Sevareid and Hanson Baldwin of the *New York Times* would gather around Colonel Eisenhower's tent for informal discussions, a bawdy joke or two, some inside dish, and a friendly drink.

Ike's easy way of dropping occasional off-the-record scoop endeared him to the press corps, and it paid off handsomely. Columnists Robert S. Allen and Drew Pearson, authors of the influential "Washington Merry-Go-Round," singled out the affable colonel with the wide grin and twinkling eyes, claiming that the man who "conceived and directed the strategy that routed the Second Army has a steel-trap mind plus unusual physical vigor." Other reporters jumped on the Eisenhower bandwagon, and Ike got the lion's share of the credit for Third Army's performance.[34]

The press was not the only one to take note of Eisenhower's performance. Before long the War Department rewarded Ike with his first star, and as General Marshall was observing the Army's next phase of maneuvers in North and South Carolina, he approached Clark and mentioned some staffing changes he was considering for the War Department. The nation's best and brightest would be needed for the Department's War Plans Division to develop strategic plans for the new divisions McNair and Clark would be training.

"I wish you would give me a list of ten names of officers you know pretty well and whom you would recommend to be the head of the Operations Division," Marshall said.

"I'll be glad to do that," said Clark, "but there would be only one name on the list. If you have to have ten names, I'll just put nine ditto marks below it."

The name?

"Ike Eisenhower."[35]

Eight days after the Carolina maneuvers ended, the Empire of Japan shocked the nation with a lightning strike on Pearl Harbor. The attack sent much of the U.S. Pacific Fleet to the bottom, and four days later, Germany declared war on the United States. War was now no longer a contingency; on two sides of the globe, it was a conspicuous fact.

Ike got the call five days after Pearl Harbor. Colonel Walter Bedell Smith, Secretary to the General Staff, rang up Ike in San Antonio and brusquely told him, "The Chief says for you to hop a plane and get up here right away. Tell your boss that formal orders will come through later."[36]

"How long?" said Ike.

"I don't know. Just come along."

Ike was puzzled, wondering what kind of clothes to bring.

"Well, what kind of duty—office duty or where?" he asked.

"The Chief said you get on a plane and get up here."

That was it.[37]

Two days later, Ike found himself sitting in a second-floor office in the old Munitions Building before the most demanding, most powerful, most intimidating man in the United States Army. A man his own mentor, Fox Conner, had called a genius. There Ike got his first taste of Marshall's management style.[38]

Skipping formalities and small talk, Marshall looked up from a sheaf of papers and came straight to the point. Sketching a broad picture in the Pacific—the Philippines, Australia, the U.S. islands, as well as the forces available to defend them, he asked the brigadier directly: "What should be our general line of action?"[39]

Ike asked for a few hours to consider this immense problem. Marshall gruffly dismissed him, his lined face falling back to the papers on his desk.

Ike hurried over to the office of his new boss—and old friend—Gee Gerow. He borrowed a desk, some maps, and any other information he could lay his hands on in the precious little time he had. As a government-issue wall clock ticked off the minutes, Ike began scribbling a list entitled "Steps to be Taken" on a yellow pad.[40]

Taking a deep breath, he marched back to the office of the man who would either keep him on the varsity team or cut short his career. Sitting stiffly before his chief, Ike advised Marshall that the Philippines probably could not be saved, though an effort to succor the islands had to be made, even a token one, as neutral Pacific nations would be carefully watching the U.S. reaction to the Japanese advance. At the strategic level, Ike continued, the Pacific theater should be held passively through Australia, the logical base for future operations, while the major Allied push should be against Hitler in Europe, for Germany was the more dangerous enemy.[41]

Ike finished. He waited.

His piercing blue eyes locked on the brigadier, General Marshall told Eisenhower he agreed with his conclusions, which were, he said, in line with the War Department's larger strategy.

The details and analysis Eisenhower had worked out merely confirmed what Marshall already knew, and Ike's ideas were unremarkable in and of themselves. But what Marshall was looking for, and what Ike seemed to offer, was a willingness to craft policy, to make decisions, without laying everything before the Chief of Staff for advice and approval. Ike intuitively understood Marshall's need for officers who didn't need close supervision, men who would free the Chief of Staff to deal with Congress, the White House, the allies, and the brass-capped prima donnas who dotted the upper floors of the Navy and Pacific command buildings.

His voice sharp and direct, Marshall said, "Eisenhower, the Department is filled with able men who analyze their problems but feel compelled to always bring them to me for final solution. I must have assistants who will solve their own problems and tell me later what they have done."[42]

Ike nodded. He had passed his first test.

A week after his appointment to the I Armored Corps, George Patton fired off a quick note to his old friend in the War Department:

Dear Ike,

After you have gotten the war plans in shape, you had better fix to get a division in the corps. . . . I further appreciate your advertising of the 2d Armored Division, and I am sincere in believing with you that it is ready to fight anywhere, any time.[43]

Like in the old days, George still wanted the Kansan fighting by his side.

As he rose through the ranks, George Patton attracted news coverage like nails to a magnet. He was a colorful man who relished his publicity, and his wife, Beatrice, faithfully clipped articles about her husband for the family scrapbook. But despite a strong narcissistic streak, George knew too much of a good thing might put a target on his back. So when *Life* decided to do a feature article on the Army's flamboyant general, George asked the editor to kill the story in a letter that revealed much about himself and the Old Army's office politics:

> *I deeply appreciate your continued interest in me and the nice things which your great magazine has said about me. But frankly, I hope you will not publish Mr. Field's article. My reasons for making this request are:*
>
> *In the first place, I do not believe it paints a just picture of me. The casual reader would think I am one of the most profane, crude, and vulgar people on earth; because the profanity of fifty years has been compressed into a few pages.*
>
> *I have always deprecated any mention of what little inherited wealth I possess because I do not believe that wealth acquired through the judicious selection of ancestors is in itself a mark of ability.*
>
> *Finally, the future of an officer who has been sufficiently fortunate to arrive at the position of a corps command, a position which, thanks to General Devers, I now hold, must depend for his future advancement upon the opinion of his military equals and superiors, not upon public sentiment. In fact, it has been my observation that untimely or excessive publicity is a great detriment to an officer's career because people are bound to believe that the publicity was asked for by the officer and that he probably dictated most of it. Now, while you and I know that this is not the case, it is none the less what other people will think. . . . [I]t is my honest opinion that to publish this article now would not only not help me, but might very well ruin my career and bring to nothing the effort of more than 30 years.*[44]

In this, George was not indulging in false modesty. He was so close to combat he could taste the cordite smoke, and the last thing he needed was a whispering campaign against him in Washington when he was too far from the nerve center to defend himself. After writing to *Life*'s editors, he penned a letter to the Army's Press Relations Officer, Brigadier General A. D. Surles, to see if Surles could get *Life* to kill the story. To cover his flanks, he wrote a second letter to his boss, General Devers, explaining that he had tried to convince *Life's* editors to drop the story, and had enlisted Surles's help to do so. The implied message to Devers was clear: The boss needn't worry about Patton trying to jump ahead of his peers by encouraging lavish press reports.[45]

Another problem Patton wrestled with was the nagging task of getting Ike transferred into his corps, and here, George was of two minds. On one hand, George would have loved to acquire Eisenhower for himself, as would any other commander of the day. He knew Ike and he would think, act, and react on parallel lines, a vital requirement for a chief of staff. At the same time, he considered Brigadier General Eisenhower his ace in the hole at the War Department, and he wasn't sure he wanted to remove a tank advocate so close to General Marshall. So after a trip to Washington in February 1942, George wrote back to Ike:

> *Of all the many talks I had in Washington, none gave me so much pleasure as that with you. There were two reasons for this. In the first place, you are about my oldest friend. In the second place, your self-assurance and to me, at least, demonstrated ability, gave me a great feeling of confidence in the future. I am very glad that you hold your present position and have the utmost confidence that through your efforts we will eventually beat the hell out of those bastards—"You name them; I'll shoot them!"*[46]

Ike was quick to oblige. *"I don't have the slightest trouble naming the hellions I'd like to have you shoot,"* he wrote back. *"My problem is to figure out some way of getting you to the place you can do it."* As for being stuck in his current staff position, he added:

> *It was a personal disappointment to me to have to come to Washington—but there are many more in the same fix. This thing is too serious to worry about anyone's preferences, so I have wrapped up in cotton-batting all my ideas about troop training and troop leadership and laid them away in mothballs. You'll have to do that end of the job. I know you'll get that whole Corps up to the 2d Division standard.*[47]

But Ike's dreams of troop command wiggled their way out of his cotton-batting, for two months later Ike wrote to George: *"Maybe I'll finally get out of this slave seat, so I can let loose a little lead with you. By that time you'll be the 'Black Jack' of the dam war."*[48]

George, now sensing that Ike, rather than he, might become the "Black Jack" of the "dam war," wrote back,

> *My feelings are identical with yours as to the pleasure of our being together. While I can appreciate your natural desires, owing to the fact that you were red-headed before you were bald, to quit your present job, I personally believe to abandon it now would be little short of a national calamity. However, being selfish, there is nothing I would like more than to be the "Black Jack" of this war with you as assistant "B.J." or even the other way around.*[49]

To this Ike replied:

> *The "baldness" you speak of was caused by you—I was constantly worried, during maneuvers [in Louisiana], that you would run down the CG in that hell and maria chariot of yours. Or that I would become important enough to justify a "price on my head" to your bullies.*[50]

Their joking aside, while Ike thought George had the plum job, theirs was becoming a symbiotic partnership. Patton, who had been assigned to establish a training center in far-off California, needed allies in Washington, while Eisenhower needed a commander who could give him a field position once he had sprung loose from the War Department. So they carried on their correspondence through early 1942, rekindling that old feeling of teamwork from the Camp Meade days. George confided to Ike in May,

> *Sometimes I think that your life and mine are under the protection of some supreme being or fate, because, after many years of parallel thought, we find ourselves in the situations we now occupy. But remember that my fate largely depends upon you, because in this distant locality, one can very easily be forgotten. . . . I stick my neck out, but I trust to your great powers of discernment and persuasion to see that no one drops an ax on it.*[51]

As America lurched into a shooting war, the Patton-Eisenhower relationship fit both men. Not like a glove, maybe, but it played into each man's strengths. Ike, the junior partner, was bred to coach a team, to assess each player's abilities, and to bend each man's efforts toward a common goal. It was a natural role for Ike, because the collective industries of an organization were a part of his core fiber since his childhood in Kansas. He had grown up in a large family, where relationships, pecking orders, playmates, fistfights, and family dinners had filled out the landscape of life. He went to public school, played football and baseball, and treasured his connection to a larger community. As a man, the simple pastimes Ike enjoyed most—bridge, golf, and tennis, for instance—tended toward the social, where banter was as important as the play. When he needed strength, he found it by drawing close friends closer. And he solved problems by linking people, people who would thrash out a consensus, people who would produce the right answers.

George, for all his family wealth, for all his sophistication, lacked the exposure to broad society that formed the chassis of Ike's machine. Growing up with few neighbors and one sibling, George drew his strength from within. His hobbies—shooting, sailing, horseback riding, and polo—centered around personal dominance and individual execution. In quieter moments, when his soul felt empty, he retreated, he read, he wrote, and prayed. Then he came back ready to fight. He was a lone knight, a weapon of single combat, and he needed a man like Eisenhower to put him on the right team, in the right place, at the right time.

While Patton was training tankers and Ike was shaping War Department strategy, Omar Bradley was putting in long hours at Fort Benning. He developed training methods for the Army's new parachute infantry regiments, he raised fitness standards, and he ran the fort like a tight ship, from far-reaching bivouac decisions all the way down to the fort's traffic regulations, which he enforced most harshly against maverick officers who, like George, loved to flout the rules of the road.[52]

Bradley's outstanding work at Fort Benning gilded his growing reputation. General Marshall, as usual, kept his ear close to the officer corps grapevine, and positive comments about Brad eventually percolated up to the cavernous office of the man who could make or break any soldier.

In 1942, during a visit to Benning, Marshall startled the left fielder with one of his typically out-of-left-field questions: "Bradley, do you have a man to take your place when you leave here to command a division?"

Brad, excitement exploding within his chest, kept his outward composure and simply said, "Not yet, sir"—but he quickly offered the name of his next choice. Within three months, that man would report to Benning for duty, and Bradley was on his way to a division command and a second star.[53]

With America's entry into the war, the Army activated three new infantry divisions, one of which was the 82nd "All-American" Division, a deactivated division whose battle flag was draped with worn silk ribbons dating back to World War I. Working from a white clapboard building on the Benning campus, Brad pulled together a division staff for the 82nd and hired two new aides, Lieutenant Lewis D. "Lew" Bridge, an outstanding athlete from Lodi, California, and Lieutenant Chester "Chet" Hansen, a former newspaper editor from Syracuse who would serve as Bradley's confidant and chronicler.[54]

Brad set to work whipping the 82nd into shape, and after four months of intense physical training, Brad felt he was ready to lead his division into battle. His tight-lipped smile betrayed his feeling that combat could not be far off. He would soon have a chance at the laurels denied to him in the Great War.[55]

But his dreams of combat command were rudely interrupted by a confidential letter from General McNair. Marshall, McNair said, valued Bradley's talents as a trainer, and right now he needed someone who could train a National Guard division that "needs help badly." The 28th Infantry Division, he explained, was in dire need of sound, mature guidance, and Marshall wanted Brad to whip those men into shape, just as he had toughened up the 82nd. Although McNair acknowledged that the assignment would be a "disappointment" to the restless commander, Marshall wanted him with the 28th, and the major general would cheerfully go along with it, whether he wanted to or not.

McNair assured Bradley, "Your ability is going to be recognized in due course, so that this particular task may be merely regarded as an incident."[56]

Brad wasn't comforted.

FOUR

STRIKING THE MATCH

You see what's happened to our dream team of twenty years ago, of going to war as a team. I'm slated to stick here to do a lot of heavy planning and operating on a global scale, but I wish you all the luck in the world.

—Ike to George, summer 1942

AFTER PEARL HARBOR, the first high-level effort to coordinate U.S.–British planning was the December 1941 conference code-named ARCADIA. Despite Atlantic-size differences over basic strategy, war aims, and command structure, the ARCADIA meeting gave the Anglo-American planning team some basic guidance in which to frame future operations. The two countries reaffirmed their "Germany first" war policy, notwithstanding intense public pressure on the Roosevelt Administration to avenge the Japanese attack. They agreed on a command structure that incorporated the army, navy, and air force chiefs of both countries, called the "Combined Chiefs of Staff," which would direct the supreme Allied commanders in each theater.[1]

As for the first major operation, the Americans proposed an invasion of France in the spring of 1943, code-named ROUNDUP, to be preceded by a buildup of U.S. forces in England, later given the code name BOLERO. They also proposed, as a contingency measure, an emergency cross-channel invasion for the fall of 1942, which was intended to pull some of Hitler's divisions off the Eastern Front if it looked as though the Soviet Union were going down for the last time. It was code-named SLEDGEHAMMER.[2]

As a matter of geography, the quickest way to Germany was through northern France. But the British insisted that the first Allied invasion, wherever it took place, must enjoy a high likelihood of success, since failure in their first joint effort would deal a severe blow to Anglo-American morale, it would boost the myth of German invincibility, and it might dishearten the Soviet Union to the point of suing for peace. The western Allies needed to launch their operation before the end of the year, for neither Stalin nor the voting public would stand for a year's inactivity. ROUNDUP, they argued, was patently infeasible in 1942. In lieu of an invasion of France, British Prime Minister Winston Churchill proposed SUPER-GYMNAST, an Anglo-American invasion of North Africa. SUPER-GYMNAST—later shortened to "GYMNAST"—was sent to Ike's planning department as another option for 1942.[3]

In the wake of ARCADIA, Ike's work piled up like a Montana snowdrift. He rarely saw his home while the sun was shining. He substituted cigarettes and blackstrap coffee for food and sleep, and he described his daily routine to a friend in the waning hours of 1941: *Just to give you an inkling of the kind of mad house you are getting into, it is now eight o'clock on New Year's Eve. I have a couple hours' work ahead of me, and tomorrow will be no different from today. I have been here about three weeks and this noon I had my first luncheon outside the office. Usually it is a hot dog sandwich and a glass of milk.* He also complained to his diary, *"Tempers are short! There are lots of amateur strategists on the job—and prima donnas everywhere. I'd give anything to be back in the field!"*[4]

As Marshall feared, the pressure was getting to Eisenhower. It only grew worse when Ike's father died on March 10; owing to the press of work, the mourning son had to miss his father's funeral. Something seemed like it would have to give way.[5]

But Ike persevered, contenting himself with small-scale outbursts that collectively forestalled a complete collapse. In his diary, he called MacArthur "as big a baby as ever," and he wrote of Admiral Ernest P. King, the Navy's incoming chief of operations, *One thing that might help win this war is to get someone to shoot King.* Despite his friend Patton's wider reputation for profanity, Eisenhower could send up a cloud of curses as thick and blue as the cigarette smoke that filled his office.

But apart from occasional outbursts in his diary, or howitzer blasts directed at staffers who turned in shoddy work, Ike swallowed his frustrations like a good soldier, put his head down, and bulled through his work. In an introspective diary entry in March, he compared his outbursts to Marshall's:

Marshall puzzles me a bit. I've never seen a man who apparently develops a higher pressure of anger when he encounters some piece of stupidity than does he. Yet the outburst is so fleeting, he returns so quickly to complete "normalcy," that I'm certain he does it for effect. At least he doesn't get angry in the sense that I do—I blaze for an hour![6]

Amidst the stress, the long hours, and complaints from seniors and subordinates, Ike, a man who prided himself on putting duty first, finally lost his temper with Marshall. In mid-March, having sensed Eisenhower's desire for a field command, the Chief casually told him one afternoon, "I want you to know that in this war the commanders are going to be promoted and not the staff officers."

Marshall let the message sink in for a moment; then he drove the point home. "Take your case. I know that you were recommended by one general for a division command and another for a corps command. That's all very well. I'm glad they have that opinion of you, but you are going to stay right here and fill your position, and that's that!"

An excruciating moment passed in silence.

The general's pitiless voice continued: "While this may seem a sacrifice to you, that's the way it must be."

Ike's great failure of 1918—his failure to leave friendly shores, his failure to fight—was about to be repeated.

The way the snide old general spoke to him, looked at him, finally got to Ike. His bald head turning crimson, Ike shot back through gritted teeth: "General, I'm interested in what you have to say, but I want you to know that I don't give a damn about your promotion plans as far as I'm concerned. I came into this office from the field and I am trying to do my duty. I expect to do that as long as you want me here. If that locks me to a desk for the rest of the war, so be it!"[7]

There was no mistaking the bitterness behind Ike's words, and he started for the door. "Already I was feeling sheepish over my outburst," he wrote. "[Marshall's] office was long, and every step I took toward the door I felt more ashamed of myself."

Grasping the brass doorknob, he looked quietly over his shoulder. The Kansan thought he saw a crack of a smile in the granite general's face.

He walked out quickly.[8]

In his flustered state, Ike didn't understand that his chief's loaded statement was not browbeating or bullying, for Marshall intended to promote him in the near future. He was giving Ike another test of character. The basic point of Ike's bitter reaction—that he would serve wherever Marshall wanted him, to hell with the rest of the war—wasn't refined or even articulate, but it was exactly what Marshall wanted to hear. Ike was committed to the good of the team, even at the expense of his own career. He had passed his second test.[9]

About three days after Ike's tirade, the Chief promoted him to major general. It was a temporary appointment, of course—Eisenhower would hold the permanent rank of lieutenant colonel until late in the war—but the twin stars made an eminently satisfying badge of office, particularly since staffers were not supposed to rate above brigadier general. And more important, it meant that if he ever knocked off the shackles of staff duty, he would probably get a division, or perhaps even a corps.[10]

In late spring, word reached Marshall that the Americans in London charged with organizing BOLERO were not doing their jobs, and the Chief dispatched General Eisenhower to kick some urgency into the American contingent. Ike packed his bags and brought along Wayne Clark, whom Marshall was sending to build a training infrastructure in England. On May 23, Ike and Clark drove to Bolling Field, kissed their wives good-bye, and boarded their plane for the first of many visits as Marshall's emissaries.[11]

After a long flight to Prestwick, Scotland, and a train ride to London through the obligatory rain, the two major generals commenced several grueling days of dawn-to-dusk conferences with their American and British counterparts. The meetings brought Ike into contact with many players in the transatlantic drama, including General Sir Alan Brooke, Marshall's opposite number in the Imperial General Staff, and the dashing Lord Louis Mountbatten. As he got to know his allies, Ike found the Britons warm, pleasant, and helpful—with two exceptions.[12]

Alan Brooke, nicknamed "Colonel Shrapnel" by those unfortunate enough to work for him, had a temper that easily matched Marshall's. The staccato-voiced Briton with the long, drooping face felt his sense of duty to country every bit as deeply as did Marshall, though added to his regular duties was the Herculean burden of reconciling Churchill's grand schemes with the art of the possible.[13]

But while Brooke had to bite his tongue with Churchill more or less stoically, he reserved a quiet, patronizing contempt for his Yankee cousins. He had a great deal of respect for the German foe, and he saw in the Americans an inexperienced, reckless bunch of newcomers whose ideas, if not checked by a veteran hand, would bring disaster to the Allied cause.

Ike tried his best to warm up the Imperial General Staff chief, but Brooke's furrowed brow and persistent look of displeasure, magnified by horn-rimmed glasses and an abrupt manner, stymied even Ike's considerable charm. Throughout the war Brooke would look upon Eisenhower as a well-meaning chap who was patently unfit to hold high military command. Eisenhower, for his part, found Brooke too wedded to the Great War approach—a view that, he felt, afflicted too many of those generals fortunate enough to have served in the First World War.[14]

Another meeting on Ike's agenda was with a short, wiry lieutenant general named Bernard Law Montgomery, commander of a British Army training center in southeastern England. Ike and Clark drove to Sussex, where "Monty" and his staff were giving a lecture to an assembled group of American officers on lessons learned from fighting the Germans. It was in Sussex where Ike got a taste of the Englishman's "house rules."[15]

Montgomery opened the meeting by remarking, "I have been directed to take time from my busy life to brief you gentlemen." He launched into a rather patronizing lecture, and after some minutes, Clark remembered, "Ike quietly fished around in his pocket, and pulled out a pack of cigarettes." Before Ike could get three puffs into his smoke, Montgomery, his dachshund-like nose wrinkling, halted the briefing and demanded, "Who is smoking?"

Ike looked up. "I am, sir."

"Stop it," Montgomery snapped. "I don't permit it."

Ike, his bald pate reddening, grinned sheepishly at Clark, looked down, and obediently stubbed out the offending cigarette.[16]

On the ride back to the hotel, Ike's driver overheard the words "Montgomery" and "son-of-a-bitch" billowing from the backseat in a harsh American dialect. As the driver later recalled, Ike was "furious—really steaming mad. And he was still mad. It was my first exposure to the Eisenhower temper. His face was flaming red, and the veins in his forehead looked like worms."[17]

By the time the car rolled up to the hotel, Ike's prodigious temper had simmered. He had done what he came to do; he had listened to Montgomery's lecture, and that was all that was required of him. With any luck, he and the condescending Briton would never cross paths again.

* * *

Returning to Washington in early June, Ike drafted a report to Marshall about the state of U.S. preparations in England. The central point of his draft report was that American officers in London, lacking both leadership and a sense of urgency, were wasting valuable time. Soon afterward, Marshall called Ike into his office to discuss the Washington side of the operations. The forbidding Chief looked at his lieutenant and asked him in his monotone, "In your opinion, are the plans as nearly complete as we can make them?"[18]

"Yes, sir," said Ike.

"That's lucky, because you're the man who is going to carry them out."[19]

It was one of those ironic moments General Marshall—a man whose sense of humor was as dry as a the desert—loved to construct for his favored soldiers. With no fanfare, no ceremony, just a seemingly offhand comment, he had propelled Dwight D. Eisenhower into the highest American command in Europe. Whatever happened in England, Ike would be at the center.

Ike went home that night giddy and nearly speechless. The best he could muster for his diary that night was the simple note, *The chief of staff says I'm the guy.*"[20]

While Eisenhower was organizing the American buildup in Europe, his friend George Patton was fighting for his ticket to the battlefield. As he scurried about the desert by scout car, jeep (or "peep," as he called it), and light observation plane, Patton kept his Indio, California, desert training center running smoothly under the scorching summer sun. His personal staff now included youthful aide Captain Richard N. Jenson from southern California, and Sergeant Alexander Stiller, a stoic, heavily armed Texan who, one aide remarked, "looks as if he were made of solid hickory."[21]

George's reputation as a training commander grew, which was important to men like Generals Marshall and McNair. But so did his itch to get into an overseas combat command. In the early summer of '42 he heard rumors that "Eisenhower and Clark will have the big jobs" in Europe, and George figured Ike's patronage couldn't hurt his chances at being the first general to hit the beaches—wherever those beaches might be.[22]

The Patton-Eisenhower friendship bore fruit that June, when the British bastion of Tobruk in eastern Libya fell to General Erwin Rommel's

Panzerarmee Afrika. The loss of Tobruk was a disaster of the first magnitude, for the collapse of Tobruk's defenses left much of North Africa open to German conquest. Roosevelt asked Marshall to do what he could to help the British, and Marshall asked Ike for his recommendation on the best man to lead a one-division expeditionary force. Without missing a beat, Ike replied, "Patton."[23]

Marshall doubted Patton would take the job, as it would involve a demotion to division commander. But Ike knew his old friend. He asked the Chief for permission to take the offer directly to Patton, and Marshall nodded.[24]

"When can we start?" thundered George into the telephone when Ike broached the subject. "To get an outfit destined for immediate battle I'd sell my soul!"

Ike explained that someone would get back with him once a specific plan was in place. But until then, George needed to be ready to fly to Washington at a moment's notice.[25]

Over the next few weeks, George and Ike caught up with each other, dashing off quick notes when the crush of work permitted. Ike, resigned to his staff position, told George he didn't see much chance of getting into a combat outfit. Reflecting on the way their paths had diverged since their Camp Meade days, he ruefully commented, *"You see what's happened to our dream team of twenty years ago, of going to war as a team. I'm slated to stick here to do a lot of heavy planning and operating on a global scale, but I wish you all the luck in the world."*

George, always the optimist, reassured his friend, *"Ike, don't give up. The basic truth of war is that the unexpected always happens. It will be a long war. We'll get together yet."*[26]

On June 21, General Marshall summoned Patton to Washington. George hopped the next plane to the capital, and the next day he found himself sitting quietly in Marshall's office while the Chief succinctly outlined the situation. The British were on the ropes, he said. From his perch in Libya, Rommel threatened the Suez Canal, and with it, the Empire's lifeline to the Far East. President Roosevelt wanted something done to help the British, but the U.S. Army could spare only one reinforced armored division, about 18,000 men. If it did, that division would be commanded by Patton. Marshall quietly sent the old cavalryman to the nearby War College to assemble maps and make preliminary plans.[27]

Turning the picture over in his mind, George concluded that the old man had it all wrong. The advantage of armor, of course, was its mobility. But one division—four armored regiments, or "combat commands"—would not be enough. With a second division, he could envelop the enemy with far greater destructive power. Do what the Carthaginians had done to the Romans at Cannae. Smash, not merely blunt. So the next day, he sent word to Marshall's office that two divisions, not one, would be required for his operation.

When Marshall's aides passed along the message, the Chief erupted. Patton had a hell of a lot of nerve asking him to double his command to a two-division corps. The precise General Marshall had specified that Patton could have ONE division, because MORE THAN ONE division would take away forces needed for other, BIGGER plans. Plans in theaters Patton knew nothing about.

"Localitis," as Marshall called it, was exactly the sort of thing he wouldn't stand for from Patton or any other man, and he decided to set Patton straight in a way he wouldn't forget. He grunted to his aides, "Send him back to Indio."

Marshall's aides politely escorted General Patton to the airport that day.[28]

George boarded the plane for California, chilled and mortified. He had just offended the Chief of Staff by presuming to change the Army's basic plans. Who knew where that would leave him? Had he just consigned himself to training duty, stateside, for the rest of the war?

As the plane bumped its way across the continent, a desperate feeling spread across George's chest. He had spent a lifetime getting to where he was—or rather, where he had been yesterday—and he had just tossed away his best, perhaps only chance at getting in on the ground floor of the greatest war in history.

Maybe it was a misunderstanding, he thought. Maybe Marshall didn't get the message right. Maybe he didn't realize it was only a *suggestion*, not a *demand*. But George knew he had to do something quickly, before Marshall's icy judgment became a professional death sentence.[29]

When he arrived back in California, he frantically telephoned Marshall's office to make amends. Marshall's secretary told him the Chief was in conference. Days ticked by, and repeated calls to Marshall went unreturned.

George was aghast. Dejected. Dumfounded. Marshall would never again trust him with a combat command. It was stupid George again—the same boy who had such a beastly time learning in school. The same George who blew it because he was "too damed military." *That* George Patton had blown it for the other George Patton, the Patton who could have been the war's greatest battlefield general.

Had he known the truth, he wouldn't have lost much sleep. True, Marshall didn't cotton to demands from subordinates. And George's appointment had rankled several War Department staffers, who disliked Patton's eccentric showmanship and his unpredictability.

But the real reason Marshall didn't use him was because the mission was infeasible. As Marshall was meeting with Patton, the War Department's planners were concluding that any U.S. assistance would not be ready until October or November at the earliest, far too late to do the British any good. The only thing Marshall could offer Churchill at the moment was a shipment of three hundred tanks and some artillery pieces, which a grateful Churchill accepted. Marshall decided to shelve the Patton mission.[30]

Marshall did not see any reason to enlighten Patton about the Department's reasons for canceling the mission, at least not yet. He knew George was an oddball fighter whose towering strengths were mitigated by exasperating weaknesses. He also knew Patton was a good soldier who sometimes needed a strong reminder of who was boss. So Marshall refused to take George's calls for several days while George stewed in his own profane juices. As Marshall wryly told his deputy chief of staff, Lieutenant General Joseph T. McNarney, "That's the way to handle Patton."[31]

After several days squirming in purgatory, Marshall let Patton off the hook. Brigadier General Floyd Parks wrote to assure Patton that he had not offended the Chief. George, heaving a sigh of relief, replied, "I was very glad to get your letter and find that I had not completely destroyed my opportunities. If the question ever comes up, you can tell all and sundry that I am willing to take anything to any place at any time regardless of the consequences."[32]

On July 11, General Devers, Patton's Armored Force boss, reiterated the message, informing Patton that the War Department was thinking of moving an armored corps overseas in September or October. Would he be willing to go?

To George, that was not much of a question. Overjoyed, he shot back: "Until getting your letter I had heard nothing of an armored corps going over seas. I appreciate you in selecting me. THANKS. I WON'T LET YOU DOWN."[33]

With this brush with disaster, George had finally learned his lesson. He would walk the straight and narrow. He would follow orders and keep his mouth shut. He would never again cause problems for the high command. Ever.

"The Chief of Staff says I'm the guy."

Eisenhower considered the duties of "The Guy"—or more formally, Commanding General, European Theater of Operations, United States Army (ETOUSA)—as he stared at a mountain of fresh responsibilities. He had to set up a new headquarters. He had to build an invading army from scratch. He had to plan three possible invasions, all of them amphibious and all of them tremendously complex. He had to integrate an American military staff with a British military staff, and he had to do it all to the exacting requirements of General Marshall, who would answer to Secretary Stimson and President Roosevelt for Eisenhower's performance.[34]

The title "commanding general" had an impressive ring, but Ike was painfully aware of the narrow confines within which "The Guy" would have to operate. A supreme commander, Ike quickly learned, was rarely supreme, at least in a coalition environment. As he wrote to his diary, *"In a war such as this, where high command invariably involves a Pres., a Prime Minister, 6 Chiefs of Staff and a horde of lesser 'planners' there has got to be a lot of patience—no one person can be a Napoleon or a Caesar!"*[35]

Ike knew he would need help, and lots of it, to handle the mounting stress of his immense jobs, and he knew this help would have to come from someplace other than a cigarette pack or an officers' club bar. Ike would need some personal companionship, and he asked Admiral King if the Navy could spare a "naval aide" for him. The man he had in mind for the job was Lieutenant Commander Harry C. Butcher, a longtime golfing buddy from CBS who had returned from the Naval Reserve to active duty. Commander Butcher, Ike explained, would be his "naval aide."

A slightly puzzled Admiral King gave his assent—it never hurt to place a Navy man in Army headquarters—and Ike gave the tall, affable "Butch" his new naval assignment, which, fortunately for Butch, had nothing to do with the Navy. Butcher's real job would be to drag Ike to a field to whack golf balls, toss a baseball with him, get him to sketch or paint (which, often as not, pushed Ike's blood pressure up), and organize long, unwinding bridge sessions with aides, deputies, Red Cross girls—anyone who could keep Ike's mind from going dull with overwork and despair.

Butcher was to provide Ike the companionship and good humor he desperately needed. As Ike wrote to his brother Milton, *"It is a rather lonely life I lead; every move I make is under someone's observation and, as a result, a sense of strain develops. . . . At home, a man has his family to go to. Here there is no one except a fine friend like Butch. . . ."* As he told several friends, *"There are days when I just want to curl up in a corner like a sick dog, but Butch won't let me. That's why I need him. To keep me from going crazy."*[36]

A second man Ike tapped for his inner circle was Colonel Thomas Jefferson Davis, an old friend from the dark days working for MacArthur in Manila. The mild-mannered South Carolinian, whom Butch described as "roly-poly, with bright, flashing brown eyes," blended Old South gentility with a quiet efficiency. T.J. would become Ike's adjutant general, the man who kept track of personnel, rode herd on the headquarters staff, and issued orders in the name of the commander. As in Manila, T.J. was a tonic in rough times, as well as a good public relations man to have in a pinch.[37]

Then there was Ike's office aide, the tall, bespectacled Captain Ernest R. "Tex" Lee. Tex's job was to ensure Ike's memoranda, correspondence, orders, and filing flowed smoothly in and out of ETO headquarters. Gifted with a booming voice and a good sense of fun, Tex rode a magic carpet of paperwork that made sure, somehow, that everyone knew what they were supposed to be doing. Like Harry Butcher, however, Tex's value was more than the sum of his duties. Though his obsession with paperwork would annoy Ike to no end, Tex was a regular face at Ike's bridge and dinner tables, and he became another of those personal friends on whom Ike would lean for support and energy during the trying times ahead.[38]

Taking Wayne Clark, who would train a corps in England, plus Tex Lee, Butch, and his orderly Mickey McKeogh, a former New York bellhop, Ike boarded a Pan Am Stratoliner on June 23 and left Bolling Field a second time for England. Mamie and Maurine Clark came to see their husbands off, and as they prepared to mount the plane's steps, Ike assured Renie Clark, "Don't worry about Wayne, I'll take good care of him." The wives watched the plane take off, then milled back to their cars. Ike and his men were on their own.[39]

The Combined Chiefs of Staff, the august body to whom Ike now reported, consisted of some of the most strong-willed, ruthless, calculating men the two nations had produced. On the British side, they included General Brooke; Admiral Sir Dudley Pound, Britain's First Sea Lord; and Air Chief

Marshal Sir Charles Portal. Their American counterparts included General Marshall, Admiral King, and Lieutenant General Henry "Hap" Arnold of the Army Air Force, all members of the nascent U.S. Joint Chiefs of Staff. In addition, both Roosevelt and Churchill had their personal representatives on the Combined Chiefs, Admiral William D. Leahy for Roosevelt, and Marshal Sir John Dill, a former Chief of the Imperial General Staff, for Churchill. Their job was to set grand strategy for the China, Pacific, Mediterranean, and European theaters. As Ike would later put it, satisfying this headstrong group was like "trying to arrange the blankets smoothly over several prima donnas in the same bed."[40]

Beyond his immediate bosses—Marshall, the Joint Chiefs, and the Combined Chiefs—Ike also had to arrange the blankets over the heads of state. Roosevelt was far too removed to see Ike regularly, and didn't meddle in operational matters much anyway, so Ike had little direct contact with him. But Ike's London residence placed him squarely within the orbit of the exasperating, brilliant, pugnacious, eccentric dynamo Winston Churchill, a man to whom meddling was second nature.

The most obvious difference between Eisenhower and Churchill, both military leaders, was their respective rank. Ike, a mere major general, held a tightly circumscribed field of authority. The Pacific was off-limits. Politics was off-limits. Industrial output was off-limits. Eisenhower was an executor, and his job was to organize whatever units and equipment the Allied governments gave him and carry out whatever operations the Combined Chiefs directed. Churchill, by contrast, had no such constraints, and he was not the sort of man to impose any upon himself. He was a politician, a head of government, and his own Minister of Defense. His authority was coextensive with the power of the Empire, and he thoroughly relished wielding it.

Throughout the war, Ike would see the many contradictory sides of Churchill: a bully, joker, historian, warrior, charmer, philosopher, storyteller, egomaniac, and political strategist of the highest order. He was a romantic whose allegiance, above all else, was to the British Empire, and this was what Ike would have to guard against.

Working with Churchill, the Combined Chiefs, Marshall, the ETO staff, and the field commanders would have exhausted a young man. But for a man of fifty-two, Ike's job was nearly lethal. The stress of conferences, requests, memoranda, personnel problems, inspection tours, press demands, social invitations, and decision making took a heavy toll on Ike's strong Kansas constitution. His front parlor and bedroom at London's stately Dorchester Hotel became office annexes, so he rarely escaped the press of business. Exhaustion began to set in.

The punishment Ike's body withstood from his hard-riding schedule was aggravated by his notoriously poor diet. Ike's lunch would frequently consist of nothing more than peanuts, or raisins, washed down with coffee or tea with milk. He increased his cigarette intake to four packs a day, which gave his doctors fits and irritated his uncomplaining orderly Mickey, who had to clean up the ashes Ike blithely tapped onto the carpet or tossed into the fireplaces, real or false, that ornamented his suites.[41]

The converging pressures of work, homesickness, and incessant meetings left Ike with chronic insomnia, bursitis, and an exceedingly bad temper. "The wrinkles deepened in his face," his driver later wrote. "He showed increasing signs of impatience and nervousness." ETO deputy chief of staff, Colonel Al Gruenther, who had last seen Eisenhower at the Louisiana maneuvers, was shocked at his old friend's appearance when he arrived in England; Ike looked as though he had aged ten years during that ten-month interval. He was no longer the smiling, vibrant Ike Eisenhower of 1941. He looked careworn; he showed signs of exhaustion. He needed help.[42]

In July Ike's spirits received a lift when he learned the Senate had confirmed his promotion to temporary lieutenant general. Soon afterward, he received a congratulatory letter from one Major General George S. Patton Jr., addressed to "Lieutenant General Eisenhower." George told Ike, without a hint of professional jealousy, *"We know each other so well that I guess you know with out my saying it how truly delighted I am at your success and how earnestly I wish you all good fortune for the future."*[43]

Ike, glad to hear from his old friend, wrote back:

Dear George:

If I were not perfectly sure that you were merely indulging your perverted sense of humor in addressing me as "Lieutenant General" I would tear up your damn letter and never answer it. As you well know, there is no one else whose good wishes mean more to me than do yours. It does look like for the past eight or nine months I have been riding the crest of a huge wave of luck—I hope it will hold together at least until we get this war won. . . .

He continued to stoke their mutual hopes:

> *It is entirely within the realm of possibility that I will need you sorely: and when that time comes I will have a battle with my diffidence over requesting the services of a man so much senior and so much more able than myself. As I have often told you, you are my idea of a battle commander, and if the fates decree that battles by big formation are to come either wholly or partially within my sphere of influence, I would certainly want you as the lead horse in the team. . . . I truly thank you for your thoughtfulness in sending me congratulations. I particularly appreciated it because you and I both know that you should have been wearing additional stars long ago.*[44]

That summer, Ike acquired a chauffeur named Kay Summersby, a woman who had driven Ike on his first trip to London. Born in Ireland's County Cork to a wealthy family, Kay worked as a model in London in 1938 and won some bit parts in films before driving ambulances during the London Blitz. Tall and attractive, she naturally stood out in drab army circles. A Red Cross worker who knew her described Kay's eyes as "rather heavily lidded, they appeared sexy . . . they were slate blue and could blaze with scorn and anger befitting her Irish ancestry." Having married a British Army officer who was serving in India, she carried on an affair with a U.S. Army officer prior to Ike's assignment to England.[45]

Courageous but somewhat cliquish, Kay joked that she was qualified to do little else besides ride a horse and pour tea properly. But as a veteran ambulance driver during the London Blitz, she knew her way around the city better than any other driver in the Motor Transport Corps pool. Ike and Kay instantly took to each other, and before long "Skib"—the staff's nickname for the girl from Skibbereen—became a close, integral part of Ike's Army family.[46]

It didn't take long for rumors of an affair between Ike and his chauffeuse to make the rounds at ETO headquarters, and from London those stories naturally worked their way through the wider Army grapevine. But for now, the pleasant company of Mrs. Summersby provided Ike with a measure of relief from the grim faces that permeated wartime London. Throughout the war, Ike valued her skills as a driver above every other member of the staff motor pool. With Kay, Butch, Mickey, Tex, and several other friendly faces among his subordinates, Ike's life would be as bearable as his wartime duties would allow.[47]

Despite the obstacles to a cross-Channel invasion, Marshall, Ike, and Admiral King clung to the belief that if action had to be taken in 1942, SLEDGEHAMMER, an invasion of northern France, would provide the greatest succor to the hard-pressed Soviet Union. For 1943 the chief goal, the Americans agreed, was to get into France and over the Rhine as quickly as possible, bypassing Africa, the Balkans, or any other scenic detours along the periphery that Churchill and his generals seemed enamored with. Marshall feared the Mediterranean would become a bottomless pit, one that would swallow up so many men and machines that an invasion of France would not be feasible in 1943. For this reason he vehemently opposed the GYMNAST landing in North Africa. Eisenhower wholeheartedly backed Marshall's conclusion, and in mid-July he wrote in his diary, "GYMNAST is strategically unsound as an operation."[48]

But it was Roosevelt, not Marshall, King, or Eisenhower, who was calling the shots, and Churchill had persuaded Roosevelt to throw his support to the North African landings. The American generals flew to London to wage a rearguard action to salvage an early cross-Channel attack. But given Roosevelt's insistence on a major operation in 1942, GYMNAST appeared to be the only feasible project, and they had little logic to support any other plan. After two days of heated arguments with their counterparts, the Americans surrendered. Marshall and Ike had lost, at least until 1943.[49]

Before Marshall and King left England, however, the British threw them a bone. Two bones, actually. First, in return for American acquiescence to GYMNAST in 1942, the British tentatively agreed to ROUNDUP in 1943. Second, they agreed to an American commander for both operations.[50]

At the conclusion of the London meetings, Marshall summoned Ike to his elegant suite at Claridge's Hotel to discuss one important detail. When Ike arrived, the august chief of staff was reclining in his bathtub, and through the lavatory door the two commanders nonchalantly discussed high-level strategy. One item splashed around by the soaking general was of particular interest to Ike; Eisenhower, the Chief said, would be the deputy Allied commander for planning GYMNAST, now renamed TORCH. Moreover, Marshall said, he and King would push for him to command the entire invasion of North Africa.[51]

With that inauspicious announcement, TORCH took center stage in Ike's life.

* * *

From his crowded desk, Ike stared at a tremendous problem. He had just been ordered to merge two large, bureaucratic armies to fight a long war, a struggle that would embroil him in at least two amphibious invasions, perhaps more. He couldn't know how many mountains he would have to climb to complete his mission, or how many young men would die fighting under his command. But he did know there would be a lot more graves if he lost his nerve or made a mistake.

History, to which Fox Conner had taught him to look for guidance, offered little help to a man welding a modern coalition army. Page after disheartening page filled Conner's history books with legends of bickering allies: Spartans and Athenians, Orthodox and Latins, Prussians and Austrians, to name but a few. During the Napoleonic wars, coalition troops were either swallowed up by a dominant army—as when German, Italian, and Spanish divisions served in Napoleon's *Grande Armée*—or simply collaborated on a battle or two, as with the Prussian march to the guns at Waterloo. In World War I, the closest analogy to which Ike could look, "Black Jack" Pershing famously kept his American forces out of the European framework, but this approach wouldn't work against a skilled, well-integrated enemy.

So Ike was on his own.

On top of his bewildering organizational problems, there was the nagging sore of Anglo-American distrust. From the chauvinistic British standpoint, the apple-green Americans were a bumbling militia of loudmouthed, overfed citizen soldiers, while Britain's veterans had been fighting the Germans for nearly three years on the Continent, in North Africa, and in the Middle East. From the chauvinistic American standpoint, the British had been beaten on the Continent, in North Africa, and in the Middle East; thus, for all their practical experience, they had little to teach the Americans except how to lose. The U.S. Army had done things its own peculiar way since 1775, and the British Army had been doing it far longer. As Ike later recalled, the two groups "came together like a bulldog and cat."[52]

As with other thorny problems, like censorship and race relations, Ike felt the best way to sort out the problem was to drag it into sunlight and address it plainly with his colleagues. In the case of nationalistic prejudices, this meant preaching—and practicing—the gospel of Allied unity. He staffed his headquarters with American deputies to British section heads, and vice versa. He demanded, and received, complete cooperation from his officers, at least as far as he could police them. Americans who insulted their

British counterparts were promptly sent home "on an unescorted boat," as Ike liked to put it. He had little direct control over his British subordinates, however, so he depended largely on the British to keep their own nationalism in check.[53]

Ike knew his Swiss-like neutrality would inflame a lot of hard-nosed Britons and Americans. American officers in particular began grumbling that Eisenhower bent over backward to favor the British. Ike even struggled to make Wayne Clark, his best friend in England, toe the line. But he ignored whatever criticism might fly his way. He surrounded himself with a cadre of men and women who were able to see past their prejudices and think of themselves as members of a unique, multinational team. There would always be the Clarks and Brookes who could see only their country's military reputations, he knew, but there would also be the Mountbattens and the Eisenhowers, and their persistent voices would grow louder in the Allied councils of war.[54]

Ike spent the early part of August assembling his senior staff for TORCH. His planning group, known as Allied Forces Headquarters (AFHQ), was a fairly even mix of British and American officers covering the air, land, and naval services, and the group set up shop at Norfolk House, a large office building in London's St. James's Square. But to keep an eye on the details as he managed the big and medium pictures, he needed a right-hand man, a motivator whose planning abilities he trusted. Casting his eye north, to the Army's English training center, Ike asked its commander, Wayne Clark, to serve as his deputy commander.[55]

Ike's old friend accepted, albeit with a good deal of reluctance. Clark was currently commanding the II Corps, a fighting outfit, and the ambitious general had little interest in the ill-defined job of second fiddle on a bloated, half-British staff. But Clark also knew that an outstanding job in TORCH would put him in the running for combat command in the next big invasion, so he accepted Eisenhower's offer, making sure Ike fully appreciated the sacrifice he was making.[56]

Clark proved a godsend to Eisenhower. He deftly handled overwhelming but vital details such as shipping schedules, ammunition stockpiles, assembly logistics, and a myriad of other problems that he neatly summarized for Ike each day. But even with Clark's help, Ike's life became one long, blurred trail of conferences, telephone calls, paperwork, more calls, and more conferences. He put in twelve-hour shifts at Norfolk House, shuttling from one meeting to the next, handing out assignments and coordinating details with a host of headstrong commanders. He smoked a lot, ate little, and had precious little time to sleep. He held conferences in his private suite at the Dorchester Hotel. When he did get a moment to relax—usually when spirited away from London by an insistent Harry Butcher—he found he could not sleep more than five hours before his brain began spinning again, winding itself like a mainspring for the next day's problems.[57]

His eyes drooped, his wrinkles deepened, his temper shortened. But through his baptism of paper, Ike learned to make quick decisions and erase bottlenecks, to know when to delegate and when to demand the impossible— or accept an obstacle and move on. With his overarching guidance, AFHQ ran as efficiently as a combat brigade under fire.

The TORCH plan, so far as any of his planners understood it, was an aggressive one, and it turned on the central assumption that control of Northwest Africa belonged to the side that controlled its ports. These coastal jewels, all held by Vichy French forces, ran from Morocco, on the Atlantic Ocean, to Tunisia's Gulf of Gabès.

Initial Allied plans called for assaults against the Moroccan port of Casablanca, the Algerian port of Oran, and the Algerian capital of Algiers. Secondary ports, such as Bône and Philippeville, might also be included in the first wave, depending on available landing craft. Once the seaports were in Allied hands, supplies of ammunition, fuel, and food could sustain the drive east as the invaders rushed toward Tunisia.[58]

Victory in Tunisia would clinch the African campaign; trapped between the Allied army in Tunisia and the British Eighth Army under Montgomery in Libya, Rommel would be compelled to evacuate the continent. Or capitulate. At least, that was what Ike's planners hoped.[59]

The plan left two major Tunisian ports, Bizerte and Tunis, under Axis guns. That worried Eisenhower, for it would not take long for Hitler to send heavy reinforcements into Africa through those ports. Unfortunately for the Allies, Italo-German air cover from Sicily and Sardinia ruled out amphibious landings east of Algeria. The Allies, therefore, would have to take Algeria, race overland through Tunisia—Rommel's back door—and capture the thinly screened ports before the Nazis could fortify them.

At the end of July, Ike sent Marshall a list of candidates to command the American TORCH forces, and he included Omar Bradley and George Patton among his four top choices. Ike wanted men he trusted leading his first divisions into combat. As he told an old football teammate, "[I have] developed almost an obsession as to the certainty by which you can judge a division, or any other large unit, merely by knowing its commander intimately." He believed any outfit led by Brad or George would perform well under fire if given a chance.[60]

But until the shooting started, Ike could only guess whether George, Brad, or any of the others would pass the test. It was another of many, many things Ike would have to wait to find out.

While Ike was welding two creaky frameworks into a single Allied force, George Patton was girding for battle. Summoned to Washington on July 30, he learned that the grapevine was on target: He would lead the Western Task Force in Operation TORCH under Ike's command. The Patton-Eisenhower team that had dreamed of fighting a big, pitched war was finally going to have its chance on the battlefield.[61]

As he considered his mission, George knew his force would grow to huge proportions, and like Ike, he picked his senior headquarters staff from men he had known before the war. First among equals was his chief of staff, Colonel Hobart R. "Hap" Gay, a jocular cavalryman whose prejudices and style mirrored Patton's own. Gay, a plain, bald man who looked more like a small-town church deacon than a corps commander, was appalled to learn he would be working for the hotheaded George Patton, and when he heard the news he frantically tried to attach himself to another boss. But after recovering from the shock of being shanghaied onto George's staff, Hap grew to admire the old general, and he would serve George faithfully until the end of Patton's days.[62]

As head whip cracker, Gay would provide direction to a core group that included Lieutenant Colonel Paul Harkins, Gay's assistant chief of staff; Colonel Percy Black, Patton's G-2 intelligence officer; Colonel Kent Lambert, his G-3 operations officer; and his resourceful G-4 logistician, Colonel Walter "Maud" Muller. In addition to his deputy, Major General Geoffrey Keyes, and his fine corps staff, George ran a personal staff that included his driver, Sergeant John Mims; his orderly, a Buffalo Soldier from Alabama named George Meeks; and his aides, Captain Dick Jenson and Lieutenant Alex Stiller.[63]

In early August, Patton received orders to report to his new commander in London, Lieutenant General Dwight D. Eisenhower. He caught the next Stratoliner and arrived in London on the sixth of August. Checking into Claridge's that evening, he spent the next day working on his part of TORCH, then rang up his old friend.[64]

"George, oh, boy, am I glad to hear your voice!" came Ike's booming reply over the phone. "Come right over and have some godawful dehydrated chicken soup with me!"[65]

George came straightaway, storming into Ike's office for a warm reunion over a bowl of soup that was exactly as Ike had advertised. The two men jawed from dinnertime into the early morning hours, musing on their chances of victory, agreeing on personnel assignments, and discussing potential flaws in the draft plan.

Looking at it from every angle, the two men agreed the mission did not seem promising. "Ike said he would be goddamned glad if someone would give him some good news, as every step in the planning process disclosed obstacles," Butcher wrote. Ike and George felt the Allies would have a better shot by cutting out the Casablanca landings and putting George down at Oran, leaving Algiers to the British, and George scribbled in his diary, *"Had supper with Ike and talked until 1:00 a.m. We both feel the operation is bad and is mostly political. However, we are told to do it and intend to succeed or die in the attempt. If the worst occurs, it is an impossible show, but with a little luck, it can be done at a high price; and it might be a cinch."*[66]

Although no one mentioned it at the time, it had worked out just as George had predicted. Ike was commanding wings of the Allied army, like a latter-day Robert E. Lee, and George was donning the calfskin gloves of Stonewall Jackson. A benign fate had thrust upon them roles tailored to their personalities, roles each had dreamed of playing since the end of the Great War. They would make a hell of a team.

A happy and energized George Patton scurried about London reviewing maps, reports, and studies of his future battlefield. He remained focused on the daunting obstacles ahead, though in his long talks with Ike, he vaguely detected what he thought were subtle changes in his longtime friend. Ike didn't quite seem to be the same old single-minded radical of their Camp Meade days; he was *"not as rugged mentally as I thought,"* George mused to his diary. *"He vacillates and is not a realist."* George commented, as if to reassure himself, *"It is very noticeable that most of the American officers here are pro-British, even Ike. . . . I am not, repeat not, Pro-British."*[67]

Their friendship, an affinity in which George had played the role of mentor for so long, was also not as rugged as Patton had thought, for it had been supplanted by a commander-subordinate relationship, which is a very different thing indeed. Sitting around the Dorchester eating soup, smoking, cursing, and plotting, the two men were still close friends. But each understood that the distance imposed by the military command chain placed invisible limits upon their intimacy. For a man in Eisenhower's position, as Butch observed, "Although friendship has a place, this is cast aside for merit and ability to get things done." Listening to Ike give directions—orders—rather than suggestions or requests, George began seeing his new boss through the jaded eye of a veteran subordinate, rather than the forgiving eyes of an unconditional friend.[68]

George's doubts sharpened when Ike brought General Clark aboard as Deputy Supreme Commander. Though he had known Wayne since he was a boy—Wayne had lived at Fort Sheridan, Lieutenant Patton's first post, when Clark's father was a major there—George neither trusted nor liked the young general, whose rise was far too rapid, and who seemed a bit slick for George's comfort.

George's private concerns growing over the junior half of the "Sacred Family," as he dubbed the Eisenhower-Clark team, grew stronger the more of Clark he saw. As he told his diary, *"I had a drink with Clark at his flat. I do not trust him yet but he improves on acquaintance. Ike is getting megalomania."* A month later, George decided that Clark did not improve on acquaintance after all. He groused, *"[Clark] seems to me more preoccupied with bettering his own future than in winning the war."*[69]

Ike had fewer reservations about George. He felt George brought a bolt of needed energy into the campaign, and he knew from his long history with the cavalryman that he could be trusted to execute his mission professionally, obediently, and perhaps even fanatically. Ike reported to Marshall that his friend had rapidly digested the essential problems of the TORCH plan, and worked with AFHQ staff in a "very businesslike, sane but enthusiastic" manner.[70]

On the seventeenth of August, T. J. Davis arranged a whimsical dinner to commemorate a 1933 meeting between Ike, George, and J. Walter Christie, the designer of a revolutionary tank suspension and well-known hater of most Army officers—Ike and George being two rare exceptions. Over dinner, drinks, and an evening of smoking, joking, and reminiscing about their sports days, the two generals and their aides talked until late in the night, bringing a badly needed glow of warmth into Ike's pressurized life.

Butcher reflected on the charming, quixotic friend Ike had brought into the war's equation: "Patton is a rugged man. Don't doubt his statement made some days ago that he can mesmerize troops into a high state of morale. His language is salty, to the point, and colorful. His swear words are frequent and expressive. No wonder Ike's so pleased to have him."[71]

In September, after extensive and contradictory instructions throughout the summer, the Combined Chiefs reconciled conflicting views of American and British planners by recommending a three-pronged attack.

The undertaking, as the Chiefs laid it out, would be one of the most complex in military history, prescribing three large landing operations, each of which required the capture of several subsidiary objectives. General Patton's Western Task Force would sail from the United States with 58,000 men, of whom 35,000 would take part in the initial assault. Patton's immediate objective would be Casablanca, and from there he would subdue French Morocco, safeguarding the Allied supply pipeline. Major General Lloyd Fredendall would command the Center Task Force. This force would sail from Scotland and land 25,000 U.S. troops at Oran, to be followed by another 20,000 in subsequent waves. From Oran the soldiers would seize control of the Tafaraoui Airfield, which would allow Wildcat and Spitfire fighters to cover the skies above Algeria. Finally, Major General Charles "Doc" Ryder, one of Ike's classmates, would nominally command 33,000 mostly British troops for the assault on Algiers. An American was designated the task force commander, as Allied experts believed the Stars and Stripes would receive a better welcome from the Vichy defenders than the Union Jack.[72]

The final directive gave Ike a definable cluster of targets, which meant his staffers could stop chasing their tails with contingency plans for Philippeville, Bône, and other possible landing sites that had been bandied about for the past month. An encouraged Ike wrote to George,

> [Y]ou can well imagine that my feelings at the moment are merely those of great relief that a final decision and definite plans now seem assured. The past six weeks have been the most trying of my life; had it not been for the fact that I had in this thing, as my two principal mainstays, you and Clark, I can not imagine what I would have done.

But thinking of the dangers facing Patton's men in the treacherous waters off Morocco, he added, *"I am searching the Army to find the most capable Chaplain we have in an effort to assure a fairly decent break in the weather when the big day comes!"*[73]

George frowned as he considered the plan from the relative seclusion of the Munitions Building. He was dubious about an operation stitched together by a patchwork quilt of Anglo-American committees, staffers, and—most horribly of all—civilian advisers. But he, like Eisenhower, had set aside his pessimism, for the lumbering enterprise had passed beyond the time to object and complain. He fired off a personal letter to Ike, reporting on a visit to Mamie and Mrs. Butcher, assuring his friend, *"It is quite useless for me to express my sincere appreciation for all you have done for me. The only way I can and will repay you is with assurance that the job you have given me will be accomplished."*[74]

This last drew a quick reply from Ike, who told him,

> *I feel like the lady in the circus that has to ride three horses with no very good idea of exactly where any one of the three is going to go. However, there is one mighty fine feature of this whole business and that is that you are on that end of it.*

Ike also admitted to the strain he was feeling:

> *I think both Wayne and I are standing up pretty well under the load, although this morning I am in somewhat of an irritable mood because last night, when I hit the bed, I started thinking about some of these things all over again and at two-thirty I was still thinking. I suspect that I am just a bit on the weak-minded side when I allow myself to do that, but any way it doesn't happen often. We are keeping our tails over the dashboard and looking forward to meeting you one of these bright fall days.*[75]

George, master of one of Ike's three circus horses, had precious little time to figure out how to crack Casablanca. He knew the invasion would take place on November 7 or 8—the first moonless nights after the invasion force could be trained, loaded, and transported to Africa. If everything worked smoothly, the Navy would pick his men up from Hampton Roads, Virginia, during the third week in October, carry them across the submarine-infested

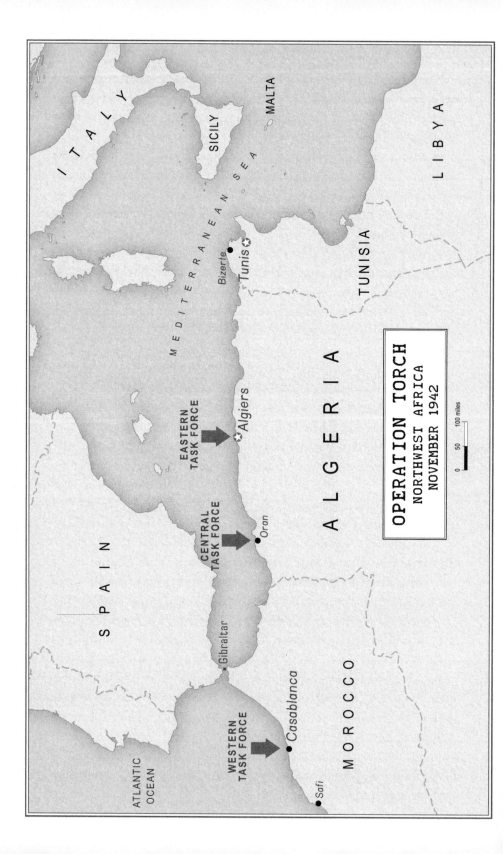

OPERATION TORCH
NORTHWEST AFRICA
NOVEMBER 1942

Atlantic, and dump them on the African coast at H-hour. For the assault force, Patton would command the 3rd Infantry Division, most of the 9th Infantry Division, the 2nd Armored Division, and two unattached tank battalions, a total of about 35,000 men and 250 tanks.[76]

It was a good corps, but like the rest of the American army, Patton's men were a deep shade of green. They were unknown quantities in a fight, and with thousands of regular French troops, a big French battleship, and rough, boat-swamping surf waiting for them at Casablanca, George wasn't about to dump everyone on Casa's bristling doorstep. That would entail too great a risk.

Instead, he broke his force into three teams that would land along the coast, capture the local airfields, and converge on Casablanca from the landward side. On the north end, Task Force GOALPOST, under Major General Lucian K. Truscott, would land just over 9,000 officers and men above Rabat, French Morocco's capital. A sort of modern-day Marshal Murat, the handsome Truscott shared George's fetish for fine military dress bordering on the outlandish; he would wade ashore in Morocco sporting a red leather jacket, a silk scarf, and riding jodhpurs. Truscott's team would capture the critical airfields at Port Lyautey and Sale, take the nearby town of Mehdia, and move south to Casablanca.[77]

Major General Jonathan Anderson would command Task Force BRUSH-WOOD, consisting of 19,000 infantrymen, plus tank, artillery, and reconnaissance battalions from Patton's old Hell on Wheels Division. Anderson's men would land at Fedala, an old fishing port about twelve miles north of Casablanca, then wheel south.[78]

Task Force BLACKSTONE under Major General Ernest J. Harmon, a hard-swearing, gravel-throated armor man—the "Poor Man's Patton," some tankers called him—would command Patton's largest division, a task force from the 2nd Armored Division under Brigadier General Hugh J. Gaffey and a regiment of the 9th Infantry Division. Blackstone's objectives were four beaches around the old Portuguese trading town of Safi, some 140 miles south of Casablanca. Though far from the principal target, Safi provided the most accommodating beach for the critical LCTs, or "Landing Craft, Tanks." Patton had reasoned that the inherent mobility of tanks would allow Harmon to move his men up from Safi rapidly in time to join Anderson's men for the final assault on Casablanca.[79]

Patton's naval support was to include one aircraft carrier, four escort carriers, three battleships, seven cruisers, and thirty-eight destroyers, as well as dozens of transports and cargo vessels. This immense fleet would steam to Africa under the guiding hand of Rear Admiral H. Kent Hewitt, a highly respected commander with a long service record going back to Teddy Roosevelt's Great White Fleet. But as schedules were drafted and landing rehearsals began, Patton's faith in the Navy withered. He found the Navy's officers "very pessimistic," and his open distrust of the fleet, bordering on contempt, came to a head during his first meeting with the genteel admiral who would command the invasion flotilla. George, being George, let his complaints about schedules, logistics, and fire support escalate into a tirade of curses better directed toward a cavalry sergeant than to a rear admiral. Hewitt, a former altar boy whose kindly features concealed an inner core of iron, didn't take Patton's tongue-lashing and bluster lying down. He remonstrated with George, then argued, then finally gave up reasoning with him and went to see Admiral King.[80]

It was George's first brush with interservice rivalry since his Academy days, when West Point played Annapolis, and this time he was in over his head. Just as George had patrons among the Army's highest ranks, Hewitt was well connected among the Navy's brass, and the Navy, in turn, was better connected with FDR's White House than was the Army. Few men could match Ernie King when it came to bare-knuckles military politics, and the admiral, exploding like a sixteen-inch shell, called Marshall to demand Patton's head.[81]

Marshall valued General Patton, but he didn't need interservice friction at a delicate time like this. He asked Eisenhower, Patton's boss, to weigh in on the cavalryman's dismissal. Ike stuck by his friend and convinced the Chief that Patton was their best hope for success at Casablanca.

To Marshall, that settled the matter. Success trumped personal burdens, whether his or the Navy's, and Patton's head would not be served up on an olive drab platter. Marshall told King that Patton had become indispensible to TORCH, and he pointed out that Patton's loud, bull-in-a-china-shop manner was the very quality that made him an effective battle commander.

King, a bull among his own china shelves, understood. Concluding that he had made his point with the Army, he didn't press the Patton matter further. The ax was put back in its rack, and George's career remained a going concern.[82]

Ike and Marshall had backed Patton this time, but the cavalryman's antics wouldn't do for a dicey operation in which air, sea, and ground forces had to work together smoothly. It was fine for George to curse the Navy when his tanks were rolling across the Moroccan desert, but for now they needed fleet officers to do a job without precedent in the history of amphibious warfare.

So Marshall let the matter officially drop, but he gave Patton a friendly admonition: "Don't scare the Navy, they are plenty scared of you."[83]

As the London summer lost its edge and fall crept over the horizon, the French and Spanish questions rose like twin storm clouds in Ike's life. Both nations were dominated by fascist tyrants, and both maintained large forces in the African theater. In the air, the Vichy regime had some five hundred planes on the North African coast, while the Allies had only 166 available aircraft to stop them. On the ground, Vichy fielded around 120,000 men from Morocco to Tunisia, so anything more than token French opposition on the first three days would doom the plan.

Multiplying the risk was the geographic fact that any air cover beyond the first wave of Spitfires and Hellcats would have to fly from Gibraltar, which lay under the guns of Spain's fascist regime. If Spain entered the war on the side of the Axis, or even allowed Germany to cross Spanish soil, then Gibraltar, with its tiny, crowded airfield, would be obliterated within minutes.[84]

The combined pressures of irreconcilable demands, his political tightrope act, and the great political, meteorological, and military unknowns built up inside Ike as predictably as steam in a boiler pipe. He confided to Marshall,

> *I do not need to tell you that the past several weeks have been a period of strain and anxiety. . . . The real strain comes from trying to decide things for which there is no decision—such as, for example, what is to be done if the weather throughout the whole region simply becomes impossible about the time we need calm seas. If a man permitted himself to do so, he could get absolutely frantic about questions of weather, politics, personalities in France and Morocco, and so on. To a certain extent, a man must merely believe in his luck and figure that a certain amount of good fortune will bless us when the critical day arrives.*[85]

Ike's handlers—Butcher, Mickey, and his driver, Kay—grew alarmed at his drawn look and tired, snappish, un-Eisenhower manner. They knew something had to be done to give the boss a respite from the journalists, servicemen, socialites, politicians, and petty royalty that littered Ike's calendar. Otherwise, that bursting steam pipe might be Ike's aorta.

So they decided to find him a secluded place in the country. After some snooping around the English countryside, in August Butch found the perfect oasis, a hedge-lined, ivy-covered Tudor house named Telegraph Cottage. "Telek," as Eisenhower's staff called the place, was a quiet three-bedroom home nestled about forty minutes west of London near Kingston upon Thames and located adjacent to two golf courses. Sheltered from the prying eyes of Londoners, Telek was the perfect retreat from the cauldron of Norfolk House.[86]

On those precious days when he could shake loose from the Dorchester and Norfolk House, Ike kept life at the cottage in line with his simple Midwestern tastes. He padded around the house in old GI slacks, a well-worn shirt, and a pair of straw slippers left over from Manila. His waiting staff served up a basic repertoire of middle-class foods—chicken, baked beans, fried egg sandwiches, beef, pork, Brussels sprouts, hominy grits—anything but the "gourmet stuff." In the evenings, he might enjoy a "sundown highball" with personal guests. He whacked golf balls, shot his .22 pistol at cans in the backyard, played bridge, and tossed the baseball with his staff. One of his pleasures, common to every man in uniform, was the occasional package from home; Mamie's regular parcels included Ike's favorite noodle soups, Old West dime novels with eye-catching titles like *Way of the Lawless* or *Gunman's Reckoning*, and socks, fresh toothbrushes, and toothpaste.[87]

One of Ike's favorite diversions arrived with four legs and a tail. He had hinted to his friends that he wanted a dog for his birthday, and he explained to Mamie, "You can't talk war to a dog, and I'd like to have someone or something to talk to, occasionally, that doesn't know what the word means!"

After Ike expressed a vague preference for a Scottie, Butch and Kay obtained a couple of likely-looking candidates, and a delighted Ike settled on a rowdy, strutting male whom he named Telek, after his slate-roofed hideaway. On October 14, Clark, Butch, Tex, Kay, and Mickey threw a "surprise" birthday party for Ike at the cottage. There they formally presented him with Telek, who sauntered into the room wearing a miniature parachute and harness made for him by the Eighth Air Force. Ike beamed with delight.[88]

Telek, who was to accompany Ike throughout the war, had few military qualities about him, and like most puppies, he was a mixed blessing for his handlers. He had a hair-trigger bladder, an abject fear of air raids, and a fondness for dragging unlit kindling from the fireplace, snaking black trails of soot for his nominal masters to sweep.

But the pint-size canine brought a touch of normalcy to Ike's pressure-baked life. He became another member of Ike's Army family, and like Butch, Kay, Mickey, and Clark, Ike needed him.[89]

A second and more substantive member of Ike's circle arrived in early September: AFHQ's much-anticipated chief of staff, Brigadier General Walter Bedell Smith. Bedell Smith—"Bedell," "Beedle," or "Beetle," as he was variously called—was a model chief of staff, which meant he was the model of ruthless efficiency. The grandson of a Prussian soldier, the tall, gaunt Hoosier had clawed his way up from buck private in the Indiana National Guard to permanent brigadier general. A master in military black arts, Beetle could be suave and persuasive on a diplomatic mission, and he could break a man's career without a second thought. He had, Kay later wrote, "all the sentiment of an S.S. general," and as one staffer recalled years later, "he was a great chopper-off of heads, I want to tell you. And he'd go off half-cocked lots of times."[90]

A combination of coxswain, *consigliere*, schoolyard bully, hatchet man, and diplomat, the chief of staff took care of the commander's dirty work, and Beetle was very good at his job. His duties required him to keep everyone moving in the right direction, and that meant he would fire, reprimand, punish, banish, or cuss any man or woman who stepped out of line. He would negotiate personnel and logistics matters with field and service commanders, attend meetings when Ike was unavailable, and act as his chief's gatekeeper and interpreter. Every now and then, Ike's instructions on a thorny problem involving the State Department, Navy, Air Force, or some other group would be simply, "Bedell, tell them to go to hell, but put it so they won't be offended."[91]

Ike once remarked that every senior commander needs a son-of-a-bitch, and Beetle was Ike's son-of-a-bitch. Beetle summarized his management philosophy to Ike's intelligence chief in plain Indiana terms: "We've hired you for your knowledge and advice. If you're wrong too often we'll fire you and hire someone else in your place." Because he was bad-tempered, abusive, dyspeptic, and highly volatile, Beetle's subordinates learned to stay out of his way whenever they could. As his secretary, WAC Captain Ruth Briggs, recalled: "He was terrifying. He would rattle off questions and orders with the speed of a machine gun. And the air would be blue with profanity." When the unfortunate Briggs poked her head through the blue air at one high-level meeting, Smith screamed at her, "Get the hell out of here!" He then explained to his colleagues, within earshot of the beleaguered woman, "You'll have to excuse her, gentlemen. She's an idiot."[92]

Yet for all the terror he inspired in his subordinates, this American Cerberus was highly respected by his American and British peers. He could be likable, even charming, when off duty, and he was a known commodity among the Combined Chiefs, for he had once served as secretary to that Olympian body. Most of all, he was prized by the men who commanded him, including General Marshall and Winston Churchill, who both fought Eisenhower for Beetle's services. As Ike later told a friend, "I wish I had a dozen like him. If I did, I would simply buy a fishing-rod and write home every week about my wonderful accomplishments in winning the war." He later remarked, "They say there's no such thing as an indispensable man, but Beetle Smith comes very close to being one."[93]

After spending an introductory day at Telegraph Cottage throwing a handball with Ike, and discussing personnel and operations over lunch, Eisenhower's indispensible man dived into his work. Within days Beetle proved himself not just a capable chief of staff, but an outstanding global strategist who could grasp the broad political and logistic pictures in addition to the operational minutiae. Amid a hurricane of details, studies, and memoranda, Beetle sorted out the immediate details and allowed Ike to train his worried mind on strategy, coordination, and the challenge of managing personalities as the clock ticked down to zero.[94]

In late August the lumbering pieces of Ike's machine were rolled into place like blocks of Cheops's pyramid. Immense stores of equipment were trucked across America and England by thousands of teamsters and railway workers, sorted by thousands of quartermasters, loaded by thousands of stevedores. Long columns of GIs and Tommies shuttled from bivouacs to training grounds to assembly areas. Trucks, tanks, food, and ammunition were "combat loaded" to ensure the first box needed on the beach would be the last box loaded onto the ship. Convoys received rendezvous dates; officers were issued embarkation schedules.

But Ike's plans, as complex, as mountainous, as meticulous as they were, would account for only half the battle. Politics was the other half, one he could not control. The French and Spanish questions particularly worried him. Nothing in his long career had prepared him for a fight like the one that would commence around one o'clock on the morning of November 8.

In the 1941 Louisiana maneuvers, Ike's closest experience to a great battle, it had all been military, like some problem typed out on purple mimeographed Leavenworth stationery. Red Army invaded; Blue Army defended. No allies, no treachery, no Navy, no unknowns. The tactics were complex, but in Wayne Clark's dress rehearsal, the big questions were elegantly simple.

Africa was a long boat ride from Louisiana. There a Red Army (Eisenhower's) would attack a Blue Army (Hitler's) and perhaps a White Army (Pétain's), which might join the Blue Army or it might join the Red Army. Or it might do nothing. The invasion might even pull in a Brown Army (Franco's), which might attack Gibraltar from both sides of the Strait. Or it might invade French Morocco. Or it might do nothing.

When Ike squinted at the situation maps, he saw clearly that if the leaders in Madrid, Vichy, or Algiers decided to throw in with the Nazis, his own men might be pushed into the sea, regardless of how carefully he planned the operation. So French and Spanish intentions were, in all likelihood, the key to the conquest of North Africa.

But who the hell knew what the French and Spanish would do? Not Eisenhower. Apparently, neither did anyone one else in the Allied camp.

Over dinner at Telek one evening, the State Department's expert on North Africa, a tall, balding career diplomat named Robert Murphy, briefed Ike, Beetle, and Clark on the tangled web that was French North Africa. The French resistance, Murphy explained, was fragmented. The largest faction was General Charles André Joseph Marie De Gaulle's Free French movement, operating from Africa's west coast. In less complicated circumstances, Murphy said, De Gaulle might be the horse to back, because he had the largest antifascist following of the bunch. The problem was, De Gaulle was considered a traitor by the Vichy government, so the Allies might stand a better chance of rallying the French Army if they backed someone less controversial. One such candidate was General Henri Honoré Giraud, the former commander of the French Ninth Army. Giraud, Murphy said, had been captured by the Germans in 1940, and had escaped from Königstein Castle in Dresden after two years in captivity. Although he opposed the current French government, his honorable war record gave him, Murphy claimed, the quiet support of many French Army officers.[95]

Among Vichy's proconsuls in Africa, the leading power figure was Admiral Jean Louis Xavier François Darlan, commander of the French armed forces and deputy to the venerated Vichy leader, Marshal Henri Philippe

Pétain. Admiral Darlan, Murphy said, was also the key to neutralizing the powerful French fleet. He was, on the other hand, an outspoken anti-Semite, and openly sympathetic to fascist aims. That was a problem, Murphy acknowledged, but the admiral was also a base opportunist. He had quietly cooperated with Roosevelt's ambassador to Vichy, Admiral William Leahy, and he intimated that he might come over to the winning side, even if it meant throwing in his lot, and that of the French Navy, with the Allies. The short, dumpy Darlan—"Popeye," Leahy privately called him—would therefore hold the trump card if things got hot. Churchill, who was considerably more worried about French ships than French garrisons, was less equivocal; in his slurpy lisp he advised Ike, "Kiss Darlan's stern if you have to, but get the French Navy."[96]

Ike, Clark, and Murphy pondered their choices. Giraud influenced the army, Darlan the navy. But after the first few hours, perhaps a day at most, the fighting would be conducted on land. Giraud was the kind of French patriot who might rally the French officer corps, and unlike Darlan, he had no fascist dirt under his fingernails. Consequently, the State Department's expert on North Africa advised Ike that Giraud, rather than Darlan or De Gaulle, represented the best hope for a quick end to Allied–French fighting.

In the final, accelerating weeks before Patton's flotilla left the Virginia coast, Ike had to umpire trade-offs over shipping tonnage, plead with service chiefs for support, and deal with problems raised by his field commanders. In many cases, he could delegate matters, but in some he had to make the final decision. Four weeks before the invasion, for instance, when Patton asked Ike for permission to bombard Casablanca with Hewitt's battleships, Ike refused to give him carte blanche to pound the city into rubble. While he did not rule it out under the right circumstances, he knew he would have to evaluate those circumstances personally when the time came. He forcefully told Patton that "no, repeat, no bombardment will be executed without prior authority from me."[97]

At the same time, Ike overruled Patton's vehement objection to a planned D-Day broadcast to the people of North Africa by President Roosevelt and the Supreme Allied Commander. AFHQ had scheduled the broadcast to run at 1:30 a.m. local time—the time of the Oran and Algiers landings, but some four hours ahead of the Casablanca H-hour. George was furious with Ike, damning the pre-Casablanca broadcast as a glaring danger to his men's security. It was, he emoted, a "breach of faith."[98]

Ike refused to be moved by Patton's histrionics. Word of the Oran and Algiers landings would surely put French forces in Morocco on alert; it was hardly reasonable for George to expect tactical surprise when the Allies were landing thousands of men to the east. Like everyone else working for Eisenhower, Patton would have to make do with the cards he had been dealt.[99]

During the last week of October, Ike's staff prepared to move him to the Rock of Gibraltar, the promontory from which he would command the invasion. To the public, and to those of his inner circle who knew he was leaving, General Eisenhower walked about London with the confident smile, resolute shoulders, and unquenchable spirit of a general who knows he cannot fail.

But beneath his cheerful countenance, Ike's nerves frayed under the oppression of a mind wrestling with thousands upon thousands of "what-ifs?"—any of which might turn out badly. For all his intrinsic optimism, Eisenhower's fast-moving brain could spin scores of permutations on the central theme of disaster. If even only a small percentage of these doomsday scenarios played out, what chance, he wondered, did the men on the beach have?[100]

As the pieces of the invasion dropped into place with emphatic thuds, Ike felt his power to influence events draining. As ships were loaded and schedules were distributed, Ike became less of a commander and more of a spectator, mediator, politician, errand boy, and cheerleader. It was a helpless feeling; the lives of hundreds, possibly thousands of men would come to an abrupt end in just a few days, and as Ike's freedom of action shrank to virtually nothing, the black gulf of anxiety that had followed him since June yawned wide. He could sit and wonder, squirm and pray, but in the end, there was nothing for him to do but wait.[101]

Before leaving London for Gibraltar, Ike, not a sentimentalist by nature, indulged a small measure of superstition. He collected six coins, representing the Allied nations, and he carried them in a little zippered bag in his pocket for good luck, rubbing the coins like rosary beads when nervous energy got the best of him.

On his last evening in England, a jittery, chain-smoking General Eisenhower, grounded by storms before the big show, sat helplessly at Telegraph Cottage with his inner circle, waiting for the weather to break so he could depart for the Rock. November's early dark fell upon London, and with nothing else to do Ike and his group donned civilian overcoats and drove incognito to Wardour Street, where they passed a few hours watching a private screening of the new Bob Hope–Bing Crosby comedy *The Road to Morocco.*[102]

Ike's own road there would be much less amusing.

George paid his final round of courtesy calls before embarking on his transport ships, relishing the violent adventure that was to come. On October 18 he had a sentimental, at times teary-eyed dinner with Secretary Stimson, Marshall, Dill, and their wives. He paid his respects to an ancient, nearly blind Pershing, and had a short farewell conference with President Roosevelt.[103]

Reporting to the White House with Admiral Hewitt, at two p.m. the men were ushered into the Oval Office. Greeting "Skipper and the Old Cavalryman" with his broad, jutting smile and cocked head, Roosevelt talked boating with Hewitt in the same blithe voice he'd used to woo congressmen, precinct bosses, industry leaders, and constituents so many times over the course of his long political career. George, placing more substance upon the meeting than did the president, tried to steer the conversation toward the overriding need to get his men ashore—a not-so-subtle dig at Admiral Hewitt. But his effort fell flat. Tossing off a noncommittal nod, Roosevelt airily asked George "whether he had his old Cavalry saddle to mount on the turret of a tank and if he went into action on the side with his saber drawn."[104]

George realized, to his disappointment, the meeting had been intended as a nice chat, an "atta-boy" for the team before kickoff, and nothing more. They exchanged pleasantries for a few more minutes, and as Roosevelt wished the two commanders an effervescent "Godspeed," the general and the admiral left the White House and went back to work.[105]

On the morning of November 5, 1942, six B-17 bombers rumbled off the runway at Bournemouth's Hurn Aerodrome carrying Ike and several staff members to Gibraltar, the temporary headquarters of AFHQ. The weather was miserable, and Ike's pilot, Major Paul Tibbets—a man who would be remembered for a more famous flight—advised against going. But Ike ordered him up, weather be damned, and after a bumpy ride, Ike's Flying Fortress, dubbed the *Red Gremlin*, touched down on one of Britain's most prized possessions.[106]

The Rock of Gibraltar commands the thin jugular of water that separates the Iberian Peninsula from North Africa, and divides the Mediterranean Sea from the Atlantic Ocean. Perched atop the Rock, one could see Europe and Africa in the same glance. The ancient monolith, mottled with vegetation and an odd mixture of migratory birds, sundry vermin, and small tailless monkeys (*Macaca sylvanus*) was, then as a hundred years before, the western cornerstone of the British Empire.[107]

Beneath the flora and fauna, Gibraltar's limestone hulk was perforated with caves and tunnels first bored by laborers around the time of the American Revolution. Since then the underground network had been enlarged to about thirty miles of tunnels some eighteen hundred feet below the mountain's peak. By 1942 His Majesty's subjects had equipped the island with communications networks, rudimentary living quarters, and a small airfield. Ike's headquarters complex was a bizarre merger of modern office suite and medieval cellar, its cramped quarters illuminated only by a string of lightbulbs. Condensation dripped down the sides of the gray walls while electric fans struggled to push the heavy, damp air through the bronchi of the cave network. "Damned well protected," a grateful Butcher noted in his diary, though Ike would remember Gibraltar as "the most dismal setting we occupied in the war."[108]

But the Rock was Ike's assigned post for now, and like everyone else, he would make the best of it. When his paperwork experts determined that enough files had made their way into the island's cramped offices, General Eisenhower opened the Rock for business. Word went out over radio and Teletype lines:

COMMAND POST OPENS GIBRALTAR, 2000 ZULU, 5 NOVEMBER. NOTIFY ALL CONCERNED.[109]

As pushpins representing Allied convoys inched their way across the Supreme Commander's map, Ike paced, smoked, and rubbed his lucky coins. The drip, drip, drip of condensation from the Rock's arched ceilings ticked off the seconds as time slowly lurched toward H-hour, the moment of decision. The moment, Ike had told Marshall, when his chances would rate about fifty-fifty.

Relieving his mind by telling the Chief what Marshall already knew, Ike wrote to Washington, *"If Patton encounters any real resistance, he is going to have a tough time of it because landing problems alone are enough to occupy his full attention. . . . We are standing on the brink and must take the jump, whether the bottom contains a nice feather bed or a pile of brickbats!"*[110]

While Ike and Clark waited for H-hour, they did what soldiers often do in the hours leading up to a risky operation: They joked, made small talk, tried to slough off the stress that wrapped them like a thick, stifling overcoat. As Butcher described the scene:

> *Ike and Clark were "opining" in our bull session that it wouldn't be long until they were either lions or lice. . . . Clark, who now plans to fly to Algiers with the advanced headquarters setup, said that if things go badly, he might just keep on flying into Central Africa, land or parachute, and keep the gobs of gold he is carrying for any contingency, including bribes to natives, if necessary. Will be a gentleman, however, and let Ike know where he is, but he'd better bring his own share of the gold swag with him.*[111]

At last, Eisenhower was snatched from nervous inactivity by news that all naval task forces were approaching the African coast. Butcher described Gibraltar on the night of the invasion: *"Hubbub and bustle around the place like Election Eve . . . We're definitely going in as planned."*

As staffers scurried about, readying radios, typewriters, pens, and encryption keys for battle, a final outgoing message clicked off the cable machines in the bowels of the AFHQ signal room. It read:

WARNING ORDER. H-HOUR CONFIRMED NOVEMBER 8. FOR EAST AND CENTER 1 A.M. FOR WEST ABOUT 4:30 A.M.[112]

FIVE

TRACKS IN THE DESERT

Ike is not well and is very querulous and keeps saying how hard it is to be so high and never to have heard a hostile shot. He could correct that very easily if he wanted to. I almost think he is timid. . . . Well in any case I would not want his job at the moment. I don't think that he or Clark have any idea of what they are going to do next.

—George to Beatrice, December 3, 1942

CHAOS REIGNED AT THE ROCK from the opening minutes of November 8. As FDR's golden voice buzzed across the radio waves to announce the landings to the world, news reached Ike from the fleet lying off Algiers: LANDING SUCCESSFUL, A, B, AND C BEACHES, EASTERN TASK FORCE.[1]

Doc Ryder had made it ashore.

At three twenty-two in the morning, the Royal Navy reported that Fredendall's initial landings near Oran had also been successful.[2]

The crescendo of coded chatter rose steadily in the Rock's communications rooms as reports poured in faster than Ike's senior men could digest them. But enough fragments of the picture filtered through the fog of war to allow Ike's mind to form a discernable image of the operation. The Oran and Algiers teams had landed. French defenders at Oran had fought back hard, slaughtering American troops trying to rush the city's harbor, but other landings were proceeding more or less as planned. Fighting was moderate to heavy, but by nine in the morning Ryder's objective—Algiers—was in Allied hands.[3]

Soon more good news filtered in: Admiral Darlan, holed up in Algiers, had been captured. Blida and Maison Blanche airfields, near Algiers, had been captured. Tafaraoui Airfield near Oran was in Allied hands. With the Stars and Stripes flying over the Algerian capital, Clark and a small nucleus of Ike's staff prepared to take their radios, files, maps, and gold swag to Algiers, where they would set up Eisenhower's advance base.[4]

The darkest cloud that long morning was the lack of word from Patton. Ike learned through naval channels that Admiral Hewitt's landings had commenced more or less on schedule, but apart from fragmentary messages from French sources referring to fighting around Safi, Ike received nothing from George all morning. Two messages came in from Hewitt several hours after the landings, but every time Ike's staff called down to Signals, the colonel on duty had nothing from Western Task Force.[5]

During the agonizing intervals between reports, an idle and more or less helpless General Eisenhower passed the time scratching out a memorandum he entitled "Worries of a Commander." The list included things like Spanish intentions, air support, and a worrisome lack of cooperation on the part of the French. The last entry, scratched in Ike's small, efficient script, read, "We cannot find out anything."[6]

Later that morning, Ike found a way he could make a contribution from his island prison: He made a run at convincing Giraud, who had been secretly ferried to Gibraltar, to throw in with the Allies. Face-to-face talks with Giraud had broken down the night before the invasion when the tall, touchy general insisted upon replacing Eisenhower as Supreme Commander and raved about an immediate invasion of the French coast.

Now, sensing Allied victory, the would-be Savior of France accepted the new reality and grudgingly agreed to Ike's terms: He would order the French Army to cease resistance, in return for which the Allies would appoint him commander of all French forces in the region and Governor of French North Africa. Ike, Commander in Chief of all Allied forces, promised to cooperate closely with Giraud as they jointly drove the Axis off the continent.

This was enough of a concession to satisfy Giraud's Gallic honor. With this awkward diplomatic lurch, Ike whisked Giraud, Clark, and the AFHQ advance team off to Algiers to bring over the French Army and Navy.[7]

No sooner had Giraud jumped into the Allied camp than Ike got the best possible news at the worst possible time. Admiral Darlan had been captured in Algiers. From house arrest, he sent word to the Allied commander that he wanted to negotiate. Having little leverage and less time to negotiate, Darlan quickly anted up his best play—the French fleet and his legal authority over Vichy Army officers. Darlan's card unquestionably trumped Giraud's.[8]

It wasn't a close call. Although Ike believed Darlan to be a fascist YBSOB—Ike's private military code for "yellow-bellied son-of-a-bitch"—he was equally certain that Darlan was the man to back. *"Kiss Darlan's stern if you have to, but get the French Navy,"* Churchill had told him. But backing Darlan meant reneging on the promise he had just given to the difficult, self-important Giraud.[9]

Straining under the invasion's crush and badly in need of sleep, Ike was beside himself when he heard the news. "Je-e-e-e-esu-ss Ch-e-ris-t!!" he sputtered. "What I need around here is a damned good assassin!"

With stress breaking like a fever, this latest political mess pushed Eisenhower to the limit of his endurance. He was livid at this quirky group of conspirators from a bad Dashiell Hammett novel, men who should have been throwing themselves at the Allied feet for the chance to liberate their country. He fumed to Beetle that he was sick of "the petty intrigue and the necessity of dealing with little, selfish, conceited worms that call themselves men," and to Marshall he complained, "I find myself getting absolutely furious with these stupid Frogs."[10]

He may have been near his breaking point with the Frogs, but the spark of optimism Ike carried in his chest, the pilot light of his soul, began to glow a little brighter as the picture crystallized. His Mediterranean forces were ashore and, thank God, they had captured enough airfields to land his Spits and Lightnings on African soil. Spanish guns had not opened up on Gibraltar's airfield—yet—which was another positive sign. Clark was setting up shop in Algiers, and the splintered French leaders from both sides were saying they wished to talk. With any luck, the French fleet would come over before long.

But where, he wondered, is Patton?

Africa's Atlantic coast has always been much more dangerous than its Mediterranean cousin. As westerly winds bear down upon the Atlantic's choppy surface, the water begins to undulate with terrible force—a force pushed up to the surface as the ocean's depth diminishes, producing great breaker waves that thunder against the beach with monstrous force. Since the summer, Allied meteorologists consistently predicted fifteen-foot swells for Casablanca on D-Day, far higher than the three-to-four-foot chops the smaller Allied landing craft could safely negotiate. More than the French, the Moroccan surf would be Patton's deadliest enemy.[11]

Through a flurry of couriers, radiograms, and message slips, what Ike needed to hear—what he was desperate for—was word from Patton's force. Rumors, some from the Axis, some from the Allies, were unsettling. He received piecemeal reports of heavy resistance from French defenders at Casablanca, Mehdia, and Fedala, and an Axis propaganda broadcast claimed that Patton was retreating to his ships under a flag of truce. Ike scoffed at this last notion, telling Beetle, "Unless my opinion of Georgie is 100% wrong, he wouldn't reembark anything, including himself."[12]

But the only definite word Ike received around the time of Patton's landing was that the battleship *Texas* was hovering off Rabat, using its radio transmitter to play "La Marseillaise" and "The Star-Spangled Banner" to confused Moroccan listeners. And that told him nothing. [13]

Where is Patton? he asked himself.

Sometime after four a.m., Admiral Hewitt radioed Gibraltar to report that the Morocco landings were proceeding on schedule. That was good news for the men on the waves, and it meant the Americans might not be fighting the heavy surf they had feared. What that meant to the men on the ground, though, no one on Gib knew.[14]

Four hours went by. Hewitt reported French opposition in all landing areas, and at least one French warship was firing on the landing flotilla. French sources implied that Vichy resistance was being snuffed out around Safi, but what was happening at Casablanca and Port Lyautey was anyone's guess.[15]

By late morning, the splintered pieces of contradictory, incomplete, and patently unreliable information left Eisenhower's nerves frazzled. George was definitely fighting for his life, but was he being driven back? Was he making headway? How bad were his casualties? Were the airfields open? What was the condition of the port?

On these critical points, the stack of decoded "URGENT" messages were resolutely silent.

WHERE THE HELL IS PATTON??

As the 102-ship armada steamed toward the Moroccan coast, George tilted between nervous energy and easy confidence. On the eve of the invasion, he sought relief from the stress by reading a detective novel and went to bed at ten thirty p.m. dressed for action—his ever-present helmet, large binoculars, and boots accenting a heavy field jacket. Armored for battle, he fell asleep.[16]

He awoke at two in the morning and clambered up to the ship's main deck. From there, he squinted through the inky night toward the glittering lights of Casablanca, an alluring metropolis that, he later remarked, "combines Hollywood and the Bible."[17]

As the flotilla approached its target, George was more interested in Morocco's surf than its exotic skyline. Breakers had been thrashing wildly against Casa's shore for several days. Meteorologists and spotter planes had checked and rechecked the breaker pattern over the last few weeks, and they had consistently reported swells of eighteen feet. The pattern was so imposing, so consistent, that Eisenhower had authorized Admiral Hewitt to put Patton's force ashore at Oran, behind Fredendall and safely inside the Mediterranean, if Hewitt felt the surf was an impassible barrier.[18]

The landing was a dangerous gamble, one no meteorologist worth his paycheck would have bet a five-spot on. But George was not the only gambler in the theater. Admiral Hewitt, carefully measuring the rolls and studying reports from his fleet's van, decided to roll the dice. He ordered his task force to go ahead with the landings as planned. They would strike the enemy at Casablanca.[19]

Hewitt's gamble paid off, and Neptune, to everyone's relief, remained docile that night. Through the rhythmic circle of a French lighthouse beam, Patton, Hewitt, and the ship's spotters could see waves teasing the shore but not hammering it. The water, so hostile to the frail Higgins boats the night before, was merely indifferent. The Americans could put ashore wherever they liked. God and His executive officer, Destiny, were still with George.[20]

The landing craft pushed off around four forty-five a.m. French shore batteries began trading shots with Hewitt's warships, and a few hours after Patton's men slogged onto wet sand, the French Navy joined the fray. As the wounded but still formidable battleship *Jean Bart* opened its fifteen-inch guns upon the Allied fleet, a line of Vichy destroyers began shelling landing craft and firing onto the crowded, vulnerable beaches.[21]

America's hard-charging battle commander would see little fighting this D-Day. George remained quietly at his command post aboard the U.S.S. *Augusta*, observing landings and staying out of the way of busy naval officers. Around eight in the morning, a Higgins boat loaded up the general's bags to take him ashore. He had strapped on his trademark six-shooters and was standing on the *Augusta*'s main deck when a French cruiser steamed within range.[22]

Hewitt's gunners swung their turrets and blasted away. The roar of the great guns blanketed all other sounds, and the concussion threw George's little transport boat off its davits, dumping its contents into the foamy sea. George's personal gear sank beneath the choppy waves as sailors scrambled to save the boat. It was an ill omen, and a disgusted George muttered to an aide, "I hope you have a spare toothbrush with you I can use to clean my foul mouth. I don't have a thing left in the world, thanks to the United States Navy."[23]

Worse than the loss of George's toothbrush was the absence of his communications gear. While the *Augusta* had loaned the Army three radio rooms to relay messages between Morocco and Gibraltar, the hammer blows of the cruiser's guns shook the delicate instruments so badly they malfunctioned. By the time the problem was diagnosed and corrected, many critical messages had been lost. Ashore, fragile tactical radios succumbed to salt water, misplaced ciphering equipment, rough handling, and countless incidents that made clear communications one of the first casualties of battle. Compounding the burgeoning communications problem, Navy dispatchers signaling Gibraltar failed to classify their messages as URGENT, and Ike's signal clerks shoved those reports beneath the hundreds of URGENT dispatches pouring in from Oran and Algiers. The chain of mishaps meant a nervous General Eisenhower would know nothing of Casablanca's fate, or Patton's, for an uncomfortably long stretch.[24]

Marooned aboard the *Augusta* for the moment, George waited while sailors fitted out another launch for him. He had a pleasant lunch with Hewitt's officers, and at noon he learned that Ernie Harmon's armored force had captured the beaches at Safi to the south. Buoyed by the expectation that Harmon's tanks would be rolling north before long, George climbed down the *Augusta*'s cargo nets into his waiting transport. Waving to cheering sailors as his boat pulled away, George and a skeleton headquarters staff made the bouncy ride to Fedala's beach and waded into the surf. George's tanker boots touched African soil at one twenty p.m.[25]

As reports filtered back that afternoon, George learned it had been a tough fight for most of his men. Harmon's landings at Safi had gone as well as could be expected, but it would take the column a day or two to reach Casablanca. Truscott's men, fifty miles to the north at Port Lyautey, had missed their landing zones. As they drove on their objective, they encountered rough terrain, stiff colonial resistance, and stiffer French Foreign Legionnaires, who fought the Americans for the approaches to Lyautey's precious airfield. Anderson's team at Casablanca, meanwhile, was facing 2,500 enemy troops at Fedala and over 4,000 enemy reinforcements. Progress, while steady, was painfully slow.[26]

*   *   *

With his radio equipment in disarray, Patton could exercise little control over his subordinate units on the morning after D-Day. The waves, which had been so lethargic the day before, were building to their typically tempestuous swells. The Americans had no land-based air support, since the closest airfields were still in French hands, so George had to rely upon carrier squads offshore to keep the skies clear. Tanks were still on ships, trucks were in short supply, and communication with Gibraltar was nil.[27]

Seeing little else he could do to affect the big picture, George launched a personal crusade to clean up the Casablanca landing zone. Using his two stars and a locked-and-loaded vocabulary to get equipment moving inland, he jumped into thigh-deep water and waded ashore a second time. Cursing and bellowing at lieutenants, beachmasters, loaders, and boatswains in equal measure, he slowly directed landing craft onto the beaches, had them unloaded, and got the empty craft shoved out to sea. Between his efforts and those of the Navy's tireless beachmasters, the Fedala beachhead was partly consolidated by the end of the ninth. A worn-out General Patton prepared for his real work the next day.[28]

It was not until November 9 that Ike finally heard from George, who reported that all beaches were in American hands. "At no time in the war did I experience a greater sense of relief," Ike wrote afterward. "I said a prayer of Thanksgiving; my greatest fear had been dissipated." On the tenth, Ike cabled his old friend, *"Georgie—Algiers has been ours for two days. Oran defenses crumbling rapidly with navy and shore batteries surrendering. The only tough nut is left in your hands. Crack it open quickly and ask for what you want."*[29]

Beneath his signature on his private file copy, Ike penned a side note on Patton's reaction: *"Will he burn!"*[30]

Beneath Ike's signature on his private file copy, George scribbled, *"The only order I got and I only got it on Nov. 23."*[31]

While Ike was relieved to hear of Patton's success in landing his men, he was heartily disappointed with the dearth of specific information reported back from Western Task Force. When Supply Services cabled from London, to ask Gibraltar whether they could begin shipping supplies and reinforcements through Casablanca's harbor, Ike had no answer for them. A squadron of P-38 fighters was ready to leave Gibraltar for Casablanca, if Patton would confirm that he had an airfield for them to land on. Again, Ike had no answer.

With the radios silent, Ike tried to reach Morocco by courier, but French interceptors turned back the light bombers that Eisenhower sent to make contact with Hewitt and George. In desperation, Ike asked his Royal Navy fleet commander, Admiral Andrew B. Cunningham, to lend him a fast ship. Harry Butcher, hovering around Eisenhower as the long, chaotic days unfolded, remarked in his diary on Ike's growing frustration with Patton:

> [Western Task Force's] appreciation of the need of the C-in-C for information is somewhat less than cooperative. They seem to think they are running a little war all their own. . . . Failure to get answers to two questions put to Patton 36 hours ago is bad. Where are his headquarters, and what is the condition of the port at Casa Blanca? Neither do we know the result of naval action in the west. Supply people in London calling for port information. Convoy sailings, loadings, timings, everything dependent on information, yet Patton sits like a lump on a log, tongue-tied. Maybe it's communications, but Christ he has planes that could fly couriers with complete dope to Gib. Incidentally, outside of Navy, particularly Royal Navy, our signals have been far from satisfactory. Biggest failure of the expedition, except Patton's silence.[32]

It was not the first time this charge had been leveled at Patton; shortly after his first engagement as a battalion colonel in World War I, George got a chewing-out from his Tank Corps commander for leaving his post and wandering around the battlefield, fixing small problems when he should have been reporting the big picture back to his boss. But George was mortified when he heard of Ike's displeasure, and tried to defuse his commander's anger with an explanation and some tongue-in-cheek humor: "I regret that you are mad with me over my failure to communicate; however, I cannot control interstellar space and our radio simply would not work any more than yours would to me. Furthermore, the only person that lost by it was myself, as by my failure to communicate with you, the press was probably unable to recount my heroic deeds."[33]

The final push against Casablanca thrust George onto the horns of an awkward dilemma. He had decided to bombard Casablanca with Hewitt's battleships and whatever airpower he could muster, then have Truscott,

Harmon, and Anderson charge in for the kill. But Ike had ordered him to obtain his personal approval before firing on the city, and Patton's radio connection with Gibraltar was virtually gone. The time to strike was now, he knew, but without a link to Gib, he would be putting his career in harm's way.[34]

He sweated out the decision at his command post: Should he wait for Ike, even if waiting meant forfeiting a golden opportunity to take the city? Or should he charge ahead and swallow the consequences? Weighing his chances, George summoned Keyes, Gay, Hewitt, and the rest and told them the *coup de main* would commence at 7:30 a.m. on November 11, George's fifty-seventh birthday.[35]

The battle lines were drawn, the tank engines revved, the gun lanyards strung for the pull. But on the morning of the assault, the French garrison commander, General August Noguès, learned of a cease-fire in Algiers. Before H-hour, word reached Casablanca that the French Navy had come over with Darlan, and Noguès joined the truce. The battle for Morocco was over.[36]

Later that day, a sullen General Noguès and his entourage arrived at Casablanca's Hotel Miramar to sign the surrender documents. Patton, resplendent in his Class-A, entered the hotel's smoking room to face his second dilemma of the day: because the French had resisted the landings, his instructions from AFHQ directed him to use "Treaty C," a harsh variation of the surrender instrument that required French soldiers to lay down their arms in complete submission. When Noguès and his delegation read this stipulation, they protested vehemently. Noguès pointed out that Morocco, a land of some eleven million restless Arabs and Berbers, was a perilous country to govern. French disarmament, Noguès warned, would lead to the collapse of French authority and invite native uprisings. The Americans would be forced to detach thousands of troops to maintain civil order— and guarantee stability along the Spanish Moroccan borderlands—while their stated business lay on the other side of the Sahara Desert.[37]

Frowning, George grasped their point immediately. Noguès was right. But he had been directed to apply the terms of the hard-line Treaty C, and orders were orders. If he dared agree to a different settlement—and if Eisenhower didn't back him—then AFHQ's staffers would set upon him like a pack of mastiffs and he might be sent home. On the other hand, his communications were compromised, and he was unable to ask Ike, or even Clark in Algiers, for instructions. Once again, he was on his own.[38]

As George's aide wrote, "It did not take him long to decide. Rising to his full height, he picked up the familiar typescript of Treaty C and tore it into small strips." He stared across the table at the French commanders. His blue-gray eyes aflame, George asked for their word of honor as officers and gentlemen that there would be no further firing on American troops, and that the French Army would consider itself bound by Patton's orders. The Frenchmen nodded. With that sweeping gesture, Morocco fell into Allied hands.[39]

George knew he was wading into political waters, and for George, political waters were always deep, murky, and teeming with carnivores. He had taken it upon himself to leave the colonial government and its army intact, contrary to orders from AFHQ, and Ike had no reason to trust Noguès, a known fascist sympathizer.[40]

George appreciated the realities of the desert kingdom. Over many decades, the French had forged an effective administrative system. Emasculating the French bureaucracy might invite a revolt that would tie down soldiers who should be kicking the hell out of the Boche in Tunisia. He knew he might get into hot water with the politicos over his deal with Noguès, but he figured that in the end, Ike would back him. After all, for a cost of eleven hundred men killed, wounded, and missing, he had delivered French Morocco.[41]

When AFHQ's staffers learned of George's "gentlemen's agreement," they were furious, and several of Ike's retainers sailed to Hewitt's flagship to straighten Patton out. Speaking to them plainly, George convinced them, at least for the moment, of the wisdom of his decision. *"A bunch of Ike's staff tried to put me on the spot for not disarming the French,"* he wrote in his diary that night. *"I assumed the offensive, showing them that to disarm or discredit the French meant an Arab war which would mobilize 60,000 as a starter. All agreed with me at last."* George then penned a personal explanation to Eisenhower. Ike sent word back approving Patton's arrangements with the French administrators and assured him, *"As reports begin to come in from your sector, it is obvious that you have done a fine job—as I knew you would! Keep it up; the one now in front of us is, in some respects, harder than the fighting. But I know you'll do it."*[42]

To this George replied, *"When I had to make the decision to form a Gentleman's Agreement without any knowledge of what was going on anywhere else, I certainly thanked the just God that I was working for a man like you, because I know many generals who would have jumped all over me for not sticking to the letter of the law."* He outlined a credible case for the way he had handled the cease-fire, and then, as he was apt to do, George tossed in an impromptu postscript that reduced his eloquent report to a lower denominator: *"On starting [to see the Sultan of Morocco] I was in such a rush that I forgot to button my fly. Keyes noted it and we closed the gap [because] it might have looked as if I was prepared to go all out in the harem to Produce allies!"*[43]

Even as he congratulated his friend and subordinate, Ike was more than a little disappointed with the cavalryman's performance at Casablanca. George had taken until D-plus-3 to capture the city, and he had neglected to keep the Supreme Commander regularly informed of his progress. This told Ike that George was not considering the larger picture.

Taking a cue from Marshall, Ike was determined to keep a tighter rein on his horse soldier in the future. As he recovered from the tempest that had tossed him since the TORCH landings, Ike sent Marshall a list of seven of the operation's "outstanding performers."

His friend's name was not on it.[44]

In the hurricane's eye, Ike had more to worry about than Patton's negotiations over Casablanca, for the political situation in Algeria was breaking down rapidly. Clark, working from AFHQ's advance post in Algiers, had managed to convince Darlan to come over to the Allied side and order French resistance to cease in return for being named civil governor of French North Africa. Giraud, whose influence over French troops turned out to be nil, exploded when he learned of Clark's negotiations with Darlan, leaving a thorny problem for Ike and Clark to work out. Adding to Ike's festering political sores, General De Gaulle notified Churchill that he wanted to send a Free French contingent to Algeria to assist the Allies. This offer placed Eisenhower between the twin forces of Churchill, who supported De Gaulle, and FDR, who thoroughly disliked the man.[45]

While the political landscape in Algeria remained foggy, the military situation to the east was clear. Sadly clear, for it was plainly falling apart. In the early hours of the invasion, word of the Allied landings reached the prominent ears of Field Marshal Albert Kesselring, a cunning, aggressive Luftwaffe commander whom Hitler had placed in charge of the Mediterranean theater. Known as "Smiling Albert" for his toothy grin and unflappable public optimism—much like his opposite number on Gibraltar—Kesselring was quick to send his warplanes into African skies. Messerschmitt fighters began arriving at Tunis the morning after the landings, followed by waves of Junkers medium bombers, Stuka dive-bombers, troop transports, reconnaissance planes, and rear-echelon personnel for the new Fifth Panzer Army headquarters. Under heavy air cover, Axis ships steamed into Tunis and Bizerte, offloading tons of ammunition, food, supplies, tanks, and wheeled vehicles to support the growing host.[46]

Before long, Smiling Al had plenty to smile about. He was winning the race for Tunisia.

On Friday the thirteenth, as Eisenhower was in the air toward Algiers, Clark and Murphy finally wrung from the Frenchmen an arrangement the Allies and French could live with. Giraud would command all French military forces in the region, but Darlan would lead the civil government in North Africa. Noguès would remain governor of French Morocco, and General Alphonse Juin, Darlan's army commander, would lead the French field forces under Giraud's overall command.[47]

As the terms of this deal were being ironed out, Ike's plane touched down in Algiers. Murphy and Clark quickly debriefed him, then ushered him into a conference room, where he briefly shook hands with the assemblage of would-be chieftains. He approved the arrangement, then departed as abruptly as he came.[48]

The war with France was over. At a cost of roughly 5,200 French, British, and American casualties, French Morocco and Algeria were in Allied hands.[49]

In approving the Darlan-Giraud agreement, Ike sensed he was skating on thin ice. The Vichy government had collaborated with the Nazis, and Darlan and Giraud, who despised each other, were bitter rivals with De Gaulle, whose credentials as a genuine resistance fighter made his anti-Darlan propaganda credible to the British and American public. AFHQ's political and public relations advisers feared it would look like Eisenhower had committed the Americans to work with a pro-Nazi, an image that would not go over well in the *Washington Post.* Ike, growing apprehensive as he thought about how the deal would look to the folks back home, hoped the firestorm would pass. But the realistic side of him feared a backlash that would reflect badly upon Marshall and the commander in chief.[50]

Ike's political instincts, as usual, were sound. In radio broadcasts, De Gaulle railed against the Allied command for bargaining with a "traitor." Radio commentator Walter Winchell called it "a deal with the devil," and *Time* accused the Roosevelt Administration of aligning itself with fascists.

From bomb-ravaged London, Edward R. Murrow boomed, "What the hell is this all about? Are we fighting Nazis or sleeping with them?"[51]

With some understatement, Ike admitted to Clark on November 18, "This case is apparently becoming one of a great deal of newspaper comment and of incessant correspondence between the Prime Minister and the President."[52]

To dampen the shock waves, the day after approving the "Darlan Deal," Ike wrote a six-page memorandum justifying the bargain on military grounds. His reasoning privately convinced FDR and Churchill, but both men publicly distanced themselves from the arrangement as popular bitterness toward the deal swelled. In a private talk with Bedell Smith, Churchill growled that he found the arrangement thoroughly disagreeable, even if he accepted the pact as a matter of military necessity. In Washington, Roosevelt tried to deflect criticism from the press, joking with reporters about an old Balkan proverb that went, "You are permitted in time of great danger to walk with the Devil until you have crossed the bridge"—though he emphasized that no decision had yet been made as to the composition of France's successor government.[53]

Even sequestered in the dark, dripping tunnels of Gibraltar, Ike began feeling the heat. Acutely sensitive to domestic politics, at least for an Army officer, Ike complained to Beetle that the high command didn't understand that the Darlan Deal was necessary to allow the Allies to turn their attention toward the Germans in Tunisia. He wrote defensively to the chief, "The authorities in London and Washington continue to suffer a bit from delusion over the extent of our military control over this country. It will be a long time before we can get up on our high horse and tell everybody in the world to go to the devil!" To Mamie, whom he knew read the editorials each day, he sighed, *Many things done here that look queer are just to keep the Arabs from blazing up into revolt. We sit on a boiling kettle!!"*[54]

Patton, sitting on his own bubbling kettle, had become convinced of the necessity of retaining the existing French administrative structure, and he firmly supported Eisenhower's Darlan Deal. Hearing of Ike's woes, he wrote a letter of encouragement to his beleaguered friend. *"As I see it,"* he told Ike, *"the French position in Morocco rests almost entirely on the mythical supremacy of France, which at the present time is represented to the Arab mind by Darlan. . . . I am fully in accord with you as to the necessity of dealing with Darlan if for no other reason than to retain this prestige. . . ."*[55]

George, it turned out, had been weathering criticism from local State Department officials, whose reaction to his policy of allowing Noguès to run the country's affairs ranged from mild disappointment to outrage. George simply shrugged. He saw the bellyaching from State as a political problem, and political problems, he felt, took a backseat to military necessity. What George saw—and what Washington and London didn't seem to grasp—was that the Allies in North Africa were not strong enough to impose martial law at one end of the continent and fight the Axis at the other.[56]

Though he felt Ike had done the right thing with Darlan, a political decision, privately George felt Ike was losing his grip on the military situation. From his post in Casablanca, George concluded that the Rock-bound Supreme Commander was too detached to command his army effectively, which should have been Job Number 1 for the lieutenant general. On November 17, after trying to make sense of Ike's directives for Morocco, he groused to his wife, Beatrice, *"I am flying to Gib . . . to see Ike. He and Clark certainly need to know the facts of life. They send some of the most foolish instructions I have ever read."*[57]

Winging his way to Gibraltar aboard a B-25 Mitchell bomber, George spent the day with his old friend, his first visit to Ike in nearly three months. On his return, he supplemented his diary entry with a short, caustic summary of his visit:

> *Flew to Gib . . . Ike lives in a cave in the middle of the rock— in great danger. His chief of staff, G-2, and G-4 are British, and so are many of his words. I was disappointed in him. He talked of trivial things. We wasted a lot of time at lunch. . . . He was nice but not enthusiastic over our war.*[58]

As George reported to Bea two days later, "Ike was fine, except that he spoke of lunch as 'tiffin,' of gasoline as 'petrol,' and of antiaircraft as 'flack.' I truly fear that London has conquered Abilene."[59]

George flew back to Casablanca disillusioned by the role that Eisenhower laid out for him. He would be in Morocco, a quiet theater, for the near future, while far to his front he could see the U.S. Army, which should be thundering into Tunisia, melting into a pot of mediocrity, swimming among two defeated allies. An army losing its identity and, perhaps, some of its honor. The very thing his idol, General Pershing, never would have countenanced.

Patton would spend the rest of the war searching for a Black Jack

Pershing within his old friend, but it was an expectation bound to disappoint. Eisenhower was a man whose horizons enveloped politics, industrial policy, planning, and diplomacy, fields as foreign to George as they were immaterial. A romantic at heart, George could not grasp that the era of the Pershings—and the Wellingtons, the Napoleons, even the Fochs—had given up its ghost on the fields of Flanders, and perhaps even earlier. Modern industrial wars were now waged by consensus; they were fought with production, alliance, and diplomacy as much as strategy and tactics. While battle captains would still reign on the battlefield, the supreme commanders in this new age would rise through their administrative, political, and diplomatic brilliance.

George couldn't fathom the demands of coalition warfare. For all his willingness to embrace military technology, he was the product of bygone times—of days when a general stood or fell on his tactical acumen, and not because of his ability to tease a consensus out of clerks and bureaucrats. For that reason, he could never fully appreciate the abilities of his old friend.

Years before, Ernest Hemingway had written of the legendary Spanish bullfighters, "Those that have known the former great ones rarely recognize the new ones when they come. They want the old, the way it was that they remember it." George had known a great one in the last war. What he could not see, what he couldn't admit to himself, was that the world no longer needed a Black Jack. It needed an Ike.[60]

While Eisenhower and Patton were hip-deep in the battle for North Africa, Omar Bradley felt the war slipping under his feet. Just as in World War I, Brad learned he was being shunted off to a division of apple-green recruits, a hard-luck bunch that General Lesley McNair had told him was in bad need of help. Turning over the 82nd to Major General Matthew Ridgway, Brad transposed his numbers and joined the 28th "Keystone" Division on June 26, bringing a skeleton staff, two aides—Captains Chet Hansen and Lew Bridge—and his driver, a bighearted Cajun named Alex Stoute, who, Brad would later appreciate, spoke French.[61]

Brad spent the next few weeks rooting out the causes of the division's many problems. It wasn't glamorous work, and he expected few plaudits from either the brass or the public. "The media were ever present," he remembered, "on the lookout for 'color' and anecdotes, always hoping, I suppose, to discover a new Patton. I think they found me disappointing." Bradley recalled one journalist writing of him, "He is not showy enough to become legend. He is not mystic enough to cause wonderment. He is tough but not cussed enough to provide narrative. In a service where personal conspicuousness is regarded with awe and something of disfavor, Bradley appears solid and stable."[62]

But even in his relative isolation, Brad's talents cut through some of the haze of obscurity that surrounded him. The reporter covering the Keystone Division cautioned his readers, "[D]on't confuse glamour with leadership. Bradley is preeminently a leader. . . . The general doesn't only command respect; he wins devotion. That, perhaps more than anything else is responsible for the heated loyalty to his command. That more than anything else is the key to his character."[63]

As 1942 slid to a close, Brad had his ear to the ground. While keeping a close watch over the 28th Division's progress, he also made time for the occasional duck hunt with the Chief of Staff, outings where his shooting prowess stood him in good stead.[64]

Through the Army grapevine, Brad learned that his division would be heading to Camp Gordon Johnston, a new amphibious training center in the warm, muggy Florida panhandle. The news delighted him, for amphibious instruction meant *real* action; a stint in Africa, perhaps, or the Pacific, or France, could not be far off.

But Brad's aptitude for training raw recruits—like Eisenhower's talent in the previous war—threatened to derail his dreams of higher command. As Marshall wrote Bradley in late 1942, "I think they have asked for you five or six times to command a corps, each of which I disapproved because I thought we must not have such rapid changes in National Guard units we are trying to build up." It looked like Brad would be stuck in Florida for the near future. But the old man admitted that he "felt rather badly" about keeping Brad at home, and he vaguely promised a "more interesting assignment" in due course.[65]

To Omar Bradley, it was 1917 all over again.

While Brad squirmed in the United States, a restless Patton fidgeted on the sleepy Moroccan front. Once hostilities there had ended, the battle lines shifted hundreds of miles to the east, along the Algerian-Tunisian border. George was left on the other side of Africa, guarding the Allied rear and playing the part of ambassador with the French and the Sultan of Morocco.

To everyone's surprise, George took to the role of diplomat exceptionally well, proving that his smooth handling of the French surrender was no beginner's luck. On the advice of Patton's intelligence officers, supplemented by his own intuition, Patton had left Rabat, the administrative and spiritual capital of the Muslim country, untouched by the invasion, which pleased the sultan and his court. George's relaxed but dignified bearing at banquets, ceremonies, dances, boar hunts, parades, and reviews impressed both Moroccan royalty and the French military, while his firm hand ensured the safety of Allied supply lines from the west. He may have ruffled a few feathers with the State Department by refusing to clamp down on the Noguès clique, but as George saw it, his job wasn't to keep the *Washington Post* happy. His job was to keep the supply terminal safe from Spanish, French, and Arab threats.[66]

That, and to make Eisenhower understand that he belonged at the front.

To get an idea of what was going on at the unimaginably distant front, in late November George squeezed his six-foot frame into the Plexiglas nose cone of a B-25 bomber and flew to Oran, then pushed on by car to see General Fredendall, commander of the Army's II Corps. Fredendall, a sour Anglophobe, didn't lift George's mood, and Oran, hundreds of miles behind the real front, seemed almost as dull and complacent as Casablanca. George fretted to himself: *"I seem to be the only one beating my wings against the cage of inaction. The others simply say how much better off we are than the people at home. I dont want to be better off—I want to be Top Dog and only battle can give me that."* He repeated his theme in a letter home to Beatrice: *"I have the most awful blues today. Nothing seems to be happening and I just sit. I suppose it is because I want to go on [campaign] and have nothing to go on with. . . . I think I will go mad if we don't get some more battles."*[67]

George's awful blues ran a deep shade of indigo around the first of December, when, over dinner with the "Sacred Family"—Eisenhower and Clark—he learned of Clark's next assignment. Clark, Ike informed him, would command the Fifth U.S. Army for the invasion of Italy.[68]

The blow hit George squarely on the chin. Clark had been a snot-nosed Army brat skipping around Fort Sheridan when George was already a commissioned officer. Now Clark, whom the War Department had promoted to lieutenant general, outranked him by a star. It was an especially bitter pill, given that Clark's army would probably requisition Patton's remaining combat troops, as well as the U.S. II Corps, which Fredendall, not Patton, would lead. Thinking of the ancient lands Clark would have the honor of conquering—lands he had studied as both child and adult—George could only plaster a counterfeit smile over his face and fervently wish the dinner would come to a rapid and merciful close.[69]

After dinner George bemoaned, *"I had expected this but it was a shock. . . . I felt so awful I could not sleep for a while."* His frustration and jealousy growing, he reacted by finding fault with the Eisenhower-Clark faction. He complained to Beatrice a few days later, *"Ike and Wayne have the inside track. Their Hq certainly is a mess and gets out contradictory orders almost daily. Some day they will be found out."*[70]

For all his complaints about his old friend, George was not blind to Eisenhower's strengths. He was proud of Ike's political talents, as well as Ike's capacity for crafting the right solution to the big Allied problems. These were gifts George knew he lacked. He admitted to himself after one dinner meeting, *"Ike certainly makes a fine impression when he talks. I was proud of him. I think that I could do better in the same job, but I seem to lack something which makes the politicians trust Ike."*[71]

The problem for George was that his feelings about Ike, like his feelings about most everything else, had no moderator. The love-hate currents that buffeted George would pitch him further and more violently over time.

Eisenhower had ordered General Anderson to run pell-mell into Tunisia and capture Bizerte and Tunis before Hitler and Mussolini could reinforce those ports. But the distance from Algiers to the Gulf of Hammamet was four hundred miles, and the dirty, primitive roads skirting Africa's coast were wholly inadequate to the task. Ike's lightning thrust to the Tunisian capital thus turned into a piecemeal, amateurish stumble. As Ike later admitted to a *New York Times* reporter, "The battle line at that time was in a hell of a mess. It was the most messed up thing imaginable. We had gambled everything sending small bits and pieces from many outfits to the front to try and take Tunis and Bizerte quickly and all of the outfits were mixed up together strung out over hundreds of miles of hills and muddy country."[72]

Once the Allies lost the race for Tunis and Bizerte, the territory east of Tunisia's Dorsal Mountains became a formidable Axis redoubt. During November, Italo-German transports shipped in 176 tanks, 131 artillery pieces, 1,152 vehicles, and 13,000 tons of supplies to the thousands of *soldaten* forming the newly activated Fifth Panzer Army. In December those numbers would grow yet again. Against this expanding force, Eisenhower fielded two overstretched groups—Kenneth Anderson's five-division British First Army, and Fredendall's four-division U.S. II Corps.[73]

Unfortunately for Eisenhower, each day's delay in the race to Tunisia meant pointed interrogatories from the Combined Chiefs, as well as "suggestions" from Allied capitals that came perilously close to telling Ike how to do his job. On November 21, after getting called on the carpet about the ill-advised publicity of his generals, he complained to Clark, "I've been pounded all week from the rear. Sometimes it seems that none of us in the field can do anything to the satisfaction of Washington and London."[74]

Partly to escape the python-like cable that bound him to London, on November 23 Eisenhower moved his headquarters to Algiers, where Clark and Murphy had been working since TORCH's early days. Twenty-seven years after he first put on a soldier's uniform, he was finally in a war zone. A convoy arrived to meet him at Maison Blanche airfield, and he moved into the Hôtel St. Georges.[75]

The St. Georges was an elegant bastion of French Old World colonialism. *New York Times* columnist Drew Middleton described it as "a white, rambling building, decorated with hideous statues and paintings, the kind of hotel favored by elderly spinsters on Mediterranean tours." Its fashionable decor, palm-lined courtyard, and polished mosaic floors—which now lay beneath a spiderweb of Signal Corps lines—seemed out of place for a wartime headquarters. But it was roomy enough to accommodate a respectable proportion of AFHQ's senior staff, which would descend like the Huns on Rome and occupy much of the city before the war's end.[76]

Two days after arriving in Algiers, Ike and his official family moved their private quarters into rented villas overlooking the harbor. His house, named Villa dar el Ouard ("Villa of the Family"), was a six-bedroom rococo mansion nestled amid a patchwork of trees not far from the St. Georges.[77]

Ike didn't like the place, and he complained that the largest room, the tile-floored bathroom, was "as cold as Greenland." Tex Lee's girlfriend, a Red Cross volunteer, dubbed the home's baroque decor "whorehouse French." But the mansion was fine for entertainment, as it boasted a library, a parlor with a grand piano, a formal dining room and, before long, a Ping-Pong table, a game Ike often played with Admiral Cunningham, Harry Butcher, and other senior visitors. A few days later, a frisky Telek arrived from London, to the delight of Ike and Kay Summersby—though the Scottie added to the burdens of Ike's other personal staffers, who considered Telek an imbecile, as dogs went.[78]

* * *

Working from the St. Georges, Ike immersed himself in the operational details that consumed his days from early morning until almost midnight. He arbitrated bombing priority disputes (Luftwaffe airfields hit first), recommended currency policy (seventy-five francs to the dollar), harangued his adjutants for better rear-area security (Eisenhower's Ford was "liberated" by passing troops), and straightened out shipping and supply tangles. He made certain the Army's equipment—half-tracks, night-fighter radars, boots, bandages, spare tires, ammunition, mess tins, plasma, shovels, and gasoline—got to the right places, and he kept in touch with the field commanders, asking what they needed, where their troops were going, and what their plan was for getting there. He described a typical day to Mamie as *"one of vexatious problems, each requiring hours of dictating, writing, scratching the head and plenty of profanity. War, politics, economics, food, munitions, jealousies, and repeat the list ad infinitum—then you have some idea of the jumble still going through my poor old head!"*[79]

Perhaps the toughest part of Ike's job was that he had to answer to so damned many people. As a U.S. lieutenant general, he had to satisfy Marshall. As the senior American planner, he had to satisfy the U.S. Joint Chiefs. As Supreme Allied Commander, he had to satisfy the Combined Chiefs, which included both the U.S. and British Joint Chiefs. As the man making interim political decisions, he had to satisfy Roosevelt and the State Department. And no matter what hat he wore, he always had to satisfy Churchill, whose reach extended to anyone connected with the Allied war effort.[80]

And those were just the people who outranked Ike. Eisenhower, like Marshall, considered headquarters to be servants of the field commanders and their troops. This meant Ike and his staff also had to satisfy Anderson's British Army, the scattered U.S. II Corps, Clark's skeleton staff for the U.S. Fifth Army, and Patton's dwindling force guarding the back door in Morocco. He had to satisfy U.S. and British navies at sea, bomber forces operating in the skies, and fighter groups defending bombers, cities, harbors, and bases. And for all these undersupplied, self-centered, squawking constituents, Ike and his staff had to come up with answers to their problems. Problems of resources. Problems of personnel. Problems of direction.[81]

The dilemmas Ike struggled with daily were enough to shorten anybody's fuse, and Ike's was never long to begin with. He had become so distracted by political matters during the first two weeks of the invasion that he hadn't devoted enough time to the military side. He bellowed to one associate, "For Christ's sake, do you think I want to talk politics? Goddammit, I hate 'em. I'm sick to death of this goddamn political question!" And he told Marshall, "I have lived ten years each week, of which at least nine are absorbed in political and economic matters." His pace was so frenetic that Marshall began to worry Ike was burning out from the "terrific pressure put on him more or less to do the impossible."[82]

One way Ike sought to escape the spiral of anxiety was to visit the front. He had always drawn energy from visits to the troops, for in the bivouacs politics was banished. Sheltered from the elements by a wood campfire and a canvas roof, Ike could feel like a real soldier again. He found he could relax as he quizzed the fighting men about their food, their equipment, their backgrounds, and their gripes. He loved to inspect what they were carrying, eat C-rations with them over a campfire, and talk to them under the shady wing of a parked Dakota. Those were the general's duties Ike relished, trips that gave him a sense of freedom.[83]

As he drove along the front in late November he saw plenty of the fighting man's problems. The worst was the Luftwaffe's ability to throw Stukas and Messerschmitts against them with impunity. Next came his army's leadership; nosing around Anderson's headquarters, Ike returned from his trip quietly worried that the pessimistic Scot was not the right man to lead the British First Army.[84]

As he took stock of his army, Ike's military worries ballooned. How, he asked himself, could he take Tunis without tactical air superiority? Would he have to abandon his cherished hopes of a "quick thrust" to the coast? How much of 1943 would be spent tied to this desert wasteland? These were the problems that bore down on Ike as he saw the front from the perspective of his field officers. By the time he returned to Algiers, he was beaten down: exhausted, depressed, and suffering from a hacking cold that worked its way deeper into his lungs with each punishing day.[85]

Back at the St. Georges, Ike saw the sand in his hourglass running low, for although 1943 wasn't quite knocking on his door yet, it was strolling past the mailbox and moving briskly toward his front steps. Desperate to break the stalemate, Ike knew he had to make something happen before year's end.

In conjunction with General Anderson, Eisenhower set a December 9 D-Day for an all-out push against Tunis. But a few days before the attack was to begin, Anderson informed Ike of a "nasty setback" along his front. Smiling Al Kesselring had launched a spoiling attack; shrieking Stukas and field artillery pounded the Allied advance posts, while Mark IVs, Tigers, and 88mm antitank guns from Germany's 10th Panzer Division inflicted heavy losses. Anderson managed to halt Kesselring's offensive by December 10, but in view of British casualties and heavy tank losses, a glum Eisenhower had no choice but to accede to Anderson's request to delay the final offensive to December 20—about the time the rainy season, with its formidable mud traps, was due to begin.[86]

Eisenhower tried to remain optimistic, but each day's worries plowed deeper the lines that creased his brow. Allied losses were mounting, and a decisive battle had not been joined. He had lost the race for Tunis and Bizerte, and now he faced a slow, bloody grind through the foothills and mountain passes of Tunisia that would cost more Allied lives. The setback might even delay the great cross-Channel invasion that he and Marshall had worked so hard to secure.[87]

Eisenhower was floundering, and he knew it. He needed a trusted pair of eyes at the front, eyes that knew armor and terrain. Looking for an experienced doctor to diagnose his army's problems, and particularly its high losses in tanks, he called Casablanca and rang up George Patton.[88]

Answering Ike's call, an energized George flew to Algiers to meet with Ike, and the two men talked until well after midnight. Ike was glad to see an optimist whose advice he trusted; his opinion of George had generally improved since he scratched the cavalryman's name off his "outstanding performers" list in mid-November. After the meetings, Ike even remarked to Harry Butcher, "Among the American Commanders, Patton I think comes closest to meeting every requirement made on a commander."[89]

The feeling was not entirely mutual. George was still wary of Ike's military prowess, and he saw the Supreme Commander letting the ground situation slip past him. *"Ike and Clark were in conference as to what to do,"* George muttered to his diary on December 13. *"Neither had been to the front, so they showed great lack of decision. They are on way out, I think. Have no knowledge of men or war. Too damned slick, especially Clark."* The day after Christmas, George sent his wife a veiled message in which he predicted the end for Eisenhower: *"I get fed up sitting here and seeing the war lost but it may all work out for the best as some goats will have to be found soon and they are all ranker than me. There are already rumors that one of them is on the way out. I fear it is the better of the two."*[90]

George's ambivalence toward the "Sacred Family" went double for

Clark, who, unlike his boss from Abilene, had few qualities George considered redemption material. In another letter home, George implied to Beatrice that Clark was somehow responsible for his remaining a major general:

> *I had my three stars but they have never arrived to date. Something failed to click. Or rather some one else filched them. However I am not sure that it is not all for the best as I am convinced that things are not going too well with and between the "boy wonders." One will cut the others throat and then break his own neck.*[91]

As December progressed without any forward movement, a frustrated Eisenhower grew bitter around his staff. He fretted to his brother Milton, who was visiting Algiers on business for the Office of War Information, "Damned if I'm not about ready to quit. If I could just get command of a battalion and get into a bullet battle, it would all be so simple." At one luncheon, he announced, "Tell everybody here that anyone who wants my job can damned well have it." Harry Butcher, Ike's emotional barometer, told his diary, *"Ike should stop saying at the lunch table: 'Ch-ee-r-i-s-t, anyone who wants the job of Allied Commander-in-Chief can have it.' Not because he isn't right, but because it may spread the wrong kind of stories of his ability to take it. . . . Milton and I agree on this."*[92]

Ike may have wanted a simple bullet battle, but inside he knew that he no longer fit the mold of a traditional field commander. Yet he wasn't exactly an armchair general, either. As he wrote to his old West Point roommate, P. A. Hodgson: *"I think sometimes that I am a cross between a one-time soldier, a pseudo-statesman, a jack-legged politician and a crooked diplomat. I walk a soapy tight-rope in a rain storm with a blasting furnace on one side and a pack of ravenous tigers on the other. . . ."*[93]

The ravenous tigers would only grow more ravenous if Ike didn't produce a victory, and by mid-December, he knew victory lay far, far beyond the forbidding Dorsal Mountains. On December 22, General Anderson launched his army on its long-awaited drive. But what neither Anderson nor Ike had counted on was Tunisia's rainy season, which turned its few roads into muddy, washed-out gullies in which trucks and men slowed, struggled, and sank.[94]

Acknowledging both the beating he was taking over the Darlan affair and the slow progress on the ground, Ike tried to remain outwardly philosophical about the whims of public opinion. To his son, John, a second-classman at West Point, he wrote, *"From what I hear of what has been appearing in the newspapers, you are learning that it is easy enough for a man to be a newspaper hero one day and a bum the next. The answer is that just as one must not let his head swell too much by a bit of acclaim, he must not be too upset and irritated when the pack turns on him."* After all, he said, a soldier's job is to do his duty, *"and not be too much disturbed about popularity or newspaper acclaim."*[95]

Ike's desire to get out of the political front and onto the battlefront was driven home by a peremptory order from Marshall. "Delegate your international problems to your subordinates and give your complete attention to the battle in Tunisia," the Chief growled.[96]

Ike took the message to heart. Sputtering from a debilitating mixture of chest cold and cigarettes, he left for the front on December 23, stuffing his lean frame into his traveling "goop suit," consisting of a pair of overalls, a field jacket, and a knit cap. He also carried his lucky coins, some reports to read on the long trip, and a dagger concealed in a swagger stick—reasoning that if the Supreme Commander's defense required anything more than a small knife, the four heavily armed escort vehicles in his convoy could provide it. Thus outfitted for battle, Ike's armored Cadillac gunned its engine and the convoy began its long, slow journey to the front.[97]

As his escort slogged its way toward British V Corps headquarters at Souk el Khémis, a relentless, pounding rain drenched the brown Tunisian countryside, hammering Ike's soul with the same thumping it gave the Caddy's metal roof. The trip was something of an education for the Allied commander, for the farther the convoy waded through the slashing rainstorm, the better Ike understood the problems facing Anderson and his beleaguered men. Rain and mud, he saw, were staking their claim to the battlefield. Ike prayed the weather would break by the time he reached the front.[98]

Rolling to a stop after a punishing thirty-two-hour road trip, he arrived at V Corps on Christmas Eve. Climbing out from his Caddy under storm clouds, both literal and figurative, Ike squinted through the lashing rain and beheld a city of slick pup tents pitched in huge brown puddles. It was an unkempt, forlorn picture that would have made Bill Mauldin's Willie and Joe grimace. Anderson's men, when they weren't huddled in their canvas tents, pinwheeled in the Tunisian mud while their vehicles wallowed like steel hippopotami in the axle-deep mire. With a wince, Ike swallowed a reality apparent only to himself, Anderson, and the 39,000 other men at the front: The Allies would not be in Tunis by Christmas, nor even by the end of the year. They would be lucky to get out of the thick, glutinous mud by then.[99]

"This was a bitter disappointment to Ike," Butch remarked with some understatement. Anderson, who had a tendency to oscillate between confidence and despair, offered to resign, but Ike shrugged him off. He had seen just enough of that impassible Tunisian goo to know that a change in the weather, not a change in command, was what the Allies needed. Until the roads congealed into passable avenues, Hannibal himself couldn't move against Tunis. His spirits as gloomy as the black African skies, Ike went into a tent and dictated a message to Washington that stuck hard in his craw:

DUE TO CONTINUAL RAIN THERE WILL BE NO HOPE OF IMMEDIATE ATTACK ON TUNIS.[100]

Ike was irritable and exhausted. He sank into a functional depression, a blue funk that allowed him to smile at his men even as his heart broke beneath his tunic. The barracks bags under his eyes grew dark, and some days he seemed to spend as much time blowing out his infected sinuses as he did sucking in nicotine. His language grew profane and violent around his staff, a fact he didn't relish but couldn't help, and the strain of keeping his pessimism hidden from his lieutenants added fresh burdens to old ones.[101]

About the only bright spot in Ike's dreary existence that Christmas was news that the troublesome Admiral Darlan had been assassinated by an anti-Vichy radical on Christmas Eve. His joke on Gibraltar about a "damned good assassin" had found a fatal punch line, and the killer's work had removed a lingering public relations problem for the Allies. Nonetheless, Darlan's demise—a relief to everyone except, presumably, the late admiral and Mrs. Darlan—was a rose that bristled with many thorns. "Popeye," for all his fascist sentiments, had honored his commitments to the Allies. Ike might be exchanging the devil he knew for one he didn't.[102]

Word of the assassination brought Ike scurrying back to Algiers, where he arrived on Christmas Day. When his mud-splattered Cadillac rolled up to Beetle's magnificent villa, Ike got out, stretched his stiff limbs, confirmed that the city hadn't descended into anarchy, then declared the war off-limits to AFHQ for a few hours. He celebrated Christ's birthday with his staff, singing carols in his hoarse baritone, and the group dined on a turkey that George Patton had shipped from Casablanca along with two complimentary tanker's uniforms—subtle reminders that a certain tanker was waiting in the wings.[103]

The endless, mind-numbing procession of troubles continued to take its toll on Ike's mind and body. Butch observed in early January, "After a solid month of colds, sniffles, and general below-par physical condition, Ike laid up in bed until lunch, then got up and sat by the fire. Had lunch with him at the house, and he feels punk and looks the same. Carpetbags under his eyes." By the middle of the month, Butch noted little or no improvement: "Ike went to bed the same day with a severe head cold and general grippy condition. Had been persisting in keeping on ever since it first struck him shortly after we arrived here 'permanently' . . . The succession of events kept him from stopping even one day to give his system a chance to throw off the cold, and the accumulated lack of rest for many months finally compelled him to give himself unto the doctors." Ike's blood pressure, his doctors told him, was running dangerously high.[104]

It was clear something had to be done to get the Allies, and the Supreme Commander, out of the quicksand, and Ike saw a direct role in the battle as his only way out. Lowering his balding head, he ground out another plan for the capture of Tunis and Bizerte, this time by an attack up the center, which he hoped would split the two wings of the Italo-German army. The offensive aimed to capture Gabès and Sfax, two Tunisian coastal towns that lay between Rommel's forces, on the Libyan border, and the Fifth Panzer Army, under General Hans-Jürgen von Arnim, in Tunisia's north. After talking over dispositions with Anderson, Ike decided to employ Lloyd Fredendall's II Corps in an attack on Gabès on the southern end of the Tunisian coast, just north of Rommel. With an American corps athwart German supply lines to Libya, they hoped that Rommel would be forced to detach troops that were badly needed for his fight against General Montgomery in Libya.[105]

To avoid losing sight of the battlefield, as he had in mid-November, Ike set up an advance post at Constantine. He appointed Major General Lucian Truscott, an old polo-playing friend of Patton's, as his eyes and ears at the front.

Ike held Truscott in high regard, though he wished he could have used his trusted friend Wayne Clark, who had left AFHQ to head up the Fifth U.S. Army, which was assembling in Morocco and Algeria. Clark had been bucking for a field command; when the Fifth Army position opened, he had lamented that, while he would prefer to be on the front lines with II Corps, he would accept the Fifth Army command as a matter of soldier's duty.

Few believed him. Ike later remarked that his schoolmate had "begged and pleaded" for the job with the more prestigious title. Butch wrote in his diary, "Ike doesn't think Clark is disappointed [to be sent to Morocco]— in fact thinks he is rather relieved as he hadn't wanted the [II Corps] particularly."[106]

About the time Clark was taking his leave of AFHQ, Ike and Marshall compared notes on their field commanders. When they got to Patton's name, Marshall, pleased and no doubt surprised with George's diplomatic aptitude, pointedly asked Ike if the cavalryman should be given command of American and French forces covering the south Tunisian front. Ike demurred, but did rate George highly among his senior generals. Ultimately, he recommended his friend for a corps command. "He does render willing and generous support to the plans of his superiors regardless of his personal views in the matter," Eisenhower wrote. "Of the approximately 150 general officers of his grade personally known to me, I would rate General Patton number 5." Completing Patton's annual evaluation form, Ike commented: "This officer is energetic, courageous, well informed, impulsive; definitely a leader type; devoted to the service."[107]

From his house in Casablanca, Ike's number five general squirmed as the war receded over the burning horizon. He fidgeted his days away on the "Ice Cream Front," shuttling between his third-floor office in the Shell Oil building and local Moorish palaces, where he did little more than put a friendly face on America's occupation. He disliked the country and its inhabitants, and his military duties were confined to keeping an eye on the Spanish to the north and protecting Casa's harbor. Important work, but it wasn't fighting.[108]

That was always the problem for George. Anything that wasn't fighting, wasn't fighting. It wasn't the center ring, the main event. The front-page news.

Patton, from an early age, had been driven by an insatiable need to be the center of attention, whether at a dinner party, a polo match, or, as he preferred, a military campaign. When he was fighting, his thoughts were focused and efficient; his blood was up, his spirits high. When he was in the grip of ennui, his thoughts turned brooding and destructive. He became depressed. He blamed his friends, sought out conspiracies against him, and denigrated colleagues behind their backs.

Succumbing to the temptation to find fatal flaws in other men, Patton reflected on Eisenhower and Clark, insisting to himself and his confidantes that the "Sacred Family," riddled with professional incompetence, would soon collapse under its own weight. *"The old sawdust basket is bound to collect a few heads soon,"* he predicted to Beatrice. *"One for sure and possibly two."*[109]

But by January 10, the Fifth Army commander's head was still attached to its corpus, and George rolled out an honor guard to greet Clark at the airport when he came to inspect the rear areas. Spending the day with Clark, George found the lieutenant general dismissive of everything other than his own career interests. Patton scribbled down his impressions of his new commander in his diary that day:

> *I took him on inspection of all local troops. He was not in the least interested. His whole mind is on Clark. We went to the house and for one hour he spent his time cutting Ike's throat. And Ike, poor fool, sent him here. Of course Clark came so that if, as most likely, the new attack fails, he can crawl out from under and land it on Fredendall. . . . It is most discouraging.*[110]

As the month wore on, George's cloaked bitterness festered. He told Bea,

> *There is so much back bighting between soldiers and also politicians or between soldiers who are primarily politicians. We have many commanders but no leaders. . . . Sometimes I wish I was retired but I guess I would not like that either. Probably I would only be content if I was god and probably some one ranks him.*[111]

After a visit with Everett Hughes, Ike's incoming deputy and an inveterate headquarters gossip, George wrote in his diary, *"We had a long talk about the glamour boys. He fears that the senior partner is on his way out due to the knife work of the other, concerning whom he has the same ideas as I have."* Following a similar bull session with his task force surgeon, Brigadier General Albert Kenner, he quipped, *"[Kenner] too feels that Ike is not commanding and that Clark is an s.o.b."*[112]

* * *

In early January, George learned that his city had been tapped to host a gathering of "VIPs" and their even loftier superiors, known around headquarters as "VGDIPs." Roosevelt and Churchill would be holding a secret summit, code-named SYMBOL, at the upscale suburb of Anfa, and for this meeting the two leaders would bring their full entourages: chiefs of staff, personal advisers, military advisers, Secret Service, press, the works. Patton, as Ike's proconsul in Morocco, would arrange accommodations, logistics, and area security.[113]

The Casablanca conference, held from January 14 to January 24, introduced George to a menagerie of politicians, allies, and generals whom he would never have met in the usual course of his work. It was much closer to Ike's world than his own, and in most cases he came away unimpressed with the civilians who claimed to run the free world. Churchill, in George's view, "speaks the worst French I have ever heard, his eyes run, and he is not at all impressive," while Giraud, George sneered, "is an old type Gaul with blue eyes and limited brains."[114]

The Americans generally fared better in Patton's estimation. Roosevelt, he decided, was "a great Statesman," while Admiral King, "when off duty, is most affable." As for Harry Hopkins, the president's close adviser, "[He] is very clever and intuitive—like a Pilot Fish for a shark . . . extremely intelligent and very well-informed." Of Marshall, a man who had fought honorably alongside Black Jack Pershing, George would never utter a word of criticism. But at the end of the day, George concluded, "The more I see of the so-called great the less they impress me—I am better."[115]

Ike arrived at the Anfa conference on January 15, winging in on a dangerously broken-down B-17 that threatened to quit in midair. His first stop was a turbulent session with the Combined Chiefs, where he patiently endured a grilling from Field Marshal Brooke over the Allied failure to reach Tunis and Bizerte. Once the scathing welcome concluded, a besieged Eisenhower shuffled from villa to villa, caucusing with Roosevelt, Marshall, and Admiral King, hoping to pick up a crumb or two of support.[116]

To Ike's quiet disappointment, President Roosevelt remained noncommittal about his performance as Supreme Commander. He offered no clearcut words of encouragement, no pledge of friendly support, and Ike began to get the distinct feeling that the Washington jury was still in the back room deliberating. Until some decision was reached on the battlefield, Ike would not hear the verdict.

What he did get from FDR was another reason to lose sleep. As they talked about the war's progress, the not-so-beaming president began pressing Ike for an estimate of the campaign's completion date.

Ike hemmed and hawed for a few minutes. There were so many variables. He had a staff of hundreds who spent their days trying to sort out the unknowns of the African campaign. And the president wanted all the variables reduced to a single date?

He did.

Ike began with qualifications, outlined his operating assumptions, gave caveats about the uncertainties and permutations. But Roosevelt, a thirty-second-degree master of obfuscation, knew how to draw out precisely what he wanted. Like a fly in a web, Ike wriggled and struggled until he saw he would not leave before he answered the question. So he hazarded a rough guess:

"Maybe as early as the middle of May. June at the latest."[117]

There. Now he had done it. He had given his commander an end date. And he knew no matter what other caveats, qualifications, or conditions he might add, only the date—the early date—would stick. The President of the United States would leave Casablanca remembering the Supreme Commander's estimate of victory by "the middle of May." May 15. Ike had just committed himself to clear Africa of some 200,000 Axis veterans within 120 days.

As if he didn't have enough pressure.

After dinner and more interminable meetings that droned well into the night, a wilted Eisenhower invited Patton to join him for a postmortem of his disastrous first day at the conference. Until half past one in the morning, the two men dissected the corpse and mulled over Army politics, military strategy, and Eisenhower's exposed political flanks.[118]

As the hours ticked by, their conversation turned, inevitably, to their colleagues. When Ike casually referred to Clark's twin weaknesses of self-promotion and ambition, George, eyeing a fracture among the Sacred Family, concluded, *"He and Clark are at outs, and he thinks his thread is about to be cut."* George plied Ike with advice, and he told himself afterward,

> *Ike was his old self and listened. I told him he had to go "to the front." He feels that he cannot, due to politics, said he had suggested to Gen. Marshall that I be made Deputy Commanding General AFHQ and run the war while he runs the politics.*[119]

Ike was under incredible strain as he presented himself to the various chiefs the next day, for he knew his fate was as much a political as a military matter. "It seemed to me," Butch commented afterward, "the absence of clear-cut words of thanks from the President or the Prime Minister showed they had their noses to the political winds, and weren't going to be caught holding the bag for a general who had made an unpopular decision and hadn't yet got Tunisia."

"I told him his neck is in a noose," Butch continued, echoing George's words. "And he knows it."[120]

The Anfa conference proved to be a boon to Patton, who had played the part of host, concierge, and security chief with the grace of an old-line Southern caterer and the decisiveness of a New York precinct boss. Cunningham, Churchill, Marshall, and others congratulated him on his fine hospitality and the men's smart appearance. Ike awarded him a second Distinguished Service Medal, and later, he repeated his ideas of making Patton his deputy commander for military strategy.[121]

But Patton aspired to something that society lunches and conferences with the top brass could never give him. He wanted a fight. To an old secretary from his Washington days, he wrote, *"[F]or the last ten days we have been very busy entertaining the leading lights of the world. It was very amusing but was not war. Personally, I wish I could get out and kill someone."*[122]

Patton's hopes were dashed when he learned that Ike's intention to promote him to deputy commander had fallen by the wayside. Under a new command structure worked out by the Combined Chiefs at Anfa, once Montgomery's British Eighth Army crossed into Tunisian territory from Libya, General Sir Harold R. L. G. Alexander, British ground commander in Egypt and Libya, would command the new Eighteenth Army Group. This group would encompass Anderson's First Army, Montgomery's Eighth Army, the U.S. II Corps, and General Juin's French XIX Corps. Patton, to his private distress, would play no part in the final campaign for Africa.[123]

George searched his soul for the reason why he, the tactical expert, the founder of America's desert training school, a pioneer in tank development, kept getting pushed aside in favor of lesser men like Fredendall. *"I wish someone would listen to me,"* he wrote. *"I have something which makes people reluctant to question me; perhaps I always have an answer based on truth and not bootlick."*[124]

Perhaps. Or perhaps Patton's truth was just a little too far removed from the truth that was accepted by the Allied command.

What Patton did not know—what few people were permitted to know—was that another, bigger assignment lay just around the corner. At the Anfa conference, FDR, Churchill, and the Combined Chiefs had struck a complex bargain that called for an amphibious invasion of Sicily, dubbed Operation HUSKY. The chiefs had placed General Eisenhower in charge of planning the operation, but this put Ike in a bind because, as the chiefs may have noticed, he was already running one campaign, and not making swift progress at that. Two campaigns, in two different lands, would be asking a great deal of any man.[125]

Stuck with these widely disparate tasks, Ike asked Patton, his most experienced amphibious commander, to plan the American side of the HUSKY invasion. George's appointment provided some direction to the U.S. ground forces, but with naval, air, and British ground chiefs reporting to him on both North Africa and Sicily, Ike's duties still stretched him to the breaking point. Marshall, quick to spot an organizational disaster in the making, urged Ike to find some "eyes and ears" to watch over the battle front while Ike took care of the big picture in Algiers. Shortly afterward, Ike cabled Marshall a list of stateside officers he wanted to help him run the theater. On his list was Major General Omar N. Bradley.[126]

As Ike adjusted to the realities of his expanded theater, a personal problem emerged in the complicating presence of his comely driver, Kay Summersby. Kay stood out in press photographs of Ike's staff, and her central position in his entourage—a position not typically occupied by a foreign driver—brewed tension on the home front. After a reference to Ike's "beautiful Irish driver" appeared in *Life* magazine, Ike had to go out of his way to assure Mamie there was nothing untoward between him and Kay—or anyone else, for that matter. He pointed out that by moving to North Africa, Kay was stationed closer to her fiancé, whom she planned to marry the following June. Shoring up his defensive lines, he answered Mamie's unspoken question by declaring, *"If anyone is so banal and foolish enough to lift an eyebrow at an old duffer such as I am in connection with Waacs—Red Cross workers—nurses and drivers—you will know that I've no emotional involvements and will have none."*[127]

Of course, regardless of the true nature of their affiliation, Ike and Kay's proximity was wonderful grist for the office gossip mill. Lord Nelson had once remarked, "Once past Gibraltar, every man is a bachelor," and now that Ike's cadre had forged well beyond that famous landmark, many an officer had stowed his wedding band or embarked upon a campaign of conquest. President Roosevelt's son Elliott, a reconnaissance pilot, was briefly engaged to Beetle's secretary, for instance, and Tex Lee quickly took up with one of the available Red Cross girls.[128]

It was hardly an unusual story, though the fact that the Kay Summersby tale implicated the Supreme Commander made the subject irresistible to much of the AFHQ staff, and even Ike's field generals. Eisenhower's deputy, Everett Hughes, for instance, included a number of references to Ike and Kay in his diary. *"Discussed Kay [with Ike],"* Hughes scribbled in one entry. *"I don't know if Ike is alibiing or not. Says he likes her, wants to hold her hand, accompanies her to house, doesn't sleep with her. He doth protest too much, especially in view of the gal's reputation in London."* Patton, who didn't like Kay, afforded her the same polite deference one would give to a venomous spider. But publicly, he and Bradley kept tight-lipped about their inferences, even though the two men saw little to allow them to certify that Ike's association with Kay was a wholly innocent one.[129]

Eisenhower, stuffed into the pressure cooker that was AFHQ, needed as much unofficial companionship as anyone; an extrovert by nature, he probably needed more than most. Whether it was playing bridge with his staff, whacking golf balls with Butch, shooting pistols with Tex Lee, or riding horseback with Kay, Ike thrived on the energy of companions, who took his mind off the business of death and acted as his sounding board from time to time. Kay's earthy charm eased Ike's mind, and his confidence in her as a driver, secretary, bridge partner, and friend made her an immovable fixture in his wartime domain. Whatever the nature of their relationship, Everett's diary hit upon the one dispositive point: *"Maybe Kay will help Ike win the war."*[130]

In mid-February, General Marshall reaffirmed his faith in Eisenhower's stewardship by promoting him to full general. Despite the lukewarm reception Ike had received at the Casablanca conference, Marshall had pressed Roosevelt for Ike's promotion when they returned to Washington. On February 11, FDR submitted Eisenhower's name to the Senate, which ratified the promotion that same day. As the twelfth officer in U.S. history to wear a fourth star—his hero Ulysses S. Grant was the first—Ike gathered his household staff together and gave them each a one-grade promotion. Patton sent Ike a warm congratulatory cable, to which Ike graciously responded, "No one else can understand as well as I how much I owe you." That evening, Ev Hughes and Harry Butcher broke out drinks to toast to Ike's good fortune, and a beaming General Eisenhower and his war family broke out the phonograph to sing "One Dozen Roses" and other popular tunes. It was a badly needed respite from the strains of war.[131]

Far to the east, a world away from the delighted notes wafting through a little villa in Algiers, tank and scout car drivers gunned engines in the darkness. Rommel's troops began assembling at jumping-off points. Gasoline was distributed. Ammunition stocks were sent forward; weapons were checked.

Under the twinkling desert stars, the enemy coiled to strike.

SIX

A LONG-LOST BROTHER

It is possible that a necessity might arise for my relief and consequent demotion.... Modern war is a very complicated business and governments are forced to treat individuals as pawns.

—Ike to his son, February 19, 1943

THE KEY TO THE TUNISIAN PORTS—that is to say, the key to victory in Africa—was control of the passes that led through the two Dorsal Mountain chains into central Tunisia. Just behind these rocky promontories lay Ike's problem. In February 1943 von Arnim's Fifth Panzer Army was poised just beyond the mountain passes, while to the south near Mareth, Rommel's *Deutsch-Italienische Panzerarmee* faced Montgomery along a strong defensive belt. For both armies, the lifeline to the Fatherland ran through Tunis and Bizerte, and without the petrol, food, and 88mm artillery rounds that Berlin funneled through those ports, Hitler's legions wouldn't last a week.[1]

On the Allied side of the Dorsals, Major General Lloyd Fredendall's II U.S. Corps, under Anderson's British First Army, manned the southern stretch along the Algerian-Tunisian border. In the center stood the French corps, and to the far north, opposite Tunis and Bizerte, Anderson's British Army completed Eisenhower's thin chain. To reach the ports, Ike needed Fredendall to hold open two Dorsal crossing points. The first pass lay at Maknassy to the south, a town that straddled a slender, miserable highway stretching toward Gafsa. The second pass, a little north, was Faïd Pass, a winding path east of the town of Sidi bou Zid. If Lloyd could push east from the hamlet of Kasserine and capture Sidi bou Zid and Maknassy, the Eastern Dorsals would be open for business; Ike could drive a wedge

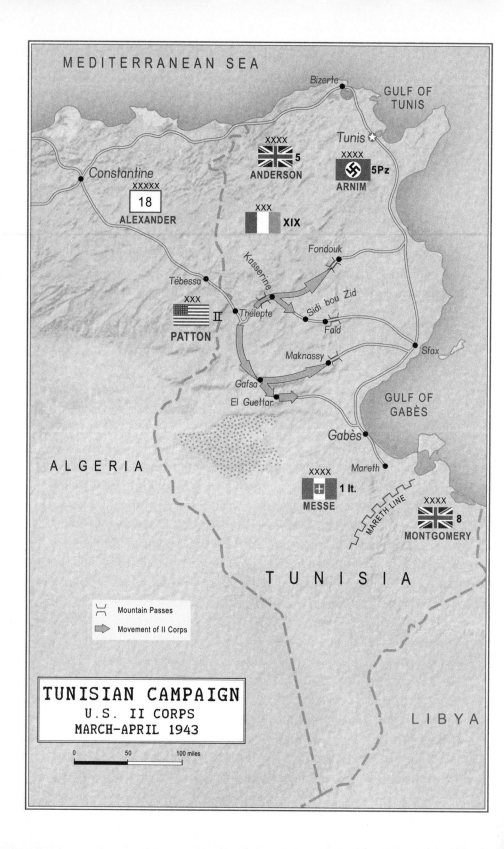

MEDITERRANEAN SEA

GULF OF TUNIS

Bizerte

Tunis

XXXX
5
ANDERSON

XXXX
5Pz
ARNIM

Constantine

XXXXX
18
ALEXANDER

XXX
XIX

Fondouk

Kasserine

Tébessa

XXX
II
PATTON

Thélepte

Sidi bou Zid

Faïd

Maknassy

Sfax

Gafsa

El Guettar

GULF OF GABÈS

Gabès

ALGERIA

Mareth

XXXX
1 It.
MESSE

MARETH LINE

XXXX
8
MONTGOMERY

TUNISIA

Mountain Passes

Movement of II Corps

TUNISIAN CAMPAIGN
U.S. II CORPS
MARCH–APRIL 1943

0   50   100 miles

LIBYA

between Fifth Panzer Army and Rommel's men, and his two British steam-rollers would crush them one at a time.[2]

But Rommel and von Arnim were not about to let the green, disjointed Americans get between them, and they prepared to hand the Yanks their first major setback. While von Arnim's vaunted 10th Panzer Division quietly moved up to Faïd Pass, Rommel's 21st Panzer Division crept northwest toward Gafsa. The German commanders planned to hit the Americans at Sidi bou Zid, overrun Allied air bases at Thélepte, then push west through Kasserine Pass onto Algerian soil, smashing the south flank of the Allied line. The two German commanders had aligned their sights on the weak link in the chain: Eisenhower's Americans.[3]

Allied reconnaissance had detected a concentration of panzers along Anderson's front, and Fredendall's hotheaded G-2 intelligence officer, Colonel Benjamin "Monk" Dickson, had warned Anderson of a probable attack from the south. But Ike's own G-2, Brigadier Eric Mockler-Ferryman, concluded that von Arnim was preparing to hit the Allies north of the American lines, at Fondouk. Because Mockler-Ferryman was one of the few men privy to deciphered German Enigma intercepts circulated under the code name ULTRA, Ike valued his prognostications over the shrill warnings of the man on the ground.[4]

Based on intelligence forecasts from AFHQ and British First Army's G-2 staff, Anderson moved a U.S. armored column north to shore up the British sector. The move drained reserve firepower from II Corps, and Fredendall further depleted his armored strength by sending other tank crews rearward to Tébessa and scattering the rest like seeds in a strong wind. Though Eisenhower had ordered him to keep a "large, central and powerful reserve" ready, Fredendall allowed pieces of his command to become isolated along the Eastern Dorsals, unable to support one another in the event of a rapid enemy strike.[5]

On February 12, Ike paid a visit to Fredendall's headquarters, a bunker complex nestled in an immense gulch near Tébessa. The command post, some seventy miles behind the front lines, had been fortified by a regiment of engineers who labored for three weeks boring deep tunnels into the Tunisian rock.[6]

Fredendall's bunker was beautifully laid out for a heroic last stand, but the compound hardly sent stirring messages of confidence to his troops. It looked more like an Alamo than the headquarters of an aggressive field commander, and enlisted men dubbed the place "Lloyd's Very Last Resort." When he glimpsed the monstrosity, Ike was visibly embarrassed, and like many first-time visitors, he made several caustic comments about the place.[7]

Leaving Fredendall and his sappers to complete their excavations, Ike drove to the front and spent the night with the scattered shards of the 1st Armored Division, one that Ike had told Fredendall to hold as a compact, mobile reserve force. What he found at 1st Armored was even more disturbing than Fredendall's bunker: Tank platoons were spread out, communications were unreliable, and the division's commander, Major General Orlando "Pinky" Ward, had been shut out of his own command by Fredendall, who despised him. Butcher said the two men were "almost high-schoolish in their criticism of one another, not only to Truscott and Smith, but to Ike." Fredendall, lacking confidence in Ward, began bypassing the division commander and issued his orders directly to Ward's combat commands.[8]

Although Marshall had warned Ike to get rid of anyone in whom he lacked confidence—and Eisenhower repeated this instruction to other generals—Ike hesitated to replace Fredendall. After all, Marshall had shown confidence in Lloyd by placing him in command of the Oran landing force, and Marshall's approval counted for a great deal in Ike's book. Besides that, Eisenhower was still feeling his way through the process of executive command. At this point, he felt he needed to give field commanders a fair chance—perhaps more than one fair chance—before casting them into the darkness. If he didn't, he worried, he would never find out who would become this war's Phil Sheridan, Stonewall Jackson, or William T. Sherman.[9]

So whistling past the graveyard, Ike hoped things in the field would sort themselves out. Before Rommel did anything dangerous.

On February 14, the Germans struck. Von Arnim's 10th Panzer Division burst through the Faïd Pass, slashing through Fredendall's thin lines around Sidi bou Zid and sending the Americans reeling west toward Kasserine. The next morning, Rommel's 21st Division rolled up from the southeast, steamrolling through Gafsa and enveloping the startled Yanks. As Fredendall's men withdrew toward Kasserine Pass, crowding the valley floor, Rommel's panzers caught up with them like Pharaoh's chariots. Germans and Italians swarmed over the high ground, sending artillery shells down upon the confused, retreating soldiers, and by February 20, Fredendall's line buckled as his men fled for their lives.[10]

* * *

Ike, following the steady retreat from his advance post at Constantine, sank into thick, black gloom with each fresh report of American losses. Losses of territory. Of men. Vehicles. Fuel.

In the first two days of fighting, Ike learned, Fredendall had ordered supply dumps destroyed, abandoned his bedrock headquarters, and lost over 2,500 soldiers, 112 tanks, and 280 other vehicles. The advance air base at Thélepte, a critical link in the Allied air defense chain, had to be evacuated. By the time Ike got back to AFHQ on February 16, he feared that Fredendall might have squandered as many as five thousand men and vast amounts of critical equipment.[11]

As casualty returns were counted and re-counted, Ike learned that American losses along the eighty-five-mile retreat were even worse than he had feared. In the end, his boys were saved only by German indecision and severe fuel shortages, which forced Rommel to pull back on the night of February 22–23. Butcher summed up the candid view among Ike's inner circle: "It's the worst walloping we have taken in this fight, and perhaps the stiffest setback of our ground forces in the war." "Headquarters," remarked Kay, "had all the cheer of an empty funeral parlor."[12]

What made Kasserine Pass particularly demoralizing for Ike was that it was U.S. troops whose teeth were being kicked in. Eisenhower may have been an Allied commander leading a multinational coalition, but these were *American* troops—*his* troops—and they had been humiliated before the world. The defeat tore a hole in American morale, from the private in the slit trench to the brass at the St. Georges; against the impersonal rumble of conversations, telephones, and typewriters in the background, Ike sank into despair. After a day absorbing reports of disaster, he slumped back to his quarters, plucking out "Taps" on the villa's piano as he stared blankly at the black and white keys. "I don't think I ever saw him lower than he was that night," his faithful sergeant Mickey McKeogh wrote.[13]

One of a commander's duties is to deliver bad news to his superiors, and Ike dutifully sent reports back to Washington and London, the capital cities where office-bound superiors in wood-paneled rooms expected the African war to be over by mid-May. Teletype lines crackled as memoranda, situation reports, and explanations buzzed from Algiers to the various Combined Chiefs. So many explanations, in fact, that Marshall shot back, "I am disturbed by the thought that you feel under necessity in such a trying situation to give so much personal time to us. . . . You can concentrate on the battle with the feeling that it is our business to support you and not to harass you."[14]

If Ike had felt a noose tightening around his throat at Casablanca, he now felt the trapdoor opening beneath his feet. The grilling from Marshal Brooke at Anfa, the tepid reception from Roosevelt and Churchill, and now the American defeat at Kasserine pointed to one conclusion he could no longer deny. Sensing his tenure as Supreme Commander drawing to a close, on February 19 Ike laid some hard psychological groundwork for his family in a letter to his son, John. *"It is possible that a necessity might arise for my relief and consequent demotion,"* he wrote. *"It will not break my heart and it should not cause you any mental anguish. . . . Modern war is a very complicated business and governments are forced to treat individuals as pawns."*[15]

But for the moment, he was still the Allied commander, and running his tired blue eyes over the jumbled situation maps, Ike wondered whether it might be time to replace Fredendall. Although Lloyd had been hamstrung by orders from Anderson, the irascible Westerner had made some terrible dispositions of his own. He never visited his front line, he'd built a hideout worthy of a Cecil B. DeMille film, and he collapsed under pressure. Then, when the extent of the defeat became apparent, Fredendall spouted off about Anderson and Ward, and why the disaster was their fault, not his. Why Ward, he contended, should be immediately relieved of command.[16]

Ike was skeptical of Fredendall's shrill protests of innocence, but he could not diagnose the problem accurately from Algiers, and he didn't have time to conduct a personal investigation. So he sent for Ernie Harmon, the barrel-chested tanker who had led the armored landings in Morocco. He ordered Harmon to stabilize the situation, then recommend whom Ike should send home.[17]

It was a delicate time for the II Corps, and Ike tried to buck up Fredendall by offering his support for any offensive action the corps commander might see fit to take. He even told Fredendall, without much sincerity, "I have every confidence that under your inspiring leadership current advances of the enemy will be stopped in place." But deep inside, Ike knew either that Fredendall or Ward was to blame for the Kasserine disaster, and someone's head had to roll.[18]

The first head, however, would not be Fredendall's. Years before, after graduating from Leavenworth, Ike had written, "Trust not the G-2 artist; he fools himself, let him not also fool you." Seduced by Mockler-Ferryman's ULTRA analysis, Eisenhower had been guilty of that sin. AFHQ and First

Army had refused to heed warnings from Fredendall's staff, warnings based on hard evidence from the field rather than jumbled radio intercepts. So Ike relieved Brigadier Mockler-Ferryman, replacing him with a capable British brigadier named Kenneth Strong. For good measure, Ike also sent one of Pinky Ward's commanders packing, along with one of the 1st Division's regimental colonels.[19]

In the midst of disaster, Eisenhower was learning the vital art of relieving subordinates. The Army's rolls boasted a thousand generals and seven thousand colonels, and though each blow of the ax pained him, Ike was learning to tap into this vast, willing pool of replacements. A few days after Rommel withdrew from Kasserine, Ike gave his friend Gee Gerow some stiff advice that reflected his current thinking:

> [O]fficers that fail to devote themselves completely and exclusively to the task must be ruthlessly weeded out. . . . You must be tough . . . [on] the lazy, the slothful, the indifferent or the complacent. Get rid of them. . . . For God's sake don't keep anybody around that you say to yourself, "He may get by"—He won't. Throw him out.[20]

"Throw him out." Ike was hearing that chorus a lot lately. Ernie Harmon, a man who had all the charm of a half-track, bluntly told Ike that Fredendall was "no damned good. You ought to get rid of him." Alexander, who took command of Fifteenth Army Group as Rommel's panzers were battering the Americans, delicately seconded Harmon's opinion. He suggested, "I'm sure you must have a better man than that."[21]

Yet for the moment Ike did nothing about Marshall's man in Tunisia. He wanted a third opinion, preferably from another Marshall man.[22]

Omar Bradley, commanding the 28th Infantry Division at Camp Gordon Johnston, was preparing his men for amphibious training, a phase he hoped would be the last step in his division's long journey from reactivation to combat.[23]

As Brad saw it, he had earned the right to lead his men into battle. Three decades in uniform seemed an awfully long time for him to wait, and his years at Benning, his years under Marshall, and his years in the War Department should have earned him command of a fighting division by now. In fact, why not a corps? After all, a third star would require only a couple of orphaned divisions in need of a good, solid commander, and Brad knew he could do the job.[24]

Bradley's dreams of higher command were stoked by a telegram from General Marshall that landed on his desk on February 12, 1943, his fiftieth birthday. Scanning it rapidly, Brad's eyes quickly lighted on the cable's concluding paragraph:

IT IS ONLY FITTING THAT YOUR BIRTHDAY SHOULD PRECEDE BY ONLY A FEW DAYS YOUR TRANSFER TO COMMAND A CORPS WHICH COMES AS A LONG-DELAYED ACKNOWLEDGEMENT OF YOUR SPLENDID RECORD WITH THE 28TH DIVISION. CONGRATULATIONS AND BEST WISHES.[25]

"Your transfer to command a corps."

It was about the sweetest thing Bradley had ever read. Words like those did not come lightly from the tight-lipped Marshall. Something, he knew, was about to happen. The message from Olympus was too specific to be anything but a harbinger of good things. Make that great things.

"To command a corps."

Three days later secret orders arrived directing General Bradley to take command of X Corps, a headquarters outfit assembling in Texas. But Brad barely had time to savor his new orders when an abrupt call from General McNair's personnel chief jostled him from dreams of a third star and a corps command:

"We're cutting orders for you today, Brad. You're going overseas on extended active duty. Not the division—just you."

The news floored Bradley. "I've just received orders to Temple, Texas, to . . ."

"Oh, that was yesterday."

Yesterday?

"Well, what kind of clothes?" Brad pressed. "Which way do I go?"

The question "Which way do I go?" was a tough one to ask a War Department staffer over the telephone. Army regulations were specific on that point—no discussing troop movements on an open line, even if it was only the movement of one soldier. Loose lips sink ships, and all that.

The reply was guarded. "Remember your classmate? You're going to join him."

Classmate?

Eisenhower.

I'm going to Africa.

Try as he might, by the end of the call, all Brad could ferret out was that he would report to General Eisenhower in Africa, and would receive an initial briefing in Washington as soon as he could get there. He could take only a couple of low-level staffers—his aides Chet Hansen and Lew Bridge, to be exact. Even his driver, Sergeant Stoute, would have to stay home for this trip. And because Brad's orders were secret, he couldn't even tell his staff where he was going.[26]

Still wondering what Marshall had in store for him, Bradley stuffed his shaving kit and a few essentials into a footlocker and suitcase; because he was going to face the German Army, the War Department also ordered him to bring along a .45 pistol, twenty-one rounds of ammunition, a helmet, and a gas mask. Thus outfitted, Brad sped to the airport, Chet and Lew in tow, and flew to Washington for an appointment at the newly completed Pentagon building.[27]

Marshall, it seems, had decided that Ike needed more professionals with him. American professionals, to be precise. Men to direct the battles at the corps and army level while Ike tangled with the Combined Chiefs, Churchill, the French, the media, and everyone else. The day before the Kasserine disaster unfolded, Marshall had cabled Ike, "I propose General Omar N. Bradley for the detail in question," and Eisenhower quickly accepted. Bradley would be the Supreme Commander's eyes on the front, the man who would give Ike his unvarnished opinion on the state of the battlefield.[28]

Reflecting on his assignment, as well as his loss of both the 28th Division and X Corps in a two-day span, Omar Bradley decided he hadn't been robbed after all. At least, not completely. His train to corps command may have been derailed for now, but he had a ticket to the front lines, which was in some ways even better. The experience he would gain would make him a natural for a corps command in the Mediterranean theater, and if nothing else, he was finally going to see some action. "For the first time in thirty-one and a half years of active Army service," he remembered, "I was on my way to a real war."[29]

After enjoying his last American meal for the unforeseeable future—a slice of cherry pie and two glasses of milk—Brad embarked on a mind-numbing ninety-hour journey to Algiers. He, Chet, and Lew touched down on February 23, the day Rommel's panzers withdrew from their Kasserine victory, and Kay picked up the trio in Ike's big armored Cadillac. She drove the tired men through the twisting streets of Algiers, and deposited them at the entrance to the Hôtel St. Georges.[30]

Bedell Smith, Prince of Algiers, greeted Brad warmly and showed the newcomers around the bustling hotel, now cluttered with phone lines, filing cabinets, couriers, and staffers scurrying about in French, British, and American uniforms. After a few brief introductions to the Allied team, the Hoosier ushered Bradley into the office of the Supreme Commander, where Brad would find out exactly why he had been summoned from sunny Florida.[31]

"In a way it was a 'get to know each other' session," Bradley recalled afterward. "Although we had known each other at West Point thirty years before, serving in the same company, we had not been close. We had seen little or nothing of each other in the intervening years. We had never served together; we had exchanged few letters. In all those years I had only seen Ike a few times, fleetingly, at class reunions or Army-Navy football games, usually with Mamie and Mary in tow. Since Mary and Mamie did not— and never would—take to each other, these occasional social meetings had not rekindled our earlier acquaintance into any sort of flame."[32]

Despite their years of separation, or perhaps because of them, Ike was delighted to see his old classmate. He had a high regard for Omar, who had outranked him when they wore the cadet shako. Ike had, in fact, written a warm tribute to Brad in the West Point *Howitzer* twenty-eight years earlier: "Some of us will some day be bragging to our grandchildren, 'Sure, General Bradley was a classmate of mine.'" In Bradley, Ike felt he had another friend in Algiers, someone he could trust, someone loyal to him. "He greeted me warmly and effusively," Brad remembered, "like a long-lost brother, and instantly made me feel at home—and needed."[33]

Their pleasantries finished, Ike got down to business. As Brad recalled, "he took the time to brief me personally (map, pointer and all) on the recent German offensive." Eisenhower outlined the disposition of the opposing armies; then he sketched out Omar's first assignment: "Just as quickly as you can," he began, "I want you to get up to the front and look for the things I would want to see myself if I only had the time. Bedell will give you a letter telling Fredendall and the others that you are to act as my eyes and ears."[34]

What struck Bradley as he watched his old friend sweep the pointer over the African expanse was how much Ike had matured. He was no longer the class-cutting, cigarette-sneaking rulebreaker from F Company whom

Brad had known so long ago. The Ike he saw pacing the office in a buzz of nervous energy was a charming, mature, almost patrician statesman with a first-rate mind and a sense of his own businesslike authority. He could charm, he could curse, he could persuade, and he could demand. The small-town Kansas linebacker had become a *commander*.[35]

But as impressed as Bradley was with Ike's poise, the Missourian also thought he sensed another Dwight Eisenhower lying just below the surface, an Eisenhower shielded from the public and let out only among those he trusted. As Ike spoke, Brad remembered later, "I noted another aspect of Ike new to me: a deep-seated, barely controlled anger. The public perceived him as smiling and genial. But I saw that he had very thin skin, a short fuse, and an explosive temper." When the conversation drifted to the Darlan Deal, Brad wrote, "Ike's anger welled up and for a very long time—overly long, I thought—he defended the deal, for which he had been severely criticized in the media worldwide. Media criticism was a new experience for Ike, as it was to all of us who had grown up in the obscurity of the peacetime Army. It was not easy for any of us to cope with it."

Over the next two days, Brad pored over situation reports and maps, acclimating himself to the headquarters and the front. One thing he immediately noticed was that "Ike brooked no American criticism of the French or British—especially the British. Any American who criticized the British stood a very good chance of being busted and sent home." He later recalled, "I came away with the opinions expressed back in Tom Handy's OPD: In his efforts to achieve harmonious 'coalition warfare,' Ike had become excessively pro-British in his attitudes and thinking. . . . I believe his close association with Kay and her family likewise contributed to Ike's pro-British attitudes, that her influence over him was greater than is generally realized."[36]

As Ike's spy, official or otherwise, General Bradley did not rate much of a welcome in Fredendall's house. Upon Bradley's arrival at II Corps's command post, Fredendall banished him to a small, windowless building— "quarters unsuitable even for a second lieutenant," Brad complained. From there he began watching and learning.[37]

Bradley and Bedell Smith spent the next couple of days listening to Fredendall and his staff expound on the many places, other than Fredendall's abandoned bunker, where the real blame for Kasserine lay. Brad found Fredendall and his staff to be "rabidly, if not obscenely, anti-British," and

Beetle snorted that the major general was "incompetent or crazy or both." Even Butcher, a novice at military matters, understood the problem. He wrote in his diary, *"If you ask me, it should have been Patton in the first place, and if it weren't for Ike not wanting to let a commander down when he is drooping, Fredendall would be out, but Ike isn't the kind to let his commander down. Ike told me a week ago he wished he had sent Patton instead, but Patton had to be held in Morocco to cover possible Spanish moves, and also for the American attack in [Sicily]."*[38]

Soon afterward, Ike paid another visit to II Corps headquarters. Taking Bradley aside, he asked his old classmate, "What do you think of the command here?"

"Pretty bad," Omar replied. "I've talked to all the division commanders. To a man they've lost confidence in Fredendall as the corps commander."

"Thanks, Brad. You've confirmed what I thought was wrong."[39]

Fredendall was out. He would get his third star, a ticket home, a hero's welcome, and an army to train in Tennessee.

But Ike needed a replacement for II Corps, someone with good organizational skills and a keen sense of urgency. He called his trusted friend, General Clark, and asked Wayne to take over the corps.

It should have been an easy move, Ike figured. After all, when Wayne took over Fifth Army, he had assured Ike, *"I hope you will consider my going as only temporary and know that I stand ready and anxious to serve you in any capacity in order to bring you the success you deserve."*[40]

But the "American Eagle" refused to take over the corps. He was concerned, he intimated, that since he was commander of Fifth Army, reassignment to a mere corps command would be perceived by everyone as a demotion. If Ike would assign an army to him, that of course would be a different story. Otherwise, he had pressing business with Fifth Army to manage.[41]

Ike was flabbergasted. He had told Marshall in 1942 that he would never, *ever* commit the sin of placing his personal ambition over the role assigned to him, even if that meant sitting out the war as an unknown brigadier, shuffling papers behind a government-issue desk in Washington. Now his best man was committing that very sin. Clark may have been a publicity hound, someone Ike had to rein in from time to time, but this was just the sort of thing he would have expected from a prima donna like MacArthur. Not Clark.[42]

Well, Ike's personal disappointment was beside the point. He would not push Clark if Clark didn't want to go. Clark could keep his "manure pile," as Ike called it. But Ike needed an aggressive leader, someone to get the American fighting man back on his feet, and he needed that leader *now*.[43]

Looking across the Sahara, Ike thought he knew the right man for the job.

George Patton had spent his weeks since the Casablanca conference much as he had spent them since the French surrender—sitting, waiting, fretting. Watching the war go by.

He might shuttle around Rabat or motor over to Casablanca in his Packard limousine. Or fly over the desert inspecting scattered remnants of his original force. But with no operations to run, nothing to plan, no enemy to fight, Patton played the comfortable but unfulfilling role of American viceroy in Morocco.

Every now and then he stirred himself and vented to his friends, usually over the way the war was being run. At the end of January, for instance, he had a long conversation with Clark, who "told me the damndest thing I have ever heard." The final attack on Tunis, Clark said, was to be carried out by two British armies, Monty's Eighth and Anderson's First—and Anderson, a Briton, would command the American II Corps! George raged to his diary: *"Shades of J.J. Pershing! We have sold our birthright and the mess of pottage is, in my opinion, the title of Allied Commander to General Marshall. I am shocked and distressed."*[44]

Personally, he was glad it was Ike's mess, and maybe Clark's, so he couldn't be blamed for whatever insults would be inflicted on American honor. *"I think that I was fortunate in not being made Deputy Commander-in-Chief to Ike,"* he told himself. *"I truly think that the whole set up is the result of clever politics by the British and selfish ambition on our part."*[45]

But the biggest threat to Patton's aspirations did not come from the British, or AFHQ, or the politicians. It came from George's own mouth, his pronouncements and witticisms rattled off with a deliberate, offending flippancy that cloaked years of thought and study.

His sharp, vulgar wit was something his father had warned him about at the end of the last war, something Katherine Marshall had chided him for during his Fort Myer days. But it was a trait George could never shake—nor did he try—and in early February, after a lunch meeting where George had run his mouth one time too many, Ike sent his old friend a personal message:

You are quick-witted and have a facile tongue. As a result you frequently give the impression that you merely act on impulse and not upon study and reflection. People who know you as well as I do are quite well aware of the fact that much of your talk is a smoke-screen, but some of those in authority who have a chance to meet you only occasionally do not have this knowledge.

Talking as a kindly parent would to a troublesome adolescent, Ike continued,

My advice is, therefore, (if you want it) merely the old saw to "count to ten before you speak." This applies not only to criticism of Allies, a subject on which I am adamant, but to many others. A man once gave me an old proverb. It was this: "Keep silent and appear stupid; open your mouth and remove all doubt." I do not mean that this applies to you, as you damn well know, but I do mean that a certain sphinx-like quality upon occasion will do one hell of a lot toward enhancing one's reputation.[46]

Ike's words cut George to the quick. Patton had taken the young officer under his wing since 1919, invited the Eisenhowers to countless lunches and dinners, introduced Ike to the right people. He had even helped Ike and Mamie remodel their family living quarters at Camp Meade. As for his own reputation, George had studied the art of war, and he practiced it better than any other officer in the service. Ike had no business telling him to shut his mouth.

Then again, George could not dismiss Ike's words lightly, especially if, as Ike said, the opinion was held by "other" people. If by "other" people Ike meant Marshall or McNair or McNarney, then George was already in trouble, and he had damned well better take Ike's lecture to heart. Mulling the matter over, George wrote in his diary that night, *"Got a secret letter from Ike in which he advises me to be more circumspect and less flip in my conversation on military matters. He means well and I certainly have thus far failed to sell myself in a big way to my seniors."*[47]

The next day, George drafted a letter to Ike thanking him for the frankness of his advice. He wrote, *"Let me start by assuring you that I want your advice. I want it for two reasons, because you are my Commanding General and because you are my friend."*

He explained to Ike that his apparently flippant manner was the result of much forethought, not a half-cocked approach to war as it might have seemed to the less perceptive. But he admitted, *"I have realized for sometime that I do not present myself in the best light to my seniors. I feel that thanks to your thoughtfulness in writing me frankly, I shall in the future do much better. At least it shall be my constant study to follow your advice."*[48]

Patton was onto something here. He might grouse about Ike to his diary, or gossip with Clark and Hughes about the miserable way Eisenhower was running the war, but deep in his heart he knew his friend "meant well," and that, to a point, Ike would protect him from wolves who wore stars. Their friendship had become exactly what George had predicted a year earlier: a symbiotic relationship in which Ike's need for George's military talents, and George's need for a protector on high, were the central pillars.

But before sending Ike the conciliatory letter, George decided he'd better sleep on it. The next day, reflecting further, he decided not to send it.[49]

At the end of January, a light flickered in Patton's long, dreary tunnel. He learned, unofficially, that he had been tapped to plan Operation HUSKY, the invasion of Sicily. Ike confirmed the news over lunch on February 3. An elated Patton gave Eisenhower the credit for his ticket out of calmed waters, and a few weeks later he gave Beatrice a revised opinion of his former Tank Corps brother: *"D. has realy* [sic] *developed beyond belief and is quite a great man. He has certainly been nice to me. In fact I seem to have got more of a job than W[ayne], but that remains to be seen."*[50]

Not that the Sicilian operation was without its drawbacks, the most obvious being its low probability of success. After all, the Allies had been given a bloody nose by a French enemy that had inwardly wanted to surrender, and Patton's phenomenal luck with the Casablanca surf was a bolt of lightning that might not strike twice. After a few weeks in Rabat, where his newly organized I Armored Corps (Reinforced) was studying the challenges of an amphibious landing, George confessed, *"We all realize it is a damned poor bet."* But he added, *"It is an honor to be trusted with the American part of the plan. I feel I will win."*[51]

While Patton was planning his "damned poor bet," he had a chance to see his British colleagues—the ones he would be fighting alongside—up close for the first time. Hopping a B-17, he flew to Tripoli for a military conference, where for three days British ground and air commanders lectured their American cousins on lessons they had learned while fighting the Germans over the past three and a half years. George scribbled down some initial impressions of His Majesty's field commanders, including Alexander ("very quiet and not impressive looking") and Montgomery ("small, very alert, wonderfully conceited, and the best soldier—or so it seems—I have met in this war"). Aside from Montgomery, whom he called "sort of a Stone Wall Jackson type"—big words from a former VMI cadet—he dismissed most of the British war chiefs as "the same non-committal clerical types as our generals." Patton's instincts told him that where fighting was to be done, he was still in a class by himself.[52]

On the fourth of March, while returning from an afternoon ride on General Noguès's big charger, a thoroughbred named Joyeuse, George was flagged down by a messenger bearing an urgent dispatch from Algiers. It was from Eisenhower. The message directed General Patton to leave for Algiers the next day for extended field service. George told his diary that night: *"I phoned 'Beetle' Smith, Ike's chief of staff, and asked what it was about. He said that I may relieve Fredendall. Well it is taking over rather a mess but I will make a go of it. I think I will have more trouble with the British than with the Boches. 'God favors the brave, Victory is to the audacious!'"*[53]

SEVEN

FORGING THE PARTNERSHIP

[Ike] was well aware of the British leaks. His failure to stop them contributed to our growing paranoia that Ike was so pro-British he didn't much care what happened to II Corps.

—Bradley

PATTON'S NEW COMMAND consisted of Terry Allen's Big Red One, Ward's 1st Armored Division, Manton Eddy's 9th Infantry Division, and Doc Ryder's 34th Infantry Division, a total of around 90,000 men. A damned fine fighting force, if properly led, he thought. George's study of history had convinced him that the American soldier was the best-equipped, best-fed, and fastest-moving fighting man the world had ever seen. The men of II Corps only needed order and discipline to lick any force that Hitler, Mussolini or anyone else cared to throw against them. And where discipline was concerned, Patton knew he was just the man to give it to them.[1]

Back in Rabat, he packed his bags, hastily leaving his deputy commander, Geoff Keyes, in charge of I Armored Corps at Rabat. Taking along Gaffey, Lambert, his G-2, Oscar Koch, and his youthful aide, Captain Dick Jenson, George flew to Maison Blanche to confer with Ike and Bedell Smith before heading to Tunisia. Ike, Beetle, and Butch met him on the tarmac.[2]

The runway conference, as Butch recorded, began as a kind of oratory contest in which George and Ike made opening statements directed at themselves as much as each other. Ike, concerned about George's attitude toward their British allies—allies with whom he would be working closely—commenced the discussion with his gospel of Allied unity, a now-standard sermon. Patton, emotional over the recent capture of his son-in-law, a lieutenant colonel in the 1st Armored Division, "damned the

Germans so violently and emotionally that tears came to his eyes three times during the short conference."[3]

Their rhetoric out of the way, both men got down to business. Ike gave Patton a handwritten letter relieving Fredendall, and sketched out Patton's duties as head of II Corps: "Patton's first and big task will be to assist the British Eighth Army get[ting] through the Mareth line," Butcher wrote. "His force is to tie up as much German strength as possible and secure Gafsa as a forward supply base for Montgomery's army."

To assist Patton, Ike also offered George the use of Omar Bradley, a sort of adjunct who would be "immediately available to you for any duty that you may desire, and will serve you cheerfully and effectively." Brad, Ike subsequently indicated, would be Patton's understudy for the first few weeks of the campaign. Once Patton had restored the American position, Brad could take over the campaign while Patton would return to Rabat, to complete plans for Sicily.[4]

Ike advised George to be "perfectly cold-blooded" about sacking officers, even old friends, who were not up to the task. He told George, "We cannot afford to throw away soldiers and equipment and . . . effectiveness" due to concern for "the feelings of old friends." Whether Ike's comment was a warning to George or a piece of friendly advice was left hanging, for the moment.

Before they shook hands and parted, Ike warned his old friend to take care of himself. "He doesn't need to prove his courage," Butch wrote. "General Ike wants him as a corps commander, not as a casualty."[5]

With Ike's words of welcome and advice, Patton sauntered back onto center stage, the place he always wished to be. But as he prepared to take the reins of his new Thoroughbred, George's lingering doubts over the man who had handed him the tether nagged at him like an itch inside his shoe. Ike had *"stressed that criticism of the B[ritish] must stop,"* George told his diary. He continued, *"I fear he has sold his soul to the devil on 'Cooperation,' which I think means we are pulling the chestnuts for our noble allies. . . . It is clear that I too must 'cooperate' or get out."*[6]

Patton arrived at Fredendall's headquarters on March 6, 1943, at 10:00 a.m. As Bradley recalled the moment years later:

> With sirens shrieking Patton's arrival, a procession of armored scout cars and half-tracks wheeled into the dingy square opposite

the schoolhouse headquarters of II Corps at Djebel Kouif. . . . The armored vehicles bristled with machine guns and their tall fishpole antennae whipped crazily overhead. In the lead car Patton stood like a charioteer. He was scowling into the wind and his jaw strained against the web strap of a two-starred steel helmet.[7]

Invading the empty French schoolhouse that housed the corps command post, Patton was appalled to find Fredendall and much of his staff still at breakfast. Struggling to remain proper with the outgoing general, George held his tongue until Fredendall had left; then he burned through corps headquarters like an African sirocco, aiming his practiced scowl and sharp tongue at clusters of lackadaisical staff officers, whom he berated into moving faster and acting more soldierly. He then moved on to visit his four divisions, sniffing out telltale signs of ineffectual leadership. The men's dress was poor. Their discipline was worse. *"34th is too defensive,"* he concluded. *"9th has 'Valor of Ignorance.' 1st is good. 1st Armored is timid. . . . I cannot see what Fredendall did to justify his existence. Have never seen so little order or discipline."*[8]

One of the many officers glad to see Fredendall gone was the new man from the States, Major General Omar Bradley. He hadn't gotten on well with General Fredendall, having spent the last two weeks in a windowless, dingy stinkhole of a mining company hotel for being one of Eisenhower's "spies," whom Fredendall would not countenance.

Neither would George, who bluntly told Bradley, "I'm not going to have any goddamn spies running around my headquarters." He snatched up the desk phone and told the operator to ring Freedom, Ike's headquarters in Algiers. Soon Bedell Smith's grating voice came on the line.[9]

"Bedell, I'm calling you about Bradley and his job up here," George said. "Look, we're awfully hard up for a good Number Two man as deputy corps commander. Bradley can fill the bill perfectly. If it's all right with Ike, I'm going to make Bradley my deputy commander. He can help us out and I'd like to have him. Okay? Then clear it with Ike."[10]

Beetle called back a short time later to relay Ike's approval. With a single phone call, George had turned Ike's spy into his right-hand man.[11]

Tromping back to his office, George sat down with his adjutant and pounded out standing orders that burned the Patton brand onto II Corps. Every soldier, including specialists such as nurses and auto mechanics, would henceforth wear the regulation helmet liner. Leggings, neckties, and polished hardware were now mandatory for all personnel, whether in combat or behind the lines. Jackets and raincoats would be buttoned up. Breakfast at the corps mess hall would be served until 6:00 a.m.; then the chow line shut down until lunch. Accompanying his general orders were bombastic instructions to junior officers mandating absolute, rigid enforcement of the Patton Dress Code.[12]

George knew that his men—officers as well as enlisted ranks—would curse, grumble, and try to shirk his regulations. That was what fighting men did. "Soldiers are always contrary," he once told his G-2, Colonel Oscar Koch. "I'd issue them coats without buttons, and I'll bet that within twenty-four hours they'd find some, sew them on, and keep them buttoned."[13]

Patton intended to use the soldier's instinct to cut corners to get in their faces, to let them know there was a new, vigorous, all-seeing sheriff in town. Patton spent the next several days scurrying from regiment to regiment in his best Black Jack Pershing style, launching surprise attacks on unsuspecting officers and leaping on men from staff cars, Bantams, tanks, and half-tracks, inspecting uniforms, giving speeches, confiscating nonregulation knit caps, handing out fines, and cursing profusely. Penalties for noncompliance ran to $50 for officers and $25 for enlisted men. George took delight in personally assessing many of these fines.[14]

"When you hit their pocketbooks," he remarked smugly to Brad after a few hours of gigging men, "you get a quick response." In mid-March he reported to Ike, *"Just soaked two officers $25.00 each for not wearing tin hats as we have ordered. I guess I am a S.O.B. but Discipline will win the war."*[15]

Patton's rules obliged everyone to wear a helmet in his sector, without exception. Even Eisenhower, who almost never wore a helmet, fell in line to show his support. While Ike's entourage was visiting II Corps headquarters at Le Ceif, Patton ran across Mickey McKeogh, Ike's batman. Scowling down at Mickey, George asked him if he had twenty-five dollars to throw away. Mickey admitted he didn't, and George warned him to find a helmet.

Afterward, Mickey mentioned the incident to Ike, who blandly nodded and told Mickey to find him a helmet, since he didn't have twenty-five dollars to throw away, either. Ike spent the rest of his visit to Patton's headquarters in canvas leggings and a steel helmet.[16]

While Patton's tough, lowbrow methods sent a clear message to the GIs in his ranks, his earthy rhetoric offended many officers, who fumed silently through George's heavily salted lectures and drill-instructor tirades. Bradley was one of them.

"While some men prefer to lead by suggestion and example and other methods, Patton chose to drive his subordinates by bombast and threats," Brad later complained. "These mannerisms achieved spectacular results. But they were not calculated to win affection among his officers or men."[17]

Pondering George's rhetoric years later, the mild-mannered Missourian recalled,

Whenever he addressed men he lapsed into violent, obscene language. He always talked down to his troops. . . . [H]is language was studded with profanity and obscenity. I was shocked. He liked to be spectacular, he wanted men to talk about him and think of him. "I'd rather be looked at than overlooked." Yet when Patton was hosting at the dinner table, his conversation was erudite and he was well-read, intellectual and cultured. Patton was two persons: a Jekyll and Hyde.[18]

To his growing distress, Omar learned that the old rooster could be downright crude to senior officers, especially when he was "onstage," which was most of the time. Once, when the two men paid an impromptu visit to the headquarters of Major General Terry Allen, the veteran commander of the 1st Infantry Division, Brad saw George eye with contempt a row of slit trenches, a common precaution against Luftwaffe attacks.

George and "Terrible Terry" had a long history. Both hailed from Civil War–era army families. Both were from the West, and both had stopped Mauser bullets in the First World War—the hole in Patton's thigh was matched by one perforating Allen's jaw. They were cavalrymen of the old style, not "Benning men" like Bradley, and the two generals, religious yet prone to curse like the horse soldiers they were, argued violently whenever they disagreed.[19]

Patton's vulgar approach toward the hard-fighting Allen boiled over on that day's inspection, and when his eyes lit on those neat slit trenches, he did something he should have regretted.

"Terry, which one is yours?" he chirped in his tight tenor voice.

Allen pointed to one trench. With a smirk, Patton walked over to the edge of the cut, unbuttoned his fly, and pissed into the trench of the general who had led the Big Red One ashore at Oran.

Closing his fly, Patton sneered, "Now try to use it."[20]

General Allen and his rumpled deputy, Brigadier General Theodore Roosevelt Jr., stood in silence under the hot sun, red-faced and insulted. Their bodyguards, cradling Thompson submachine guns, glared menacingly at the erratic corps commander.

George sensed he had crossed a line, but he stiffly shrugged off the icy looks. He turned on his heel and marched off, a visibly embarrassed Bradley in tow.[21]

Brad was stunned by George's grotesque display. Shaking his head in disbelief, he later wrote, "At times I felt Patton, however successful he was as a corps commander, had not yet learned to command himself."

Sure, Brad would have enforced helmet rules, just like he would have enforced speeding rules. But neckties? Early breakfasts? Slit trenches? Years afterward, he commented, "For my taste, it was all excessively harsh; but intentionally or unintentionally, excess was Patton's style. A firm but more mature and considerate discipline would no doubt have achieved the same results. But he was the boss, and the stage was his." Brad felt George treated subordinates like idiots, ruling them in an iron-fisted, almost Prussian manner. Except that Prussians were too dignified to talk like George.[22]

Brad's style was much more low-key. He wore a simple uniform—a plain helmet, plain clothing, no Sam Brown belt or dress cap—and his only concession to George's affectations was a simple walking stick given to him by a former Pennsylvania congressman. While Patton mounted two ivory-handled revolvers on a thick gun belt with an oversize buckle—his "wrestling belt," Brad's aides chortled—Brad toted the same old, heavy Colt automatic he had been issued as a lieutenant.[23]

Brad's language was moderate, his tenor voice almost shy, and he got along better with his peers than George did because he sounded a lot less presumptuous. Like George, Bradley's Missouri twang seemed incongruous with his six-foot, muscled frame, though the contrast between sight and sound was not so pronounced as in Patton's case. George compensated for his nasal tone with profanity, wit, or both, while Brad compensated with gravitas and modesty. As war correspondent Ernie Pyle commented, "His voice was high-pitched and clear, but he spoke so gently a person couldn't hear him very far. . . . He always put people at their ease."[24]

Brad enjoyed movies, drank Coca-Cola by the case, devoured ice cream by the tub, and littered his oratory with Southernisms like "cain't" and homespun phrases like "fighting to beat the band." His language and gestures, such as his furrowed brow and use of understatement, stressed sincerity in contrast to George's artifice. Bradley occasionally swore, as did most generals, but he did not curse nearly so much as Patton or even Eisenhower; Brad's utterances also lacked the premeditated violence and scatological vulgarity of his immediate boss. In victory or crisis, the man seemed imperturbable, a sea captain who could be seen calmly loading his pipe on a ship's deck while the vessel rocked in a hurricane.[25]

There was one other difference. Unlike George, Bradley cared nothing for publicity. To Omar, the measure of a man was his results, not how he looked in a column for *The Saturday Evening Post*. "Any day I can stay out of the newspapers," he once told his staff, "is a day to the good." It was vintage Bradley.[26]

Brad's public image as an even-tempered "regular guy" bore a much closer resemblance to the Eisenhower model. But, unlike Patton, Brad was quick to sack deputies whose performance was less than stellar, and despite his egalitarian public image, he played favorites among those compelled to salute him. It may have been something he picked up from Marshall, but Bradley also deliberately wielded his natural talent for making subordinates feel ill at ease. It was something about his weathered look, those steel-rimmed bifocals, his tight grimace. The look of an old schoolmaster eyeing a lackluster student as the reproach was forming in the master's throat. "Despite his mildness the general was not what you would call easygoing," Pyle wrote. "People who worked with him had to produce or get out. They didn't get the traditional Army bawling-out from him, but they did get the gate."[27]

In a curious way, the differences between George and Brad were summed up in their boots. Bradley, like Ike, was an infantryman at heart. He wore the infantryman's high-cut russets and leggings—those coarse canvas leggings, straight-laced with seventeen maddeningly inconvenient grommets, that foot soldiers loved to bitch about. The leggings did little to ward off the cold, but they kept out most of the mud and some of the dirt. Made for the workingman, they didn't look good on a parade ground, but they were functional. Useful. *Reliable.*

Patton, like his brother horsemen, wore cavalry boots, knee-high brown leather with brass buckles running up the sides. The kind of boots an aide could shine and shine until they held a mirror finish. Boots that caught the light. Boots you could see in hundreds of oil portraits of field marshals from the nineteenth century. Boots for a Duke of Wellington, or a Marshal Murat, a J. E. B. Stuart. Or a Patton.

Boots Omar Bradley would not be caught dead wearing.

As much as he tried in later years, Brad could not fathom what made George tick. The gulf of upbringing, training, and personality that divided them was too vast for even Bradley's incisive mind to cross, assuming he ever had the time and inclination to measure the gap. Omar came from a small, poor family, a home where swearing and alcohol were both officially and unofficially forbidden, a home that had lost its patriarch when Omar was a boy. George's cloistered, wealthy upbringing, and the love and support of a successful father, had imbued him with a social confidence that bordered on megalomania and frequently crossed that fine boundary. Before the war, while George was hosting lavish dinner parties, shuttling polo ponies around the country, and sailing his yacht to Hawaii, Brad and Mary had struggled to make ends meet on a modest officer's salary and Brad's poker winnings. Where George excelled at individual contests, like track and fencing, Bradley was a team player, at his best when he stood upon the pitcher's mound, the leader of a cohesive nine-man organization.

For all the Army's efforts to standardize its officer corps, Omar Bradley embraced a philosophy of tactics that was very different from the methods of his boss. Brad had learned his trade in the infantry, a conservative branch wedded to dogma that harkened back many centuries. Brad's spirit of "fire and maneuver" was tempered by a doughboy's keen appreciation for the vulnerability of the human body when facing tanks, machine guns, howitzers, and mortar fragments. Going off half-cocked was a mortal sin among the old-line footsloggers; most infantry generals lived by the dictum of Confederate General James Longstreet, who once advised an attacking subordinate, "Hit hard when you start, but don't start until you have everything ready."[28]

Brad's prewar duties as a mathematics and tactics teacher at West Point and Benning reinforced those conservative instincts. He had spent most of his career laying out ground rules for students to follow in this physically hazardous profession. To Omar, an officer should never deviate from the Army's tried and tested rules unless the benefits of breaking them were clear and demonstrable. Those who broke the rules would answer for the results at their own peril.[29]

Bradley, like Eisenhower, also felt a particular sensitivity toward logistics, which usually governed his actions. As he once outlined his philosophy to his headquarters team:

> I explained to my staff that G-2 [intelligence] existed to tell me what should be done on the basis of information concerning the enemy. G-4 [logistics] was to tell me what could be done in view of our limitations on supply. Then once I made my decision, G-3 [operations] was to do it. Thus a timid G-4 could directly restrict the scope of his commander's operations. And similarly a resourceful G-4 could expand it.[30]

In short, tactics to Omar was a type of mathematical problem solving. Like a scholar working an algebraic proof, Brad took the known x and y factors—logistics and intelligence—and used them to derive z, the field operation. If everyone did their job, the course of events would fall into place naturally and predictably. The secret to Bradley's success, the engine of his genius, was his ability to grasp all parts of the equation on a monstrous, moving battlefield, and derive from them a plan in which the foot soldier on the line could have confidence.

Patton, by contrast, would never think of putting his staff in the driver's seat and sitting back like a figurehead. Driven by a sense of self-aggrandizement, an insatiable thirst for approval, and an overpowering feeling of destiny, George invariably turned toward the offense, the G-4 man be damned. He broke away from his command post, led from the front, and disregarded rules when they stood between him and his objective. His preferred method—"bypass, haul ass, send for the infantry," in the thumping GI cadence—was the same doctrine George had preached when he and Ike took on the Army establishment back in 1920. It was this same method the Germans had put to good use in Poland, France, the Low Countries, and Russia during these last three and a half years. His outstanding performance at the Louisiana maneuvers taught George that accepted doctrine was a fine thing to follow until it conflicted with the requirements of victory; once that happened, doctrine would invariably get the boot in favor of whatever worked.[31]

Patton's ability to look beyond the rules—a sixth sense built over years of study, experimentation, even prayer—was what gave him his touch of genius. Where Bradley saw logistics and enemy defenses as limitations on his freedom, Patton, who had outflanked everything from spelling deficiencies to cavalry dogma, conceded none. Where audacity was George's watchword, realism was Brad's.

These differences, glaring though they would seem in later years, were matters of degree, of course. Bradley understood and appreciated the need for an offensive spirit, even if opportunity implied risk, and he was ready to propose bold measures, especially when he sensed his foe was on the ropes. And while Patton never conceded the supremacy of logistics in battle—he had argued the point with Ike too many times before—he grasped the basic limits imposed by lines of communication, he coveted fresh intelligence, he carefully husbanded artillery and engineer support, and he rarely exceeded his logistical means. Though he might belittle staff functions over dinner and cigars, he kept a highly skilled team of planners by his side. He trusted his senior men to do their jobs quietly and effectively, and he listened to them when they spoke. As Major General John P. Lucas, a confidant of both Ike and George, wrote in his diary, "[Patton] strives to give the impression of doing things in an impulsive and 'on the spur of the moment' manner but in back of all his actions in war is very careful staff planning and much thought."[32]

Patton's crass conduct during his first weeks with II Corps planted seeds of discord that would later bear bitter fruit. But for now the two men worked well together. During combat, they would take turns managing operations at headquarters; one would visit the front while the other minded the shop. Bradley considered the pairing "a very fine association" at the beginning, and George, who had no inkling of Bradley's dark feelings toward him, told his diary that Brad was a "swell fellow" and a "great comfort." Not long afterward, George would write to his understudy, "I want to repeat that I never enjoyed service with anyone as much as you."[33]

Another event George enjoyed occurred on March 12, the day the 9th Division's General Eddy called him to say that the radio was reporting that General Patton had been awarded his third star. It was unofficial for now; George's dream would not become a reality—at least so far as the Army was concerned—until a few days later, when the Senate confirmed FDR's appointment. But George didn't worry with formalities in this instance, and that evening his quarters flew a three-star flag that his devoted aide Captain Dick Jenson had been saving for the occasion.[34]

Bradley, fully expecting George's promotion—after all, a corps command entitled him to it—teased Patton as he pinned on his own third star, pointing out that the new rank would not become effective until it was approved by the Senate.

"The hell you say," George retorted, grinning. "I've waited long enough for this one."[35]

The Californian's last words of the day reflected an intoxicating mixture of satisfaction and unquenched ambition. *"When I was a little boy at home I used to wear a wooden sword and say to myself 'George S. Patton, Jr., Lieutenant General,'"* he told his diary. *"At that time I did not know there were full generals. Now I want, and will get, four stars."*[36]

His journey to that fourth star would be a remarkable one.

When Patton assumed command of II Corps, the western components of Alexander's Eighteenth Army Group formed a north-south line facing the Dorsal Mountain range, which guarded the coastal cities of Gabès at the extreme south, Sfax above Gabès, and the two critical ports, Tunis and Bizerte. The 90,000 Americans of II Corps guarded the southern end of Alexander's line, abutting the 50,000 underequipped men of General Juin's French XIX Corps. North of the French stood Anderson's 120,000-man British First Army. Some two hundred miles southeast of Alexander's Dorsal line lay Montgomery's British Eighth Army, driving northwest from the Libyan frontier, slowly pushing the Germans back toward Tunis.[37]

Isolated and hard-pressed, the Axis armies in North Africa were still a force to be reckoned with. On the southeastern side the First Italian Army, a permutation of Rommel's *Afrika Korps*, still held Montgomery's Eighth at bay along the Mareth Line. East of the Dorsal Mountains, opposite Patton, Juin, and Anderson, sat von Arnim's Fifth Panzer Army, another fearsome foe.[38]

On March 9, Rommel returned to Germany for a long-overdue sick leave. Command of the Axis armies in Tunisia thus devolved upon von Arnim, who reported back to "Smiling Al" Kesselring in Sicily. As Brad remembered, "We believed we were still up against the champ." George, who was itching to test his mettle against the famed "Desert Fox," would not learn of Rommel's recall until later.[39]

For the final push for Tunisia, Alexander and Ike considered two options. Alexander could use II Corps to drive a wedge between the two Axis armies, then send Anderson's First Army to smash Fifth Panzer in the north while Montgomery hit First Italian from the south. Alternatively, Alexander could squeeze both enemy armies together like a giant, crooked accordion, allowing Montgomery to drive northwest while Anderson, Juin, and Patton pushed east. This second option would be a longer, harder road to victory, they acknowledged, but it was less risky in Alexander's mind.[40]

With Ike's consent, Alexander took the second path. The U.S. showing at Kasserine had convinced Alex and many other British officers that the American fighting man was all talk and no skill. A wedge that imperiled a dozen desperate Axis divisions simply would not work when its linchpin consisted of four divisions of green Americans who had been roughed up by just two panzer divisions a few weeks before.

No, Alexander decided, Patton's men would be given something simpler, something more adequate to their capabilities: They would make a "demonstration"—a loud feint—north of the Mareth Line, capturing the town of Gafsa and tying down Axis reinforcements while Montgomery and Anderson did the heavy lifting. Once Monty had broken through the Mareth Line and was chasing the Jerries up the Tunisian coast, Patton and his men could ride alongside Eighth Army and guard Monty's flank, or something inconsequential like that. In any event, Alexander's orders were clear: The Americans were not to advance beyond the Eastern Dorsals, and certainly they would not drive east to the Tunisian coast.[41]

Patton was naturally unhappy to see his men shunted aside in the Tunisian theater. In the privacy of their headquarters, he and Bradley groused about their secondary role. But they kept their feelings to themselves, and Brad had an inkling that a cautious approach was the better part of valor. "We were both disappointed," Bradley recalled, "but we took it with good grace. Alexander was right, II Corps was not then ready in any respect to carry out operations beyond feints."[42]

George and Brad sat down with their staff and planned their new mission, code-named Operation WOP. Terry Allen's Big Red One, driving southeast, would take Gafsa and the mountain pass of El Guettar, then send scouts to feint southeast toward the coastal city of Gabès. "Pinky" Ward's 1st Armored Division and a regiment of Manton Eddy's 9th would push up from Gafsa toward Maknassy, as if to drive toward Sfax on the Tunisian coast. The bulk of the 34th and 9th Divisions would be held in reserve, ready to blunt the inevitable German counterattacks. The drives toward Gabès and Sfax, they figured, would threaten Rommel's road to Tunis, forcing him to pull troops off Monty's back to deal with the American threat.[43]

Patton spent his nights leading up to the battle exhorting anyone within earshot to do their damnedest. The night before the offensive, he gathered his staff into a dilapidated hotel room near Thélepte and gave them their final briefing, concluding with the benediction, "Gentlemen, tomorrow we attack. If we are not victorious, let no one come back alive." As he dramatically tromped off to his private quarters to pray, his staff looked at one another, shaking their heads. Bradley later wrote:

> The contradictions in Patton's character continued to bewilder his staff. For while he was profane, he was also reverent. And while he strutted imperiously as a commander, he knelt humbly before his God. And while that last appeal for victory even at the price of death was looked upon as a hammy gesture by his corps staff, it helped to make it more clearly apparent to them that to Patton war was a holy crusade.[44]

On March 17 Patton launched his attack, and on the battle's opening day, Eisenhower and Alexander decided to join him. *"Ike and Alex were both telling me to stay back, which cramped my style,"* George complained to Beatrice, though his style recovered when the Supreme Commander formally pinned a third star onto Patton's collar—a star matching the three already stitched on each epaulet of his jacket. George and Brad left a fine impression on a helmeted General Eisenhower, who wrote a friend in Washington that *"[Patton] is in good fettle and it is a real pleasure to see what he has accomplished in a very short time. Bradley is equally on the job. What a godsend it was to me to get that man!"*[45]

The two partners survived close calls over the next few days; Brad's jeep ran over a land mine, while George survived a near miss by an Arab sniper. But both men were in high spirits after their corps captured Gafsa. Seeing Patton's initial success, Alexander spooled II Corps a longer leash, authorizing Patton's armor to seize Maknassy and press past the oasis of El Guettar toward Gabès, to enlarge the American threat.

Patton's infantry rolled out like clockwork, capturing El Guettar, and Ward's tanks snapped up Sened Station, the gateway to Maknassy Pass. In fact, the only serious limitation on Patton's freedom of movement was Alexander's stipulation that "large forces" were "not to drive beyond the Eastern Dorsals." Alexander needed to hold open a wide, clear lane as Montgomery's Eighth Army drove north toward Tunis, and he didn't want to risk Patton getting run over by Monty's freight train.[46]

For George, that was the real sticking point. The American role, in

Alexander's mind, was strictly secondary, so Patton would be obliged to stay out of Monty's way. Still, George thought, if Ward could open the Maknassy Pass—technically a violation of Alexander's orders—he could then petition Alexander for a more prominent role. Perhaps even a bite toward the coast.[47]

Unfortunately for Patton, Pinky Ward's 1st Armored ground to a halt before the rain-soaked roads and mired walls of Maknassy Pass. As a result, the critical gap, undefended on March 21, was crawling with Germans by the time Ward ordered his tanks to move on it.[48]

Because Ward's caution, combined with miserable weather and axle-deep mud, allowed the enemy to fortify his position, George was fighting mad. Livid at the delay, George ordered Bradley to give Pinky some personal motivation. Slinging an old Springfield rifle over his shoulder, Brad hopped a jeep over to 1st Armored's command post.[49]

Bradley was fond of Ward, a fellow Missourian with whom he'd worked at the War Department. He saw Pinky not as a slow mover, but a casualty of George's excessive ambition, a good soldier plagued with bad weather, who paid the price for Patton's deferred glory. He later recalled, "Patton was furious, blaming not the rain but Ward. . . . Patton impulsively concluded that Ward and the 1st Armored Division, still skittish from the defeat at Kasserine Pass, were lacking in aggressiveness. Nothing I said would change Patton's mind." Years later he told his biographer that when George heard Alexander might relent and allow a drive to the coast,

> I could almost see him licking his lips in anticipation. The problem was, however, that the armor required for this proposed mission— Ward's—was still bogged down in the mud and had not even captured the assigned heights at Maknassy. Ward was holding everything up, a harsh reality encroaching on Patton's John Wayne fantasy of a cavalry dash to the sea! Red-faced with rage, Patton blistered Ward.[50]

George found more success to the south, where Terry Allen's 1st Division had occupied El Guettar and was staring down the highway to Gabès. On March 23, von Arnim moved up his 10th Panzer Division—the same Visigoths who had smashed through Faïd Pass in February—and flung his Mark IVs and Tigers against Allen's infantrymen, who were dug in on a hill outside El Guettar. Terry's men, flush with howitzers and antitank guns, threw back the assault, knocking out thirty panzers in the process. When Allied code breakers picked up German orders for a second, infantry-led assault, they routed word to Patton, who made sure that Terry was waiting on hills above the attack route, his big guns well sited among the rocky slopes. When the screening infantry came within range, Allen's arm-droppers sent round after round of high explosives and white phosphorus into the German columns, cutting down *panzergrenadiers* right and left.[51]

George Patton, the highest-ranking irrelevancy once the battle started, sat on a hillside with Allen and Roosevelt, elbows resting on the sandy lip of a trench as he peered through his oversize binoculars. With no role in the fight, he wasn't really a general. He was a spectator, watching the opening notes of an extraordinary symphony dedicated to Mars. As the baritone sounds of howitzers mixed with the tympanic echoes of exploding ordnance, George grinned with delight. Flowering black bursts knocked over squads like tenpins, scattering men and limbs along the desert floor. When the Germans pulled back, George could make out through his binoculars khaki-clad corpses strewn everywhere—men who had been full of life moments before, now left to rot alongside the panzer carcasses that littered the valley floor like dead Carthaginian elephants.[52]

George was, if anything, taken aback at the lopsided result of his handiwork. Disappointed, even. The battle was nothing like a rapier duel among master swordsmen, something he would have expected from the Desert Fox. No cut and thrust, no parry. No fine moves accented with courtly bows. Thanks to Allied intelligence and Allen's savvy gun placement, the battle was an American-style turkey shoot, a loud, unrefined slaughter.[53]

"They're murdering good infantry," George muttered, his high regard for Rommel fading. "What a helluva way to waste good infantry troops."[54]

Brad, who had joined Patton for the battle's second act, remarked afterward, "Patton just hated to see good infantry men murdered that way. But they were Germans, you see, but I mean, he could appreciate well-trained infantrymen though he had been a cavalryman all his life."[55]

The Battle of El Guettar, minuscule by the standards of the war, carried tremendous significance for the Americans, because it was the first real triumph of green Yanks over their German foes. Brad christened it "the first, solid, indisputable defeat we inflicted on the German army in the war," and to Brad, George, and Ike, the victory was a harbinger of greater achievements to come.[56]

Patton had every right to be pleased with Terry's performance, and he was delighted to receive a message from Ike congratulating him on the battle's result. But before George could rest on his laurels—or even count them—he had to deal with Pinky Ward, who was still mired down at Maknassy Heights.[57]

"What's wrong with that Goddamn 1st Armored Division??" George barked to his staff. Furious with the slow pace of his armored force, he rang up Ward's headquarters on the twenty-fourth and demanded, "Pink, you got that hill yet?" After listening to Ward's breathless explanation for about ten seconds, George cut him off, bellowing into the receiver, "Goddamn it! I want that hill in front of you. Get off your ass; get a pistol in your hand, and lead that attack yourself."[58]

Sitting down at his desk that night, George told his diary:

> *After dinner I found that the 1st Armored Division had still failed to get the heights . . . so I called Ward on the phone and told him to personally lead the attack on the hills and take them. Now my conscience hurts me for fear that I have ordered him to his death, but I feel that it was my duty. Vigorous leadership would have taken the hill the day before yesterday. I hope it comes out alright.*[59]

Ward complied with Patton's order and led the attack—his face was smashed up in the process—but despite his personal leadership, the division ground to a halt. Two days later, on March 27, George paid a call on Ward, hoping to put more fight into him. He told his diary:

> *Visited 1st Armored Division near Maknassy and talked with Ward, explaining the ensuing operation. I also told him that he lacked drive and trusted his staff too much in that he presumed orders were carried out and did not take the trouble to find out that they were. He admitted this. I also told him that if he failed in the next operation, I would relieve him. He took it very well. I decorated him with the Silver Star for his action in leading the attack. I believe his action would have merited the DSC except for the fact that it was necessary for me to order him to do it.*[60]

On the second of April, Ike sent Patton a short cable passing along Alexander's disappointment with General Ward. George needed little convincing that Ward had to go, and over breakfast on April 4, he handed Omar a particularly distasteful assignment.[61]

"Look, Brad," he explained, "you're a friend of Pinky Ward's. Go up there and tell him why I've got to let him go."[62]

Brad nodded, a dutiful deputy executing the wishes of his commander. But inside he seethed. He had been at 1st Armored's command post when Ward—his face a Picasso painting of bruises, blood, and sulfa powder— reported back from the charge up Maknassy Heights. Ward's failure, he felt, was not from lack of trying; George was simply unwilling to admit that sometimes plans failed through no fault of the local commander on the ground. It wasn't fair.[63]

What irked Brad more than the injustice to Ward was that George had ordered him to do the dirty work. "This bravest of all battlefield warriors could not summon the personal courage to confront Ward face-to-face," he later vented. "Instead, he asked if I would do it!"

Here, Bradley had a point. George knew what had to be done; he knew that Ward had to go. But under George's gruff exterior lay a softhearted man who could not bring himself to dismiss a subordinate easily. He had given Ward several chances, spoken to him several times, and still he didn't want to face Pinky when the time came to drop the ax. George's coward-ice in the face of a tough personal decision, as Brad saw the episode, was another crack in the bridge of their relationship.[64]

Perhaps it was something about George's sense of loyalty. Or an unwrit-ten code among soldiers of the Old Army. Ike once recalled a similar inci-dent that spotlighted the yin and yang of George's personality:

One of his poses, for example, was that of the most hard-boiled individual in the Army. Actually he was so soft-hearted, particu-larly where a personal friend was concerned, that it was possibly his greatest fault. Later in the war he once vehemently demanded that I discharge eighty of his officers because, as he said, of inefficiency and timidity bordering on cowardice. He was so exercised and so persistent that I agreed, contingent upon his sending me a report in writing. Apparently astonished by my acquiescence, he began post-poning from week to week, on one excuse or another, the submission of his list. Finally he confessed, rather sheepishly, that he had recon-sidered and wanted to discharge no one.[65]

Brad handed Ward his walking papers, but the job shook him badly, just as it had shaken his faith in George Patton. After meeting with Pinky at 1st Armored headquarters and breaking the news to him, Brad left almost in tears. "[Bradley was] much more upset than I," Ward wrote in his diary that night. It was a dark day for Bradley.[66]

George's darkest day in North Africa fell on April 1, the day Captain Richard Jenson, the young aide he was so fond of, was killed. George had sent Dick out with Bradley to an advance command post when a squadron of Junkers bombers flew overhead, disappeared, then returned out of the sun. Brad, Dick, and the rest of the party dived into slit trenches as five-hundred-pound bombs rained among them, throwing sand, flames, metal fragments, and shock waves in all directions. When the explosions stilled and the hum of bomber engines faded into the distance, the party began climbing out of their trenches.[67]

Except for Dick.

It was the concussion that got him. When the aides found him, his head was snapped back in an awkward position. He lay curled in his trench, a lifeless doll with an innocuous bruise on his forehead and a scarlet thread of blood seeping from the corner of his mouth. His wristwatch had stopped, marking the moment of his death.

The intense fright of the attack gave way to a resigned sense of the tragic. Bradley, whose trench was only about fifteen feet from Jenson's, quietly ordered his aides to load Dick's body onto a jeep and take the lad back to Gafsa.[68]

Dick had been like a son to George, and the news cut him to the bone. When Bradley's aide arrived with Dick's body, the old horse soldier fell to his knees over the corpse and wept like a child. Choking with emotion, he pushed aside flowing tears and withdrew a pair of scissors from his pocket. He clipped a lock of Jenson's hair to send to Dick's mother, put the lock into his wallet, and left, to struggle privately with his grief.[69]

"Blood and Guts" Patton may have been, to the reading public, the face of U. S. Grant, Wyatt Earp, and the Green Hornet. But his emotions—rage, exuberance, dejection, sorrow, pride—always bubbled dangerously close to the surface. Though he lived for battle, or so he told himself, he bit his lip whenever he had to face the awful consequences of war, be they enlisted men moaning in a hospital tent or the broken body of a young friend. Dick's death struck close to his heart; the man who loved war could only shake his head in sadness as he wrote in his journal that night,

"I can't see the reason that such fine young men get killed. I shall miss him a lot."[70]

Since his assignment to II Corps, George had been working hard "keeping my temper with the B's," as he told Beatrice. But nightly Luftwaffe raids, bitter mountain fighting, and patronizing British attitudes from Alexander, Montgomery, and Anderson shoved him against his psychological limit. On more than one occasion, he had pulled his pistols at the sound of a Daimler fighter engine, and Brad had unslung his Springfield more than once to take a shot at an enemy fighter. These were hazards British Tactical Air was supposed to protect them from.[71]

George's mind kept coming back, with growing heat, to the British-led XII Air Support Group, which was supposed to intercept the big Junkers locusts that regularly sought out and claimed men like Dick Jenson. "You can't get the Air Force to do a Goddamned thing," Monk Dickson remembered George complaining. George fumed to his diary, *"Our air cannot fly at night, nor in a wind, nor support troops. The Germans do all three."*[72]

It was no wonder George's pot boiled over the day Dick's heart went cold.

All headquarters units regularly sent their parent commands situation reports, or "sitreps," to keep the higher echelons informed of their progress. In the case of II Corps, sitreps went out each day to Eighteenth Army Group headquarters, with a copy to Eisenhower. On April 1, George, grieving over the news of Dick's death, sent a routine sitrep to which he appended the note, "Total lack of air cover for our Units has allowed German air forces to operate almost at will."[73]

When George's sitrep hit the Allied command desks, it set off a string of firecrackers among British airmen, particularly Britain's tactical air commander in North Africa, a Pattonesque air marshal named Arthur "Mary" Coningham. Smoking with rage over George's written criticism of his fliers, the mercurial Coningham sent a reply message to every senior commander in the Mediterranean. Lampooning Patton's sitrep as a bad April Fool's Day joke, the air marshal implied that Patton was employing the "discredited practice of using the Air Force as an alibi for lack of success on the ground." If the sitrep were not intended as a joke, Coningham continued, "it can only be assumed that Two Corps personnel concerned are not battleworthy in terms of present operation." Coningham's message concluded, "Air Support Command have been instructed not to allow their brilliant and conscientious support of II Corps to be affected by this false cry of wolf."[74]

Before long, the war of words spread like a tavern brawl. Headquarters staffs were in an uproar, and Eisenhower's American air commander, General Carl "Tooey" Spaatz, joined the fray, cabling to Coningham that he took "gravest exception" to comments by the commander that "are entirely outside his competence." It looked like an Anglo-American, Army–Air Force fistfight would break out among the Allied generals.[75]

The "Sitrep Incident" was a crisis Ike didn't need, and it flared up at a particularly distressing time. Ike was already frustrated by a blasé assumption back home that the war for Tunisia was as good as over when, in truth, the Allies were facing a large, desperate force of crack veterans. He had just recovered from the fallout over the Darlan Deal and his icy reception from the British chiefs at Casablanca. He had spent countless hours trying to keep peace between Patton, Spaatz, Fredendall, Brad, Alexander, Coningham, and Anderson. Now his official G-3 spy, Major General Harold R. "Pink" Bull, was telling him about some damned fool message wired to everyone but Hitler by the hardheaded Mary Coningham—sent in response to an equally tactless signal from the hardheaded George Patton. All this on the very day Ike had complimented his RAF air chief, Air Marshal Arthur Tedder, on the effectiveness of Coningham's force.[76]

"Ike apparently took the incident very, very hard," Brad commented later. To Ike, the "Sitrep Incident" was symptomatic of the hopeless mess into which he had gotten himself, a monster that grew and snarled despite Ike's best efforts at peacemaking. He had lectured Patton and every other American general time and time again about keeping their mouths shut around the British. To tolerate their allies. To help Ike win the war, for heaven's sake, and to win it by mid-May, as he had promised Roosevelt. Now his carefully brokered peace was falling apart. If he could not even command his own generals, he had to wonder how in hell he could conquer Tunisia in the next forty-five days.[77]

For Ike, the Sitrep Incident was the last straw. Fed up with his generals and their antics, he drafted a cable to Marshall asking to be relieved of command, citing his inability to get his commanders to drop their national prejudices and work together for the common good—the one condition, Fox Conner had lectured him years before, that was indispensable for victory.

A shocked Bedell Smith intervened with the kind of persuasion he was best at. Using a mixture of logic and charm, Beetle convinced Ike that the damage to Anglo-American relations could be repaired. Ike, he pleaded, was the right man for the job, and needed to stay where he was, for the good of the Allied cause. Beetle managed to arrest Eisenhower's self-immolation, and Ike's telegram was never sent.[78]

Mollified for the moment, a thoroughly frazzled Eisenhower sent Tedder and Spaatz to Gafsa to smooth things over with George. They arrived at II Corps headquarters two days after the Sitrep Incident, ostensibly to discuss the larger air cover issue. As the chiefs were listening to the cavalryman's harangue about inadequate protection from the *Luftwaffe*, four Focke-Wulf fighter-bombers roared over the street outside Patton's headquarters, dropping bombs and strafing soldiers.[79]

Amid the explosions, the roar of radial engines, and a light dusting of plaster from the office ceiling, the British air marshal sat, quietly loading his pipe, his tight lips cracked into an ironic smile. Spaatz looked at George incredulously and asked, "Now how in hell did you ever manage to stage that?"

George, grinning ear to ear, shook his head. "I'll be damned if I know, but if I could find the sonsabitches who flew those planes I'd mail them each a medal."[80]

At the insistence of Ike and Alexander, Marshal Coningham made a fence-mending visit to Patton's headquarters. After a shouting match in which each man defended the honor of his men, the two commanders cooled down and Coningham offered to make amends in a telegram of retraction. *"We parted friends,"* George wrote, *"and I think we will now get better air support than ever before. I was rather proud of myself, as I was firm, but moderate. I doubt he ever sends the telegram of retraction because Ike will tell him it is not necessary."*[81]

Coningham circulated a cable blandly withdrawing his earlier signal, but Patton, as he had foreseen, was not placated. He wrote Ike a letter, telling his old friend he was "quite mad and very disgusted" by Coningham's "altogether inadequate apology to the United States troops."[82]

Ike demurred in his reply. He acknowledged that George had a right to feel "some public retraction or apology was indicated," but reminded him that "the great purpose of complete Allied teamwork must be achieved in this theater." He wrote the irate horseman that Allied victory would *"not be furthered by demanding the last pound of flesh for every error,"* and advised the Californian, *"if we will only take the trouble to seek a frank and friendly exchange of views, rarely, if ever, will there be any real differences of opinion or any irritations develop."* He also assured George that if his British counterparts gave him any trouble, General Alexander could be relied upon to clear up the matter fairly and objectively.[83]

If Ike ordered Patton to swallow his pride, he would do it. It was just another distasteful part of his job. George obediently accepted Coningham's apology and responded with a cordial letter of his own. He also sent a gracious letter to Alexander praising the air support his corps was receiving.[84]

But if Ike thought he could inject any real balance into George's pro-Army, pro-American bias, he was wasting his time. George was chafing at Alexander's un-American habit of telling him both what to do and *how* to do it, and Ike's international approach to war foreshadowed more trouble down the line: *"I feel all the time that there must be a showdown and that I may be one of their victims,"* he wrote in his diary. *"Ike is more British than the British and is putty in their hands. Oh, God, for John J. Pershing."*[85]

In just a few short months, George Patton and Omar Bradley had become of one mind about their friend's attitude toward the British. On April 3, as his fight with Coningham was reaching its crescendo, George ranted in his diary:

> *The U.S. troops get wholly separated and all chance of being in the kill and getting some natural credit is lost. Bradley and I explained this to Ike and he said he would stop it. He has done nothing. He is completely sold out to the British. I hope the Press at home gets on to it. Brad and I have decided to saw wood and say nothing. If he falls, it is not our fault. I hope the Boches beat the complete life out of the [British] 128th Brigade and [British] 6th Armored Division. I am fed up with being treated like a moron by the British. There is no national honor nor prestige left to us. Ike must go. He is a typical case of a beggar on horseback—could not stand prosperity.*[86]

His rantings about Ike and the British were simply his way of blowing off steam, but in the wake of Dick Jenson's death, George could not get Ike's pro-British bias out of his head. Nor did he try. Two days later, he grumbled that Ike's attitude

> *is, I think, unfortunate. He is very critical of all we do and is very prone to argue in favor of the British. Bradley and I . . . feel that*

the U.S. is being sold out for a theory, and that the theory is bad. There is no attempt to aggrandize the American Army. We have fought continuously for 19 days and have never given ground. The Eighth Army has fought for five days. We have pulled the 10th and 21st Panzer off them and it is gently—not too gently— intimated to us that we are not doing our best. . . .[87]

He also complained, *"One can only conclude that when the Eighth Army is in trouble, we are to expend our lives gladly; but when the Eighth is going well, we are to halt so as not to take any glory. It is an inspiring method of making war and shows rare qualities of leadership, and Ike falls for it. Oh! for a Pershing."*[88]

To make matters worse, on April 10, Alexander's chief of staff called to tell Patton that Alex was going to place II Corps under Anderson's command once again. The logic was simple, and it appealed to staff officers who enjoyed clean, straight Order-of-Battle tables: Eighteenth Army Group, they pontificated, should be commanding armies, not individual corps. The final push on Tunisia should therefore be made by the British First Army in the north and Monty's British Eighth Army in the south, with the American and French corps to be directed by Anderson, as the closest army unit.[89]

Hearing of this, George blew his stack. He flew to Alexander's headquarters to talk him out of it, but Alex wouldn't budge. George huffed to himself that evening, *"God Damn all British and all so-called Americans who have their legs pulled by them. It will be that Ike does nothing about it. I would rather be commanded by an Arab. I think less than nothing of Arabs."*[90]

The Supreme Commander and General Marshall had exchanged secret cablegrams over the roles George and Brad should play in the final stages of the campaign, taking into account the slow progress of the HUSKY project in Rabat. Ike had been thoroughly pleased with Bradley's performance as George's deputy, and he told Marshall, "[Bradley] has been a godsend in every way and his utter frankness and complete loyalty are things that I count on tremendously."[91]

But the Tunisian theater called for only one capable general, not two, and Ike had to decide which man to send to Rabat to complete the HUSKY planning. Before the Gafsa attack, when Omar was visiting Ike in Algiers, the Kansan had asked his classmate what should be done about Patton.

"Well, I would think George ought to go back and resume his Sicilian planning," Brad said. "After all the I Armored staff is his own. He could get much more out of them than I could."

"That's just the way I feel about it, too," Ike replied. "When this Gafsa phase is completed, you'll take command of II Corps and we'll send George on back to Rabat."[92]

So George was out, and Brad was in. It was an honest deal, one George had assumed from the start. And it was in the best interests of both II Corps and the HUSKY team. Ike made it clear to Alexander, Anderson, and the other generals that he felt Patton had done his job well. Once Bradley was ready to take over the corps, Patton would resume the urgent business of reducing Sicily.[93]

Patton did not blow up over his relief from a combat command, though he knew the public, unaware of his limited orders, would think he had been fired for failing to reach the Gulf of Gabès. On the eighth, he told Beatrice, *"If the papers say I have been relieved, don't worry. I was only pinch hitting here. Bradley will take over the trouble. He is a swell fellow."* In his diary, he told himself, *"I would like to finish this fight, but shall not argue, as it seems to me that I am in the hands of fate, who is forging me for some future bigger role."*[94]

The next day he scribbled, with a hint of glee, *"Saw Clark—he was sour as a pickle. I think I have passed him, and am amused at all the envy and hatred I wasted on him and many others. Looking back, men seem less vile."*[95]

A Missouri backwoodsman from childhood, Omar Bradley was used to all sorts of snakes. He knew in his home country, for instance, there were four basic types of venomous serpents. He knew how to identify them, and he knew how to avoid getting bitten by them. They were known, accepted risks, and over time he had learned to deal with them rationally and with confidence. Snakes in the Old World, by contrast, were mysterious and unfamiliar to him. He knew serpents of various malignities probably slithered around Africa, and they very likely slithered around Britain, too. But, having no experience with any of those species, it would have been in Brad's nature to handle any snake very carefully—if he had to handle them at all—and take exquisite care not to get bitten.

When he learned of Alexander's plan to bury II Corps within First British Army, under the dour Anderson, Bradley saw fangs, and he reacted violently. The II Corps was his inheritance, and he refused to let it become a sideshow. Behind closed doors, Omar and George, who had not yet returned to Rabat, worked each other into a froth. "Every time I thought about it, I seethed with anger—I more so than Patton," Bradley said later. "Both Patton and I were speechless with rage. But since we were under strict orders from Ike to do what Alexander told us to do, we raised no objections."[96]

With George's endorsement, on March 22 Omar flew to Algiers for a heart-to-heart talk with his old classmate. Years later, Bradley presented his version of the conversation that would do much to fix the role of American arms in the final battle for Africa. He claimed he told Ike:

"The people in the United States want a victory, and they deserve one. After playing an important part in the North African invasion and in the early Tunisian campaign, they would find it difficult to understand why the American forces were squeezed out in this final campaign."

"That's probably true, Brad," said Ike. "I hadn't thought of it in that light."

"The war's going to last a long time, Ike. There'll be a lot more Americans in it before we're through. I think we're entitled to function under our command without being farmed out forever from ally to ally. Until you give us the chance to show what we can do in a sector of our own, with an objective of our own, under our own command, you'll never know how good or bad we really are. And neither will the American people."

"What do you have in mind?"

"Move the entire II Corps up north, not just the 9th Division. And then let us go after Bizerte on our own."[97]

On April 14, Ike flew to Haïdra, a Tunisian hamlet that was home to the Eighteenth Army Group, Alexander's headquarters. There he met with his lieutenants to sort out the American role in the final campaigns for Tunis and Bizerte. He wanted Patton and Bradley there because he felt it would be a good time to show them how to deal with their allies, speaking plainly and assuming best motives and good faith.[98]

Because of their greater numbers on the front and their longer commitment to the war, Eisenhower felt it was important for the British to take the lead, and it was a foregone conclusion that the British would add Tunis to their battle honors. But given the need to manage American public opinion—a task that required an easily understood, definite U.S. contribution—he told Alexander he wanted Bradley's corps to have a shot at capturing the secondary port of Bizerte. Alexander agreed, and when the meeting was over, Butcher wrote, "Both Patton and Bradley expressed themselves as delighted and satisfied with the conference."[99]

If Ike came away with the same conclusion, he was far off the mark; Butch's observation was a measure of how guarded Brad and George had become when talking about British plans around Eisenhower. In reality, George left the meeting characteristically sullen, grousing, *"Ike talked a lot and let Alex do just what he wanted to. Ike said that he 'did not come as an American but as an ally.' And he told the truth. What an ass and how tragic for us."*

Over the next two days, as he stewed among his like-minded confidants, Patton grew more and more venomous. After another evening with Ike, George ranted in the privacy of his diary:

> *It appears to me that Ike is acting a part and knows he is damned near a Benedict Arnold, and is either obeying orders (if so, he does it in a soldierly way without squealing) or else the British have got him completely fooled. In any case he is usually not telling the truth. He is nothing but a Popinjay—a stuffed doll. . . . Bradley, Everett Hughes, General Rooks, and I, and probably many more, feel that America is being sold. I have been more than loyal to Ike and have talked to no one and have taken things from the British that I would never take from an American. If this trickery to America comes from above, it is utterly damnable. If it emanates from Ike, it is utterly terrible. I seriously talked to Hughes of asking to be relieved as a protest. I feel like Judas.*[100]

Judas would blow off steam about Benedict in the privacy of his diary. But there was something about the two men's late-night discussions that never failed to revive the best in their friendship. So it was on this occasion. On the eve of Patton's departure, he and Ike spent the evening together and talked as friends, much as they had twenty-three years earlier during quiet spring evenings at Camp Meade. As they talked, Harry Butcher made a short, insightful record of their conversation:

"While Ike and Patton discoursed on the need of the toughness to build and run an effective army, they agreed that utter ruthlessness, even to their best friends, was mandatory," Butcher wrote that night. "Troops had a right to good leadership, and it was up to top commanders to relieve any officer who failed to provide it."[101]

But Butch wryly added:

I could not help but comment that both gave every exterior indication of toughness but actually were chickenhearted underneath. Scarcely had I made this comment when Patton recalled that before leaving the II Corps headquarters, he had taken time to pick some wild flowers and place them on the grave of his aide. As he recalled the incident, he said: "I guess I really am a Goddam old fool." His voice quivered, tears ran down his cheeks.[102]

The next morning, Tex Lee called Patton to tell him of a congratulatory cable from Marshall commending General Patton for his outstanding work commanding II Corps on the Tunisian front. Seeing Ike's hand behind the message, George, his nasal voice tinged with emotion, told Ike, "I owe this to you."

"The hell you do," a proud Ike replied.[103]

George truly felt indebted to Ike, and Ike was truly proud of his friend. But the tired old subject of Anglo-American relations would rise again like the Tunisian sun, for the framework of an alliance simply would not permit Ike to be the kind of supreme commander—a nationalist, chauvinist, American commander—George longed for.

This scar running down the once-smooth skin of the Patton-Eisenhower friendship grew thicker and more pronounced the longer the war dragged on. *"Talked very plainly to Ike this morning,"* George wrote after leaving Algiers in mid-April. *"I told him he was the reverse of J. J. Pershing. He quoted the time in March 1918 when Pershing put every American at the disposal of Foch. I countered with the time of August in the same year when General Pershing told Foch that unless he issued orders for the concentration of an American Army, Americans would not fire a shot nor move a vehicle nor train. St. Mihiel was the result."*[104]

Neither man budged. It was not in their nature, and even if it were, they had long ago fixed their eyes on two radically different paths to victory. Ike looked at a map of the world and saw a new kind of war; a war not found in the history books, a war that required close, seamless movement among American, British, and French allies if the coalition were to defeat a ruthless, industrialized enemy. But to George, you could not put an American soldier under a foreign leader any more than you could hitch a wildcat to a chuck wagon. A competitor at heart, George was convinced that allied forces worked best when they worked independently, each army seizing whatever share of glory it could grab. And if the Americans were capable of winning the lion's share of that glory, why should any patriotic American stand in their way?

With decidedly mixed feelings, George bade his friend good-bye and hitched a plane to Rabat, his thoughts already swirling with the details of the next invasion. But before leaving, he wrote Bradley a warm, complimentary letter and took him aside for a last, private exchange about how things were being run at AFHQ. He never recorded what he told Brad that day, but whatever he said to Omar prompted the Missourian to tell George to "button his lip, to stop criticizing Ike and the British."

A few days later, George dropped Bradley a personal note, assuring him, *"I have continued to take your advice and say nothing. In other words, I act like the three monkeys."*[105]

EIGHT

"MISSION ACCOMPLISHED"

Had I followed Ike's suggestion—it was tantamount to an order—I feel
certain we would have suffered another Kasserine Pass.

—Bradley

WHEN OMAR BRADLEY TOOK COMMAND of II Corps on April 16, he was
blessed with a 90,000-man force that had regained its morale after the losses
at Kasserine Pass and Sidi bou Zid. His division commanders, Terry Allen,
Manton Eddy, Doc Ryder, and Ernie Harmon, were a tough but generally
obedient bunch—Terry was the least pliant of all his generals, but Brad felt
he could handle the unkempt general.[1]

He also had every right to be pleased with his headquarters team, whom
he had gotten to know and appreciate over the past two months. With the
exception of his incoming chief of staff, an abrasive tyrant from the Keystone Division named Bill Kean (nicknamed "Captain Bligh" by terrified
staffers), Brad kept the corps staff intact. As with Ike and George, Brad had
also cultivated a reliable, fanatically loyal "war family" that included aides
Chet and Lew, his stateside driver, Alex Stoute, and a crackerjack orderly,
a Michigander named Corporal Frank Cekada whom Brad had picked up
after moving to Africa. It was a solid cadre, he thought, and as the time to
assault Bizerte approached, Bradley worked alongside his men with a calm,
unruffled confidence.[2]

Soon after he took the reins of II Corps, Bradley decided to loosen up some
of Patton's old edicts. Breakfast, for instance, would henceforth be served until
8:30 a.m., a move he believed "vastly improved the efficiency of command at
headquarters," whose personnel often worked deep into the morning hours.

★ 163 ★

He had no time for the "hat patrols" and other pointless minutiae of the Patton regime, and he scaled back George's uniform policies. With everyone out from under Patton's boot heel, Brad figured he could get more work out of his corps if he backed off the spit-and-polish stuff for a while.[3]

If anything began to rub Bradley the wrong way, it was Eisenhower's well-intentioned meddling in corps business. For a man who had never commanded troops on a battlefield, Brad thought, Ike dispensed an awful lot of tactical advice. When he read Ike's first official letter to the incoming corps commander, Brad found it patronizing in its tone. Ike's suggestions about troop dispositions, he felt, were poorly conceived, even dangerous. On the whole, Ike's comments convinced Brad that his old classmate had little or no understanding of battlefield tactics. With more than a wisp of contempt, Brad took note that Ike was pressing him to attack along the Tine River valley in his southern sector with tanks in the lead. That route—a funnel-like defile under enemy guns, nicknamed "Mousetrap Valley"—smacked of old Fredendall's Waterloo just a few months before. Turning over Ike's letter in his head, Brad concluded Ike's proposal would lead to disaster. He later told his biographer, "Had I followed Ike's suggestion—it was tantamount to an order—I feel certain we would have suffered another Kasserine Pass."

Omar wanted no part of another low-ground debacle, so he quietly ignored Eisenhower's advice, ordering the Big Red One out to clear those heights before he sent his tanks into a Nazi shooting gallery.[4]

With the attack set for April 23, Bradley and his staff polished their plans to a mirror-like finish. Nothing was left to chance, and if Brad was nervous, he showed little sign of it. But at a conference of Anderson's corps commanders on April 18, the confident tactician had the first of many awkward moments among his more worldly European counterparts. During the planning meeting, General Louis-Marie Koeltz, commander of the French XIX Corps, began to outline his group's objectives in his native tongue. "I tried to follow him as best I could with my rusty West Point French," Bradley recalled. "When Koeltz apologized for not presenting his plan in English, Anderson waved him airily on. 'Of course, everyone here understands French,' he said. I didn't—but I suffered in silence." George had studied *la langue française* since before the First World War, and Ike had a squad of translators at his beck and call. Bradley wished he had his French Acadian driver with him, but for the moment he had little choice but to stand among the erudite commanders in uncomfortable silence, a backwoods provincial among the profession's elite.[5]

Fortunately for Bradley, Koeltz's Frenchmen lay on the far side of Anderson's Britishers, so it would be Anderson, not Bradley, who would need to know what was happening on the French side.

On D-minus-one, his plans for Bizerte approved, Brad unrolled his maps and outlined his strategy to a group of reporters. It was his first press briefing as an operational commander, and the man with the round spectacles and gentle twang skipped the theatrics. Standing before an easel, he gave his presentation "with no more panache than a teacher outlining the curriculum for the new semester." But, for the schoolteacher's son, what he said was far more important than how he said it.[6]

The plan to capture Bizerte was as straightforward as the man himself. Eddy's 9th Division would attack "the other fellow," as he often called the enemy, from the north, while Allen's 1st Division would attack from the south. Doc's 34th Division would neutralize an Axis redoubt designated "Hill 609," near the center, while part of Harmon's 1st Armored Division would roll forward on Doc's right. The rest of Ernie's tankers would be held in reserve, ready to exploit any breakthrough.[7]

The approach carried risks, of course, but when Bradley's mind was engaged in planning, his gray matter focused on the objective, not the flesh and blood behind or before it. He did everything he could to minimize loss of life, of course, but, as his aide wrote, when Bradley was planning an attack, "troops become blue and red symbols on a sheet of acetate as he jockies for thrusts into the enemy weak positions." Men were, as near as Brad could make them, simply inputs into an equation.[8]

To keep up with Brad's progress, Eisenhower sent his official spy, Major General Harold "Pink" Bull, to act as his eyes and ears at II Corps—just as he had sent Bradley before. Then, as the opening salvos were about to begin, Ike and his retinue joined Bull and Bradley at II Corps, along with a small group led by Lieutenant General Lesley McNair, who was in Africa as Marshall's eyes and ears. Thus, Brad's headquarters was crowded with official spies, as well as spies spying on the men to whom other spies reported— all out in the open with everyone aware of one another's presence.[9]

For Bradley's first offensive, Ike and his entourage became a distraction he neither needed nor wanted. The influx of "visiting firemen" obliged him to give the brass a corps-level briefing before shuttling everyone over to Terry Allen's command post, where the group sat in on Allen's final briefing of the 1st Division staff. It made little military sense to put on these dog-and-pony shows, but it was part of the game. Brad tolerated it, and Ike came away well pleased with his friend's performance.[10]

H-hour arrived at half past three on the morning of April 23. By then, even the imperturbable Bradley began showing signs of nervousness. During the lull between the attack's step-off and the initial reports, he fidgeted around the command post until, sick of the four walls of his office, he suggested to his two aides that they take a short walk. The trio strolled out to a nearby gulch at the desert's edge, where the general, unslinging a carbine, shot at rocks tossed into the air. Firing off a few light rounds seemed to settle Brad's nerves, and he returned to his command post, ready to run the battle.[11]

For the first few days, Bradley's offensive went smoothly. Each morning, he would wake at the crack of dawn and, lying in bed, he would telephone each division commander for an oral report before heading into the office.[12]

But on the third day Brad's corps hit a brick wall—or rather, the tall, rocky prominence of Hill 609, the objective assigned to Doc Ryder's 34th Division. The hill, over eighteen hundred feet high, dominated the routes into Bizerte, and Axis guns posted along its ridges pounded the Big Red One every time General Allen's men ventured toward their target. Brad knew that if he wanted to capture Bizerte, he would have to plant the Stars and Stripes atop that hill.[13]

Brad watched Ryder's troops assault the hill three times, only to scurry back down under withering German fire. Momentarily stumped, Bradley hit on the solution; he supplemented his infantry with a company of Ernie Harmon's tanks. Using Harmon's Shermans as mobile howitzers, Ryder's men took the summit on their fourth run, on April 30; they consolidated their position the next day, and with Hill 609 in Allied hands, the road to Bizerte lay open.[14]

Picking their way over scrubby, rock-strewn terrain, Brad's riflemen had to take their objectives slowly. But slow and careful was fine with the methodical Omar Bradley, who directed the battle from his command post, seated in a metal folding chair in front of a giant situation map. He was a patient man, and he knew the end of Bizerte must be in sight.

It was an article of faith that Brad would not rush his men into untested defenses when a more careful, disciplined approach would save lives. As he saw it, his job was to take Bizerte, and whether he took it on May 1 or May 15 made no difference to him unless the risks and effusion of blood were even—and they rarely were.

Patience was a lesson he had learned in his early childhood. As a young boy hunting squirrels with his father, little Omar had fidgeted and squirmed as his father lined up his rifle sights on a squirrel. Unable to contain himself, Omar threw a rock at the animal, which ran off before his father could fire; the pair returned home without their quarry. This lesson stayed with him as he grew up, and he carried that bit of backwoods wisdom into battle.[15]

But while the delay didn't affect his strategy with the enemy, it gave General Anderson time to infuriate Bradley with a request for a U.S. regiment to be placed under his First British Army command. It was a dangerous precedent, one Bradley and Patton had railed against in private, and Brad was determined to spike Anderson's guns, even if it meant running to Ike for protection.[16]

When Ike visited Brad's command post the next day, Omar brought up the subject. He made his case forcefully against the transfer of U.S. troops to a Briton, and to his relief, Ike assured him, "Stand your ground, Brad. I'll see Anderson this afternoon and back you up."[17]

Perhaps George's polemics about Black Jack Pershing and American prestige had made an impression on Eisenhower after all. Perhaps Ike sensed that, with the eyes of Marshall looking down on him, he needed to let Bradley wave the American flag for a while. Whatever the reason, Ike was dead set against the move, and Anderson had no choice but to back down. Bradley, like the revered General Pershing, had kept all his troops under one flag.[18]

With Anderson, Montgomery, and Bradley in position, Alexander ordered the final push to begin on May 6. Ernie Harmon, whom Bradley considered foulmouthed and boastful but a superb division commander, was to take the lead with his tanks. Eddy's 9th, Allen's 1st, and Ryder's 34th Divisions would support the breakout.

The plan worked almost perfectly, Bradley's only complaint being that Terry Allen had ordered an unauthorized attack, which was repulsed with heavy losses. It was just the kind of move Patton might have attempted, although George, Brad knew, would have had better luck. "From that point forward," Brad said, "Terry was a marked man in my book. I would not permit him or his division to operate as a separate force, ignoring specific orders from above."[19]

Despite local setbacks, Ike was happy with Brad's progress. He visited the front three times after the offensive was launched, and he joined Brad in regular briefings. He assured Bradley, *"You must know that everything you are doing excites not only my great admiration but my very deep appreciation."* On the seventh, Ike visited the II Corps command post at Sidi Nisr, a town mispronounced "Sneer" in Bradley's Missouri twang. At Sneer the two old classmates, unfolding their spectacles, pored over huge, acetate-covered maps marked with arrows and circles as they speculated about the final end of the Fifth Panzer Army. The West Pointers were happy men.[20]

The day after Eddy launched his final assault on Bizerte, the lead elements of his 9th Division broke into the city. On May 9, his position untenable and his back to the sea, German General Fritz Krause, commander of Bizerte's defenders, accepted Bradley's terms of unconditional surrender. The fighting was at an end.[21]

The death of an army is a somber, awe-inspiring sight, much like the image of a still-smoldering woods after a forest fire, or the smashed carcass of a coastal city after a hurricane has swept through. It begins with a lull in the fighting, followed by uncertain, hesitant steps by the bravest men, men who risk death at the hands of nervous victors to walk across No-Man's-Land. As word spreads through the defeated ranks, clusters of exhausted men rise from their trenches and begin walking, limping, carrying friends and personal belongings toward their armed captors and the yawning mouths of the steel enclosures that await them. As the unfamiliar stillness thickens, undulating columns of men—some sullen, some smiling with relief, some stonefaced—lengthen and swell like swarms of locusts as sergeants, MPs, and company-grades herd their human spoils into one giant cage after the next. For the victors, the unshaven men cradling M-1s and Thompsons by the side of the road, it is a sight never to be forgotten.

The last hours of Fifth Panzer Army were no different. Upon confession of defeat, Axis prisoners, most of them sick of war and thankful to escape death, began pouring into Brad's makeshift POW camp on bicycles, motorcycles, donkeys, half-tracks, and German trucks stenciled with the faded palm tree and swastika of the *Afrika Korps.* The prisoner haul, some forty thousand men, was so copious that Brad's provost marshals had to conscript German engineers to help build larger enclosures to house their countrymen.[22]

To Bradley, this victory, the product of his planning, his sweat, his leadership, was the most thrilling moment of his war service. "No other single incident of the war brought me the elation I experienced in viewing this procession of PWs," Bradley later recalled.[23]

It was a triumph he would savor for the rest of his days. His tight, inscrutable smile cracking just a bit, the proud Missourian cabled his old classmate a simple message:

MISSION ACCOMPLISHED.[24]

Shortly after the twin victories at Tunis and Bizerte, George Patton paid a visit to Algiers to make good on an old bet with Ike that the Allies would not drive the enemy out of Africa until June 15. George was good-natured about losing, and in his usual theatrical style, he stomped ostentatiously into Ike's office with a five-hundred-franc note on a silver tray and red rose, bellowing, "Hail, Caesar!"[25]

The two men talked for some time, smiles beaming right and left. But George left Algiers a little perplexed and annoyed over Ike's lack of appreciation for the fine work of Bradley's illustrious predecessor. The man who had rebuilt II Corps and smashed the Germans at El Guettar and beyond. He commented later that day:

> [Ike] walked the floor for some time, orating, and then asked me to mention how hard he had worked—what great risks he had taken—and how well he had handled the British, in my next letter to General Marshall. I wrote a letter which largely overstated his merits, but I felt that I owe him a lot and must stay with him. I lied in a good cause. As a matter of fact, I know of no one except myself who could do any better than Ike and God knows I don't want his job.[26]

As the Tunisian campaign shuddered to its denouement, the Supreme Commander was hailed on three continents as the hero of the hour. He was careful, however, to spread the credit among his senior generals, particularly the Missouri crack shot who had busted open Bizerte. He told Brad, "I am bursting with pride over you and the magnificent fighting team you are commanding," and in a letter to Marshall, Ike privately recommended Bradley for promotion to lieutenant general. When a waggish classmate bestowed the nickname *"Ikus Africanus"* on Eisenhower, Ike pointed out several other Class of '15 graduates who had contributed to the North African campaign, even suggesting the title *"Omar Tunisus"* for his II Corps commander. The day after Bizerte fell, *The New York Times* introduced its readers to Omar Bradley. Ike gave his prized corps commander a further boost by advising a hovering war correspondent named Ernie Pyle to "go and discover Bradley." Before long, Brad would be basking in well-crafted praise from the prolific writer, whose columns touted the soft-spoken Missourian as the "GI's General," a nickname that would stick with the public.[27]

With the end of the North African campaign, Ike was finally able to lift the lid on press restrictions about the names of his senior commanders, including Patton and Bradley. Accredited journalists, who could always count on splendid copy from Patton, naturally wanted to know why Ike had relieved Old Blood and Guts in favor of Bradley. Ike repeated the official line at his next press briefing: Bradley's background was in infantry, "and therefore more suitable for mountainous fighting." Patton, he explained, was a tanker at heart, and the man for the job when the war rolled across the flatlands to the south.

After giving them the official line, Ike took the assembled journalists off the record and explained that Patton would take part in the next big operation, and had only left the Tunisian campaign to go back to his headquarters to concentrate on the assault. Ike could not, of course, tell the press where that assault would take place. Everything was under wraps for now, he cautioned, because he didn't want Hitler finding out where the Allies would strike next.[28]

The press, and Hitler, would not have long to wait.

NINE

LOOKING NORTH

I can't make out whether Ike thinks Bradley is a better close fighter than I am or whether he wants to keep in with General Marshall, who likes Bradley. I know that Bradley is completely loyal to me.

—George, July 5, 1943

SICILY IS AN ANCIENT ISLE, thick with cliffs, mountains, and scrublands that make the promontory a defender's dream. Shaped like a rough triangle—the Greeks called the island Trinacria—its principal cities frame the tricorn: Palermo in the northwest, Syracuse in the southeast, and Messina to the northeast.

Of these three gems, the great prize was Messina, a port city on the island's northeastern point that faces the toe of the Italian boot over a two-mile channel. Capture this small corner, and you control Axis movement between Sicily and Italy, as well as the sea-lanes along Italy's Tyrrhenian and Adriatic coasts. For the defenders of Sicily, the Strait of Messina was the gateway for reinforcements, and the escape hatch in case of disaster. It was the key to Mussolini's island, and for that reason Messina became George Patton's obsession.

As he immersed himself in the invasion's basics, Patton realized that he had drawn a plum assignment. He would hit the beach at the head of a reinforced armored corps, which was almost as good as an army, while in North Africa AFHQ was cannibalizing Clark's Fifth Army, stripping Clark of his landing craft, staff, training facilities, and units, giving some to Patton's corps and sending others back to train in the U.K. Through the Army's grapevine, George learned that his stock with Ike had jumped when he agreed to take on the II Corps in Tunisia, a post Clark had turned down.

With more than a hint of rough glee, George told Beatrice, *"It now appears that W was given a chance to take Lloyd's place in the beginning but refused to go as a corps commander. Now he is about nothing, and I think knows it."*[1]

In the celebration over the Tunisian victory, though, George struggled with his disappointment over being left out—cut out, actually—from the campaign's final act, a dissatisfaction that did not diminish when Ike invited George and Brad to the victory parade in Tunis. Contemplating the mental picture of Ike on a reviewing stand, surrounded by his smiling British generals, snubbing his American colleagues, George grumbled, *"AFHQ is really a British headquarters with a neuter general, if he is not pro-British. It is a hell of a note."*[2]

Patton's mental picture of the victory celebration turned out to be just about right. Ike met George and Brad at the airfield, but he had little time for them because of the press of British and French officers, diplomats, and other applauding dignitaries jockeying about the Supreme Commander. The reviewing stand, flanked by two British Churchill tanks, wasn't especially large, so Bradley and Patton were relegated to a lower dais, where they stood in the sweltering heat among African and French field grades—the "upper middle class frogs," George called them. Ike, Giraud, Churchill's representatives, British generals, and a company of nodding, smiling politicians stood proudly on the reviewing stand with Eisenhower as a 14,000-man British contingent dwarfed the much smaller U.S. and French contingents.[3]

It was a "goddamned waste of time," Patton spat, and he wrote Bea that *"Omar and I were very mad and chagrined, for reasons you can guess, and they were not selfish ones either."*[4]

But George, outraged though he was over the second-class status given to the Americans, held his tongue around Eisenhower. Ike had told him to lay off the British, and George knew Ike was dead serious. Besides, as George had told himself a few days before, *"[Ike] needs a few loyal and unselfish men around him, even if he is too weak a character to be worthy of us."*[5]

Bradley felt the same way. The parade, Brad thought, was arranged "to give the British overwhelming credit for victory in Tunisia. For Patton and me, the affair seemed to reinforce our belief that Ike was now so pro-British that he was blind to the slight he had paid to us. . . ."[6]

For Eisenhower, the celebration in Tunisia was overshadowed by Sicily, an operation that would require him to best six second-rate Italian coastal divisions, four regular Italian infantry divisions, and two formidable German divisions. As usual, he was up to his neck in details, and he was beset on all sides by well-intentioned advice, some of which came perilously close to being orders. Marshall, for instance, advised him to rush Sicily before the Germans had a chance to recover from North Africa, and he heard rumors that Churchill had complained to President Roosevelt that he should have followed up Tunisia with a quick leap against the island. This armchair quarterbacking was fine in theory, Ike thought, but a "Notre Dame Shift" was an impossible play given the dearth of landing craft, the need to refit divisions in Tunisia, and the Luftwaffe stronghold at the nearby island of Pantelleria.[7]

In late January, to a man Ike's subordinates believed a June landing was out of the question, and Ike had to break the unwelcome news to the Combined Chiefs. After his draft invasion plan was circulated on February 12, a wave of objections poured in, and Ike told Marshall in late March that changes were being made to the plan to satisfy Alexander and Montgomery. "I didn't like it," Ike said, "but it seemed to me there was no other course."[8]

A wave of planners, liaisons, and politicos pressed upon Eisenhower from all sides that spring, cluttering his already-cluttered days with questions, comments, and respectful demands. Ike, looking for a sympathetic ear, complained to Mamie,

> In my youthful days I used to read about commanders of armies and envied them what I supposed to be great freedom in action and decision. What a notion! The demands upon me that must be met make me a slave rather than a master. Even my daily life is circumscribed with guards, aides, etc, etc, until sometimes I want nothing so much as complete seclusion.[9]

Gazing up toward a cloud-cloaked summit of hard decisions, Ike sank into another bout with anxiety. He began waking at four in the morning, unable to sleep, his mind turning over one seemingly insoluble problem after another. "He scarcely ever has had a feeling of self-satisfaction," observed Harry Butcher. "He becomes impatient and irritated because of the slowness with which the next phase can unfold. He makes himself quite unhappy." He had once suggested to Butch that they both "get good and drunk when Tunisia is in the bag," but now that Tunisia was in the bag, his crowded schedule prevented him from sharing even that traditional right of soldiers.[10]

* * *

Ike's official family tried to keep their leader on an even keel, but the Kansan was prone to explode in a cloud of profanity and heat. One of his public relations specialists, the faithful Butcher, had to continually blue-pencil a pamphlet's worth of "hells," "godawfuls" and "damns" out of magazine articles profiling the Allied Commander in Chief, as he didn't want the Allied leader's vocabulary becoming too widespread a topic.[11] To complicate things further, Kay, whose fiancé was killed during a mine-clearing sweep after the fighting in Africa had ended, drew closer to Ike amid her grief. This, of course, stirred up fresh rumors about the Supreme Commander and the girl from Skibbereen.[12]

For Ike, the messy planning for HUSKY was little different from the messy planning for TORCH. Maybe a bit more refined, but still the same deranged muddle. The invasion was supposed to be phased in over five days, with nine divisions—five British and four American—landing on the island's southern, eastern, and northwestern coasts. General Alexander and his Fifteenth Army Group would command the operation, while the I Armored Corps (Reinforced), under General Patton, would land on the island's northwest corner near Palermo. The star of the show, Britain's Eighth Army, would land on Sicily's southeastern coast, near Syracuse, and the Eighth would be led by General Montgomery.[13]

Sir Bernard Law Montgomery, a master of tactics if not tact, was the one man upon whom George, Brad, and Ike could agree. A son of a bishop—though Ike privately called him a son of something else—Monty was the United Kingdom's preeminent battle commander, a legend whose wounds at Ypres in 1914 had left scars as deep as his immovable beliefs in his own preeminence. A teetotaler who cited Scripture as unabashedly as did George, Monty's abstinence from vice was more than offset by an acerbic temper, a towering ego, and an effortless, natural condescension. Standing five feet, seven inches and looking down his prominent nose at men physically taller than himself, the self-assured Ulsterman never seemed to notice that he became a lightning rod for everything he touched.[14]

Montgomery had performed brilliantly during the Eighth Army's Libyan and Tunisian campaigns, and the British documentary *Desert Victory*, released in April 1943, made the victor of El Alamein an instant hero in the United States and Great Britain. But Monty's irascible personality would also give his legion of critics no shortage of grounds, rightly and wrongly, for bitterness. Whether it was insisting on the correct course in the most offensive way, or simply sticking his beak into political questions best left to others, Montgomery's answers, so often militarily correct, were prone to become lost in the bile he stirred up.[15]

Ike had taken a disliking to General Montgomery during their first meeting in the summer of '42, when the haughty Briton dressed down the Kansan for smoking in his presence. After this inauspicious start, Kay wrote, "the relationship between the two men never got any better; in fact, as the war progressed, Monty's self-righteousness and rigidity often had the General gasping in anger." As Ike wrote in a secret letter to Marshall, "[Montgomery] is so proud of his successes to date that he will never willingly make a single move until he is absolutely certain of success—in other words, until he has concentrated enough resources so that anybody could practically guarantee the outcome."[16]

Ike's colleagues at AFHQ—particularly Air Marshals Tedder and Coningham and Admiral Cunningham—loathed Montgomery so much that he generally avoided meetings at AFHQ, and would frequently send a surrogate in his place—a tacit acknowledgment that his personal presence would be counterproductive. Monty's refusal to leave his "home field" was invariably taken as aloofness in the other camps, and it only deepened the resentment felt by Eisenhower's other generals.[17]

Monty, for his part, had little use for America's smiling chairman of the board. He sneered to Brooke that Ike's "high-pitched accent and loud talking would drive me mad," and he commented that while Ike was "probably quite good on the political side . . . he knows nothing whatever about how to make war or fight battles; he should be kept away from all that business if we want to win this war."[18]

But while Ike disliked Montgomery, he recognized he was the best available man for the combat job, and that was all that mattered. He would get along with Montgomery, and so would each of his subordinates.

Besides, as Supreme Commander, Eisenhower necessarily focused on supplies, air cover, landing craft, politics, and Italy, not the specifics of what division went where. It would therefore be Patton—or rather, Patton, Alexander, Tedder, Cunningham, Beetle, among others—who would have to bear the cross of El Alamein.

Since their meeting in February, Patton and Montgomery had begun a cordial relationship that would evolve into cordial loathing, mostly because, in a perverse sort of way, they were two of a kind. Both were nationalistic bigots, incapable of seeing the larger picture, and each was intensely convinced his own army could win any campaign without help. Both generals were cursed with high-pitched voices, a fetish for headwear, and a grandiose sense of self. Montgomery's edge over Patton was his wider experience in fighting the Germans, while Patton's, incredibly, was his tact. When word reached Montgomery that Patton had been little impressed by one of his post-Tunisian seminars, Monty is said to have replied, "The next time I see Georgie Patton, I'll have just three things to say to him: Get out of my way, take your troops back and train them, and leave me your petrol."[19] But through their formal disdain for each other emerged a kind of grudging respect. Knowing a talented prima donna when he saw one, George remarked privately, "Monty is a forceful, selfish man, but still a man. I think he is a far better leader than Alexander and will do just what he pleases, as Alex is afraid of him." His suspicions of the Montgomery-Alexander dynamic were confirmed at a later meeting, when Patton complained to Montgomery about an order from Alexander's headquarters. "George," a bemused Monty replied, "let me give you some advice. If you get an order from Army Group that you don't like, just ignore it. That's what I do."[20]

Patton was perfectly willing to keep his men in Palermo, on the opposite side of the island from Montgomery, and he bluntly told General McNair, "Allies must fight in separate theaters or they hate each other more than they do the enemy." But George's splendid isolation shattered as the HUSKY plan was overhauled with round after round of staff analysis and high-level amendments. The original plan had called for landings on the east, near the open land around Catania, and in the northwest, near Palermo. But under pressure from the air services, the Combined Chiefs also required the British Army to land on Sicily's southern coast and seize the airfields at the towns of Gela and Licata. Landings there would stretch Montgomery's Eighth Army around Sicily's southeastern corner, and Montgomery hated being stretched.[21]

It was hard enough for Ike, a natural balancer, to reconcile these irreconcilable interests on a purely military basis. But throw in the sharp personalities of Air Marshal Tedder, Admiral Cunningham, Patton, Alexander, and Montgomery, and the tug-of-war became a blood feud. Tedder demanded the southern airfields on D-plus-1 to dominate the skies over the battlefield. Cunningham sided with Tedder, not relishing the idea of Stukas taking off from those same fields and screaming down on his warships. Alexander tried to bring the two sides together, but he had little luck. The battle for landing sites on the ten-thousand-square-mile island was reminiscent of the transatlantic old arguments over Bône, Philippeville, Casablanca, and Tunis. Another geographic card game.

I'll trade you Gela for Palermo. I'll see your Syracuse, and raise you two airfields at Licata. Call. All in.

Before the end of April, Eisenhower was fielding complaints from three different continents, and he still had to manage the last phase of the shooting war in Tunisia. With his generals deadlocked, Ike called a meeting on the second of May with Montgomery, Tedder, Cunningham, and a few other interested parties in Algiers to decide what to do. Bad weather kept Alexander from attending the meeting, and before the conference began Montgomery accosted Bedell Smith in the men's room of the St. Georges. There, standing among toilet stalls and sinks, he pitched his plan to Beetle. Breathing on the lavatory mirror, he drew a crude map of Sicily, and he outlined in simple terms his proposal to land the British in the east and the Americans in the south.[22]

Beetle, blind to nationality when it came to military operations, knew the plan made sense. Though he also knew it would spark a firestorm among Ike's anti-Montgomery clique, he took it to Ike with his endorsement. Eisenhower agreed, and that evening Beetle was on the phone to Patton explaining that AFHQ would be making some big changes to the invasion plan. He invited Patton to come to Algiers the following day to hear Monty out and voice any concerns, and George promised he'd be there.

Next morning, George attempted to fly in for the meeting, but heavy spring rains grounded his plane. He packed Colonel Muller and his aide, Captain Stiller, into a car and set out for Algiers over washed-out roads and crooked highways jammed with supply trucks. He showed up at Ike's headquarters at five thirty that evening, worn out and frustrated, and apologized for missing the meeting. Ike assured him, "Oh, that's alright, I knew you would do what you were ordered without question."[23]

Ike called in Alexander, Hughes, and Beetle to bring George up to speed. Palermo, he said, had been scrubbed. Instead of landing on the northwest corner, Patton's force would hit the southern shore, capturing Gela, Scoglitti, and Licata, as well as three airfields on the outskirts of those towns. Monty would land in the east, capturing the ports of Syracuse and Augusta; then he would move north against Catania, and from there to Messina.[24]

So where, exactly, did that leave Patton?

The American force, Beetle said, would be supplied through Syracuse. The problem, as Beetle acknowledged, was that Syracuse was large enough to service the British forces, but not big enough to supply all of Patton's force in addition. Patton's men would have to make do as best they could with supplies dumped onto the beaches around Gela.

That didn't look promising, but George put on a brave front and refused to jump openly into the anti-Montgomery fray. When Kent Hewitt approached him about protesting to his old friend Eisenhower, Patton puffed up and replied, "No, goddammit. I've been in this Army thirty years and when my superior gives me an order I say, 'Yes, sir!' and then do my goddamndest to carry it out." And he intended to.[25]

But that night, Patton again raised the "British issue" privately with his old friend. After a late-evening dinner with Ike and Kay, he and Ike talked until half past one in the morning. *He is beginning to see the light but is too full of himself,* George remarked afterward. *I was quite frank with him about the British and he took it.* To George, it was a mote of progress, though only a mote. Perhaps what Ike lacked was moral courage. *I think D sees the light a little but fears for his head if he stands on his feet,* he wrote.[26]

While George worried about Ike's fears for his head, one bright spot emerged. Going over the composition of Patton's corps—an armored corps that would command an infantry corps—Ike casually remarked, "Perhaps Western Task Force should be made an army."

George's ears perked up. He was wary of who his new army commander might be, and shook his head. He bluntly told Ike that he did not want to serve under Wayne Clark.

Unflustered, Ike replied, "I don't mean that." He said he was considering upgrading I Armored Corps to full army status.[27]

Shortly afterward, Ike called Patton at Mostaganem to officially notify him that I Armored Corps (Reinforced) would become the Seventh U.S. Army on D-Day. George was elated. The promotion—and in George's eyes, that was exactly what the redesignation was—put him on equal terms with both Montgomery and Clark, a fact that delighted him to no end. As he told Beatrice: *It seems probable that I will not have the I Armored Corps much longer, but as our British friends say, 'I am happy about it.'* You can guess *the rest. W will be very mad indeed, but I am not taking over his number. As a matter of fact, we get on fine. He is much chasened."*[28]

Throughout the late spring, George tried to stay out of trouble, but he couldn't help drawing attention to himself. He had a gift for capturing the fickle spotlight, which made him a hero when he was engaged in battle. Waging a fast, hard-fighting campaign, his exploits would stand out among those of the thousand other general officers on the Army's rolls.

But when he was not engaged in combat, a bright light on Patton was never a good thing.

This time, the light was flicked on by one of his task force censors. In late May, Marshall learned of a letter sent home by Patton's G-3, Colonel Kent Lambert. In his letter, Lambert told how a previous letter to his wife describing the TORCH operation was forwarded by censors to Patton because it violated security regulations. Lambert escaped punishment, he later claimed, because "my friend Patton said, 'Nuts, file it.'" General Marshall, Ike learned, was in a rage over the high-level breach of security, and he wanted the matter investigated.[29]

Calling him into his large office, Ike told George somewhat apologetically, "I have got to give you hell about Lambert." He laid out the story as the Chief related it, underscoring Marshall's fury at Lambert's lapse and at Patton's apparent cover-up.[30]

George, on the defensive, denied sweeping anything under the rug. He disputed Lambert's version of events, pointing out to Ike that "'nuts' was about the only expletive I did not use." He said both he and Hap Gay had taken Lambert to the woodshed over the incident—Gay formally, and George using his extensive library of expletives other than "nuts."[31]

Eisenhower, who was coming down on his friend only because Marshall ordered him to, took no further action, and George left, more or less unindicted of the crime. Reviewing the matter with Hughes afterward, George came away with the impression that Ike was simply *"doing a little face-saving at my expense."*[32]

He had dodged a bullet. With any luck, the Lambert incident was behind him, and he could go back to Mostaganem and train his thoughts on the mission at hand.

But with this shot across the bow, a first from Ike Eisenhower, George resolved to use better judgment, at least around the upper echelons. On

June 2, Marshall, Clark, and a platoon of generals arrived at Patton's head-quarters to see how things were going. Before Clark left, George went out of his way to tell Marshall how helpful Clark had been. *"I am getting tactful as hell,"* he told his diary, *"and in this case it is true. I think that if you treat a skunk nicely, he will not piss on you—as often."*[33]

Patton's thoughts, on war at least, had a beautiful clarity about them. They were as straight and unyielding as the saber he had designed for the cavalry. War began with discipline. Then violence. Then one side bled to death, or gave up. Nothing more complicated than that. Everything else—the weapons, the tactics, the logistics—were just means to an end. Things other men allowed to obscure their vision of war's true essence.[34]

Patton's plan for HUSKY reflected his simple philosophy. He would land one division at Scoglitti, one at Gela, and a reinforced division at Licata, and he would drop a regiment of the 82nd Airborne behind the beaches. His men would then push forward until told to stop.[35]

Patton's largest component, the VI Corps under Major General Ernest Dawley, fielded some good division commanders, including Major General Troy Middleton, an old Leavenworth classmate who had left the Army in the late thirties to help run Louisiana State University. A favorite of Marshall's, Middleton had come out of retirement to command the 45th "Thunderbird" Division, a National Guard outfit training in the United States. Now in his mid-fifties, Middleton had the look of a big-city banker until he opened his mouth and a thick Mississippi Delta drawl sauntered out of his throat.[36]

Major General Lucian Truscott, his polo-playing cavalier from Casablanca, was another crackerjack general of like mind with Patton. A hard driver of men, Truscott once told his son, "Wars aren't won by gentlemen. They're won by men who can be first class sonsofbitches when they have to be. It's as simple as that. No sonofabitch, no commander."[37]

Truscott would command the overstrength 3rd Division, Fred Walker would lead the 36th Division, and Matt Ridgway, who succeeded Bradley when the 82nd Division went airborne, would round out his division commanders. At Patton's headquarters swirled the usual crew—Keyes, Gay, Muller, Koch, and Stiller—as well as newcomers Colonel Halley G. Maddox, his operations head, and aide Charlie Codman, an old-line Bostonian, decorated World War I aviator, and former wine dealer, who took the place of the deceased Dick Jenson.[38]

Patton was satisfied with his headquarters team, which he had trained in Morocco. He was also reasonably satisfied with his major generals and their divisions. But the more he thought about Bradley's performance in Tunisia, the more he liked the idea of bringing Brad's II Corps into the fight. He told himself that Ike "wanted to get Omar a chance as [Marshall] likes him," but the truth was that Patton knew and respected Bradley. In Brad, Patton's army would be getting a first-class corps commander who could bring his hardened veterans along for the ride.[39]

Not that it would be an easy sell to either Ike or Brad. Dawley was a favorite of Marshall and McNair, and Brad's II Corps was refitting from their long, hard struggle for Bizerte. Brad's men were also busy herding thousands of Italian and German prisoners west, and his battalions would need time to rest, replace losses, and train for a new invasion. Their respite, from mid-May to early July, allowed them only seven weeks.[40]

Still, it couldn't hurt to lay some groundwork, and George broached the idea in mid-April, as he was taking his leave of II Corps. Pulling Brad aside, he asked, "Bradley, how would you like to go with me and take II Corps into Sicily?"

"In place of Dawley?"

Patton nodded. "I've worked with you and I've got confidence in you. On the other hand, I don't know what in hell Dawley can do. If you've got no objection, I'm going to ask Ike to fix it up."[41]

Despite the obstacles, it was an offer Brad couldn't refuse. As the shooting in Bizerte stopped, he wrote Patton, *It will be a pleasure to again serve under your command.*"[42]

After two days of briefings by Alexander's staff, Bradley flew to Mostaganem to set up his command post. Patton greeted him like a conquering hero, meeting him at the airport with an honor guard and throwing a luncheon for him, where he broke out two bottles of champagne to toast the "Conqueror of Bizerte." It was a bit over-the-top, but it was genuinely felt. Patton, still somewhat hurt that Ike had never really congratulated him for the Battle of El Guettar, was determined to see that no man could lay the same charge against him. To George, a gentleman in spite of himself, it was the proper thing to do.[43]

But George's deference to the Conqueror of Bizerte vanished when Brad's staff asked permission to set up II Corps command post near Patton's seaside headquarters. Patton's commandant nixed the request, and told them to set up shop sixty kilometers to the south at Relizane, a dust-streaked hamlet on the edge of the Sahara Desert.[44]

What was the guy thinking? Brad wondered when he saw the place. It was late May, and the thermostat in North Africa hovered somewhere between "blistering" and "broiling." His men were garbed in their woolens from the mountains of Tunisia, and to ship them next door to a desert, subjected to the relentless Sahara sun, was a recipe for mass heatstroke.

Flabbergasted, he appealed to George.

"Why, Brad," said George with a chuckle when Brad made his case, "if you set up shop on that beach, the Krauts might slip ashore some night, cut your throats, and make off with our plans." II Corps would stay in Relizane.

Bradley was not amused. He could almost see that smug, bucktoothed grin on George, a telephone in one hand and a cigar in the other, sunlight gleaming off the brass of his "wrestler's belt" and the polished silver of his six-shooters.

Brad never forgave George for what he later called "this petty, demeaning and wholly unnecessary discomfort to my men." But he had no choice. With an acrid taste in his mouth, he called his advance team and told them to go ahead with the relocation to Relizane. Brad and his inner circle lodged in a house owned by an elderly French couple. He, Chet Hansen, Lew Bridge, and the rest warded off the summer heat with the sole luxury of a swimming pool. His soldiers had none.[45]

Poring over a huge topographical model of Sicily while their Coca-Cola bottles sweated in the heat, Brad, Monk Dickson, and the II Corps operations staff had a bad feeling about HUSKY. The difficulties of any amphibious operation were self-evident—enemy subs, beach obstacles, landing site mix-ups, air vulnerability, and a host of other problems to fret over in due course. But the Americans had to cover forty-seven of the sixty-nine miles of landing zones; Brad's men would be spreading themselves dangerously thin and inviting a counterattack, most likely at the middle of his line. Of the two hundred thousand Axis troops in Sicily, Monk warned, two divisions were front-line German units, "strictly hot mustard." The question was not *whether* those German divisions would attack, but *where*, *when*, and *how hard*.[46]

During May and June, George and Brad spent their waking hours hammering the out details of the landing. On the right, the men of Middleton's 45th Division would assault at the fishing village of Scoglitti, next door to

Montgomery's Canadian contingent. Their job would be to capture the Axis airfields at Comiso and Biscari. In the center, Allen's 1st Division and two battalions of Rangers under Lieutenant Colonel William O. Darby would hit Gela and the Ponte Olivo airfield. After taking the airfields, these men would move northwest toward Caltanissetta, a road juncture in the middle of the island that would allow Patton's men to drive either east or west, as events dictated. On the left, Truscott's 3rd Division, a combat command from the 2nd Armored, and a reinforced Ranger battalion, nearly 50,000 men together, would land at Licata, capture the airfield there, then push north. Bradley would command the right and center, while Patton would supervise Truscott's division and the spare armor on the left. He would also keep an armored combat command and a regiment from the 1st Infantry Division in his back pocket as a floating reserve. Meanwhile, Manton Eddy's 9th Division would hang back in North Africa, ready to add weight to the attack when the time was right.[47]

Patton also had at his disposal a division of paratroopers, the 82nd Airborne. He had enough planes to drop one reinforced regiment on D-Day, and he trusted Bradley to designate their place of attack.

"On the air drop we get 220 C-47s to land four battalions of infantry and another pack of howitzers," he told Bradley. "Where do you want to use them?"

"In the high ground behind Gela where they can protect that beach from counterattack by the reserves waiting farther inland," Brad said.[48]

Fair enough, Patton thought. A regiment of the 82nd would drop in front of Gela ahead of the Allied landings. He would bring the rest in shortly after D-Day.

While he smarted over his banishment to Relizane, Brad was not entirely unhappy with his Tunisian mentor. Professionally, the horseman and the infantryman understood each other well by now. Their instincts were, more or less, predictable and harmonious, like a pair of temperamental musicians working separate instruments to create a surprisingly good melody. Brad kept his feelings about George's personal style to himself, and after one long talk, George remarked that Brad "grows on me as a very sound and extremely loyal soldier."[49]

The tough part of their invasion, both acknowledged, would be the long, tenuous supply line. Divisions require immense quantities of supplies—the 45th Division alone would carry almost a million pounds of

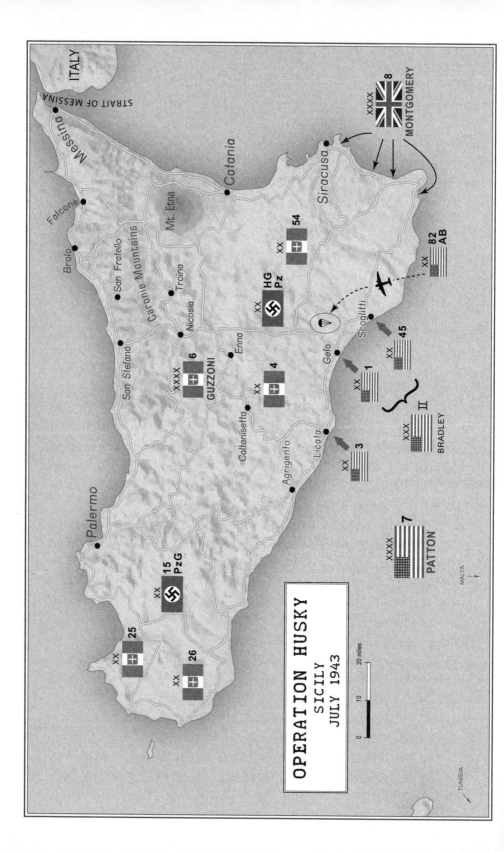

OPERATION HUSKY
SICILY
JULY 1943

equipment ashore—and the tonnage needed to keep the men shooting and scooting stretched Patton's meager port facilities to their limits. Any fuel, food, ammunition, or equipment Patton or Bradley needed would have to come through Syracuse, Monty's port, and those follow-up supplies would not arrive until D-plus-14. Even when Syracuse was open for business, a glance at the map told them the goods would have to be carted over 140 miles of notoriously bad roads to reach the American quartermasters and their customers.[50]

For George, the problem of supplies, like the problem of preeminence in battle, came down to a lack of backbone on the part of one man: Eisenhower. *"Under the present arrangement for Husky,"* he groused, *"we have a pro-British straw man at the top, a British chief admiral and senior vice admiral . . ."*[51]

His mind wandered back to this theme a few weeks later after he and Gay attended a church service led by a new chaplain. *"He preached on the willingness to accept responsibility, even to your own hurt,"* George wrote. *"That ability is what we need and what Ike lacks."*[52]

George was a devout Episcopalian, and his thoughts would turn toward a benevolent, omnipotent God when his spirits needed sustenance. But marring his smooth, theological tonic was the recurring presence of Ike and Clark, whom he could never fully trust. *"In spite of the fact that Ike and Wayne have both cussed the other out to me,"* he wrote in his diary, *"there is still some sort of an unholy alliance between them. I should not worry as I seem to be doing nicely, but I do worry. I am a fool—those two cannot upset destiny. Besides I owe each of them quite a lot, but of course don't know to what extent they have undercut me."*[53]

To keep tabs on Patton, in early June Ike detached his new deputy commander, Major General John P. Lucas, to act as his "eyes and ears" in Mostaganem. Lucas, a bald, kindly-looking man with a corncob pipe fixed in his smile, talked straight and enjoyed a high reputation among Ike, George, and Marshall. Though Lucas was another of those official spies, Patton saw no need to co-opt Lucas into his organization, as he had with Bradley; he frequently called on Lucas for advice, and he used Lucas as a filter to convey information to Ike, as he sometimes did with Ev Hughes or Harry Butcher. Lucas sympathized with George's complaints about Eisenhower, or so George thought, and he told his diary, *"Lucas too feels that Ike is just a staff officer and not a soldier. Too bad. When Lucas came over, General*

Marshall said to him, 'The situation at AFHQ is not satisfactory, or I should say it is very dangerous.'"

Patton added, *"Myself, Bradley, or Keyes could do the job. Personally I don't want it."*[54]

While Patton and Bradley mused over their landings, Eisenhower spent his long days settling squabbles among the vast network of headquarters spread out between Amilcar (Ike's command post), Algiers (AFHQ), La Marsa (the air command center), Bizerte (the British land command post), Malta (the advanced naval center), Cairo (Montgomery's headquarters), and Mostaganem (Patton's headquarters). He waded into questions of logistics, air support, naval coordination, and weather conditions, leaving a trail of cigarette butts and swear words in his wake. "Every indication," he wrote Marshall with growing pessimism, "is that HUSKY is going to be a difficult and hazardous operation. Progressively our daily planning reveals the seriousness of obstacles to be overcome. . . ."[55]

One of those obstacles was HOBGOBLIN, the Allied code name for the island of Pantelleria, a rugged listening post off the Tunisian coast garrisoned by a 10,000-man Italian contingent. The craggy chunk of volcanic rock was occupied by the Italian Army in 1926, and since then the Axis had fortified the island with a U-boat refueling depot, airfields capable of servicing eighty Messerschmitts, and some one hundred gun emplacements. HOBGOBLIN would pose a reconnaissance, air, and naval threat to the HUSKY team, and Ike wanted this particular thorn clipped off before he flung George and Monty onto Sicily's shores.[56]

Talking matters over with his air chiefs, Ike proposed a novel approach to the island's reduction: He would bomb the defenders senseless. Operation CORKSCREW, as the air campaign became known, would be "a sort of laboratory to determine the effect of concentrated heavy bombing on a defended coastline." If the bombings were successful, he could send a brigade to wade through the wreckage and pick up any survivors. If not, then at a minimum the shore defenses should be thoroughly softened up.[57]

This was Eisenhower at his optimistic best, and few of his advisers agreed with him. His pipe-smoking air chief, Marshal Tedder, and his naval commander, Admiral Cunningham, voiced skepticism over Ike's proposal, while Alexander begged him not to throw men against the fortified beach. Against this advice, Ike had his way. CORKSCREW would go forward on June 8; the landings would proceed three days later.[58]

* * *

On the appointed day, Ike joined Admiral Cunningham aboard his flagship, the cruiser H.M.S. *Aurora*, where the two men watched the bombardment. Seeing the island engulfed in a wall of fire loosed by sixty-four hundred tons of high explosives, Ike joked to Cunningham, "Andrew, why don't you and I get into a boat together and row ashore on our own. I think we can capture the island without any of these soldiers."[59]

For all Ike's bravado, he was terrified by staff predictions of horrendous casualties. Pounding the coastline with bombs and shells from air and sea was one thing; sending flesh-and-blood men onto beaches studded with mines, mortar emplacements, and machine gun nests was a different, much deadlier game. Just before the landings, Ike, Butch said, "has been going through the same type of jitters and worries which marked the days immediately preceding our landings in North Africa." He got little sleep the night before his men hit the beaches.[60]

On D-Day, June 11, Ike awoke early. The news from the front stunned him: The island's garrison had surrendered en masse. Italian soldiers, pleading lack of water, began pouring into POW cages, and before long Ike would call on Churchill to collect a wager of one Italian cent for every prisoner over three thousand. When the final tally of eleven thousand prisoners was counted, Churchill was delighted to send Ike the $1.60 balance to satisfy his debt. Ike, breathing a sigh of relief, was happy to have guessed correctly.[61]

Pantelleria was one thing. Sicily was another prospect entirely. Most divisions manning Sicily's coastline were weak units composed of local conscripts whose willingness to die for *Il Duce* was questionable. However, Hitler and Mussolini could ferry 40,000 men from the toe of Italy to Sicily in a day's time, and there were several Axis units in Sicily that kept Ike awake at night. Allied code breakers in London's Bletchley Park intercepted radio transmissions revealing that Marshal Kesselring's commander on Sicily, Italian General Alfredo Guzzoni, had deployed the *Hermann Göring* Panzer Division and the best Italian unit, the 4th *Livorno* Division, in the island's southeastern sector. He also held the German 15th *Panzergrenadier* Division to the west, near Palermo. From their dispositions, it appeared that Kesselring and Guzzoni hoped the German units would put some iron into the five Sicilian coastal divisions and four regular Italian divisions that formed the bulk of his defenses. If they did, the Italians might put up a serious fight.[62]

The final HUSKY plan called for an armada of three thousand ships from the United States, Great Britain, Malta, Algeria, and Tunisia to converge upon Sicily and disgorge their landing craft. Some 149,000 men would hit the beaches during the first wave, spreading out along an eighty-mile arc under cover of naval gunfire, tactical air cover, and paratroop drops behind enemy lines. General Montgomery would command four assault divisions, some armor, commandos, and glider troops who would land behind Syracuse. Patton's men would land on the southern coast and drive north and west, protecting Montgomery's flank until they reached the Yellow Line, their final HUSKY objective.[63]

After that, the plan for Sicily became rather vague. Montgomery would presumably push through Catania along the east coast, keeping to the right of Mount Etna, and Patton would presumably move north, to meet Monty at or west of Messina. At least, those were the presumptions Alexander's ground plan suggested. But as D-Day approached, none of these presumptions had been settled. Or really even discussed.

The collective nervousness in the run-up to HUSKY deepened the cracks in the Eisenhower-Patton-Bradley partnership. In mid-June, Ike prepared a secret memo in which he analyzed his subordinate commanders. Of Patton, he commented: *"A shrewd soldier who believes in showmanship to such an extent that he is almost flamboyant. He talks too much and too quickly and sometimes creates a very bad impression. Moreover, I fear that he is not always a good example to subordinates, who may be guided by only his surface actions without understanding the deep sense of duty, courage and service that make up his real personality. He has done well as a combat corps commander, and I expect him to do well in all future operations."*[64]

For Bradley, Ike's case was much simpler: *"About the best rounded, well balanced senior officer that we have in the service. His judgments are always sound. . . . I have not a single word of criticism of his actions to date and do not expect to have any in the future. I feel that there is no position in the Army that he could not fill with success."*[65]

Patton tended to stay out of Ike's way, communicating with his commander through Hughes, Lucas, Hewitt, and others when he could. But on July 5, the two men argued over whether Allen's 1st Division was up to the task of landing on Sicily's defended beaches. Ike, having listened to many complaints about the division from Bradley and Lucas, declared that the Big Red One was so undisciplined that its combat effectiveness had necessarily become impaired. Patton, privately wondering about Allen's fitness himself, disagreed. He told Ike in no uncertain terms he was wrong about Allen and the Fighting First. "Anyhow," Patton argued, "no one whips a dog just before putting him into a fight."[66]

George won the argument. But Ike insisted the division needed different leadership, and the best George could do was delay Terry's relief until after the landing phase of the operation was over.[67]

The two men discussed air cover and a few other neutral subjects. Then Ike turned to Patton's role in Sicily. As George remembered the conversation:

> I told him that I was very appreciative of being selected. He said, "You are a great leader but a poor planner." I replied that, except for Torch, which I had planned and which was a high success, I had never been given a chance to plan. He said that if "Husky" turned into a slugging match, he might recall me to get ready for the next operation, and let Bradley finish Husky. I protested that I would like to finish one show. I can't make out whether he thinks Bradley is a better close fighter than I am or whether he wants to keep in with General Marshall, who likes Bradley. I know that Bradley is completely loyal to me.[68]

Ike spent his last days before the invasion visiting troops, checking weather, and worrying about enemy dispositions. But there was surprisingly little else for him to do. He wrote a rambling letter to Mamie, telling her, "In circumstances such as these men do almost anything to keep from going slightly mad. Walk, talk, try to work, smoke (all the time)—anything to push the minutes along to find out a result that one's own actions can no longer affect in the slightest degree. I stand it better than most, but there is no use denying that I feel the strain."[69]

On July 6, his lucky coins tugging at his pocket, Ike boarded a B-17 and flew to the island fortress of Malta, where Alexander had set up the advance headquarters of the Fifteenth Army Group. Ike's office, a fourteen-by-ten-foot room, was little better furnished than his cadet barracks at West Point, and Malta's thick, salty moisture assaulted his lungs almost as savagely as did his damp Camel cigarettes. As the warm Mediterranean sun baked the island's surface, Ike and his subterranean companions wore overcoats in the cold, dripping tunnels, one of which led from Ike's bedroom to a medieval dungeon. The scene would remind Ike of his anxious days at another

British island fortress. It was only eight months ago, yet it was barely visible through the haze of memory.[70]

So much had changed since he had bent his head beneath the tunnels of Gibraltar. He was a different man. His army, his job, the faces he worked with, they had all changed. Only a few vestiges of his life before TORCH remained. The insomnia, the jitters, the crush of duty. Those things never left his side.

In the palace that was once home to the Knights of Malta, Eisenhower and his lieutenants spent the night of the invasion tuning in to distressing reports of a gale sweeping the Mediterranean. As darkness enveloped the ancient fortress, the man from Kansas motored to the southern end of the island, where he hoped to catch a glimpse of the transport planes carrying paratroops and pulling gliders.[71]

The tight, worried look that spread across his face said it all. Ike muttered a quick but fervent prayer for the safety of his men, then sent word to Marshall that the operation was on.[72]

Omar Bradley learned of his promotion to lieutenant general on June 10, and the following day Ike awarded him the Distinguished Service Medal for his work in Tunisia. But apart from a brief party thrown by his harried staff, he had no time to savor either honor. The weeks leading up to HUSKY were jammed with training exercises, conferences with division commanders, and fretting over small but crucial details, most of which involved the Navy's most cherished acronyms: LST (Landing Ship, Tank), LCI (Landing Craft, Infantry), LCT (Landing Craft, Tank), LCVP (Landing Craft, Vehicle or Personnel, the "Higgins boat"), and DUKW (an amphibious truck whose acronym GIs naturally shortened to "Duck"). Brad was pulled in 151 separate directions as he played umpire to the shrill demands of each II Corps unit on his extremely limited shipping space: Artillery chiefs wanted more guns ashore, and were willing to cut out the engineers to get their tubes on the first wave. Engineers wanted more bridging and corduroy materials, even if that meant cutting back on antiaircraft guns. The AA bosses demanded more batteries and more ammunition—cut out the quartermaster, why don't we? And on it went. There was only one premise on which every commanding officer agreed: If each didn't get his way, the invasion would be in grave danger.[73]

A typical dustup began when Air Support Command, the men who would repair the airfields that provided tactical air cover, demanded room on the first wave for 660 vehicles, bulldozers, heavy trucks, and the like.

Brad's entire force was permitted only 4,500 "vehicles," including towed antiaircraft and antitank guns, so the request was preposterous.

"You'll have to cut it down," Brad quietly told the colonel representing the air wing. "That's almost as much as we can allow for an assault division." Surely, he said, some of those bulldozers could come in on the second wave, after the airfields had been captured.

The colonel was unmoved. "Six hundred and sixty is rock-bottom," he insisted. "We can't go in with anything less."

Brad, more than a little annoyed by now, gave the petulant colonel a hard look. "Very well, then," he said testily. "You make the assault with your six hundred and sixty trucks. Clear the beach for us and we'll come in on a later lift. It's either you or the infantry. There's not lift enough for both." With that, he dismissed the man.

The next day Brad got a call from Patton.

"Brad, the air force is up here raising hell," said George. "They tell me you're pretty tough to get along with."

"Not half as tough as I will be, George, if they don't come down out of the clouds and play straight with us on this business of lift."

George listened respectfully as Brad outlined the problem. He might play games with Bradley on headquarters locations or command style, but this landing craft allocation was serious business. If Brad picked a fight with another outfit, he probably had a very good reason.

"I know what you're up against," George said at last. "Handle them any way you want. I'll back you up."[74]

When Brad learned that General Marshall and his retinue would be flying in from Algiers, he staged a landing exercise by Allen's 1st Division to show the brass what his men could do. The June 2 landing would lack live fire, and there would be no opposition, of course, but it would be a stressful exercise, for joining Bradley on the beach would be his boss, General Patton; his boss's boss, General Eisenhower; and his boss's boss's boss, General Marshall. And each of these luminaries brought his own squires and attendants to watch the show. If Brad had been nervous about Ike's "visiting firemen" looking over his shoulder in Tunisia, it was nothing compared to the pressure of this audience.

On the appointed day, the assault convoy steamed in. To the sound of rattling davits and the splash of Higgins boats—"puppies," George called them—the first wave motored up to the beach. Down dropped the metal ramp doors, and out stumbled the infantrymen, who sloshed through the surf and onto the beach.[75]

The loose pack of generals milled about the beach and squinted through binoculars as wet soldiers bent low and fanned out. Suddenly Patton, frowning at a nearby squad of crouching riflemen, politely excused himself and jogged over to the enlisted men.

"And just where in hell are your goddamned bayonets?" Patton bellowed to the startled men.

The riflemen stared at him. They hadn't expected the beach to be defended by a three-star general.

Inclining his long frame forward, George let loose with a loud, violent harangue on why a fighting man needed cold steel at the end of his rifle. He gave it to the privates and corporals full-bore, all within earshot of the startled generals.

Ike stood in embarrassed silence as George lashed his men with colorful vivid obscenities. He might have thought the outburst was for Marshall's benefit, except that it was so characteristically George. "Pink" Bull, standing nearby, nodded to Marshall, who looked at him but said nothing. Then Pink turned to Brad and whispered, "Well, there goes Georgie's chance for a crack at higher command. That temper of his is going to finish him yet."

George, sand flicking with each stride of his boots, rejoined his fellow brass with a smug, toothy grin.

"Chew them out and they'll remember it."[76]

On June 27, Bradley's men broke down their headquarters and the senior team moved to Oran. After seven days attending to last-minute details, he drove over to the harbor of Mers-el-Kebir, where his ship awaited. At its moorings sat the U.S.S. *Ancon*, a converted passenger liner that would serve as Brad's floating home and command post until he hit the beaches. On the Fourth of July, Rear Admiral Alan R. Kirk, commander of the ninety-six-ship Scoglitti strike force, had Bradley piped aboard *Ancon* in the Navy's best traditional style, though Bradley, uninitiated in the ways of the Navy, was unsure whether he should salute the officers, shake hands, or wait for an invitation to his quarters. Eventually, he and his gear ended up in the right place, and he settled uncomfortably into his cabin to await orders to attack.[77]

To the same traditional piping, General Patton thumped up the gangplank of the U.S.S. *Monrovia*, a transport ship that would serve as Western Task

Force's floating headquarters as well as his hotel at sea. It was his second time aboard a ship bound for a foreign beach, and he shared few of Bradley's apprehensions about naval etiquette.[78]

As the resident Army commander, George Patton had little enough to do while the task force was at sea. He argued with Admiral Hewitt over the timing of the naval bombardment, and he spread the word to antiaircraft units that a wave of Matt Ridgway's paratroop transports would follow up sometime after D-Day. But by and large, he was a general without portfolio. Until he and his men were on solid ground again, he would simply be one of the hundreds of lubbers wandering about the *Monrovia*'s immaculately swabbed decks.[79]

As Hewitt's flotilla pulled away from Algiers at five in the afternoon on July 6, George stood on the *Monrovia*'s deck to watch the armada of transports, cruisers, destroyers, battleships, minesweepers, and supply vessels picking their way through the harbor's channel. The late-summer dusk slowly engulfed the shoreline, throwing a purplish, peaceful hue over the city, while George gazed across to the far side of a continent he had first seen eight months earlier.

As the briny waves lapped at the steel bellies of the Allied fleet, the underemployed Patton grew anxious. His fate, and the lives of his men, were now in the hands of men he would never meet. *"It is a moving sight,"* he wrote of the armada, *"but over all is the feeling that only God and the Navy can do anything until we hit the shore. I hope God and the Navy do their stuff."*[80]

Three nights later, to the soothing rumble of the ship's engines, George lay on his bunk, dressed for the next day's battle like a stone effigy of a medieval knight. A nervous sort of quiet settled over him on the eve of battle, and he lay there clinging to the burdens of the morrow, yet trying to shed those cares for just a moment. The knight slowly drifted off to sleep, *Monrovia*'s hull rocking him into a dark, sweet slumber.

Behind his closed lids, in the recesses of his dreams, a black kitten purred its way toward him. As George looked down at the deck, the kitten was joined by a dozen cats swarming around him, arching and spitting. Hissing. Then, without warning, they turned, ran down a flight of stairs, and were gone.

George sat up and looked at the clock. It was time.[81]

TEN

UNDER FIRE

When we left General Patton I thought he was angry. Ike had stepped on him hard.

—Harry Butcher, July 13, 1943

ABOARD THE WOOD-FRAMED HIGGINS BOATS, the men of the beach assault teams, packed three dozen to a box, rode out four-foot waves in a fog of anxiety. As they stood inside their floating sardine cans, they fidgeted, vomited, muttered, and prayed. They stared at red arcs of tracer rounds flying from six-inch naval guns. They heard the screams of projectiles, and they squinted against searchlights that swept the dark sea.

But mostly, they waited. For until their coxswains dropped the eight-hundred-pound steel ramps, until the time came for them to sprint forward and fan out from the boat's vulnerable mouth, until the time came to face the machine guns, mortars, and shelling, there was nothing these men could do but wait in purgatory. Like their commander, they could only place their faith in God and the Navy. And pretty soon the Navy would be out of the picture.[1]

Under a black canopy of space, Patton wedged himself onto the ship's crowded bridge. He stood alongside Admiral Hewitt, Johnny Lucas, Hap Gay, and a cluster of khaki-clad officers, watching his men ride those bouncing puppies to Gela's foam-flecked shore. High above them flashed a thatched roof of fire arcing from the guns of *Monrovia* and her sisters, their strawlike fingers snuffing out enemy searchlights and probing the coast for anything that resembled a bunker or dugout. Wherever the light beams lit, the land soon burst open in short, beautiful blossoms of white and yellow, followed several seconds later by a soft, concussive boom that was swallowed up by the next salvo.[2]

Into this light show went Darby's Rangers; in went Allen's assault teams. In they went, weathering fire that glittered along beaches festively designated Red, Green, Yellow, Blue, Red 2, and Green 2.[3]

The invaders, threading their way through dancing lights of fire, moved rapidly through Gela and pushed out the city's defenders. The beaches were not yet quiet when engineering teams began staking out wire-mesh paths over the dunes and posting colored beach markers, while armbanded shore police directed troops and supply vehicles inland.[4]

God and the Navy had done their stuff.

As the clock ticked off the minutes, Patton received his first reports. Truscott, commanding his division from the flagship *Biscayne*, radioed that the landings at Licata were a "magnificent" success; before lunchtime, the town would be in American hands. Terry Allen was also making good progress at Gela, except around that damned Yellow Beach; his landing craft were also hitting thickets of mines around Blue and Red 2, and enemy panzers had been spotted rolling toward town. No word yet from the paratroopers, and Bradley was overseeing Middleton's Thunderbird Division off Scoglitti.[5]

With so many pieces in wild states of flux, Patton's first order of business was to get everyone into a solid line and deploy his reserves, something he could best do from his command center on *Monrovia*. With more than a hint of embarrassment, he confessed to his diary that night, *Things were so complicated here that I did not go ashore. [I] feel like a cur, but I probably did better here.*[6]

One of George's complications was the knotty problem of getting the second wave of Ridgway's 82nd Airborne onto Sicily safely. The airborne commanders, Ridgway and Colonel Reuben H. Tucker of the 504th Parachute Infantry Regiment, worried about friendly fire from jittery antiaircraft crews, and their fears grew acute when Troop Carrier Command took until late in the game—July 5—to get its final flight path to Seventh Army. Five days before the landings, Patton had sent a signal to Bradley, Middleton, Allen, Gaffey, and Truscott warning them to expect flights of friendly troops around midnight during one of the first six nights of the operation, and Hap Gay reiterated the orders with Seventh Army units.[7]

But no one could be sure the word had gotten around to every AA gunner who would be tracking the unarmed planes as they flew into Sicilian airspace.[8]

Brad spent the early morning hours of July 10 curled up in his bunk, hurting like he had never hurt in his life. During the rolling voyage through the Mediterranean gale, amid cramped quarters and thick Navy chow, he had come down with a piercing case of hemorrhoids that was as excruciating as it was untimely.[9]

With D-Day drawing near and the pain becoming insufferable, Brad made the command decision to go under the surgeon's knife, which put him out of commission during HUSKY's opening hours. A sympathetic Chet Hansen jotted in his diary that day, *"The general is ill in his room, confined there by an inopportune local operation. Compelled to lie in bed, he soon became quite ill in the pitching sea. Chafed because he has been confined to his quarters and is unable to view the start of the campaign."*[10]

For a man of Brad's work ethic, lying on his stomach during the invasion was almost as distressing as the pain itself. Almost.

The naval bombardment proved devastating, and as fragmentary reports chirped into the *Ancon's* command center, Brad breathed a sigh of relief: The enemy had made no real effort to stop him on the beaches. Despite a few delays and some missed landing zones by Middleton's Thunderbirds, a queasy Omar Bradley was pleased to signal Patton's command ship that six battalions were firmly ashore, and the rest of the 45th Division was on the way. By two in the afternoon Middleton's men, most of them dumped onto the wrong beaches, broke into Scoglitti and began pressing the enemy toward Comiso airfield. The landings weren't pretty, but they were wholly successful.[11]

The same could not be said for the 1st Division's Gela landings. Shortly after the city fell, panzers from the *Hermann Göring* Division came clacking over the hills to the north and began firing into Allen's men before they had unloaded their antitank guns. In the confines of his small bunk, a doubled-up Bradley frowned at reports passed to him describing touchy resistance along the high ground behind the town. His quarry was evidently turning on him, fangs bared and ready to lunge. Taking Gela, Brad realized, was the easy part; holding the high ground just behind it would be the real test.[12]

By the time Allen's men had wrested a foothold on Gela's beaches, Bradley had recovered just enough to hobble up the steps to the bridge, suck in a mouthful of fresh air, and survey the chaos through his binoculars. He said a silent prayer of thanks, then got down to business.[13]

Like Patton, General Bradley spent the rest of a chaotic D-Day coordinating movements by radio, accounting for his jumbled battalions, and trying to make out where the enemy would strike next. With 15th *Panzergrenadier* and *Hermann Göring* out there, Bradley was looking for any sign of the gathering blow.

But as the thin blue curtain of dusk rose from the east on the tenth of July, his beaches held. A limp, miserable Omar Bradley prepared to leave the *Ancon* for Mussolini's island.[14]

At eight o'clock on the morning of July 11, a nervous General Patton ordered Ridgway to jump his 504th Parachute Infantry Regiment onto the 1st Division beachhead that night. To avoid the prospect of friendly fire, he sent *Monrovia*'s overburdened communications room a top-priority order warning subordinates—especially antiaircraft commanders—that the 82nd was coming. He paced the flagship's decks, fretting over his tenuous grip on the beaches, and he listened to ominous reports of Italian and German tanks converging on Gela. By nine, the fidgeting man decided he couldn't stay aboard ship any longer, and he loaded up Gay, Stiller, and a few aides into the admiral's barge for the ride ashore. Wading the last few yards in knee-deep surf, Patton hit the gritty beach by ten.[15]

Unlike his landing at Casablanca, this time George came ashore dressed for history. His star-studded helmet, oversize binoculars, and ivory-gripped revolver were set off by soaked jodhpurs, tall cavalry boots, and a riding crop that he pointed in the general direction of Gela, delighting a troupe of Signal Corpsmen who snapped pictures and rolled camera footage of the Seventh Army commander in his element. While a beach crew scrambled to de-waterproof his jeep and adorn it with a bold three-starred banner, George puffed away on a long *presidente* cigar, strolled the beach, and conspicuously ignored the sound of enemy shells.[16]

Also unlike Casablanca, for this round Patton did not have time to play three-star beachmaster. Mounting his jeep, he spent the day dashing around Sicily's southern coast looking for Lieutenant Colonel Darby and General Allen. He raised hell and pushed his men forward, called in naval gunfire, deployed his armored reserves, and shoved every tank-busting contraption he could find up to Allen's hard-pressed perimeter. He bypassed

Bradley and ordered Terry Allen to send a regiment inland to make contact with Truscott's division to the left, which would give Seventh Army a solid, coherent line. And he tried to make his presence felt among his smaller units. The way a general ought to.[17]

For reasons having more to do with Seventh Army's spirited defense than with Patton's personal presence, by two in the afternoon the *Hermann Göring*'s commander called off the counterattack. While Patton could not take much personal credit for the outcome of Gela, his hands-on leadership had certainly helped; John Lucas, whom Ike had attached to Patton's command, later quipped, "I am convinced that his presence had much to do with restoring the situation."[18]

George returned to Hewitt's flagship that evening, wet, tired, but pleased with the day's fighting. His army had lost more than 2,400 men in the counterattack, but he had taken more than 4,400 prisoners and gained an unbreakable grip on Sicily's lower coast. With a measure of self-satisfaction, he sat down at his cabin desk and wrote, *"This is the first day in this campaign that I think I earned my pay. I am well satisfied with my command today. God certainly watched over me today."*[19]

As George dried out from the rolling surf, his biggest worry remained those damned paratrooper runs. The more he thought about them, the more apprehensive he grew, and by eight that evening he made up his mind to scrub the operation.

But by then it was too late. In the midst of the invasion, communications from ship to shore to airfield were too jumbled to allow even the Seventh Army commander to stop the mission. As he told his diary, *"Went to office at 2000 to see if we could stop the 82nd Airborne lift, as enemy air attacks were heavy and inaccurate and army and navy anti-air was jumpy. Found we could not get contact by radio. Am terribly worried."*[20]

He had good reason to be worried. That night, some 2,000 men of the 504th flew overhead in their slow, twin-engine transport planes. As fate would have it, they arrived on the heels of the largest Axis bombing raid of the battle. The lumbering transports had just crossed the beach line when a single gun shattered the night, sending every AA cannon on ship and shore into wild spasms of reactive fire. Yellow-orange rays split the night and tracer fire perforated wings and hulls. The lumbering transports broke formation at once and scattered like frightened geese.[21]

By the time the staccato bursts died down, twenty-three American planes had been shot out of the sky, six of which came down before their troopers had time to jump. Another thirty-seven limped back to Africa in various states of mutilation. The brief, violent fratricide took the lives of 141 men. Another 177 were sent the field hospitals to dress wounds and splint limbs.[22]

As he turned in for the night, knowing nothing of the fate of the paratroopers, George felt pleased with what his men had done. On the right, Middleton's 45th had taken Comiso and wedged itself against Montgomery's Eighth Army. In the center, Allen's 1st Division and Darby's Rangers had taken Gela, then fought off a vicious counterattack by Hitler's best panzer division. On the left, Truscott's 3rd Division was holding an easy line at Licata, while the Hell on Wheels Division was rolling off the boats to give the Americans some heavy long-arm punch. By the end of the first day, Patton's men had taken some four thousand prisoners, and George was sure plenty more would be counted by the time the day's action was sorted out. He had done a damned fine job.[23]

Unfortunately for Patton, that's not the way Ike saw it. The Supreme Commander had spent several anxious, coin-rubbing days in the "Wake," the naval headquarters section on Malta where messages would first arrive. With the initial stress of the operation breaking like a fever, the Eisenhower temper percolated up to the surface and began seeking out an object of wrath.[24]

Several days of enforced radio silence had been absolutely necessary, but the silence had worked Ike into a high state of uneasiness. Now that the shooting had started, he was receiving neat progress reports almost hourly from Eighth Army. Patton's reports, by contrast, were sparse, infrequent, almost nonexistent. Why? he wondered. Didn't George want air support? Did he plan to overrun Sicily all by himself? How was the Supreme Commander supposed to report back to the Combined Chiefs if his Army commander kept him in the dark? As Harry Butcher noted midmorning on D-Day, "We had no news from the U.S. forces, and it is important that the good old USA do well . . . but cripes we were eager for information."[25]

News arrived soon. Signals from the *Monrovia* told Ike that Patton's men had landed at Gela. They had faced shore opposition but, thankfully, no mines, no enemy surface ships, no hostile aircraft. Butcher, working his Navy connections, learned Allen's 1st Division had taken Gela and its aerodrome, news that gave Ike a real lift.[26] But the report raised other questions in Ike's mind: What about Truscott? What about Middleton? How were their divisions holding up? Were Darby's Rangers—the glue holding Patton's front—standing firm? Where were the paratroopers? Ike hadn't a clue.[27]

Ike knew *Monrovia* had been specially fitted with enlarged communication and coding facilities, unlike Patton's command ship at Casablanca. So this time, the problem clearly did not lie with the Navy. Restless and uptight, Ike knew it had to be George's fault. So after pacing around the Wake for a day and a half, Ike decided to pay a visit to the Seventh Army commander.[28]

In the deep, dark hours of July 12, Ike boarded a Royal Navy destroyer, the H.M.S. *Petard*, and took the four-hour trip to rendezvous with *Monrovia*. He brought along Harry Butcher, several British officers, some aides, and a couple of journalists, and the *Petard* shoved off around two o'clock in search of the elusive Seventh Army commander.[29]

At six, the *Petard* steamed alongside Hewitt's flagship. Under gunmetal skies, Eisenhower and his retinue were piped aboard with stiff salutes from Admiral Hewitt and General Patton. Ike conferred with Hewitt over a short breakfast; then he marched off to George Patton's war room for a status report.[30]

George, blissfully unaware of the friendly fire on his paratroopers, was beaming as he showed Ike maps of his army's progress while his chief of staff, Hap Gay, looked on. Truscott and Middleton, he explained, had exceeded their objectives and were moving up the island's center. The Comiso airfields, with 125 planes, had fallen to the Americans. Allen's 1st Division was having a tough time around Gela, having been jumped by Italy's *Livorno* Division and the *Hermann Göring* panzers, but they were pushing back the Eyeties and the Huns. They had every reason to be pleased.[31]

No, they didn't, Ike snapped. Drawing himself up to full height, he unleashed a furious burst of Eisenhower temper on his bewildered friend. Seventh Army reports, he declared, had been far from satisfactory. The Eighth Army was sending in detailed, hourly reports, and Patton's transmissions were sparse and pathetic by comparison. The Germans, as George well knew, had been *expecting* a landing; now that they knew exactly where Patton's army was, they were rushing reinforcements to smash Truscott and the rest in the flank. How the hell was he supposed to order air interdiction if the Germans knew where George's men were but he didn't? And why, he demanded, had George left his command post to play squad leader on D-plus-1?[32]

George, caught completely off guard, was mortified. But he didn't argue with Eisenhower. Red faced, he snapped to attention and took the tongue-lashing like a plebe cadet. When Ike paused, George turned to General Gay and ordered his staff to provide AFHQ with three daily reports in addition to the regular 4:00 p.m. situation reports. But even this submissive response drew a dressing-down from an irate Supreme Commander, whose broadsides burst out anew. As George complained, *"Ike also told me that I am too prompt in my replies and should hesitate more, the way he does, before replying."*[33]

The mix of tension and collective embarrassment grew thicker when General Gay, sent to find his G-2, G-3, and G-4 chiefs to provide details, proved unable to track them down. Butcher, one of George's best friends among Ike's inner circle, commented afterward, "Gay seemed in a fog. I took a rather 'poor view' of his management ability and reluctantly took a similar view on General Patton's bumptious but rather disorganized executive management." The interview showcased George at his worst.[34]

Ike spun on his heel and left the steel-walled room, leaving a shaken Patton to stiffen in the now-frigid air. For George, a man who craved the approval of his superiors, it was a terrible blow.

Ike's outburst seemed to be reactive, coming without warning, and members of his staff privately thought he was being too tough on Patton. "Ike stepped on him hard," Butcher acknowledged. "There was an air of tenseness. I had a feeling that Ike was disappointed. He had previously said that he would be happy if after about five days from D-Day General Bradley were to take over because of his calm and matter-of-fact direction."[35]

Butch's sympathy for George grew when he learned from his Navy contacts that messages had been running as much as seven hours behind in *Monrovia*'s overburdened communications center, a department under Hewitt's control, not Patton's. Ike's spy John Lucas missed the incident but witnessed the fallout, writing afterward in his diary,

> *I didn't hear what he said but he must have given Patton hell, because George was much upset. Having just come from the beach where there had been terrific mortar fire, he might well have been upset anyhow. The British apparently keep Ike better informed than the Americans but our situation reports go through General Alexander and what happens to them I don't know. Anyway I checked them myself and they seemed to me to be as complete as they could well be under the circumstances.*[36]

But what Lucas and Butcher and the rest of the staff thought meant nothing. Eisenhower was the boss, and the boss seemed to have it in for George. Not long afterward, Lucas wrote in his diary, *"Saw Ike again. Smith was present part of the time. Both said that Bradley and Truscott have been the outstanding figures in this operation. Without disparaging either, I don't see what this is based on. I think many people are jealous of Patton."*[37]

Why had Ike come down so hard on George? He didn't say. Maybe it was to keep the old dog on a short leash. After all, Marshall had said that was the way to handle Patton. And in the end, a short tether might be a good thing for George, to keep him from digging under the fence and scaring the neighbors.

Or maybe it was because Ike knew that George Patton was one of the few people on earth who would let him blow off that much steam and still remain as loyal as a brother—a surly, vain, jealous brother perhaps, but a brother he could always count on when the dice were in midair.

Or it may have been Supreme Commander Eisenhower stretching his wings, showing everyone he was willing to push people, even old friends, to make sure his quarterbacks ran the plays as he called them. Whatever the reason, it didn't sit well with George.

As he slunk back to the silence of his cabin, thinking about the bawling-out Eisenhower had just given him, thinking about where he stood in the eyes of his superiors, George must have looked wistfully upon those bucolic days that followed the War to End All Wars. The days when he could enthrall a young, smiling lieutenant colonel with stories of combat, of what it was like to hear the ping of Mauser bullets bouncing off the hull of a tank, of the roar and smoke of the Meuse-Argonne and St.-Mihiel. Or even those days a few short years ago, when a frustrated, deskbound Eisenhower was begging him for a colonelcy in the Armored Force.

However those days used to be, and however George remembered them to be, they were long gone now.

The incident aboard Hewitt's flagship was one of those jarring moments when an intimate relationship becomes merely a close one, the kind of transformative moment when a man promoted to supervisor or shift foreman has to drop the hammer on an old chum. A time when, once and for all, the bond of friendship gives way to the chain of command.

It may not have been the death of that bond between Ike and George, but both men understood from then on that their friendship would have its limits.

Well, what the hell, thought George. He had work to do. He told his aides to gather his personal gear for the short trip to his headquarters at Gela. The boat was readied, and he climbed down *Monrovia*'s rope ladder for the last time.[38]

When Eisenhower arrived back at Alex's command post, his fury at George, which had subsided during his return trip, came roaring back with news of the airborne fiasco. *Twenty-three transports* shot down over American lines? What the hell was wrong with Seventh Army? Why hadn't George gotten the word out to his AA units? And why didn't George tell him about the disaster that morning aboard the *Monrovia*? His bare brow tightening and muttered curse words forming on his lips, Ike bellowed for an aide and dictated an immediate dispatch to the Seventh Army's commander.[39]

A glum George Patton told his diary he "received a wire from Ike, cussing me out" for the airborne fiasco, a tragedy he hadn't known about until shortly after Ike had left the ship. Ike's cable warned, "If the cited report is true, the incident could have been occasioned only by inexcusable carelessness and negligence on the part of someone." Ike wanted someone's head, not a whitewash, and to keep Patton from burying his order in some adjutant general's paper-shuffle game he added, "I want a statement of the disciplinary action taken by you."[40]

Patton, having issued repeated orders warning ground and naval units that friendly transports would be overhead, felt there was no point in trying to nominate a scapegoat. He quietly refused to do anything more than initiate a pro forma inquiry and allow Ike's investigator to nose around harmlessly. His conscience, he decided, was clear on this point: *"As far as I can see, if anyone is blamable, it must be myself, but personally I feel immune to censure,"* he wrote. *"Perhaps Ike is looking for an excuse to relieve me. I am having a full report made but will not try anyone. If they want a goat, I am it."*

His bitterness smoldering, he added, *"Men who have been bombed all day get itchy fingers. Ike has never been subjected to air attack or any other form of death. However, he is such a straw man that his future is secure. The British will never let him go."*[41]

Omar Bradley set foot on Sicilian soil on the morning of July 11, grimacing with every bump of the boat that carried him in. He was in agony from his hemorrhoidectomy, and he spent the next few days sitting awkwardly on an inflatable life jacket, shifting his weight every few minutes to dull the pulsing knife thrusts that shot through his rectum as a surprisingly large congregation of nerve endings stitched.[42]

But if one overlooked his custom seating and saw only his plain jacket, leggings, and pot helmet, the bespectacled man with the homely, weather-beaten face looked like any other middle-aged officer on a sprawling headquarters staff. He posed for no pictures; he waited for no three-starred jeep. His aides simply flagged down a passing Duck, and he hitched a painful, bone-shaking ride into Scoglitti, where busy staffers were setting up his new command post.[43]

As he settled into an old, dilapidated *carabinieri* headquarters that would become his new office, he heard an insistent, rhythmic rumble of howitzers booming from Terry Allen's direction. When he learned from frantic Signals men that his waterlogged radio set would not be sending or receiving that day, he reluctantly saddled up for another painful trip. He headed for Gela.[44]

As his jeep bounced toward Gela's outskirts, Brad saw the Big Red One fighting for its life. Panzers were pressing against the division's eggshell perimeter at the village of Piano Lupo, and Brad ordered his driver to burn rubber to Allen's headquarters.

"Do you have it in hand, Terry?" Brad asked in his plain drawl as the jeep rolled to a stop.

Exhaustion covered Allen's face. A cigarette held on to Allen's lower lip for dear life. He nodded. "Yes, I think so, but they've given us a helluva rough time."[45]

The Fighting First had indeed been given a helluva rough time. But Allen's brawlers gave as good as they got, a fact not lost on Omar Bradley. Bradley, a man who had built his reputation by doing things by the book better than anyone else, disliked the unkempt general and his unruly division. Watching Allen's men slug their way through a vicious panzer attack, he realized that Patton had been right to insist Terrible Terry lead the charge up the center. "In doing so he may have saved II Corps from a major disaster," Brad later conceded. "Only the perverse Big Red One with its no less perverse commander was both hard and experienced enough to take that assault in stride."[46]

But Bradley's respect for Patton's foresight withered when he learned his boss had countermanded one of his orders to Allen. After Brad had ordered one of Allen's regiments to sit tight until an adjacent enemy pocket had been cleaned out, an impatient Patton had ordered Terry to push the regiment forward. When the regiment was threatened with annihilation, Bradley had to beg George to send a part of the 2nd Armored Division reserve to the regiment's relief. George had interfered with Bradley's orders and placed men's lives in danger.[47]

An incensed Brad confronted George about his sin in breaking the Army's sacred chain of command. George apologized, which at first smoothed Brad's ruffled feathers, but Brad later found out that George had complained privately to Ike that his corps commander was "not aggressive enough" during the Axis counterattack.

This was a remark that cut Bradley to the bone. His personal courage should not be in question—he had taken up a carbine and gone hunting for a sniper holding up a sector he was passing through, a gutsy move for any man—and he felt he was professionally correct in firming up his line before pushing inland. But George's thoughtless comment was calculated to damage Brad's standing with their mutual boss. The remark, and Brad's learning of it, was a jagged gouge in the smooth if unlikely partnership they had forged in the days of Tunisia.[48]

As the ground campaign revved up to full speed, Brad took the reins of Patton's eastern forces and drove them north. His surgical pain slowly subsiding, he moved into a converted Army truck that would become his home for the balance of the campaign. In the back, crosswise behind the cabin, sat a low bed covered with a wool West Point blanket stenciled U.S.M.A. Over the bed, Bradley had painted the beginning and ending dates for the North African campaign, and underneath them, D-Day for HUSKY. The Sicilian campaign's end date was left blank, for the moment. One side of the truck was filled with a desk; its drawers were crammed with orders and reports, and it was flanked by a heavy black field telephone hanging in a leather case. The other side of his rolling apartment was fitted with a small closet and a washbasin, over which hung a large map of Sicily he would study alone at night.[49]

On campaign, Brad and George worked well together, just as they had in Tunisia. Patton trusted Bradley enough to let him run most of his own show without too much topside interference, and that laissez-faire management allowed Seventh Army to get the most out of Bradley and his men. But before long their diverging styles began to rub both men the wrong way, just as they had rubbed each other the wrong way at times in Tunisia.

In mid-July, for instance, Bradley stormed into George's headquarters in a hot fury. Incensed, he relayed a report of a rogue American captain who had gunned down some fifty Axis prisoners "in cold blood." To make matters worse, Brad said, the obedient prisoners had been lined up for march behind American lines when the captain massacred them.

George just shrugged. *"I told Bradley that it was probably an exaggeration, but in any case to tell the officer to certify that the dead men were snipers or attempted to escape or something, as it would make a stink in the press and also would make the civilians mad,"* he told his diary.[50]

It was not the answer Brad was looking for.

Another time, Brad asked Patton for a replacement colonel to command a regiment of Middleton's 45th Division. The current CO was not up to snuff, Brad said, and he wanted the colonel tossed. He asked Patton to replace the man with Lieutenant Colonel Darby, the Ranger battalion commander who had fought like a lion around Gela.

George duly offered Darby a promotion to full bird colonel if he would take over Middleton's regiment. Darby, fond of his Rangers, begged off. "Maybe I'd better stick with my boys," he said, and George, privately impressed with any man who would turn down a promotion to stay in a fight, did not insist. Brad, however, was miffed that the famously tough George Patton had given Darby a choice in the matter. The perceived slight would rankle him for years.[51]

Other flashpoints cropped up over an old bugaboo, their logistical tail. Sicily was an unruly island, and under any circumstances moving ammunition, fuel, and food along rugged highways from Gela to the front would have been difficult. Lacking a major port in Patton's territory, the problems multiplied. Patton's staff, fixated on Gela's beaches as its starting point, therefore assigned the II Corps supply mess to an engineer beach battalion, a unit well suited to getting goods ashore, but inept at pushing them forward to the frontline troops. The result was a black eye for the Ordnance Department.[52]

"On the several occasions I appealed to Patton for more supply support," Brad wrote later. "He would respond as though I had come to chide him on a minor detail and he would brush my complaint aside. Although Patton ran his Army tactically with an iron hand, he remained almost completely indifferent to its logistical needs. In war as Patton knew it there was little time for logistics in the busy day of a field commander." As Bradley recalled, George's stock answer whenever he raised a supply question was, "Have your people take it up with my G-4. Now let's get back to this scheme of attack. . . ." When he complained to Lucas about Seventh Army's neglect of supplies, Lucas agreed with him, sympathetically remarking that George "never bothers his head about such things."[53]

While Patton and Bradley were moving off the beaches, General Montgomery was running into a figurative brick wall near the town of Catania. The figurative brick wall was, unfortunately, backed by a literal brick wall—or rather, a rock-and-lava cone named Mount Etna, the chief obstacle on the British coastal road to Messina. Soaring eleven thousand feet into the Mediterranean sky, Vulcan's mythical forge anchored a defensive belt that commanded the highway running up the east coast. Tough German *Fallschirmjäger* troops, a panzer division from Italy, and a scratch collection of Italian brigades manned a strong, protective ring around the volcano's base, and by mid-July Monty realized he was in for some impossibly hard fighting at the Etna Line.[54]

Few of the G-2 wizards had foreseen stiff resistance here. Before D-Day, Eisenhower's staff had predicted that fighting would be heaviest around Patton's Seventh Army, since most of Guzzoni's strongest units had been stationed on the island's west and center. With the Germans bearing down on Seventh Army, Monty should have been shielded in his drive for Messina. Even Alexander conceded, "The American troops were being given the tougher and less spectacular task."[55]

But General Guzzoni's few mobile troops had outmaneuvered Eighth Army, and before long Montgomery was scanning the map for a way around the Etna Line. Going west, the only way around Etna, would take him deep into Bradley's territory, but Monty needed a route to outflank the volcano's defenders, and the Americans held the only open highway, known as Highway 124. So early on July 13, Montgomery sent a corps toward Highway 124 near the crossroads town of Enna, then directed his nominal commander, General Alexander, to redraw the boundaries between the American and Commonwealth forces to give the coveted highway to Eighth Army.[56]

Thirty hours after Ike "stepped on George hard," the stepped-on general was jolted by a surprise visit from Alexander, who politely ordered him to surrender Highway 124. The boundary lines were being modified, he explained, and Eighth Army would go around both sides of the mountain to secure Messina. Bradley's corps would have to move out to make room for the incoming 1st Canadian Division.[57]

Before the invasion, George and Brad had assumed the two armies would move in tandem toward Messina to cut off the Axis retreat. That seemed to make good military sense, and it was consistent with the original plan to land George's U.S. troops at Palermo and march them eastward along the north coast to Messina, converging there with the Commonwealth forces. Alexander never confirmed this supposition—incredibly, there was no firm plan beyond the initial HUSKY objectives—but the two American generals had assumed their men would be given an equal shot at the final kill.[58]

So when Alexander directed the Americans to step aside to give the British an open shot at Messina, George had every reason to be furious. After all, Montgomery had supplies from Syracuse, he had the eastern road, and he had the Seventh Army watching his back. What more did he need? Was Alexander's job to make sure Monty snatched every last laurel of victory for the British Empire?

Then again, George was in no position to argue. The Supreme Commander had just jacked him up over Seventh Army's reports, and the friendly fire on Ridgway's paratroopers had driven George deep into Ike's doghouse. He worried, with some justification, that Ike was going to fire him. Ike had lectured him for months on the necessity of complete and seamless Allied harmony, and he had personally warned Patton that he would send home any general who failed to cooperate. Now, George fretted, Ike seemed to be looking for an excuse to fire him and replace him with someone more pliable. Someone like Omar Bradley.[59]

It was no time for George to open his mouth, and he knew it. Seventh Army would comply fully with Army Group orders, he assured Alexander. If called to do so, the Americans would be Monty's shield, and that was that. All a wounded George could do was sound off to his staff afterward and complain to his wife about Ike's complicity in Montgomery's devious games. He would confine his temper to his diary and confidants.[60]

With Alex's departure, George called an aide and told him to have General Bradley come to army headquarters. They needed to talk.

ELEVEN

CRACKS IN THE WALL

I disliked the way he worked, upset tactical plans, interfered in my orders. His stubbornness on amphibious operations, parade plans into Messina sickened me and soured me on Patton.

—Bradley, postwar interview

"My God, you can't allow him to do that!"

Brad was livid. "This will raise hell with us," he protested. "I had counted heavily on that road. Now if we've got to shift over, it'll slow up our entire advance."[1]

Brad could not believe his ears. His sole job—in fact, the only apparent reason for his corps being in Sicily—was to move north, toward Sicily's coast, for moving there would put him in position to get in on the final kill for Messina, similar to his capture of Bizerte in the African campaign. He had counted on Highway 124 to keep Middleton's division moving forward, and George had just told him he was losing his most precious piece of real estate.[2]

"May we at least use that road to shift Middleton over to the left of Terry Allen?" Brad pleaded, looking to salvage something of his battle plan.

George shook his head. "Sorry, Brad, but the change-over takes place immediately. Monty wants the road right away."

"But that leaves us in a pretty tough spot. Middleton is now within a thousand yards of that road. If I can't use it to move him over to the other side of Allen, I'll have to pull the 45th all the way back to the beaches and pass it around Terry's rear."[3]

No, George said, that ship has sailed. Monty wants it and Alex ordered it. So Monty gets it. The II Corps would have to play musical chairs with some 30,000 men.[4]

With look of gloom on his face, Brad drove back to his command post, furious with both Alexander and Patton. Later he would call Alexander's order "the most arrogant, egotistical, selfish and dangerous move in the whole of combined operations in World War II." He was especially flabbergasted to think that some British aristocrat named General Sir Harold Rupert Leofric George Alexander, K.C.B., G.C.B., D.S.O. and S.O.B., had faced down "Blood and Guts" Patton and shoved his *American* 45th Division to the side. How could George, of all people, have taken this kind of insult?[5]

"By all rights, he could have been expected to roar like a lion," Bradley griped. But for some reason, Patton swallowed the order as meekly as a plebe cadet.[6]

When Brad arrived at his command post at Gela, Monk Dickson needed little of his considerable intelligence-gathering acumen to know that Brad was "as hot as Mount Etna" over the highway switch. Livid with Alexander for playing the same game he tried to play in Tunisia, Bradley also blamed Eisenhower for letting him get away with it. So did John Lucas, who flew to Algiers on George's behalf to enlist Ike's help.[7]

Eisenhower, wary of Montgomery's hold over Alexander, was sympathetic, but he refused to intervene. Having gone to bat for George on other occasions, Ike refused to countermand Alexander's tactical order. Ike tried to get Lucas to see things from the British point of view, pointing out that Alex had formed his first impression of the American soldier during the Kasserine Pass debacle, and, right or wrong, the awful repulse at Kasserine had shattered Alexander's confidence in the American fighting man.[8]

Ike figured George's steam-gauge needle was stuck well into the red by now and, under pressure from Marshall to defend American prerogatives, encouraged George to stand up to Alexander—though he'd have to do it without any overt support from AFHQ. In a voice bereft of conviction, Ike told Lucas "to see that Patton was made to realize that he must stand up to Alexander." But he added, "He didn't mean [Patton] was not to obey orders, of course." This was mighty cold comfort, and a disgusted Lucas reported back to George at Gela, complaining later to his diary that criticizing the British to Ike was "like talking to a man about his wife."[9]

Right or wrong, the whole exchange had become academic. By the time Ike offered his highly conditional support, the American engine had been shifted into reverse. Montgomery was pushing his Canadians up Highway 124, and Middleton was pulling his 45th Division back to the beachhead.

Ike's dicta affected nothing, and to Bradley's dismay, George obeyed his orders with an uncharacteristic quiet.

But when George was quiet, he usually had something up his sleeve.

The Seventh Army commander had been complaining to Army Group since April about his supply lines. It wasn't that his army lacked the stockpiles, but Patton couldn't roll nearly enough ammunition, food, and equipment over the rutted beaches at Gela; Licata was too small for his supply ships, and he hated being at the mercy of Monty's logistics men, who decided what to forward him through Syracuse, some 140 miles to the east.

But to the west, just beyond his army's boundary lines, lay the tempting little fishing village of Porto Empedocle, a small but adequate harbor town on the seaward side of the ancient city of Agrigento. To relieve the strain on his supply lines, George suggested, why couldn't he try for Agrigento's modest port, just a little farther west?[10]

Alexander, his mind fixed on matters closer to Messina, politely told George that if he could capture Agrigento with limited forces—say, in the nature of a reconnaissance in force—he had no objection to the proposal. George immediately drove over to 3rd Division headquarters and told Truscott to push like hell toward Agrigento and Porto Empedocle with whatever "reconnaissance in force" he needed to storm the place.[11]

George understood that with a modest supply base in western Sicily, it would be a small matter to push up to Palermo. The itch to take Palermo, the island's capital, was an almost unbearable obsession for him; as Truscott remembered it, "It was the glamour of capturing Palermo—the biggest city in Sicily—that attracted Georgie Patton." To reach Palermo, he formed a provisional corps under his deputy, Geoff Keyes, and reared back to hurl it like a javelin at the ancient city. On July 14, the day after his visit from Alexander, the cagey general wrote in his diary. *"When the present line of the combined armies is secured, which will probably be around the 19th, it will be feasible to advance rapidly with the 3d Division and 2d Armor and take Palermo. I will bring this question up to General Alexander when the time is ripe."*[12]

Truscott, reliable and aggressive, took his orders to heart. Driving his soldiers forward on a five-mile-per-hour march pace—the "Truscott Trot," his soldiers called it—he captured Porto Empedocle by July 16 and reported to Patton that Agrigento, enveloped from all sides, was about to fall. The time to speak with Alexander was ripe.[13]

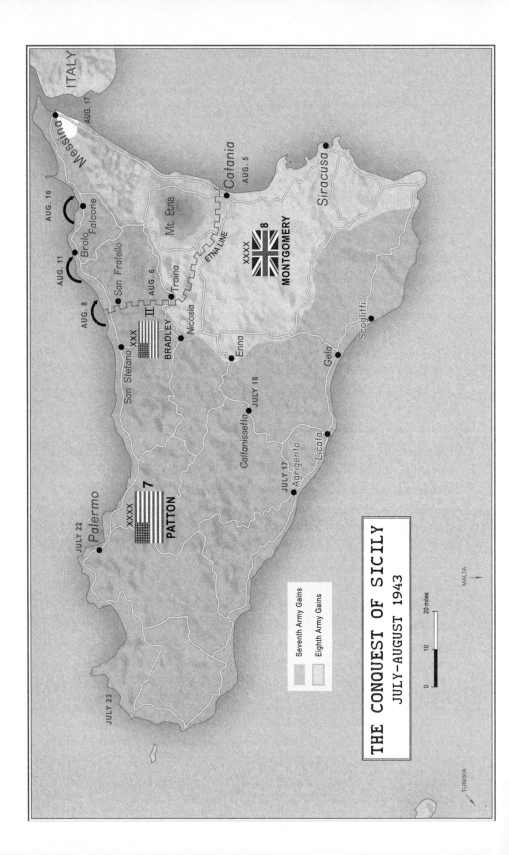

THE CONQUEST OF SICILY
JULY–AUGUST 1943

Seventh Army Gains
Eighth Army Gains

0   10   20 miles

* * *

As he stared at the grid-lined operations map, a jittery General Alexander saw an Italian menace lurking to the west. He fretted over the need to keep Montgomery's left flank anchored as the British and Canadians enveloped the Etna Line, and his mind kept coming back to what would happen if General Guzzoni made a hard drive from Palermo through the thinly spread Americans into Eighth Army's rear. So late on the sixteenth Alexander ordered Seventh Army to resume its watch over Montgomery's perimeter.[14]

In glancing over Alex's order, George's eyes lit on one particularly ugly sentence: "SEVENTH ARMY WILL PROTECT THE REAR OF EIGHTH ARMY." In his diary, he spat, *"General Alexander . . . directs that the Seventh Army protect the rear of Eighth Army, thus putting the Americans in a secondary role, which is a continuation of such roles for the whole campaign and may find the war ending with us being overlooked."* It was intolerable to a man of Patton's prejudices that the Americans should be chained to Monty's backside, and he decided to remedy that grave injustice before Alex's habit of handing the war to Montgomery on a silver platter turned into an unalterable pattern.[15]

"I am flying to Tunis to see General Alexander," George wrote in his diary on the seventeenth. *"I am sure that neither he nor any of his British staff has any conception of the power or mobility of the Seventh Army, nor are they aware of the political implications latent in such a course of action. I shall explain to General Alexander on the basis that it would be inexpedient politically for the Seventh Army not to have equal glory in the final stage of the campaign."*[16]

Watching events from distant Algiers, Butch noted the following day, "General Patton made a quick trip to La Marsa in a B-25 yesterday. He wanted to see General Alexander, to clarify the order to the Seventh Army. He was mad as a wet hen because the order said the Seventh Army would protect the rear and flank of the Eighth Army and left the American in an inferior position."[17]

Actually, George did not intend to "clarify" the order, as Butcher suggested. He intended to rewrite it.[18]

While he might sound off recklessly to his diary, or bitch in violent terms to close friends, when it came to high-level meetings George was always tactful, businesslike, and well prepared. He studied up on his tonnage requirements, enlisted a friendly War Department witness, Brigadier General Albert C. Wedemeyer, marked up his map, and hopped a medium bomber over to Tunisia.[19]

The Battle of La Marsa went better than George had expected. At Alexander's headquarters, George lobbied the waxen general to let Bradley's II Corps drive to the north coast, splitting Sicily in two and giving the Americans control over the island's western half. With no real progress along Montgomery's front, Alexander simply nodded his assent, with the stipulation that Patton's men must cover the road net around Montgomery's flank. That was easy enough, thought George. He would have his coveted Palermo.[20]

Omar Bradley gritted his false teeth and surrendered Highway 124 to the Canadians, just as Patton had ordered. He couldn't understand how, without a word of protest from George, American forces had been cut out of the picture. With II Corps relegated to covering Monty's western flank, the Missourian saw slim pickings for his men, mostly "the capture of hills, docile peasants and spiritless soldiers." George, it seemed, was treating Brad's corps with benign neglect, just like Eisenhower, and just like the British.[21]

Stomping back to his command tent, he directed an astonished Troy Middleton to break contact with the enemy and reverse course toward Gela. Troy was no happier about the move than Brad was, since he and Eighth Army were about to put the XIV *Panzerkorps* out of business, and he probably gave Bradley the same hot flak Bradley had given Patton. The Army chain worked that way, too. In the end, though, Middleton obediently withdrew his confused men southwest toward Gela, then sideslipped them around the rear of the 1st Division. Away from the fighting.

Before long Middleton, as capable a coach as either Brad or Ike, had his men pushing north again, leapfrogging regiments toward Sicily's north coast. As GIs covered in sweat and dust pounded roads once trampled by Greek hoplites, the colors red and blue began to dominate a huge map of Sicily that Brad kept in his operations tent—blue representing territory captured by the Americans, red showing land captured by Monty's men. The blue field dwarfed the red, a pointed reminder to visitors and himself which nation was winning the battle for Sicily.[22]

As George and Brad picked their way through central Sicily, the Supreme Commander struggled to keep his head above the political entanglements that were part and parcel of his office. In late July, President Roosevelt sent Ike a rebuke in response to a groundless rumor that AFHQ had formally recognized De Gaulle's French Committee of National Liberation, and to counteract De Gaulle's influence, Roosevelt gave Ike an impossibly tall order to supply Giraud's men liberally with war matériel. Secretary Stimson began pressuring Ike to make sure the Americans did not take a backseat to the British in Sicily—probably in response to complaint letters from Patton and other grumbling Anglophobes who had the secretary's ear. To please his American bosses—Marshall, Arnold, King, and the rest—he had to make a record of complaint letters to Churchill and Brooke about the pro-British slant in BBC reports, which always seemed to overlook or even denigrate American contributions. Finally, whenever Ike had time, which was never, he had to straighten out a thousand administrative problems growing like weeds from his bloated headquarters: Judge Advocate, Military Police, Supply, Personnel, Transportation Corps, Civic Administration, and countless other departments where Ike alone had to make important calls, ranging from affirming death sentences to allocating supply tonnage.[23]

If there was one bright spot in Eisenhower's dreary sky, it was that, as far as he could tell, his lieutenants were working more or less harmoniously, for George, Brad, Monty, and Alex all seemed to be getting along. For now.

In western Sicily, George drove Truscott's men north toward Palermo, a move that aggrieved Bradley, since his 45th Division had been promised the honor of taking that city. But Patton had bigger things to worry about than Bradley's ire; having finagled Alexander's paper-thin acquiescence to operations in the west, George fretted that Fifteenth Army Group might cut him off again, before he could leave his mark on the campaign. He was certain that armored mobility and the hustle of the "Truscott Trot" would take him all the way to Messina if Alex weren't so damned timid, and perhaps thinking of the swift "foot cavalry" of his hero, Stonewall Jackson, George grumbled, *"Alex has no idea of either the power or speed of American armies. We can go twice as fast as the British and hit harder. . . ."*[24]

George's fears proved prescient, for a day after turning him loose, Alexander sent a cable to Seventh Army headquarters imposing debilitating constraints on Patton's drive to Palermo. Directing him to devote most of his force to building a defensive perimeter from Agrigento in the south to Campofelice in the north, Alexander gave George a laundry list of objectives he must take *before* striking out for Palermo. In other words, Seventh Army would become Montgomery's shield once again.[25]

This time George ignored Alexander's order, possibly because he never received it, or possibly because he let it be known around Seventh Army headquarters that he didn't want any such orders to reach him. George's loyal chief of staff, Hap Gay, interpreted the order as a confirmation of Alexander's oral directive, the order's peremptory language notwithstanding.[26]

Geoff Keyes, commanding Truscott, the airborne, the Rangers, and Hugh Gaffey's 2nd Armored Division, began the race for Palermo on July 19, and Patton finally saw events moving in the right direction. *"Now I am trying to get Gaffey loose,"* he exulted to Beatrice the following day. *"If I succeed, Attila will have to take a back seat."* On July 21, while Monty was still struggling at Catania, Gaffey reported that the 2nd Armored would be in Palermo by the following morning. EXPEDITE REPLY URGENT. CAN WE MAKE TOUCHDOWN ON OUR OWN INTITIATIVE? Keyes wired Patton.

George's reply: YOU HAVE THE BALL, CALL THE TOUCHDOWN PLAY.[27]

The next day, Shermans of George's beloved Hell on Wheels Division clattered down the wrecked streets of Palermo to the cheers, stares, peace offerings, and quizzical looks of the city's four hundred thousand inhabitants. The battle for Sicily's capital had cost George's army a grand total of 272 casualties, and his men had killed some 2,900 enemy soldiers and captured another 53,000. He gleefully dashed off a note to Beatrice just ahead of the official press release, joking, *"By the time the censor sees this the name of the town will be in all the papers so he can fill it in here* _____."[28]

George arrived in Palermo deliberately late on the evening of July 22. In a rare instance of public modesty, he wanted to avoid overshadowing Geoff Keyes, whom he decreed would have the honor of taking the city's official surrender. Casting his blue-gray eyes over the crumbling stone buildings dotted with white sheets, American flags, and vandalized fascist banners, George beamed with delight. American men, under his leadership, had liberated an ancient enemy capital![29]

It was something he had dreamed of for years. Something to be savored. Something that would elevate Patton and his Americans to the ranks of the Greeks, the Carthaginians, the Romans, Normans, Byzantines, and Neapolitans as conquerors of that fabled piece of volcanic rock.

Something to cement his reputation among his peers.

Something to show the world Lieutenant General George S. Patton Jr. was Top Dog.[30]

The momentarily satisfied Top Dog installed his new headquarters in the opulent palace of the King of Sicily, a beautiful, dilapidated mongrel building that, like Italy's tottering government, was as regal in ornamentation as it was decrepit at its foundations. Ignoring fascist salutes from palace servants, which were obviously a matter of habit, George set up his office in a cavernous state apartment adorned with crystal chandeliers, heavy upholstered chairs, classical oil paintings, and a giant rosewood desk. From here, under a ceiling frescoed with rococo cherubs, he would plan the conquest of the rest of Trinacria. It was an altogether fitting venue for a man with George Patton's deep sense of history.[31]

To his immense delight, George soon learned that events around Mount Etna were bringing Bradley's troops back into the show. With Montgomery locked in battle at the Etna Line, Generals Eisenhower and Alexander reached the conclusion that Middleton's Thunderbirds might help Monty crash through the enemy's front. On July 20, Montgomery sent General Oliver Leese to work out road rights, and General Clarence R. Huebner, Eisenhower's unofficial eyes and ears, came to George on his own initiative, and he strongly advised George to insist to Alexander that Seventh Army get both north coast roads for the drive to Messina. Alexander, believing the Americans could be of real help to Montgomery, readily confirmed that Seventh Army would make a cautious, exploratory probe toward Messina, and on the twenty-third, Alexander's new orders appeared to put George's army on an even footing with Montgomery's.[32]

The next day, Alexander ordered Patton and Montgomery to meet him the following morning at Cassibile airport, south of Syracuse, where they would hash out the details.[33]

"I fear the worst," confessed George, *"but so far have held my own with them."* As he told Beatrice, *"I always feel like a little lamb on such occasions but so far I have gotten by."* He obediently hopped onto a plane the next day and touched down on Monty's home turf.[34]

It was an oddly informal meeting, one of the few times Patton and Montgomery would meet as equals. Monty drove out to the airstrip at the appointed hour, his slightly baggy British trousers set off by a rumpled, unmarked shirt, the sleeves rolled up to his bony elbows. The only hint of Montgomery's military occupation was his trademark Royal Tank Corps beret, and he fit Chet Hansen's description of him as "a poorly tailored bohemian painter." George, for his part, stepped off the plane wearing a plain khaki uniform, his trademark steel helmet replaced by a simple garrison cap. No pistols, no campaign ribbons, no riding crop. Just old George, his deputy G-3, and his aide Charlie Codman. He hurried to meet

Montgomery, who reciprocated by stepping up his pace to shake hands with his fellow army commander.[35]

With Alexander running late for the meeting, Monty spread a huge map of Sicily over the hood of his tan staff car and the two men negotiated their own boundaries. As Monty smoothed out the worn contour map, there was little of the usual leaning forward and pointing to features, or running fingers along roads and lines of communication while squinting at tiny place names. This day it was much simpler. There were four roads leading toward Messina—two to the northwest, in George's area, and two to the southeast, in Monty's. Seventh Army, they agreed, would get Highway 113, the north coastal road, and Highway 120, the parallel route. Monty got the two southern roads.[36]

On the flight to Syracuse, George had steeled himself for some hard bargaining. But Montgomery, faced with a bloody, uphill struggle, was glad to let Patton take Messina if that was the fastest way to wrap up an all-too-sanguine campaign, though it was understood by both men that Monty would try to get there first. *"He agreed so readily that I felt something was wrong, but I have not found it yet,"* George mused afterward, but this time his suspicions were off the mark. Monty, like George, may have been personally vain, but he was intellectually honest enough to recognize that pressure from Seventh Army would, in the end, save Allied lives.[37]

When Alexander finally arrived, he was visibly irritated at being left out of the discussion. *"He looked a little mad and, for him, was quite brusque,"* George quipped that evening. *"He told Monty to explain his plan. Monty said he and I had already decided what we were going to do, so Alex got madder. . . ."* But the issue had been decided at that point; Montgomery told Alexander what he and George had agreed to—recommended, technically—and with a few face-saving modifications, Alex capitulated.[38]

George climbed into his C-47 and flew back to Palermo a happy man. Monty had asked the Americans to help out their British cousins, and for once, George was truly happy to oblige. By the time he reached the Royal Palace, he had worked out a new set of orders for the star of his next show: Bradley.[39]

Brad's map-lined truck rolled north over wagon-rutted hills, following the general lines of Terry Allen's 1st Division on his right and Troy Middleton's 45th on the left, and before long he set up a command post in a gaudy baroque palazzo in Caltanissetta. He was naturally unhappy at being squeezed out of the capture of Palermo in favor of the 2nd Armored Division—Patton favored his horses, whether iron or flesh—but he was pleased to learn that George was sending him additional artillery and a few more regiments. When George directed Brad to turn his corps ninety degrees and hit the enemy at Troina, a fortified mountain town on the middle road to Messina, a dutiful Bradley fired off fresh orders to both divisions. He sent Middleton east along the coastal road, and Allen in a roughly parallel direction toward Troina, between the craggy Caronie Mountains and the looming Mount Etna. Bradley's G-2 forecast little German resistance at Troina, and Brad reasoned that a breakthrough there would open up his colored map of Sicily to a lot more blue shading.[40]

For the better part of a week Allen's regiments pushed and prodded at Troina's well-prepared perimeter, looking for a way to cut off the defenders or cave in their flanks. But the Germans there were a desperate lot, and they counterattacked every time Allen's veterans began to waver. It took eighteen battalions of howitzers, three squadrons of fighter-bombers, and many blood-soaked assaults to eject the defenders, who began to evacuate the city on August 6. Later that day, as the Stars and Stripes snapped over Troina's central piazza, Bradley planned his next move. He also turned his attention to the problem of the 1st Division's commanding general.[41]

Brad had been stewing over "Terrible Terry" for some time. The man was good, very good, but he was impossible to control: too foulmouthed, too boastful, and too aggressive to make a good team player. From under the rim of his lopsided helmet, Terry winked at violations of Army regulations that he didn't deem critical to his division's combat effectiveness. A guy who thought the 1st Division was the only division on the island, Allen seemed to think that because his men had seen more combat than anybody else, they were excused from the rules everyone else had to follow, and Terry's personal example, especially his fondness for bourbon, would weaken the fabric of his division. On at least one occasion, the Army telephone operator overheard a greatly agitated Bradley saying, "Allen, let me remind you that I am your Corps commander," to which Allen responded by hanging up.

Allen's self-centered outlook was, Brad thought, a lot like George Patton's, except that Brad had to put up with George, and he didn't have to put up with Terry. Allen's gregarious deputy commander, Brigadier General Theodore Roosevelt Jr., was also indifferent to discipline, which aggravated the problem. "The men worship Ted," Bradley told Ike, "but he's too soft-hearted to take a division—too much like one of the boys."[42]

When he took the reins of II Corps, Ike had warned Brad to be tough on his subordinates. Bradley, a disciple of Marshall, didn't need that kind of advice from Ike, for he had a hair trigger when it came to inefficiency, real or perceived, and he could be as ruthless as Bedell Smith when he had to. So by the middle of July, Brad decided that Terry and Teddy had to go.[43]

He laid the necessary groundwork with the higher-ups. He wrote Ike in late July that the 1st was "battle weary. I suspect that it is more Terry and Ted than it is the division as a whole." Ike agreed that Allen could use a rest, thinking he could contribute plenty to the divisions forming back home.[44]

After clearing it with George, who formally cleared it with Ike, Brad's adjutant prepared the orders relieving Terry and Teddy. But through a typical bureaucratic screwup, the orders relieving the division's commanders were sent to Allen's headquarters through the routine mail pouch and arrived while Allen was in the midst of the battle for Troina. He telephoned Bradley, who assured him the orders were premature, but on the sixth of August Brad called Allen and Roosevelt over to his command post at Nicosia, sat them around a camp table, and told them he was relieving them.[45]

Though they knew orders had been cut, the grizzled veterans were floored. They could not believe they were being fired after another hard-fought victory. Didn't twenty-eight days of solid fighting in Sicily, and an African campaign from Oran to Bizerte, count for anything?

Their appeals fell on deaf ears. To Omar Bradley it was not about their track record, brilliant as it was. It was about playing on a team. In the campaign for Messina, and in larger battles in Italy or France, every division would have to play on a team; there could be no mavericks, because in war mavericks cost lives. Allen's independent spirit made the Big Red One an exceptional division for a one-on-one match, which was why his men had broken out of the slugfest at Gela against the *Hermann Göring* panzers. But one-on-one matches don't win wars—at least, not wars against the forty-odd Nazi divisions holding France. Men's lives were at stake, and Bradley, a baseball player at heart, didn't tolerate independence in his subordinates. So, for the good of the division, for the good of the corps, Allen and Roosevelt had to go.

While the decision to relieve the two generals originated with Brad, the move fit within a larger reorganization Patton was working into the Seventh Army. George, less dispassionate than Bradley, felt uncomfortable relieving an old friend who had fought a good fight—a brilliant fight by most accounts, even Bradley's. He wrote a glowing commendation for Allen (toning it down a bit at Brad's request), and gave the old horse soldier a pep talk at his headquarters before sending Terry down to Algiers until Ike could figure out what to do with him. When he learned that Roosevelt would be relieved with prejudice to his future command prospects, George told himself, *"While I think General Roosevelt is not the best general in the world, particularly for organization and disciplinary purposes, he none the less, is a gallant soldier who has fought well. . . ."* He decided to *"talk to Ike about doing the right thing by Teddy R.,"* and eventually got Roosevelt relieved on the same nonprejudicial terms as Allen.[46]

To Ike, George's success validated his judgment in sticking with the controversial tanker. Butcher's diary noted: "Patton's great progress gives Ike a warm glow, as there are many Army officers who could not see through Patton's showmanship and boisterousness to discern his fine qualities of leadership, on which Ike banked so strongly." In contrast to his mid-July cable to Marshall, where he sounded high praise for Brad but only grudgingly conceded that George was "doing well," in early August a beaming Ike reported, "The Seventh Army has been performing magnificently. It has marched over long distances, supplies itself under most difficult circumstances, fought many sharp and successful engagements, and is now in a prominent place on the battle line hammering away to drive the enemy out of the island. It is really difficult to give it sufficient credit for its accomplishments to date." He was glad to see George avoid another sitrep showdown over Alexander's orders pushing Bradley aside, and he felt his friend had done a masterful job moving a provisional corps of infantry and tanks against Palermo. The capture of the ancient capital made headlines around the world, George's scowling face appeared on the cover of *Time* and *Newsweek*, and Secretary Stimson sent a cable to AFHQ crowing about how "his ex-aide Geo P jr" was "doing right well." To Ike, George, Brad, and their division commanders had brought the American Army back from the stigma of Kasserine Pass. Perhaps that was their most important achievement of the war so far.[47]

Despite Seventh Army's performance in Sicily, Ike's opinion of George's management style did not change fundamentally. He knew George was the same old impulsive, socially reckless showboater, and the day after Palermo's fall he told John Lucas to stay close to Seventh Army headquarters and keep an eye on how it functioned. But as the impact of George's campaign set in, the tone at AFHQ toward the cavalryman made a subtle shift. Staffers smiled more when they spoke of Seventh Army, and Ike and Beetle began talking of awarding George another Distinguished Service Cross for his actions at Gela during the counterattack. Lucas, a reliable barometer of Ike's mood, quipped, "Something has happened around here" in regards to Patton.[48]

The political repercussions of Patton's tear through western Sicily made life easier for Eisenhower. The day after Palermo's capture, Rome's Grand Council of Fascism ejected Mussolini and replaced him with Marshal Pietro Badoglio, who immediately dispatched secret peace feelers to the Allies. This was tremendously important, since Ike knew well that political results were much better understood in Washington and London than military results. It was a matter of personal pride to him that the Allied High Command could report, "Scratch one dictator."[49]

Notwithstanding *Il Duce*'s early retirement, the military picture in Sicily fell far short of Ike's expectations. On the German side, Smiling Al Kesselring was fighting a delaying action to move troops and equipment off the island, and it was obvious to everyone that the better way to bag the defenders would have been to cork the bottleneck, Messina, rather than start at the bottle's base and flush the Germans out the neck, where they would live to fight another day.[50]

Beyond Sicily and its next logical step, Italy, the future held little joy for Ike. Word had begun trickling back that he would be swapped out for Marshall, who would lead the invasion of France, and his heart sank every time he heard the rumor. He had outwardly presumed that Marshall would command the invasion, but deep down the very thought of returning to a desk job, even one as prestigious as Army Chief of Staff, revolted him. After several visitors brought Ike the same repetitive prognostication, he privately blew his stack. "Goddammit," he told Kay Summersby, "I've had a bellyful of every Tom, Dick and Harry coming here from Washington and telling me I'm about to be stuck behind a desk in the Pentagon."[51]

By the end of July, George Patton, America's great charging bull, was ready for his final drive on Messina some 150 miles to the east. He told Truscott over drinks that he "would certainly like to beat Montgomery into Messina," and he sent President Roosevelt a well-thumbed engineering map of Sicily highlighting the territory under American control. At the map's eastern tip, a blue-pencil arrow pointed to Messina underneath Patton's handwritten inscription, *"We hope!"*[52]

It was a race George desperately wanted to win. He was running for American honor, and he was running for long-denied recognition from Ike and his British entourage. *"BBC just barely admits we exist,"* he groused to Beatrice, and he felt just as neglected by the one man in the theater whose approval he craved most. He told Bea, *"FDR sent me a signed picture of he and I, and the PM has wired congrats, but Divine Destiny* [D. D. Eisenhower] *is still mute,"* he complained.[53]

On July 31, as the race for Messina was getting under way, Ike flew to Palermo for lunch with the Seventh Army commander. Patton greeted him at the airport with an honor guard from the 15th Infantry Regiment—"the only unit he ever commanded," George noted—as a polite nod to Eisenhower's field experience. He and Ike climbed into a waiting staff car, and George gave the Supreme Commander a tour of the city, pointing out the progress his engineers were making in getting Palermo's water and lights back on, and paying high tributes to Seventh Army's fighting men and subordinate commanders.[54]

Winding back through Palermo's narrow streets, they motored back to the palace, where the two old soldiers shared a quiet lunch of fried Spam. As their forks clinked on china emblazoned with the Savoy coat of arms, Ike told George he was "anxious that there be no misunderstanding between Alexander and Patton as to plans for the attack." George, he stressed, was to continue his methodical and steady advance, while Montgomery was to lay on all he had and try to break through the Etna Line on the east. It was hardly a rousing call to arms.[55]

When Ike left, a slightly deflated George reported: *"He was quite relaxed but did not compliment us. He did say that I had moderated, which he thought was a compliment, but which I regret. I tried to get him to stay all night so I could show him the truly appalling nature of the mountains, but he had to leave. . . ."*[56]

Perhaps sensing that he had not done much to lift his friend's spirits, two days after his lunch meeting, Ike sent George a letter that did the trick:

"The Seventh Army has already made a name for itself that will live in American history," he wrote. *"Within the next few days it will add immeasurably to the luster of its fame. I personally assure you that if we speedily finish off the German in Sicily, you need have no fear of being left there in the backwater of the war."*[57]

Ike's praise meant George was out from the shadow of his mid-July chewing out. George scribbled "whoopee!" under Ike's signature and underlined it three times before dropping the letter into his "to file" box. Reviewing his Sicilian campaign with a self-satisfaction he rarely admitted, he channeled Ike's words of support into a confidence—a hubris, in fact—that would soon bring him to personal grief.[58]

By the last week of July 1943, Patton's Seventh Army held the Messina road from San Stefano, the midpoint on Sicily's north coast, and he controlled the highway leading from Troina. Now, George thought, was the time to put some fire under his generals, especially Bradley and Middleton, who might be getting a little "sticky" in their pace. George's fervor to reach Messina intensified when, on August 5, he learned that Catania, the great roadblock to the east, had at last fallen to Montgomery's troops. "This is a horse race in which the prestige of the US Army is at stake," he told Middleton. "We must take Messina before the British. Please use your best efforts to facilitate the success of our race."[59]

Trouble was, Patton's men were staring at the same problem Monty's men had confronted for the last three weeks: To the east, the neck of the island narrowed so sharply that George's two roads were squeezed together like spaghetti noodles in a funnel, which provided little or no room for the kind of mobile operations at which George excelled. The Germans, experts at interior defense lines, made the most of their cramped quarters, and they were determined to fight like Spartans at Thermopylae for every inch of the way back to Messina. So when Middleton's men marched up to the seaside town of San Fratello, they hit an unyielding wall of fire and steel that filled the hospital tents with the wounded and the dying.

The solution, George thought, was an amphibious left hook. If he and Bradley could load a few tanks and enough troops on boats—say, a battalion or two—they could flank the Axis line and catch the defending 29th *Panzergrenadier* Division from behind. From his advance command post in an olive grove at San Stefano, near the front lines, George picked up the phone and called Bradley.[60]

When Bradley and Patton had discussed the concept of an amphibious landing in late July, Brad convinced George to let him control the timing of any such movements. Bradley's confidence in his own ability was growing, and even though he would be using Truscott's 3rd Division veterans, whom George was bringing in to replace Middleton's Thunderbirds, Brad worried that his high-strung commander might order a beach assault without first making sure everything was ready. Brad and Truscott discussed the matter at length, and once they agreed on the correct time and place for an amphibious end run, Bradley set to work leapfrogging the San Fratello Line with a passion. Like George, the Missourian was anxious to beat Monty to Messina, not least because his soldiers were still steaming over BBC reports trumpeting the heroic exploits of the British Eighth Army while claiming, erroneously, that the Americans had been "swimming" and "eating grapes" in western Sicily. San Fratello, Brad thought, was the perfect place to show the British what their resourceful cousins were capable of.[61]

Brad's amphibious end run, launched on the night of August 7–8, was a solid local success. The gravel-voiced Truscott timed the landing to coincide with a big frontal push; the one-two punch forced the grenadiers back, and the operation took three Axis tanks and a respectable number of *soldaten* out of circulation. It was a beautiful local maneuver, Brad thought, a model for future West Pointers to learn from.[62]

Though the landings did little in the larger scheme of things—the Germans were pulling out from the San Fratello Line anyway—George, elated by the operation's success, wanted to try it again, and this time, he arranged to have the press cover his next tactical victory. As the attack hour approached, his impatience festered like a boil, since Montgomery, now beyond Catania, was sending cables announcing his swift progress toward Messina. Now beyond Etna, now through Randazzo, George absorbed every Eighth Army dispatch with an eye for where Montgomery was in relation to Messina—and in relation to him. Anxious to get moving, he fretted on the night of August 9, "*We are trying to get out another landing operation for tonight, but I am afraid that the 3d Division has not progressed far enough.*"[63]

The British, he learned, were passing through Bronte. Montgomery was closing the gap. He *had* to get beyond the next German line.[64]

After a day's delay courtesy of a Luftwaffe bombing hit to one of his precious LCTs, an impatient George waited for Truscott to launch another planned leapfrog up the road, around the Germans holding the little coastal town of Brolo. On the morning of August 10 he barked for Sergeant Mims and jumped into his car for a drive over to II Corps headquarters, where he had Brad issue orders to Lucian Truscott. From there he returned to his forward command post at San Stefano, stopping on the way to visit an evacuation hospital, where he dealt with an alleged case of battle fatigue in the simple, direct Patton style.[65]

Although General Truscott supported the idea of an amphibious landing, he knew his main force was too far back to support the landing party when it came under fire; isolated on the rocky beaches, the beach team would be sitting ducks when the Germans responded to the threat. Truscott rang up Bradley, who agreed with him, and at seven fifty in the evening Truscott phoned George's headquarters and told the army commander he and Brad wanted to delay the attack for a day. The delay was necessary, he explained, to give the infantry on the road time to prepare a big frontal assault, so the main force would be in position to link up with the beach team before things got too hot.[66]

Patton was unimpressed by Truscott's logic. There were few things that could justify postponing an attack, George thought, and he turned down Truscott's request in no uncertain terms, declaring, "Dammit, that operation will go on!"[67]

After hanging up on Truscott, George reflected on the reluctance of his two senior lieutenants. Orders were orders, and his directives would be obeyed, but to make sure the job was done right, the Seventh Army commander felt the situation required some Black Jack–style elbow grease. He drove over to Truscott's headquarters, giving hell to everyone from the MPs to the chief of staff, and when the hard-bitten Texan again tried to talk Patton out of the operation, George's anger got the better of him. "Goddammit, Lucian, what's the matter with you?" he demanded. "Are you afraid to fight?" The mission had been delayed long enough. It was going forward. His men would hit the beaches on the morning of August 11, exactly as ordered. If Truscott didn't want to pull off the landing, George would relieve him. Truscott politely dared him to do it. George told his diary that day: *"[A]t 8:00 Omar and Lucian both called to say it was too risky. I told them to do it and that if it failed I was responsible and that if it worked they got the credit. . . . I had to get pretty tough and ask how they would like to have stars turn out to be [colonel's] eagles."*[68]

* * *

Brad slammed down the phone, ready to spit nails. This was ridiculous. George was being pigheaded, looking to do something flashy, even rash, when the situation demanded a more conservative approach. Didn't he realize the geography, the enemy, the whole picture around Brolo was entirely different from at San Fratello? Geography dictated the tactics, not history, and damned sure not flashy publicity.

"I was more exasperated than I have ever been," Brad wrote later. He had strongly suspected that George's decisions since the capture of Palermo had more to do with self-aggrandizement and his childish race with Monty than with sound military judgment, and every one of Patton's boneheaded orders since early August reinforced Brad's suspicion. The man was creating Gold Star Mothers just to feed his vanity.[69]

Just as Brad had predicted, the landing, though successful, proved costly. Shortly after a task force from Truscott's 30th Infantry Regiment waded ashore, German defenders pounced on them. Self-propelled guns bogged down on the beaches, tanks were knocked out, and the enemy pounded the invaders from the high ground. Truscott's men fought through the day and night under a hailstorm of shell and mortar fire, and it was not until the next morning that the 3rd Division managed to punch its way through to his struggling men. By then, 167 of the initial 650 soldiers were lying on the beachhead, dead or wounded. Nearly 30 percent casualties.[70]

All for what?

Bradley was getting fed up with George's antics. The Seventh Army headquarters staff, following their commander's lead, never seemed to think of what the GI on the front lines needed to survive. Artillery ammunition was in desperately short supply, while small-arms ammunition piled sky-high, but Seventh Army didn't care. Seventh Army didn't run its communications wires as they should have; Brad's signalmen had to do it themselves. Seventh Army didn't give the corps any procedure for summoning air support—or even for avoiding friendly fire from confused air support. Brad's overworked men had to figure it out themselves or, more often, just do without.

For all the fine press Old Blood and Guts was getting, a lot of important stuff was falling through the cracks. Since George didn't give a damn about these "details," his staff didn't, either. As Brad later fumed, "Patton was developing as an unpopular guy. He steamed about with great convoys of cars and great squads of cameramen. . . . To George, tactics was simply a process of bulling ahead. He never seemed to think out a campaign. Seldom made a careful estimate of the situation. I thought him a shallow commander."[71]

George's showboating also rubbed Brad the wrong way. His dashing around in a parade of star-spangled squad cars, MPs on motorcycles and jeeps. His clueless driver blowing that earsplitting siren as they roared past weary foot soldiers. "Canny a showman though George was," Brad later concluded, "he failed to grasp the psychology of the combat soldier. He traveled in a platoon of command cars and surrounded himself with nattily uniformed yes-men. His own vehicle was decked with red flags and oversize stars and the insignia of his command. These exhibitions did not awe the troops as perhaps Patton believed. Instead, they offended them as they trudged through the clouds of dust left in the wake of that procession." It just wasn't Brad's style, and never would be. To the Missourian with the Middle America twang, George's pageantry was as foreign and disconcerting as the fascist pomp in Rome and Berlin they used to show on the old black-and-white newsreels before the war.[72]

But his most unforgivable sin, Brad thought, was that George was more obsessed with getting to Messina ahead of the British than with saving men's lives. Brad recalled running into Patton and Senator Henry Cabot Lodge on the coastal road the morning after the Brolo fiasco. As Bradley recalled, "[George] wanted me to get to Messina as quickly as possible, [said] that he was determined to get there ahead of the British. He told me that if I could get there one day earlier by losing additional men, I was to lose them. He said he had a bet with 'Monty' and wanted to win it."[73]

War, Brad believed, was not about preening like a fighting bantam. It was a sober, methodical exercise in which the goal was to accomplish an objective while expending the fewest possible lives. It required careful management and meticulous planning, not a flick of the riding crop or a profanity-laced speech inspired by William the Conqueror or Pompey the Great or some other fellow who had turned to dust a thousand years before they invented the gasoline engine, the M-1 rifle, and the wireless. This was one lesson Brad had learned through years of study, teaching, observation, apprenticeship, and combat experience. If George could not understand it by now, he and Brad weren't speaking the same language.

Well, Brad thought, no sense hiding the truth from the brass. If George wanted to run the war for his own glorification, II Corps sure wouldn't cover for him. The rotten fruit would fall off the tree soon enough.

On the night of August 14, when Ike's official spy, John Lucas, stayed over for a visit, Brad unloaded his frustrations and gave Lucas every complaint he had been sitting on since the campaign began. There would be plenty for Ike to chew on.[74]

By mid-August, Smiling Al had pulled nearly everything that would move off the island. Militarily, Messina held little value now, since the Germans and any motivated Italians would be off the island long before the Allies could stop them.[75]

But thirty-odd miles from the gilded prize, Patton was not about to let Monty get there first. To George, the quest for Messina was a race—a race far nobler than even his 1912 Olympic run. It was a race for the finest prize of them all: the capture of the last enemy stronghold. With the eyes of history looking down on him—as well as those of his celestial ancestors—George Patton would not allow any man, be he German, Italian, British, or American, to get in his way.

Rising from his four-poster bed after three days of fighting a high fever, an irritable, much-fatigued Patton flew to Truscott's command post on the afternoon of August 14 to order another amphibious movement. Meeting Bradley there, he assured his senior lieutenant that the leapfrog landing would be bigger than the last, so there was no need to worry about the safety of his men. This time, George promised, the Navy would give them enough boats to land an entire regiment, Middleton's 157th Regiment, to be precise.[76]

Brad simply shrugged. It didn't matter, he told George. He had already spoken to Truscott, who had assured him they could get up the road faster by simply kicking in the rickety front door. "The Kraut's got nothing out front to stop us," Truscott had promised. In fact, Truscott was worried that his infantrymen, hearing voices in the dark, might fire on the invaders. They should continue pushing forward rather than waste time putting soldiers on and off landing boats.[77]

Horseshit, George thought. Since when was flanking a worse idea than a frontal assault? At a minimum, it would put more troops closer to Messina.

George was getting put out by commanders who constantly questioned their commanding general. Bradley had balked at the Brolo landings, and he was balking again. Well, like it or not, he told Bradley, the landing was going forward, and this time George would assume direct command of Middleton's regiment.[78]

"Very well, General," Brad replied, his voice growing colder. "Mount this operation if you want to. But we'll be waiting for your troops when they come ashore." Brad left to push Truscott's men up the road.[79]

We'll be waiting for your troops. Bradley's men were now "we," and George's men were "your troops."

Brad's nuanced comment was another chip at their working relationship, one that didn't bode well for either general or for the men who served them. It was the rub that had been building for half a year, the time when the Missouri teacher and the California polo player had to face the truth that they would never see eye-to-eye. They were born different, grew different, yet they were both lieutenant generals, both on the same team, both placed in a pressure cooker like meat and potatoes. The question for them was whether their sense of duty would hold them together long enough to complete their mission of liberating a big part of Europe, and that question would not be answered until the Third Reich had been destroyed.

If George noticed the change in Brad's tone or his choice of words, he never mentioned it. In time, he would learn to listen more carefully.[80]

On the night of August 15–16, Patton's amphibious regiment landed at the tiny village of Falcone, thirty-two miles from Messina. In the darkness, infantrymen splashed ashore amid the rush of foaming surf. Their pathfinders spread out, and they crouched down, fingering their triggers at the sound of approaching men. They were soldiers wearing olive drab, carrying lanterns and calling to the invaders—in English. They were Lucian Truscott's guides, waiting for them, just as Brad had promised.[81]

The next evening, Truscott's reconnaissance patrols cautiously probed their way into Messina's outskirts. Except for the occasional crack of a sniper's rifle and the usual fusillade in reply, the air was quiet and the road was littered with the detritus of a retreating army: jerry cans, ammo crates, dead pack animals, burned-out vehicles, broken bicycles. A few bodies in charred gray uniforms.[82]

Truscott sent word to Patton, who called Brad at three in the morning to tell him that Seventh Army would formally enter Messina seven hours later. George dressed quickly—pistols, helmet, the rest of his battle regalia—and told his aides to get him a Cub to fly to Truscott's command post.[83]

Throughout the night and early morning, elements of the 3rd and 45th Divisions pushed through dust, rubble, and craters churned up by bombs and shells and converged on Messina's bomb-scarred city hall. Civil authorities, thankful for an end to the devastation, came out to welcome Truscott, who, more or less, took the city's surrender.[84]

But the capitulation had to remain unofficial for the moment, as Truscott was under strict orders from the Seventh Army's commanding general: There was to be no formal surrender until the commanding general arrived to lead the parade. As the morning air began soaking up the August heat, Truscott's tired men waited for Patton.[85]

"I'll be damned. Now George wants to stage a parade into Messina." Bradley shook his head in disbelief. George's megalomania knew no bounds, Brad thought. "I disliked the way he worked, upset tactical plans, interfered in my orders," he recalled. "His stubbornness on amphibious operations, parade plans into Messina sickened me and soured me on Patton. We learned how not to behave from Patton's Seventh Army."[86]

Brad briefly considered driving to a street corner along George's motorcade route, just to infuriate the old peacock, but he decided that any juvenile theatrics on his part would just be "playing Georgie's game." But he wouldn't follow George on his victory parade, either, so he skipped the festivities.[87]

Instead, Brad made a mental note to speak with his old West Point classmate about the problems he and his staff had endured, the supply and ordnance snafus—things General Eisenhower would no doubt find unsettling. The five weeks of hard fighting in Sicily had permanently ruptured Bradley and Patton's relationship, and Brad's dim view of the brash cavalry commander, a picture he had first glimpsed in Hawaii in the late 1920s, gave him plenty of ideas of how different things would be if *he* were in charge.[88]

"What in the hell are you all standing around for?" piped the squeaky voice from the big staff car.[89]

On cue, Sergeant Mims gunned the loud engine of the converted Dodge command car. Horn blasting, he led a procession down the crumbling streets as George, his best war scowl strapped on, surveyed his conquest. Like a Roman emperor for whom the Senate had voted a triumph,

General Patton rolled past cheering civilians into the city's central piazza, Truscott at his side, and there he accepted the surrender of Messina, Signal Corpsmen snapping photos all the way.[90]

It was the greatest day in George's long life, the zenith of a lifetime of work, study, and worship at the altar of Mars. It was a victory won despite the best efforts of the Germans, the Italians, the British, and the Supreme Command. To top everything off, the old Californian had the pleasure of greeting a small commando party Montgomery had sent scurrying ahead of his armor columns to stake the British claim to Messina. An exultant George recorded the moment in his ever-present diary that night:

> [D]rove to . . . top of hill overlooking Messina. Bradley not there—must have failed to get the message. This is a great disappointment to me, as I had telephoned him, and he certainly deserved the pleasure of entering the town. We started into town about 1010. . . .
>
> In the town of Messina we met three British tanks and a few men who had arrived at 10:00 under the command of a general. It was very evident that Montgomery sent these men for the purpose of stealing the show. . . . I think the general was quite sore that we had got here first, but since we had been in for 18 hours when he arrived, the race was clearly to us.[91]

It was George's hour of triumph, the moment where his brilliance as a tactician shone for all to see. Like a messiah in khaki, in thirty-eight days George had scoured the island and cleansed it of its sin. He had captured an enemy capital and made a name for his army. This moment, he knew, would be the finest moment in his life, and one of the proudest in the annals of the United States Army.

Laurels flowed into the Mediterranean, and the greenest wreaths naturally landed on George's rosewood desk. Within days of the island's pacification, FDR sent a cable echoing his praise of the Palermo conquest: ALL OF US ARE THRILLED . . . MY THANKS AND ENTHUSIASTIC APPROBATION.[92]

Marshall's message read, YOU HAVE DONE A GRAND JOB OF LEADERSHIP AND YOUR CORPS AND DIVISION COMMANDERS AND THEIR PEOPLE HAVE MADE AMERICANS VERY PROUD OF THEIR ARMY.[93]

Admiral Cunningham cabled: IT HAS BEEN A JOY TO WATCH THE SPEED AND DASH OF THE SEVENTH ARMY.[94]

Alexander signaled: YOUR COUNTRY WILL BE VERY PROUD OF YOU AND SO AM I TO HAVE THE HONOR OF HAVING UNDER MY COMMAND SUCH MAGNIFICENT TROOPS.[95]

Even Katherine Marshall sent her congratulations on "your magnificent campaign in Sicily." George's face was splashed across the covers of newspapers and magazines. It was a grand time to be Lieutenant General George S. Patton Jr.[96]

Until a message from Ike stopped him dead in his tracks.

TWELVE

AVALANCHE

Georgie is one of the best generals I have, but he's just like a time bomb. You can never be sure when he's going to go off. All you can be sure of is that it will probably be at the wrong place at the wrong time.

—Ike to Kay Summersby

A GRAPHIC REMINDER OF THE COSTS OF HIS DECISIONS, the hospital tent is a place no general is eager to visit.

In the safe confines of headquarters, casualty returns prepared by company commanders—present, absent, killed, wounded, missing—represent a running ledger of the unit's business. Of men lost, some for a time, some forever. But those tabulations are silent numbers, recorded on clean sheaves of neatly lined paper—paper that can be filed in a drawer, or handed off to the adjutant general, or passed up the chain to someone else, like so many other reports that cross a general's desk each day.

Inside the warm canvas walls of the field hospital, a commander cannot pretend the price of his calculations is a mathematical abstraction. In the receiving tent, a man sees, hears, and smells the butcher's bill, splashed in blood, in stench, in sickening sights and cries wrenching to the ear. The field hospital houses no glory; it offers none of the distractions of battle. It is simply a warehouse of misery.

More than most senior generals, George made a practice of visiting the wounded. His aides kept pocketfuls of Purple Hearts, Bronze Stars— anything he was permitted to award—and when he came to a first-aid station or an admitting tent, he liberally pinned medals on shirts or pillows of men wounded in the line of duty. Men who had not let their comrades down. Men who had done their country proud.[1]

★ 234 ★

But George's emotions always lurked just below his leathery skin. His tears flowed easily at the sight of suffering—tears of admiration as much as sorrow—and the passions swirling within his warrior's breast were hardest to control when he saw younger men maimed and dying. One of his diary entries described a typical visit: *Stopped at an evacuation hospital and talked to 350 newly wounded. One poor fellow who had lost his right arm cried; another lost a leg. All were brave and cheerful.* During another visit, George wrote, *"One man had the top of his head blown off and they were just waiting for him to die. He was a horrid bloody mess and was not good to look at, or I might develop personal feelings about sending men to battle. That would be fatal for a General."* At one hospital filled with bandaged amputees, he excused himself to the latrine, where an orderly found him sobbing uncontrollably.[2]

Visits to the hospital were an ordeal to the spirit, but George felt they were expected of a great general. No less than fearlessness in battle, he believed compassion for the wounded was part of the example a commander must set. So when George, John Lucas, and a few aides showed up at the receiving tent of II Corps's 15th Evacuation Hospital near Nicosia around noon on August 3, Patton expected that the commanding general's presence would encourage the brave men, alleviate a bit of their suffering. Show them their leader cared for them and respected their valor.[3]

He moved deliberately from bed to bed, chatting genially with men wrapped in bandages, men hooked to plasma bottles, men missing limbs. Soon he came to a forlorn-looking private from Indiana named Charles Kuhl. Amid antiseptic and oxygen masks, the man seemed out of place. He sat upright, looking feverish and exhausted, but showed no visible signs of injury.

Frowning, George asked him what was the matter.

"I guess I can't take it," Kuhl said.

Can't take it?

To George, the man's words were a bald confession of guilt—of treason, even—and they took a moment to sink in. But sink in they did, and George's pulse began to race; his eyes narrowed, his breath became shallow. Inside his head one could almost hear the click of a gun being cocked to fire.

Two or three heartbeats later, the monster roared.

Leaning his six-foot frame into the young man, George began screaming at the bewildered private. Cursing, calling him every type of blasphemous coward in the endless Patton lexicon, George slapped Kuhl across the face with his gloves. Working himself into a frenzy, George grabbed Kuhl by the collar, yanked him to his feet, and shoved him out the tent's doorway, swinging his boot-clad leg into the lad's backside and sending him into the arms of some nearby corpsmen, yelling and cursing all the while.[4]

Can't take it, indeed.

After a few moments, George's breathing slowed, his pulse relaxed, his fury ebbed. He stood quietly in the midst of the shocked hospital staff until, with an imperious air, he marched out of the tent, ignoring indignant looks and shaking heads in his wake.

That night, taking up a heavy, emphatic pen, George told his diary:

> *In the hospital I also met the only arrant coward I have ever seen in this army. This man was sitting, trying to look as if he had been wounded. I asked him what was the matter, and he said he just couldn't take it. I gave him the devil, slapped his face with my gloves, and kicked him out of the hospital. Companies should deal with such men, and if they shirk their duty, they should be tried for cowardice and shot.[5]*

On the afternoon of August 10, as a tired, frustrated General Patton was trying to goad Bradley and Truscott into the Brolo landings, he paid an impromptu visit to the 93rd Evacuation Hospital at Sant'Agata di Militello, midway between Palermo and Messina. This time, his eyes lit on a twenty-one-year-old named Paul Bennett, an artilleryman who had been ordered to the rear by his battery's medical officer. Bennett, like other skulkers George had seen, was sitting on the bed, huddled up and shivering, but still in uniform, even wearing his helmet liner. There wasn't a damned thing wrong with him. George knew a cowardly rat when he saw one, and he was looking at one now.[6]

George strode up to him, halted, and asked him what was wrong.

"It's my nerves," Bennett said, his face tightening up.

George's face tightened up, too. "What did you say?" he demanded, his adenoidal voice rising.

The private sat at attention. "It's my nerves," he said. "I can't stand the shelling anymore." Bennett's eyes fluttered, and sitting there he began to cry.

George wheeled on the admitting doctor. *"What's this man talking about? What's wrong with him, if anything?"*

Without waiting for an answer, George, working himself into a full-bloom rage, spun on the young patient. *"YOUR NERVES, HELL!"* he bellowed. *"YOU ARE JUST A GODDAMNED COWARD, YOU YELLOW SON-OF-A-BITCH!!"*

Bennett sat there, tears running down his cheeks as George leaned over him and slapped him across the face. Bennett sobbed.

"Shut up that Goddamned crying!!" Patton roared. *"I won't have these brave men who have been shot at seeing a yellow bastard sitting here crying!!"*

The livid general swiveled back to the stunned admitting officer and screamed, *"Don't admit this yellow bastard; there's nothing the matter with him! I won't have the hospitals cluttered up with these sons of bitches who haven't got the guts to fight!"*

His blue-gray eyes burned as he turned them back on the pitiful man. *"YOU'RE GOING BACK TO THE FRONT LINES AND YOU MAY GET SHOT AND KILLED, BUT YOU'RE GOING TO FIGHT. IF YOU DON'T I'LL STAND YOU UP AGAINST A WALL AND HAVE A FIRING SQUAD KILL YOU ON PURPOSE!*

"IN FACT," he continued, reaching for his pistol, *"I OUGHT TO SHOOT YOU MYSELF, YOU GODDAMNED WHIMPERING COWARD!"* The hospital's commander, Colonel Donald Currier, came running to the scene of the ruckus. What he saw took him completely off guard.

"I WANT YOU TO GET THAT MAN OUT OF HERE RIGHT AWAY!" George was bellowing to everyone and to no one. *"I WON'T HAVE THESE BRAVE BOYS SEEING SUCH A BASTARD BABIED!!"*

George began to storm off as Bennett sobbed harder. After a few steps, his mind frozen, he turned back and lunged at the bawling private, slapping Bennett so hard his helmet liner rolled across the floor.

The medical staff, nurses, and patients stared at the three-starred maniac, stunned. Dr. Currier, an old friend of Beatrice's family, slid between George and his patient and guided the general to the door with respectful, soothing assurances. But George was in no mood to be soothed, and he left the place in a cloud of curses, Currier following close behind. He continued to scream, to no one in particular, ***"SEND THAT YELLOW SON-OF-A-BITCH BACK TO THE FRONT LINE!!!"*** until he had passed from view.[7]

His temper receding, Patton completed his hospital tour without incident. But before leaving, he warned Currier, "I meant what I said about getting that coward out of there. I won't have these cowardly bastards hanging around our hospitals. We'll probably have to shoot them some time anyway, or we'll raise a breed of morons."[8]

Back at Palermo's dark palace that night, George truly did not know what to make of the unnamed man he had so violently excoriated. *"Saw another alleged nervous patient,"* he told his diary. *"Really a coward. I told the doctor to return him to his company and he began to cry so I cursed him well and he shut up. I may have saved his soul if he had one."*[9]

Two days after Patton's visit, Brad's chief of staff, Brigadier General William Kean, brought his boss a report from an outraged doctor in the 93rd Evacuation Hospital. It was a complaint against the Seventh Army's commanding general.

Brad read the summary.

George had done it this time. *Slapping an enlisted man, kicking him out of the hospital tent?* Striking an enlisted soldier was a court-martialing offense. What could George have been thinking?

More to the point, what was he to do with the report?

Had it been up to Bradley, he would have fired George on the spot. But it wasn't up to him. Army procedure called for General Bradley to forward the report to his superior, General Patton. Of course, that would do nothing except circulate the incident to a larger staff within Seventh Army headquarters, creating problems, gossip, and no solutions.[10]

He could bypass Patton and send the report directly to Eisenhower. That would ensure the matter was treated properly, and it would probably mean the end of George Patton's career. But, reflecting further, Brad felt he couldn't do that to him. George had pulled him into Sicily, and George had lavishly commended his work in Africa. For all Patton's exasperating flaws, for every time Brad's blood pressure shot up over one of his stupid, vainglorious orders, Brad was not going to take the drastic step of bypassing his superior and cutting his throat. He owed George more than that.

He locked the report in his office safe and left it there.[11]

Back in sunbaked Algiers, Ike was wrestling with a barrel of problems that ranged from the profound to the mundane. His bowels were recovering from a hideous case of the African trots. The invasion of Italy would take place the next month—a good bit later than Churchill and Marshall desired—and Ike had to make sure Clark's Fifth Army was ready for that daunting task. Churchill, FDR, Stimson, and Harry Hopkins were pulling him in different directions over the Balkans, De Gaulle, Giraud, and the French coast. Press relations were a never-ending chore, administrative work was piling up, and the country seemed to have naively assumed the war in the Mediterranean was as good as over.

Then, on the morning of August 17, about the time Patton's scout car was rolling through Messina, Brigadier General Frederick Blessé, AFHQ's chief surgeon, asked for a moment of the Supreme Commander's scarce time to talk about a rumor Ike had asked him to check out.[12]

General Patton, it seemed, had caused a row at a pair of II Corps hospitals, cursing and striking two enlisted men and riling up the doctors and nurses. Blessé handed Ike a detailed investigative report by a II Corps surgeon describing one of George's tirades. The report, and the problem, now sat in Ike's lap.

Dammit, Georgie. Can't you stay out of trouble for one campaign?

All right, Ike told Blessé. "I guess I'll have to give George Patton a jacking up." Standard procedure for bringing the old cuss back into line. Ike said he'd look at the report and take care of the situation, thank you very much.[13]

But the more Ike thought about it, the more the incident bothered him. His thin lips curling downward, he ordered Blessé to keep the episode under wraps, at least for now. "If this thing ever gets out," he cautioned Blessé, "they'll be howling for Patton's scalp, and that will be the end of Georgie's service in this war."[14]

Leaning back into his desk chair, Ike put on his reading glasses and pored over the report, turning it over in his hands as he considered what to do. The document described Patton's outburst in clinical detail, slap by slap, curse by curse. Set out on paper, the incident was more damning than it had first sounded; his old friend had committed a court-martialing offense, and Ike realized George would need more than just a garden-variety jacking up. Over the next three days an unsettled Ike flailed, smoked, paced, and talked to himself as he tried to figure out what he should do.

It should have been an easy matter to replace George, or to wash his hands of the incident with a quick referral to the War Department—which would be the same as replacing George, though the hands gripping the ax haft would belong to a Department IG man, not Ike.[15]

But to Ike, it wasn't that simple. And it wasn't just that their friendship went back more than two decades, or that George had been the first general to offer Ike the combat command he had desperately craved before the war.

No, it was a hard call because the Allied crusade needed a difficult man like George Patton. A man who would bull through any obstacle just to prove he was America's greatest battlefield general. A man whom Ike would one day call "the finest leader in military pursuit that the United States Army has known."[16]

What was it Ike had said before the war? That he could judge a unit merely by knowing its commander intimately? If that were the case, and Ike firmly believed it was, then any army commanded by George Patton would be a formidable one.[17]

Distilling George's value into concrete terms, Ike explained to Harry Butcher that "in any army one-third of the soldiers are natural fighters and brave. Two-thirds inherently are cowards and skulkers. By making the two-thirds fear possible public upbraiding such as Patton gave during the campaign, the skulkers are forced to fight. . . ." George's method, he said, "was deplorable but his result was excellent." Ike had even told Dr. Blessé that "Patton is indispensable to the war effort. One of the guarantors of our victory."[18]

It was an extraordinary word, "indispensable," since an article of Army faith dictates that no man is indispensable. Arlington Cemetery, they say, is filled with indispensable men.

But in Ike's estimation, George came pretty close. Sure, he might bruise morale from time to time with his martinet act, but most of the grousing, Ike figured, was nothing more serious than the normal soldier complaints. Patton was a successful general, and the bottom line, he told Butcher, was that "soldiers love and respect a successful leader. Nothing breeds confidence like success."[19]

But something had to be done about this outburst, and Ike saw that as clearly as anyone. If the press got wind of this—to say nothing of what Marshall would do when he found out—George Patton would be finished.

Of course the press got wind of it. It always did. General Patton was a popular hero, a man larger than life, and the cycle of great American fables was to build up a hero, then tear him down, then—maybe—raise him up again.

Patton himself had recognized this cycle back in Tunisia when he had written Beatrice in April, *"I am too popular with the press but now I think they will take a crack at me."* Four months later, they had their chance. Hot on the heels of Ike's meeting with Blessé, a trio of correspondents—Demaree Bess of the *Saturday Evening Post,* "Red" Mueller of NBC, and Quentin Reynolds of *Collier's*—rang up Eisenhower's headquarters, demanding that Butcher set up an appointment with the Supreme Commander to discuss a serious matter involving General Patton.[20]

"I know what you're coming to see him about," Butcher told them as he penciled in the time. "The general hasn't slept for two nights worrying about it."[21]

On August 20, the newsmen met with Eisenhower behind closed doors. The press, they said, was in an uproar over Patton's abuse of his enlisted men. It wasn't just a sanctimonious feeling of indignation on the part of liberal journals, they stressed; Patton had committed serious a court-martialing offense, and he was becoming a drain on the army's morale. Quent Reynolds even went so far to claim that "there are at least 50,000 American soldiers who would shoot Patton if they had the slightest chance." To the reporters covering the Mediterranean theater, it was not about a witch-hunt, or even good copy for their papers. It was a question of Patton's fitness to command.[22]

Eisenhower and the press had enjoyed a relationship of trust going back to the Louisiana exercises of 1941, where his judicious censorship policies had convinced the newsmen that the man from Abilene was an honest fellow who would not squelch the truth, even if it meant revealing problems that gave Uncle Sam's army the occasional black eye. And despite their addiction to stories of military incompetence and abuse, the newsmen accredited to the theater were patriots who, as much as the foot solider, understood that the overriding goal of everyone was the defeat of Hitler and his Nazi thugs.

Sitting behind his desk, Ike pored over the political landscape like a general surveying his battlefield. Then he took a calculated risk. "You men have got yourselves good stories," he said, cracking a knowing smile, "and as you know, there's no question of censorship involved." He assured the newsmen he would not quash any reports they chose to file about the incident. Then he sat back quietly and awaited their response.[23]

The gambit worked. The journalists were proud of the role they had been selected to play, and they wanted to show Eisenhower that the guardians of the Fourth Estate were just as committed to the war effort as the men in uniform. They rallied around Eisenhower's standard, and they met him more than halfway. Bess, speaking for the pool of forty-plus reporters, emphasized that they were Americans first and journalists second. If Eisenhower felt the story would damage the war effort, he said, they would kill it. Red Mueller went even further, adding, "They were not only going to kill the story but deny it if any of the correspondents broke it."[24]

For the moment, Patton's skin was intact. Ike had exerted no pressure on the press, made no threats, held out no offers. He simply read the journalists like bridge players and played square with them, knowing they would respond with fair play of their own. A grin and an unspoken request were all Ike needed to save Patton's career.

A tired Ike shuffled back to his villa that night, sipping nervously a potent cocktail of frustration and worry. Although he sent George the "sternest letter of reprimand he had ever written an officer," he fretted over what would happen to them on the inevitable day of reckoning, the day when word leaked out and they both had to face the music. Even with his deal with the reporters, he might, he confessed, "have to send Patton home in disgrace."[25]

But what else could he do? Patton had just orchestrated one of the most brilliant military operations of all time, a campaign Ike predicted would be studied as "a model of swift conquest by future classes in the War College." George was the best ground-gainer in the Allied army, precisely because he demanded so much from his grumbling GIs and their shrugging officers. Friendship aside, Ike believed the Allies couldn't afford to lose a valuable asset like George. Once victory was assured, and only then, George's many flaws could catch up with him. But not yet. Not if Ike could help it.[26]

As George perused telegrams of congratulation in his crimson-carpeted palace, General Blessé arrived from Algiers with a personal package from Ike. The packet contained a short report. It also contained a terse letter that sent a stab of pain through George's chest:

Dear General Patton:

> *I am attaching a report which is shocking in its allegations against your personal conduct. I hope you can assure me that none of them is true, but the detailed circumstances communicated to me lead to the belief that some ground for the charges must exist. I am well aware of the necessity for hardness and toughness on the battlefield. I clearly understand that firm and drastic measures were at times necessary in order to secure the desired objectives. But this does not excuse brutality, abuse of the sick, nor exhibition of uncontrollable temper in front of subordinates. . . .*

[I]t is acutely distressing to me to have such charges as these made against you at the very moment when the American Army under your leadership has attained a success of which I am extremely proud. I feel that the personal services you have rendered the United States and the Allied cause during the past weeks are of incalculable value; but nevertheless if there is a very considerable element of truth in the allegations accompanying this letter, I must so seriously question your good judgment and your self-discipline, as to raise serious doubt in my mind as to your future usefulness. . . . In Allied Headquarters there is no record of the attached report or of my letter to you, except in my own secret files. I will expect your answer to be sent to me personally and secretly. Moreover, I strongly advise that, provided there is any semblance of truth in the allegations in the accompanying report, you make in the form of apology or such other personal amends to the individuals concerned as may be within your power, and that you do this before submitting your letter to me.

No letter that I have been called upon to write in my military career has caused me the mental anguish of this one, not only because of my long and deep personal friendship for you but because of my admiration for your military qualities; but I assure you that conduct such as described in the accompanying report will not be tolerated in this theater no matter who the offender may be.

Sincerely,
Dwight D. Eisenhower[27]

Leaning back into his desk chair, George removed his reading glasses and turned Ike's letter over in his hands as he considered what to do.[28]

George, you really screwed up this time.

Sitting before his diary that evening, George penned a half confession on the subject:

General Blesse, Chief Surgeon AFHQ, brought me a very nasty letter from Ike with reference to the two soldiers I cussed out for what I considered cowardice. Evidently I acted precipitatly and on insufficient knowledge. My motive was correct because one cannot permit skulking to exist. It is just like a communicable disease.

I freely admit that my method was wrong and I shall make what amends I can. I regret the incident as I hate to make Ike mad when it is my earnest study to please him. . . . I feel very low.[29]

The next day came an "eyes only" cable from Algiers, which read:

GENERAL LUCAS WILL ARRIVE AT PALERMO AIRFIELD BETWEEN FIVE AND FIVE THIRTY THIS AFTERNOON. IT IS HIGHLY IMPORTANT THAT YOU PERSONALLY MEET GENERAL LUCAS AND GIVE YOUR FULL ATTENTION TO THE MESSAGE THAT HE WILL BRING YOU. IN THE EVENT THAT IT IS ABSOLUTELY IMPOSSIBLE FOR YOU TO MEET HIM PERSONALLY, BE CERTAIN TO HAVE TRANSPORTATION AWAITING HIM AND LEAVE WORD AS TO THE PLACE WHERE HE CAN REACH YOU QUICKEST.[30]

That didn't sound good.

George sped to the airport and waited. And waited. After an hour, an ungainly olive drab transport appeared in the distance. It waddled down to the runway and rolled to a reluctant stop. Out from the gangway came Johnny Lucas.[31]

In sympathetic but firm tones, Lucas told Patton he had royally screwed up. Ike had called the outbursts in the hospital tents inexcusable, and the press was screaming for his scalp. Lucas described the torch-and-pitchfork mob calling for his head, and he warned his friend not to underestimate the trouble he was in. It was exceedingly unlikely his career could survive this blow, he said, even with Seventh Army's victories at Palermo and Messina, unless he fixed a massive public relations problem.

George swallowed hard. What was he supposed to do?

Apologize, Lucas told him. Apologize to the enlisted men, the doctors, the nurses, and, though Ike didn't ask for it, to every damned division in the Seventh Army, since they all probably knew about it anyway. And don't ever, ever, *ever* let it happen again, he said, or Ike would bust him to permanent rank and send him home for trial.[32]

A sickened George Patton replayed those words as Sergeant Mims drove him back to the palace. He understood the gravity of the matter, or so he thought, although he still didn't fully appreciate the grease pit into which he had dropped his friend and commander.

Fighting off a thundercloud of self-pity, Patton quietly ordered his aides to track down Private Bennett and bring him to his opulent office. On Saturday, August 21, beneath rococo frescoes of cherubs and angels, George Patton commenced his apology tour.

He first met with Bennett. As he told his diary, *"I explained to him that I had cussed him out in the hope of restoring his manhood, that I was sorry, and that if he cared, I would like to shake hands with him. We shook."* The transaction completed with the warmth of a real estate closing, George's aides had Bennett sent back to his unit.[33]

The next morning, Patton had the doctors, nurses, and enlisted men who witnessed the affairs report to his office. Dr. Currier grumbled that from behind Patton's "impressive desk" he offered what seemed to be "no apology at all," but simply "an attempt to justify what he had done." On Monday, George called in Private Kuhl and apologized to him, too.[34]

Wondering whether Ike would throw him to the wolves, George sat in his office, a badly shaken man. To George, it wasn't just the humiliation of an apology, for he had been apologizing to enlisted men since his second lieutenant days at Fort Sheridan, and his ego was big enough to say "sorry" to an inferior grade. What haunted him was the fear that the skulkers, pressmen, and bedpan commandos would get him crucified. That the big show would go on in Europe without him. That he would be left out of the greatest fight in man's long, violent history.[35]

To contain the flying shrapnel, George tried a little quiet public relations work of his own. The night after his apology session with Private Bennett, George turned on his most ingratiating, self-effacing charm at a dinner with USO comedian Bob Hope's entertainment troupe, which was working the Mediterranean and foxhole circuits and happened to be in Sicily. Afterward, Hope recalled Patton taking him aside and asking him in a somber voice, "I want you to tell the people that I love my men."

The comedian said, "I looked at this guy and I thought he was suffering from some kind of battle fatigue. And I said, 'You're the biggest general in our country. You're in the headlines all the time. . . . You don't have to worry about anything.' He said, 'No, I want you to go on radio when you get back. I want the people to know that I love my men.'"[36]

His apologies made, his contrition expressed, George hoped his fence-mending efforts would kill the controversy. He hoped Ike wouldn't be too sore at him.

He hoped he hadn't blown his chance at Army Group command.

* * *

To make certain Ike knew he was duly penitent, George took Lucas's advice and made a whirlwind tour of the entire Seventh Army. He gave his divisions a stump speech that was part pep talk, part eulogy to the fallen, and part vague reference to certain regrettable actions.

He didn't have to spell it out for the men, for the grapevine's shoots extend deep into the field, and his soldiers knew exactly what he meant. At some assemblies the men cheered him, but in most cases they didn't much care; they simply stared, waited for their commanding general to ride off in his big staff car, then went back to their campsites to resume their daily lives.[37]

George completed his sentence in purgatory by writing one final, expiatory letter to his commander. Disregarding the advice of Everett Hughes, who warned him not to justify his dumb conduct with dumb excuses, George wrote,

> *I want to commence by thanking you for this additional illustration of your fairness and generous consideration in making your communication personal. I am at a loss to find words with which to express my chagrin and grief at having given you, a man to whom I owe everything and for whom I would gladly lay down my life, cause for displeasure with me. I assure you that I had no intention of being either harsh or cruel in my treatment of the two soldiers in question. My sole purpose was to try and restore in them a just appreciation of their obligation as men and soldiers. In World War I, I had a dear friend and former schoolmate who lost his nerve in an exactly analogous manner, and who, after years of mental anguish, committed suicide. Both my friend and the medical men with whom I discussed his case assured me that had he been roundly checked at the time of his first misbehavior, he would have been restored to a normal state. Naturally, this memory actuated me when I inaptly tried to apply the remedies suggested. After each incident I stated to officers with me that I felt I had probably saved an immortal soul.*[38]

Mercifully, by the end of August it looked as if George had cleared his name, at least for the moment. On August 30, he met Ike, Bradley, Montgomery, Keyes, Truscott, and a gaggle of lesser luminaries at Catania for a victory luncheon hosted by General Montgomery. After Eisenhower decorated Monty with the Legion of Merit, George slipped Ike his letter of explanation.

"He just put it in his pocket," George wrote, concluding with a literary sigh, *"Well, that was a near thing, but I feel much better."*[39]

Taking Patton aside, Ike asked him to visit Wayne Clark, who was neck-deep in planning for the Italian operation. The implied message, that he might step in as Fifth Army's deputy commander, boosted George's spirits. *"[Ike] said that he may lose Bradley, Clark may be killed, and I will have to take over,"* George wrote, his confidence returning. *"I seem to be third choice but will end up on top."*[40]

Although he had managed to keep the Patton problem within the "Mediterranean family," Ike continued to toss and turn over what to tell Marshall. Debating the question with his inner circle, Butch wrote, "Ike said Patton's method was deplorable but his result was excellent. He cited history to show that great military leaders had practically gone crazy in their zeal to win the fight. Patton is like this. . . . Yet Ike feels that Patton is motivated by selfishness. He thinks Patton would prefer to have the war go on if it means further aggrandizement for him. Neither does he mind sacrificing lives if by doing so he can gain greater fame. So Ike is in a tough spot; Patton is one of his best friends . . . but friendships must be brushed aside."[41]

Friendships brushed aside, General Marshall would want Ike's recommendations on Patton, Bradley, and his other commanders, so the War Department could decide where to place them for the next big show. With Patton, Ike knew he had to walk a very fine line. He could not whitewash the slapping incidents, but he didn't want to raise too many red flags, either.

Thinking it over carefully, he drafted an accurate but discreet letter to the Chief that did not hide the incidents, but it did not draw too much attention to them, either. In his report he told Marshall that Patton

has conducted a campaign where the brilliant successes scored must be attributed directly to his energy, determination and unflagging aggressiveness. The operations of the Seventh Army in Sicily are going to be classed as a model of swift conquest by future classes in the War College and Leavenworth. The prodigious marches, the incessant attacks, the refusal to be halted by appalling difficulties in communications and terrain, are really something to enthuse about. This has stemmed mainly from Patton. . . . Now in spite of all this—George Patton continues to exhibit some of those unfortunate personal traits of which you and I have always known and which during this campaign caused me some most uncomfortable days. His habit of impulsively bawling out of subordinates, extending even to personal abuse of individuals, was noted in at least two specific cases. I have had to take the most drastic steps; and if he is not cured now, there is no hope for him. Personally, I believe that he is cured—not only because of his great personal loyalty to you and me but because fundamentally he is so avid for recognition as a great military commander that he will ruthlessly suppress any habit of his own that will tend to jeopardize it. Aside from this one thing, he has qualities that we cannot afford to lose unless he ruins himself.[42]

The shock waves of the slapping incidents would continue to rumble and clang for the next few months. Around the first of September, Ed Kennedy, the AP's local bureau chief, perked Ike's nervous ears with some harsh comments he had picked up from stateside journalists about General Patton. Kennedy told Ike he was worried that the press corps in Algiers would be accused of whitewashing the slapping scandal, which it had, or that AFHQ would be accused of censoring the story, which it hadn't.

Though Kennedy and most other journalists accepted Ike's word that Patton was too valuable to cashier over this double incident, Ike, shaken by Kennedy's comments, mulled over the idea of making Patton hold a news conference to explain what happened, to tell his side of the story, and to apologize once again. But Butcher, calculating the news cycles, convinced Ike that a press conference would do more harm than good. After all, he pointed out, the next few months would create fresh headlines that would push the slapping story off the front pages.[43]

So Ike let the matter go for the moment, hoping it would drift away. But he continued to toss and turn over the repercussions among George's men. Lucas, back in Algiers, wrote in his diary:

> *Ike is still worried about George. The rumor is spreading all over North Africa, he says, that George is brutal to his men. The newsmen may have started the story, I don't know, but there it is. . . . [I]f the higher ups and, above all, the lower-downs, lose confidence in him, his usefulness will be impaired, to say the least. As Ike says, George has never grown up.*[44]

Ike gave George his final trip to the woodshed on September 2, a 105-minute lecture in Algiers that covered the waterfront of judgment errors and verbal slips that he would no longer tolerate. Over lunch with Lucas and Everett Hughes, another trusted friend who, like Lucas, acted as an Eisenhower-Patton intermediary from time to time, George unloaded his troubles, stressing other reasons for his temporary residence in Ike's doghouse. "Ike has ordered him to apologize to Montgomery for losing his temper," an astonished Hughes told his diary afterward. "Ike says that Geo. has ruined Monty's career by getting Messina first, that Ike is going to send an IG to Sicily to ask soldiers what they think about their Army commander."[45]

The story about Monty was undoubtedly one of George's occasional exaggerations, but the Inspector General's investigation was real enough. The IG report urged Ike to forward the whole story to Marshall, and Lucas spoke to Eisenhower about the morale problem their friend was wallowing in. Ike's reply was terse: "Tell George to sit tight and behave himself."[46]

For all the lingering fury over the slapping incidents, as far as Ike was concerned, the gnawing question of his prodigal brother was settled. Ike continued to promote his friend's interests, and on September 6, when he cabled Marshall on the subject of permanent promotions, he wrote, "With respect to Patton, I do not see how you could possibly submit a list for permanent Major Generals, on combat performance to date, and omit his name. His job of rehabilitating the Second Corps in Tunisia was quickly and magnificently done. Beyond this, his leadership of the Seventh Army was close to the best of our classic examples."

George's battlefield performance was exemplary. But given his personal track record, Ike felt he had to edge a bit closer to full disclosure. So he penned an important caveat:

It is possible that in the future some ill-advised action of his might cause you to regret his promotion. You know his weaknesses as well as his strength, but I am confident that I have eliminated some of the former. His intense loyalty to you and me makes it possible for me to treat him much more roughly than I could any other senior commander, unless my action were followed immediately by the individual's relief. In the last campaign he, under stress it is true, indulged his temper in certain instances toward individual subordinates who, in General Patton's opinion of the moment, were guilty of malingering. I took immediate and drastic measures, and I am quite certain this sort of thing will never happen again. You have in him a truly aggressive commander and, moreover, one with sufficient brains to do his work in splendid fashion.[47]

There, he thought. He had made a clean breast of it, more or less. In Ike's view, if the Chief wanted to know more about Patton, he could ask. Otherwise, Ike would let the matter drop.

The more Ike reflected on George, the more he was sold on Patton's unique value to the Allied team. A few weeks later, he sent Marshall a follow-up cable. "[In England]," he suggested, "I gather you are to have *two* Armies. I think you should consider Patton for command of one of those Armies." Patton's strength, he explained, "is that he thinks only in terms of attack as long as there is a single battalion that can keep advancing. Moreover, the man has a native shrewdness that operates in such that his troops always seem to have ammunition and sufficient food no matter where they are."[48]

But a recommendation for army command, Patton's position in Sicily, was as high as Ike would go. An army commander's job was to take large-scale objectives as directed by the army group commander. Here's a city; capture it. Here are the enemy; kill them. An army command in ordinary circumstances required a cup of finesse and a bucketful of drive.

An army group commander's duties, by contrast, required diplomatic forbearance, strategic farsightedness, and an ability to balance. These salubrious qualities George Patton plainly lacked, at least in the same quantities other men seemed to possess. So Ike told Marshall, "Personally, I doubt that I would ever consider Patton for an army group commander or for any higher position, but as an army commander under a man who is sound and solid, and who has sense enough to use Patton's good qualities without becoming blinded by his love of showmanship and histrionics, he should do as fine a job as he did in Sicily."[49]

While George and Ike were drawing fire over the slapping incidents, Omar Bradley was savoring the fruits of a beautifully executed campaign. His performance had evidently pleased General Patton, and despite their arguments over the Brolo landings, George sent the Missourian a formal letter expressing his *"admiration for and appreciation of the magnificent loyalty and superior tactical ability you have evinced throughout the Campaign of Sicily."*

With considerable exaggeration, George wrote, *"Beyond question, your capture of Troina is the outstanding tactical operation of the Campaign, and is so far as I am aware the most important military victory gained so far during World War II."*[50]

Eisenhower's confidence in his old classmate also bloomed. A week after Messina fell, Ike reported to Marshall, "There is very little I need to tell you about [Bradley] because he is running absolutely true to form all the time. He has brains, a fine capacity for leadership and a thorough understanding of the requirements of modern battle. He has never caused me one moment of worry. He is perfectly capable of commanding an Army. He has the respect of all his associates, including all the British officers that I have met. I am very anxious to keep him in this theater as long as we have any major operations to carry out." Two weeks later, when discussing permanent rank promotions with the Chief, Ike said of Bradley, "He is, in my opinion, the best rounded combat leader I have yet met in our service. While he possibly lacks some of the extraordinary and ruthless driving power that Patton can exert at critical moments, he still has such force and determination that even in this characteristic he is among our best. In all other things he is a jewel to have around. . . ." By the time Ike was through singing Brad's praises, the Army's schoolmaster was being considered for the biggest show of all: next spring's invasion of France.[51]

As the smoke cleared over Messina, Bradley's public reputation seemed to break out of the confining shadow of Old Blood and Guts. News stories by Ernie Pyle, Hanson Baldwin, and other big-name journalists put the "GI's General" under the blazing spotlight of public view for the first time in his life. *Time* praised the "tall, tough commander of the Army II Corps in Tunisia and Sicily," and before the end of the year the provincial from Missouri would find himself invited to Buckingham Palace for an elegant gala thrown by King George VI. Even his daughter, Elizabeth, a junior at Vassar College, had become a minor celebrity as word of her now-famous father spread, and her name, and Mary's, began turning up in news and society columns. The chickens, on which Bradley had never been able to count, were finally hatching.[52]

Now all Brad had to do was get away from the rooster in Palermo.

Eisenhower's letters to Marshall had driven home one point: Both Bradley and Patton were eminently capable of commanding armies. But at the army group level, where logistics had to be balanced among competing armies, where moves had to be coordinated with allies, teamwork was paramount. An army group commander, Ike knew, needed diplomacy and perspective as much as tactical expertise. More, in fact.

This was where, in Ike's mind, Bradley made the better choice. Ike and Brad had learned to work together on the Academy's football squad so many years before, and Brad, like Ike, had grown up on baseball, a team sport. Brad's outlook reflected team play, the kind of play Ike appreciated. George, by contrast, was a track runner and a fencer, a one-man show whose prodigious energies worked in one direction and in one gear. Patton would run fast and strike hard, but his talents, impressive though they were, had to be harnessed within the broader framework of Allied strategy to be useful, for Ike knew the upcoming campaign would be a team effort dominated, in the end, by team-oriented American generals. If the Battle of Waterloo had been won on the cricket fields of Eton, the Battle for Europe would be won on the gridiron of West Point.

Marshall agreed Bradley was the better choice for an army group, though for the moment that particular appointment could be deferred. Right now he needed someone setting up an army headquarters in England, and he knew who that someone would be. On August 25, eight days after the last shots were fired in Sicily, he named the man he wanted to set up the American army headquarters in England. "My choice has been Bradley," he said. "Could you release Bradley for this command?"[53]

Although he had suggested the appointment, Ike was reluctant to see Brad go to England. He had done a damned fine job as George's understudy in Tunisia and Sicily, and he was a formidable commander in his own right. Ike was learning to rely on Brad, both in and out of the formal command chain, and he wished he could keep the Missourian in his back pocket in case something should happen to Clark in Italy, just as he had considered moving Bradley into the top spot in Sicily once George had set his GIs down on HUSKY's beaches.[54]

So in his response letter to Marshall, Ike backtracked a bit, cautioning the Chief that Bradley "has some little experience in planning amphibious operations, but his function in preparing for the Sicilian show was a subordinate one, especially with respect to all the intricate cooperations with Navy and ground forces." To remain completely candid, he added, "As you can see, I am personally distressed at the thought of losing Bradley because I have come to lean on him so heavily in absorbing part of the burdens that would otherwise fall directly upon me. . . . This very reason probably makes him your obvious choice for the other job; but if you should take Clark, I could shove Bradley into command of Fifth Army."[55]

The day after sending Marshall his cable, Ike reconsidered his lukewarm comments about Bradley and his disingenuous suggestion that Marshall take Clark instead. To clear his conscience, he dictated an addendum: "The truth of the matter is that you should take Bradley and, moreover, I will make him available on any date you say. I will get along. I hope my former telegram did not sound weaseling to you."[56]

Why not Patton for the army post? After all, Patton had commanded the Casablanca and Sicily landings, the latter as a coequal with Montgomery. His Seventh Army had captured over 122,000 enemy soldiers and liberated most of the island, and he had executed three tactical landings along Sicily's north shore. A Francophile with experience fighting in the Ardennes, George seemed a natural for a job of commanding mobile armies in France; it would be like handing Tommy Dorsey a fifteen-piece band and telling him to blow the house down. At the very least, George deserved to be in the discussion.

Problem was, Ike didn't think much of Patton's planning or logistical skills. George did little to make his peers believe he cared about logistics beyond the current day's stock of ammunition, and Brad's complaints to John Lucas, as well as Ike's personal observations, had convinced Ike that Patton was a limited asset outside an attack-and-pursuit role. Downplaying his work in the TORCH and HUSKY planning phases, he wrote Marshall, "[Patton] has planned two operations but, as you know, he is not as strong in that phase of the work as he is in the actual attack."[57]

So Brad, not George, was going to England.

The morning of September 2 found an unsuspecting Omar Bradley bouncing up the coastal road toward Messina. He was going to meet Lieutenant General Oliver Leese, a decent enough Britisher whom Brad had gotten to know during the Sicilian campaign. Leese's XXX Corps staff had informed Bradley that the corps artillery would be firing across the Strait of Messina in support of Monty's army, and Leese cordially invited Brad to watch the fireworks.

Four hours after his two-jeep convoy set out for Messina, it was buzzed by the *Missouri Mule*, Brad's personal Piper Cub. The *Mule* landed in a nearby field, and Chet Hansen jumped out with an urgent message from

Army HQ; Bradley was to return to his command post immediately, where General Patton would send him instructions about a "short trip."[58]

It was not what Bradley had been expecting, but few things about the Army were predictable, even for an old foot soldier. Well, he mused, Leese's arm-droppers would have to start the show without him.[59]

Hitching a ride aboard the *Mule* to his headquarters at Campofelice, Brad telephoned Patton, who told him Ike wanted to meet with him the next day. George was in fine fettle, notwithstanding his woodshed trip to Algiers, and he offered Brad the use of his C-47 to make the trip. Bradley got up at four thirty the next morning, and drove to Palermo for breakfast with George before flying out.[60]

When Patton's Gooney Bird lumbered to a stop on the runway at Cassibile, near Syracuse, Bradley climbed out and Eisenhower's aides escorted him to a cluster of camouflaged tents that formed the Fifteenth Army Group's command post. Bradley waited patiently for Ike, chatting amiably with a disheveled Bedell Smith, who had been wrangling with Italian emissaries over the terms of a secret armistice.

After a while, Ike emerged from a tent and apologized to Brad for keeping him waiting. With a grin he came straight to the point: "I've got good news for you, Brad. You've got a fancy new job."[61]

"I guess I'm the luckiest man in the world," Brad told Tex Lee. And he might have been, at least for that moment. He had just won one of the war's top prizes: command of the First United States Army, the spearhead of the Allied invasion of Western Europe, the invasion everyone had been talking about for years. For staff he would get his pick of the litter, and he was at last out from under Patton's heavy thumb. Brad was holding a winning hand, and all that remained was to play out the final round. He issued orders to himself to report to Eisenhower on "temporary duty," and, as a courtesy, he called on George Patton, to let him know he was moving on with his life.[62]

While Brad's visits with George always remained outwardly cordial, behind those steel-rimmed glasses the Missouri sharpshooter held a quiet loathing for his former mentor. The man's strengths were exaggerated, and his faults—*gosh!* how he detested those faults—were a ball and chain to Bradley and his loyal staffers. In the swirl of the slapping incidents, Brad's aide Chet Hansen penned his own feelings of disgust, feelings that undoubtedly mirrored those of his boss:

*Hoped the seventh army would be disbanded and
repudiated. . . . Talk of army is now smoldering and vicious.
Even the nurses in for dinner are swapping stories on Patton, all
of them bad. Klotz from 1st tells of Pat. visit to that Division and
the stony silence that greeted him. Profanity and vulgarity. Men
don't like it. Officers detest it. Hospital story resulted in rumor
that General Patton would be court martialed. Officers ask us.
Glad above everything else to get out from under his army as is
everyone else. They all ask why aren't people wise to the Green
Hornet—newspaper men are. They roundly dislike him.*[63]

Stopping at Carthage on the first leg of his roundabout trip to England, Bradley caught up with Ike at his villa overlooking the Gulf of Tunis, where he found Ike "in a dither" over the Salerno operation. They shared a late lunch, in which Ike gave Brad some last-minute guidance, and Brad flew to Algiers, where he met Bedell Smith, who plied him with more advice. Armed with this accumulation of wisdom, Brad boarded his plane and took the monotonous, winding journey to the United Kingdom via Marrakesh and the eastern Atlantic.[64] Arriving in Prestwick, Scotland, Brad, Bill Kean, and Chet Hansen hopped a short commuter flight to London. The welcoming committee that met them at the airport included the current head of ETOUSA, Lieutenant General Jacob L. Devers. Over several conversations with Devers, Brad learned that an invasion of northern France—formerly ROUNDUP, now rechristened OVERLORD—had been developed over the preceding year by a group called Chief of Staff, Supreme Allied Commander, or COSSAC. Working from the COSSAC outline, Devers and Bradley began putting meat on the plan's loose-jointed bones.[65]

Although he had known Jakie Devers since his West Point days, when a youthful Lieutenant Devers had managed the Point's varsity baseball team, Bradley was underwhelmed with the man who had become the highest-ranking American soldier in Britain. For one thing, Eisenhower had despised Devers ever since he published writings in Washington critical of Ike's handling of North African operations. Ike's distaste for Devers rubbed off on Brad, who later described the artilleryman as "overly garrulous (saying little of importance), egotistical, shallow, intolerant, not very smart, and much too inclined to run off half cocked." Another thing that bothered Bradley was that Devers gave the impression of a highly ambitious man who was trying to parlay his position at ETOUSA into a monopoly over the invasion's forces.[66]

In addition to refining the American side of the OVERLORD plan, Bradley's other job was to prefabricate an army group headquarters that would direct U.S. operations once the Americans fielded two full armies on French soil, which planners estimated to occur about a month or so after D-Day. To prepare for this, Brad's advance men would spend the next several weeks trucking their charts, file drawers, typewriters, and maps over to Bryanston Square in London's West End, where they became the advance guard of the First U.S. Army Group, abbreviated FUSAG. Other staffers, working under tighter deadlines, invaded the Gothic halls of Clifton College at Bristol, on England's western coast, where they set up the First U.S. Army headquarters, or FUSA. Bradley's driver, the faithful Alex Stoute, drove Brad to Bristol to survey First Army's new bivouac in one of the college's large boarding houses. As he rode to Bristol crisp Channel winds already growing cold, Bradley found himself startled to hear the rare sound of church bells ringing throughout the countryside.[67]

The idea of landing in Italy had never appealed to the Americans. To Marshall, King, Ike, and others, an Italian adventure was just another uncertain step into a Mediterranean sinkhole that would siphon off resources needed for an invasion of France. But it took until the spring of 1943 before the Americans could wring from Churchill and the British chiefs a commitment to launch OVERLORD by the spring of 1944.[68]

The price of Churchill's commitment to OVERLORD was an invasion of Italy, which was a logical next step after HUSKY, anyway. The Combined Chiefs ordered Eisenhower to land an army as far up the Italian boot as air cover would allow, with an eye toward the capture of Rome and its large, strategic air bases. This order meant an Apennine-size mountain of work for the Supreme Commander and his beleaguered staffers as they analyzed the composition of available forces, leaders, landing craft, and objectives. After weeks of studies by Eisenhower, Alexander, Clark, Montgomery, and their staffs, the CCOS settled on landings at two sites. The first operation, codenamed BAYTOWN, would put the Eighth Army ashore at Calabria, on the toe of the Italian boot opposite Messina. A week later, Clark's Fifth Army would land at Salerno, take Naples and the nearby Foggia airfields, then push on to Rome. The code name for Clark's operation was AVALANCHE.[69]

The many problems these landings posed, both logistical and tactical, put Ike under another dreadful strain. Landing craft were in dangerously short supply, and Ike's veteran divisions had not fully recovered from Sicily.

Clark's battle plan was particularly troubling; Wayne intended to throw out two corps, the U.S. VI and the British X, along a thirty-six-mile front around Salerno, with the two halves of his army divided by the Sele River. The strategy, which sounded ominously similar to McClellan's disastrous Peninsula Campaign strategy in the American Civil War, kept the two wings of his Fifth Army from supporting each other in case of a German counterattack.[70]

To make matters worse, Ike would not receive the air support he felt he needed for the landings. He had asked the Combined Chiefs to allocate him four squadrons of medium bombers to provide tactical bombing for Clark's invading infantry, but General Devers, head of ETOUSA, argued against the transfer and it was refused. To Ike's fury, a self-important Devers told the Supreme Allied Commander, "I must consider the overall war effort"—as if there were much to the war effort in September 1943 of greater importance than the invasion of Italy. To add to Ike's troubles, the Combined Chiefs turned down his request to use an additional eighteen LSTs en route to England from India, which would have allowed Clark to land additional armored units behind the first assault waves. To Eisenhower, this much belt-tightening by the high command left his men with an uncomfortably thin margin.[71]

Political uncertainties also clouded Ike's forecast, just as they had before TORCH. Although Mussolini's successor, Marshal Pietro Badoglio, was negotiating with Beetle over Italy's surrender, the Chiefs had given Ike a very tall diplomatic order: He was to induce the Italian government to sign "unconditional surrender" instruments at a time when German divisions were streaming over the Bremer Pass into northern Italy.[72] On September 3, Badoglio's emissaries finally signed secret surrender documents, though it took some hard-nosed threats from Ike and Beetle to force a frightened Badoglio to stick to the agreement. The Italian marshal, his eyes fixed along the Alps passes, knew any armistice would turn his country into a battlefield if the Allies couldn't move north and eject the Nazis *molto presto*.[73]

The public announcement of Italy's capitulation five days later was greeted with joy among the Allies, and it was a victory, though a messy one, for Eisenhower. Throughout England church bells—including those of the Bristol cathedral near Bradley's headquarters—pealed in celebration. In Italy, they rang out in alarm.

Montgomery's BAYTOWN invasion, launched on September 3, went reasonably well; his force met little resistance, and by September 9, the day Clark's force landed, Montgomery controlled the peninsular foot from toe to heel. But Clark's army, hitting the lower shin, had a hard, bitter struggle from the beginning. The Germans held the high ground around the beaches and pounded the invaders with their heavy guns, while panzers moved up to contain the landing zone. Kesselring's LXXVI Corps quickly exploited a six-mile gap between the British and American forces along the Sele River; Allied losses mounted, and an anxious General Clark began contingency planning to evacuate the U.S. VI Corps, under Major General Ernest Dawley. Over four stomach-churning days, VI Corps fought for its life, and Clark convinced Eisenhower to call in the 82nd Airborne to bolster Clark's thinning ranks. The American line, out of immediate danger, settled in for a long, violent struggle with Hitler's men in gray.[74]

As Allied casualty lists lengthened and Clark sent back pessimistic situation reports, Ike grew "tremendously worried" that Clark might be pushed off the peninsula. He told the Combined Chiefs that Salerno would be "a matter of touch and go for the next few days," and he openly fretted that Clark was losing his nerve, grumbling to confidants that he would be "out" as Supreme Commander if Clark were driven into the sea.[75]

As his eyes swept over the situation map in central Italy, Ike quietly wondered whether he had made a mistake in using Clark instead of Patton. By September 16, Clark's army had taken some nine thousand casualties—over a third the number lost during George's entire Moroccan, Tunisian, and Sicilian campaigns combined—and as Ike's companion Harry Butcher pointed out, "In case of evacuation, it would have suited Patton's personality and philosophy as a fighter to have been the last off the beach, if indeed he came off at all as he would prefer to die fighting." For his poor showing at Salerno, Ike busted General Dawley to his peacetime rank and sent him home. Having made that human sacrifice at the corps level, he tried to protect Clark's flanks as best he could in his reports back to General Marshall. But the best thing Ike could say to the Chief was that while Clark was "not so good as Bradley in winning, almost without effort, the complete confidence of everyone around him," and while Clark was "not the equal of Patton in his refusal to see anything but victory," he was, at the moment, "carrying his full weight and has, so far, fully justified his selection." For Eisenhower, it was a thin, strained endorsement.[76]

The Chief didn't buy it. He hadn't become head coach of the American team by allowing his quarterbacks to throw to receivers who couldn't catch the ball. On September 23, he shot back a sharp cable chiding Ike for failing to get his beachhead pushed out before the enemy could box him in. He offered no encouragement or support, because so far he saw nothing tangible to validate Ike's feeble hopes.[77]

Marshall's rebuke stung. Already under tremendous strain from the uncertainty of the invasion and the certainty of heavy casualties, Ike lost his appetite after he received the cable. Just as George coveted Ike's praise from time to time—and became sullen when he didn't get it—when the chips were down Ike needed a good word from the man he most respected. Butcher and Beetle spent a good part of the afternoon trying to cheer him up.[78]

Unfortunately for Ike, criticism of Clark's generalship would mount, and sharp cables from Marshall began landing on Eisenhower's desk with distressing regularity. That dismal autumn, the Italian front would unfold in slow, bloody steps that Ike would be obliged to recount to the Combined Chiefs in painful detail. In October, when the Allies finally captured Naples, Eisenhower warned the Chiefs that even with the Foggia air bases in Allied hands, "there will be very hard and bitter fighting before we can reach Rome." His natural optimism more subdued than ever, he ordered his staff to plan new landings around the coastal town of Anzio, thirty-five miles southwest of the Italian capital.[79]

"We are fiddeling while Rome burns, but only in metaphor, for I doubt if she burns—not for quite a while any how."[80]

That was how George Patton saw the struggle up the bloody stump of the Italian leg during the fall of 1943. While Clark's men were slugging it out at Salerno, and Brad was assembling his new staff in England, George sat on the sidelines, stuffed into his antique home like a dusty old book no one cared to read.

On September 2, Eisenhower's headquarters informed Patton that the Seventh Army would be formally dispersed, its troops parsed out to First and Fifth Armies. General Bradley, the message told him, would be sent to England to plan the cross-Channel invasion.

George took the blow hard. He spent the next two days in his gilded cage recovering from his trip, hoping against long odds that Ike's words were simply predictions of which way the wind might blow—winds that could change at any moment if his destiny, and Divine Destiny, remained in his corner. To get back in Ike's good graces, he even tried to convince Harry Butcher to come to Sicily on leave, where George could wine and dine the Supreme Commander's shadow from exile. (Butch, who admired Patton, dryly commented, "As I have no desire either for a leave or, if I had one, to spend it in Sicily, I rejected the suggestion when it was related to me by Ike."[81])

In a blue funk, George told Beatrice, *"It always takes me about three days to get over a trip to Alger. One should wear chain mail to avoid the knife thrusts. . . . I was told that I was too impetuous to do what Omar has to do apparently I am a man of deeds not words. Except when I talk too much. Speaking of which reminds me that some of the damndest lies are being circulated about me. . . . Ike has been fine but if George [Marshall] ever believes half the lies I will probably be in position to recommission the 'When and If.'"*[82]

George's hopes for battle command, fragile as they were, collapsed like logs on a dying fire when two coded messages arrived from AFHQ on September 6. The first told him in no uncertain terms that the Seventh Army would not be reconstituted. The second confirmed that Bradley would get the top U.S. combat command in England.[83]

It was this second message, George wrote, that "ruined me." By all rights Lieutenant General Patton, the man who had led the TORCH and HUSKY invasions, the man who had pushed his way into the history books by capturing nearly all of Sicily, the man who had picked up a stumbling corps in Tunisia and pushed it to victory, should lead that invasion. Not his understudy.[84]

As if George didn't have enough misery for one day, his bitter cup ran over that same afternoon when two investigators from AFHQ showed up to grill him about the slapping incidents and Seventh Army's care of Italian prisoners in its custody. *"[Ike] said he did it on my behalf, to counteract untrue stories,"* George wrote dubiously. *"I think this may be true but fear that it is to protect Ike."* To an old friend of Charlie Codman he spat, "You know what's happened to me now? I've just had my ears pinned back. All they do is pin my ears back. You know what they've pinned them back for? It seems I haven't given the Italian prisoners enough latrines. God damn it, they didn't know what a latrine was until I built one for them."[85]

In a shaking hand that night, he flipped open his diary and scribbled, *"It is very heartbreaking. The only time I have felt worse was the night of December 9th, 1942 when Clark got the Fifth Army."*[86]

The next day, when Brad came by to pay his respects before leaving for England, he found Patton wallowing in a full-blown depression. George kept up a pleasant front during the interview—he arranged for an honor guard and a band to salute Bradley, hosted a luncheon for him, shared some ideas about the Normandy invasion, and generally tried to send his former deputy off to England on a positive note. It was not just a matter of friendship or good manners, they both knew. *"Bradley has a chance to help or hurt me with General Marshall,"* he told his diary. *"I hope he chooses the former course, but I did not ask him to."*[87]

It was not much for George to pin his hopes on, and he knew it. His goose might not have been cooked, but it was sitting in a cast-iron pot next to a warm stove. In the evening's personal sitrep, he wrote, *"I have to keep working on my belief in destiny, and poor old destiny may have to put in some extra time to get me out of my present slump."*[88]

The saturnine general spent the next two months coming to grips with his status as an unemployed soldier, and he spent much of his time battling lethargy, anger, and depression—as well as his inability to understand why he was being shelved. His life took on the suspended pattern of those achingly dull months at Casablanca, but his days were made infinitely worse by the gnawing fear that his indiscretions at the hospitals had condemned him to the sidelines for the rest of the war. He complained frequently, disliked his surroundings, and told his brother-in-law, *"Sicily is the dirtiest place I have ever been, its inhabitants of the lowest type. I feel that I must return to Africa to apologize to the Arabs for what I thought of them."* With the steady departure of his field commanders, sent off to other adventures, he told Bea, *"I felt like the Ancient Mariner: 'Alone alone all all alone. . . .' I am approaching an irreducable minimum but it has happened before and I have survived."*[89]

As weeks passed with no urgent calls from Algiers, George desperately scrounged around AFHQ for a ticket to the battlefield. He wrote wildly obsequious letters to Beetle Smith, and he tried to ingratiate himself with members of Ike's inner circle, beckoning several to come visit him in Sicily. But he only managed to cajole a visit from Kay, whom he favored with gifts of liberated silk stockings, drinks aplenty—the "Patton 75," a mongrel concoction akin to fraternity punch—and a tour of ancient Palermo.[90]

George's depression deepened every day he was overlooked by his superiors—something a showman such as himself could not bear for long. Added to his frustration was the miserable fact that no one else seemed to understand was that George was a *fighting* bull, an animal specially bred animal for the *plaza de toros*, not the pasture. Despairing of holding high command again, he asked his friend for the unthinkable. *"I told Ike I was willing to fight a corps under Clark,"* he wrote in his diary on September 17. *"I would serve under the Devil to get a fight."*

Ike demurred. A glum George told his diary, his slashing script softening: *"He said Clark and I were not soul mates so he could not do it."*[91]

A fair point, but one that didn't make George feel any better.

George's confidence revived itself in early October, when President Roosevelt nominated him to the permanent rank of major general, a promotion the Senate would likely take up the following month. Ike, who had accurately if reluctantly referred to George as "surplus in this theater," sensed the acute pain his friend had endured for the previous six weeks. In early October Ike sent him a cable to lift his spirits. *"I am highly delighted that the War Department and the President have recognized the value of your war contributions by nominating you as a permanent major general,"* he told George on the day he learned of Patton's nomination. *"You have lived up to every one of the expectations I have held for you during the past 25 years, and I know that every job the government may give you during this war will be performed with the same dash, energy, and determination that have characterized all your action during the past 10 months."*[92]

Warming up to Ike again, George replied with a theme he had voiced in early 1942: *"It is my personal conviction that you, and you alone, are responsible for the promotion, as you have been for every other promotion I have received. I have run out of proper words to thank you, so you can just put the nth power on my remarks and let it go at that."*[93]

While Ike was quick to praise Patton to General Marshall, he also saw in Georgie an *enfant terrible* who needed to be kept on a tight leash. Occasionally, Ike would give that leash a sharp jerk, to remind George who was boss. Over dinner in Algiers one evening with George, Hughes, Kay Summersby, and Hughes's secretary, Ike, in Patton's words, *"gave a long monologue on himself and his early training. He then said I was always acting a part, that it was probably due to my having an inferiority complex. This amused me a lot but I agreed. The truth is that I have too little of such a complex—in fact I look down my nose at the world and too often let them know it."*

George had learned not to challenge Ike at times like this, moments when the Supreme Allied Commander was flexing his muscles. Afterward Hughes told George that, in his opinion, "Ike's trouble is that he is not humble," and because Ike "did not dare to cuss out or criticize the British," Hughes said Ike took it out on his American friends, proving the adage, "the better he knows a man, the more he preached to him."[94] George agreed.

* * *

Looking at the two old friends now, one would never know how close they were back in the days when officers wore Sam Brown belts and broad-brimmed campaign hats. By the fall of 1943, George's run-ins with the Navy, the British, tactical air, the hospital staff, and Bradley had stripped the Patton-Eisenhower relationship of its old stability. While the friendship remained real and personal, very much a living organism, the weakened bond between them would sway one way, then the next, like a metronome, as Eisenhower absorbed oscillating rays of brilliance and imbecility from his friend.

The basic personalities of the two men hadn't changed much since they first met. Patton was the same blustering, bloodthirsty martinet who strutted into Camp Meade in the fall of 1919. Eisenhower was still the same old chain-smoking workaholic with the effortless ability to charm.

But some things were different now.

One difference, of which their trappings reminded them every minute of every day, was the positions into which they had been thrust. As an Army commander, Patton could, in a sense, look out only for Patton. His job was simply to destroy whatever Ike told him to destroy, and in his army he ruled the roost. He was a commanding general, and cloaked in this authority, Patton held near-absolute power over anyone with the Seventh Army pyramid stitched onto his left shoulder.

Ike, by contrast, lived in a world of fewer absolutes. As Supreme Commander, he didn't rule the Allied force the same way Patton ruled Seventh Army. In fact, he directly ruled very little. He had to cooperate, even bow to outside forces—be they physical, such as the carrying capacity of a landing ship, or political, as when Jake Devers vetoed his bomber support. Despite his lofty title, Ike's dictatorial powers were much more circumscribed than Patton's.

Ike's job was also broader, for unlike Patton, Ike had to keep the whole Allied ship afloat, not just the American side of it. Neither side could afford to unbalance the other, which meant that if Patton was standing in the boat and leaning too far to one side, it was Ike's job to whack him with an oar and tell him to sit down. Ike spent a lot of time doing that.

A second departure from the Old Days was that Ike's way of looking at problems had matured, while George's had not. Back when the two young officers were tinkering with Renault tanks and debating armor doctrine,

George believed he knew more than anyone else about military tactics. He had, in fact, believed it since his West Point days, and he spent his succeeding years learning the same way he had learned as a child—by reading history books and listening to his inner voice, not learning from his contemporaries. That was why Patton so often flouted Army doctrine. That was why he felt free to criticize his superiors. That was why he wasn't tops in his class at Leavenworth.

That was why the George Patton of Sicily, 1943, was little different from the George Patton of Camp Meade, 1920.

Eisenhower, a much more pliable man in many ways, was receptive to instruction. He learned from Conner; he learned from the Leavenworth faculty. He learned from politicians and he learned from sergeants. He even learned from MacArthur.

In the process of absorbing these lessons, Ike changed. He was no longer the eager, single-minded tank zealot of 1920. By 1943 General Dwight D. Eisenhower had become the hub of a military-political wheel that spun at rates Patton never tried to keep up with, much less master.

George had seen these changes coming since before the war, but he still found it hard to adjust to the differences in his old comrade. To George, Ike was like the young blond-haired boy with freckles and torn pants that a man sees and leaves and doesn't see for another thirty years. The boy grows and matures into an adult, his belly paunches, his hair thins, his chin sags, and his talent for business or medicine or craftsmanship blossoms. But the older man still carries around in his head a picture of the young, blond-haired boy with freckles and torn pants he knew decades before. Despite all the letters and dinners and phone calls and planning sessions, despite the high rank both of them had earned, despite the late-night predictions of "I'll be Jackson, you'll be Lee," George Patton was still having trouble shaking loose the picture of a young, smiling lieutenant colonel in a Sam Brown belt and broad campaign hat.

By late October, George believed Fortune had begun to smile on him again. At the very least, it winked, though Patton should have known by now how deceptive a wink can be. On October 25, nine weeks after Messina's capture, Ike summoned George to Algiers "for a tactical reconnaissance." In Algeria's capital, Ike invited him to attend a play and have lunch with him, which should have been a harbinger of good news—some problem that only an old warhorse like George Patton could handle. The meal was pleasant, Ike was in a good humor, and George was anxious to get to the point of the meeting.[95]

"Ike was his old self," George remarked that night, with some relief. *"Beedle Smith told me that I am to get an Army in England. He said he had told General Marshall that I am the greatest assault general in the world and should lead the attack."*[96]

Of course, there were always caveats to good news, especially when Ike brought along Beetle. The Machiavelli from Indiana related a conversation with General Marshall in which Marshall agreed with Beetle that George was the country's best combat leader—but he added that he didn't trust George's staff. Beetle claimed he told Marshall, "Well, they have always succeeded," to which the old general replied, "I have been told that in Sicily the supply was not good. I have my own means of knowing."

"That," concluded George, *"means either Wedemeyer or Bradley or both."*

After lunch, Beetle dropped the boom on George: Instead of leading an invasion of France—or the Balkans, for that matter—the Allies would use Patton's reputation to draw Axis attention away from the French north coast. To Corsica. George would be the decoy, not the fighter.[97]

"This is the end of my hopes for war," he muttered.[98]

THIRTEEN

KNIGHT, BISHOP, ROOK

Regret trouble I am causing you. Will abide implicitly by your instructions.

—George to Ike, November 25, 1943

GEORGE'S HOPES FOR WAR WERE DIMMING, but for reasons other than Beetle's perfidy, or Bradley's backstabbing, or Ike's Anglophilia. Although journalists in the theater had kept their promise to lay off the slapping story, rumors of an incident involving General Patton and a hospital began circulating in press circles back home. *The Washington Post*'s Drew Pearson began sniffing around, and in mid-November he broke the story on his syndicated radio show. Pearson dished to his national audience a detailed account of General Patton's physical abuse of his enlisted men and claimed General Eisenhower had "severely reprimanded" the Seventh Army commander. Pearson urged the Senate's Truman Committee to investigate a "high-ranking officers' self-protective club" that covered up injustices within the officer corps, and newspapers across the country picked up and amplified Pearson's report. Outraged mothers wrote their congressmen about the sadistic general who should have been court-martialed for striking young men, and editorial boards from coast to coast railed against Patton. Congressional Republicans, smelling blood, called for a formal investigation of the incident.[1]

Eisenhower and his PRO wizards should have forecast this typhoon from the time Ike first met with Bess and Reynolds, but for some reason AFHQ was caught flat-footed. In a press statement, Army headquarters categorically denied that General Eisenhower had reprimanded General Patton over the incident, though when the press corps demanded a detailed explanation, Beetle admitted that Eisenhower had written Patton a "personal" though not "official" reprimand. As one reporter quoted "a high-ranking officer," Beetle, "General Patton was mercilessly berated by General Eisenhower," though nothing had been placed in Patton's official personnel file.[2]

This too-clever game of Army semantics gave the press fresh meat to latch onto, and before long public outrage shifted from Patton's slappings to Eisenhower's ham-fisted attempt to cover for his high-strung friend. Congressmen, newspaper editors, and, most important, senators, who were considering Roosevelt's military nominations, began calling for Patton's court-martial. A beleaguered Secretary Stimson, one of Patton's oldest and strongest protectors, ordered Eisenhower to prepare a full report of the incident, and the press began beating down Ike's doors for further comment. As domestic news reports forwarded by the Office of War Information began flooding Algiers, Ike publicly distanced himself from his old friend while doggedly insisting George was too valuable to discharge from the service.[3]

To Ike, it was like the Darlan Deal all over again, and to make matters worse, General Joseph T. McNarney, an officer whom Marshall had called "a merciless man, a true hatchetman," began firing off cables to Algiers demanding a explanations of Eisenhower's actions on a variety of subjects. Added to Patton's personal humiliation over the incident was the feeling that he was bringing down his friend. Watching events unfold from distant Sicily, a glum George concluded, *"I seem to be the means by which McNarney is trying to hurt Ike so as to become Chief of Staff in the event that General Marshall leaves."*[4]

Sticking by his convictions, Ike refused to send George to the scaffold. He wired Secretary Stimson a full report that did not excuse Patton's conduct, which he called "unseemly and indefensible," but it expressed his firm conviction that Patton's personal drive—a drive inseparable from his other, more destructive instincts—had been the key to Seventh Army's swift conquest of Sicily. Eisenhower had to weigh "losing to the United Nations his unquestioned value as a commander of an assault force" against the damage to the Army's public image, and he told Stimson the Allied cause was best served by retaining General Patton for future operations. Putting his own neck alongside George's, Ike signaled that he would not willingly part with him. His corrective measures were adequate, Ike felt, and he was not going to sacrifice his best ground-gainer to appease shortsighted congressional demands or assuage momentary public fury. Stimson agreed.[5]

* * *

From his villa in Algiers, Ike had sensed what his old friend was going through. Exiled to Sicily, pacing the volcanic island uselessly from one end to the other while his army was cannibalized, a "KICK ME" sign pinned to his back, George was on the ropes, and Ike felt the time was ripe for another Eisenhower pep talk, which in Patton's case meant assurances of more fighting. Eisenhower understood George needed pep talks, just as he needed, for his own good, an occasional jacking-up. On October 4, before the Pearson broadcast, Ike had assured George, *"You have lived up to every one of the expectations I have held for you during the past 25 years, and I know that every job the government may give you during this war will be performed with the same dash, energy, and determination that have characterized all your action during the past 10 months."*[6]

But the Drew Pearson report was a stark reminder that Ike needed to keep George on a very short leash, for his own good as well as the Army's, and in November, he sent another "eyes only" letter to Palermo:

> *The flood of newspapers accounts in Washington concerning incidents . . . has continued today. It is my judgment that this storm will blow over. . . . I must stress again to you the necessity for acting deliberately at all times and avoiding the giving way to impulse. . . . If any inquiry is made of you by the press, I insist that you stick to the facts and give a frank exposition of what occurred. In addition, you could, I think, invite any such press men to the units still under your command to determine for themselves the state of morale. I do not desire that you make a formal statement for quotation at this time.*[7]

George had no intention of making a statement about anything to anyone. On November 25, he cabled back: REGRET TROUBLE I AM CAUSING YOU. WILL ABIDE IMPLICITLY BY YOUR INSTRUCTIONS.[8]

The near miss to his career left the idled horseman feeling lower than ever, and each new cable informing him of the loss of another division was a crisp, shiny nail in his psychological coffin. Unable to resist stories about himself—most of which excoriated him—he felt acutely the stabs of newsmen and politicians who didn't even know him. Worse, he darkly suspected, one of those blades might have Bradley's fingerprints on the knife's grip. Perhaps even Ike's.[9]

Self-pity and depression, two demons he regularly banished in the rush of battle, returned, made themselves at home, and became his unwanted houseguests. He spent his days fidgeting, reading history, ambling about the island, writing letters, and searching for ways to occupy a mind that begged to be occupied. He moped, slept late, cursed and brooded, twisting the knife deeper into his own wound. At one point, an engineer walked into George's imposing office and was astonished to find his commander "literally cutting out paper dolls" with a pair of scissors.[10]

George's friends pleaded with him to be patient, but they might as well have been telling a bull not to snort. On his fifty-eighth birthday, George told Bea that Everett Hughes had advised him to "keep my shirt on and sit tight." Feeling that Everett gave Ike the benefit of too many doubts, George replied, "hair shirts scratched," and "I had been kicked in the tail so much that I had a hard time sitting at all."[11]

He summed up his mood in a diary entry for November's final Thursday: *"Thanksgiving Day. I had nothing to be thankful for so did not [give thanks]."*[12]

But George had one thing to be supremely thankful for: Eisenhower's loyalty, a loyalty based on cold, military calculation that dovetailed with his personal feelings. The two men may no longer have been Huck and Tom, but so long as there was fighting to be done, Ike would see something in George few others could discern: that beyond the staged scowl, beyond the riding crop and the outlandish command cars, lay a man to whose judgment the Allies could entrust men's lives.

Deep down George knew Ike was not going to throw him to the wolves. But to play it safe, in late November George sent Ike a wildly obsequious letter promising to write a history book grandly entitled *The Greatest Conquest,* covering Eisenhower's military campaigns from November 1942 to November 1943.

His bootlicking was entirely unnecessary. Ike had sent Beetle to Washington to boost George's chances for future command, and if George needed another augury of Ike's support, he received it on the first of December, when a personal letter from the Kansan reassured him,

The furor at home over the incidents of last August is, I think, dying down a bit; however, we may yet have a lot of grief about it. I want you to know that I think I took the right decision then

and I stand by it. You don't need to be afraid of my weakening on the proposition in spite of the fact that, at the moment, I was more than a little annoyed with you.[13]

By mid-December, the wave of indignation over the slapping incidents seemed to have receded in Washington officialdom as well as in the papers, just as Butcher had predicted. Ev Hughes noted in his diary a Gallup poll that showed four out of five Americans favored keeping General Patton in the ranks. In the end, Ike passed off the matter philosophically, telling his former division commander that the slapping incident was *"just another one of those irritating and needless things that occur to make everybody's job a little bit harder."* Patton, he reiterated, *"is a gorgeous commander when the going is tough. He has more 'drive' on the battlefield than any other man I know."*[14]

Before setting up shop in England, Omar Bradley flew to Washington for two weeks of planning and briefings. His itinerary included a short meeting with President Roosevelt, who, to Brad's amazement, casually discussed an extraordinary bomb project that used nuclear fission rather than explosives. Brad spent several hours riding with General Marshall on a plane to Omaha, Nebraska, during which he briefed Marshall on his Sicilian experiences—and pulled no punches as he unloaded the many sins of George's headquarters.[15]

Bradley returned to England in October, about the time ETOUSA activated the First U.S. Army Group. He immediately took the helm of FUSA and FUSAG, even though Devers failed to issue any written orders appointing General Bradley to either post. As Group headquarters was filled with men from ETOUSA chosen by Devers—men whom he didn't know well enough to trust yet—Bradley set about cleaning house. He liberally raided his old II Corps headquarters staff, even stripping the headquarters of its nicer furniture, and before long he had a fine skeleton team working on the invasion's details.[16]

FUSAG commenced its work in a row of West End flats with ornate rococo interiors and blackened windows guarded day and night. Though FUSAG had no armies, no mission, and, courtesy of a subsequent Luftwaffe raid, few intact offices, Bradley was perfectly happy to oversee the nascent organization, since acting command of the army group would give him a leg up when Marshall cast around for a permanent commander.

Working from a hideously painted office with a large dent in its floor—the result of a dud bomb, courtesy of Hermann Göring—the businesslike Bradley brought together the infrastructure of an organization that would govern at least two American armies, the First and Third, and perhaps others. When not working at FUSAG, he wore his First Army hat. He lived with his top lieutenants at a large country home outside Bristol with Chet Hansen and the remainder of his personal staff, while work proceeded at nearby Clifton College.[17]

Looking at his fine new command posts, Brad knew he had finally made it. His little egg had finally hatched, and the bird inside had grown into an eagle that would land in France in about five months and astound the military world.

Among the many blessings of his new assignment, Omar Bradley didn't have to stand in anyone's shadow, least of all George Patton's. In fact, it was unlikely he would ever see Patton again, since Ike, like most everyone else in the American command, seemed pretty sour on old Georgie right now. With no distractions from a blowhard cavalryman who had little appreciation for logistics and teamwork, Bradley could get down to the business of running his war by method, rather than by impulse.

While Bradley assembled the nucleus of the First U.S. Army, the Allied High Command struggled over critical points of grand strategy. Stalin, hardened by two and a half years battling four million Axis soldiers, castigated the Americans and British over their failure to open a true second front. The Red Army had chewed up Hitler's mammoth tank offensive at Kursk in early July, then launched its own counteroffensive. In that slaughterhouse, the Soviet Union had lost 800,000 men, three thousand tanks, and two thousand aircraft. *Now*, Stalin insisted, was the time for the Allies to step forward and open a second front. An invasion of France.[18]

The Western powers agreed in principle, though British consent came with strings attached. In Churchill's mind the Balkans, the Aegean, and the Italian boot all competed for priority with OVERLORD. On the American side, Marshall and Admiral King prepared for Anglo-American conferences in Cairo, as well as a "Big Three" conference to begin on November 28 in Tehran, on the assumption they would have to fight like devils to hold OVERLORD's May 1, 1944, target date.

To the surprise of the U.S. chiefs, the British joined the Americans in assuring Stalin they were serious about opening a true second front in the spring. The cagey dictator, unwilling to put much faith in Anglo-American promises, insisted that his allies name a supreme commander for OVER-LORD. Roosevelt promised to announce the appointment within a few days, after he and his advisers conferred in Cairo.[19]

Ike played no role in the Tehran discussions. He spent his days sitting on a pincushion of anxiety at Amilcar. He later compared himself and Marshall to "two pieces in a chess game, each compelled to await the pleasure of the players."[20] But as far as Ike could see, in the next round he wouldn't be the rook, knight, or bishop. Or even a pawn. Instead, he would be pushed off to an entirely different board: Marshall would get the top spot in the OVERLORD invasion, and because Roosevelt had promised Churchill that a Briton would command the Mediterranean theater, Eisenhower would probably be sent to Washington around the first of January. It was a prospect he considered with the enthusiasm of a condemned man scanning the calendar.[21]

Before his swan song, Ike had to play host to another bevy of VGDIPs making their way to the Cairo and Tehran conferences. On November 19 he flew to Oran, where President Roosevelt arrived the next day in grand style aboard the battleship *Iowa*. From there, he accompanied FDR's entourage—Marshall, King, Harry Hopkins and the rest—to Amilcar aboard a C-54 Skymaster, nicknamed the *Sacred Cow*.[22]

During FDR's stopover, Eisenhower took the president on a driving tour of the Tunisian battlefields, Kay at the wheel. As they rode past the detritus of wars recent and ancient, of battles joined in space but separated by millennia, Roosevelt's mind began to wander to the legacy of his own generals. Generals who one day would elicit comparisons to Scipio, Hannibal, and Caesar. Generals who fought their wars from behind desks with pen and telephone instead of gladius and musket. Turning his aged face to Eisenhower, he mused, "You and I know who was Chief of Staff during the last years of the Civil War, but practically no one else knows, although the names of the field generals—Grant, of course, and Lee and Jackson, Sherman, Sheridan and the others—every schoolboy knows them. I hate to think that fifty years from now practically nobody will know who George Marshall was. That is one of the reasons why I want George to have the big command. He is entitled to establish his place in history as a great general."[23]

Marshall and King billeted at Ike's villa outside Tunis. As Eisenhower was getting ready to leave for a private dinner with the president, the top brass lounged around the living room, sipping glasses of sherry. Walking Ike to the door at the appointed hour, Admiral King, puffing away on a cigarette, casually remarked, "I hate to lose General Marshall as Chief of Staff." Ike looked at him, saying nothing. King continued, as if Marshall were not in the room, "My loss is consoled by the knowledge that I will have you to work with in his job."[24]

Marshall stood with them, silent as the Sphinx while King insisted that Marshall's place was in Washington. "You, Eisenhower," he declared, "are the proper man to become the supreme commander for the Allies in Europe."[25]

Ike, taken aback at the way this delicate issue had been lobbed at him, simply mumbled, "The President has to make his own decisions," hoping it would end the matter. But King, trying to be polite in his rough way, ignored the invitation to drop the subject. After a moment Marshall in his usual brusque manner, shut down the discussion. "I don't see why any of us are worrying about this," he growled. "President Roosevelt will have to decide on his own, and all of us will obey."[26]

Marshall was correct, as usual, and Ike's heart sank lower, if that were possible. He always knew he might be recalled to Washington. After all, four-star generals could not be easily wedged into a tight command structure, even in Europe. Ike's own letters had reflected his assumption since early autumn that Marshall, not Ike, would be running the European show in 1944. But to *suspect* bad news was one thing; to *hear it* from the mouth of a four-star admiral was another.[27]

It was a blue season for Ike Eisenhower, and he bitterly told his close friends that if he were sent back to Washington, "I'll be carried up to Arlington Cemetery within six months." Remaining a field commander was all he was asking for in return for eighteen months of thankless work under the criminally misleading title of Supreme Commander. Was it too much to let him serve where the fighting was raging, where he knew the staffers, the generals, the leaders better than any other man in uniform? How was he going to handle the personalities and issues that Marshall had mastered in four years on Mount Olympus—Congress, MacArthur, Stilwell, Chiang, the Joint Chiefs, the Central Pacific, appropriations, the draft, production, and who knew what else? And, at a personal level, how would he adjust to life back in the States?[28]

These were the questions that gnawed at Ike's gut, questions he had been able to brush aside for months under the press of work, a lake of coffee, and a mountain of cigarettes. Now he had to face them.

But inside his small, half-veiled box of emotion, Ike knew he was being selfish. The War Department had given him unprecedented opportunities. He had led the two greatest amphibious invasions the world had ever seen, and he had ordered the most decisive tactical bombing operation in history. Like the good soldier he was, if the War Department wanted him in Washington, that's where he'd go. He only hoped Marshall would let him bring Beetle back, though he knew he'd probably have to fight both Churchill and the Chief to get him.[29]

As staffers in England began moving Marshall's personal effects to London, Ike made plans to come home. He gave valedictory statements to his staff stressing his gratitude for their services, and he began outlining plans for a Far East tour to confer with MacArthur and Lord Mountbatten. He quietly offered Kay Summersby to Everett Hughes, "with the [Cadillac] thrown in," and he heeded Marshall's advice to take a few days off—a sightseeing trip to Luxor, the Valley of the Pyramids, and the Holy Land with Kay and a few close associates.[30]

Winging its way back from the Tehran conference, the *Sacred Cow* touched down on the dusty Tunisian airfield on the second anniversary of Pearl Harbor. The Skymaster was stopping to refuel on its return flight to Oran, where President Roosevelt would reboard the *Iowa* for his journey home. General Eisenhower dutifully saluted the president's party as it emerged from the big plane, and he walked alongside the president as the Secret Service escort wheeled him into the backseat of Ike's Caddy.

Shifting from his wheelchair into the car's cavernous backseat, a grinning Roosevelt came right to the point: "Well, Ike, you are going to command OVERLORD."[31]

FOURTEEN

ENGLAND

If I have to apologize publicly for George once more, I'm going to have to let him go, valuable as he is. I'm getting sick and tired of having to protect him. Life's much too short to put up with any more of it.

—Ike to Brad, April 1944

ON CHRISTMAS DAY, 1943, Ike flew to Tunis to meet his successor in the Mediterranean, British General Henry "Jumbo" Wilson. The baton was passed at an awkward time, as Churchill had been pressing for a second landing in Italy. Eisenhower's team had planned an assault against the coastal city of Anzio, whose defenses would be manned by a formidable twenty-three German divisions. Ike had serious misgivings about the Anzio plan, and he expressed them to a dismissive Churchill. But Anzio would be Wilson's cross to bear, not Ike's, and the lame-duck theater commander went along with the plan, dubious as it was.[1]

The Anzio landings proceeded with predictable results. Clark's frontal assault met with a bloody check, and his amphibious force, led by General Lucas, quickly fell under the guns of 70,000 enemy troops massed over the high ground. The Italian campaign would degenerate into one of the most sanguinary struggles in the west. As Churchill summed up the operation's first painful weeks, "We hoped to land a wild cat that would tear out the bowels of the Boche. Instead we have stranded a vast whale with its tail flopping about in the water."[2]

Bidding good-bye to his AFHQ staff, Eisenhower left the Mediterranean for a short visit to the United States on the first of January. At Marshall's insistence, much of Ike's trip was recuperative, and in Washington Mamie and Ike spent a few precious hours reacquainting themselves.[3]

★ 275 ★

Mamie, who hadn't seen her husband in a year and a half, instantly noticed unsettling changes in her man. Months of excessive smoking, late-night conferences, early-morning inspection trips, and endless, endless worry had etched deep lines into a once-cheerful face that was veiled with distraction. Ike tried to give Mamie his attention and affection, but he knew crucial decisions on landing craft, air strategy, and the movement of men—twelve thousand at a time—awaited his return.

Like the moonlight that follows a man as he walks through the woods at night, Ike could not for a moment escape the European theater. His body in America but his mind in England, Ike was restless, abrupt, far less approachable than the bright-eyed major general who had kissed his wife good-bye at Bolling Field in the summer of '42. Mamie saw, to her quiet distress, that the portrait of a husband she had carried in her head since that bittersweet day had become dated. It was hard for her to redraw that picture in her mind's eye.[4]

After a twelve-day respite that was too short for Mamie and too long for Ike, the new Supreme Commander, Allied Expeditionary Forces, boarded a plane for Prestwick and arrived in Scotland on the evening of January 7. With Butcher and his British aide, Lieutenant Colonel James Gault of the Scots Guards, he sped to London in a teak-walled luxury train car specially allotted to him. The next day, he moved into his new office at 20 Grosvenor Square. It was as if he had never left.[5]

OVERLORD's top appointments—the naval, air, and ground commanders—were not Eisenhower's to make. The British had grudgingly agreed to OVERLORD in 1944, they knew the territory better than the Americans, and they would supply more than half the assault divisions for Operation NEPTUNE, OVERLORD's crucial amphibious landing phase. Thus, while Eisenhower would serve as the Supreme Allied Commander, the critical air, ground, and sea commands would be dominated by Britons.

The highly capable Admiral Sir Bertram H. Ramsay, Admiral Cunningham's right arm in TORCH and HUSKY, would command the invasion fleet for NEPTUNE. The air force command, including fighters, strategic bombers, fighter-bombers, and paratroop transports, was more complicated. These forces would all be placed under the command of Air Chief Marshal Sir Trafford Leigh-Mallory during the NEPTUNE landings. However, the strategic bomber commanders—General Spaatz and RAF's Air Chief Marshal Sir Arthur "Bomber" Harris—had for many months argued that the war could be won by simply turning their fleets of Liberators, Lancasters, and Flying Fortresses against German cities, factories, airfields, and oil refineries. The bomber advocates, Ike realized, would be impatient to get their fleets out of Normandy's skies and back over Berlin.[6]

For ground commander, the role occupied by Alexander in HUSKY and AVALANCHE, the British choice was General Montgomery.

Monty. The same Bernard Montgomery who had dressed Eisenhower down for smoking in His Majestic Presence. The same Montgomery who had insisted Ike give him an American bomber for his personal use after Tunisia. The same Montgomery who had strong-armed Alexander into shunting Patton's Seventh Army off to western Sicily. The same self-assured Montgomery whose peacock style was the polar opposite of Ike's trusted lieutenant from Missouri. *That* Montgomery would be Ike's ground commander.[7]

Plenty of American generals, Ike and Brad among them, would have preferred to see Alexander at the helm. Bradley particularly smelled a rat, for he saw Montgomery pushing the Americans into a supporting role in France, just as he had with Patton. As he later wrote, "Had Alexander commanded the 21st Army Group in Europe, we could probably have avoided the petulance that later was to becloud our relationships with Montgomery. For in contrast to the rigid self-assurance of General Montgomery, Alexander brought to his command the reasonableness, patience, and modesty of a great soldier."[8]

Ike privately agreed with Bradley. But Sir Alan Brooke, the Imperial General Staff chief, held a dim view of Alexander's leadership skills, and he pushed hard for Montgomery's appointment. Churchill, who preferred Alexander, uncharacteristically declined to press the point, so the Allied ground commander would be the hero of El Alamein.[9]

Although he couldn't touch the senior Allied appointments, Eisenhower had a free hand in selecting the staff of Supreme Headquarters, Allied Expeditionary Forces, or SHAEF, as it was universally known. As the senior American general in Europe, he was also entitled to appoint or veto any American division, corps, or army commander who wanted to work in Europe, subject only to Marshall's concurrence.

Learning from his past experiences with Fredendall, Clark, and Mockler-Ferryman, Eisenhower was not about to let anyone he didn't completely trust near OVERLORD. From his office in London, he reached down to Algiers and stripped away the cream of the Mediterranean crop, starting with Beetle Smith, his chief of staff. Marshal Tedder, Ike's quiet, pipe-smoking air chief in the Mediterranean, would serve as deputy supreme commander and de facto air coordinator. To manage the theater's logistical octopus, Ike appointed the imperious Lieutenant General John C. H. Lee as head of the Army Supply Corps, a branch everyone still referred to by its old name, Services of Supply, or, in GI jargon, "Shit on a Shingle" (the foot soldiers' affectionate name for government-issue chipped beef on toast). Before long, Pink Bull, Ken Strong, T. J. Davis, and the rest of Ike's inner circle at AFHQ had rejoined their captain under the SHAEF umbrella. Eisenhower retained COSSAC's incumbent midlevels—assistants to the assistants, deputy assistants to the assistants, and the like—but he banished to the Mediterranean the ETO's senior American, General Devers, whom he didn't want around his headquarters.[10]

As for his field generals, Ike already had the reliable Omar Bradley firmly ensconced at First Army, and on December 23 he asked Marshall to assign Bradley command of the U.S. army group once it was activated. After a good deal of discussion, Marshall agreed, and Ike and Brad spent several weeks selecting generals for key command positions. They agreed that Courtney Hodges, in whom Brad reposed much confidence, would lead First Army when Brad moved up to army group, and he would act as the army's deputy commander until then. Gee Gerow, Ike's close friend, would command V Corps, one of the two assault forces. For the other assault corps, Ike and Brad interviewed several promising candidates before settling on Major General J. Lawton "Lightning Joe" Collins, a veteran of the horrific battles of Guadalcanal and Guam. Digging below corps level, Brad and Eisenhower worked through their lists of potential division leaders until they had the NEPTUNE command chain filled out.[11]

Notwithstanding the bad press he attracted like rusty nails to a magnet, George Patton, Ike decided, would command Bradley's second American army, the flanking force that would come ashore once First Army had created enough running room for an attack against Brittany. Ike wanted a hard fighter on his team, and in meetings with Marshall in Washington he once more went to bat for his trusted warhorse. When Marshall wondered aloud whether George could subordinate himself to Bradley and Montgomery, Ike insisted that Patton was the man for his job. He wrote substantial checks on his credibility account with the War Department to vouchsafe Patton's future conduct, and he assured Secretary Stimson, "It is my conviction that [Patton] has really learned his lesson and I expect him to do such good work in the future, that his past offenses will be forgiven, even by his most severe critics."[12]

Ike had been aware of OVERLORD's broad outline since mid-October, and he hadn't liked what he had seen. Based on estimates of landing craft then available, the COSSAC plan called for three divisions to assault the beaches around Caen, in the French province of Normandy. The flaws in a three-division invasion of a coastline defended by fifty divisions were so obvious that, he later confessed, he wasn't even sure he wanted the job of Supreme Commander.[13]

Eisenhower and Montgomery independently concluded that the plan needed more muscle up front, and Ike and his staff spent the next several weeks recarving OVERLORD's basic parameters from recommendations by Montgomery, Beetle, and others. As usual, it was a question of optimizing trade-offs, the biggest one being over the size of the beach assault. Eisenhower's insistence on OVERLORD's expansion to five divisions from the original three better guaranteed success of the landings. But it also carried a price—a delay from May until early June, which might make operations later in the year more difficult.

The invasion's date and composition were two of the many thorny compromises that piled upon each other and exponentially sharpened the risks. The amendments to the COSSAC plan also created uncertainty among his planners, and Ike was determined to avoid the problems that had plagued his staff during the run-up to TORCH. So after listening to competing views, he announced he would convene a meeting of his ground, air, naval, and logistical chiefs on January 21 to lay down the invasion's broad structure.[14]

On the appointed morning, Kay drove Ike to Norfolk House, his old headquarters from the pre-TORCH days. There, consistent with military protocol, the MPs had marked parking spaces assigned in order of seniority; Ike, being Supreme Commander, was assigned the Number One slot, the parking space closest to the door, and Kay in her usual businesslike fashion drove toward the building's entrance. But when Kay wheeled the olive drab Packard into the parking lot, she and Ike saw a huge, shiny Rolls-Royce parked in spot Number One. Monty's car.

Kay began to growl in her low, Gaelic tone, and she made ready to hammer things out with Montgomery's impertinent chauffeur. But Ike, not wanting things to get off on the wrong foot, told "Skib" to let it drift.

"That's okay now," he cautioned her. "Don't say anything. It just doesn't matter."[15]

It would be a long meeting.

By the time Allied planners had finished their long meeting, OVERLORD called for airborne night drops and a five-division assault against beach sectors designated SWORD, JUNO, GOLD, OMAHA, and UTAH. On the American side, the first order of business would be to capture Omaha and Utah beaches, then secure the large port at Cherbourg on Normandy's Cotentin Peninsula. Cherbourg, in turn, would allow the Allies to land reinforcements and supply the armies as they drove toward Paris and beyond. From the Cotentin, Bradley's forces would move southwest into Brittany, capture the port of Brest, then turn east to drive the Germans against the Seine River near Paris.

The British and Canadians would operate on the east side of the Cotentin. Storming ashore at Sword, Juno, and Gold, Montgomery's Second British Army would capture the critical road juncture at Caen on the first day, then press toward the open country near Falaise. Montgomery, in charge of the overall plan but naturally more focused on the British side, cautioned that the Germans would put their strongest forces before Falaise. The best the British and Canadians could probably hope for, he suggested, was to pin down the enemy's mobile reserves while the Americans broke out of the beachhead.[16]

Though Hitler fielded over fifty divisions scattered throughout France and the Low Countries, it was an article of faith among SHAEF planners that they could win the battle for Normandy if the Germans could not throw more than thirteen divisions against them by the operation's third day. The key was to get off the beaches and push inland before Rommel's reserves, ten panzer and *panzergrenadier* divisions and seventeen field infantry divisions, converged on the fragile beachhead.[17]

In the flurry that followed the January 21 conference, Ike Eisenhower had a lot on his plate and very little time to think of himself. But in his few moments of quiet he began wondering of what the world—the Western world, anyway—thought of him. He was so often characterized by the press as a "smiling chairman" or "coordinator," rather than a soldier or general, that he wondered, with more than academic detachment, whether his legacy would be political rather than military. After all, a big part of his job was playing peacemaker between British and American, air and ground, field and logistic, and a host of small yet vital cogs that drove the giant Allied machine. His own job description, set forth in a SHAEF memorandum that March, listed eleven responsibilities of the Supreme Commander; more than half of those jobs began with the word "coordinate." Ike complained that British newspaper columnists "try to show that my contributions in the Mediterranean were administrative accomplishments and 'friendliness' in welding an Allied team. They dislike to believe that I had anything particularly to do with campaigns. They don't use the words 'initiative' and 'boldness' in talking of me, but often do in speaking of Alex and Monty."[18]

If they only knew, thought Ike. He had ordered the attack on Pantelleria. He had stiffened the Americans at Kasserine. He gave the go-ahead for AVALANCHE and HUSKY. "It wearies me to be thought of as timid, when I've had to do things that were so risky as to be almost crazy," he grumbled.[19]

By February, Beetle's advance men had erected enough temporary buildings to move SHAEF into Bushy Park, a former Eighth Air Force headquarters near Kingston upon Thames. Surrounded by an eight-foot-high stone wall and guarded with white-helmeted MPs dubbed "Ike's snowballs," Bushy Park lay not far from Telegraph Cottage, of which Ike had many fond memories from 1942, and before long he and his entourage—now expanded to include a mess sergeant, a waiter, a cook, and a tailor—moved the Eisenhower household back into the cottage.[20]

At his new headquarters, code-named WIDEWING, Ike settled into Building C, a corner shack with a tin roof and oppressive fluorescent lights. His Spartan office featured a desk with two telephones, pictures of his mother, Mamie, and John, and drawers filled with boxes of cigarettes. Heating, aside from the cigarettes, was nonexistent, and in the winter months Butch's teeth chattered, aides piled on coats and scarves, and secretarial fingers grew numb. Ike seemed to have a hospital nurse treating him for a throat cold or some similar affliction nearly every day, and he struggled through the dreary winter months without even the small comfort of Telek, who was stuck in mandatory quarantine for six months after his return from Africa. The Scottie's place was taken, temporarily, by a scrawny housecat named Shaef.[21]

Ike sure missed his dog.[22]

It was a complicated time for him professionally, and Ike struggled to keep his head above water. Staring down from the apex of a pyramid that incorporated over seven thousand ships manned by 195,700 sailors and merchant mariners, Eisenhower's ground force consisted of thirteen U.S. infantry divisions, ten British infantry divisions, eleven armored divisions, four airborne divisions, and innumerable commando, Ranger, supply, and engineering brigades. His British air force boasted 226 squadrons of heavy bombers, light bombers, fighters, night-fighters, photo-reconnaissance craft, and troop carrier planes, while his American force included another 161 squadrons. And every man in every unit had to be fed, housed, cared for, trained, supplied, paid, led, and kept out of trouble.

The challenges were massive, almost incomprehensible, and were far more intimidating than those that Ike had wrestled with before the TORCH landings. But over the months of peaks and valleys, Ike had learned to become a dogged optimist. He kept his mind fixed on the progress of the moment, not the mountains behind the mountains that faced him, and in this way he moved from one precipice to the next, like a mountaineer scaling a thousand-foot cliff ten feet at a time.[23]

At least the tired old issue of "British versus Americans" seemed to have been settled—in Eisenhower's house, anyway. The British worked hard to accommodate their American counterparts, and the Americans developed an appreciation for British planning methods. Each day the staff had American coffee at eleven and British tea at five, and these traditional breaks gave everyone time in which to resolve issues on a friendly, informal basis. The blended customs and Eisenhower's personal example cemented the bonds of cordiality, even friendship, among the men who wrote the orders for OVERLORD.[24] Ike hoped his field commanders would take the hint.

One old, personal matter that kept hounding Ike, though he refused to acknowledge it, was Kay Summersby. He had had Kay transferred back to England to serve as his driver, and most of Ike's colleagues, including some of his field commanders, found his friendship with her inappropriate. He had invited Kay to dine with him and Roosevelt back in Tunisia, and he brought Kay, who lacked high security clearance, to top secret meetings, responding to subtle hints from other attendees by declaring, "We have no secrets from Kay."[25]

"I *do* have secrets from her," Patton grumbled to himself. But George, like most other intelligent generals, played his cards close to his vest on personal matters involving his direct superiors. He said little of importance around Kay, and he made a studied habit of staying on her good side. Bradley, for his part, thought Ike's relationship with Kay was foolish—though not really any of his business. Jimmy Gault warned Ike that his conspicuous association with Kay would uncork talk best avoided. But whatever Ike's true feelings might be, he kept his own counsel on Kay Summersby.[26]

Brad spent the early months of 1944 organizing his command and noodling over how to put 50,000 men on a shore bristling with machine guns, mortars, mines, and artillery.

As commander of First U.S. Army, the plan called for him to work under Montgomery during the campaign's opening phase. But once he had liberated enough space to move a second army onto the Continent, Brad would move up to army group command, which would put him out from under Montgomery's thumb. Because of the role it would be expected to play, First Army was under enormous pressure to assemble the requisite divisions and train them for amphibious landings in an uncomfortably short time. To meet the OVERLORD schedule, General Kean, First Army's chief of staff, drove his men at a merciless pace to get ready for the big day.

FUSAG, or First U.S. Army Group, had more lead time than First Army, and it moved at a more deliberate pace. Its staff, under Chief of Staff Leven C. Allen, another friend of Brad's from Fort Benning, was, Brad remembered, "mild, unhurried, and unworried except during an occasional tussle with Monty." Bradley allowed his staffers to dress casually, no neckties or spit-polished shoes. His dim view of Patton's management style in Tunisia had given him plenty of ideas about how he would run things if *he* were in charge, and now he was in charge. Things would be different without George around.[27]

In stark contrast to his personal feelings about Patton, Brad was delighted to bring aboard Lieutenant General Courtney Hicks Hodges, the man who would command First Army when Brad moved up to Group. Bradley had idolized Hodges, who had worked his way through the enlisted ranks to become Fort Benning's commandant, and later, commander of the stateside Third U.S. Army in February 1943. Brad valued Hodges for his skill as a balanced commander, a man who, unlike Patton, had lost neither common sense nor dignity when the Army pinned a star on his shoulders. "I had implicit faith in his judgment, in his skill and restraint," Brad later claimed. "Of all my Army commanders he required the least supervision."[28]

"I personally assure you that if we speedily finish off the German in Sicily, you need have no fear of being left there in the backwater of the war."

It had been almost five months since Ike had written those words to George, and during that interminable wait George had undeniably been left in the backwater of the war. Ike and Brad were holed up in England, preparing history's greatest invasion, and George was fading into oblivion amidst a crumbling palace of despair.

As often happened when he was shunted to the sidelines, Patton's fitful energy gave way to a sense of persecution and self-pity. His blue eyes lost their old sparkle, and his thin lips curled into a scowl that was more genuine than staged. When the Fifteenth Air Force commander, Jimmy Doolittle, stopped by to pay his respects, George, feeling particularly sorry for himself, let his emotions pour forth. Doolittle recalled Patton choking back tears, saying, "I didn't think anyone would ever call on a mean old son-of-a-bitch like me." To Bea he wrote, *Send me some more pink medecin. This worry and inactivity has raised hell with my insides.*[29]

It would take quite a bit of pink medicine to quell George's insides, for he was becoming irrelevant, and he knew it. He knew he had himself to blame, and he freely admitted to Kay, "I always get in trouble with my goddamn mouth."

He clung tightly to his faith in an inalterable destiny, and with Bea's long-distance support he tried to remain philosophical about the limbo in which he had been left to dangle. "Very few of us fail to make mistakes," he told an old acquaintance. "This does not excuse mistakes, but it at least puts us in good company."[30]

Well, there was nothing he could do for the moment but wait. He had given the roulette wheel a hard yank, and now he would have to wait for the wheel to stop.

By late 1943, Fate's wheel had begun to slow perceptibly. As it turned on its axis, George Patton sat behind his rosewood desk and fidgeted. A prisoner on Sicily, he had nothing to do but stare at the wheel and wait for it to stop. He watched and watched as the numbers crept by—numbers that cared nothing for the man staring at them so intently.

Click, click, click, click . . .

Of course, as with many things in life, it was only the last number that mattered. Where one ended up, not the bumps and potholes along the way. Until the magic wheel stopped for good, to await someone else to grab the handle, none of the numbers ticking by made a damned bit of difference.

But it was hard for George to remember that, shunted off with worry raising hell on his insides. In an old, dilapidated palace on an island that was yesterday's news.

Click. . . Click . . . Click. . . .
Click.

Finally, in December 1943, George saw events moving in his direction. On the seventh, Assistant Secretary of War John J. McCloy told Patton that Ike had been selected to command the cross-Channel attack. The next day, when President Roosevelt stopped in Sicily on his way back from Cairo, the brass turned out in force to shake hands with their commander in chief. As George's turn came, the president took his hand, held it for a moment, and confided, "General Patton, you will have an army command in the great Normandy operation."[31]

The news sent a jolt through George's large frame, and moments later he unobtrusively broke away from the crowd and quietly moved into a nearby room. After glancing around to assure himself that no one was watching, he broke into sobs. He wept for several moments. Then, composing himself, he wiped his cheeks clear and defiantly marched to the officers' club for reception cocktails.[32]

Things were finally turning around. His destiny—and Divine Destiny— had protected him, and he would soon be saddling up for the biggest fight of his life. But as December lurched into January with no formal word of his new assignment, George feared he would fall victim to Army politics and bad luck. Two days before Christmas he told Beatrice, *"Destiny has never backed me up nor will it,"* and four days later he fumed to his diary, *"I wish to God Ike would leave and take Smith with him. They cramp my style. Better to rule in Hell than serve in Heaven."*[33]

On January 18, just after breakfast, his orderly came down to report that the BBC had announced that General Bradley had been appointed commander of all U.S. ground troops in England. Patton had little to say publicly, though the announcement set off a lengthy diatribe in his journal. Taking the measure of his former deputy, he wrote:

> *Bradley is a man of great mediocrity. At Benning in com-*
> *mand, he failed to get discipline. At Gafsa, when it looked as*
> *though the Germans might turn our right flank on April 5th*
> *and 6th, he suggested that we withdraw Corps Headquarters to*
> *Feriana. I refused to move. In Sicily, when the 45th Division*
> *approached Cefalu, he halted them for fear of a possible German*
> *landing east of Termini. I had to order him to move and told him*

that I would be responsible for the rear, and that his timidity had lost us one day. He tried to stop the landing operation #2 east of Cape D'Orlando because he thought it was dangerous. I told him I would take the blame if it failed and that he could have the credit if it was a success. Finally, on the night of August 16-17th he asked me to call off the landing east of Milazzo, for fear our troops might shoot at each other. He also failed to get word to all units of the II Corps of the second paratroop landing.

On the other hand Bradley has many of the attributes which are considered desireable in a general. He wears glasses, has a strong jaw, talks profoundly and says little, and is a shooting companion of the Chief of Staff. Also a loyal man. I consider him among our better generals.

I suppose that all that has happened is calculated to get my morale so that I will say "What the Hell! Stick it up your ass and I will go home," but I won't. I still believe.[34]

Around that time Bradley, still bitter toward George, sent Patton his first personal letter since leaving Seventh Army and since the story of the slapping incidents publicly broke:

Dear George:

I was sorry to see you get so much unfavorable publicity lately. I do hope they have found something else to write about and that your future career will not be affected. . . .

I was back about two weeks during which time I was kept very busy in Wash. except for two days at Governors Island and at West Point. I was supposed to stay more or less under cover, but then Gen. Marshall introduced me to the American Legion Convention at Omaha. I had to ride out with him to get a chance to talk to him. . . .

I hope this lull in the action is not getting too tiring. I sure have been kept busy here. I had rather be in the field than fighting on paper.

Best of luck.
Sincerely,
Brad[35]

Given Brad's feelings toward Patton at the moment, it was unclear whether the letter was intended to rub George's nose in his sorry plight, or simply catch up with him. But whatever message he was sending, George didn't have long to consider Brad's intentions. On January 22, orders finally arrived in Palermo directing Patton to report to Algiers, and thence to Britain, for further orders. On the morning of January 25, he and Charlie Codman bade their final farewells to the remnants of the Seventh Army staff in Palermo, turned the outfit over to Clark, and took the day's last C-54 to Prestwick.[36]

After a pea-soup flight to London, George was greeted at the airfield by Harry Butcher and Lieutenant General John Clifford Hodges Lee. Cliff Lee, a fifty-six-year-old classmate of George's, had Patton's penchant for self-aggrandizement and an appetite for creature comforts that dwarfed George's living standards. He assigned himself a beautifully furnished personal train to move about the country, his helmet was decked with triple stars front and back, and he defended his perquisites like Rommel with his back to the sea.[37]

Supply never gets good billing, but Lee's self-indulgences, his backroom politicking, his ostentation, and the natural inefficiency of a system supplying millions of men made him one senior general whom all field commanders could hold in quiet—and sometimes not-so-quiet—contempt. After working with Lee for a few months, George would subscribe to one officer's description of him as "a pompous little son-of-a-bitch only interested in self-advertisement," and it didn't help George's temperament when, on his arrival in London, Lee's SOS men had quartered him in a hotel room that resembled a garish bordello, its boudoir featuring a white bear rug, nickel-plated furnishings, and a satin-sheeted bed perched low under a lewd ceiling mirror.[38]

Patton's first day at his new job was not auspicious. He reported to Ike and received what he described as "a severe bawling out" for not counting to ten before making his typically abrupt comments. Ike wanted George to remember who was the boss was, and he wanted to make sure his pursuit general didn't behave like a bull in a china shop while in England.[39]

Having given George's leash another hard yank, mostly to set the ground rules, Ike informed George that he would command Third U.S. Army, a force that would follow Bradley's army onto the Continent. The basics laid out, Ike invited him to dinner at his place with Kay, Butcher, Jimmy Gault, and a few others. During the meal, Ike again berated George, chiefly to rub in the reality of who was running the European theater. Patton wrote that evening, *"Ike very nasty and show-offish—he always is when Kay is present—and criticized Lee for his flamboyance which he—Ike—would give a million to possess."*[40]

To Eisenhower's provocations, George remained contrite and obsequious. Butcher noted that every time Ike argued a point, Patton found a reason to agree with him. "He is a master of flattery and succeeds in turning any difference of views with Ike into a deferential acquiescence to the views of the Supreme Commander," Butch concluded. When the subject of George's temper came up, recalled Butch, Patton swore that "hereafter he certainly would be more careful as to the place he has a tantrum and certainly will not choose a hospital."[41]

Office politics never rests, even in wartime. As he established himself in England, Patton kowtowed to everyone in Ike's inner circle. He gave Butch his opinion that Ike was "on the threshold of becoming 'the greatest general of all time—including Napoleon,'" a message intended for Ike's ears. He also remained polite and deferential to Kay when, at Ike's request, she gave him a driving tour of bomb-ravaged London. Though he disliked Beetle intensely, he shifted his bootlicking campaign into high gear for Ike's Lord High Executioner. In one of his first staff conferences where Beetle was present, George wrote, *"I had the opportunity of letting him advertise himself. I let him do all the talking and played him up. Washed out mouth later."*

A month later, after seeing a post doctor about an infected lip, he said to himself, *"After all the ass kissing I have to do, no wonder I have a sore lip."*[42]

If Omar Bradley was unenthusiastic about Monty's arrival in the ETO, he was even less pleased with Ike's decision to bring George Patton aboard. "I did not learn that Eisenhower had proposed Patton as an Army commander until Ike arrived in England," he wrote years later. "Had it been up to me," he told Chet Hansen, "frankly I would not have chosen Patton. I had so many misgivings about Patton. I had seen so many things he had done in Africa and Sicily—particularly Sicily. . . . [I]n Sicily, there were a lot of things in which I thought he was not too much of an Army commander. . . . He did things almost one hundred eighty degrees different from the way I did them."[43]

To Brad, it was like drafting a middleweight boxer to play shortstop.

His experience with Seventh Army left him with the unalterable impression that George was long on tactics but hopeless on logistics. Brad held little respect for Patton's staff, and he was quick to offer his negative opinions to Ike and General Marshall. "I did not dispute George's brilliant dexterity in gaining ground," Brad recalled, "but even this striking talent of Patton's could not offset the misgivings I felt in having him in my command."[44]

Ike assured Brad that George would play ball. "All he wants is the chance to get back into the war," he explained. When Brad realized that Ike's mind was made up, he resigned himself to working with the boisterous cavalryman. But, as he later wrote, "I feared that too much of my time would probably be spent in curbing his impetuous habits." He later recalled, "Ike and George had been friends ever since they were lieutenants or captains together . . . been together a long time, well, ever since the first World War anyway when they were mixed up with tanks. So Ike got him back to England as the next Army commander. . . ."[45]

Well, he might have to put up with George, but he sure didn't have to put up with George's mouth. Patton's bloodthirsty speeches to his troops were alleged to have prompted at least one massacre of German prisoners in Sicily, and Brad fretted about what his loudmouthed companion would say to the English press. "It was this unhappy talent of Patton's for highly quotable crises that caused me to tighten the screws on press censorship at the time he joined my command," Brad wrote afterward. "Public relations will cuss me for it," he told Bill Kean, "but the devil with them. I'll take the chance. Tell censorship that they are not to pass any direct quotes from *any* commander without my approval. And I want to see those quotes myself."[46]

He had little time to review press quotes, however, as planning chores were endless for the man who wore two hats. For Operation NEPTUNE, Brad's First Army would land three infantry divisions between Caen and Cherbourg, a prized port city whose capture would give the Allies the means to push farther into France. The assault force would land on two beaches separated by an eighteen-mile gap around the Carentan estuary. The Big Red One and part of the 29th Division would land on the British right, at Omaha beach. The other beach, designated Utah, lay along the east shore of the Cotentin Peninsula near Cherbourg. The green 4th Division would assault there. Gee Gerow, an old friend of Eisenhower's and a solid soldier, would command the V Corps at Omaha and push inland to the road network at St.-Lô, while Lightning Joe Collins would command the VII Corps

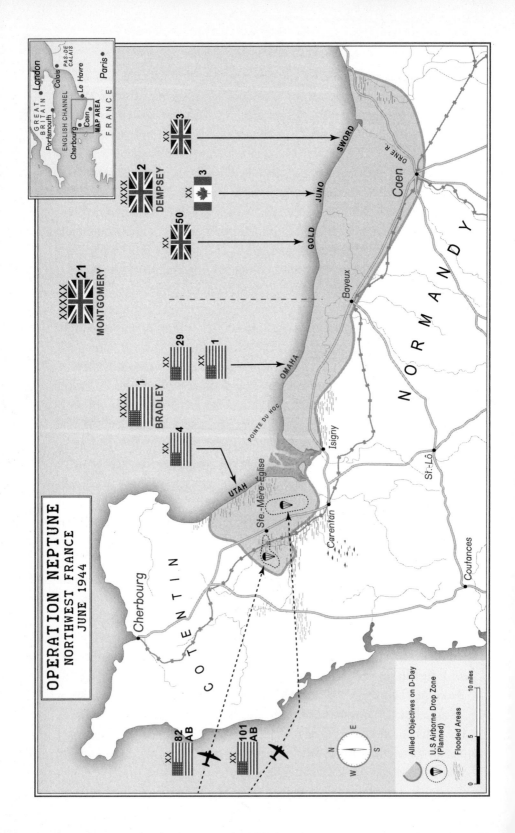

OPERATION NEPTUNE
NORTHWEST FRANCE
JUNE 1944

MAP AREA

GREAT BRITAIN — London, Portsmouth, Cherbourg, Caen, Calais, Le Havre, Paris
ENGLISH CHANNEL — PAS-DE-CALAIS — FRANCE

21 MONTGOMERY

2 DEMPSEY
3
50
3

SWORD
JUNO
GOLD

1 BRADLEY
29
1
4

OMAHA
POINTE DU HOC
UTAH

Ste.-Mère-Église
Carentan
Isigny
St.-Lô
Coutances
Bayeux
Caen
ORNE R.

NORMANDY
COTENTIN
Cherbourg

82 AB
101 AB

N
W E
S

Allied Objectives on D-Day
U S Airborne Drop Zone (Planned)
Flooded Areas

0   5   10 miles

at Utah beach, pushing toward Cherbourg. Once Cherbourg had fallen, Brad's army would receive reinforcements through that port until he had enough divisions to form two full armies. At that point, Brad would move over to FUSAG and run the American side of the adventure, while Montgomery would command the forces of the Commonwealth.[47]

To sort out NEPTUNE's details on a battalion-by-battalion, boatload-by-boatload basis, Brad's staff worked with a "planning syndicate" set up by Montgomery. Brad; Hodges; his G-2, Monk Dickson; his logistics head, the oddly nicknamed "Tubby" Thorson (Tubby was no more than average size); and the rest of First Army's staff spent hours poring over maps and schedules working out a fourteen-hundred-piece jigsaw puzzle whose final picture changed many times as the puzzle was assembled.[48]

While the invasion was, for the moment, a matter of troop lift, reinforcements, air cover, and supplies, Brad and his team knew the output of their work would be measured in blood spilled and lives lost. They took their jobs seriously, and their attitudes were reflected in their collective phobia of security leaks. Just to set foot in Brad's planning sections required BIGOT clearance, a super-secret classification for those select individuals entitled to know the invasion's two most critical details: the *where* and the *when.*

When Brad learned that an Air Force major general, an old friend of his since West Point, had let slip during dinner conversation that the OVERLORD invasion would take place before June 15, Bradley quickly informed Ike, who had the general broken to his permanent rank and sent home within twenty-four hours. "There were officers who afterward contended that Ike had acted with unnecessary harshness but I was not among them," Brad said later. "Had I been in Eisenhower's shoes, I would have been no less severe. Although no damage had been done, the penalty proved that rank has no privileges where the safety of men's lives is at stake."[49]

While Eisenhower operated at two levels above Bradley, a mere army commander, the classmates saw each other several times a week over lunches, meetings, dinners, and private chats, and they spoke several times a week on the telephone. They attended dinners with King George VI, Churchill, and Marshal Brooke, among others, and they often inspected Allied units together, sometimes with their usual retinue, other times joined by Churchill and Brooke.

Brad's friendship with General Eisenhower also entitled him to go directly to Ike with his problems from time to time, which was fortunate, since Brad considered the elusive General Montgomery aloof, overly theatrical, and quick to deride any suggestion that did not emanate from himself. Montgomery of El Alamein left Omar of Moberly, Missouri, with the distinct feeling he was simply tolerating a provincial bumpkin in the name of Allied harmony, much the same way he had with Eisenhower two years before. While Bradley was perfectly correct to Monty in public—he dutifully referred to him as "sir" or "General Montgomery" before others—in the privacy of his headquarters he winked at snide and insulting remarks of his staffers directed against the British general, just as he had with Patton in Sicily.[50]

On April 7, General Montgomery hosted a top secret conference to acquaint his many field generals with the overall plan. His staff set up a giant relief map of Normandy in a lecture hall at London's St. Paul's School, Montgomery's alma mater and the Twenty-First Army Group headquarters. There the diminutive general, wooden pointer in hand, strode over the map as he explained the OVERLORD plan in eloquent, authoritative detail, pointing out phase lines where he expected the front to run from D-Day to D-plus-90, the date the Allies would occupy Paris. After taking Caen on D-Day, he calmly told the audience, he would turn loose his armored divisions to run deep behind the front lines to "crack around Falaise" to the southeast. The Americans would take the port of Cherbourg, break out of the Cotentin's peninsular neck; then the two follow-up armies, Patton's Third U.S. and H. D. G. Crerar's First Canadian, would join the show.[51]

Montgomery's virtuoso performance at St. Paul's encouraged and impressed his audience, particularly the doubters in the American camp. Monty, they realized, was the genuine article, whatever his eccentricities and affectations. But the presence of those phase lines angered Bradley, and after the presentations, he asked for a private word with Montgomery.

He reminded Monty that he had previously asked him to discard phase lines, at least in the American sector, on the grounds that the lines tended to limit initiative. Once phase lines were reached, he had argued, commanders felt their jobs were finished until time to move against the next imaginary line. On the other hand, the lines could become setups for failure, since an army that didn't make its phase line objective looked as though it had suffered a check, which was not always the case. Montgomery had previously agreed to delete the lines, so Bradley thought, but across his great map snaked the lines Bradley had asked him to erase. General Collins, who had overheard the conversation, recalled afterward that a petulant Montgomery backed down, adding that it was the "first sign, but not the last, of Bradley's irritation with Montgomery."[52]

In late April, Bradley hosted Tedder, Ike, Gerow, and a bevy of lesser brass at Slapton Sands, near Plymouth, to watch Exercise TIGER, a dress rehearsal for the 4th Division's Utah Beach assault. As the exercise commenced, the generals crowded the deck of an LCI, salt spray lashing them as they squinted through binoculars at the huge invasion fleet. The naval bombardment began right on schedule, and the water was perfect, but to Brad's chagrin, H-hour was postponed, which left LCTs and other craft milling around, waiting for someone to give them the order to proceed.[53]

The exercise did not bode well for either Bradley or the 4th Division's men. The air strike had run late, and the clouds lay thick and low. "If they make a pass this late," Brad remarked to Lieutenant General Lewis Brereton, Ike's tactical air commander, "they may hit our troops."[54]

Soon the bombers screamed overhead. Ike, watching the bomb sticks fall, was more optimistic. He remarked to Brad that Bradley's rule of keeping troops fifteen hundred yards short of the bombing zone seemed a bit cautious: Why not move them in closer, say, five hundred yards, to take advantage of the confusion and immediate destruction the bombs wreaked among the defenders?

Just as Ike had uttered the words, an errant bomber unloaded its payload about five hundred yards short of the target. Ike let the matter drop.[55]

That evening, on the train ride back to London aboard *Bayonet*, his private car, Ike, Brad, Tedder, and Gerow discussed the problems elucidated by Exercise TIGER. The engineer organization had broken down, and air support had generally failed. Bradley solved the first problem by firing the beach engineering commander, but the second problem, air support, lay outside Bradley's control. After sampling the things that could go wrong for him on Omaha Beach, Gerow was so pessimistic that Ike had to give him a separate pep talk, reminding Gee that he would have the greatest assemblage of firepower in history behind him when the invasion began.[56]

Despite TIGER's cautionary tale, Bradley felt strangely confident, much more so than before HUSKY, when George had been at the helm. "When OVERLORD was widened to a five-division assault, skepticism went out the window and our tails went over the dashboard," he wrote. "This time I was afflicted with none of the doubts that had assailed me on the Sicilian invasion, for I had weathered the first and was rid of squeamishness on this second go-around."[57]

Before January was out, Patton had set up shop outside Knutsford, an old Cheshire city southwest of Manchester. His Third Army command post, code-named LUCKY, was set in a Georgian-Tudor mansion named Peover Hall, a country estate whose melodic English pronunciation was quickly corrupted to "Piss-Over Hall" by Patton's less-refined Yanks. Before long, familiar faces began turning up at Piss-Over Hall as George convinced Beetle to pull some of his Seventh Army staffers out of the Mediterranean and reassign them to Third Army. With Beetle's help, Patton expected to get most of his Sicilian staff—Koch, Muller, Maddox, and a few other trusted lieutenants—back into the fold.[58]

The sticking point was Patton's trusted chief of staff, General Hap Gay. To George, Hap was a solid chief, a loyal friend, and the perfect instrument for his plans. Ike agreed that Hap was a good egg, but neither he nor Beetle saw Hap as a smooth administrator, a leader up to the management of an army on the scale they contemplated for France and Germany. Ike urged Patton to remove Gay and appoint their old friend Everett Hughes as Third Army's chief of staff.[59]

Eventually, Ike decided to retain Hughes as his personal representative to Third Army. He told George he would not order him to fire Gay, but he wanted George to remove him anyway, as Hap simply wasn't the right man for the job. To George, however, firing Hap would be a breach of faith to a loyal friend, a friend whose record with Seventh Army was exemplary. When he balked, Ike admonished him, "You are fundamentally honest on the larger issues but are too fanatical in your friendships." To that George fumed, in the privacy of his diary, *"It is a good thing that some one is."*[60]

George knew his career was hanging by a thread, and he couldn't afford to antagonize Eisenhower further, at least until he had racked up some victories. *"Of course I was originally selected for 'Torch' through the direct action of Ike and therefore I owe him a good deal,"* George told himself. *"On the other hand, I have paid my way ever since. I am very reluctant to supersede Gay, but it looks to me and to Hughes, and others with whom I have talked, that if I don't I will be superseded myself, so I will have to make the change."*[61]

While he concluded he could not defy the "most powerful man in the world," his conscience bothered him, and he told Bea, *"I really believe I would retain more self-respect if I resigned, but I am not quite that big-hearted."* He went along with Ike's recommendation as a matter of self-preservation, but he felt like a heel for doing it. A few days later, still not having told Hap of his decision, he confessed to his diary, *"I feel very bad over this damn chief of staff business. I must do it in a way not to hurt Gay's feelings. . . ."*[62]

In the end, George buried the issue under a layer of Army bureaucracy. To appease Ike, he formally replaced Hap with Hugh Gaffey, a fine field general and a good friend of Gay's. But he moved Gay into the deputy chief of staff spot, which would keep him around until he could safely restore Gay by sending Gaffey back into the field with an armored division. By binding Gay to the altar, but not plunging the knife, George defused a potential bomb in his relationship with Eisenhower, but the incident was, to George, an object lesson about the lack of value Ike placed on personal loyalty. Henceforth, he would have to tread lightly with Ike and Brad.[63]

FIFTEEN

FIX BAYONETS

[Ike] has an unfortunate habit of under-rating all Americans who come under him and overrating all British and all Americans who have served elsewhere. I wish to God he was more of a soldier and less of a politician.

—George, February 18, 1944

THE FRENETIC PACE GREW MORE FRENETIC as D-Day drew near. Settling into their respective commands, Bradley and Patton recovered a fraction of the old camaraderie they had lost during HUSKY.

But proving the adage that complaints and orders travel in opposite directions, George's private thoughts were drawn to the many faults he found in higher echelons, particularly Bradley's. *"This outfit is not very clever,"* George wrote, referring to Brad's staff at First U.S. Army Group. *"They plan too minutely on some things and not minutely enough on others. They suffer from not having anyone in command."*[1]

It wasn't just Bradley whom George found wanting, for he was also concerned, as both friend and subordinate, with the way the pressure seemed to be getting to Ike. Waiting in Ike's office with Bradley one afternoon, George overheard his old friend bellowing to Air Marshal Tedder, "Now, listen, Arthur, I am dealing with a lot of prima donnas. By God, you tell that bunch that if they can't get together and stop quarreling like children, I will tell the Prime Minister to get someone else to run this damn war. I'll quit." George told his diary on March 1, *"Ike and I dined alone and had a very pleasant time. He is drinking too much and is terribly lonely. I really feel sorry for him—I think that in his heart he knows he is not really commanding anything."*[2]

But the prospect of real action in the near future blew fresh wind into his sails, and his private life was enlivened with the arrival of a four-legged aide-de-camp, a fifteen-month-old bull terrier whom he christened Willie. Like Telek, Willie was tenacious and loyal, traits George admired. Not that he was an easy dog to keep up with—Willie snored in his sleep, and amorously pursued bitches and pups alike. But he proved to be a better fighter than Ike's scrappy Scottie. His favorite pastimes, to Patton's delight, included chasing cars, waiting for George to flick him a table scrap, and being swung around in the air with his jaws clamped onto a tree branch. (Later, they would include hiding under the furniture whenever Germans shelled his master's headquarters.[3])

Like Bradley at II Corps, George felt at peace amid the familiar surroundings of his headquarters. In contrast to his stage persona—the helmeted general waving a riding crop at Gela—the relaxed George Patton did not march around Peover Hall ramrod straight, did not curse profusely. He ordinarily left his ivory-gripped pistols at the office and carried a small holstered automatic as his required sidearm. With Willie at his heels, he would shuffle about the grounds of Peover Hall, his beefy fists thrust into the front pockets of his overcoat, a stogie jutting from his pursed lips. He was busy, so he was happy.[4]

On April 7, the evening after Montgomery's brilliant exposition on the OVERLORD plan, George had dinner with an elite group of U.S. officers that included Ike, McNarney, Bradley, Beetle, and Assistant Secretary McCloy. There George made a pitch for overstrength divisions, in light of the casualties he expected to take, but he could not make any headway. *"That is because none of our topflight generals have ever fought,"* he complained. *"As usual, Bradley said nothing. He does all the getting along and does it to his own advantage. . . . All of them but me are scared to death."*[5]

As dinner progressed, the topic of conversation turned to the Inspector General's investigation into the prisoner killings Brad had brought to George's attention in the first days of the Sicilian operation. The lawyer for an American sergeant being tried for the murders claimed that General Patton's fiery speeches had influenced him to kill without mercy.

All agreed the charge was baseless, but to Ike, Patton's notorious speeches gave the claim a veneer of plausibility. He bluntly warned George to scale back his remarks to the troops.

George replied that he would stop giving strong speeches to the troops if Ike ordered him to do so. "Otherwise," he said, "I will continue to influence men the only way I know, a way which has so far produced results."

Ike frowned. He needed George, but he didn't need collateral damage from the 280mm howitzer that George called a mouth.

"Go ahead, but watch yourself," he said at last.

It was obvious to everyone that, in addition to his thousands of other worries, George's next outburst loomed large in the Eisenhower windshield. Patton's presence in England was, for the moment, a well-known secret, and his affiliation with Third Army was supposed to remain a secret for many weeks after D-Day. An open secret, George Patton, and a roving press corps was hardly a recipe for success.[6]

Over the next several weeks, George's opinions of his fellow ground commanders ebbed and flowed according to his erratic moods. On April 11, looking back with admiration on Bradley's accomplishments, he wrote to Beatrice, *"One year ago to day I turned over to Omar in Tunisia. I did not realize how great he was going to be at least for a while."* Two days later, though, he told his diary, *"I have a feeling, probably unfounded, that neither Monty or Bradley are too anxious for me to have a command. If they knew what little respect I have for the fighting ability of either of them, they would be even less anxious for me to show them up."*[7]

Occasionally McCloy, McNarney, or Hughes would stop by Piss-Over Hall, ostensibly to see how Third Army was doing, and while there the emissaries would remind Patton of Eisenhower's dire warnings. McCloy, for example, knew how Secretary Stimson doted on Ike's *enfant terrible*, and how "now and then when Patton would get in trouble Stimson would ask me to go out and calm him down or patch up the difficulty."

But since it was Ike who would be hung out to dry if George ran amok and smashed the china on the shelves, he asked McCloy to make it his special project to keep George out of trouble.

McCloy remembered that Ike "was very partial to Patton. Eisenhower saw his virtues and his qualities, and but for his rather tenacious confidence in Patton, and also the fact that the Secretary of War several times intervened with Marshall, who I think was on the verge from time to time of at least considering whether Patton wasn't more of a nuisance than he was worth, though Marshall was also aware of Patton's qualities. But it was primarily Eisenhower's confidence in Patton that kept him at the front. . . ."[8]

As McCloy recalled one incident shortly before D-Day:

Patton wasn't scheduled to take part in the original landings and he was making all sorts of noises about it. . . . Eisenhower got hold of me one time and said, "I know you've helped save Patton's skin, thanks to the Secretary of War, two or three times. . . . You go down and tell Georgie, I'm trying to get him, I'm going to get him in where he's going to have all the fighting he wants, but in the meantime you go down there and tell him to keep his God damned mouth shut!"

McCloy duly drove out to Peover and, after a lunchtime meeting, he maneuvered Patton into a small room where they could talk one-on-one. McCloy told George he was "getting to be quite a nuisance, that he was causing Eisenhower a lot of trouble and doing himself no good."

George drew himself up to his full height, chest out, war scowl in bright, fearsome bloom. "You're taking a great deal of responsibility on yourself, Mr. Secretary, to come here on the eve of battle, and to destroy a man's confidence in himself who is about to face the enemy," he said.

McCloy was taken aback. George wasn't supposed to argue with his superiors. After all, when Eisenhower had called him out on the carpet, George was the soul of contrition. But that, apparently, was only for Ike. Mere mortals got the Act.

McCloy coolly replied, "Listen George, if I thought I could destroy your confidence by anything I might say, I would ask General Eisenhower to remove you."

George, ruffled to the core, withdrew behind a sullen scowl. He muttered, "Well, you'll never hear another word out of me."[9]

"You'll never hear another word out of me."

George had meant what he said. After SHAEF announced General Patton's presence in England in mid-April, he knew the press would be after him for quotes, and he knew he'd have to take particular care to keep his words from biting him where it counted most. So to play it safe, he would simply stick to kind, polite things. Positive, cheerful things. Unquotable things. Words nobody could raise a ruckus over. While he'd always be Blood and Guts to his public, he would make damned certain the public saw the benevolent side of George Patton, the affable fellow who hosted dinners for Bob Hope and loved his dog and treasured the lives of his men. The man who refused to say anything worth printing.[10]

Patton found an opportunity to play goodwill ambassador on April 25, when he received an invitation to speak at the opening of a Welcome Club in Knutsford. To play it safe, he showed up for the event fifteen minutes late, hoping any journalists in attendance would think he had skipped the party and would leave early. But when he arrived, he saw photographers snapping his picture, and he made them promise not to publish the photos. The austere chairwoman who introduced General Patton reiterated the unofficial nature of his visit, which George took to mean that any reporters would consider his remarks "off the record" and keep them out of the papers.[11]

Thus insulated from danger, George flashed his bucktoothed smile as he marched up to the podium. Shooting for a fine diplomatic performance, he began his remarks with an upbeat if well-worn quip:

"I feel that such clubs as this are a very real value, because I believe with Mr. Bernard Shaw, I think it was he, that the British and Americans are two people separated by a common language. . . ."

Smiles, a few polite nods from the audience.

"Since it is the evident destiny of the British and Americans, and, of course, the Russians, to rule the world, the better we know each other, the better job we will do."[12]

Smiles, a few more polite nods.

George made a few more pro forma remarks about everyone doing their part for the war effort, goodwill among allies, and so on. Then, with a smile, he ceded the floor. He shook a few hands, the band played "God Save the King," and the audience dispersed to admire the new Welcome Club.[13]

A nondescript reporter sitting in the nondescript audience recorded Patton's "rule the world" comment without including the words "and, of course, the Russians." He filed his story with the censors, who passed the article because the speech raised no apparent security issues. The story was scheduled to run the next day.

Knowing nothing of the reporter or his story, George went to bed that night confident that no one could possibly misconstrue such dull, pedestrian remarks. *"I was really trying to be careful,"* he told his diary.[14]

* * *

In Washington two days later, General Marshall opened his newspaper to read that General Patton had announced that Britain and the United States—not their Soviet allies—were destined to rule the world.

He couldn't believe it. Flipping to the editorial pages of *The Washington Post,* the capital's most conspicuous political weather vane, he read the column on his general. The press was howling once again about General George Patton, the loose cannon who had the temerity to suggest the postwar world order. Republicans eyeing the 1944 elections seized on George's comments as another example of the Roosevelt Administration's inept handling of the war. Alluding to the slapping incidents, the *Post* editorialized, "General Patton has progressed from simple assaults on individuals to collective assault on entire nationalities." Echoing the words of George's father a quarter-century earlier, the influential paper declared, "We think that Lieutenant Generals . . . ought to talk with rather more dignity than this. When they do not they risk losing the respect of the men they command and the confidence of the public they serve."[15]

The Chief, sitting upright in his overstuffed War Department chair, called for a stenographer. He had a message for General Eisenhower.

While Ike was at Slapton Sands observing the TIGER exercise, a cable from Washington landed in his "eyes only" box in London. Beetle read the cable. It seemed George had given an informal talk to a British service club and declared that Britain and America, and not the Soviet allies, would rule the postwar world. It was, Marshall noted, not only a huge diplomatic gaffe, but it handed the Republicans a new stick with which to bludgeon the Roosevelt Administration. To make matters worse, a long list of permanent promotions—a list that included George S. Patton Jr. and Walter Bedell Smith—would be held up in the Senate indefinitely until the furor died down. "We were just about to get confirmation of permanent makes," Marshall complained to Ike. "This I fear has killed them all."[16]

Ike blew his stack when Beetle called to relay the news. Even under a secrecy injunction, George was like a bull elephant that had to trumpet every now and then, just to let everyone know he was there. When Ike had to deal with Patton's squabble with the Navy he was merely concerned. When he brokered a peace between George and Tactical Air he was upset. When he had to pass judgment on the slapping incidents, he was anguished.[17]

Now he was simply tired—tired and angry. Tired of the same old story, tired of the same blister rubbing and swelling and bursting. As Supreme Commander, there were some nuisances he shouldn't have to bear, and one of those nuisances was George's six-month calendar of sin and penitence.[18]

Back at Widewing, Ike stomped around his office, swearing and chain-smoking as he decided what to do. "I'm just about fed up," he told Bradley. "If I have to apologize publicly for George once more, I'm going to have to let him go, valuable as he is. I'm getting sick and tired of having to protect him. Life's much too short to put up with any more of it."[19]

Brad nodded. Patton had to go, he agreed, since there were plenty of other commanders in the theater who were team players, plenty of generals who wouldn't burden their superiors with the theatrics George excelled at. Life, in or out of uniform, was indeed too short to put up with the man's antics. It was time to get rid of him, this time for good.[20]

On April 29, Eisenhower cabled Marshall to complain that Patton was *"unable to use reasonably good sense in all those matters where senior commanders must appreciate the effect of their own actions upon public opinion and this raises doubts as to the wisdom of retaining him in high command despite his demonstrated capacity in battle leadership. . . . I have grown so weary of the trouble he constantly causes you and the War Department, to say nothing of myself, that I am seriously considering taking the most drastic action."*[21]

Through the grind and frustrations of work that day, Ike's mind kept drifting back to George's inability to stay quiet. Ike couldn't get the irritation out of his head, and that afternoon he supplemented his earlier cable to Marshall with an even more blunt message:

> *Frankly I am exceedingly weary of his habit of getting everybody into hot water through the immature character of his public actions and statements. In this particular case investigation shows that his offense was not so serious as the newspapers would lead one to believe, and one that under the circumstances could have occurred to almost anybody. But the fact remains that he simply does not keep his mouth shut.*[22]

At the same time, Ike squirmed at the thought of losing a heavy hitter like George. When the Nazis counterattacked in France, Ike knew he might live to regret his decision—and some men might not live to regret

Ike's decision. Moreover, Ike's political weather vanes didn't seem to point toward Patton's relief. Marshall told Eisenhower it would be the Supreme Commander's call whether to give George the boot, though the Chief acknowledged, "Patton is the only available Army Commander for his present assignment who has had actual experience fighting Rommel and in extensive landing operations followed by a rapid campaign of exploitation." Marshall seemed content to keep George for the good of the operation, if Ike was correctly reading between the lines, and Churchill, to whom Ike had mentioned the incident, waved it off as a tempest in a teacup; good men were hard to find. (Though he didn't mention it to Ike, the headstrong prime minister had privately made the same boast a year earlier.[23])

George learned that his remarks had found their way into print when SHAEF's public relations office called Hap Gay on April 26 to ask what Patton had said—and whether he had included the Russians in his "rule the world" remark. The next day, Bedell Smith, invoking Ike's authority, called to chew him out, remarking bitterly that George's "unfortunate remarks" had cost them both their promotions. He ordered George never to speak in public again, even to his divisions, without submitting his statements in writing to Ike's office in advance.[24]

George bit his tongue and played the part of a penitent sinner. He knew there was no point in arguing, and he couldn't afford to provoke Beetle further. But after he hung up with the Hoosier, his fury erupted and he spewed venom to his confidants. *"As far as I am concerned every effort is made to show lack of confidence in my judgment and at the same time, in every case of stress, great confidence in my fighting,"* he wrote. *"None of those at Ike's headquarters ever go to bat for juniors, and in any argument between the British and the Americans, invariably favor the British. Benedict Arnold is a piker compared to them and that includes Lee as well as Ike and Beedle. . . . 'God show the right' and damn all reporters and gutless men."*[25]

What was so frustrating was that he *wasn't guilty* of this particular sin. Or at least, he didn't think so. He immediately dispatched associates to contact several of those present at George's speech, and obtained signed statements from the chairwoman of the event, a Royal Navy officer, and U.S. and British aides certifying that he had included the Russians in his "rule the world" reference.[26]

Beyond that, George could only hope Ike wasn't through with him.

The first step in Ike's now-standard "jacking-up" process was to send

George a harsh personal letter. The tone of this one was little different from the one he wrote the previous August:

> *My attitude with respect to this case is not so much concerned with the effects of this particular incident as it is with the implications that you simply will not guard your tongue in spite of the most drastic instructions and orders. I have warned you time and again against your impulsiveness . . . and have flatly instructed you to say nothing that could possibly be misinterpreted. . . . You first came into my command at my own insistence because I believed in your fighting qualities and your ability to lead troops in battle. At the same time I have always been fully aware of your habit of dramatizing yourself and of committing indiscretions for no other apparent purpose than of calling attention to yourself. I am thoroughly weary of your failure to control your tongue and have begun to doubt your all-round judgment, so essential in high military position.*

His verbal flogging administered, Ike hedged. *"My decision in the present case will not become final until I have heard from the War Department,"* he told George. *"I want to tell you officially and unofficially that if you are again guilty of any indiscretion in speech or action . . . I will relieve you instantly from command."*[27]

When Ike's letter hit George's desk, the old soldier was horrified. Worse than enduring the humiliation of another jacking-up was the knowledge that he had imperiled other officers who were up for their hard-earned permanent promotions. To George, that was not just an indiscretion; it was a betrayal of his brother officers, and he placed a call to the reliable Ev Hughes and asked to have Ike withdraw George's name from the promotion list. He groused, "You are probably damn fed up with me, but certainly my last alleged escapade smells strongly of having been a frame-up in view of the fact that I was told that nothing would be said, and that the thing was under the auspices of the Ministry of Information who was present. . . ."[28]

Hughes tried to reassure George, telling him that Ike had drafted a cable to Marshall sending him home, but after reading the witness statements, simply muttered, "Oh, hell," and tore the message up.[29]

Perhaps the worst was over. But Patton's sixth sense told him that danger lay ahead. Besides, Hughes, one of Ike's "old guard," was not always the most reliable source around SHAEF these days.[30]

Sinking into a great, sucking hole of self-pity, George again saw himself as a victim. He wrote his daughter Ruth Ellen, *"I have caught nothing but hell for nearly a year now. All I want to do is win the war and everyone seems to think that all I want is notoriety which I despise. . . . [T]he soldiers think I am wonderful, but the Press??? Bah! Jesus only suffered one night but I have had months and months of it, and the cross is not yet in sight, though probably just around the corner."*[31]

Returning from church on the last day of April, George received a call from SHAEF ordering him to report to Ike's office in London. The next morning, a very worried George caught a train for the five-hour trip.[32]

Ike told Harry Butcher, "he was afraid Patton's goose was cooked. Patton had violated Ike's order, i.e., no public speeches and interviews for the press. . . . The furors raised by the Press and in Congress simply emphasized Patton's instability and Ike was fearful that he would be unable to save him this time. In fact, Ike said Patton's chance of retaining his command was only one in a thousand."[33]

As a tired Eisenhower told Marshall,

> *After a year and a half of working with him it appears hopeless to expect that he will ever completely overcome his lifelong habit of posing and self-dramatization which causes him to break out in these extraordinary ways. Starting with the incident involving censorship and Colonel Lambert in January of '43, I have time and again earnestly advised and instructed him along this one line and finally went to the point of giving him unequivocal orders and warnings. . . . [H]is whole record combined with the explosive effect his latest outbreak is having in the United States, leads me to believe that disciplinary action must be taken. It is a pity but that is the way I feel about it, and, as I said before, my decision will be along the lines indicated except in the unlikely circumstance that Patton can produce additional mitigating evidence.*

He concluded: *"I have sent for Patton to allow him the opportunity to present his case personally to me. On all of the evidence now available I will relieve him from command and send him home unless some new and unforeseen information should be developed in the case.*"[34]

The "new and unforeseen information" Ike was looking for had nothing to do with George's remarks, and everything to do with his replacement. Lucian Truscott, who commanded the Third Division in Sicily, was the obvious choice. An aggressive, old-school cavalryman who had orchestrated amphibious landings in Morocco and Sicily under Patton's tutelage, Truscott, like George, was adept at rapid pursuit, but he didn't have George's political baggage. Or George's mouth.[35]

Old Blood and Guts squirmed nervously in Ike's waiting room as the minutes ticked by. In his creased jacket, riding breeches, steel helmet, and tall cavalry boots, he had the look of an overdressed cadet reporting to the disciplinary board—or the guest of honor at a military funeral.

Ike kept him waiting in his antechamber a long time—a very long time for a man who was unsure what rank he would hold when he left the Supreme Commander's office.

As the morning clock's hands edged their way toward eleven, Eisenhower's secretary ushered George into Ike's office. The door closed, and the two men stood alone, face-to-face, Ike's cigarette silently releasing its wispy ribbon of smoke.[36]

"George, you have gotten yourself into a very serious fix," Ike began.

George cut him off. "I want to say that your job is more important than mine, so if in trying to save me you are hurting yourself, throw me out."

Ike shook his head. "I've got all that the Army can give me. It's not a question of hurting me, but of hurting yourself and depriving me of a fighting Army Commander."

His temper growing, Ike told George that General Marshall had become fed up with his lapses. The Kent Lambert incident, the hospitals in Sicily, now this. His outbursts had "shaken the confidence of the country and the War Department." The Republican opposition was making an election issue of George's words and outbursts, claiming that even if General Patton were the best tactician in the world, his actions plainly showed that he lacked the judgment to command large bodies of troops. Ike said he had wired Marshall to wash his hands of his old friend.[37]

As Ike later recalled, George stood at attention during the tirade, shoulders back, eyes fixed. But as Ike drew out the moment, painting with sharp, cutting syllables a vivid picture of George's excommunication, the older man's emotions overcame him. His blue eyes welled with tears. Ike's message had broken through the tough exoskeleton George had painstakingly built since childhood and was tearing his insides apart.

Toward the end of the harangue, when Ike's tone, and perhaps hesitancy, implied some hope, George seized on it like a pauper begging his king for clemency. The old general swore he would use complete and sound discretion from that day on. Never again would he burden Ike, Marshall, or the War Department with his stupidity.

"In a gesture of almost little-boy contriteness," Ike wrote years later, "he put his head on my shoulder. . . . This caused his helmet to fall off—a gleaming helmet I sometimes thought he wore in bed. As it rolled across the room I had the rather odd feeling that I was in the middle of a ridiculous situation . . . his helmet bounced across the floor into a corner. I prayed that no one would come in and see the scene. . . . Without apology and without embarrassment, he walked over, picked up his helmet, adjusted it, and said: 'Sir, could I now go back to my headquarters?'"[38]

Ike told a SHAEF public relations officer after Patton's helmet fell off, fresh tears ran down George's cheeks. "I could no longer stand it," Ike guffawed afterward. "This was too much for me! I stretched out on the couch in my office and burst into laughter, which I now regret for it was, in retrospect, cruel. General Patton stood at strict attention, not even looking at me lying on the couch, laughing."

After George left his office, Ike said, "I had to tell someone, so I called in Beetle and told him what had happened. It is probably the only time in all the years of my long experience with Smith that I saw Beetle really lose himself in laughter!"[39]

The scene wasn't as far-fetched as it sounded, at least not to those who knew George. "Patton always lived at one extreme or the other of the emotional spectrum," Ike wrote many years later. "He was either at the top of his form, laughing and full of enthusiasm, or filled with remorse and despondency." George often wept at the sight of wounded men, of great deeds. And his own screwups.[40]

George left Ike's office, eyes rimmed red, his sagging cheeks more flushed than usual. He boarded the next train home, silently running over lines of poetry to keep his mind from drifting into black thoughts as the wheels clicked along the tracks. Although his contrition, charm, and combat value had gotten him out of an ocean of hot water since 1918, he had no idea whether Ike would have to throw him to the wolves. He scribbled in his diary, "I feel like death, but I am not out yet. If they let me fight, I will; but if not, I will resign to as to be able to talk, and then I will tell the truth, and possibly do the country more good. . . . My final thought on the matter is that I am destined to achieve some great thing—what I don't know, but this last incident was so trivial in its nature, but so terrible in its effect, that it is not the result of an accident, but the work of God. His Will be done."[41]

George spent the next day wondering whether His Will was to kick him home in disgrace. The more he contemplated his predicament, the more he must have felt like a Spanish fighting bull that has been stabbed and jabbed by the circling picadors, bloodied but unbowed, waiting for the matador to prance into the ring to deliver the final blow. From where he was standing, George couldn't see the name stitched on the matador's cape, but at this point the most likely name was SMITH, or perhaps MARSHALL. Maybe even EISENHOWER.[42]

While an unconcerned Willie lounged by his desk, George slipped into another black spell of distraction and uncertainty. The day after his meeting with Ike he wrote Beatrice, "I had a pretty terrible day yesterday. . . . If I survive the next couple of days it will be O.K. . . . But still I get in a cold sweat when the phone rings. . . . Well, we ain't dead yet."[43]

And he wasn't. Though George didn't know it, Ike was looking for a way to keep him on the team. For all George's blasted indiscretions, when it came to attack and pursuit, Ike had more confidence in George Patton than in any other senior commander.

"The flashy, publicity-seeking type of adventurer can grab the headlines and be a hero in the eyes of the public, but he simply can't deliver the goods in high command." Ike had written these words during the darkest days of the Tunisian campaign. "On the other hand, the slow, methodical, ritualistic person is absolutely valueless in a key position. There must be a fine balance. . . . To find a few persons of the kinds that I have roughly described is the real job of the commander."[44]

Ike had plenty of generals, but the overwhelming majority fit the "slow, methodical," Leavenworth mold. Most lacked Patton's hell-for-leather drive, his willingness to berate, curse, and threaten to get his men across the finish line. They lacked the single-mindedness, the familiar comfort with risk that was second nature to Patton. Ike couldn't find the methodical commander in George any more than he could find the flashy adventurer in Bradley. He needed both men.

On May 3, seven days after George's ordeal had begun, Ike sent his friend another "eyes only" cable. He told George, "I am once more taking the responsibility of retaining you in command in spite of damaging repercussions resulting from a personal indiscretion. I do this solely because of my faith in you as a battle leader and from no other motives." As Ike's press officer remembered, Ike followed up his cable with a personal call, concluding, "I expect, George, from now on that you will please keep your goddamned mouth shut. When it is time for you to speak, I will tell you! I intend to use you to the fullest—you will have every opportunity to get into all the combat you ever dreamed of. That is all for the moment!"[45]

For all Patton's gaffes, for all the times he had stepped in horse manure, Eisenhower retained just enough confidence in his old friend's discretion that he would allow George to make occasional low-profile remarks to his troops. He had warned him to keep his mouth shut, but he gave George just enough leash to do his job. Or hang himself.

Ike's shadow, Commander Butcher, penned the epilogue to the Knutsford story in another entry for Eisenhower's diary: "Patton's skin has been saved again. Ike told me last night that he had written a blistering letter to Patton and although he told him it would be placed in his official record, actually it had not been."[46]

"I am once more taking the responsibility of retaining you in command. . . ."

George's eyes zeroed in on that sentence. When a condemned man gets to the part where the court uses the words "reprieve," or "stay of execution," his interest in the rest of the court's decision drops perceptibly. He doesn't much care about the flowery language or the rigid logic that got the court to the place where "reprieve" or "stay" comes in. The other words are abstractions; "reprieve" is his reality. So it was with George.

But he read the rest of the cable anyway, and after discovering no land mines buried within the message, he called Gay, Stiller, Gaffey, and Charlie Codman into his office for a celebratory drink. He probably would have invited Willie if Willie weren't partial to water.

"Sometimes I am very fond of him and this is one of those times," George remarked of Ike. Relieved, he wrote Beatrice, *"Everything is again O.K. because divine destiny came through in a big way . . . but I was really badly frightened."*[47]

Of course, just because George had walked down the scaffold steps didn't mean he was off death row. There is a big difference between a reprieve and a pardon, and he had only won a reprieve. To keep his command, he understood he would have to guard his words carefully, lest anything get back to Ike, for God only knew how many more lives the California cat had left. Probably none.[48]

A letter from Secretary Stimson, one of Patton's most loyal and important supporters, drove home the message. Praising Ike's courage in keeping George on the team, Stimson warned him, "Each time you have acted or spoke in this irresponsible, reckless, and arrogant way, you have laid an additional burden on his back. The only way you can hereafter justify yourself and your commander is to keep your mouth absolutely shut until you have reached the beachhead and then, by successful drive and successful fighting, win your reputation back again as a soldier who can contain himself as well as conquer the enemy."[49]

Every now and then, Ike would send George a reminder of his tenuous hold on command. One day, while George was in London on business, a SHAEF colonel stopped by George's flat with a message from Ike. General Eisenhower, the colonel said, had asked the colonel to remind General Patton that he and his staff were to refrain from making any further public statements.

"What did Ike really say?" George pressed the colonel.

"He said you were not to open your goddamned mouth publicly until he said you could."

George burst into laughter.[50]

There was, Ike knew, one way in which Patton's flamboyance could be put to good use. In 1943, COSSAC planners had worked up an elaborate deception plan called FORTITUDE. The premise of FORTITUDE was that the German High Command, like everyone else in Western Europe, knew the Allies intended to invade the Continent, for the preparations were being made on such a vast scale they were impossible to hide. The German High Command, or *Oberkommando der Wehrmacht*, knew as well as anyone that an Allied invasion would require the capture of a major French port, and that port had to lie within range of Allied air cover. That meant the Allies would either hit the French coast around Calais, or slightly south, in Normandy, near Caen or Cherbourg. Thus, the only variables Ike and his planners could hide from Hitler were the exact date of the invasion and the particular stretch of beach they would hit.[51]

Allied planners knew the Germans fielded fifty-five divisions in the west. While many of those divisions were understrength and immobile, a few, like the *Panzer Lehr* and 10th SS Panzer Divisions, were real monsters. Field Marshal Erwin Rommel, whom Hitler had assigned command of the Atlantic Wall, deployed nine of his mobile divisions around the port city of Calais, while Rommel's boss, Field Marshal Gerd von Rundstedt, held his heavies, the I SS *Panzerkorps*, farther back toward Paris. Twelve German reserve divisions was the maximum number COSSAC planners believed the Allies could take on successfully at the outset; if the panzers managed to pounce on the five divisions struggling to get off the Normandy beaches, OVERLORD would be in deep trouble.[52]

To keep those panzers away from Normandy, Ike approved a deception plan that aimed to hold the imposing Fifteenth Army around Calais as long as possible. Tapping into Patton's notoriety, in February SHAEF submerged his army command under a press blackout and placed Patton in command of the First U.S. Army Group, a real headquarters commanding a phony invasion force based in East Anglia. A small army of carpenters and movie propmasters augmented Patton's force with a formidable array of inflatable tanks and trucks, stage-prop Higgins boats, empty tents, barbed-wire fences, and a constant stream of meaningless radio traffic to give German listeners the impression that something big pointed toward the Pas de Calais. Despite the skepticism of his fighting generals, Ike and his staff dearly hoped FORTITUDE would convince the Germans that the real blow would fall at Calais until Montgomery and Bradley could establish a safe beachhead.[53]

Patton would take no part in any army group planning, and he had no authority over a single soldier in the real army group. But SHAEF's choice of Patton was an inspired one, and George played the part magnificently, ensuring the public glimpsed him scowling for the cameras, Willie by his side. He wore his FUSAG patch and at various times he let slip tantalizing allusions to Calais as he visited real units. For military theatrics, George Patton was the best thespian this side of MacArthur.[54]

The Fifteenth Army notwithstanding, it was clear to Eisenhower that, as at Casablanca and Sicily, the unpredictable monster that would give him more grief than anything else on June 5, the presumptive D-Day, was the weather. In early June, the Atlantic blows mild and it blows harsh, as high and low pressure systems clash from the Azores to the Arctic. The winds churned up from these collisions stirred waves that could swamp the stoutest landing boat. As the competing systems twisted and pirouetted, making their way east, the Allies kept a close watch on the meteorological dance steps, for they held the fate of the Allied cause.[55]

To predict the weather's path, every Monday Ike and his senior commanders would meet with their weathermen and select an imaginary D-Day a few days hence. The meteorologists would give Eisenhower their forecast for Normandy on the target date, and Ike would make his hypothetical decision to invade or stay in port. The results of these games were not encouraging, but Eisenhower came away from these exercised with a thorough understanding of factors that would dictate the clouds, waves, and winds along the coast.[56]

"It is the same old story of gambling on the weather and knowing there is nothing that can be done about it," wrote an unhappy Harry Butcher. "This has always been the most anguishing period for Ike and now is no exception."[57]

It was not hard to see the effects of the grinding stress. Ike looked old, his left eye hurt from too much reading, and he couldn't shake a high-pitched ringing in his ear. Pressure was beginning to mount within Dwight Eisenhower again. Something would have to give, and soon.[58]

Omar Bradley shook his head when Ike reversed his decision to bust George. Why not make him MacArthur's problem, or let him blow his smoke to draftees in Louisiana?

Brad was smart enough to accept Patton's obvious value as a pursuit captain, but there were limits. The Army functioned as a team; you were either on the team or you weren't, and if you weren't, there were a thousand general officers on the Army's rolls who would kill to take your place. To Bradley, the question of George Patton, or for that matter, any man above lieutenant colonel, was that simple.

What galled Brad was that Ike never consulted him. After all, George Patton would be Brad's cross to bear, not so much Ike's, since George would be working for Brad. After railing about how life was too short to work with George Patton, the least Eisenhower could have done was talk to him about keeping the man on Bradley's team.[59]

Well, no use complaining, Brad knew. Few commanders get to pick their subordinates, and Brad had already spent enough time on the subject. He had an invasion to plan.

* * *

The more he saw of Rommel's defenses, the more Brad frowned at his chances. Allied intelligence now estimated that by the end of spring the "other fellow" would have fifty-eight divisions in France, including ten panzer and panzergrenadier divisions and fourteen to seventeen front line infantry and parachute divisions. On the American beaches, which aerial photos showed to be heavily mined and studded with obstacles, Bradley might face as many as four infantry divisions, and he would have to rush at least four batteries of heavy coastal guns. To top it off, the two American beaches were separated by the swamp-logged Vire Estuary, which would make cooperation among the assault divisions difficult.[60]

The planning phase, at least, had a familiar ring to Brad. It was not so different from an Academy exercise, where obstacles were set up and overcome on paper—papers not so different from those that crossed Brad's desk every day.

But planning was one thing. Execution—that was the rub, because the Germans had a say in how the battle would go once his men's feet were on the sand. H-hour, Brad knew, would simply be the opening, a king's pawn two to king's pawn four. Then Rommel would get his turn.

The solution to this unknown—at least, the best solution Bradley knew—was to find commanders who would make the right decisions, who would react quickly and whom he could trust to fight within the framework that he and his staff laid down. That was why a team was so essential, and that was why George Smith Patton was not cut out for a Bradley team.

As D-Day approached, Brad became tired, irritable. His quiet demeanor, legendary around his staff, gave way frequently to hard questions and implied threats. It didn't improve Bradley's mood that he would miss his daughter Lee's wedding in May, and around his staff he made no secret of his disdain for the unstable former Seventh Army commander whom Ike had decided to keep on the team.[61]

The boss's attitude naturally filtered down through First Army's janissaries, who loved to recall Patton's humiliation over the slapping incidents. Brad's aide Chet Hansen noted in his diary, "Never knew anyone in such complete disrepute as George." The captain of the MPs, Hansen wrote, "threatened to knock him down if he as much as spoke, and everyone ducked out for dinner the night he was here, especially Red O'Hare who dislikes him violently." During a dinner with Bradley, Hansen narrated how Brad's staffers lampooned a publicity photo of George. "His picture was ridiculous with the wrestling belt, the pearl handled revolver, chin back, staring at the sun," Hansen wrote. "Monk says it looks like the photos of Musso we saw in Sicily. I saw it and it does with the chin." Bradley laughed about the picture the next day, though he did remark that he was glad Patton had spent so much time with him, as he knew George's weaknesses better than anyone, and could keep the man in check once they were on the Continent.[62]

But Brad's first task was to get on the Continent, and stay there.

To complicate an already complex plan, General Bradley requested airborne drops at Carentan, near the juncture of Utah and Omaha beaches, and at the village of Sainte-Mère-Église, behind Utah beach. The air drops made military sense to a ground commander, since his paratroopers would shield the exits from Utah beach until the 4th Division could get its boots onto green grass. But to Brad's surprise, the air drop request put him at loggerheads with Ike's tactical air commander, Air Chief Marshal Trafford Leigh-Mallory.[63]

Leigh-Mallory, a dour sixty-four-year old Cheshire native with an acute sense of cost but little appreciation of benefits, feared the airborne landings would incur unacceptable losses and he vehemently protested the air drop portion of the operation. So much so, in fact, that at a planning meeting at Montgomery's headquarters, Bradley and Leigh-Mallory got into a shouting argument that was settled only when Montgomery sided with Bradley.[64]

Not content to let the matter rest with Montgomery, eight days before D-Day Leigh-Mallory ran to Ike with a balance sheet that projected 50 percent casualties among the paratroopers and 70 percent among the glider troops. Ike called Brad into his office and told him of Leigh-Mallory's objections.[65]

"It's risky, of course," Brad conceded, "but not half so risky as a landing on Utah Beach without it."[66]

Ike, ears ringing with prophecies of doom, later reflected, "It would be difficult to conceive of a more soul-racking problem." Once again he had to weigh two different approaches to minimize the butcher's bill in an operation where the butcher's bill would be unavoidably high. Between Brad's prediction of disaster without the airborne and Leigh-Mallory's warning of disaster with the airborne, Ike had to consider whether the Utah landings would become another Dieppe, another Kasserine, another Anzio.

Then again, Ike thought, Bradley hadn't steered him wrong yet. Eisenhower put a lot of stock in Brad's judgment, and when it was time to ante up, Ike would back Brad's play. He took a deep breath and announced that the airborne landings would go as planned.[67]

Brad spent his last few days in England ensuring that the plans, the arrangements, the logistics, all stuck. He visited the men who would pay victory's price, giving words of encouragement that, in their brevity, contrasted sharply to the bombast, profanity, and fluency of Old Blood and Guts.[68]

But if Patton had a history with terrible press quotes, Bradley was learning to watch his own back around the growing horde of reporters who would test the vigilance of his censors. During a visit to the 29th Division, Brad gave a pep talk to soldiers where he belittled rumored estimates of 90 percent casualties on D-Day. "This stuff about tremendous losses is tommyrot," he told them. "Some of you won't come back—but it'll be very few." Several days later he learned that his off-the-record remarks turned up in stateside papers alongside warnings of high casualties that Roosevelt, Churchill, and Marshall issued to temper public expectations. Embarrassed at the disparity, Brad punished the censor, raised hell with SHAEF's public relations office, and resolved to watch his words in public, even when reporters didn't seem to be hanging around.[69]

On June 1, Brad and George rode over to Montgomery's tactical headquarters outside Portsmouth for dinner with Monty and the two Commonwealth army commanders, General Crerar of the First Canadian Army and General Miles "Bimbo" Dempsey of the Second British Army. The gathering was congenial, almost lighthearted, considering the lake of blood that was to flow four days hence. It was the type of social gathering perfectly suited to George, a personality everyone took note of. There was much talk of where they would be "if all goes as planned," a caveat Patton had learned to distrust, and buoyant Montgomery predicted that the war would be over by November 1.[70]

When it was almost time to go, Monty's orderlies brought out glasses of port, and Montgomery proposed a toast to his army commanders, to whom they all drank. When no one jumped to respond, George stepped forward and raised his glass of the sweet, tawny liquid. "As the oldest Army Commander present," he said with a smile, "I would like to propose a toast to the health of General Montgomery and express our satisfaction in serving under him."[71]

George's compliment was not perfectly sincere—"lightning did not strike me," he remarked with mock surprise—and the toast did not endear him to Bradley, who was, though he didn't say it, not satisfied serving under Montgomery. But it was a fitting curtain call to an evening of Anglo-American camaraderie, a brotherhood all too likely to splinter once the men were on the Continent.[72]

George's good-bye to his Missouri comrade the next day was suffused with quiet emotion. His face growing red, George turned to Brad, took his hands in his own, and said, "Brad, the best of luck to you. We'll be meeting again—soon, I hope."[73]

Throughout southern England, dry runs were wrapped up, and Brad's men were herded into their staging areas, known around headquarters as "sausages" for the fat, oval shapes they made on operations maps. Though the plan called for Bradley to watch and coordinate troop movements from the U.S.S. *Augusta*, Patton's old command ship for TORCH, the bulk of First Army's command apparatus would be with Hodges aboard the converted freighter *Archerner*. Ike wanted Brad to stay with him at Plymouth, the invasion's command center, but Brad politely refused. "If we run into trouble on the landing, the decisions are going to have to be made aboard Kirk's flagship," he pointed out. "Our communications are all tied in there and that's where I belong."[74]

Ike nodded in agreement, and on June 3 Lieutenant General Omar N. Bradley carried his duffel bags aboard the *Augusta* for another ride to a foreign beach. "For the first time since Sicily," he wrote afterward, "I buckled on a pistol and bent my neck under the weight of a steel helmet."[75]

Bradley walked past a row of blue-jacketed salutes from the *Augusta*'s crew as his First Army "family"—chief of staff Bill Kean, intelligence chief Monk Dickson, operations head Tubby Thorson, Chet Hansen, and some signal officers—dragged up bags and footlockers stuffed with waterproof gas masks, pistols, Mae West jackets, vitamin pills, toilet paper, and sewing kits. The embarkation to Normandy was exactly as Brad wanted it to be. No ceremony, no fanfare. Just the straightforward business of war.[76]

SIXTEEN

PASSWORD: "MICKEY MOUSE"

I'm delighted with the performance of you and your troops.

—Ike to Brad, June 18, 1944

IKE STARED AT HIS WET, soapy hands as they scrubbed the dishes. *Lather, around in circles, rinse. Back in the rack, then on to the next dish.* Simple. Mechanical. Just like any of the Army's ten thousand other machines.

It had been years since Ike had had to wash his dishes. The dishes, like a lot of domestic accoutrements that cluttered his life, were the province of Marty Snyder, his mess sergeant, or when Marty wasn't around, Mickey, or Moany, or Hunt, or the other valets, orderlies, and aides responsible for that type of chore. They could do it better than Ike could, because that was what they did.

But as the invasion loomed, Ike's hands grew restless. His thoughts kept spinning over factors he could not control. Air superiority. Beach obstacles. Panzer divisions. The weather. His mind spun itself into a barrier no sleep could penetrate, and his body, denied the rest it craved, grew thin and threadbare. After tossing under the sheets nightly in search of the elusive slumber, he often quit trying. He would find himself up before daylight, shuttling a spatula across a cast-iron skillet with the deftness of a blackjack dealer while eggs sizzled or flapjacks browned.[1]

Stove to medium, add butter, crack the eggs, cook, and flip. Wash up.

The ritual seemed beautifully straightforward.

Eisenhower's other skillet was painfully overloaded with ingredients that probably did not mix—many of which he would never see, because they had

★ 317 ★

been added weeks or months earlier by thousands of nameless cooks somewhere up the line. And it was too late to do anything about those ingredients. Monty's men were embarked. Brad's men were embarked. Spaatz's air crews were standing by. Ramsay's fleet was ready. Patton had played his part in FORTITUDE, and the supply transports were loaded. Every one of the roughly two million men in Ike's command knew what he would be doing on the morning of June 5, 1944.

All but one.

As June dawned, the bright, clear English skies smiled at Ike's men, veiling a dark storm system crossing the North Atlantic. As a blissfully unaware General Eisenhower informed Marshall that the weather looked good for a June 5 landing, low-pressure fronts rolled like Thor's hammer toward the North Sea. Picking up the storm system at the beginning of June, the best meteorologists from Newfoundland to Scapa Flow studied every twitch and jig to figure out where the storm would land, when it would land, and whether it would be a puff or a howl. Timing was crucial, since the Allied force had only three days in early June when the tides and moonlight would accommodate the divergent demands of the Navy, airborne, ground, and Air Force: June 5, 6, and 7.[2]

Late on the third of June, Ike took the twenty-minute drive from his small trailer to SHARPENER, known more familiarly to its owners as Southwick House, a tall, ivy-covered mansion overlooking the Portsmouth Harbor, where ashen-faced weathermen talked pressure drops and Ike's senior commanders gathered to receive their final "go" order. Sitting in the high-ceilinged library, Ike opened the conference with a flat, businesslike tone.[3]

"Well, gentlemen," he began, "this decision, in the last analysis, depends on the weather, so I suggest we bring in the meteorologists right away."[4]

The lead meteorologist, RAF Group Captain J. M. Stagg, shambled into the room like a man being led to his own hanging. In his Scotch brogue, Stagg delivered some sobering news: a low-pressure area forming over the Shetland Islands would draw high waves and low clouds to the French coastline during the next few days, creating conditions far short of the minimum parameters for invasion.[5]

The admirals and generals set upon Stagg with questions about wave height, cloud ceilings, winds, and tides. Ike listened to the back-and-forth among them for several minutes. Finally, in a voice weighed down with care, he provisionally decided D-Day would be postponed for twenty-four hours.

Eisenhower's decision to postpone the mission would remain a tentative one, subject to revision if conditions changed, and he asked his college of cardinals to return at half past four the next morning, June 4, for another reading of the winds. At that time the high command would have one half hour in which to render a decision, so the fleet's sailing orders could be reliably canceled by six a.m.[6]

At the appointed hour, the soothsayers returned with their consensus: the wind, waves, and low clouds would make air missions impossible on the morning of June 5. Eisenhower paced the great room, hands clasped behind his back, chin set into his chest as he spun the variables to himself. His head would jerk up as he fired off a question to one commander or another, then he would lower his head, frown, and continue pacing. He asked his senior men for their views. The Navy and Air Force, the services most affected by weather, were convinced the show must be postponed. Among Eisenhower's advisers, only Montgomery was willing to launch the great crusade that day.[7]

As Ike told Butcher afterward, "Probably no one who does not have to bear the specific and direct responsibility of making the final decision as to what to do can understand the intensity of these burdens." Ike's besieged mind longed for an end to his ordeal, for himself and for the thousands who struggled under the tyranny of the wait. But the stronger part of Ike admitted that without clear skies for his air force—to say nothing of beach conditions afflicting the Navy—the operation was militarily unsound.[8]

Scanning the faces of his lieutenants, General Eisenhower quietly gave his final order: Operation NEPTUNE would be postponed for at least twenty-four hours.[9]

For most of Sunday, June 4, rain lashed the English coast, and as Ike was about to retire for a few precious hours of sleep, he learned from Butcher that the Associated Press had inexplicably issued a statement announcing that Allied forces had landed along the French coast. The AP retracted the story twenty-three minutes later, but not before CBS, Moscow, the Germans, and the rest of the world got wind of it.

It had been Eisenhower's worst nightmare, or one of them, but by now he was so exhausted, it didn't seem to matter. He could do nothing about it anyway. "He just sort of grunted," said Butcher. Then he fell into his bunk to sleep.[10]

As he trudged through the fourth of June, the man from Abilene sank into a depression as thick as the clouds blowing in from Iceland. He was killing time, waiting for the next caucus of his commanders, set for that evening. Ike walked the pebble-lined paths of his trailer grounds with NBC's Red Mueller, murmuring to himself as he squinted into the forbidding, spitting sky. He looked, said Mueller, "as though each of the four stars on either shoulder weighed a ton."[11]

As each hour passed, as each tankard of coffee went from pot to cup to stomach, Ike wrecked himself. His headaches ebbed and flowed. He battled an eye infection and high blood pressure. The ringing, the damned ringing in his ears, gave him no peace. "Ike could not have been more anxiety ridden," wrote Kay, who overheard him muttering, "I hope to God I know what I'm doing."[12]

Stove to medium, crack, scramble, cook. Keep the skillet hand steady. Try not to burn them to cinders.

As thick raindrops drummed against the tall French doors of Southwick House at half past nine, Group Captain Stagg strode into the dark, heavy library with a surprising announcement for Eisenhower's commanders. Unbelievable though it might seem, a "bubble" of high pressure had formed over Iceland and was moving toward the coast, carrying a brief window of clear skies. Beginning Monday night, June 5, the storm would abate just enough to make the invasion feasible on June 6. Barely.[13]

Ike's mind raced over the competing factors. Cloud ceiling, tides, rain, loading schedules. Naval bombardments. Moonlight, breakers, bomber cover. The matrix of conditions swirled through his thoughts like a Kansas twister. He spoke quietly, talking to himself, though others in the room heard him mumble, "The question is, just how long can you hang this operation on the end of a limb and let it hang there?"[14]

It would have eased Ike's troubled soul had he another half day to weigh the variables, but the sand had run out. Admiral Ramsay, the man charged with putting the soldiers ashore, gave voice to the deadline Ike knew was upon him: "[I]f OVERLORD is to proceed on Tuesday, June 6, I must issue provisional warning to my forces within the next half hour."[15]

Eisenhower sat in the Southwick library, among friends, yet a thousand miles distant. "I never realized before the loneliness and isolation of a commander at a time when such a momentous decision has to be taken," recalled Ike's unsentimental hatchet man, Bedell Smith. "He sat there quietly, not getting up to pace with quick strides as he often does. He was tense, weighing every consideration of weather as he had been briefed to do during the dry runs since April."[16]

After several moments of silence, the tension in Ike's face broke. "I am quite positive we must give the order," he murmured. "I don't like it but there it is. . . . I don't see how we can do anything else." His mind snapped to attention. It was all clear to him now.[17]

"O.K., we'll go," he said.[18]

With "Godspeeds" and "good lucks," the group broke up and men dashed to their command posts. OVERLORD was on, and events were no longer in the Supreme Commander's restless hands.[19]

"HORNPIPE-BOWSPRIT."

The laconic message clattered across the Teletype page in the signal center of the U.S.S. *Augusta* in the early morning hours of June 4. The message, forwarded to the First Army commander, told Brad that NEPTUNE would be postponed for twenty-four hours—a decision he understood but regretted, for it meant another long day of seasickness, tension, dank air, and unbearable waiting. His heart had jumped every time he saw a break in the clouds, only to plunge again as another rank of thunderheads swallowed up the sun's feeble rays.

Admiral Kirk had assigned Bradley the captain's cabin—a room occupied by President Roosevelt during his Atlantic Charter rendezvous with Churchill in 1941—but for all its comforts, Omar Bradley, like all infantrymen, felt vulnerable when packed like a sardine aboard a large, slow, floating target.[20]

To add discomfort to anxiety, just before the invasion Bradley's sharp nose welled up with a painful boil that forced him into the infirmary. To avoid a potentially debilitating infection, the *Augusta*'s doctor strongly recommended lancing the swollen welt, and Brad was forced to wear a sterile gauze bandage for the next few days as the wound healed. The man with the false teeth naturally felt a bit ridiculous, but he tried not to let it bother him. His image-conscious aides shunted camera-toting reporters away from their commanding general until his proboscis returned to normal, and Brad kept a show of good spirits throughout the day as the ship's clock crept forward at a snail's pace.[21]

Like every other officer, Brad passed the time worrying about details he could not control, and making small talk with the ship's company and his staff. He and Hansen revisited Patton's glorious entry into Messina—even on the eve of invasion, George's pomposity still rankled him.[22]

Waiting patiently for new orders to come in, Brad's mind spun through the countless details he would have his staff check and recheck. His war room, a cramped sheet-metal shed assembled on the afterdeck, lay uncomfortably close to a loud antiaircraft gun that required aides to tape lightbulbs, clock faces, and anything else prone to shatter when the gun went off. A Michelin map of France hung on one wall alongside beach maps featuring ominous red semicircles that showed fire arcs of coastal guns. Web gear littered the floor, typewriters lined one wall, and rags for wiping grease pencil marks off the maps accumulated in the room's corners in an entirely un-shipshape fashion.[23]

Of more concern to Brad than the mess strewn about the war room was his G-2's assessment of the weather that awaited the argonauts on the Channel's far side: *Low clouds and reduced visibility. Winds at seventeen to twenty-two knots. Choppy water. Five-foot breakers. Four-foot surf.*

"Doesn't look good," said Brad.

Monk nodded. "It stinks."[24]

Twenty-four hours later, *Augusta* and her sister ships were still bobbing atop the Channel's waters. Given the forbidding look of the western skies, Brad and his team were convinced Ike would signal a second postponement, to June 7, the last available day until late in the month. But when word reached the ship that Eisenhower had decided to forge ahead on June 6, Brad retired belowdecks. He yanked off his life jacket and fell asleep, uniform and shoes on, his mind slowly releasing its grip on the wind, surf, and cloud cover.[25]

There was no point in thinking of such things, anyway. Ike couldn't control them, and Ike outranked everyone. At least, unlike Sicily, Brad wouldn't ride in on a pillow cushion.

At 3:35 a.m., Bradley roused himself. As his mind shook off the shallow slumber, he heard the clang of the ship's bell and the call to general quarters. He slipped a Mae West over his shoulder, buckled his helmet, and hustled up the steep stairs to Admiral Kirk's darkened bridge, a heavy pair of binoculars swinging from his neck.[26]

The morning wind bit into the men's faces as they stuffed cotton wads into their ears, protection from the thunder of the Navy's big guns. There, off Omaha Beach, the man from Moberly would have a ringside view of the greatest amphibious invasion in history.[27]

* * *

What Brad saw didn't encourage him. The skies were dark and overcast. The surf was choppy, and the landing craft would have a heck of a time dog-paddling their way to the beaches. Worse yet, at the eleventh hour Monk had learned that the powerful German 352nd Division had been moved up to Omaha Beach, too late for anyone to do anything about it.[28]

But none of that mattered now. The airborne was already on the ground, and his men were going in, come what may. Brad's authority was now limited to the reach of his voice, and his job was to encourage everyone around him. So a tight, unfamiliar smile wedged itself onto Brad's face, concealing his feelings at the impending deaths of hundreds, maybe thousands of young men, and for the families back home who would soon receive a telegram from the War Department and a gold star for their window.[29]

NEPTUNE was a panorama no man that day would ever forget. Thirteen hundred RAF bombers threaded their way across the indigo sky, a thick, speckled ribbon of aluminum geese returning home after brutalizing the French coast. In the other direction came low-flying Spitfires, the van of a wave of 480 twin-tailed Liberators flying inland to deposit another 2.5 million pounds of explosives. Beneath them sat hundreds and hundreds of ships: landing ships, support ships, battleships, hospital ships, screening ships. Ships to land soldiers, ships to land tanks, ships to land bulldozers, bridging spans, and signaling stations.

It was the smallest of these craft that worried Brad the most, the boxy Higgins boats with their thirty-two sardines, and the experimental dual-drive Sherman tanks that plowed into the sea with only thin canvas walls to hold back the waves. Brad and Tubby shook their heads as they squinted at the breakers.[30]

Well, no point in worrying too much, Brad reminded himself. His men were far beyond the control of generals milling aboard their command craft. It was up to the men with rifles, men with mortars, men killing, men dying, men hiding behind beach obstacles and men calling the out-of-place challenge "Mickey," and the response "Mouse," with deadly earnestness. *Those* men, not Eisenhower or Montgomery or Bradley, would decide the battle. For the next few hours, Omar would watch and wait while the Navy's guns pounded the pillboxes and the soldiers did their bloody work. He had called the play, and the game was on.[31]

It was not until about ten that morning that the first reports began crackling in from Gee Gerow's V Corps. Gerow's report was not encouraging. It read, "OBSTACLES MINED, PROGRESS SLOW . . . DD TANKS FOR FOX GREEN SWAMPED."[32]

It was the "progress slow" part that worried Brad the most, because the battle raging on the beaches was not to hold Omaha's sand and shingles, but to reach those four vital exit roads leading to green grass and open country. Something more useful than a beach.

Though he tried not to show it, Brad's nerves wore thin as he learned of unexpectedly fierce German resistance at Omaha. When he considered how few troops stood between him and the expected German counterattack, his stomach tightened. From the moment the Allied fleet was spotted, time began working against the Americans; some 34,000 men and 3,300 vehicles formed Omaha's first attack wave, and behind them steamed a second echelon, 26,500 men and another 4,400 vehicles. The follow-up force would be knocking at Omaha's door by the next tide, and if the first wave didn't secure the beach by then, a traffic jam like no one had ever seen would clot the dangerous seas.[33]

There was little he could see through his field glasses from the *Augusta*'s deck, but as an infantryman, Brad could envision the foot soldier's bitter fight for the beach: the assault teams wading through neck-deep water, men staggering onto the beaches, their waterlogged kits, ammunition, and clothing pulling them down to the gritty sand as they entered the killing zone. Mortar shells bursting right and left, spraying steel fragments. The spasmodic zipping of the dreaded MG-42, served by unseen crews who played their bullet hoses across the open sands in methodic, crisscross directions. The din of explosions and the screams. Fountains of blood. Noncoms and junior officers crouching low, looking for men they recognized, trying to establish order. Trying to survive.

By noon Gerow pronounced the situation off Omaha "critical," and when Chet Hansen returned from a reconnaissance dash with a gloomy report of swamped boats and bodies blown sky-high, Brad briefly considered abandoning Omaha and diverting his second wave to Utah. So worried was he during those critical moments that two days later he confided to Montgomery, "Someday I'll tell General Eisenhower just how close it was those first few hours."[34]

But at one thirty that afternoon, Bradley and his command team learned Gee's men had broken through to the beach exits and were pushing inland. A firsthand report from Bill Kean confirmed Omaha was in

American hands. Brad heaved a sigh of relief, then settled into the business of directing bulldozers, artillery, men, and plenty else onto French soil.[35]

When he turned in around midnight, Brad could look with satisfaction on his handiwork. He and his lieutenants had put some 50,000 men onto Hitler's "Fortress Europe" and had pushed them six miles closer to Berlin. It was a great start.[36]

"If all goes right, dozens of people will claim credit. But if it goes wrong, you'll be the only one to blame." That was what Kay Summersby had told Ike the night he approved the invasion. Ike had a long, quiet June 5 to think about how much blame he would shoulder if the landings failed. If the airborne were torn to shreds. If the waves swamped the landing craft. If his intelligence misplaced the *Panzer Lehr* or 12th SS Divisions. If he fell victim to bad luck.[37]

Of course, there was no point in speculating. There wasn't any point in anticipating what might happen, since there were about a dozen echelons between Ike and the private who would have to deal with the problems as they arose. So he paced, smoked, visited soldiers, including the airborne boys Leigh-Mallory had pronounced doomed. He scratched off a draft announcement accepting defeat—a message he hoped he'd never send—and he muttered to himself throughout the evening, as if the answers to his questions were lurking on some desk or behind some bookshelf in South-wick House.[38]

Ike, this is pointless. Get into bed and shut your damned brain off.

He stepped into his trailer and closed the door behind him.

At six forty on the morning of June 6, the Supreme Commander's green-handled scrambler phone rang at Sharpener, Ike's forward command post. Butcher, who was answering Ike's phone while the general caught some sleep, picked up. The news was good; Leigh-Mallory was calling to tell Eisenhower that the airborne had made land with no serious casualties. Butch sent the irrepressible Mickey McKeogh to wake the Supreme Commander.[39]

A trepid Mickey cracked the door to Ike's trailer to find his boss sitting up in bed with a Western novel, awake and haggard, a thin cigarette jutting from his stubble-creased jaw. An ashtray next to his bed spilled over with cold butts, and a pile of delicate ash flecked the ashtray's base like snow on a miniature train village. Ike looked like a man who hadn't slept, which made sense, because he hadn't.[40]

"His face was drawn and tired," Mick remembered, "and he had only a half smile." But when Mickey asked him how he felt, Ike croaked, "Not too bad, Mickey." Mickey passed along some good news that had just come in from the Navy, and Ike, brightening up, emerged from his trailer a short time later, a shave, coffee, another cigarette, and news of the paratroopers buoying his spirits.[41]

"Dozens of people will claim credit," she had said.

Well, based on Montgomery's initial reports, Ike knew those dozens would be lining up to claim their share before long, which was just fine with him. Driving to Montgomery's command post, he met with his senior ground commander and picked up more good news from the Commonwealth side; Sword and Gold Beaches, the British ones, looked good, although the Canadians were having a tough fight for the high ground behind Juno. Not a bad start.

As D-Day wore on, Ike became enmeshed in the same worries that had shaken him on Gibraltar and Malta: Where were Bradley's reports? Ike's closest aides were working feverishly to put together a coherent picture for the Supreme Commander, and his loyal Scotsman, Jimmy Gault, got on the scrambled phone with the Navy while Ike strained to listen in. "God, this must be bad," Ike surmised as he listened to Gault's end of the conversation.[42]

Throughout June 6, a sober cloud hovered over Ike's crew. "Nobody made any of the silly little jokes we usually made," remembered Mickey. "We just waited." As the battle unfolded, Dwight Eisenhower fretted and fidgeted without a peep from the U.S.S. *Augusta* and her three-starred Army commander.[43]

Where the hell was Brad?

Well, Ike thought, he would find out. Late on the morning of June 7, he and his retinue pulled away from the coast aboard H.M.S. *Apollo,* a three-stack minelayer, for a personal visit to Bradley's command ship. As the *Apollo* steamed toward Omaha Beach, the messy scene—landing craft, oil slicks, supply ships, troop ships, battleships, artificial breakwaters, supply dumps, destroyers, barrage balloons, and those lines of tiny, olive-drab ants swarming all over the beaches—amazed even the architect of this great enterprise.[44]

But he had little time to take in the spectacle. The *Apollo* pulled alongside the *Augusta*, and soon the coxswain of Bradley's landing boat was asking permission for General Bradley to come aboard.[45]

"Golly, Brad," Ike said as he shook hands with his old classmate. "You had us all scared stiff yesterday morning. Why in the devil didn't you let us know what was going on?"

"But I did," said Brad, his alarm growing. "We radioed you every scrap of information we had. Everything that came in both from Gee and Collins."

"Nothing came through until late afternoon—not a damned word. I didn't know what happened to you."

"But your headquarters acknowledged every message as we asked them to. You check it when you get back and you'll find they all got through."[46]

Ike shrugged the matter off. He'd have someone get to the bottom of this. In the meantime, he had plenty of questions for General Bradley.

The culprit, Brad later found out, was Montgomery's overburdened command post, the proper channel for reports emanating from First Army. The British decoding system had broken down shortly after the landings, and Montgomery's "brass pounders" were running twelve hours behind in their coded messages.[47]

But it was small comfort to Bradley, who knew he had added to his old friend's anxiety on the biggest day of their lives.[48]

Like George nearly a year before, Brad was chagrined at Eisenhower's rebuke, and he was more than a little miffed at the petty complaints over his slow reports. Brad was, after all, the general who had put 50,000 soldiers on *Festung Europa*, and that should count for something.[49]

On June 9, First Army's advanced command post crashed ashore. Bradley's industrious headquarters engineers set up a small tent-and-trailer city in an apple orchard just behind Pointe du Hoc, the battleground wrested by Rangers three days earlier. Montgomery's men, now firmly ashore at Gold, Sword, and Juno Beaches, were having a tough time closing in around Caen, one of Monty's D-Day objectives. On the American side, Brad remained optimistic, though he knew the area south of Omaha and Utah, the neck of the Cotentin Peninsula, would remain hot for some time.[50]

The gap between Omaha and Utah was closed on June 12, and Bradley rumbled off in a jeep with Chet Hansen to scan the front near the old village of Auville-sur-le-Vey. It was the way he liked to get around—a jeep with a padded seat, a good driver, and a load of K-rations for lunch. No flags, no sirens, none of Patton's parade of showboats and sycophants.[51]

Brad, Chet, and their driver, Alex Stoute, bounced down a worn road toward the village and soon pulled to the roadside to watch an armored car turning its 37mm cannon on a concealed sniper. Amid the noise and smoke, another jeep roared up to Brad's vehicle, bearing a worried-looking brigadier general.[52]

"You're crazy as hell to go through, sir," the general shouted at Bradley above the thirty-seven's thumps. "The road may be mined. Let me go on in front."

Brad, calculating risks to himself and the brigadier, shook his head. "Nope—but thanks anyhow," he told the general. "I'm not going to go through." Stoute swung the jeep around and the threesome sped back to the beach.

"We'd better stick to the PT boat until Carentan is opened," he told Hansen as they returned to the command post. Dangerous showboating was for other generals. Not Bradley.[53]

"All the so-called information we get over the radio is imaginary, as, from my previous experiences in landings, I know that were I on the beach I would not know a damn thing at this time of the operation, so how can the commentators know anything?"[54]

That was George's D-Day experience. An old man sitting by the radio, listening intently as events—great events—passed him by.

Thinking it over, he sank back into his chair. That day, he wrote Beatrice, *"It is Hell to be on the side lines and see all the glory eluding me but I guess there will be enough for all."* He penned in his diary, *"I started to pack up my clothes a little bit, always hoping, I suppose, that someone will get killed and I will have to go."*[55]

Many men did get killed that day. Several thousand of them, in fact. But to George, none of the dead men were the right ones. No lieutenant generals, no major generals, not even brigadiers. No one George could reasonably replace. The Nazis would have to aim higher up the chain if Patton were to get to France soon.

So he sat there by the radio, listening intently as events—great events—passed him by.[56]

As George was listening to the wireless, Bradley was hurrying reinforcements ashore, working them into the line, pressing them toward Cherbourg. His most conspicuous job was keeping the fires lit under his corps commanders—Collins, Gerow, and Major General Charles H. Corlett, commander of the newly arrived XIX Corps—but the jobs that took up most of Brad's time were logistics and personnel. To Brad, this last duty meant that all combat commanders who couldn't cut the mustard when the shooting started must be sent back to the minor leagues immediately, and he made his opinions crystal clear to his corps leaders. At the request of Lightning Joe, he sacked the commanding general of the poorly trained 90th Division, even though the general had been in office for only a short time. When that general's replacement did no better, Brad relieved the whole division and replaced it with the 79th, and less than a month after firing the first commander of the 90th, he fired the replacement commander, too. Shortly after VIII Corps arrived under Troy Middleton, he also relieved the 8th Division's commander.[57]

It was a pattern that would repeat itself as the war dragged on. As he later summed up his philosophy of responsibility,

There were instances in Europe where I relieved commanders for their failure to move fast enough. And it is possible that some were the victims of circumstance. For how can the blame for failure be laid fairly on a single man when there are in reality so many factors that can affect the outcome of any battle? Yet each commander must always assume total responsibility for every individual in his command. If his battalion or regimental commanders fail him in the attack, then he must relieve them or be relieved himself.[58]

Brad's was a tough, intolerant approach that many generals thought unnecessarily harsh, and Ike had already lectured Bradley on the need to rehabilitate, rather than fire, deficient commanders. Brad saw it differently. To Bradley, war was an unforgiving teacher, and anything less than immediate replacement of generals found wanting would court failure and create unnecessary Gold Star Mothers back home. And that he was not willing to do.[59]

Tactics were another matter in which Brad played a close, active role. In Corlett, Gerow, and Charles H. Gerhardt, commander of the aggressive 29th Division, Bradley had three commanders itching to dash for St.-Lô, an essential road juncture at the neck of the Cotentin Peninsula. Take St.-Lô, the men urged Bradley, and you open the exit door from the Cotentin.

Bradley, envisioning insurmountable logistical problems, refused to turn his generals loose until Joe Collins captured his assigned port. With his head stuck down a rabbit hole, rooting around for Cherbourg, Brad wasn't going to let Farmer Adolf come along with a hoe and whack him on the back of a long, exposed neck. As he told his operations man, Tubby Thorson, his corps commanders "want to go like hell. I've got to stop them, get them solid and dug in. He's going to hit us hard and I don't want a breakthrough." Corlett and Gerow, he said, would "hold their ground even if we've got to take their ammunition away to make them do it. Nobody's going anywhere until Joe gets Cherbourg."[60]

Events vindicated Brad's caution a few days later when a smiling Monk Dickson sauntered into the mess tent with the happy news that the Germans outside Cherbourg were pulling out of the peninsula. Obviously the Hun couldn't find a chink in Brad's armor, and Bradley now owned the Cotentin, or most of it, without spreading his men dangerously thin. The next day Joe Collins's men sealed off Cherbourg, which he expected to fall soon, and Brad decided to make his first big press announcement the next day.[61]

First Army's personnel staff had pulled together casualty figures for the first ten days on the Continent. The classified numbers showed approximately 15,000 killed, wounded, or missing, which was far less than anyone had expected. They validated Brad's pre-invasion press comments about losses that had gotten him into warm water at home. Why not share the good news with the American people? his staff asked him. It would let the public know that the Normandy landings were not the bloodbath they had been told to expect.[62]

Brad approved the disclosure, since it was good for morale, and made good sense.

Not to everyone, however. SHAEF's intelligence officers, who were paid to piece together enemy strength from a variety of sources, worried that the Germans could make a fair estimate of First Army's strength based on the casualty figures Brad had released. One of them called Montgomery's staff to complain, and Monty, Bradley's superior, placed an icy call to Brad, chiding the junior American about his security lapse as only Montgomery could chide.[63]

Bradley and Montgomery never spoke of the conversation again. They were too professional to harp on something where the matter was academic or settled, at least so long as a war was on. But the abrupt warning from Montgomery put Omar Bradley on notice that the Englishman in baggy pants was going to run his armies with a tight, unyielding fist.

At least, until Brad found a way to get out from under him.

* * *

By mid-June, Eisenhower was beginning to wonder whether the wizard who bounded across the giant relief map of Normandy was ever going to crack the Cotentin Line. The city of Caen, over which the swastika still flew, had been Montgomery's D-Day objective. The land Caen screened would provide beautifully clear, flat space for airfields and logistical dumps, and its eastern roads led to the Seine, Paris, and Orléans. It would give the Allies room to fire up their tanks, and it anchored the left flank of the Allied line.[64]

Montgomery's failure to capture Caen on D-Day, or the next week, or the next week, began incubating a virulent strain of anti-Montgomery sentiment at SHAEF. While some of these complaints carried a vague undertone of national prejudice, Monty's biggest critics were Royal Air Force marshals such as "Mary" Coningham, Patton's hot-tempered antagonist in North Africa, and Arthur Tedder, Eisenhower's right-hand man. Montgomery's penchant for infuriating his colleagues outside Twenty-First Army Group meant there would be plenty of rock throwers waiting for him to stumble.[65]

An unruffled Montgomery concluded that the large German armored force to his front made an assault on Caen impractical for the moment. Instead, he suggested, he would "pull the enemy on the Second Army," loosening up Brad's front so the Americans could drive south into Brittany. With Ike's blessing, Montgomery ordered Bradley to attack toward Coutances, a coastal town at the base of the Cotentin neck.[66]

Ike's ever-present optimism was dealt a severe blow on June 19 with the unexpected arrival of a torrential gale. The three-day tempest, one of the worst to lash the Norman coast in twenty years, capsized or beached some eight hundred ships and wrecked the artificial harbor engineers and seamen had constructed at Omaha Beach. It would be days, maybe weeks, before Ike and his staff could calculate the impact of this disaster, and Ike quickly realized that this one storm was a setback far worse than anything the Germans had inflicted.[67]

As the strain on Eisenhower was rebuilding, the War Department provided him with a bit of personal relief when it authorized a two-week leave for his son, John, a newly commissioned second lieutenant, and provided the young officer with transportation to England to visit his father. Arriving on the thirteenth, John was greeted at the docks in Scotland and whisked off to Ike's headquarters at Southwick. For the first time since the previous Christmas, he saw his father, who was, at that moment, cursing J. C. H. Lee over the telephone.[68]

The man John saw that busy day in June was very different from the one who had left the States in the summer of 1942. He was abrupt, almost rude. While Ike would always remain a devoted father, now that John was an officer, Ike's parental love was tempered by his position as John's ultimate superior. At Telegraph Cottage, he picked at his son for making poor plays at bridge, and in response to his son's question about military protocol among officer ranks, he curtly remarked, "John, there isn't an officer in this theater who doesn't rank above you and below me." Before long John would be out of the theater, reassigned to his unit, destined to return the following spring.[69]

As usual, Eisenhower was at his most relaxed over late-night conversations with old friends. It was one way he shook off the stress of the war, and sometimes his official visits were really an excuse to escape his command post and find people who would rejuvenate his spirit. One evening he decided to settle in for a spell with Bradley at First Army's mess tent. Pulling the blackout flaps as the sky outside darkened, Brad had an orderly bring up a liberated bottle of French wine and the two comrades talked until long after dark. As usual, their late-night conversation was a hodgepodge of business, gossip, and anecdotes that, often as not, went nowhere.[70]

In one conversation, for instance, Ike told Brad how he had run into a soldier from Kansas who was a wheat farmer. The lad said his family's twelve thousand farm acres produced forty-one bushels apiece, a claim Ike didn't find credible.[71]

"When I was a kid," he mused, "two hundred fifty acres of Kansas wheat land would have represented an honest ambition for any Abilene boy. Yessir, it would have looked mighty good to me—and I guess to you too, Brad."

As Brad later remarked, "In Moberly I would have settled for one-sixty."[72]

Homilies like this one were one of the many ways Eisenhower, Bradley, and many others in their positions kept life bearable. Ike may have had more history with George, but in Brad he found a comfortable friend, one who didn't wear him out with the pomp and bombast and when-is-the-next-disaster of a George Patton. Bradley was not a king of the pursuit of warfare, and he did not make life so interesting as George did. But like the Eisenhowers of

Abilene, Bradley hailed from Middle America. He was someone with whom Ike could share a relaxed moment, knowing that when there was fighting to be done, the unflappable Omar Bradley would push as hard as military sense would permit. With Ike's help, the two of them could handle Montgomery, Patton, and the enemy.

SEVENTEEN

SLOW MARCH

Neither Ike nor Brad has the right stuff. Ike is bound hand and foot by the British and does not know it. Poor fool. We actually have no Supreme Commander.

—George, July 12, 1944

TIME WAS EISENHOWER'S OTHER ENEMY. According to the OVERLORD plan, the plan his bosses undoubtedly checked each day, the Allies should have broken into open country by the end of June. Instead, his men were penned behind swamps, hedgerows, and thick German defenses. Aggregate levels of soldiers, equipment, and supplies brought into France had fallen hopelessly behind SHAEF planning schedules, and his beachhead—a month into the invasion, it was still just a beachhead—was too thin for maneuver, too thin to bring reserves from England, too thin even to get his equipment off the beaches in an orderly fashion. So thin, in fact, that his only big prize, Carentan, still lay under German artillery fire. So thin, in fact, that a man could stand on the airstrip at Isigny, watch the P-51s take off, drop their wing bombs on the enemy, and bank toward the airstrip to return for more bombs, without ever losing sight of the planes.[1]

Why was the great Allied crusade, the operation his staff, Montgomery's staff, Bradley's staff, and a hundred other staffs had labored on for half a year, becoming a Great War stalemate? It wasn't supposed to play out that way.[2]

Well, he could blame the big storm. That gale had played hell on the engineers and longshoremen who swarmed over the makeshift docks. He could blame the mud and he could blame the hedgerows, those ancient bulwarks that lent their formidable weight to the defender. He could even blame Montgomery for moving too slowly.[3]

But Ike knew no one in London or Washington would blame the hedgerows. Or the weather, or Montgomery. They would blame the Supreme Commander.

So Ike had to get out of Normandy, and soon.

The beleaguered general had two ways to break out of his congealing cement shoes, and both options required additional ports. He could move north, sending Monty toward the Seine ports of Le Havre and Rouen, which would open the Channel and the Low Countries. Or, he could move south toward Brittany, aiming Bradley at St.-Nazaire, Lorient, and Brest. Once those ports were open for business, then ammunition, fuel, and replacements from the United States and England would be plentiful. Patton's Third Army could take the field, and the frontline forces could turn the rear areas over to General Lee's supply troops—"one a-shootin', ten a-lootin'," as the GI phrase went. Then Ike could begin thinking about Paris, the Rhine, and Berlin. And home, Mamie, and his six-month fishing trip.

But it all started with a breakthrough.

After studying the little red rectangles on his G-2 maps, Ike concluded that Bradley, not Montgomery, was in the better position to break out. While the Germans had about 35,000 men opposing either Allied army, the panzer group facing Dempsey's Second Army fielded more tanks, more flak, thicker artillery, and loads of those "screaming mimi" rocket batteries the Germans called *nebelwerfers*. As a result, Monty hadn't managed to seize Caen on D-Day and then "crack around Falaise," as he had promised at St. Paul's. It was nearly D-plus-30, and the swastika still fluttered over Caen's city center; this was not only an embarrassment to Montgomery—it was a worrisome drain on limited British manpower. With greater relative mobility to the south, Ike reckoned, Brad should be able to smash through the weakening German crust and explode southward into Brittany. This approach was, in fact, consistent with Monty's pre-invasion orders, and it had made the most sense from the beginning.[4]

Not that Brad would have an easy time breaking out. The Cotentin was a devilish place for offensive operations, since the peninsula was hedgerow country, except where it was swamp country. Sluggish, muddy streams and deep drainage ditches crisscrossed the region's neck, making movement arduous even for foot soldiers.[5]

And then there was the stubborn problem of Cherbourg, which was holding out under an airtight siege by Joe Collins and his VII Corps. The port city had long been a vital OVERLORD objective, a requirement for movement inland, and until that splinter had been extracted from First Army's backside, the Allies couldn't turn their attention to the east.

Worse yet, the enemy Bradley's men would face wouldn't be those second-rate static divisions of the coast. Instead, Brad's opponents in the next round would be veteran, well-equipped infantry, grenadier, panzer, and paratroop units, all of which had been baptized in hard fighting on the Russian Front. Though Bradley commanded thirteen full divisions—nine infantry, two armored, and two airborne—most of his incoming regiments hadn't been blooded yet, and his airborne was due to rotate back to England to refit for its next jump.[6]

But Ike saw no other choice. The north was too heavily guarded, and the Allies had to break out before the entire damned *Wehrmacht* sealed them off. So, placing his chips on the better of two risky hands, Ike handed the ball to Brad and told him to run with it. The Allies would break out to the south, and Lieutenant General Omar Bradley would be Eisenhower's new running back.

Since von Rundstedt could not afford to have British Cromwell tanks rolling behind Falaise, Omar Bradley was hopeful that the panzer divisions along Dempsey's front wouldn't shift south in time to prevent him from getting through the Cotentin swamps to the open south and west. His fingers crossed, Brad's breakout plan was a massive twelve-division offensive that would open a giant hole leading to Brittany, the Loire, and the Seine.[7]

It was a good plan, a realistic one, Brad thought. But the timing of his attack, June 30, worried both Bradley and his bosses, as SHAEF and everyone else figured that Rommel and von Rundstedt were bringing up reinforcements from Paris. As June waned, Monty advised Bradley that German heavy panzer divisions—around 200 Mark IVs, 150 Panthers, and 80 Tigers—were assembling west of Paris for a "full blooded counterattack." A nervous Monk Dickson predicted that the II SS Panzer Corps, formerly homesteaded on the Eastern Front, would arrive by July 3, and those SS panzers, everyone knew, were not to be trifled with. To make matters worse, a corps from Fifteenth Army, around Calais, was spotted moving south, and Brad worried that Hitler's hotshots might hit First Army's exposed flank once the breakout began. With jitters spreading through SHAEF, Ike personally asked Brad to rush preparations for the attack "with all possible speed." Writing Bradley on the twenty-seventh, Ike gave thin encouragement to his friend, telling him, *"I feel very sure that a strong attack on your side will go with a bang once it gets started."*[8]

Under this sort of pressure, Brad really, *really* wanted to kick off his attack by the end of the month. But during the last week of June, his staff convinced him that everyone would have to hold their horses for a few more days. Artillery ammunition and infantry were simply in too short a supply to support a simultaneous breakout to the south and the reduction of Cherbourg to the north. His divisions were in the process of absorbing replacements, Middleton's VIII Corps artillery was stranded in England due to the storm, and reserve ammunition had to be dragged forward from the beaches. Adding to the rear-echelon chaos, Lee's SOS people had neglected to send First Army the ship manifests that would allow Brad's quartermasters to identify artillery ammunition among of the cityscape of crates piling up on Omaha's sands.[9]

On this last count, Brad complained bitterly to Ike, who broke open the bureaucratic logjam within a few days and assured Bradley that heads would roll if improvements weren't forthcoming. But for the other appalling problems confronting Bradley, there was little either man could do for the moment. First Army was in no shape to launch an attack by the end of the month, and on the twenty-ninth, Brad swallowed his pride and set his pen to letters to generals Eisenhower and Montgomery:

"I am very sorry to make this postponement but . . ."[10]

News that Brad's attack would be deferred to July 3 hit Ike in the gut, since it came on the heels of Montgomery's announcement that he would sit where he was until an expected German counterattack ran its course.[11]

Shaking his head, Ike told Everett Hughes, "Sometimes I wish I had George Patton here." But Patton was in England, not France, and by now disappointment had become Ike's long-term houseguest. He resigned himself to another few days squirming at his headquarters desk, anxiously reviewing weather reports, and waiting for those panzers to come rolling in from Paris.[12]

With his armies immobilized, Eisenhower took on the old, familiar role of football coach, moving up and down the sidelines, exhorting his backs to give it their best shot. On the first of July, he flew to Normandy for a four-day visit to Brad's headquarters. Promising himself to rough it—no four-star treatment this time—he wrote Bradley, *"I am counting on going over with nothing but a bedroll. . . . I want nothing but a slit trench with a piece of canvas over it. If you attempt to move out of your caravan I won't stay."* Brad courteously interpreted Ike's stipulation as a preference for a tent, rather than a trailer, and he was happy to accommodate his old friend.[13]

Ike came ashore at Omaha Beach with Mickey and Jimmy Gault, and stowed his traveling gear in a tent at Bradley's campsite. His four-night stay at First Army's rude headquarters was a fine trip for a man who loved the invigoration of field life. He slept on a cot (red pajama bottoms, no top), washed himself in cold water, used the latrine behind a hedgerow, and dined on beans 'n' weenies and Army coffee, just like the enlisted men.[14]

His orderly later remarked that Ike went to a lot of trouble to live in a tent. But the man who devoured Western novels by the bushel couldn't shake his romanticized image of camp life. *"Where the buffalo roam," as it were.* Ike loved being around fighting men, and he understood that while he did not face the hardships of his GIs, he could share some of their travails, even if it was but a token gesture. Bradley's aide later wrote, "There's something about the guy, the way he brushes along, the way he breaks out in a big grin, the way his voice, harsh and loud, cracks out, that disarms all within his vicinity. Stand at attention if you wish, let your heart thump if it must, but there's no getting away from the feeling of 'easiness' that pervades his presence. . . . That's the way he is, gay, loud, democratic, dynamic, thinking fast, acting fast, spreading confidence." In some ways, his sideline visits brought out the Middle American best in Dwight Eisenhower.[15]

Bradley, slightly closer to the men on the scrimmage line, had no such romanticized illusions about either outdoor life or the slit trench. For all the "GI's General" press Ernie Pyle dished out to his readers, Brad never attained the "common touch" Ike exuded when he visited soldiers in the field. While Brad was universally regarded as friendly and unassuming— "plain as an old shoe," his aides used to quip—he had little capacity for humor. Ike believed papers like *Stars and Stripes* performed an important service to a citizen army, by allowing citizen soldiers to air their gripes. Bradley, "top brass" by any standard, retained the high command's traditional distrust of the press, whether Army-sponsored or private. He had no time for the human-interest stories of the everyman soldier, and he refused to pose for photographs with soldiers the way Ike did, at least when those photos were intended for publication. "Goddammit, I'll stand here for your pix but I will not pose," he once bluntly told photojournalists who asked for a picture of the commanding general shaking hands with his soldiers.

To Bradley, public relations were someone else's problem. He was a military commander; political officers like Ike could handle the politics.[16]

The next day, July 2, Ike and Brad drove over to Montgomery's command post, an apple orchard some fifteen miles from St.-Lô. Under a mottled sky of camouflage netting, the two men found the British general in fine spirits. Monty claimed he was pleased with his army group's progress, and to the astonishment of his American guests, he suggested abandoning the southern breakout and making an all-out drive for heavily defended Calais. Such a move would, of course, liberate the largest Channel port and eliminate the launching sites for the V1 "doodlebug" rockets that were raining down on London with frightening regularity—this last consideration being one of particular importance to Winston Churchill, the principal object of said doodlebugs.[17]

Ike was diplomatic, and he nodded in agreement with most of what Monty said. But Monty's suggestion about Calais, Ike knew, was preposterous, and when he returned to his tent at *Chez Bradley*, Ike told Brad he was disappointed with Monty's general preoccupation with avoiding defeat, even at the expense of victory. This was war, after all, and there was a place for unreasonable, brutal drive. Montgomery didn't seem to understand that. All Monty wanted was a "tidy" logistical tail and a set-piece play, which naturally gave the Krauts as much time as they needed to move up panzer divisions for a counterattack. He was, he told Brad, particularly unsettled over Monty's habit of blaming the Air Force, an interservice criticism Ike somehow had kept below the boiling point ever since the row between Patton and Coningham back in Tunisia.[18]

But Montgomery was the one man in the theater whom Ike could not fire, no matter how many sparks the Ulsterman threw off. So he sighed, and continued to push Bradley for more progress.

Ike, who had been looking for an offbeat adventure for some time, was delighted to get a break from the war—sort of—when Major General Elwood "Pete" Quesada, commander of the IX Tactical Air Command, offered him a flight over the Allied beachhead in a special two-seater P-51 Mustang. Other than the press, nobody was happy about it, because no local commander wants the top dog killed, accidentally or otherwise, in his sector. But Ike liked to tell his staffers that the Supreme Commander was the one man whom no one could ground, and he ignored Bradley's pleas to stay away from the front lines. "All right, Brad," he assured his lieutenant, "I'm not going to fly to Berlin."[19]

With Quesada at the controls, Ike took a short flight over the battle-fields, banking sharply so as to view the terrain over which his trucks and jeeps were rolling. As the Mustang returned and rolled to a stop, he and Pete climbed out of the cramped quarters into a battery of flashbulbs, look-ing, to Bradley like "sheepish schoolboys caught in a watermelon patch." For that stunt, Ike knew he'd catch a little hell from Marshall, and from Mamie, too. But the Mustang flight, like his tent trip to Brad's headquar-ters, was one of those small risks Ike yearned for after weeks behind desks, on telephones, and in conferences. They were a way he could share a frac-tion of the risks his soldiers were taking every day, and they were a sorely needed antidote to the sterile atmosphere at SHAEF Main.[20]

But the magical Mustang was parked and silent, and after sliding off the fighter's wing, it was back to the dreary business of war management. Back to London, back to supply estimates, back to weather reports, and back to shipping tables. Back to hell.

As he had been in Tunisia, Brad was growing more than a little annoyed with his old friend's Anglophilia. On the afternoon before Brad's big July offensive, Ike, lounging around headquarters, began to wax enthusiasti-cally about FORTITUDE, a plan designed and largely implemented by his beloved allies. The plan was working wonders, Ike said, and the Americans could learn something from the British about diversionary and counterin-telligence operations.[21]

Even more galling to Bradley was Ike's delight that, through FORTI-TUDE, George Patton had pinned the Fifteenth Army all by himself, all by his reputation—a fact that, Ike claimed, hadn't escaped the rank and file of First Army. Word on the beaches, Ike said, was that Patton's army had captured Norway in a couple of days; Patton, so they said, had offered Ike a thousand dollars for each week that Eisenhower would push up the date of his army's move into France.

This was one of those times, as in Tunisia, when Eisenhower seemed to Bradley a bit pontifical for someone who had never commanded fighting troops in battle. When Ike suggested to Brad that it might be a good idea to second promising division commanders as deputy corps commanders, to speed their development into corps commanders, he added: "You learned things with II Corps that you never would have learned in a division." The implication that Bradley had something to learn from George during the horseman's five weeks in Tunisia must have stuck in his craw. *"Brad, to my mind, never needed to learn,"* snorted Bradley's aide Chet Hansen.[22]

Well, Brad figured, he might as well let Ike ramble on. It made no difference to him what George did with his phony army, or what he had done in Tunisia, because when George came over, George would be working for him, not Ike. And George would come only when Bradley sent for him.

Bradley's great breakout offensive finally pushed off on July 3. The plan was a basic echelon attack, with Troy Middleton's VIII Corps leading the advance by moving south along the Cotentin coast toward Coutances. The next day, Lightning Joe would drive on a parallel route, Corlett's IX Corps would move against St.-Lô, and Gee Gerow would maintain the link with the British right flank. After breaking through the shell of the "other fellow's" lines, Brad's men would wheel counterclockwise, threaten the rear of the Germans facing General Dempsey, and open enough real estate to bring over Patton's Third Army.[23]

From the opening barrage, Brad's offensive fell apart like a wet biscuit. Although he had assured Middleton that VIII Corps would get all the tactical air support it wanted, heavy rains had scrubbed ground-support missions for the first two days of the attack. Struggling through mud, thick hedgerows of what the French called the *bocage* country, and well-sited German observation posts, Middleton made only a thousand yards a day for the ensuing two weeks. Brad's other corps commanders did little better.[24]

Bradley brought in more troops, shuffled divisions, fired generals, and changed corps boundaries, but nothing worked; Middleton's corps alone paid for seven miles of useless hedgerow country with ten thousand casualties. On July 14, a disappointed Bradley called Middleton and Collins and told them to sit tight for the moment; over the next five days, Corlett achieved only modest success in capturing the city of St.-Lô, a D-Day objective, at a cost of five thousand men. All told, Brad had advanced the Allied line about seven miles, but he had paid for it with forty thousand battle casualties—not including cases of combat fatigue, which weren't officially reported but probably accounted for another ten thousand ineffectives. Other than a memorable photo opportunity of himself pulling the lanyard on an artillery piece to celebrate the Fourth of July, a superficially pleased General Eisenhower looking on, the great July offensive was a bust.[25]

For Omar Bradley, Marshall's protégé and one of the Army's top performers, it was a crushing setback, and it kicked around his gullet like a lump of old chipped beef. He had been checked before—Troina, for instance, and at Cherbourg—but then only briefly. Now he was well and truly stalemated, and the price in blood was becoming intolerable. He could bemoan the lack of replacements and underpowered tank guns, and he could blame the weather, which had scrubbed 50 percent of his air support. He could stare blankly at those impenetrable hedgerows, every one of which seemed to conceal a Kraut machine gun and mortar team. But in the end he knew the blame would only rebound upon one man: himself.[26]

His spirits, sagging under the weight of his failed offensive, received a nudge from a sympathetic General Marshall, who had read a report from Eisenhower blaming Brad's rough start on factors beyond his control. The Chief wrote Bradley: "The weather has treated you badly, particularly considering the character of the terrain you have been trying to break through. However, it seems to me that things have gone extraordinarily well and that the German dilemma must be a nightmare for them." Montgomery, still stuck at Caen, was also a good sport and a supportive teammate. When, at Montgomery's headquarters, Bradley admitted that his initial progress had not been as rapid as he had hoped, Montgomery reassured him that the British would keep the Jerries pinned down until the Americans could get clear of the Cotentin. They'd be fine, he said.[27]

It was a nice assurance, but Bradley didn't need cheerful words from Monty, or even from Marshall. He needed victory. He needed his men to push more intelligently. Relieving colonels, brigadiers, and major generals sent a strong message to his division commanders, but the past two weeks had taught him that the Allies had not yet derived the formula for a breakout. They needed to learn to fight smarter; after all, combat is a notoriously unforgiving teacher.

He would learn. He would do better next time. Hopefully there would be a next time.

George Patton arrived in France on July 6, with Stiller, Codman, Willie, and his jeep in tow. He kept his trip under deep cover, as the Germans still believed he commanded the First U.S. Army Group, a mighty host poised to cross the Pas de Calais and battle the German Fifteenth Army. As his staffers scouted ahead for Third Army's headquarters site, Patton called on Brad and Troy Middleton, whose VIII Corps would move over to Third Army when Patton's command was "hatched."[28]

George was still highly unpopular within Bradley's clique. In his diary Hansen, unimpressed as ever, growled,

> *Shortly before noon Patton came in with Codman and a medico. Jaunty and well dressed in green jacket with the bright buttons and in ice cream pants with the fancy leather belt though I did not notice the pearl handled revolver which has been put under bans it was so highly publicized. Chastened as a result of this experience with the newspapers but he is still basically the same showman.*[29]

The chastened showman spent a long, pleasant afternoon with Bradley, who narrated First Army's experiences in the hedgerow country. From Sherman weaknesses to the flooded swamps at the Cotentin base, he outlined the many difficulties Third Army would face when it debouched from its camps in England.[30]

After listening to Brad and his corps commanders for a day, George came away unimpressed with American performance to date. He saw few sound tactics at the army level; Brad was scattering his divisions like seeds in a stiff wind, not concentrating his force. To George, Brad was doing it all wrong, trying to bust through the German lines everywhere. And *en échelon*, no less. How the hell did he think he would put one over on Rommel that way?[31]

Musing over what he had learned about the campaign, George thought he discerned another problem. Collins, he concluded, was quick to bust his division and regimental commanders, and Bradley was too quick to support him. He told his diary, *"Collins and Bradley are too prone to cut off heads. This will make division commanders lose their confidence. A man should not be damned for an initial failure with a new division. Had I done this with General Eddy of the 9th in Africa, the army would have lost a potential corps commander."* While George was ready to give at least one corps commander the boot because of his inexperience in combat, he commented, *"One should never penalize a commander for making mistakes that were due to audacity, even where it was carried to the point of rashness, but only for failing to take risks—so often in war the apparently rash move came off."*[32]

As Bradley's July offensive ground to a halt about seven miles from its starting point, George's opinions grew more venomous. As he muttered in his diary in mid-July, *"Brad and Hodges are such nothings. Their one virtue is that they get along by doing nothing. I could break through in three days if I commanded."* As the stalemate hardened, Patton's opinion of the high command did not improve. On the twelfth, he wrote that confusion on the beaches and Allied disorganization were *"the result of lack of one responsible commander. Neither Ike nor Brad has the right stuff. Ike is bound hand and foot by the British and does not know it. Poor fool. We actually have no Supreme Commander."*[33]

For all their scathing missives and grousing to their staff, Brad and George respected each other. They had come up through the Old Army together, and neither man felt the other one had risen to his rank on favoritism or politics. Though different, they were each the genuine article. But the vast gulf that separated their personalities, their outlook, their styles, meant they would fail to appreciate each other's talents unless they were working closely enough to appreciate each other's strengths. Or saw a common enemy.

What brought the two men close in the spring of 1944 was the dominating presence of General Montgomery, a man they could both abhor with beautiful sincerity. The day after Patton's "ice cream pants" arrival at Brad's headquarters, Patton and Hugh Gaffey came upon Monty as he was decorating U.S. soldiers under a field battery of movie cameras commanded by a former Hollywood director. *"There were at least twenty-five camera men of various types,"* George noted in his diary with contempt. *"Also a loudspeaker on a pole was held over Montgomery's head so his priceless words would not be lost."* As the lights snapped off and the cameramen began packing up their equipment, Brad, George, and Monty retired to Brad's "war tent," where Montgomery and his staff, in George's words, *"put in several hours explaining why they had not yet taken Caen, their D-Day objective."* When Montgomery sidled up to the topic of Third Army's activation, he left George with the distinct impression that he didn't want Third Army in France until sometime in the future, say, when Middleton's VIII Corps took Avranches. Bradley, said George, *"refused to bite because he is using me as a means of getting out from under the 21st Army Group. I hope he succeeds."* A few days later, George penned a personal explanation for why Third Army was still sidelined:

> *Brad says he will put me in as soon as he can. He could do it now with much benefit to himself, if he had any backbone. Of course, Monty does not want me as he fears I will steal the show, which I will.*[34]

* * *

With Brad's offensive a bust, Eisenhower looked to Montgomery's front with the longing eyes of a sick man waiting for the doctor. Daily G-2 reports showed panzers and infantry piling up along an Allied line that had hardly moved since June, and Ike foresaw a hardening stalemate that might require a McNair or an Alexander, maybe even a Jake Devers, to pull his chestnuts out of the fire. So on July 7, after conferring with Beetle and Tedder, Ike wrote Montgomery again to urge him to use "all possible energy in a determined effort to prevent a stalemate" on the Continent. He promised Montgomery the full support of SHAEF, Air Force, and First Army as needed.[35]

"I am, myself, quite happy about the situation," Monty airily replied the next day. The Germans were, after all, hurting far worse than the Allies were. As the Allies had recently learned, an enraged Hitler had fired von Rundstedt at the end of June, replacing him with another field marshal named Günther von Kluge. Montgomery assured Ike and his critics at SHAEF that he had "a very definite plan" for breaking out of the hedgerow country, and he wrote to Eisenhower, "Of one thing you can be quite sure, there will be no stalemate."[36]

Monty's very definite plan, Operation GOODWOOD, envisioned a three-division armored thrust from Caen over the Orne River. He would seize the German-held Caen suburbs and move south toward Falaise, isolating the frontline Germans in a pocket from which they would not escape. The innovative part of the plan, Monty told Ike, was the use of heavy bombers as flying artillery to smash the outer German defenses. He promised Eisenhower the "whole eastern flank" would soon "burst into flames" under the weight of his assault. GOODWOOD, Monty predicted, would give the Allies the "decisive" victory they so desperately needed.[37]

As Ike read Montgomery's letter, he became electrified at the possibilities. Words like "decisive" held special meaning for men steeped in the quest for the fabled "decisive battle." A *decisive* blow would give his tankers space to maneuver, give his airmen bases, and, most important, give him room to field two more armies. After telling Montgomery how "pepped up" he was about GOODWOOD, he gushed that the British triumph "will make some of the 'old classics' look like a skirmish between patrols." Ike needed Brittany and the rest of Normandy, and GOODWOOD seemed his best hope.[38]

Montgomery launched GOODWOOD on July 18 with an air bombardment that opened the vomiting mouth of hell, or the nearest facsimile Bomber

Harris could arrange. Nearly seventeen hundred planes from RAF Bomber Command and the U.S. Eighth Air Force, plus another four hundred mediums and fighter-bombers from Ninth Air Force, sailed over the German lines and dropped seven thousand tons of high explosives on the huddled men below. The British moved out behind the smoldering plowline of death, and Ike was delighted to receive a report that Montgomery was "very well satisfied" with his men's progress. Later that day Monty predicted his three armored divisions would soon be "threatening Falaise." These were just the words Ike wanted to hear.[39]

But Montgomery's satisfaction proved premature. German defenders, fully conscious that an attack was in the works around Caen, quickly recovered from the shock of the bombing and threw in eight battalions from the 1st SS and 21st Panzer Divisions, blunting the British thrust. Antitank crews rushed in to halt the British Shermans, and by July 20, when a heavy storm halted further advance, Dempsey's Second Army had moved little over six miles forward at a cost of some four hundred tanks—nearly a third of all British tanks in France—and some six thousand Tommies and Canadians. A German counterattack the next day sealed off the advance, and the exhausted Commonwealth soldiers fortified their positions, to await the next big idea from the brass.[40]

If Montgomery's true object was to break out of the confining beachhead, then GOODWOOD was a failure. The press thought so, RAF thought so, and so did Ike. Although the operation had drawn more panzers onto Caen, and away from Bradley's sector, Monty had promised a "decisive" breakthrough. When Ike reflected that the Allies had dropped over seven thousand tons of bombs to move less than seven miles, he wondered how long they could afford to spend a thousand tons of bombs per mile. The current pace was unacceptable.[41]

In the wake of GOODWOOD, Monty's critics drew their daggers. A groundswell had been building against him at SHAEF, 10 Downing, and elsewhere since late June, and SHAEF office gossip turned to who would replace the condescending little snit when Churchill and Brooke sacked him. Tedder, whose favorite topic of conversation seemed to be Montgomery's relief, claimed the British Chiefs of Staff would support any recommendation that Ike might care to make with respect to the aloof general's reassignment. He urged Ike to displace Monty and assume direct command of the ground war, *now*.[42]

* * *

For Eisenhower, the situation at home was also getting dicey. The public was reading of a titanic offensive by the Red Army that was liberating thousands of square miles and chewing up German divisions by the dozen. In Italy, the capture of Rome had been followed by a hasty German retreat to the Gothic Line, and in the Pacific, Admiral Chester Nimitz was announcing landings in Guam, another stab into the Japanese defensive perimeter. What, the public would ask, was General Eisenhower doing about France? Every day Caen's road net remained in German hands, every day they failed to bust out of Normandy, was seen by Ike's bosses as a failure, a failure to be laid at Ike's door. Ike, Butch remarked, was "blue as indigo over Monty's slowdown."[43]

But what to do about it? The Washington establishment, including Roosevelt, Stimson, and Marshall, felt Eisenhower needed to move his headquarters across the Channel and exercise personal control over the ground campaign. There was also a rumbling on the American side that Ike was wasn't being firm enough with the plodding Montgomery. As Harry Butcher quipped, "Monty has issued directives as lofty as the Ten Commandments but has so far not carried through on them except as performed by Bradley and then only by Ike 'pushing the reins' with Bradley, for whom Ike feels not only responsibility but authority to press."[44]

As in the early days of the North African campaign—or for that matter, his early days at the War Department, or his nights fretting over TORCH and CORKSCREW and HUSKY and BAYTOWN and AVALANCHE and OVERLORD—Ike's health suffered. Late-night conferences, incessant smoking, a haphazard diet, pacing, cursing, worrying, physical and mental wounds—these demons drove his blood pressure to life-threatening levels, which, he learned, explained the ringing in his ears. As the rush of D-Day settled into a slog of attrition, the pressure squeezed Ike like a famished python. The pressure was consuming him, making his head spin, driving him into an early grave.[45]

"It ain't good," Butch said of Ike's health, recalling sadly how General Teddy Roosevelt, who had survived North Africa, Sicily, Utah beach, and the hedgerow fighting, died of a heart attack one month into the Normandy campaign. "[Ike's] troubles are not from physical exertion, but they are from the mental strain and worry," he wrote. "What a blow it would be to the world, not mentioning that to his personal followers, if he should pull a Teddy Roosevelt!" The key to avoiding Ike's becoming a high-ranking casualty of the war lay in the best way to get Montgomery's forces moving south, toward Brittany, then east to the Seine.[46]

Ike's relationship with Bernard Montgomery remained distressingly awkward. On one hand, something of the same intimidated major general, whom Monty had dressed down for smoking in his regal presence back in 1942, still lingered. Ike treaded lightly with the man, as Monty was not only a highly popular figure in America and Britain, but he was a favorite of Brooke, and, from time to time, of Churchill. Ike also knew Monty could show true military brilliance, as he had amply demonstrated at El Alamein and in the planning phase of OVERLORD. The trick with Monty was waiting patiently through the uncomfortably slow intervals of deliberation that separated his penetrating flashes of genius.

Montgomery, for his part, sensed that SHAEF was a lions' den, with the lions—Ike's air marshals, admirals, and American generals—licking their chops for a bite at the Hero of El Alamein. Reasoning that his chief of staff, Major General Francis de Guingand, was better liked and less of a lightning rod than he, Monty usually sent "Freddie" to SHAEF whenever he had to deal with Eisenhower & Company. Before long, though, his modus operandi backfired. While De Guingand was an undeniably talented diplomat, well liked by everyone, Monty lacked the foresight to see that a *personal* engagement of the Allied board of directors would be indispensible if he were to remain in the tactical driver's seat. Either that, or a great victory, which he didn't have at the moment.[47]

Notwithstanding the indecision at Caen, Ike was not about to succumb to calls for Montgomery's head, at least not at the moment. He had stuck by George, who had gotten him into hotter and deeper water than Monty ever would. As Brooke liked to remind him, Montgomery did have the heavier weight of German armor covering his front, as Eisenhower had intended, and it would not be realistic to believe that a Red Army–like offensive could be launched around Caen in the face of this much enemy armor. More to the point, Ike knew it would be unpalatable for an American general to relieve a British general, especially as the British censorship policy restricted the pool of generals known, and therefore acceptable, to the British public.[48]

So Monty's job was secure. Ike would have to content himself with letters assuring Montgomery that he needn't fear an imminent German counterattack, and politely suggesting that he should push Dempsey forward as soon as First Army launched its next offensive.[49]

To Eisenhower, GOODWOOD was a bitter disappointment in a campaign littered with bitter disappointments. And dead men.

He understood why Bradley was stuck in the hedgerows, and he understood why Dempsey was stuck around Caen. There were reasons, perhaps compelling reasons. But knowing *why* his soldiers were stuck didn't bring him much comfort. After all, the word *"why"* came up often when generals, historians, and politicians discussed failed campaigns. And failed generals.[50]

Well, that was the nature of the beast, and there was little Ike could do about it now. Napoleon had Borodino, Grant the Wilderness, and Ike had the endless line of Norman hedgerows and swamps in which his troops were now stuck. It was a leafy green cross, one of many that Ike, Brad, and their men would have to bear a little longer.

Fretting as he shuttled between Widewing and Sharpener, Ike pushed thoughts of past setbacks out of his head, though he knew the ghosts of those setbacks would haunt him as his armies marched into the winter. *Stick to the plan,* he reminded himself, *and you'll make it.*

Besides, he remembered, Bradley had told him of another card they could play. A pretty good card, though it would require a hell of a lot of bombers and tanks. A project called COBRA.

He tucked that one into his brain before falling asleep.

EIGHTEEN

OPEN FOR BUSINESS

For God's sake, Brad, you've got to get me into this fight before the war is over. I'm in the doghouse now and I'm apt to die there unless I pull something spectacular to get me out.

—George to Brad, July 1944

BRADLEY'S JAW CLENCHED as he walked past the large operation maps that hung from the wall of his paneled trailer. Cluttered with lines, circles, arrows, and little rectangles, together they detailed his army's excruciating progress toward St.-Lô. It was a remarkably short distance in which to amass forty thousand battle casualties. Every glance at those maps gave him the same knotted, helpless feeling in his gut that a boy gets when he runs into the neighborhood bully and knows he's about to be picked on and taunted. To a commanding general, that was what those maps were— perfectly drawn, neat, categorized taunts. Taunts updated continuously by three lieutenant colonels whose sole reason for being was to keep the big maps up-to-date and blissfully free of extraneous information. Taunts that reminded him that, in spite of his beautiful July 3 battle plan, he was still stuck in a Norman prison and would not bust out anytime soon.[1]

What had gone wrong?

Well, terrain and rain and supplies and men and, of course, the Hun— that was what had gone wrong. But as Bradley donned his teacher's cap, he saw something else, a flaw in his plan's basic conception. Something that, by gum, he had taught countless West Point students never to do: He had dispersed his striking power over a broad line, which didn't leave much punch to ram his armor deep into the German defenses.

* * *

By the second week in July, Brad felt the germ of an idea sprouting in the back of his head. If properly executed, the move might get his men out of the Cotentin, where they could snatch up those coastal ports and drive their tanks into open country. But to flesh out that idea, to turn the vague concept into something worthwhile, he needed to retire to his map room.

The map room was Bradley's inner sanctum, his temple on the mountaintop. It wasn't really a room, but a long, canvas mess tent where the biggest map of Normandy his G-2 men could find covered an entire wall. The place was his office, his workshop, his monastery, because to Brad maps, like the Good Book, would tell you a lot if you were willing to spend time thinking about them.

Over two nights, Brad's boots clunked over the tent's planked floors as he penciled, rubbed out and penciled more lines, an Einstein in olive scribbling and scratching out theoretical formulae. As rags smudged with pencil grease piled up in the corners of his tent floor, Brad traced and retraced road networks and studied the land around them. The black lines took shape, and Brad's dark eyes brightened as he awoke to possibilities spread along the Cotentin's old, rutted roads.[2]

After wrestling the problem down to a workable concept, Brad asked Hodges and Collins for their thoughts. Then, on July 12, he invited Bill Kean, Tubby Thorson, Monk Dickson, and his corps commanders to critique his work. They shuffled into Brad's office like a panel of drab professors assembled for a master's thesis, and emerged with a plan.[3]

Plan COBRA, as Tubby dubbed it, was an American-style solution to the hardening stalemate. Like GOODWOOD, Bradley's campaign would begin with a saturation bombing in lieu of the conventional artillery barrage. The difference between COBRA and GOODWOOD was that First Army would use infantry divisions, rather than armor, to punch a narrow hole in the enemy lines around St.-Lô. The infantry would hold the shoulders while an entire corps of armor and mechanized infantry rushed through. With luck, the three mobile divisions would blast their way to Coutances, where they could pivot, then encircle the German defenders. If events so dictated, Brad could send his armor toward Avranches, at the base of Brittany's peninsula. Once in Avranches, he would have enough space to bring Patton's army into the fray, and Brittany, with its fat, juicy ports, would be his for the taking.[4]

It was a risky plan, Brad acknowledged. Hedgerow country went back

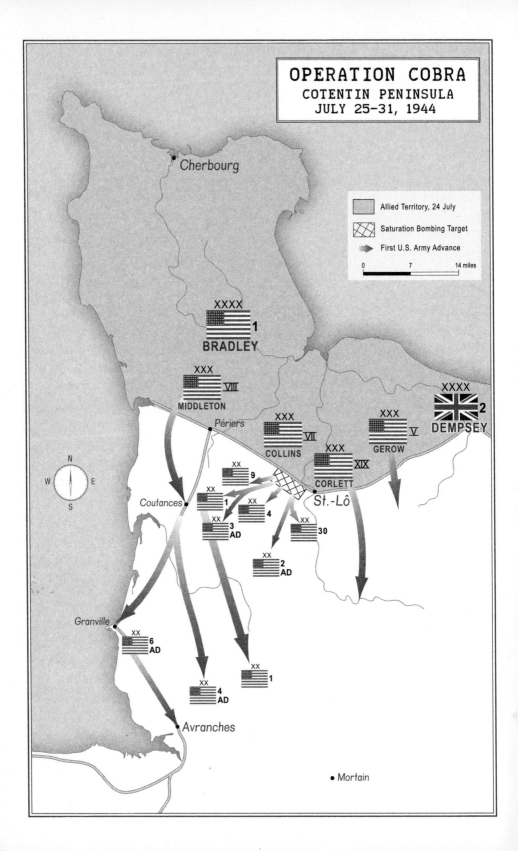

OPERATION COBRA
COTENTIN PENINSULA
JULY 25–31, 1944

Cherbourg

Allied Territory, 24 July
Saturation Bombing Target
First U.S. Army Advance

0   7   14 miles

XXXX
1
BRADLEY

XXX
VIII
MIDDLETON

Périers

XXX
VII
COLLINS

XXX
XIX
CORLETT

XXX
V
GEROW

XXXX
2
DEMPSEY

XX
9

St.-Lô

XX
1

XX
4

Coutances

XX
3
AD

XX
30

XX
2
AD

N
W   E
S

Granville

XX
6
AD

XX
1

XX
4
AD

Avranches

• Mortain

another forty miles, and until his tanks reached the fruited plains beyond they would be highly vulnerable to infantry, land mines, and antitank attacks. There was also the matter of fuel, food, and ammunition supply, which First Army would have to channel down two long, fragile arteries running from the beaches to the front. Those roads would be choked with supply trucks bumping up against the attacking army, and something as simple as a stalled truck or a lost convoy could shut down his advance as effectively as a counterattack. "Of course you are going to end up with a hell of a scramble. We will have to unscramble our divisions when we get through [the hole]," Brad admitted to his concerned staff.

He also acknowledged that he would be placing his chips on two relatively untested infantry divisions that would hold open the hole; any screwup by those divisions could bring down the whole show. As he summed up his theory in a soft Missouri drawl, "The whole thing depends on certain assumptions—move boldly and be ready to take stiff losses if necessary."[5]

Yes, the plan put a lot of people in harm's way, and it violated many canons he had preached at West Point and Benning. But the alternative— a return to the slugging match of the last two months—was unpalatable, especially with the large, menacing Fifteenth Army posted up around Calais waiting for Patton's army. He knew they wouldn't wait forever.

In final form, COBRA looked just like any plan does before the shooting starts: neat and feasible. The operation would commence with a massive air bombardment of a rectangle seven thousand yards wide and twenty-five hundred yards deep, just south of the Périers-St.-Lô highway. On the heels of the air bombardment, three infantry divisions, the 4th, 9th, and newly arrived 30th, would punch a three-mile hole between Marigny and St.-Gilles. The penetrating force, consisting of the Big Red One, the 3rd Armored, and Hell on Wheels, would race toward Coutances and run behind the six weakened German divisions facing Middleton's VIII Corps. Then the turkey shoot would begin. Middleton would push forward and liquidate the pocket, clearing the base of the Cotentin neck, and Bradley's armored column would drive south, eating up French real estate as it pushed the Germans back. The Americans would own the coast all the way to Avranches, and then Third Army would come aboard for the dash into port-rich Brittany.[6]

The weather was the wild card, as it always was. When heavy rains began to drench Normandy in the middle of July, roads became muddy troughs and Brad's timetable became hopelessly deranged. On July 20, Eisenhower came to Bradley's headquarters to watch the assault commence, only to be told by a sheepish Brad that the big push would be delayed until the next day on account of rain. Bradley's mood darkened after another day of pluvial weather, which forced him to postpone COBRA one more day, then another, then another.[7]

"Dammit," Brad grumbled to an aide after several days of rain, "I'm going to have to court-martial the chaplain if we have very much more weather like this."[8]

Rotten weather notwithstanding, the eleven days between COBRA's conception and jump-off were Omar Bradley's moment to shine. His staffers prided themselves on meticulous planning, and as the planning phase of COBRA rushed toward its climax, Brad buzzed about his headquarters like a spinning gyroscope, demanding obedience to COBRA's holy principles while letting his staff and field officers work out the details. It wasn't the kind of work that made headlines, and it wasn't something an artist would depict in bold colors for *The Saturday Evening Post.* But Bradley's genius burned brightest in the creation of a complex operation, and he poured his heart and soul into the details of this breakout. When his men stepped off, he wanted to rest assured that he had done his best for them.

As COBRA's D-Day drew near, Bradley's spirits rose again. One reason for his brimming confidence lay in the corps commander who would throw the first punch, Lightning Joe Collins. With a square jaw and youthful eyes that gave him the self-assured look of a star high school quarterback, Collins had plenty of drive, and Brad could see many of George Patton's best qualities in the young general. But unlike Patton, Lightning Joe's enthusiasm was tempered with sound judgment and an ability to play on a team. In assigning him the lead role in COBRA, Brad knew he could give Joe considerable leeway in directing the block-and-run play without fear that VII Corps would send its tanks halfway to Berlin and let them run out of gas.[9]

Bradley's incoming headquarters, designated Twelfth U.S. Army Group, as well as Patton's Third Army staff and two new corps headquarters, were all setting up shop by the time COBRA was finally ready to kick off. It was almost time for Bradley take his place as an army group commander, a position that had effectively not existed since the Civil War. Ike gave the Missourian the authority to activate Twelfth Army Group and Third Army at the time of his choosing, and the two men agreed that the first of August would be about the right date. Turning the controls over to his protégé, Eisenhower sent Bradley a valedictory letter on the day the COBRA was to strike: *"My high hopes and best wishes ride with you in your attack today. . . . Speaking as the responsible American rather than Allied commander, I assure you that the eyes of our whole country will be following your progress, and I take full personal responsibility for answering to them for the necessary price of victory."*[10]

But as D-Day approached, one unfamiliar detail began to weigh on Brad's mind: How close could he move his soldiers to the bombing zone?

Brad obviously wanted to keep his men out of harm's way, but he didn't want them so far back that the Hun could regroup before his foot soldiers took them at a rush. So he selected a "safety zone" of eight hundred yards, and on June 19 he flew to Allied Expeditionary Air Forces headquarters in Stanmore, north of London, to personally explain COBRA's requirements to the air lords—Trafford Leigh-Mallory, Quesada, and others. One condition, he told them, was that the bombers must approach the target parallel to the enemy lines, rather than over the heads of the infantry, to avoid the risk that they might accidentally drop their eggs on friendly foxholes.[11]

On the question of approach, the AEAF barons demurred. They agreed that Bradley had selected a sound target, and they assured him that nothing would be left standing in that rectangle when they were finished. But they were unwilling to risk their bombers by concentrating them along a narrow corridor lined with German AA guns, and they calculated that they could not physically run the number of planes Bradley wanted through a narrow rectangular chute within the one hour the COBRA plan allotted. Given their approach requirements, they pointed out that an eight-hundred-yard gap between Brad's riflemen and the Germans was too close to guarantee the safety of everyone wearing olive drab. If Bradley wanted a carpet of high-explosive bombs, they insisted that he would need a fifteen-hundred-yard safety zone for his men.[12]

Dissatisfied with the airmen's reply, Brad refused to pull his troops more than 1,250 yards from the highway that marked the border of the bomb zone. Sure, there was a risk of short drops, he acknowledged, but the greater risk, as he and Collins saw it, was that the Boche would reset their MG-42s and mortars while the Americans were picking their way forward. Blowing a hole in an enemy line was good only if the hole was still there when the foot soldiers arrived. Holding men too far back in 1915 had condemned thousands of Tommies to death at the Somme, and Bradley was not one to repeat the mistakes of the past.[13]

By the end of the meeting, Brad secured a compromise: The more precise Thunderbolt fighter-bombers at Quesada's Tactical Air Command—"*jabos*," the Germans called them—would take care of the closest targets, letting the big Forts and Liberators work on the rectangle's deeper targets. The question of running parallel to the lines, Brad felt, was also settled in his favor, although Leigh-Mallory, running late for his next meeting, left the conference before it had ended, and they never got back to that point in detail. Brad left Stanmore satisfied that he had gotten his way.[14]

It was a dicey proposition. Flying boxcars cruising at high altitudes were notorious for scattering their explosives all over creation, and the bombing runs on D-Day and at Slapton Sands did not make Brad swell with confidence. To cut his margin even closer, he planned to have his infantry move up to the highway at the end of the heavy bomber strike, while fighter-bombers were still bombing and strafing the near zones. "We're taking a helluva chance—much more than I want to take with only a mile between my front lines and the target," Bradley said. It was a gut feeling similar to the one that had struck George Patton the night his paratroopers climbed aboard their transports for Sicily. But Bradley was confident in the end result.[15]

Threading his way gracefully among the tents and mobile trailers of his new command post, Patton felt he was safe from danger. Not the shooting kind of danger—for he still wanted a piece of that, though he had stopped kidding himself long ago that a three-star general would see much hostile fire. No, the danger he was worried about was the kind a general faces when he opens his mouth to a man holding a pen or a microphone. The kind of danger that becomes obvious only when General Marshall or Bedell Smith picks up the newspaper with his morning coffee.[16]

For the time being, George figured he was safe from this occupational hazard. He had kept his word to Ike about no press quotes. He had kept his trademark pistols in the office, mostly, and censors dutifully blacked out newspaper photos of Patton's Third Army insignia. So a phone call from Bradley's headquarters on July 17 rattled him. Journalists attached to Third Army were evidently telling their buddies at First Army that they knew all about First Army's big plan, a secret Brad had withheld from First Army's press pool.

What the hell was going on? Brad demanded. COBRA was one of the Army's most jealously guarded operations, and someone, evidently Patton's Press Relations Officer, Colonel Charles Blakeney, had been speaking out of turn to the bullpen.[17]

George was horrified, particularly as the war might be over before his beautiful killing machine got into the thick of it. He quickly called Bradley back, apologized, and promised to cut Blakeney from his team. "For God's sake, Brad," Bradley remembered him pleading, "you've got to get me into this fight before the war is over. I'm in the doghouse now and I'm apt to die there unless I pull something spectacular to get me out."[18]

Bradley accepted George's explanation and his remedial action. But he made no guarantees about future adventures. If he had his way, Rommel, Hitler & Co. would be out of business before long.

George surmised that Third Army correspondents, rivals with their counterparts in First Army, had bragged about some First Army secrets they knew, secrets it took no time for First Army's reporters to uncover. It was bad enough that George got into trouble when he opened his own mouth to reporters, and he didn't need his staff to dump him in hot water for their own mistakes. He rounded up his correspondents and gave them a sober lecture on the stakes of this leak. "I haven't got the words to express the danger which this violation of orders and trust may have on the lives of soldiers," he told them. "It is perfectly possible that through loose talk by some of you, thousands of your countrymen or Allies may be killed. It is perfectly possible that as a result of what has happened a very great operation may come to nothing."[19]

The clouds were damnably thick and low that Monday, and at the last possible minute, Bradley learned that Leigh-Mallory, who had flown to France to make a firsthand assessment of bombing conditions, had postponed the air attack. Knowing the bombers wouldn't come, Bradley also issued orders to stand down. But come they did, and as they reached the target, the lead planes unloaded some 685 tons of explosives on the box below the Périers-St.-Lô highway. Those behind them followed suit, and then the earth erupted in a torrent of smoke, dirt, flying debris. Just as planned.[20]

Not quite as planned, Brad realized. The bombers were supposed to run parallel to the infantry lines, but they were approaching on the perpendicular, from behind Bradley's infantrymen. It also didn't appear that the whole complement of bombers was attacking. And the bombs were landing closer than they should have been. Leigh-Mallory had a lot of explaining to do.[21]

Bradley's staff began frantically calling air headquarters to find out what was going on.

News came in spasmodically to the little stone house Brad had commandeered for his observation post. Leigh-Mallory, who had arrived in Normandy that morning to find the clouds impenetrable, had tried to cancel the air mission. Some air crews got the message, and some didn't. As a result, half the fighter-bombers stayed home and none of the mediums showed up. The remaining bombers arrived from the north, perpendicular to the line, instead of parallel to the German line as Bradley had requested. To make matters worse, the lead bombardier on a formation of sixteen bombers jammed his bomb release; trying to free the mechanism, he dropped a portion of his load on the 30th Division. The fifteen heavies flying behind him followed suit—that's how it works with bombers: the lead goose drops its eggs, everyone behind follows—and the unfortunate 30th suffered 156 casualties, including as many as thirty dead.[22]

Chaos reigned at VII Corps headquarters. Just before the bombardment, Collins had pulled his men back from the highway to avoid being in the bomb target area. Then General Bradley's headquarters told him the air and ground missions were canceled. But then the bombers did their work.

Did that mean COBRA was back on? Or was the bombing run an aerial snafu?

Collins called First Army to find out whether COBRA had been postponed: Were both the air and ground portions canceled, or did Bradley want him to go ahead behind the half-baked bombardment? If the game was off, Collins would have to move his infantry up to their regular line before the Germans figured out what they were up to, and the Americans would also lose the priceless element of surprise. On the other hand, if the operation were on, he would be sending infantry across a field only partly saturated, where there would be a lot more defenders left than advertised. Whatever his orders, he insisted, *somebody has to tell me what to do.*

At his command post, Bradley paced around wildly, purple with rage. The air forces had agreed to run in from the side, not over the heads of his troops. At least, that was what he had *thought* they had promised when he left Stanmore after the July 19 conference. So, apparently, did Pete Quesada, whose fighter-bombers had run in from the lateral. Now, he learned, that cowardly s.o.b. Leigh-Mallory, the same snob who had tried to scrub his D-Day airborne operation, came running to his command post pleading ignorance over the approach direction. To Brad, it wasn't negligence or ignorance; it amounted to a serious breach of good faith by the air brass.[23]

Well, no time to throw around accusations, Brad thought. He could take the matter up with Ike later. Right now, with one hundred thousand men waiting on him, he had to make a decision, one of those snap decisions portrayed in Hollywood but rarely made in a real-life operation.

Bradley wanted a rapid, blitzing attack, but he wanted it done right. Patton used to say that a good plan now was better than a perfect plan next week, but Brad saw it differently. Given the choice, he'd take perfect execution tomorrow over poor execution today. So he confirmed his postponement order: COBRA would commence the next day, Tuesday, July 25. In the meantime, Collins could move his men back to the Périers-St.-Lô road.[24]

Maybe tomorrow would be better.

For a second straight day, Bradley pricked his large ears for the drone of aircraft, this time with the Supreme Commander at his elbow. Because Bomber Command could not formulate and issue orders to change their route without delaying COBRA yet again—something neither Ike nor Brad would countenance—a reluctant Bradley was compelled to let the bombers fly in the same way: perpendicular to his lines.[25]

This time the full bomber complement, over fifteen hundred Forts and Liberators, waddled over the targets, slow and low, where they dropped more than three thousand tons of high explosive and fragmentation bombs on the unfortunate *Panzer Lehr* troops who inhabited Brad's rectangle. Another 380 mediums came in, dropping 650 tons of high-explosive and fragmentation bombs; this wave was followed by a swarm of fighter-bombers, which screamed in with another two hundred tons of HE bombs and a horrifying jellied gasoline that Ordnance was calling "napalm." The earth shook, flew up, settled, then flew up again as wave after wave of flying killers turned defense positions into freshly plowed fields. The impact was so violent that a mile from the front, the lace curtains hanging from the hut in which Brad and Collins conferred trembled with each concussive thud. Those sticks, they thought, were landing awfully close.

Before long, dust-covered aides arrived to report bad news from the forward posts.

"Oh, Christ," Brad muttered. "Not another short drop."[26]

* * *

Ike was gratified that Bradley was willing to launch COBRA despite the risks, and he harbored guarded hopes that the payoff would be substantially higher than GOODWOOD. The accidental bombing of the 30th Division the day before had worried him; he had often feared that airmen, flying high over clouds and smoke, jittery about antiaircraft fire, anxious to drop their load so they could return home, might drop their bombs short, into the tightly packed infantry below. When word came of the attempted scrubbing of the bomb runs on the twenty-fourth, followed by the postponement of COBRA and the casualties among the Americans, he began to wonder whether heavy bombers were the wrong animal for ground support. Before leaving First Army headquarters to return to Sharpener, Ike had told Brad he had "lost all faith in bombers acting in support of the ground force. . . . I gave them a green light this time. But I promise you it's the last."[27]

The next day's bombing, however, seemed to come off splendidly. Early reports of the devastation within Bradley's rectangle augured swift success for the foot soldiers, at least locally. Then he got the news: The Air Force had done it again. In three separate incidents, bombs had landed on friendly forces, killing 111 and wounding 490. The stunner was that one of the casualties—a death, not an injury—was none other than Lieutenant General Lesley J. McNair, head of Army Ground Forces and Patton's replacement as commanding general of the fictitious First U.S. Army Group in England.[28]

"Whitey" McNair, a close colleague of Marshall's, had been one of the Army's all-stars long before the Louisiana maneuvers. That afternoon, he had the honor of becoming America's highest-ranking fatality, thrown eighty feet from his slit trench and identified by three stars found on the shoulder of a shred of a corpse. To add insult to mortal injury, Ike could not even give McNair, or the little that was left of him, a decent burial, as McNair's presence in France was a carefully guarded secret, just as Patton's presence had been earlier in the month. So Whitey went to his grave accompanied only by a few senior officers and former aides, his next of kin blissfully ignorant of his fate.[29]

Back in Portsmouth, Ike slunk around Sharpener "terribly depressed," according to Kay. Thunderstruck by the loss of the Army's most senior general in Europe, Ike told Marshall that he had warned Whitey on several occasions about taking unnecessary risks, since the roving McNair had been wounded in Tunisia, again under Eisenhower's watch.[30]

Far worse than the loss of a single general, as COBRA's D-Day wore on Ike learned that the bombing didn't seem to have the advertised effects. Follow-up reports indicated that German artillery was still strong, and on the first day of the offensive, VII Corps managed to push only a little beyond its starting point. Commanders and enlisted men had been expecting an afternoon stroll south of the Périers-St.-Lô highway, and their disappointment in finding Germans very much alive threw a wet blanket over American élan.[31]

That evening, Bradley rang up Sharpener to report opening day's initial progress: The 9th Division had made a twenty-three-hundred-yard gain, and his other two assault divisions, the 4th and 30th, advanced just over half that distance.

The first day being something of a bust, Ike could see another expensive plan grinding to a dispiriting halt. Nevertheless, Ike kept faith with his Missourian. As with other generals, when the chips were down he reassured Brad that, despite the slow progress on his flanks, "I am perfectly certain that you are going to make the grade."[32]

But beyond a little high-level cheerleading, there was little Ike could do. Back in southern England, he could only hope that Omar would continue to push—and take risks, if need be—until something happened. Bradley assured him he would.[33]

Although COBRA's opening day was a disappointment, Bradley saw a few glints of sunlight among the clouds. The infantry had not fully secured the shoulders of the rectangle, but the prisoners taken from *Panzer Lehr* sure looked like they'd had their bells rung but good by the bombers. South of the Périers-St.-Lô road, German resistance was light, which could indicate that the Hun was on his heels. Or it could indicate that the "other fellow" had pulled back and was ready to pounce on Brad's armor the minute it came rolling down the road to Coutances.

Brad didn't know which was the answer, but late in the afternoon of July 25 a decision was made for him. Although he didn't fully own the "shoulder" towns of St.-Gilles and Marigny, Collins decided to go for broke: The roads, he reported, were clear enough for his armor, and he was committing his Shermans slightly ahead of schedule, at first light on D-plus-1. As American infantry broke the back of German resistance at the gap, the tanks rolled through, and Omar Bradley was about to collect his payoff.[34]

The payoff, Brad found, was not as large has he had hoped, at least not immediately. Because Huebner's 1st Division made slow going due to road congestion and savvy German resistance, the Big Red One was unable to reach Coutances in time to capture the city or bag the Germans lined up between him and Middleton. But over the next two days, Middleton's corps lunged forward and the armored column Collins had launched slammed into the rear of a retreating enemy. Brad's 2nd and 3rd Armored tankers put their Shermans into high gear and slashed their way south, deepening the hole in the German left flank and encircling the German LXXXIV Corps. Brad's haymaker had caught von Kluge square on his left jaw, and now his men were rolling into open country.[35]

Brad's blood was up. Within a week of COBRA's abortive first notes, his men flew past Coutances and drove on toward Avranches with a vengeance. They sent nearly twenty thousand prisoners into Allied POW cages, and as the German line crumbled, Brad threw Corlett and Gerow into the battle to block any further German retreat. He was conquering land he and Ike had been salivating over since D-Day. Around headquarters Bradley began talking of the "unconditional surrender" of German armed forces in France. On the twenty-eighth, three days into the COBRA offensive, Bradley wrote Ike, *To say that the personnel of the First Army Headquarters is riding high tonight is putting it mildly.*[36]

In the full bloom of confidence, Omar on the first of August assumed command of Twelfth Army Group. The mild-mannered teacher's son was showing the world what he could do.[37]

The Plan—the OVERLORD plan that had framed Dwight Eisenhower's life since December 1943—called for the Allies to be in Paris by D-plus-90, or around September 4. It was an assumption that mocked Ike during June and July as Montgomery, then Bradley, then Montgomery, then Bradley again, tried to break out of the corral in which Rommel, von Rundstedt, and von Kluge had penned them.[38]

But COBRA changed everything. By the end of July, Bradley had captured Avranches. He had almost taken enough French real estate to give Third Army some running room. Once Brittany had fallen—easy pickings, it now seemed—the port of Brest would give the Allies a second major supply artery. German resistance in France was crumbling, and an attempt on Hitler's life in late July, with its inevitable military purges, underscored Ike's early prediction that the war in Europe would be over before the end of 1944. Even Montgomery was getting into the act, for on July 28 he informed Eisenhower that he had ordered General Dempsey to take risks, accept casualties, and "step on the gas."[39]

So as August opened, a weary but exuberant Eisenhower told Harry Butcher, "If the intercepts are right, we are to hell and gone in Brittany and slicing 'em up in Normandy." He joked with Bradley that Churchill was so happy he was apt to come down to Twelfth Army Group headquarters and give Brad a kiss on both cheeks. Patton, in turn, wrote Ike, *Bradley has done a wonderful job. My only kick is that he will win the war before I get in.* George hailed Brad's plan as "a great military conception," and the self-centered publicity hound told visiting reporters that Bradley "hasn't gotten the praise he should have for having done it."[40]

As Sherman tanks roared out of the hedgerow country, Eisenhower began spending more and more time with his favorite subordinate, bumping elbows with Bradley as the two jostled about Brad's map trailer to get the latest updates from the front. Ike played late-night rubbers of bridge with his old friend and stayed for dinners and overnight visits whenever possible. When not talking business, the two men swapped gossip, reminisced over Army football games, talked over who needed promoting and who needed relieving. When traveling to meetings with "outsiders" like Montgomery and Devers, they often shared a car, working out their ideas together before proposing them to others. They were close, Kay remarked, "almost like brothers," and Ike commenced a letter-writing campaign to urge General Marshall to promote Bradley to permanent major general.[41]

To keep pace with his advancing armies, on August 7 Eisenhower had a small staff of deputies move his advanced command post to the bucolic little village of Tournières, not far from Bayeux, the city for which the famed tapestry was named. His new post, code-named SHELLBURST, was set up in his preferred fashion: simple Army style, with a few rudimentary sleeping trucks and slit trenches ringing a cluster of plank-floored office tents. Ensconced in a tangle of hedgerows and telephone lines, Ike felt he could better appreciate firsthand the terrain over which his men were fighting. From Tournières he would fight one last battle with Winston Churchill, over Operation ANVIL.[42]

ANVIL, later renamed DRAGOON, was a landing in Southern France under the command of General Devers. It would bring additional divisions onto the Continent, and just as important, it would give General Lee's SOS people two major ports, Marseilles and Toulon, through which to supply the growing Allied host. Churchill vehemently disagreed with the concept, and on August 5 the English bulldog showed up at Shellburst and spent the next several days badgering General Eisenhower into scrubbing DRAGOON. An exasperated but confident Eisenhower refused to budge, and the DRAGOON landings went forward as planned on August 15. Before long, General Truscott's VI Corps and the French First Army liberated Toulon, Marseilles, and Grenoble, and Ike was pleased to see his newest legions do the Truscott Trot up the Rhône Valley to join forces, where they would link with Patton's Third Army.[43]

While Truscott's men were stampeding across the French Riviera, Ike had to deal with a serious uproar in the press. Some jackleg reporter from the AP, it seemed, had managed to slip past the censors a story that Eisenhower was demoting General Montgomery from chief ground commander to mere army group commander. British newspaper editors, sensitive to the patriotism of their subscribers, voiced their indignation in loud, unqualified tones. SHAEF attempted to clarify the situation by announcing that Montgomery would continue in command of all ground forces for the time being, but that announcement created a backlash in the American press and stirred up great concern among both Stimson and Marshall.[44]

Since the early days of OVERLORD, the plan had called for Montgomery to relinquish his role as ground commander to the Supreme Commander and take the reins of Twenty-First Army Group on a full-time basis. The story of Montgomery's "demotion" was, therefore, hardly newsworthy to Ike and his planners. With six armies operating on the Continent—Second British and First Canadian under Monty, First and Third U.S. under Brad, and First French and Seventh U.S. under Devers—it seemed natural to Ike that he should become his own ground force commander.

But that story, unknown to the British public and press, inspired an outcry that Monty did nothing to check. Eisenhower and Bradley were soon caught in a nasty cross fire between Fleet Street, which called for the retention of Montgomery as Allied ground commander, and the U.S. press, which accused the British of running the show on the backs of the American soldier. "Goddammit," Ike emoted, "the British have never understood the American system of command."[45]

That was certainly part of the problem. Commanders in the American army traditionally set the objectives, but defer the *how* and the *when* to their subordinates; Bradley's COBRA directive, for example, was a page and a half of instructions, with one diagram illustrating what he wanted his divisions to do. The rest was a matter of trust, or clarification. If Ike could trust Bradley, Montgomery, and Devers to do their jobs faithfully and efficiently, the Allies would not need a separate ground commander.

The British model, with which Montgomery, Churchill, and the British press were better acquainted, encouraged detailed instructions set out in pages of paragraphs and subparagraphs. Thus, in Montgomery's army group directives, a large serving of the *how* and the *when* was ladled out with the *where* and the *whom*. Montgomery referred to this concept as "tight battle grip," and many British chieftains, both uniformed and civilian, had a hard time understanding Eisenhower's laissez-faire attitude toward operational details.

It was a hopeless scuffle among journalists and politicians, but with two great democracies as co-belligerents, neither country's high command could afford to ignore the question. As a sop to the king's subjects, Churchill promoted General Montgomery to field marshal, equivalent to an American five-star general. Ike, trying desperately to right the boat, sent his warm congratulations to the prickly marshal, but refused to alter the command arrangements to maintain Montgomery's position as his top lieutenant.[46]

The Battle of the Ground Commander hammered home another wedge between Montgomery and the American generals, and Bradley in particular. Before long, Montgomery began complaining about Bradley to Eisenhower, and he would begin complaining about Eisenhower to Marshall. The Americans didn't buy it, and the Chief and Ike remained Bradley's strongest backers. But the inescapable fact was that the Allied command in Europe was rupturing. Brad concluded with the benefit of hindsight, "The unfortunate August split never completely healed."[47]

Patton, invested on the Continent with four dormant corps headquarters and some thirty thousand French irregulars, squirmed impatiently as Brad's COBRA slithered toward Avranches without him. Waiting for his activation orders, he fretted that command politics might get in the way of sound operations. He also worried that Bradley was just a bit reluctant to activate Third Army, since it would bump him up to army group commander and move him farther from the front lines, where the action was. *"In this I can sympathize with him,"* George remarked.[48]

But on the last day of July, Third Army's incubation period was over, and the chicken was ready to peck its way out of the egg. Though he would not officially become Third Army's commanding general—LUCKY SIX—until the following day, Patton proceeded to move his headquarters, LUCKY MAIN, up to the Coutances-St.-Lô road. From his advanced command post at LUCKY FORWARD—which included a van with living quarters, secure phone lines, and a glass-topped desk—he ordered General Middleton to move his stalled VIII Corps over the Selune River and into Brittany.[49]

George's war was about to begin. Again.

The Team: George, Brad, and Ike on German soil, 1945.

Cadet George Patton in his first class year, 1908–09.

Cadet Omar Bradley on West Point's 1915 baseball team.

Cadet Dwight Eisenhower on the Point's football team.

Patton and a Renault light tank, summer 1918.

Eisenhower and a light tank, 1919.

Patton models a tank uniform of his own design. He insisted it was better than the one issued by the Ordnance Department, but the "Green Hornet outfit" spent the war in George's closet.

Bradley (*standing, second from left*) and General Marshall (*seated, center*) on the Fort Benning faculty, 1930.

Patton and Ike, together in the center, pose for a group photo of the U.S. Tank Corps, Camp Meade, Maryland, 1920.

Ike plots the destruction of Second Army during the 1941 Louisiana war games.

Eisenhower and his staff in London, 1942 (*from left to right*): his driver, Kay Summersby; his orderly, Sgt. Mickey McKeogh; his deputy commander, Lt. Gen. Mark W. Clark; his naval aide, Cdr. Harry Butcher; and Gen. Smith, who would serve him until the German surrender.

Walter Bedell Smith, Eisenhower's chief of staff. Ike considered "Beetle" his one indispensable man.

Eisenhower and Kay Summersby on the road in North Africa, 1942.

An American tank destroyer group advances cautiously in Tunisia, 1943.

Admiral François Darlan of France.

Eisenhower, Gen. Harold Alexander, and Patton confer at II Corps headquarters, March 1943. In Patton's territory, even Ike wore a helmet.

Eisenhower pins a third star on Patton, March 1943. Note that George's jacket already had a third star sewn onto the shoulder.

Bradley and Maj. Gen. Terry Allen confer as fighting rages in Gela, Sicily.

Patton shows Gen. Bernard Montgomery the big picture.

Ike and Patton in Sicily, September 1943, shortly after the "Slapping Incidents."

President Roosevelt and Eisenhower during the president's visit to the Mediterranean.

Lt. Gen. Mark W. Clark.

American infantrymen, on alert for snipers, advance down an Italian street. Caiazzo, 1943.

Lt. Gen. William Simpson.

Maj. Gen. Manton Eddy.

Brig. Gen. Hobart "Hap" Gay.

Eisenhower, Churchill, and Bradley try their hands with Army carbines. Their scores were classified as military secrets.

Patton and Secretary of War Henry L. Stimson. Stimson was Patton's patron and protector in Washington.

Lt. Gen. Lucian Truscott.

Maj. Gen. John P. Lucas.

Admiral Ernest King.

Bradley piped aboard the USS *Augusta*, his command ship for Operation NEPTUNE, the amphibious phase of OVERLORD.

Troops wade ashore at Normandy's beaches.

Brad, Ike, Maj. Gen. "Gee" Gerow, and Maj. Gen. J. Lawton Collins after the fall of Cherbourg.

Eisenhower visits troops in Normandy.

Collins describes the fighting around Cherbourg to Bradley.

Brad, Patton (*head of far column*) and Lt. Gen. Courtney Hodges (*head of near column*) lead the funeral procession for Maj. Gen. Theodore Roosevelt Jr.

Brad at his command trailer desk.

Patton, Brad, and Monty share a forced smile for the camera.

An American patrol labors through the blasted ruins of Saint-Lô.

Crowds celebrate the liberation of Paris, August 1944.

Ike waves to Paris crowds after the city's liberation.

Monty and Ike butted heads over questions of supply, strategy, and ground command.

Bradley, Beetle Smith, and Montgomery's chief of staff, Maj. Gen. Francis de Guingand, leaving a contentious meeting in September 1944. Brad and Monty would clash over troop allocation and basic strategy.

Patton and Bradley share a ride in a C-47 over Brittany.

Hodges, Bradley, Patton, and Maj. Gen. Hugh Gaffey, Patton's chief of staff, at the "Communion Rail" in Brad's command trailer.

Ike and George at Third Army headquarters, October 1944. Ike cut Third Army's troop and supply allocation to make progress along Montgomery's front.

Brad, Hodges, and Ike tour the Remagen bridgehead with the commanding general of III Corps, Maj. Gen. John Millikin.

Shortly after Third Army's Rhine crossing, Ike and George share a joke. Brad and Hodges look on.

Ike confers with Field Marshal Brooke and Prime Minister Churchill on the banks of the Rhine River, March 1945.

The master and his cavalier: Ike and George, March 1945.

Patton's troops push past "dragon's teeth" in the Siegfried Line.

Fired: Patton bids his Third Army farewell, October 1945. Behind George is his friend and successor, Lt. Gen. Lucian K. Truscott.

Ike (*right of center*), Patton (*behind Ike*), and Bradley (*near Ike's left*) look on in horror at the Nazi handiwork, April 1945.

The last salute: Ike, Patton, Truman, Stimson, and Bradley (*front row, left to right*) salute the Stars and Stripes at the Potsdam Conference in 1945.

NINETEEN

"WE MAY END THIS IN TEN DAYS"

George is used to attacks from a single division. But he's not used to having three or four divisions hit him. He doesn't know what it means yet.

—Brad, August 2, 1944

Bradley came down to see me, suffering from nerves. . . . His motto seems to be "In case of doubt, halt."

—George, August 15, 1944

IN BRAD'S MIND, George didn't appreciate the need to take the Nazis seriously. On the Continent, where the enemies were Germans, not French or Italians, attacks came at the Allies by corps and divisions, not by battalions. Yet Patton's first edicts as Third Army commander told him that George was still playing by the penny-ante rules of North Africa and Sicily.[1]

Bradley viewed George and his many deficiencies in planning in stark contrast to Hodges, who was appropriately aggressive, but prudent and attentive to detail. As Brad later contended, "Whereas Patton could seldom be bothered with details, Hodges studied his problems with infinite care and was thus better qualified to execute the more intricate operations." On the other hand, as Chet Hansen opined to his diary, *"Bradley . . . has had difficulty keeping Patton on the plan. Pat[ton] more interested in fighting for headlines than soundly."*[2]

To Brad's surprise, George quickly fell in line, just like a good old soldier. Or, at least, a soldier who knew he was one step away from being sent back to Palermo. George had always respected the civilities between senior generals, the "gentleman's code" of the military nobility—the salute and the "sir" and the small honors, like motorcades and honor guards—and these

★ 367 ★

social rules gave way to a comradely informality only when the two men were in private, or accompanied only by their trusted retainers. Another sure sign that George knew who was boss was his ham-handed bootlicking campaign directed at his Group commander; shortly after arriving in Europe, George began to refer to Bradley as "the Eagle," and he sang loud praises of Brad's military acumen to Brad's aides, fully expecting the message to get back to Bradley as a burst of spontaneous sincerity. Just as he did with Eisenhower in Sicily and England.[3]

Privately, however, George *knew* that Bradley, like his understudy Hodges, lacked drive and imagination. They lacked a willingness to take risks. Brad didn't appreciate the need for improvisation, something vital in a fluid battle, especially when the enemy was on the run. With the collapse of German resistance after COBRA, George thought it made sense to chuck the playbook and hound the Kraut all the way to the Rhine. Rather than squeeze his entire army into the Bretagne peninsula, why not cut off Brittany at the neck, clear out the interior with armor, then dispatch bottled-up defenders in the ports with an infantry division while sending the rest of his army toward Paris? To George, who tended to think in great, sweeping movements, throwing off division-size flank protection as he drove into Brittany seemed a huge waste of effort.[4]

Troy Middleton was the first commander caught in the Patton-Bradley cross fire. On his way to executing Bradley's orders to take St.-Malo, Middleton received a message from General Patton ordering him to bypass the town. "There is nothing there anyway," George assured him. "There aren't 500 troops in there." But when Middleton tried to bypass St.-Malo, the town garrison—estimated by G-2 at three to six thousand strong—showered his men with an artillery serenade that stopped his armor until Middleton sent the 83rd Division in to put a stop to the nuisance. In the end, the 83rd captured some fourteen thousand Germans there; Middleton never knew how many they killed.[5]

So much for Patton's famous instincts.

As Middleton's VIII Corps was battering its way toward Brest, Bradley stepped in personally to countermand George's orders. It was the very sin he had been furious with George for in Sicily, but as Bradley saw it, he had to insert himself into George's business to stave off disaster. Middleton recalled:

The confusion lasted for several days. For instance, Bradley told me, "When you get out through Avranches to the south, be sure to guard the south flank very heavily because it's wide open not only to the south but in the direction of Paris. There was a town named Fougères; I was ready to send the Seventy-Ninth Division there to block when Patton came along. "Hell, no," George said, "we're going to Brest."[6]

Shortly afterward, Bradley motored over to Middleton's command tent, where he found the normally quiet Louisianan complaining about Patton's orders.

"I'm wide open here," Middleton groused in his Mississippi Delta drawl, and he explained to Bradley that his corps front faced west rather than east, where the main enemy force was hunkered down. "I'd hate to attack with enemy at my rear and with my rear exposed the way it is. If he cuts through the hinge, I'd be stuck."[7]

Brad exploded when he heard the news.

"Dammit, I'm not interested in making news," he said, his brow furrowing over his steel-rimmed spectacles. He ordered Middleton to send the 79th Division to shore up the corps rear at Fougères, and he lectured the college president on Patton's limitations:

[The] Germans could hit us with three divisions there and it'll make us look very foolish. It would be embarrassing to George. George is used to attacks from a single division. He's buttoned up well enough for that. But he's not used to having three or four divisions hit him. He doesn't know what it means yet.[8]

White hot under his three-starred collar, Bradley had Sergeant Stoute drive him over to Lucky Forward to set the ground rules. "For Christ's sake, George," he began, "what are you going to do about this open flank you have; I've sent the 79th down there and I hate to have to bypass a commander, it's your army." He proceeded to lecture Patton on the need to keep his eastern front secure while Middleton was doing his job in Brittany.[9]

Patton, unbeknownst to Bradley and Middleton, had already sent the 5th Armored Division to Fougères to protect his flank. But he simply grinned at Bradley and told him he would make sure the 79th got there without delay. As Brad later recalled, George put his arm over the Missourian's shoulder and said with a lop-eared grin, "Fine, fine, Brad. That's just what I would have done."[10]

On the drive back to Army Group headquarters, Brad commented that George would probably call him a son-of-a-bitch behind his back for breaking the chain of command and reaching down to George's corps. And why shouldn't he? Bradley had felt the same when George did it to him in Sicily. But Brad also knew he was right in this instance. "Hell, there's no telling what might happen if we didn't button up there," he explained. From his close work with Patton, he knew the Californian needed discipline from above, as George was not the man to see, much less curb, his impulsive excesses. "If George were hit by three divisions, he might lose two of his own and that'd be terribly embarrassing. It'd cost him his job. He should thank me for doing what I did."[11]

George never thanked Brad. Instead, he recorded a different version of his talk with Brad in his diary. He wrote that Bradley,

> with some embarrassment, stated that he had been waiting for me at the VIII Corps, and as I had not arrived there, he had taken the responsibility of telling Middleton to move the 79th Division to the east. . . . He said he knew that I would concur. I said that I would, but that I did not agree with him and feared that he was getting the British complex of over-caution. It is noteworthy that just about a year ago to the day I had to force him to conduct an attack in Sicily. I do not mean by this that he is avengeful, but he is naturally super-conservative.[12]

"Super-conservative" is, of course, a relative term, and in comparison to George's philosophy, it must have seemed that way. To Patton, in a war of maneuver the flanks would take care of themselves. "Some goddamn fool once said that flanks have got to be secure," a reporter quoted George saying. "I don't agree with that. My flanks are something for the enemy to worry about, not me. Before he finds out where my flanks are, I'll be cutting the bastard's throat."[13]

It was Pattonesque overstatement, of course; on the day he assumed command of Third Army, George threw out an infantry division to protect his armor's flanks, and he often shifted infantry to cover worrisome gaps when he could not get reliable tactical air cover. But George's comment summed up his basic approach to war, and it reflected the cavalryman's philosophy that an army's strategic momentum should always be driven forward. That was where he and Bradley still differed, if only in degree. He had told Brad that he had to do something spectacular to get out of the doghouse; as Brad reflected years later, Patton had little to lose and much to gain by taking spectacular risks in the open country of France.[14]

Worried about the pace of his Brittany campaign, which he felt was headed in the wrong direction anyway, George threw his men into the peninsula in piecemeal fashion. He sent the outnumbered 6th Armored Division against Brest, he flung the 4th Armored against unknown defenses at Lorient, and he split the 5th Infantry Division between Angers and Nantes. It was, George knew, the kind of approach that gets students failing grades at Leavenworth. *"I am doing this without consulting General Bradley,"* he wrote, *"as I am sure he would think it too risky. It is slightly risky, but so is war."*[15]

While Middleton's men were scrambling up the Breton neck, Bradley and Patton were thinking about Paris, the Seine, and beyond. Patton urged Bradley to toss the Third Army portion of the OVERLORD plan and let him move east. He could, he argued, leave Middleton's corps to clean up Brittany, and send the rest of his army toward Germany, rather than the Atlantic Ocean. Bradley, having reached the same conclusion, agreed; with the Normandy beaches piling high with supplies and Brest a complete wreck, the Breton ports were becoming logistically unimportant. To Bradley, the job in Brittany had become a matter of pride rather than strategy. As he later confided to George, "I would not say this to anyone but you, and have given different excuses to my staff, but we must take Brest for the honor of the U.S. Army." (At this George quipped, *"More emotion than I thought he had."*[16])

The matter decided, Bradley pressed Ike to let him hold Brittany with as few men as possible and turn the bulk of Patton's army—the XII, XV, and XX Corps—against the Seine. Ike, elated by the success of COBRA, agreed.[17]

Third Army's spearhead was its three-division XV Corps, commanded by Major General Wade Haislip. Haislip, a fighter whose jolly-looking features concealed a killer instinct, had set up shop on the Continent in mid-July. His tanks primed, a happy George Patton hustled Haislip's divisions through the Avranches neck and directed them to the open country to the southeast.[18]

Before long, Haislip's XV Corps and the newly arrived XX Corps, under Major General Walton "Bulldog" Walker, were barreling into the belly of the German Seventh Army. By August 7, Patton's men were driving toward Le Mans and dashing along the Loire River. It was a pace a little too reckless for Bradley, a little too timid for George. But it produced results, and it opened other delicious possibilities from Bradley as the Battle of France entered its critical phase.[19]

Thus, by early August, a hundred miles from the edge of the OVERLORD map, Bradley was about ready to give Patton an assignment every general dreams of. But first he needed Ike's blessing.

Eisenhower was finally seeing a light at the end of the tunnel. Patton had been brought into the fight, Hodges was moving east, and the Breton ports looked ripe for the plucking. Confident in his armies, Ike began thinking of the next stage, the war beyond OVERLORD's boundaries. He joked with Brad that he would enjoy nothing better than to be in Paris for his birthday, October 14. "We'd take over the biggest hotel, close it off to everyone else, and have the biggest party in the world until everyone got tight," he chortled as Brad's tanks fought their way into the open.[20]

As delighted as he was with Bradley, Ike was also elated to watch Patton's progress as the cavalryman busted out of Brittany and into central France. His thrust toward Le Mans was going so fast, Butcher noted, that "communications simply can't keep pace. Even the correspondents are writing in ecstasy about the speed." The velocity of Patton's attack forced Ike to cancel a paratroop drop west of the Seine, and Ike was more amused than angered by reports from a hot General Lee that George's men had commandeered supply trucks to move their soldiers forward. [21]

George's *Tour de France* boosted Ike's spirits, and he was happy to give George a fat slice of the credit. But he didn't want to lift the press blackout on Third Army just yet, no matter how much George would have loved the publicity. When Butcher brought up the subject, Ike asked, "Why should I tell the enemy?" To Bradley, though, he explained his reasons for keeping George quiet in terms the Missourian could appreciate: "I won't save his scalp. [I] only have gray hairs left on this poor head of mine after the hard time I had when he started and I mean to get him for it!"[22]

Bradley's clenched jaw began to loosen that summer as George plowed through Brittany and drove his remaining corps east. Ten days after COBRA, he was finally reaping the fruits of his labors since Bristol, and the thought of what he had accomplished since the day he heard the church bells ring exhilarated him.

Filled with confidence and excitement, Brad lay awake in his bunk night after night, unable to sleep soundly as his mind spun within the solitude of his trailer. As his tanks drove through Avranches, he told Chet Hansen, "When I go to bed I find myself thinking on this thing, and I cannot get to sleep without planning in my mind through half the night." Bleary-eyed from sunup to sundown, Brad eventually asked his aide to requisition him some sleeping pills from the infirmary.[23]

During August, Bradley crisscrossed western Normandy in a converted truck half the size of a Pullman car, which had an attachment to hook up his old deuce-and-a-half living quarters. At Ike's suggestion, he soon had an even larger trailer rigged up with Plexiglas skylights, long fluorescent lamps, mahogany wall paneling, thick carpeting, and of course, more maps. Inside, a cherry-stained wooden bar resembling a Communion rail separated Bradley's inner sanctum from the visitors' antechamber, and on his desk lay a red leather folder containing photographs of Mary and his daughter, Elizabeth. Scattered around his office like crystalline candles were empty Coca-Cola bottles, legacies of Bradley's favorite drink, which orderlies would clean periodically during the long, hot August days. Outside the trailer, until they wandered off with passing soldiers, were two stray headquarters pups named Omaha and Utah, who passed their free time scampering up and down the camouflage netting that veiled Brad's headquarters trucks.[24]

As he looked at the progress neatly summarized on his maps, Bradley saw mixed results. First Army, under Hodges, confronted heavy resistance from four panzer, one panzergrenadier, and two infantry divisions, and Courtney's men found the going slow on the roads near Mortain and Vire. Patton, by contrast, seemed to be making better progress, owing to fewer German defenders spread out over a wider area. He was in his element, driving recklessly, afraid of nothing. And that was the problem, for Brad was acutely aware of things George should have been afraid of. Things like vulnerable flanks and panzer movements from the east. Things like the uncomfortable fact that Third Army's thin supply lines ran around a narrow pass between Mortain and the sea.[25]

The real danger, however, lay in front of Hodges, not Patton. First Army's front erupted into flames in the early morning hours of August 7, when von Kluge launched Operation LÜTTICH, a two-army counterattack toward Mortain and Avranches. Von Kluge's intention was to smash VII Corps and cut Third Army's supply lines, forcing Third Army to withdraw to the Cotentin. If successful, von Kluge would stuff the cork back into the Cotentin neck, reversing the losses in territory since the American offensive of July 25 and trapping the Americans in the bocage again.[26]

LÜTTICH fell with unaccustomed ferocity. Beset by four panzer divisions, Lightning Joe ground to a halt as German reinforcements shot their way to within a dozen miles of the Allied hinge at Avranches. Behind them were several infantry divisions, as well as a scratch collection of battle groups from the remnants of the bombed-out *Panzer Lehr* division. It was the first serious counterattack against the Americans since D-Day.[27]

With Third Army's carotid artery running through Avranches, Bradley worried that Patton's army would be cut off from the main Allied body. If the "other fellow" reached salt water, the American force would be split, Patton would run out of gas, and Third Army would take a walloping.

But reflecting further, Bradley recognized the boon Hitler had just handed the Allies. The Mortain counterattack, he soon realized, was piling irreplaceable German tank divisions into the pocket of a giant Allied baseball glove, between the British to the north, and Patton to the south. All that remained was for Brad to close the glove.

Bradley grew excited about the prospect of a double envelopment, the holy grail of military tactics. His mind scratching out possibilities on a giant mental map, Brad jumped back into the First Army driver's seat and attached neighboring divisions to VII Corps, to allow Collins to run the defense plays. That, he figured, would hold von Kluge's panzers for now. Having attended to Avranches, he then rode over to Lucky Forward, Patton's tactical headquarters, to discuss where to halt Patton's drive east.[28]

After discussing the problem with Patton, he ratified the general's order to hold back three divisions close to Mortain as insurance against a widening German offensive. With the rest of Patton's men rushing east, parallel to the Loire River, Bradley was faced with two risky, and therefore unpleasant, choices: He could keep Patton moving ahead, which would expose his troops to the risk of isolation and destruction if Avranches fell, or he could order George to pull everyone back to Avranches, which would reverse the progress of the last seven days and probably expose him to criticism from SHAEF. His inclination was to take the bolder approach, but given the stakes, it was not a decision he wished to make alone.[29]

After conferring briefly with Montgomery, Brad arranged to meet Ike, who was touring the front, on the road near Group headquarters. He drove out to find Ike's big Packard Clipper sitting on the roadside, Kay at her usual place behind the wheel. Brad climbed into the Packard, and the two men rode to Coutances, where they conferred on the German penetration. After discussing the balance of forces and the reinforcement situation in detail, they arrived at the same general conclusion: A Boche breakthrough to Avranches was possible, though it looked probable that Collins would hold the line west of Mortain. No guarantees there, but if the Germans reached the Bay of Mont-Saint-Michel, Ike promised Bradley that Air Transport would fly in two thousand tons of supplies per day, enough to keep Patton in business. Given those probabilities, the two bridge players made an aggressive bid. They would call von Kluge's bluff, and Patton would keep moving east.[30]

Having decided to keep George in the game, the two generals tossed around the "how" and "where" of the encirclement. Patton's preference, not surprisingly, was for a "long hook" dash—a run to the Seine, then hang a left until hitting the English Channel. George claimed the maneuver would bag every Kraut west of Paris. That was the "cavalry way" to do it.

Ike and Brad liked this concept, but it invited some rather obvious risks. George could run out of gas, and even if he didn't, his lines would be weak everywhere, inviting a breakout and considerable loss of life. If Hitler were shifting divisions from the Eastern Front, there would be hell to pay.[31]

On the other hand, Ike and Brad figured Patton might try a "short hook" toward Argentan and Falaise, the natural escape route for those German divisions piling into the baseball glove. This play would require Patton to leave only his three divisions behind to hold the Avranches corridor. He could turn Haislip north from Le Mans toward Falaise, link up with the British, and *presto!* some twenty German divisions, give or take, would be bumming smokes from PW guards before week's end.[32]

Military protocol required Bradley to call Montgomery, the lame-duck ground commander, and ask permission to move Haislip north. For the plan to work, Monty would also need to push his men south from Falaise, where they would link up with Haislip to close the bag south of Argentan. Brad rang up Monty's headquarters.[33]

It was not so much a request for permission as a polite notification of American intentions. Bradley told Montgomery that General Eisenhower was in the room with him, and that the two of them had agreed on a

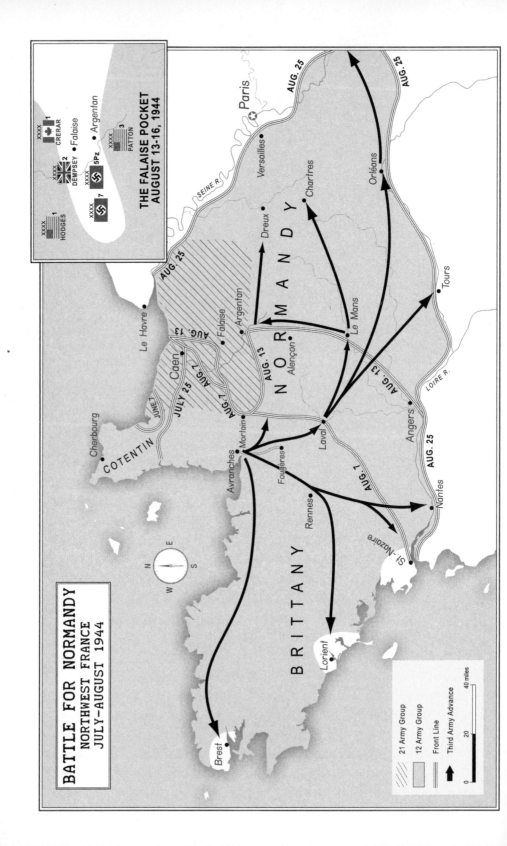

BATTLE FOR NORMANDY
NORTHWEST FRANCE
JULY–AUGUST 1944

THE FALAISE POCKET
AUGUST 13-16, 1944

21 Army Group
12 Army Group
Front Line
Third Army Advance

0   20   40 miles

plan to block the German retreat around Argentan and Falaise. With little choice in the matter, Montgomery authorized Bradley to hit the flanks and rear of the enemy and assured him that General Crerar's Canadians would press from the north. Together, they would close the jaws of a great vise between Falaise and Argentan and shut down the Seventh and Fifth Panzer Armies.[34]

With a steady hand to keep Patton focused on the team's goal, Brad knew the encirclement would be a brilliant end to a brilliant operation. As he told one distinguished visitor, the Allies had "an opportunity that comes to a commander not more than once in a century. We're about to destroy an entire hostile army. . . . We'll go all the way from here to the German border."[35]

On Brad's orders, Patton moved Haislip forward, ready to pivot around the enemy flank and rear toward Argentan. Glad to see the Allies "hold 'em by the nose and kick 'em in the pants"—with Third Army doing the kicking—Patton quietly ordered XV Corps to halt at Le Mans and swing north to make contact with the Canadians at Argentan.[36]

It was a sound maneuver, Patton knew, but inwardly he was more than a little disappointed with Brad's caution. The "short hook" was the safe play, hardly a grand envelopment worthy of a Marshal Murat. A deep envelopment along the Seine was perfectly feasible, George thought, given the desperate state of the enemy to his front. Better, he thought, to move east toward Orléans, then down the Seine to Paris, then from Paris to the sea. He complained to Ev Hughes about the "doughboy fashion" tactics Bradley had ordered and how plodding they were, knowing the message would get back to Ike.[37]

Still, bagging two German armies was a pretty fat score, one no general who wore a battle helmet could turn down. So having complained, cajoled, and sounded off to his friends, Patton ordered Haislip to make the short hook.

The question left open by Bradley's short-hook order was where, precisely, the Americans and Canadians would close the pocket. Falaise and Argentan, the north and south shoulders of the German exit, lay within Twenty-First Army Group territory. At the time Brad and Monty agreed to close the bag, they concluded that it would be easier for Crerar's Canadians to reach Argentan from the north than for Patton's troops to get there from the more distant Le Mans. Montgomery ordered General Crerar to drive through Falaise into Argentan and link up with the Yanks somewhere to the south.[38]

But as Crerar's Canadians pushed south toward Falaise, they ran into determined German opposition, resistance far stiffer than that facing their American cousins to the south. By August 13, First Canadian Army was still several miles north of Falaise, while Patton's tankers were almost to Argentan. As a result, the bag Bradley was desperate to close had a twenty-mile open mouth—the German-held ground between Haislip's XV Corps at Argentan and the Canadians, just north of Falaise. George, whose tanks were ready to advance north, had a fist wrapped around the drawstring. The question was whether Monty and Brad should order George to yank the bag shut.[39]

Bradley discussed the matter with Monty that afternoon. The two men pored over a map spread across the back of a jeep, much as Monty had done with Patton before the race to Messina. The two generals agreed that as long as Haislip's corps met little or no opposition, Patton should let Haislip push forward slowly, regardless of the formal army group boundaries.[40]

He had been given license to close the bag, but something dark stirred in the back of Brad's searching mind. The Germans, he thought, must have known they were surrounded on three sides. By now, they also knew they couldn't punch through at Avranches. Even as Haislip was threatening to cut off their retreat, still they hammered at Mortain. It made no sense. What was their game?[41]

"Either they are crazy, or they don't know what is happening," he muttered to Hansen.[42]

But von Kluge wasn't crazy, as Brad well knew. The Germans had twenty-plus divisions stuffed into the sack, and those divisions were waiting for something. What, he couldn't tell.

Patton fancied himself a high-stakes risk taker, but even he had to pause when he looked at the map. He had Haislip's corps driving east, with its right flank in the air and its left flank twenty-five miles from the nearest M-1 rifle. A first-year cadet could see the danger.[43]

It was no surprise, then, that on the night of August 12 General Haislip, fighting his way through Alençon toward Argentan, called Patton and pleaded for a halt. His corps was extended from Le Mans to Alençon to Argentan to Falaise, and he warned Patton that his men might not hold if the Boches hit him hard in the flank. At the very least, he said, he needed additional troops to help block the east–west roads north of Argentan.[44]

In a nod to Haislip's concerns, Patton moved an infantry division forward to shelter Haislip's left. But the whole point of the short hook was to bag the two armies inside the pocket, which would not happen if he waited until the everyone had moved into position; by then the Krauts would be unrolling their sleeping bags on the other side of the Seine. So, in the early minutes of August 13, he ordered Haislip to keep pushing tanks to the front. Take Alençon; take Argentan.

Hell, go to the English Channel if you have to. Just bag those Germans.[45]

As August 12 became August 13, the phones rang off the hooks at Eagle TAC and Lucky Forward. Bradley, deciding he had been somewhat ambiguous the night before, had his chief of staff, Lev Allen, call his opposite number at Third Army, General Gaffey, to make sure Patton understood Twelfth Army Group's intentions. Allen told Gaffey unequivocally that XV Corps was to halt on the army group boundary, just below Argentan. Patton was not to attempt to close the Falaise Gap.

Patton couldn't believe it when he heard the news. Stumped, he called Allen back and pleaded his case like a jailhouse lawyer. The Germans, he argued, had to man a long perimeter against four Allied armies; they did not have enough forces to stop him. Pushing Haislip forward was the surest way to close the bag, which was what Bradley wanted in the first place—a double envelopment. Otherwise, he said, the Germans would run out the back door. Would Bradley reconsider?[46]

Allen said he'd get back with George.

Allen phoned back later. Neither Montgomery nor Bradley, he said, was interested in having Haislip drive against Falaise. The army group boundaries would remain where they were, and there would be no appeals. Haislip's XV Corps would halt and consolidate its position.[47]

"We now have elements in Argentan," Patton told Bradley over the scrambler phone when he finally reached him.[48]

The announcement was premature, since as Patton spoke, a scratch collection from two panzer divisions was driving Haislip's advance parties from Argentan's outskirts. But Haislip had fought his way through Alençon, a short hop south of Argentan, and the mighty Third Army was ready to snap the trap shut. With Bradley's blessing, George promised, those two German armies were as good as gone.[49]

Bradley had been worried about friendly fire between the converging ranks of Canadians and Americans, and he told George that Twelfth Army Group's G-2 had forecast a big German attack toward Haislip, which would make any further advance a lethal mistake. It wasn't hard to foresee a violent lunge at the XV Corps flank if Haislip pushed himself between one hundred thousand soldiers and their freedom. How could one overstretched corps hold off two desperate German armies?[50]

"You're not to go beyond Argentan," Brad said, settling the argument once and for all. "Just stop where you are and build up that shoulder. Sibert tells me the German is beginning to pull out. You'd better button up and get ready for him."[51]

As Bradley later put it, "I much preferred a solid shoulder at Argentan to the possibility of a broken neck at Falaise." Besides, Brad thought to himself, that arrogant Montgomery said he would take Argentan. Brad was not about to capture one of Montgomery's objectives just to help the Englishman reach his goal. "If Montgomery wants help in closing the gap," he resolved, "let him ask us for it."[52]

George was furious. He scribbled in his diary that day, *"I am sure that this halt is a great mistake, as I am certain that the British will not close on Falaise."* He privately attributed the halt order to "the 21st Army Group," claiming it was *"either due to jealousy of the Americans or to utter ignorance of the situation, or to a combination of the two."* He fumed to Gaffey that the decision to stop Haislip would be condemned by history, and he ordered Gaffey to put the stenographic record of his conversation with Allen into the Third Army's historical files, so the world would know that the charge of timidity could not be laid at George Patton's doorstep.[53]

The gap was closed on August 21. By then von Kluge's replacement, Field Marshal Walter Model, had used his few remaining tanks to hold open a door for some twenty to forty thousand soldiers, who escaped and took refuge beyond the Seine. But in turning back the Mortain offensive, the Allies captured around 50,000 enemy soldiers, while another 10,000 of Hitler's *Übermenschen* lay in tangled heaps in ditches flanking the roads east.[54]

It was an incomplete victory, or a partial failure, depending on how one looked at it, and Bradley immediately blamed Montgomery. As ground commander, Montgomery hadn't asked or even suggested that he would alter army group boundaries to allow Bradley to move Haislip north.

Moreover, instead of running his Canadians behind the Boche and trapping them in the pocket, Monty had pushed his main force up the middle, squeezing the Germans out of the pocket like toothpaste from a tube. As Bradley wrote afterward, "General Eisenhower, Patton and I were all disgusted with the way Montgomery made his attack."[55]

But afterward Brad wondered whether he had made the right decision. Should he have called Montgomery personally and asked permission to push forward to Falaise? Should he have pressed his views upon Ike or Monty? Was he really using Monty as a scapegoat for his failure to make a decision, or to propose a solution? Brad would spend the rest of his days looking for a satisfying answer to these troubling questions. But for now, he had a war to run.[56]

When Brad learned that German units were pulling out of the Falaise pocket, he ordered Patton to send Haislip's corps east to the Seine, then turn left, facing Le Havre on the Channel coast. Having rejected the "long hook" approach the week before, he was now placing his chips on the same strategy, hoping he could race east fast enough to bag the Germans as the Commonwealth flushed them out like hounds on quail.[57]

To give impetus to his movement east of Argentan, Patton flew to Eagle TAC. There, under the camouflage netting, he talked Bradley into sending the XX Corps, under the pugnacious "Bulldog" Walker, toward Chartres, southeast of Paris. They agreed that XII Corps, under Major General Gilbert Cook, would push toward Orléans, almost due south of the French capital, while the rest of Haislip's corps would advance upon Dreux, west of Paris. Having spread his army in this fashion, he cut across virtually the entire American front lines west of Paris, pushing Hodges into the second row.[58]

"It is really a great plan, wholly my own, and I made Bradley think he thought of it," George wrote after leaving Bradley's headquarters. *" 'Oh, what a tangled web we weave when we first practice to deceive.' "*[59]

Though he had hailed Bradley as the war's greatest general, much as he hailed Eisenhower as history's greatest general, Patton's hidden disaffection for both deepened. To George, the failure to close the Falaise pocket was another classic example of high-command gutlessness.

As if to confirm Doc Patton's diagnosis of a failure of the stomach, on August 15 Bradley ordered George to pull Haislip's eastbound divisions back to Argentan, to reinforce the gap's shoulders against an expected breakout attempt. Dipping his pen into a well of contempt, George scribbled in his diary,

> *Bradley came down to see me, suffering from nerves. There is a rumor, which I doubt, that there are five Panzer Divisions at Argentan, so Bradley wants me to halt my move to the east. . . . His motto seems to be "In case of doubt, halt." I am complying with the order, and by tomorrow I can probably persuade him to let me advance. I wish I were Supreme Commander.*[60]

Well, George wasn't Supreme Commander, and he would follow orders handed down to him, whether shrewd or stupid. But his displeasure with Ike softened in mid-August, when SHAEF finally released the names of Third Army and its commanding general to the public. The next day, as if on cue, the Senate confirmed George S. Patton Jr. to the permanent rank of major general, bumping him two grades in the same day and erasing, sort of, the shame of the Knutsford and slapping incidents.[61]

To remind him that all was neither forgotten nor entirely forgiven, however, Ike passed a terse message to George through Brad's chief of staff, Lev Allen, who told Patton:

"General Eisenhower phoned me and asked that I get this message to you:

"Congress has acted favorably on your promotion.

"General Marshall has asked that you not spoil the record of a magnificent job by public statements.

"Gen. Eisenhower asked that 'you avoid making any public statements and keep out of photographs.' He wished this emphasized.

"Also no statements for press to be made by any general officer unless approved by General Bradley."[62]

Whatever the flaws with the Falaise campaign, Ike hadn't exactly rung lemons. His armies had killed or captured some 60,000 German soldiers, and while small elements of seven panzer divisions had escaped, the *Heer* had written off thousands of irreplaceable vehicles and artillery pieces. Captured officers were telling Monk Dickson that the Seventh Army was effectively destroyed, and prisoner interrogations suggested that Hitler lacked sufficient troops to man Germany's "West Wall" defenses along the Franco-German border.[63]

To see the battlefield himself, Ike toured roads littered with charred corpses, the detritus of the Fifth Panzer and Seventh Armies. Bloated, blackened carcasses of horse and human lay thick as far as the eye could see, strings of corpses punctuated by burned and abandoned equipment. As one officer attached to Bradley's group described the scene:

It was as if an avenging angel had swept the area bent on destroying all things German. . . . I saw no foxholes or any other type of shelter or field fortifications. The Germans were trying to run and had no place to run. They were probably too exhausted to dig. . . . They were probably too tired even to surrender. I left this area regretting I'd seen it. . . . Under such conditions there are no supermen—all men become rabbits looking for a hole.[64]

Credit for much of the slaughter, Ike felt, belonged to his Twelfth Army Group commander. Bradley was doing a magnificent job driving Hodges toward the Seine and sending Patton's flying columns toward Orléans, Chartres, and Dreux. He was a remarkably stable general, and Bradley's recent successes confirmed in Ike's mind the value of Brad as a group commander, strategist, and tactician of the highest order. Ike knew he had been right to lobby Marshall for Brad's promotion to major general on the permanent list.[65]

While Bradley was Eisenhower's man at the top, he was by no means Ike's only success story. Capping off a remarkably successful August, on the twenty-sixth Eisenhower received a delightfully Pattonesque missive that read, *"Dear Ike: To-day I spat in the Seine,"* a reflection of the astonishing pace of George's advance through enemy country. Once Patton's name was released to the press in mid-August, the public had an opportunity to appreciate Ike's foresight in keeping the abrasive fighter on the team. Looking back on Ike's loyalty to George, the *New York Herald Tribune* editorialized, "To say that 'Old Blood-and-Guts,' or the 'Son-of-a-Gun General,' whichever popular designation one prefers, has justified his classmate's faith in him is to put it mildly."[66]

His faith in the men he trusted amply repaid, Ike could now fix his sights upon the enemy at the Seine River and beyond.

* * *

The Seine, that fabled, dirty, broad river which meanders through France's breast, posed fresh problems for Ike. It was a natural defensive line for the enemy to take up, and on its banks stood Paris, the center of French hopes and the symbol of liberation.

To Eisenhower, Paris was just another large city, a road and rail juncture that could be driven through or bypassed on the way to Berlin. He was perfectly aware of the city's symbolic value to forty million Frenchmen, to say nothing of Allied soldiers who considered Paris second only to Berlin in their quest to liberate Europe. But Ike was running a war, not running for office, and he prided himself on placing military strategy over symbolic or political considerations. The Germans were in headlong retreat to the Siegfried Line, and Ike's first job was to destroy Hitler's fleeing supermen while their Mauser rifles were pointed in the wrong direction. As his troops blew through France with the August winds, Ike had neither the time nor the spare soldiers to parade through Paris on a victory tour.[67]

What also worried Ike, as the man in charge of everything behind the advancing front lines, was the two million civilians living in and around the City of Light. His supply lines were stretched to the breaking point; he could not afford the four thousand tons of supplies per day Bradley estimated it would take to feed the hungry Parisians—a commitment nearly large enough to keep a full Allied army on the move.[68]

But Charles De Gaulle, the de facto French head of state, had other ideas. Showing up at Shellburst on August 20, he dispensed that insistent French insolence Ike had found so wearisome in November of '42. After listening patiently to De Gaulle's fervent warnings of Vichyite and communist saboteurs—as well as the Frenchman's threat to order French forces under Bradley to break away from the fighting and march on Paris—a reluctant Eisenhower concluded that the politics of coalition warfare required him to take the French capital. While it meant diverting huge amounts of food, coal, and medical supplies from desperate troops to desperate civilians, this Gallic peacock wielded a great deal of influence over many of the forces he needed to keep within the Allied fold. Ike didn't feel he had much choice.[69]

On August 22, Ike had Bradley come over to Shellburst to discuss the thorny question. Brad claimed the Germans had nothing to stop them out front, and he had recently joked to newspaper correspondents that they had enough manpower to walk in and take the place whenever they felt like it.[70]

Although it complicated Bradley's lines of advance, the honor of liberating the city would go to Major General Jacques Leclerc's French 2nd Armored Division, which Bradley had transferred from Patton to Hodges. After a bumbling start, the city fell on August 25. The Tricolor again flew over Paris, and the French capital, for better and for worse, was in Ike's hands.[71]

Although he had promised the Combined Chiefs he would not visit Paris unless military exigencies compelled him to go, Ike, Kay, and Jimmy motored over to Eagle TAC at Chartres on August 26 to arrange a trip to the newly liberated capital. Learning that the master of the house out at Brest was expected to return before long, Ike and his troupe settled comfortably into a trio of chairs outside Brad's trailer until he returned. If Brad was surprised at finding his boss ensconced in camp, he was perplexed by Ike's invitation to join him in Paris the next day, ostensibly to meet with De Gaulle and General Gerow, who was setting up his V Corps headquarters at Les Invalides.[72]

Bradley was unenthused about the visit, as it was a detour from business east of the Seine, and one to which they'd have to invite Montgomery. But Ike pressed him. "It's Sunday," he pointed out, with the tone of a boy playing hooky at the fishing hole. "Everyone will be sleeping late. We can do it without any fuss."[73]

With no immediate need to remain at headquarters for the moment, early the next morning the two classmates piled into Ike's olive drab Cadillac, a behemoth with British, French, and American flags sprouting like a bouquet from its radiator cap. Ike's motorcade—armed scout cars sandwiching a line of sedans—merged into a nondescript convoy heading into the city. At Brad's suggestion, they took a southern route into the city, since snipers were still hot to the south, and Bradley, like most infantrymen, loathed snipers. Kay Summersby, the Caddy's enthusiastic pilot, honked the car past pedestrian and bicycle traffic as the motorcade wove toward the Prefecture of Police, De Gaulle's makeshift headquarters.[74]

Pulling away from Les Invalides, Ike and Bradley rode down the Champs-Elysées for an informal tour of the city center. The crowd of resistance fighters, gendarmerie, churchgoers, merchants, and ordinary citizens that had gathered to watch the motorcade grew enthralled when they learned that one of the occupants was the famous liberator of Europe. As the throng's emotion grew proportionate to its size, the rippling chant of *"Eisenhower! Eisenhower!"* filled the Place de la Concorde. Needing little prompting, Ike obliged the Parisians with a broad grin and the V-for-Victory sign from his sedan. Then, joined by a bevy of French, British, and American generals, Ike and Brad rode toward the Arc de Triomphe, where a giant Tricolor rippled in the summer breeze amid a collage of British, French, and American flag bunting hanging from what seemed like every window in Paris.[75]

Against this dazzling impressionist backdrop, a battalion of military policemen strained to hold back the sea of bodies as Generals Eisenhower and Bradley and their retinue dismounted to salute the Tomb of the Unknown Soldier. The crowd went wild. As Ike and Brad threaded their way back to the Cadillac, the helmeted cordon broke and the crowd spilled forward, cheering, shouting, laughing as hands spilled forth to touch the famous American liberator. Perspiring MPs forced open a winding, undulating escape route for the commander in chief, but Bradley, marooned in the crowd, broke off and shoved his way to the anonymity of an escort jeep, his only battle scar being a smear of dark red lipstick across his face. Ike was less fortunate; before he could dive into the open Caddy door, a huge Frenchman managed to encircle his neck with burly arms and plant Saint Bernard–like kisses across Ike's reddening cheeks.[76]

If Ike was unnerved by the barrage of smooches he received in Paris, he knew he'd face no such danger at Montgomery's headquarters, where he planned to speak with Monty about strategic aims. Since July, SHAEF logistics analysts had predicted a fuel and supply shortage east of the Seine, and Ike knew that shortfall was about to force a hard choice upon the Allied command: Either all groups must slow their pace of advance, or one group could charge ahead at the expense of all others. The Nazi collapse in western France had given Bradley and Montgomery a sterling opportunity to knock the enemy around east of the big river. But beyond that point SHAEF could not hope to supply both groups adequately over the bombed-out French rail network and old, winding roads barely wide enough for American deuce-and-a-halfs. That reality would put Eisenhower on a collision course with Montgomery.[77]

It was a complex problem, for it wasn't just distance and terrain that fouled up Ike's logistics. Part of the problem in "Com-Z," as the Communications Zone was known, lay at the top, with a Services of Supply general whom Ike could neither fire up nor fire. Lieutenant General J. C. H. Lee, or "Jesus Christ Himself" Lee, as some officers called him, seemed more interested in indulging his own vanity and lodging his men in the finest Parisian hotels than moving supplies to the fighting man at the front. When word of SOS men driving luxury-size cars and hoarding consumer goods reached an infuriated General Eisenhower, he ordered Lee to move his men out of their posh quarters, as soon as comparable supply facilities could be found elsewhere.[78]

This last part of Ike's order was the rub. Paris, with its road and rail networks, boasted the best supply facilities in Western Europe. There were no "comparable facilities" for Lee's logistics men, so a besieged Lee and his Com-Z staff held their 167-hotel battle line with grim determination. In the face of withering telegraphic barrages from Ike and Beetle, and verbal flank assaults from Allied field commanders, Lee's troops defended their posts at the King George V and Astoria hotels to the bitter end.[79]

Eisenhower lamented the effects of Lee's drain on the supply system. It was SHAEF's bleeding ulcer. But since he knew Lee to be a favorite of Marshall and Lieutenant General Brehon Somervell, chief of Services of Supply, he didn't take the advice of Beetle and Ev Hughes to kick Lee to the curb. When Hughes told Ike in no uncertain terms that SOS was falling apart and that Lee was to blame, Ike threatened Lee, he cursed, he pounded his desk. But he did nothing.[80]

Supplies. Public opinion. Occupation, strategy, politics.
The French, the Germans, the British, the Air, and the Navy.

This was the cohort of foes the Supreme Commander faced every morning when he rolled his legs off the bed. The pressure from these and other wellsprings of irritation, of uncertainty, pressed down upon Ike relentlessly as he came upon a fork in the road, a fork created by a shortage of gas and ammunition.

And at this crossroads two men beckoned him through the clouded distance. Along one fork stood Bernard Law Montgomery. At the other stood Ulysses S. Grant.

TWENTY

P.O.L.

If Ike stops holding Monty's hand and gives me the supplies, I'll go through
the Siegfried Line like shit through a goose.

—Patton, September 1944

IKE COULD SMELL VICTORY. The kind of sweet, sticky scent that reaches
deep into the nostrils and makes you smile all day long. A delicious blend
of history, of universal approval, of a job damned well done. That was what
the man from Abilene inhaled as his armies crashed over the Seine.

Not that Ike was naive about the war's end. The Big Prize, Berlin, was
just a hypothesis for the moment, since the only way to take Berlin was to
move his armies there, and the only way to move his armies there was to
push forward immense stockpiles of food, ammunition, and, most important, P.O.L.—Supply's jargon for "petroleum, oil, and lubricants." While
longshoremen had piled great mounds of everything along the Normandy
coast, that cornucopia lay deep within the corpulent belly of General Lee's
Com-Z, some three hundred miles behind the rapidly moving front lines.
And the farther and faster Ike's troops advanced to the Meuse, the Moselle,
and the Lower Rhine, the longer it took to move their fuel and ammunition to the front.[1]

In mid-August, none of that seemed to matter. True, the Boche had
given Bradley a mauling in the bocage, and at Mortain they proved they
hadn't lost all their teeth. But they hadn't come close to inflicting a fatal
wound. Bradley and the DRAGOON forces had cleaned out southern France,
and Montgomery's group was ripping its way up the Channel coast toward
the Low Countries. By September 14, D-plus-100, the Allies would be

sitting about where embarrassingly conservative SHAEF forecasts predicted they would be in May 1945. In the east, the Red Army had liberated Belorussia and destroyed Hitler's Army Group Center in seven weeks—a feat even more impressive than the Battle of Normandy, one that would surely cripple Germany's ability to shift troops to the west. It looked like the war would be over by Christmas of 1944. Maybe sooner.[2]

Victory disease, being highly communicable, spread through Eisenhower's headquarters like the GI trots on vegetable stew day. His G-2 chief, Kenneth Strong, boasted that "two and a half months of bitter fighting have brought the end of the war in Europe within sight, almost within reach." Beetle Smith told an interviewer, "Militarily, the war is won." In the field, Generals de Guingand and Crerar were predicting that the war would end in three weeks, and Bradley's men were in the full bloom of summer confidence. Brad and George were poring over maps of German territory that Third Army would occupy when the fighting stopped. "Everything we talk about now is qualified by the phrase 'if the war lasts that long,'" Chet Hansen wrote.[3]

While he wanted to believe the war's end was in sight, Ike tried to tamp down public expectations of a quick victory. He warned Marshall that his supply lines were growing long and thin, and he held a press conference to castigate the armchair generals back home who predicted the war's end within weeks.

But by mid-September, even Ike was euphoric about the war's drawing curtain. He had predicted in January that the conflict would be over by the end of '44. In June, when his armies were stuck in the bocage, Ike looked like a blind, raving optimist. Now that he was past the Seine, he looked woefully underconfident. Now, staring victory in the face, he quietly told his lieutenants it was time to begin thinking about the final assault on Berlin.[4]

The road to victory had been a long-running debate among Allied planners. Germany's western frontier ran from Switzerland to the North Sea in a line twenty-five to fifty miles west of the Rhine River, *das Vaterland*'s traditional border. Germany enjoyed the natural protection of the Vosges Mountains near the Swiss Border, the Moselle and Saar rivers in the south, the Ardennes Forest in the center (called the "Schnee Eifel" on the German side), and the intricate grid of rivers that sliced across the Netherlands. Germany's frontier boasted the fortress city of Metz, a bastion on the Moselle,

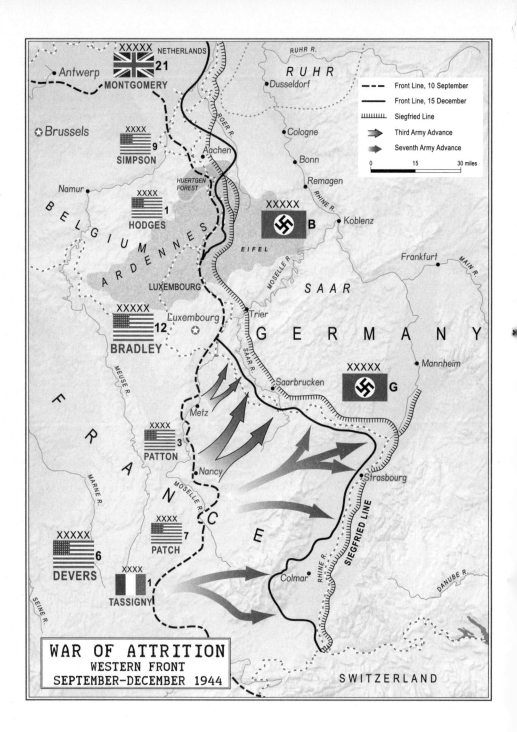

WAR OF ATTRITION
WESTERN FRONT
SEPTEMBER–DECEMBER 1944

as well as the Siegfried Line, a chain of pillboxes, antitank obstacles, and gun emplacements running along what the enemy called the "West Wall." Once an attacker cracked the hard shell of the Siegfried Line, he still had to cross the Rhine, the broad, imposing river that, since the time of Julius Caesar, presented a formidable barrier to the West.[5]

The month before D-Day, SHAEF planners had gathered in their Holiest of Holies to present General Eisenhower with four options for the war's post-Normandy phase. Ike rejected two of them, which focused upon Berlin as primary objective, and instead considered two options that took him through the Ruhr River valley, a steel, manufacturing, and refining region ringed by Cologne, Düsseldorf, Essen, and dozens of smaller factory towns. SHAEF's rationale convinced the professional logistician in Eisenhower: the Ruhr was Germany's industrial heart. Take the Ruhr, Ike's advisers told him, and Hitler will have no Porsche tanks, no Messerschmitt fighters, no Krupp cannon. The Krauts will be throwing rocks at us, and the war will be over.[6]

But the Ruhr was a compact, obvious target, which meant Hitler wasn't going to let the Allies waltz on in. Furthermore, moving a million soldiers was a lot more complicated than simply pointing to a spot on the map and saying, *"There!"* It required road networks, defensible supply lines, and protected flanks. With the thick Ardennes Forest blocking the southern approaches, the region would not accommodate the entire weight of the Allied host. That meant only a portion of the Allied strength could be profitably employed against the Ruhr.

So Ike looked to the southern end of his lines, where Patton's army strained against its reins, and he considered piercing the Siegfried Line around the Saar River valley, a secondary industrial pocket. Charging through the Saar would open a secondary route through Frankfurt, which would allow the Allies to cut Berlin off from southern Germany and Austria—another line of advance rife with possibilities.

After a hard look, Eisenhower settled on a "broad front" approach. He would send one army group, Montgomery's, north of the Ardennes, through Belgium and the Netherlands. He would send Bradley's northern armies through the center—roughly Belgium and Luxembourg. Once the Allies penetrated the Ruhr's outer defenses, Bradley and Montgomery would turn toward each other in an immense double envelopment, pinching off the Ruhr and destroying any forces trapped inside the giant pocket. Meanwhile, the armies to the extreme south—Patton's Third Army and Lieutenant General Alexander "Sandy" Patch's Seventh Army, operating under Devers—would move through Verdun, Metz, and the Saarland to pin and destroy the enemy, sweep up other heavy industries, and pry open a southern route to Germany's still-beating heart.

Chomping on a cigar deep in the background of Eisenhower's strategy was his hero, General Ulysses S. Grant, the unassuming Midwesterner who hammered the Confederacy into submission back in 1864. Grant had recognized that with the North's greater industry and its deeper manpower pool, the surest way to victory was to hit the Confederates with everything, everywhere, at every moment, leaving Johnny Reb no chance to regroup, shift his forces, gather supplies, or fortify his positions. Keep 'em off balance, Grant argued. That was how to fight an outnumbered foe.

Ike agreed with old Hiram. By the autumn of '44, the Allies had over two million men and four hundred thousand vehicles on the Continent. Allied fighters ruled the skies over Europe, and the bomber barons were smashing Germany's factories, refineries, and railyards with near-impunity. Keeping the enemy off balance by hitting him everywhere, all the time, was the best way to prevent the Models, von Rundstedts, and Kesselrings from shifting their few mobile reinforcements from crisis to crisis. With Monty rolling through Calais, Antwerp, and the Ruhr Valley from the north, Hodges pushing against the center, and Patton shooting through the Saarland, the Wehrmacht would be compelled to retreat. Or fight and die.[7]

Montgomery, who was not privy to SHAEF's original "broad front" planning, had his own ideas about how to finish the job. Appreciating the disorder that must be endemic among the *heer*'s ranks, Montgomery believed the war could be won quicker by letting Twenty-First Army Group take the lead from the north. In his view, the fastest way to victory was up the Channel coast, through Holland, over the Ardennes, through the Ruhr, then through Hamburg and Berlin. Bradley, he concluded, should move alongside Twenty-First, guarding the British flank and leaving the Alsace-Lorraine region—Nancy, Metz, and the Saar—more or less inactive.

This strategy made logistical sense to Montgomery because, contrary to OVERLORD's assumptions, Hitler had not obliged the Allies to fight a pitched battle along the Seine, which would have given the Allies a chance to move forward supplies and replacements until they could advance upon Germany in overwhelming strength. Peripheral armies, meaning Patton and Devers, should therefore remain where they were, to conserve petrol and ammunition for Monty's group.[8]

Montgomery was reluctant to leave his command post, code-named

LION, to sell Eisenhower on his vision. He never grasped that in a coalition setting, a personal relationship with the "chairman of the board" was critical to convincing Eisenhower of the wisdom of his strategy. When the basic questions of a broad or narrow front came to a head, instead of coming to SHAEF he dispatched his popular chief of staff, Major General Freddie de Guingand, to carry his torch. From August 20 to 22, de Guingand pitched the field marshal's master plan to Ike and Beetle, and on August 23 the two generals traveled to Condé-sur-Noireau, Montgomery's tactical headquarters, to settle plans for operations beyond the Seine.[9]

At Condé, Montgomery asked Ike for a meeting outside the presence of Beetle and other witnesses. With Ike sequestered, Monty pressed his case for the "single thrust" strategy. He argued that the Allies lacked the supplies needed for a broad push into western Germany. The Empire's replacement situation was becoming critical, he said, and the British Army was cannibalizing divisions to keep others in the field. He lacked the manpower to clean out the Channel ports, secure Antwerp for forward supplies, and guard his long, exposed flank.

Bradley's First Army, he strenuously argued, was in the perfect supporting position. Best to let Hodges cover Montgomery's flank, under Montgomery's direction, until the Allies were up to the Ruhr, or at least to Antwerp. Keep the focus on the north, he argued. Besides, he told Ike, he had spoken with Bradley about this a week earlier, and at the time Bradley had agreed that Twenty-First was the horse to back.[10]

Ike considered the idea. It went against his gut instincts, but Montgomery's logic seemed sound, given the swift victory in France. The pursuit had run far ahead of OVERLORD's timetables, supply shortages were reaching alarming proportions, and Brad's armies were too far from their supply dumps to deliver a killing blow in one rolling operation. On the other hand, Montgomery wanted the entire First Army placed under his command, and Ike knew neither Marshall nor the American public would countenance this.[11]

Ike knew the American commanders would complain bitterly when the big show went to Montgomery. Beetle, a realist who paid scant attention to questions of national pride, later called Montgomery's narrow-front proposal "the most fantastic bit of balderdash ever proposed by a competent general." But, Ike figured, once Montgomery pried open the great port of Antwerp, supplies would pour in for everyone. Then he could give Bradley a longer leash—if Germany didn't surrender first.[12]

During their meeting, Montgomery brought up another delicate matter, one dear to his heart and one on which there could be no compromise. Although SHAEF plans called for Eisenhower to take charge of the ground war once communications were set up on the Continent, Monty insisted that Ike retain a full-fledged ground commander, a land battle captain who would dictate strategy to all army groups in the European theater. The person for the task obviously was Montgomery, by right of seniority, depth of experience, and the winning record the Allies had enjoyed while they were under his command.[13]

By the end of August, the communication network Ike needed to run the land battle from France was nowhere near complete. But the American press—reacting in part to Fleet Street's clamor over Montgomery's "demotion" to Bradley's level on August 1—had taken up the cry that the British were running the ground war on the backs of American soldiers. This message, Ike knew, was being heard loud and clear in Washington. Montgomery's argument for his retention as ground commander—chiefly, that the victories of August were because he was commanding all ground forces—was, Ike thought, unsound. Bradley had been operating independently of Montgomery during the breakout campaign. Besides, the front was so long it required someone whose attention would not remain focused upon any one sector. Montgomery didn't need the title of ground commander to accomplish his objectives, and the only obvious use for an enlarged authority would be to shut down his allies while his own army group raced for Berlin.[14]

Ike, for political, personal, and professional reasons, had no intention of letting Montgomery call the Allied plays. On September 1, he took formal command of the three army groups. Montgomery, whom Churchill immediately promoted to field marshal, would remain one of three army group commanders on Ike's team, commanding the most critical segment of the front. *Primus inter pares* he was—but *pares* nonetheless.[15]

As to ground strategy, Ike agreed that Montgomery needed American help for the long sweep northeast. He spared a corps from First Army and an airborne corps from England, and agreed to give priority of supplies to Twenty-First Army Group while Monty's troops were moving toward Antwerp. He also gave Montgomery "operational coordination" over the northern thrust, which meant Monty could use the left wing of Bradley's group—that is, First Army—as his flank protection, while the army would remain under Bradley's command. But that was as far as he would go. Brad would build up Patton's forces for a big push toward the Saar River, while Patch's Seventh Army, under Jacob Devers, would push through the south to protect Bradley's right.[16]

To Ike it was the best possible compromise. He couldn't shove the Commonwealth armies onto the sidelines, as Twenty-First fronted three important objectives: the V-1 sites, Antwerp, and the Ruhr. But the "narrow thrust" approach Montgomery advocated would invite a lethal flank attack that his other armies, lacking fuel, would be unable to ward off. Beetle's staff was convinced Montgomery's plan was infeasible, for logistical reasons; furthermore, they argued, Montgomery's temperament wasn't right for the strategy. In any event, Eisenhower could hardly tell Marshall the million-plus men the Army had drafted, trained, and shipped to Europe were going to sit on the sidelines while Montgomery crept through Germany, demanding American divisions by the handful to protect his flanks.[17]

There was also a personal side to Ike's calculations; he wanted Bradley to obtain some of the recognition Brad so richly deserved. Bradley was the architect of the COBRA breakout, the operation that dramatically altered the Battle of France, and Eisenhower wrote Marshall in mid-August, "[I]t would be a great pity if Bradley failed to get the full credit due him for his brilliant performance merely because general instructions and policies he has pursued have been channeled through Montgomery."

It would also be a great pity if, as in Tunisia, the Allies lost another race to a weakly held German position, and Montgomery did not strike Eisenhower as the sprinting type.[18]

So Ike tried to keep everyone happy, issuing polite orders to a bunch that knew how to play the game of stretching authority to the breaking point. He held his breath, and he hoped the unity of the NEPTUNE days would hold out, just a little longer.[19]

The compromise, like most wartime compromises, infuriated everyone. To Bradley, who held a particular loathing for Montgomery by now, the thought of the Briton climbing back into the driver's seat was enough to send him into fits. In his field trailer with Ike, he blew up when his classmate toyed with the idea of leaving Monty in command of the ground war. Brad was still fuming over the missed opportunity at Falaise. Echoing George's claims, though in more civilized language, he argued that a "Monty-first" strategy would sacrifice splendid opportunities in the center and south.[20]

To the north, Montgomery rambled about his canvas-and-truck city, furious with Ike for keeping the armies to the south in play. The fact that the other armies were American was irrelevant to Montgomery's calculations, as his sole concern was that militarily, the American armies were poorly positioned to outflank the Siegfried Line. He insisted that a "full-blooded thrust" across the north to Berlin was the fastest way to end the war. In a private letter to Marshal Brooke, an agitated Montgomery complained, *"Ike is apt to get very excited and talk wildly—at the top of his voice!!! He is now over here, which is a very great pity. His ignorance as to how to run a war is absolute and complete; he has all the popular cries, but nothing else."*[21]

Montgomery cared not a whit for the political repercussions his strategy might spark, whether in the United States or among the Combined Chiefs. Just as Patton had little concept of the role of public support in a democratic war effort, Montgomery saw only the fruits of a military harvest; he was oblivious to the need to keep the Americans on the front pages, a need acutely felt by Roosevelt, Stimson, and Marshall.

Ike had tried to hammer the point home with Monty before. As he once lectured Monty, "Public opinion wins wars."

"Victory wins wars," Monty retorted. "Give the people victory and they won't care who won it."[22]

Of course, *Monty* cared who won it.

So did Brad, George, and Ike.

Adding to Ike's troubles, in early September he managed to wrench his right knee—his "good" one—when his observation plane was forced into an emergency beach landing in bad weather. The injury was serious enough to put Ike's leg in a cast, but the business of war couldn't wait for Ike's knees to repair themselves, and neither could his ground commanders.[23]

During these days of uncertainty, days when the Allied vision was not so crisp and singular as it once was, Ike's unrecorded discussions with Montgomery blurred into different—bitterly different—notions of what exactly they had agreed upon. Eisenhower, much like President Roosevelt, had a habit of nodding frequently and avoiding needless confrontation during conversation. This might mean he agreed with the speaker, or it might mean he simply acknowledged receipt of the information.

Whatever the reason, in early September Ike sensed that he might not be singing the same hymn as Montgomery, and two weeks after their meeting, as vague notions of a "broad front" were reduced to written directives, Eisenhower cabled Montgomery to clarify his position on European strategy. Although he had temporarily given priority to Twenty-First Army Group's front, he told the field marshal, "We must immediately exploit our success by promptly breaching the Siegfried Line, crossing the Rhine on a wide front and seizing the Saar and the Ruhr." As he reiterated in a private memorandum, *"I see no reason to change this [broad-front] conception. . . . I now deem it important, while supporting the advance on eastward through Belgium, to get Patton moving again so that we may be fully prepared to carry out the original conception for the final stages of this campaign."*[24]

On September 10, Ike rose from his on-again, off-again sickbed to ensure that Montgomery would tow the line. His knees—one of them encased in a cast—shrieked every time they bore his weight, but he felt it imperative to work out any differences of opinion with Montgomery on a face-to-face basis.

Montgomery, as usual, wired that he could not leave his headquarters. Ike, despite his knee problems, agreed to meet him at Twenty-First Army Group's headquarters in Brussels. Barely able to walk, he asked Montgomery to meet him on board his plane. Monty agreed, an unusual concession for a man of Sir Bernard's temperament.

The meeting began cordially enough. They discussed Montgomery's daring plan to force a bridgehead over the Lower Rhine at Arnhem using tanks and airborne, and they discussed the limitations Ike would place on the other army groups so that Montgomery's attack would have the best chance of success. But as they spoke, Montgomery must have wondered whether the uproar in England over the "demotion" of Britain's most popular general had left Ike politically crippled. Sitting forlornly in his plane with injured legs, Ike certainly looked the part.

It was not long before Montgomery's impetuousness churned and bubbled until it pushed back the pot's lid. With growing indignation, he began criticizing directives coming from SHAEF. When these remarks went unchallenged, he turned up the thermostat from "warm" to "insulting." Whipping out a sheaf of SHAEF transmissions, Montgomery read them back to his commander with the disdain of a schoolmaster dressing down a floundering student. He picked apart SHAEF's broad-front plans, snapping off their many potential flaws, and he and Ike went around and around over the meaning of the word "priority" in Ike's recent orders. He hectored Ike for an ironclad commitment to make Twenty-First the exclusive agent of the Allied offense, and tiring of his less-than-competent superior, he condemned Ike's most recent signals as "balls, sheer balls, rubbish!"[25]

Ike strained to hold his temper. A past master at diplomacy, Ike had dealt with tough, selfish characters before: Giraud, Churchill, De Gaulle, MacArthur, and plenty others. But those men were his superiors, or arguably so. He had never been dressed down by a nominal subordinate.

He contained his growing anger throughout the conversation, and he held his tongue as the field marshal's outburst reached a brief pause. Then, as Monty regrouped his thoughts, Ike leaned forward, calmly put his hand on Montgomery's knee, and said, "Steady, Monty. You can't speak to me like that. I'm your boss."

"I'm sorry, Ike," Monty said.[26]

The meeting adjourned on a cordial note, but Ike knew, or thought he knew, that the field marshal had pinned a target on his back, for Monty's brazen outburst could mean only that he had declared war on Eisenhower. That, or he was politically clueless. The day after the runway meeting, Admiral Ramsay stopped by Shellburst to see Ike. The Supreme Commander presented a rather pitiful sight; he lay in his bed, his knees shot, raving about his selfish man in Brussels who was undoubtedly trying to undercut him among the Imperial General Staff. Ramsay wrote in his diary that Eisenhower "is clearly worried and the cause is undisputably Monty who is behaving badly . . . [Ike does] not trust his loyalty and probably with good reason." Ike would come to wish heartily that he could have replaced Monty after the Normandy landings succeeded.[27]

Ammunition, C-rations. P.O.L. Tonnage estimates, not comfortable maps, not battles, were what Omar pondered as the Germans fled east.

Bradley's staff had drafted an operational plan in late August, one his G-3 section modestly entitled "Blueprint for Victory." The Blueprint, conceived after productive meetings with Ike and less productive meetings with Monty, envisioned a big push through Lorraine, the German frontier, and the "Frankfurt corridor," an arrowshot that ran up the Moselle Valley into the guts of the Third Reich. As Bradley envisioned the campaign, Hodges, with the bulk of his group's supplies, would play the starring role in the effort, though Brad would keep Third Army pushing forward along the Moselle and Upper Rhine. The Siegfried Line would be rolled up like a rug, and Germany's heavy industries along the Saar River would be in Allied hands.[28]

It was an exceptional plan, crafted in the slashing style of Bradley's military hero, General William Tecumseh Sherman, and it promised a quick, destructive penetration of central Germany. But Brad worried that Eisenhower, seduced by a northern route to the German capital, would give Monty all of SHAEF's limited supplies, leaving the Americans no shells to shoot, no fuel to move. Darned if Ike might not even put Hodges permanently under Montgomery's command, a possibility he and George had worked themselves into a froth about more than once. "I get along fine with Monty," Brad declared in late August, stretching the truth. "But we've got to make it clear to the American public that we are no longer under any control of Monty's."[29]

Brad's uneasiness with the Eisenhower approach burgeoned when Ike told Brad that Patton's army was to halt at the Moselle River. Hodges, Ike said, would assist Montgomery's northern effort to bridge the Rhine, and only after Monty was safely on German soil would Third Army be authorized to move forward again.[30]

Sensing an abandonment of the Americans, Brad fought a rear-guard action for the broad-front strategy. Montgomery, he pointed out, was facing the bulk of the German armor, and the northern route was ribboned with large, meandering rivers that the Germans would undoubtedly defend with their usual ferociousness. But to the south, Bradley's G-2 section was telling him that portions of the Siegfried Line lay unmanned; the list of German divisions under the heading "DESTROYED" was growing long, and Patton's army was, for the moment, facing only the equivalent of five enemy divisions.[31]

Five divisions. At the very least, Ike ought to let George pin the Germans to the south and have Brad push First Army toward the Ruhr with Monty. As Brad wrote to Ike on the thirteenth, *"The situation in front of Patton looks very hopeful this morning. I believe that he has written off a lot of Boches during his fighting here in the last few days."*[32]

He hoped the good news from the south would encourage Eisenhower to build upon American successes, rather than start from scratch in the north. But it was no use; Ike had decided to give Montgomery the big chance. SHAEF would allocate Twenty-First Army Group nearly everything, and whatever was left for Twelfth Army Group would be earmarked, for the most part, to Hodges—to support the British.[33]

The much-anticipated liberation of Antwerp on September 5 didn't do Bradley any good. Through a phenomenal lack of appreciation at SHAEF and Monty's headquarters, no one looked downriver to consider the Scheldt Estuary, a low, swampy delta that controlled access to Antwerp from the North Sea. The Germans, it turned out, didn't need Antwerp to deprive the Allies of the port, so long as they controlled the Scheldt. So Bradley would spend the foreseeable future arguing with Ike and his staff over howitzer shells, gas, food, and replacements. He badgered Ike for airlift space, and he badgered Ike for fuel. But he didn't get very far, since Ike was concentrating all his guns—and their projectiles, and the trucks that carried those projectiles—on Montgomery's front.[34]

The "northern priority" put Bradley and his logistics men in a colossal jam. Because a single day's ration for Third Army weighed a thousand tons, and a half unit of artillery fire (around sixty-two rounds per howitzer) cost another two thousand tons, cutting Patton's supplies below three thousand tons didn't leave much room for gasoline. All this forced the G-4 men at Twelfth Army Group to cut, scrape, and do without. "To make up for the British deficit in trucking we were forced to divert vehicles from Hodges," Brad later wrote. "Then to keep Hodges rolling we hijacked trucks from Patton. As a consequence, George soon found his advance choked off by a shortage in gasoline."[35]

His hands tied by scarcity, Brad found himself arguing in both directions of the command chain. He warned Ike, *You cannot cut Patton much below the 2,500 tons [per day] he is receiving,* knowing that every slash in Third Army's P.O.L. supplies would be followed by a visit from George and his G-4 man, both of them screaming like Fay Wray for gasoline. Ike insisted that First Army's mission to cover Montgomery's flank took priority, and a reluctant Bradley obeyed. He didn't like it much, but he would pull rank on George to keep Third Army in line with the broader strategy, and at the end of August Bradley's headquarters announced the allocation between Third and First Armies: two thousand tons per day for Patton, five thousand for Hodges.[36]

Bradley soon discovered that much of his time would be spent frowning over logistics and keeping the peace between two suspicious competitors. The factions—Hodges and his staff, Patton and his staff—could be as territorial as two junkyard dogs marking the same fireplug. As Brad griped to Patton's chief of staff, "I have a helluva time getting help between two Armies. After all, we are all Allies. Every time I try to get help between two divisions, one asks for too much and the other hates like hell to give anything."[37]

* * *

Throwing scarce fuel on the fire, General Dempsey of Montgomery's Second British Army infuriated Bradley with press remarks in which he blamed the Americans for wandering across his front as the Falaise Gap closed, throwing a forty-eight-hour delay into the British pursuit of the Germans. Bradley was incredulous; the Americans had driven two-thirds of the way to Le Havre, cleaning out a large portion of the enemy in front of Second Army. If the Americans were not blocking the British, it would have been the Germans blocking the British—and shooting at them, to boot. Dempsey should be thanking him, not castigating him.[38]

Brad immediately rang up Lion TAC and took up the matter with Montgomery, who brushed off the controversy as a typical press misquote. Monty apologized privately on behalf of Dempsey, but he did not order Dempsey to retract his statement. A sullen Bradley huffed around Eagle, furious with his cousins, then barked for a stenographer. He fumed to Ike, *"I consider General Dempsey's statement to be a direct criticism of American forces and very unfair. It will certainly leave a wrong impression in the minds of those who read it and do not know the true facts in the case. I believe that some action should be taken to correct this false impression, either by another statement by Dempsey himself or by other means which will give the true facts in the British press."*[39]

The "GI's General" was seeing himself as the champion of the GI's place in the history of the war. And the more he saw himself that way, the closer he edged to the Anglophobia he and George had shared in Tunisia and Sicily. That would create problems for his old classmate.

"This is the last day that Montgomery commands the U.S. Troops, for which we all thank God!"[40]

That was how George ushered in the first of September.

Since the fall of Paris, Patton spent his days pushing against ineffective resistance by the Nazis, and slightly more effective resistance by SHAEF. He didn't really blame Bradley for his debilitating supply cuts, at least not too much. While Brad was hardly the model of audacity—George sometimes code-named him "Modesty" or "Omar the Tent Maker" in his diary and letters home—"Modesty" was coming around to George's jaded view of their supreme commander. On August 22, George flew to Bradley's headquarters to make a pitch for a drive to the Moselle River, and on his return he told his diary, *"Bradley was waiting for me on his way to see Ike and Monty.*

He was quite worried, as he feels that Ike won't go against Monty and that the American armies will have to turn north in whole or in part. . . . Bradley was madder than I have ever seen him and wondered aloud what a 'Supreme Commander amounted to'—nothing."[41]

The problem, as George saw it, was chronic British influence over the peacemaker from Abilene. *"Montgomery,"* George wrote,

> *has some power to talk Ike to his own way of thinking. As Supreme Commander Ike is useless. I told Bradley that if he, Hodges and my self offered to resign unless we went east, Ike would have to yield but [Bradley] would not agree and said we owed it to the troops to hold on. I feel that in such a showdown we would win, as Ike would not dare to relieve us (no guts!).*[42]

Bradley shrugged off the offer, and George didn't press the point alone. You couldn't please everyone, he knew, for big part of war was not having enough to go around. Not enough gasoline, not enough ammunition, not enough good soldiers. Choices had to be made, and George would go along with whatever Ike and Brad decided. His army was now trimmed to seven divisions in two corps, but at least Bradley had given him a green light to move east, and he assured Patton that four more divisions would join Third Army as soon as they could be moved forward.[43]

But even these limited orders to advance were riddled with ifs, caveats, and conditions. One morning, after haggling with Bradley, George found himself grumbling, *"I had to beg like a beggar for permission to keep on the line of the Meuse. What a life."*[44]

Another thing Patton would have to beg like a beggar for was gasoline, which began to run short during the last week in August. For the first week in September, Third Army received about two-thirds the P.O.L. it required to move forward, and about half the fuel it needed to pursue the enemy beyond the Moselle. George cut food for his army to make way for fuel, and he ordered his field commanders to drain gas from half-empty tanks to get the remaining tanks to the Moselle. Visiting XII Corps, now under the command of Major General Manton Eddy, Patton learned, to his intense displeasure, that his army had once again been shorted. He immediately set out for Brad's headquarters at Chartres to plead his case. "Dammit, Brad," he hummed in that nasal voice of his, "just give me 400,000 gallons of gasoline and I'll put you inside Germany in two days."[45]

Though prone to exaggeration and bluster, Patton had a point this time. Third Army's tanks had just rumbled through Verdun, and were now only thirty-five miles from Metz, the great fortress city on the Moselle. His G-2 was telling him the Siegfried Line was unmanned and the Saar, the last river barrier before the Rhine, was theirs for the taking. All they needed was four hundred thousand gallons of gas.[46]

Bradley, dressed plainly in his combat jacket, fatigue trousers, and jump boots, nodded sympathetically. As much as anyone in the theater—other than Patton—he wanted Third Army moving and he didn't like to pull it back. On the other hand, he couldn't let George get too far ahead of everyone else, so he didn't order Patton to stop where he was; he knew Third Army would be stopped before long by empty gasoline tanks. He also asked George to come back to Chartres the next day, September 2, when Ike was scheduled to visit Eagle TAC. Ike would undoubtedly want to hear George's views.[47]

Patton knew his job, as Ike's friend and Bradley's ally, would be to yank Eisenhower off the British bandwagon long enough to get his Shermans over the Moselle. He buttoned on his immaculate uniform and prepared to put forth his best case. Arriving at Chartres just after noon, he found Ike, Bradley, Hodges, and Hoyt Vandenberg, commander of the Ninth Air Force, in the midst of a discussion of strategy for the push to the Rhine.[48]

"Ike was very pontifical and quoted Clausewitz to us," George noted afterward, wondering what a defeated nineteenth-century staff officer could tell either of them about armored, airborne, and amphibious operations, all of which, as far as George knew, Clausewitz had never seen. There was plenty of polite back-and-forth, but when the smoke had cleared, Brad and George had to settle for a draw. As George wrote,

> *We finally talked him into letting the V Corps, First Army, and Third Army attack the Siegfried Line as soon as the Calais area stabilizes. Until this is done we will not be able to get gas or ammunition for a further advance. He kept talking about the great battle of Germany . . . we assured him that the Germans have nothing left to fight it.*[49]

George left the meeting in a foul mood, a feeling shared by his fellow field commanders. *"Ike is all for caution, since he has never been at the front and had the feel [of combat],"* he complained. Ike seemed intent on swallowing all of Montgomery's platitudes and handing the British the Big Victory. And George's men would pay for Monty's Big Victory by Sitting On Their Asses along the Moselle.[50]

As the battle for Europe became a war of petrol allocation—"You know we can't piss in these tanks," Patton bitterly told reporters—his outlook toward his old friend grew blacker. While touring some French villages in the 80th Division's sector, he noted bitterly,

> *On top of Mt. Seg is a huge war memorial to our dead at St. Mihiel. Ike supervised its building after the war, his only experience of that incident. His present delay will probably justify more monuments to American dead. Every hour costs lives.*[51]

On the fifteenth Patton, his aide, Al Stiller, and his bull terrier, Willie, paid a visit to Bradley's command post, a circus of tents, tangled phone lines, and narrow trailers ringed with barbed wire on the outskirts of Verdun. Sloshing through the mire that passed for paths between tents and trailers, Patton climbed into Bradley's command truck to find Brad in a heated argument with General Bull, Ike's stern-looking operations chief whose unhappy duties included breaking bad news to Bradley. Bull and Bradley, George wrote,

> *were having quite an argument. Monty does what he pleases and Ike says yes sir. Monty wants all supplies sent to him and the 1st U.S. Army, and for me to hold. Brad thinks I can and should push on. Brad told Ike that if Monty takes control of the XIX and VII Corps of the First Army as he wants to do, he, Bradley, will ask for a leave. Bull says that Ike feels that we think he is selling us out but that he has to as Monty will not take orders so we have to. Bradley said it was time for a showdown.*[52]

As Patton watched the argument unfold, Bull insisted that Com-Z lacked the infrastructure to get supplies to Third Army. He suggested, disingenuously, that if Third Army would capture Nancy, it could use the rail lines that led there to disperse more ammunition, food, and gas. Cracking that nut, not complaining about SHAEF supply, would be a better way to get stocks rolling to the front.

The words had hardly left Bull's mouth when Lev Allen walked in to announce that Third Army had just taken Nancy.

"Damn, how do you like that!" a smiling George bellowed, flashing his bucktoothed grin around the room. "Better congratulate me!"[53]

A frowning Bull, seeing he was getting nowhere, sullenly took his leave and headed back to Versailles.

"Goddammit, Brad, you kept the flag waving," George bellowed after Bull left. "I'm proud of you!" Once again, he offered to resign with Bradley, and once again, Bradley backed down. Regardless of who ran Twelfth Army Group, regardless of any personal threats George or Brad might make, Ike had made up his mind, and the great push would go forward in the north. So Montgomery's Netherlands operation rumbled into its uncertain fate, and an embittered Brad and George spent the afternoon deriding Montgomery's "dagger-thrust" into the heart of Germany as the "butter-knife thrust."[54]

Well, it was a bad bargain for the Americans, George thought, but the capture of Nancy put him in high spirits. Wrapping up his business at Eagle TAC, he called for Willie—warning Bradley, whose staff kept a few dogs, "[Willie's] a sodomy son-of-a-bitch. Keep him away from the pups. Goddammit, Willie—get out of here!!"[55]

With that elegant benediction, George Patton marched out to his car, grinning aides and the roving Willie in tow.

George returned to camp thinking he would be better off ignoring the northern end of the Allied line and doing his own thing, with orders or without, on the assumption that once he was committed to battle, the higher echelons couldn't pull him back. *To hell with [Monty]," he vowed. "I must get so involved that they can't stop me."* On the seventeenth, he spilled his frustrations to a sympathetic Omar Bradley, who agreed to wait a couple of days before calling Patton with new orders. With the phone lines quiet, both men would see what George's army could do on its own.[56]

While Patton defended his supply lines from the insatiable Twenty-First Army Group, he learned of a new threat from the south. Word through the grapevine was that Jake Devers, commander of the Sixth Army Group, was bragging to his friends about how many divisions he would pull from Third Army, which was a critical problem for Patton, since Bradley had already taken away Middleton's VIII Corps and given it to Hodges. After losing his second veteran corps—he had lost his prized XV Corps to Hodges shortly before Paris—George was not going to let anyone filch a third.[57]

Confident in Ike's antipathy toward Devers, George flew to Paris on September 21 to *"see Ike and spike [Devers's] guns as Ike hates him."* The two men had a pleasant lunch, and as they ate, Ike vented about his British field marshal, whom he called a "clever son-of-a-bitch"—an encouraging sign, George thought, at least for the moment. Ike also couldn't stand Devers, a feeling that dated back to Jake's criticism of Ike's Tunisian campaign in 1942, and his refusal to lend Ike four badly needed bomber groups for AVA-LANCHE in 1943. Like any good political operator, Eisenhower had a long memory for slights, and he was not above holding long grudges. He had even told Bradley he would have given Seventh Army to Brad, except that it would leave Devers commanding only Frenchmen, which wouldn't do politically for an American army group.[58]

Over the lunch hour, Ike kept Devers and Sandy Patch, the Seventh Army's commanding general, waiting in his office antechamber for almost two hours—*"a good omen,"* concluded George. He returned to Chalons well pleased with his politicking, and remarked to his diary with a conspiratorial air, *"One has to fight one's friends more than the enemy."*[59]

But George, like Montgomery before him, had misread his friend. Eisenhower, it turned out, was not as hostile to Devers as George had thought, and Devers had assured Ike that Sixth Army Group's supply lines, which ran back to the immense port of Marseilles, could support two more divisions, which was certainly more than Bradley could claim. George's back-office campaign flopped, and Third Army had to surrender its 7th Armored Division to Hodges and hand two other divisions to Devers.[60]

It was another low point for George Patton, and there wasn't a damned thing he could do about it except grouse to himself and Bradley—and hope the Germans would give Devers a stiff beating. *"May God rot his guts,"* he spat.[61]

One reason Ike could start thinking of that fishing trip he'd take when the war ended was a plan of Montgomery's to cross the Rhine through Holland. The plan merged two complex operations: Operation MARKET, a five-division airborne strike against Dutch bridges over the Lower Rhine, and Operation GARDEN, a narrow armored thrust toward Arnhem to relieve the paratroopers and force open the door to the Ruhr. The scheme went against everything Ike had been taught since his days sneaking smokes behind Thayer Hall, but it was the kind of brilliant, unorthodox gamble that might hasten the war's end.

MARKET-GARDEN promised huge rewards, if it worked, but Ike was sober about its prospects and acutely aware of its costs. The road network to Arnhem was tight, and Allied experiences with combat air drops in Sicily and Normandy had been a mixed bag. The air transport Monty needed for MARKET would strip planes carrying supplies to other parts of Monty's army, and three newly arrived U.S. divisions would have to be immobilized to provide the trucks needed to carry an additional five hundred tons of supplies to Montgomery's forces. As Ike told General Marshall in a top secret cable, "I have sacrificed a lot to give Montgomery the strength he needs to reach the Rhine in the north and to threaten the Ruhr." With expectations in Washington and London running high, Ike needed a victory at Arnhem, and he needed it fast.[62]

Eisenhower threw his weight behind MARKET-GARDEN, despite its heavy price tag. He had been looking for a role for his airborne divisions, one of Marshall's pet projects, and he saw in Montgomery's proposition a bold, almost wildly aggressive plan that promised sweeter fruit than Monty's other, more conservative efforts. The operation might bog him down within the Dutch river network, but it also might give him an easy path across the Rhine, around those dragon's teeth and the pillboxes of the Siegfried Line. Eisenhower was a gambler, and if he had learned anything from those countless nights staring at bridge hands, it was that sometimes you had to take risks to get the trumps.

So with a deep breath, he approved MARKET-GARDEN, and he braced himself for the inevitable howls from Brad, George, and the rest.[63]

MARKET-GARDEN failed. The lightly armed airborne troops—two U.S. divisions, one British division, and a Polish brigade—were pounced on by a heavy SS panzer corps, and Montgomery's supporting armor could not negotiate the narrow roads in time to rescue the hard-pressed paratroopers holding the bridges. The paras suffered massive losses as they doggedly fought and died around Holland's bridges. On September 25 Montgomery canceled the operation, recalling his surviving paratroopers to lick their wounds, and a dispirited Ike went back to his office to figure out the next step.

As the battle for the bridges raged, Ike's staff moved SHAEF headquarters into the Hôtel Trianon in Versailles, where his communication network improved and he had room to accommodate most of his London-based general staff. Ike's office, a former Luftwaffe office suite, consisted of a huge, dark room with a fireplace at one end and a plywood partition creating a crude antechamber for his secretary, Kay. A terrible typist, Kay was now a second lieutenant in the U.S. Women's Army Corps, and her duties centered around keeping Ike's calendar, arranging his social events, answering his fan mail, and keeping tabs on his office life.[64]

For his personal living space, Ike's staffers set up his residence at a large though not opulent home in a Parisian suburb, one formerly occupied by his counterpart, von Rundstedt. Before long, Eisenhower's household would expand to include orderlies, aides, tailors, valets, cooks, and wait staff, as well as two Norman cows named Maribell and Lulabell, who preserved their hides by obliging Ike's mess with fresh milk and butter. The mess sergeants traded the excess milk to Bradley's cooks for fresh eggs, and the barter system kept both generals well breakfasted.[65]

And in the midst of a circus of death, Ike smoked, fretted, and nursed his aching knees.

TWENTY-ONE

TO THE RHINE

We roll across France in less time than it takes Monty to say 'Regroup' and here we are stuck in the mud of Lorraine. Why?? Because somewhere up the line some son-of-a-bitch who never heard a shot fired in anger or missed a meal believes in higher priorities for pianos and ping-pong sets than for ammunition and gas.

—George to Charlie Codman, 1944

IT WAS A GOOD ALLIANCE, and like all good alliances, it was based on a measure of fear. Fear of the British, fear of Devers, fear even of what Ike might do if Monty convinced him to stake everything on a northern thrust. Fear that the Americans under their command would be marooned in eastern France while British troops hacked their way down the long, slow, bloody road to Berlin.

In early September, Brad and George pleaded in unison for ammunition, fuel, and supplies. Bradley was becoming a tonnage umpire among his two hungry armies, and when Ike paid a visit to Eagle TAC, Brad made his best case for a modest increase in supplies. Adding his voice to Brad's, George declared that he didn't need a greater supply allocation to reach the German frontier; he could get by if Ike would simply protect his existing tonnage. "If you don't cut us back," he hummed in his rough tenor voice, "we can make it on what we're getting. I'll stake my reputation on it."

"Careful, George," Ike said, his eyebrows rising. "That reputation of yours hasn't been worth very much."

George's face broke into a toothy grin.

"It's pretty good now."[1]

To Bradley, whether George had a good, bad, or indifferent reputation was not the point. The point was that while Brad was fighting the Germans to the east, he was fighting two other battles, one with SHAEF over supplies, and one to retain control of his First Army, which Montgomery treated as colonial auxiliaries whose chief mission was to protect the British flank.[2]

In mid-September a glum Omar Bradley, crushed between Monty and Ike to the north, Devers to the south, and an indifferent Com-Z to the rear, paid a visit to Eisenhower to lobby for the lead offensive after the Ruhr was captured. By now, he was worn down from butting his head against Eisenhower's political convictions, which he understood but could never share. After conferring with Ike and de Guingand at Versailles on September 22, a visibly depressed Brad wrote to George to tell him Third Army would have to give up two divisions to Hodges. Third Army would also have to assume a defensive role, making do on thirty-five hundred tons per day, so First Army, with five thousand daily tons, would have enough supplies to advance on Monty's right.[3]

The news brought Patton to Eagle Main like a genie popping out of a bottle, and while George was at Verdun, Bradley unloaded some of his own troubles on his erstwhile ally. Ike, he said, had again instructed him to put First Army in a supporting role, guarding Montgomery's flank and doing Montgomery's bidding. He told George supplies in the theater were so short that if George could not get his Third Army across the Moselle within the next two or three days, George would have to settle down for a defensive lull while Montgomery regrouped to the north.[4]

With their tonnage whittled down to the little end of nothing, Brad and George commiserated. As George wrote, *"[Bradley] was feeling very low because Montgomery has again put it over on Ike and demands the assistance of the First Army in a push over the Ruhr. . . . Going on the defense and having our limited supplies cut still more is very discouraging. Bradley and I are depressed."* The two generals, moping together, mused how much better life would be in China, or maybe even in the Central Pacific sector run by Admiral Nimitz.[5]

Given Ike's orders, there was little Brad could do to help Patton. But seeing something to be gained by keeping the stove set to "warm" for the moment, he quietly gave George permission to make small, local attacks to "straighten out his lines." Although George predictably interpreted this as a prelude to a mass offensive, Brad relayed his instructions to Eisenhower in more guarded terms:

In accordance with instructions I received at your headquarters the other day, I have ordered the Third Army to assume the defensive. At the same time, however, I have authorized George to make some minor adjustments in his present lines. . . . I am doing this in the belief that it complies with the spirit of your directive to assume the defensive in order to save supplies for the First Army.[6]

A week later, Bradley accompanied Ike on a visit to Patton's headquarters. Eisenhower, knowing full well the grousing that must be going on behind closed tent flaps, outlined in broad terms the coming blow against Hitler. The British, he said, had reached the end of their manpower pool. Any new divisions would be American, and as Americans they would naturally go to Twelfth Army Group. As Antwerp and Marseilles opened up, Twelfth Army Group would receive enough supplies to make the main thrust into Germany. But for now, Twenty-First would lead the pack, and Ike warned Patton's men that he would not tolerate any grumbling or banter about "who was winning the war." Save it, he told them, for the boat ride back home.[7]

The roles Ike, Brad, and George had played since those long-ago days in the States had turned and twisted as Allied generals collided on different axes like balls on a billiard table. Ike was firmly in charge of strategy, Patton of execution, and Bradley hovered in the middle. In the fall of 1944, Ike told Brad when to move, though he solicited Bradley's advice and preferred the informality of discussions over bridge or highballs to conference rooms and tightly worded memoranda. By the same token, Brad called the shots within his group, but he treated George respectfully, solicited Patton's advice, and never broke his habit of saying "sir" to George in mixed company.[8]

In this old, familiar triangle, the higher man pulled rank, and the complaints sprang from below. Ike, Brad felt, didn't fully appreciate the capabilities and needs of Twelfth Army Group, while Bradley, in George's view, didn't have enough faith in Third Army. It was the time-honored tradition; Patton's corps commanders felt the same way about Patton, the division commanders griped about corps, and on it went, probably ending with a private somewhere in France bitching about the stupidity of everyone.

Well, things were getting better with George, Brad thought, an unexpected state of affairs given their history in Sicily. When Patton first shipped over to France, he worried that George would be an impossible subordinate, both by temperament and from their stormy relationship in the Mediterranean.

But as the threat of Montgomery eclipsed the threat of the Germans, the two men circled their wagons. After the war, Bradley wrote,

> George soon caused me to repent these uncharitable reservations, for he not only bore me no ill will but he trooped for 12th Army Group with unbounded loyalty and eagerness. . . . Before many more months had passed, the *new* Patton had totally obliterated my unwarranted apprehensions; we formed as amiable and contented a team as existed in the senior command. No longer the cocky martinet who had strutted through Sicily, George had now become a judicious, reasonable and likeable commander.[9]

George reciprocated Brad's public displays of courtesy. He always referred to Brad as "sir" or "General Bradley" in public, and he often kept his ivory-gripped revolvers at the office in favor of a more subdued .38 automatic. He had, evidently, learned something from the slapping and Knutsford incidents, and he spent as much time telling Third Army's journalists not to quote him as he did telling them about the war. For George, it was as a matter of self-preservation more than any newfound humility, for even cats only have nine lives, and Patton had burned through about seven or eight of his.[10]

Bradley's close companion Chet Hansen, who had loathed Patton since Sicily, found the Third Army commander surprisingly measured. He wrote in his diary:

> *Patton's stature has increased immeasurably in this campaign and everyone has a far higher regard for him than they did in Sicily. Combines the aggressive instinct that makes him good with a more realistic moderation. General Bradley acts as the leveler here and figures out the combinations and tactics necessary to make the Armies move with such perfect coordination. Patton, too, is less bombastic—appears to have fitted himself well to General Bradley's authority. . . .*[11]

He may have been the junior partner now, and perhaps a bit less bombastic, as Hansen thought. But because Patton was the group's peacock, the three friends followed the unspoken rule that Bradley and Ike would play the straight men when George was "onstage" around guests, so long as he behaved himself. During a luncheon given by Eisenhower and Bradley in honor of King George VI, Ike remembered the king engaging George in casual conversation. Always solicitous to his American allies, His Highness politely asked General Patton how many men he had killed with his ivory-gripped revolvers.

"About twenty, sir," Patton said.

"George!" Ike snapped.

"Oh, about six," George said, changing his story without a trace of embarrassment.

Ike, his son remembered, was sure the answer was zero.[12]

Patton went along grudgingly with Eisenhower's "defensive" mandate throughout late September. Even if Ike had given him permission to advance, German resistance had stiffened along the Moselle; with supplies chronically short, George had to content himself with small, local attacks. He allocated most of his supply tonnage to gasoline rather than ammunition—no need for ammo when you can't reach the enemy—and he shut down all unnecessary rear-echelon traffic with the zeal of his "hat patrol" days in Tunisia.[13]

Besides that, what else could he do? Bridges, railyards, and rolling stock had been bombed into the Stone Age before D-Day, so nothing was going to ride the rails. Air transport, the portion not allocated to Montgomery, could hardly put him over the Rhine, and after October, everyone knew Normandy's beaches would no longer be usable. The Red Ball Express, a dedicated highway running from St.-Lô to Soissons, made great public relations, but it was even more inefficient than the air drops, since the trucks required tires, spare parts, and tons of gasoline to move the fuel they were supposed to be hauling.[14]

In the quiet of his trailer, George wondered whether Ike was cutting his supplies so Third Army's big attack could not take place before the November elections, but even he dismissed that theory as too fantastical. In the end, he concluded that the problem was just the usual screwed-up Army supply system. "We roll across France in less time than it takes Monty to say 'Regroup' and here we are stuck in the mud of Lorraine," he sounded off to an aide. "Why? Because somewhere up the line some son-of-a-bitch who never heard a shot fired in anger or missed a meal believes in higher priorities for pianos and ping-pong sets than for ammunition and gas."[15]

Despite chronic shortages, George managed to get a toehold over the Moselle River near Metz in mid-September, an achievement he refused to let the press corps overlook. His army was doing the heavy lifting, he insisted, since the wide, meandering Moselle was a "son-of-a-bitch through all history." So was his next obstacle, the city of Metz.[16]

An ancient fortress that had last capitulated to the Huns in 451 A.D., Metz was the anchor of the Franco-German frontier. On the east bank of the Moselle River, the bastion had been improved by Holy Roman Emperor Charles V in the 1500s, upgraded by the legendary French engineer Vauban a century later, and expanded still further by the French over the next two centuries. After France ceded it to Germany at the end of the Franco-Prussian War, the city's defenses were further refined by the Germans. Metz's approaches were studded with barbed-wire entanglements, pillboxes, broken ground, river obstacles, and an interlocking network of forts with odd-sounding names like Driant, Kaisersmacker, Saint-Quentin, and Plappeville. Metz survived repeated assaults during two world wars, and if the title "impregnable fortress" could be laid on any place, it would be the city on the Moselle.

Patton originally intended to bypass Metz. It was a hard nut to crack, one that would require huge stockpiles of supplies and three days of good weather if losses were to be kept to a minimum. Having recently told reporters, "I am not going to get soldiers killed, in spite of being a son-of-a-bitch," George was determined to avoid a slugging match on ground that favored the defender.[17]

But Bulldog Walker, commander of Patton's XX Corps, underestimated the determination of the German garrison. He insisted on reducing the bastion with air and infantry, and managed to hook Patton on his operation, code-named THUNDERBOLT. Brad, having assured Ike that Third Army would soon have substantial forces across the Moselle, encouraged the operation.

On September 29, Ike paid a visit to Patton's forward command post, a small house in Étain, and the two old colleagues squinted at maps and plotted the Metz campaign, giving encouragement to each other just as they did during their armchair-general days at Camp Meade. It was not long before George, his blue eyes fixed on the "impregnable" fortress, was pursuing the old bastion like it was Captain Ahab's whale.[18]

Despite thorough planning, the late-September assault on Metz soured into a minor disaster. Minor, that is, only in comparison to the larger disasters facing Montgomery at Arnhem and the Scheldt. For a month, Patton and Walker tried to bludgeon Metz into submission, but as a glum George admitted to Jimmy Doolittle, *"Those low bastards, the Germans, gave me my first bloody nose."*[19]

As casualty returns trickled in from Étain, Bradley thought it might be time to put a stop to the effort. "For God's sake, George, lay off," he eventually told Patton. "I promise you'll get your chance. When we get going again, you can far more easily pinch out Metz and take it from behind. Why bloody your nose with this pecking campaign?"

"We're using Metz to blood the new divisions," Patton explained nonchalantly, showing Bradley that his attacks had been limited, small-scale ventures, battalions and such. Nothing too risky.

Brad shrugged it off. The men kept fighting.[20]

Around this time, Patton made another slip that, while trivial, underscored to Ike his lack of good judgment. This time George intruded on rear-area policy, a field in which Eisenhower was the acknowledged master and needed no advice from his old friends. As George wrote in his diary on October 17, *"I told [Ike] that some one in his office had told the French to prevent our soldiers from using their whore houses. He had never heard of such an idea which is absurd and will result in a very bad situation."*[21]

Absurd, perhaps; against human nature, certainly. But when George suggested in a letter that Ike unofficially supply French brothels with penicillin, Ike blew his stack. It was just like George, he thought, to say something stupid, to sound off in mixed company just for the hell of it. But it was out of character even for him to put a bad idea into an official letter. Imagine what those mothers and wives back home would be saying—to say nothing of the War Department—if the Army distributed penicillin to French whores while American soldiers died of infection in the field. *It was just another instance of George opening his mouth and saying the damndest, most ill-conceived things.*

"I most emphatically do not agree with the idea of furnishing penicillin to any of these places," he wrote George in late October. *"To run the risk of being short in this important drug merely in order that brothels in France may be supplied with it is absolutely unacceptable to me."*[22]

Statements like this one reminded Ike that he would have to keep a close eye on his prodigy and problem child. While George was a magnificent fighter, the man obviously lacked sound discretion when idle. Ike would have to be very careful whenever George was behind the lines and away from combat.

*　　*　　*

In early October, George devised an ambitious plan to cross the Moselle north and south of Metz, push his army over the Saar, and drive through the Siegfried Line. His two attacking corps would move out under heavy air and artillery cover. Engineers would bridge the river, infantry would open the hole, and those fast, tough Shermans would exploit the rupture. If all went well, George would be flush against the Rhine before any commander, Allied or German, knew what was happening.[23]

On October 7, Patton briefed Bradley and a visiting General Marshall on his plans for Metz, and ten days later he made a similar presentation to Ike and Devers. He fired off a "My dear General Bradley" letter to push the Missourian into letting him also move against the Saar River, then sent his deputy G-3, Colonel Paul Harkins, to Bradley's new headquarters at Luxembourg to carry a personal plea for the deeper drive on George's behalf. To succeed, George stressed, Third Army wouldn't have to empty SHAEF's limbers. His only requirement, he said, was twenty-one hundred tons of ammunition, and a like amount of fuel each day.[24]

Three days later, George had his reply. Stopping at Nancy for lunch with his chief of staff, Lev Allen, Bradley remarked that there was enough ammunition available for only one of his three armies to attack. Patton would have to hold his fire for now. But before long, he assured George, the Allies expected to have enough for a big push, all armies abreast; then Patton could move forward.

George pressed him. Third Army could jump off on two days' notice, he claimed, and the time to push onto the Saar was now. If Brad would just give Third Army priority for once in the war, his men could crack that line.

Nope, said Brad. Twelfth Army Group didn't have the supplies or manpower yet, and neither did SHAEF. When the time was right—sometime in early November, most likely—Twelfth Army Group would launch another big offensive, pushing the British and First, Ninth, and Third Armies simultaneously. But not yet.[25]

After this disappointing meeting with Brad, George lamented, *"Bradley is too conservative—he wants to wait until we can all jump together by which time half our men will have flu or trench foot. . . . I wish he had a little daring."*[26]

Patton wasn't sure why a younger man like Bradley would be more conservative than an old codger like himself. Perhaps it was lack of confidence, or maybe Brad's uncomfortable status as the junior leader among Monty and Ike. One difference, undoubtedly, was their background, for George's training as a cavalryman had taught him that speed was everything. Horses were big, heavy targets, easy to bring down if they didn't keep running; to Patton, armies and corps were not all that different from horses. You had to feed them, you had to keep them shod, and they wouldn't last long in battle if you sat on them without moving.

Why Brad and Ike couldn't see this simple truth mystified George.

With MARKET-GARDEN a bust and the airborne divisions out of the picture, Omar Bradley thought the time had come to ask Ike for his chance at a breakthrough, another roundhouse punch like COBRA that would dovetail nicely with Ike's "broad-front" strategy. He had been the American advocate of a broad-front approach to the Ruhr, and U.S. successes in Normandy and eastern France, he figured, had earned the GI a place at Ike's table. With Hodges closing in on Aachen, the first German city within Allied reach, Brad figured the moment to push his classmate for an American show had arrived.[27]

At a major strategy conference in Brussels on October 18, Eisenhower approved a late autumn campaign plan that called for a double envelopment of the Ruhr. Because Montgomery's Job Number One was the clearing of the Scheldt, the main effort for November, he decreed, would be led by the First and Ninth Armies, with Patton's Third Army in support. While the Ruhr, Monty's show, would be the focal point of Allied strategy initially, Ike's long-term plan also called for the capture of Frankfurt farther south, which implied that Third Army was still in the game. This was anathema to Montgomery's conception.[28]

To implement Ike's strategy, Brad proposed that his two northern armies, the First and Ninth, would advance north of the Ardennes, through the Huertgen Forest, over the Roer River, and into the German cities of Cologne and Bonn. Farther south, Patton's two Third Army Corps would cross the Moselle, push past Metz, and move into the Saar River valley. Given supply schedules, Brad figured the northern assault could push off around November 5, and George's supporting force would go forward about November 10.[29]

It would be a magnificent advance, Brad thought, aggressive yet nicely balanced. And it might be his last chance to clear the Rhine by year's end. Ike's invitation to fight naturally pleased Bradley, and after the conference he spent the weekend with Ike and Beetle hunting pheasant, playing bridge late into the night, sleeping well into the morning as Ike's houseguest.[30]

What disconcerted Bradley was Eisenhower's Faustian bargain with the British that neither friendship nor an appeal to Ike's American sentiments could alter. Because the Brussels strategy departed from Ike's earlier policy of letting Twenty-First take the lead against the Ruhr, Eisenhower planned to give Montgomery another shot at the Rhine if Brad couldn't score a touchdown on the next play. To this effort Monty would have the use of one American army.[31]

Brad dearly wanted to hang onto all three armies under his command. But if he had to give up one of his children, he preferred that it would be Lieutenant General William H. Simpson's newly arrived Ninth Army. Bradley had planned to wedge Ninth Army in between Hodges and Patton along the quiet Ardennes sector, but since it was the least experienced outfit at the army level, it would be the smallest loss to him if Montgomery poached a U.S. Army. So, with Ike's blessing, Brad began shifting Ninth Army from its central position in Luxembourg to the northern end of the American line, so that it rubbed shoulders with Montgomery's Second British Army. To man the Ardennes, he assigned Middleton's VIII Corps. The move into the Ardennes stretched Middleton's four divisions over a ninety-mile front, clearly too thin a screen to withstand any serious attack. But it was adequate, Bradley thought, and it substituted an unlikely German threat for one very real British threat; if Monty poached any of his men, he would get the green Ninth, and Bradley could keep his First and Third.[32]

It was a heck of a disposition to have to make against one's friends.

Patton had been itching to put on a big show since early September, and had been badgering Bradley for permission to drive to the Rhine since early October. Back then he got nowhere, because Bradley wanted to bring up more supplies to the First and Ninth, so that the offensive would employ three supported armies rather than one. To Brad, a larger offensive made perfect sense in the big picture.

As usual, George didn't give a damn about the big picture. After poring over maps and staff studies at his headquarters, he concluded that Third Army could get across the Moselle with just one reinforced corps, regardless of what Bradley's other armies could or couldn't do. He would send Eddy's beefed-up XII Corps over the Moselle, past Metz, and drive it toward the

Rhine. Walker's XX Corps, meanwhile, would envelop and reduce Metz, then bridge the Saar River behind the city. All told, seven infantry divisions, three armored divisions, fifty-two battalions of artillery, tanks, and tank destroyers, three cavalry groups, and fifteen battalions of combat engineers—a quarter million men—would move on Patton's command.[33]

It would be a hell of a battle, and when he broached the plan to Bradley, he argued that it fit into Brad's big picture, dovetailed with Ike's bigger plan. Brad approved George's proposal on October 21, the two men agreeing that Third Army would cross the Moselle and Saar and drive toward Frankfurt, or cross the Rhine between Mainz and Worms, as the situation dictated.[34]

But as D-Day approached, a hitch developed. Second British Army, Brad told George, would not be ready to jump off in a peripheral supporting role on time, and First Army would be delayed until Monty returned two U.S. divisions that had been on loan to him since October. That meant any movement by Third Army would not have the benefit of Allied flank support, a dangerous move given fierce resistance along the German frontier. His dark eyes flashing with utter seriousness, Brad asked Patton if his men would be willing to start the offensive alone.[35]

George knew an uncoordinated kickoff would pose serious and perhaps grave risks, for if the other armies didn't move out soon after he stepped off, the Boche would converge upon him like a pack of wolves. But George was an inveterate optimist, and he knew a solo attack would garner magnificent laurels for Third Army and its commanding general. So he promised Bradley the offensive would go off by November 8, rain or shine, air cover or no, flank support or no. Brad nodded his assent, and George left feeling forty years younger.[36]

But as the day of battle drew near, that old, stifling feeling once again wrapped itself around Patton's broad chest. His breath lurched in short, loud huffs. His stomach tightened; his heart pounded. Nerves, he knew. Just the nerves of an approaching battle.

George reminded himself that this was normal for him. When the time came, he knew that he, like everyone else, would do his job. During November's opening days he indulged himself in a few distractions—church, the Bible, Rommel's *Infantry Attacks*, a USO show starring Marlene Dietrich ("very low comedy, almost an insult to human intelligence," he remarked). But whatever the distraction, no matter how many battles he fought, he always felt the same queasy presence as the time for killing drew near. Nerves.[37]

George's stomach tightened every time he looked out the window at the black clouds descending on the Moselle line. The rains began on the fifth of November and pounded the lush region day after day, turning paths into quagmires and puddles into ponds. Rain fell in buckets, the Lorraine sky swirled, and the Moselle rose to a fifty-year high.[38]

Air support was out. A quick river crossing was out. Tank movement was questionable. All the elements of George's plan were thrown into uncertainty. What was certain was that an attack under these conditions would be difficult, perhaps impossible—facts stressed by two of Patton's most trusted lieutenants, General Eddy and Major General Robert Grow, commander of the 6th Armored Division. Both men asked Patton to delay the planned assault until the weather cleared.[39]

But George had promised General Bradley—and the press—that he would jump off on the eighth, and this was a promise he intended to keep. On November 7, in the midst of the deluge, he ordered Signals to send XII Corps headquarters his favorite code words: PLAY BALL.[40]

For George Patton, the battle for Germany had begun.

At five in the morning of November 8, George awoke with a start as thunder from four hundred artillery tubes shattered the dawn, taking the 46,000 *soldaten* manning the Moselle line by surprise. Despite the rain, despite the mud, he knew that within minutes, assault boats and DUKWs loaded with men huddled below the gunwales would be motoring over the river. They would climb out on the opposite bank, spread out, and move into a forbidding enemy country. As bullets whined and mortar shells crashed, the men of the Third Army would bite off another bloody piece of the Third Reich.[41]

Three hours later, Bradley rang up Lucky Forward to ask whether the attack had gone forth. Patton was pleased to report that his men had stepped off at the appointed hour, and as they spoke, a familiar Midwestern voice broke over the line.

"George, this is Ike," the voice said. "I expect great things of you. Carry the ball all the way."

"Thanks, General, I will," George replied.[42]

Afterward, he mused, *"I wonder if [Ike] ever made a decision to take risks when his best men advised caution. I doubt if he ever has."*[43]

* * *

As so often happened, George's moment of triumph was marred by a small, disconsonant note. This time, it was an irate Omar Bradley, who called to dress him down for committing one division that Twelfth Army Group had ordered to be held in reserve. After casually inquiring how Third Army's attack was going, Bradley expressed his displeasure about Walker's commitment of the division. George, who later found out that the division was not used as a spearhead, but as a follow-up force as directed, protested that Bradley was misinformed. But Brad persisted, and Patton finally remarked, "If you are going to personally command the division, it had best not be used."[44]

While this jibe at Brad's micromanagement put an end to the argument, Bradley nevertheless yanked the division from Walker and transferred it to First Army. George, who gave little thought to long-term reserves, sneered in the privacy of his diary, *"I suppose that Hodges and Middleton have been working on Brad for a week and this, added to his natural and frequently demonstrated timidity made him make a fool of him self."*[45]

Reserves, in general, were virtual strangers to Patton. His army was customarily stretched so thin that "strategic comfort" was a luxury he had learned to live without. After a subsequent phone call with Major General Lowell Rooks, a favorite of Ike's, George outlined his views on the subject in his diary. *"Rooks has an unfortunate academic mind,"* he wrote. *"Among other gems of thought he gave me was that an Army should always have a corps in reserve. I told him that in all my fighting I never had more than a platoon, and that while it is desireable to have a reserve, battles are fought with what one has and not with what one hopes to have."*

To George, the key to this war was to attack with everything, everywhere, as hard as humanly possible. Not as far as *comfortably* possible. General Bradley's order to hold a division in reserve was not only an encroachment on Patton's jurisdiction as an army commander—it was an encroachment on his way of war.[46]

Like Bradley's COBRA, Patton's Moselle attack opened slowly. His riflemen paddled their assault boats and slogged through the mud. His engineers bridged the swollen river, and his cannon cockers blasted the eastern slopes. It was hard going, but in the offensive's first three days, his troops captured one of the Metz forts and had liberated a dozen towns. As men wearing steel-pot helmets poured over the river, George Patton, a man in his element, began to relax.[47]

He remained at Nancy on the eleventh, and his section chiefs threw him a birthday party at Colonel Koch's quarters. Bradley called to wish George many happy returns, and Ike wired his congratulations. Bradley's aide Chet Hansen whimsically noted the day's dual significance:

> *November 11, 1944. Armistice Day and Georgie Patton's birthday. The two are incompatible.*[48]

On the fifteenth Eisenhower and his retinue, which included Kay and little Telek, visited Patton's end of the long, bloody line. Ike, a fanatic about troop welfare, nodded approvingly when he saw Patton's officers combating trench foot with liberal supplies of dry socks, in large part due to a rush shipment of socks George had asked Ike to send him before trench-foot weather set in. Trudging around with his overcoat buttoned to the top, the Supreme Commander, George told Beatrice, *"seemed well pleased and got copiously photographed standing in the mud talking to soldiers."*[49]

George, outwardly charming as always, hosted lunch for the group back at his headquarters, and he even banished his bull terrier, Willie, from the mess room in deference to Telek. As the group dined, however, a loud, animal racket broke out under the table as the Third Army pit bull and the SHAEF Scottie banged and tumbled against legs and chairs. Willie had launched a surprise counterattack, and the two dogs were going at it, heedless of the high-ranking company.

Startled guests kicked their chairs back from the table and dived below to see what on earth was going on. A few emptied water glasses at the snarling animals to separate them, and George, jumping from his chair, ordered his aides to break up the dogfight, using language more familiar to himself, his aides, and his dog.

As George looked on in mock mortification, Patton's batmen finally corralled the snapping Willie long enough to drag him out of the room. George apologized profusely to Ike for the ruckus.

"This is Willie's home," Ike replied, equally embarrassed. "We should lock up Telek."

"No sir!" George replied firmly. "Telek outranks Willie, so Telek stays right here. Willie is confined to quarters, under arrest."

He couldn't help adding, "But my Willie was chewing the bejesus out of your Goddamned little Scottie—rank or no rank."[50]

In spite of the battle of the mascots and a mishap at Eisenhower's hotel—Sergeant McKeogh attempted to light a wood fire in the hotel's fake fireplace—the visit was reminiscent of old times. The two balding, aged men stayed up until two thirty in the morning discussing Army gossip, their old antics, and a little bit of Army business. The friendship born in 1919 had weathered the repeated assaults of time, distance, politics, a reversal of seniority, and the fortunes of war. Yet it had survived, and each of these late-night visits breathed a little more life into their kinship. Ike left Nancy the next morning with one of his "George Patton hangovers," that grumpy, exhausted fog that stunted his brain a morning after staying up way too late talking with his old comrade.[51]

Ten days later, Ike and Bradley showed up at Lucky Forward, where Ike decorated Patton with the Bronze Star. He quipped, "George, I seem to have spent most of this war pinning things on your chest." Ike's remark pleased George to no end, as Ike knew it would. Patton had earned a pat on the back, Ike figured, as he had done what he was supposed to do—attack relentlessly, and keep his mouth shut. Ike was happy to oblige.[52]

Patton kept up the fight for orders to push beyond the Moselle, phoning Bradley on November 19 that Metz was finally in Allied hands—another exaggeration, for the fortress would not fall for three more days. With the bleeding sore of Metz stanched, he began making plans to use Haislip's XV Corps, which he expected Ike to transfer from Seventh Army, to establish Third Army's beachhead over the Saar River.[53]

He showed his plans to a visiting Ike and Bradley on November 24. Ike seemed to like the plan, but Brad found fault with it, arguing that they could reach the same result by giving Devers some of Patton's territory.[54]

George amiably told Ike and Brad, "I'll ask for everything I can get and be perfectly satisfied with what you give me," but he was not perfectly satisfied the next day when Bradley called to tell him that Devers had talked Ike out of letting Third Army use the XV Corps. A slice of Third Army territory, as well as the XV Corps, would go to Devers, just as Bradley had suggested the day before. George argued his point vehemently to Brad, but it was no use. He fumed to himself,

Evidently Devers talked Eisenhower out of letting me have the XV Corps. Well, it can't be helped, but I hate it, and from

a military standpoint it is stupid. I called Bradley and protested but got nowhere. . . . Bradley is without inspiration and all for equality—he may also be jealous.[55]

A few days later, as his army pressed against the Siegfried Line, George met with Devers to discuss coordination between Third Army and its southern neighbor, Seventh Army, which would be keeping Haislip's corps for the immediate future. Coming away from the meeting, George remarked that Devers had *"promised complete cooperation, and so far seems to have given it. I am not sure that as the lesser of two evils it might not be better to be in his Army Group. He interferes less and is not as timid as Bradley. It would perhaps be a mercy if the latter were 'gathered'—a fine man but not great."*[56]

While George was slogging through the Moselle mud, the fine man's Cadillac rumbled beneath dark, forbidding skies to Spa, a French resort town a dozen miles from the German border. He was going to visit Hodges, who had taken over the town and had recently set up his headquarters in the Hôtel Britannique. It was November 14, six days since Patton had launched his attack and three since First Army was supposed to jump off. The weather was atrocious, and under low clouds Brad's massive air support—heavy bombers and plump *jabos*—sat on their runways, their engines cold, their bomb shackles empty.[57]

Omar's mood was as foul as the weather that gray day. His armies were behind schedule, he had slept little, and his face was swollen and red, the accidental product of one of his many food allergies. The weather ruled his life. The skies told him when he could attack, when he had to lie still, when he could fly, when he could not. And right now it was telling him he could do none of those things. He spat to an aide, "This is a goddamn shame. Here the German is moving his stuff around just as we are and there is nothing we can do about it."[58]

Two days later, the clouds retreated, the big orange ball showed itself, and First Army attacked. Army Air Force and RAF bombers pounded the ground ahead of Hodges's men, and, as in COBRA, Lightning Joe's VII Corps stepped off to tear a gash into the German lines. First Army's other corps followed suit, and Hodges was off to the races.

Then things went sour. Despite the war's heaviest ground-support bombing, Hodges's divisions bogged down in the fields commanded by minefields, gun emplacements, mortar pits, and machine gun positions. Casualties mounted. Trench foot, which struck frontline infantrymen disproportionately because they lived in foxholes, added another twelve thousand names to the casualty lists. There would be no COBRA breakthrough this time.[59]

Brad had known it would be a hard fight into the Rhineland. The "other fellow" was still largely a foot-and-hoof force, and COBRA had shown the world what would happen when Brad's Shermans broke into open country. Brad worried that the enemy would hole up in their pillboxes and trenches, and his men would have to dig them out, just like they did in the Pacific. He longed for a fresh German offensive, like the fight at Mortain, so he could smash the German's teeth in and run him back over the Rhine in a battle of tank versus horse. When Beetle and Ken Strong, Ike's G-2, raised the possibility of a German counteroffensive, Bradley replied, "Let them come." He wished the other fellow would come out from his defenses, for his men could kill more of the enemy if they could see them.[60]

But to be on the safe side, he ordered his supply dumps to remain behind the defensible Meuse River. Just in case.[61]

The open country between the Roer and Rhine rivers, about thirty miles deep, was beautiful tank country, well suited to Allied mobile warfare. But as Hodges advanced to the Roer, one terrain feature bothered Bradley: a cluster of dams that, if destroyed at the right moment, could top riverbanks and unleash a mile-wide flood that would destroy every bridge, vehicle, and man in its path. The Egyptians at the Red Sea, on a grander if less biblical scale.[62]

To capture those dams and protect First Army's right flank, Bradley and Hodges concluded that Joe Collins would have to clear out the nearby Huertgen Forest, a dense, primeval thicket south of Aachen that looked like a haunted woods from a Grimm Brothers fairy tale. The Huertgenwald lacked any inherent significance, but Bradley and Hodges were loath to leave the forest in enemy hands, for they knew it would become an open sore that might conceal a lethal host. The mission of the VII Corps, they decided, would be to clean out the forest before moving against Cologne, on the Rhine.[63]

The battle for the Huertgenwald, if the ill-defined tangle of skirmishes, consolidations, and renewed attacks could be called that, ran almost continuously from mid-September until early December. It was a defender's dream, and the Germans, smelling an opportunity to bleed First Army without risk to a critical sector, showered the attackers from high, concealed positions as the Americans struggled through a second Anzio. Hodges, never one to engage in fancy maneuvers like George, committed successive divisions to the meat grinder; having made the decision to capture the forest, he would not call off the operation while the Germans held the high ground. As Tubby Thorson later put it, "We had the bear by the tail, and we just couldn't turn loose."[64]

Before it was over, Hodges and Collins would throw four infantry divisions, an armored division, a regiment of tanks, a Ranger battalion, and an armored infantry battalion into the ghastly woods. By mid-December, Hodges had lost some 31,000 men. He won the battle, but after paying the butcher's bill, he could boast no road network, no industrial zone, no Roer dams. Hodges owned a dark, deathly quiet stretch of dying trees and blood-soaked undergrowth.[65]

The weather, the battles, and the constant infighting were taking their toll on the Missourian. He looked tired; the furrows that snaked across his brow and jowls deepened, and his eyelids drooped. By the end of November, he simply couldn't function properly. Stumbling back to his bed at Luxembourg, he secluded himself in his room for nearly six days, a victim of a cold, hives, sinus infection, and physical and mental fatigue. As the winter storms gathered outside his frosted windows, Brad spent his days wrapped in a West Point robe, slippers and a kerosene heater at his feet, a glass of grapefruit juice perched precariously on the edge of a small table. Unable to focus on his work, he wrote letters home and admitted few visitors until December 6, when he emerged unsteadily, tired and irritable, to face a new round of political and logistical prizefights.[66]

The bloodletting at Huertgen, Bradley knew, would simply bolster Montgomery's case for land battle commander, notwithstanding the relative sizes of their army groups. From his sickbed Brad wrote to Monty that he would not reduce Patton's army to reinforce the north. Despite his threats to resign if placed under Montgomery—"it would be an indication that I have failed as a separate Army Group Commander," he declared—Brad worried about how the endgame played out. He worried that Ike would abandon him at a key strategy conference with the Army Group leaders, scheduled for December 7 in Maastricht, as he seemed to have done in earlier stages of the campaign.[67]

But from under the pall of sickness and low spirits, Bradley thought he saw a ray of light when Ike called to say he'd like to visit with Bradley at Eagle TAC the day before the Maastricht meeting. When a frowning Eisenhower showed up in Luxembourg with Tedder in tow, Brad knew he had a fighting chance, for Tedder loathed Montgomery almost as much as Bradley did. Brad's hopes rose again when Ike told him that the bomber barons had agreed to support a southern push into Germany; while their main job was, always had been, to bomb the hell out of German industry, they said they would be happy to lay out another bomb carpet if it would get Bradley to the Rhine.[68]

The two classmates retired to Bradley's office, where they sat before his giant map and reviewed their battle strategy for the next day. Eisenhower, his wrinkled head jutting from a fur-lined flying jacket, slumped on Bradley's low office couch, speaking in low, conspiratorial tones to the bespectacled Omar, who leaned forward, gesturing to the map with a long pointer. When they were finished, they knew exactly what they needed to get from Monty.[69]

Ike slogged, slipped, and slid through months of October and November, sometimes more literally than he would have liked. His weak knees took a pounding during visits to frontline troops, and the stress of dealing with massive problems of black marketeering, port tonnage, desertion, trench foot, Com-Z, brothels, rape trials, the French, captured liquor, concentration camps, politics—and yes, even war strategy—piled atop a diet of cigarettes and rations that bludgeoned his heart, lungs, and limbs. Adding personal sorrow to Ike's official burdens, Sir Trafford Leigh-Mallory, his sincere if pessimistic air chief, was lost when his plane disappeared over the French Alps.[70]

Even one of his few perks of office, Kay Summersby, was becoming a problem again. Her commission as a WAC lieutenant, her status as Ike's secretary—no longer a mere driver—and her prominent role as one of his three constant traveling companions continued to raise eyebrows. Once, after a formal luncheon at Reims that found Second Lieutenant Kay Summersby sitting near the head of a table that included the Prime Minister of Great Britain, the Chief of the Imperial General Staff, and the Allied Supreme Commander, Marshal Brooke noted privately, "I was interested to see that Kay his chauffeur, had been promoted to hostess. . . . In doing so Ike produced a lot of undesireable gossip that did him no good."[71]

Ike's separation from Mamie, and Mamie's natural concern for the integrity of their marriage and the safety of their only child, were other back currents of anxiety in Ike's sea of troubles. In mid-November, a lonely, frustrated Mamie lashed out at Ike by letter, accusing him of doing nothing to keep their only son away from combat hazards. The charge stung him deeply. From his command post at Greux, Ike shot back,

> . . . it always depresses me when you talk about "dirty tricks" I've played and what a beating you've taken apparently because of me. . . . It's true we've now been apart for 2½ years, and at a time under conditions that make separations painful and hard to bear. . . . Don't forget I take a beating every day. Entirely aside from my own problems, I constantly receive letters from bereaved mothers, sisters, and wives, and from others that are begging me to send their men home or, at least outside the battle zone, to a place of comparative safety. So far as John is concerned, we can do nothing but pray. If I interfered even slightly or indirectly he would be so resentful for the remainder of his life that neither I (nor you, if he thought you had anything to do with it) could be comfortable with him . . . please try to see me in something besides a despicable light and at least let me be certain of my welcome home when this mess is finished.[72]

On the last day of November, a fidgeting Montgomery, emboldened by cautious support from Brooke, tore the still-congealing scab off the fundamental question of the broad-front approach. In a letter to Ike, he declared that the Allies had "failed badly" in their quest for the Rhine and Ruhr; that "we have no hope" of invading Germany through the north; and that the Allies had "suffered a strategic reverse" because the Allies—meaning Ike—had insisted on attacking in too many places. He told Ike that he and Bradley had been a good team when Bradley was under Montgomery's command until September, and that "Things have not been so good since you separated us." To straighten out the ground strategy, Montgomery suggested a follow-up meeting, adding, "I suggest that we want no one else at the meeting, except Chiefs of Staff: who must not speak."[73]

The month before, Montgomery had made another attempt to rewrite the Allied command structure to place himself in command of the land battle. After a tiresome exchange of letters, Eisenhower put down the insurrection by threatening to take the matter to the Combined Chiefs. But the situation kept rearing its head over and over again like some bad Boris Karloff monster, and Ike was furious. He hated Monty's arrogance, and he hated the way Monty insisted on his own infallibility. "He's a psychopath," Ike sputtered to a postwar interviewer, his anger burning brightly after many years. "He is such an egocentric that the man—everything he has ever done is perfect—he has never made a mistake in his life. . . ."[74]

As he read Montgomery's letter, that Eisenhower temper—the red face, the bulging veins, the shaking cigarette hand, and the loud, Old Army vocabulary—burst forth.

Calling for a stenographer, Ike dictated his reply. He toned it down over a couple of drafts, then sent it.

In his letter, Ike firmly refuted any notion of changing either tactics or command. He told Montgomery that persuasive information from Kenneth Strong, his G-2 chief, showed Germany was about to crack. He argued that the September stalemate was little different from the situation in Normandy prior to Bradley's "brilliant break through" in July—a mild slap at Monty— and while he agreed that the Allies should not push their southern attacks senselessly, he declared, "I have no intention of stopping Devers and Patton's operations so long as they are cleaning up our right flank and giving us the capability of concentration." Ike agreed that a personal meeting was warranted, but he flatly declared that his chief of staff would say anything he felt compelled to add. "Bedell is my Chief of Staff because I trust him and respect his judgement," he wrote. "I will not by any means insult him by telling him that he should remain mute at any conference both he and I attend."[75]

Ike's letter jarred loose another conciliatory response from Montgomery, who quickly backtracked on his characterization of the last few months. Ike was satisfied by the reply, though his office diary, kept by Kay, noted, *"Monty is most anxious to have Bradley under his command, keeps on saying that there would be a lot of advantages, etc., of course he is completely crazy to even think of such a thing."*[76]

After a long talk with Beetle about Montgomery's reply, he carefully welcomed Monty back into the fold with a face-saving letter. He gave Monty his "prompt and abject apologies for misreading your letter of 30th November," and assured him, "I'm sorry if my letter gave offense."[77]

On December 7, Eisenhower convened a strategy discussion with Tedder, Bradley, and Montgomery in Maastricht, Montgomery's turf. Montgomery, arriving in his trademark beret, a long scarf, and a fur-lined bomber jacket, championed the northern, "narrow thrust" approach. He wanted airborne and land reinforcements, he said, as well as the direct support of a ten-division American army. He wanted Bradley's group shifted north. He vehemently objected to any drive by Patton toward Frankfurt or Kassel—or any other place south of the Ardennes—and he opined that any effort in that sector could never be "decisive." During the meeting, Ike made a number of big concessions. He ceded the Ninth U.S. Army temporarily to Montgomery's group, and he promised Montgomery that the northern effort would command the highest priority. But, as before, Ike refused to shut down operations in the south. Patton and Devers, he said, would keep pushing toward the Saarland.[78]

An unimpressed Montgomery didn't see Ninth Army as much of a concession, and he insisted that Ike split command so that Twenty-First Army Group controlled all forces north of the Ardennes. This would require Ike to give him First Army as well as Ninth, and leave Brad covering a region he had just characterized as irrelevant. So Eisenhower refused to budge further.[79]

Ike framed his arguments in military terms. The Ruhr, he contended, was not the final objective, and he would not make the Ruhr the basis of an army group dividing line. But the underlying reasoning behind his refusal was precisely what Ike had told Montgomery he wouldn't accept as a basis for strategy: nationalism. Whatever the flaws or merits in Monty's claims to First and Ninth U.S. Armies, the fact was, neither Marshall nor Bradley—to say nothing of Patton, Devers, the U.S. press, or the Roosevelt Administration—would stomach Montgomery commanding American troops for long.[80]

On this, Ike would never back down, and Montgomery knew it. Stung, Monty retreated.

After the meeting, Ike knew Montgomery would be out for his scalp, or at least the part of his scalp that lay north of the Ardennes. To ensure the ground beneath his feet didn't turn into quicksand, on December 12 Ike launched a spoiling attack against Monty's natural base of support. Taking Tedder with him, Ike flew to London for a briefing with Prime Minister Churchill and his senior staff, where he laid out his case for a two-pronged offensive against the Ruhr. Brooke, a Montgomery partisan, naturally gave Ike hell during the meeting, but Ike put the case to Churchill in his straightforward Kansas manner, laying out the military side with just enough hints of the political so that Churchill could easily grasp the need to do it Ike's way. By the time he returned to Versailles, Ike had accomplished what he set out to do: win over the English bulldog.[81]

Aside from Montgomery, Ike found December to be a welcome relief from the wet, dreary fall of 1944. Hodges and Collins were just about through the Huertgen. George told Ike the enemy would soon crack along his line. Ammunition and fuel stocks were growing, Monty finally cleared the Scheldt, and SHAEF was planning a big lunge into Germany come mid-January. The German was beaten, according to Ken Strong; Hitler was losing twenty divisions a month, and he could muster only a dozen new ones to replace them. Things were so quiet in Montgomery's sector that Freddie de Guingand took a short leave in England on December 15, and Montgomery asked if Ike would object to his spending Christmas in England with his son. The war's end was at last in sight.[82]

After the Maastricht conference, Ike drove down to Luxembourg to stay overnight with Brad at Twelfth Army Group, where the two men looked over the American lines with relative satisfaction. Patton was beyond the Moselle, Simpson was sitting pretty along the Roer, and Hodges, licking his Huertgen wounds in the center, still had two corps ready to strike beyond Aachen. Middleton's corps in the Ardennes looked thin, to be sure, but Bradley assured Ike he could pull troops from elsewhere if that sector were attacked, and there was nothing west of the Ardennes worth attacking. To the south, George, with plenty of action along the Siegfried Line, was behaving himself, and in a recent list of officers whom Bradley considered the top contributors to the war effort, George ranked sixth, behind Beetle, Tooey, Hodges, Quesada, and Truscott. (Brad, always in step with his commander, ranked Devers twenty-first, behind nearly every army and corps commander.)[83]

All told, Ike thought, it was not a bad situation. Not bad at all.

On the sixteenth of December, Ike learned that President Roosevelt had formally nominated him to the rank of General of the Army, a new five-star status he would share with Generals Marshall, Arnold, and MacArthur. While he took pains to keep his correspondence on the matter proper, the promotion thrilled the soldier who had warned his family years earlier that he would probably not get "made" beyond colonel. Three years, three months, and sixteen days from lieutenant colonel to five-star general. "God, I just want to see the first time I sign my name as General of the Army," he admitted to Chet Hansen.[84]

And while it was another imposition on his schedule, Ike would also have the pleasure—one of his few genuine pleasures that year—of throwing a wedding reception for his faithful aide, Sergeant Mickey McKeogh.

Mickey, the cheerful Irish face among Ike's inner family, had fallen head over heels for a WAC driver from Minnesota named Pearlie Hargrave, and the couple obtained Ike's permission to wed in Marie Antoinette's beautiful Royal Chapel in the Versailles Palace. On the sixteenth of December, Ike's entourage turned out in force for the event. Those present in dress uniform smiled broadly, shivered in the chapel's frosty air, and sniffed back a few tears as the beaming couple took their vows. The bride and groom kissed, to the applause of the audience, and the wedding party retired to Ike's spacious villa for a reception with cake, music, champagne, and, most treasured of all, a blissful respite from a world at war.[85]

Ike, Supreme Commander of the celebrants, pumped Mickey's hand in the reception line, kissed the bride, and presented the newlyweds with a hundred-dollar war bond as a wedding present. He wished them well on their Paris honeymoon—Butcher had loaned them his hotel suite—and basked in the glow of a day not entirely dominated by what the Germans were doing, or what the French were doing, or what Monty or Lee or Devers were trying to pull over on him. To the east the skies were dark, but the few hours of celebration brightened Ike's afternoon with the warm rays of hope.[86]

As champagne flutes clinked amid the laughter of the reception, TWX machines buried deep within the Trianon's signal rooms sputtered to life. Something was going on at the front, though exactly what, the chattering machines refused to say.

Kay Summersby's diary for that day concluded with the words, *"The German has advanced a little."*[87]

TWENTY-TWO

A FOREST, A CROSSROADS, AND A RIVER

By God, Ike, I cannot be responsible to the American people if you do this.
I resign!

—Brad to Ike, December 20, 1944

BRAD LOOKED UP AND DOWN HIS LINES. They were a damned mess, that's
what they were. Hodges had battered six German divisions in the Huertgen
Forest, but five of his own had taken a beating, and their losses were felt disproportionately among the rifle companies. Huertgen and the Moselle Line
had been infantry battles, and Brad's armies were running low on the men
who shouldered the M-1 and lurched forward. The men with the thousand-
yard stare who squinted into trees and windows and scanned every fold
in the ground. The men who flanked and charged and called in the arm-
droppers and crawled around pillboxes. The hard men who did the killing.[1]

Brad knew, for First Army and SHAEF had told him so, that von Rundstedt was massing his panzer strength for some kind of attack. Hodges would
need more replacements, especially riflemen, to keep pushing east, for it was
with infantry that the war would be won. If the Americans were going to push
through Germany in January, Brad reckoned SHAEF would have to start
bringing in those replacements *now*. That meant it was time to pay a call on Ike.

It was Saturday, December 16.[2]

After breakfast, Omar Bradley and his burly Irish personnel chief, Brigadier
General Joseph O'Hare, climbed into the rear seat of Brad's big white-starred
Cadillac and set off for Versailles. From the warmth of the Caddy, Brad peered
out at a low, thick sky. Chet Hansen had told him that air cover was washed out

for the day—no surprise there—and the generals rode for five hours as the car ran the 250 icy miles from Luxembourg City to SHAEF Main.[3]

After lunch, Ike chaired a meeting with Bradley and the senior SHAEF brass in the Map Room to discuss replacements, which had become a sticky matter with the War Department. As the speakers droned on about replacement, shipping, and truck schedules, a nervous-looking brigadier general slunk into the meeting with an urgent message for Major General Strong, Ike's G-2. Moments later, the bug-eyed Strong interrupted the discussion and announced in his low, Scotch brogue that the Germans had hit First Army along the Ardennes Forest at five separate points. It was unclear exactly what von Rundstedt's intentions were.[4]

Bradley was concerned but not alarmed, since the Hun clearly lacked the resources for a full-fledged offensive. The threat, he opined, was exaggerated. Both Twelfth and Twenty-First had agreed that Hitler could no longer afford a mobile, offensive battle, so it was unlikely von Rundstedt aimed to bring the Allies to a decisive engagement. Monk Dickson, First Army's G-2, had been squawking about a possible Ardennes offensive, but these days Monk was viewed as an alarmist—and Monk, who had been running intel for Bradley since Tunisia, had been drinking too much lately. Most likely, the "other fellow" was launching a spoiling attack to keep Hodges and Patton pinned down.[5]

That night Brad joined Ike, Everett Hughes, and a few other friends for a bottle of champagne to celebrate Ike's promotion to General of the Army. The generals played five rubbers of bridge and killed a bottle of Highland Piper before retiring for the night. Without further information, there was little Bradley could do except wait for fresh reports to come in. He had a fitful night's sleep.[6]

By the time he awoke the next morning, Kenneth Strong had identified at least seventeen German divisions on Hodges's front, far more than Brad had thought possible. Though Brad still clung to the hope that it was a spoiling attack, ULTRA decrypts of von Rundstedt's attack order read:

THE HOUR OF DESTINY HAS STRUCK. MIGHTY OFFENSIVE ARMIES FACE THE ALLIES. EVERYTHING IS AT STAKE. MORE THAN MORTAL DEEDS ARE REQUIRED AS A HOLY DUTY TO THE FATHERLAND.[7]

That was not the kind of order for a diversionary attack.

On Saturday the sixteenth, the Fifth and Sixth Panzer Armies had smashed into First Army's spine at its weakest vertebrae, the four thinly spread divisions of Troy Middleton's VIII Corps. No one had seriously thought they'd hit there. As Bradley and his staff saw it, there were no strategic prizes to be gained—no fuel dumps, no ports, no railyards. If the Germans came, they would hit in the north, near the Ruhr, or in the south, in the Saar Valley.[8]

But the Ardennes region? What could they possibly want with that?

For most of Sunday, December 17, a calm Omar Bradley remained convinced that the fireworks were just a spoiling attack, probably to keep George from amassing enough strength to punch through the Siegfried Line. But as reports trickled in from First Army, it looked like a formidable assembly of SS panzer, infantry, and *volksgrenadier* divisions were crunching their way toward St. Vith, Bastogne, and Spa, First Army's headquarters. Two American divisions in the path of this steamroller were still depleted from Huertgenwald; one of these, the 4th Infantry, was so desperate it began throwing cooks, typists, translators, and bakers into the line of battle. The other two divisions, the 99th and 106th, had never been blooded.[9]

It was the real show, and by Sunday everyone at SHAEF knew it. Beetle, who had sent Strong to discuss the panzer buildup with Brad back in November, saw Bradley that morning and quipped, "Well, Brad, you've been wishing for a counterattack. Now it looks as though you've got it."[10]

"A counterattack, yes," Brad acknowledged. "But I'll be damned if I wanted one this big."[11]

Damned if he had. Hodges was fighting for his life, and Bradley desperately needed to plug the Ardennes Line before it ruptured. The question was, with what?

Ike, who was asking himself the same question, inquired of Bradley what Twelfth Group had available to stem the advance. But Brad had never asked Hodges or Middleton what the defense plan would be in case they were attacked there. Brad told Ike he could pull the 7th Armored Division from the north and the 10th Armored from Third Army in the south—though if he asked George for the 10th, Brad noted, Patton would probably throw a fit.[12]

"Tell him that Ike is running this damned war," Eisenhower spat, and he ordered Bradley to get the 10th Armored right up to Bastogne. The German breakthrough was a strategic lunge, and strategic matters were not in

BATTLE OF THE BULGE
DECEMBER 1944

Patton's job description. An army commander was too far down the chain to have any say in the Allied response.[13]

At Luxembourg City that day, Bradley walked stiffly into his war room, his grimace more pronounced than usual. Ignoring the salutes of guards and aides, he bounded over to the situation map where Lev Allen was watching G-2 men mark the locations of identified German divisions.

One, two, three, four . . . fourteen so far.

And those were just the ones G-2 had positively identified. Who knew what else von Rundstedt was holding in his back pocket beyond the Schnee Eifel.

Brad sure didn't like the look of the grease-pencil arrows that splayed out from the Eifel into his lines, and Hodges and Bill Kean painted a dark picture of what was going on around them.[14]

"Pardon my French," he asked Lev Allen, "but just where in hell has this *sonofabitch* gotten all his strength?"[15]

Allen nodded. It was a big one, all right.

The Americans were rattled, rattled like they hadn't been in a mighty long time, and huge red holes were being torn through Middleton's defenses. Bradley was working on little real sleep, and he looked tired as he moved troops about the map. To Harry Butcher, Twelfth Army Group headquarters resembled II Corps during the Kasserine crisis.[16]

The news from First Army was worse. Teletype lines between Spa and Luxembourg went out, then came back on, then went out for good. First Army's staff had to pull a crash evacuation, burning files and pulling out just ahead of the ravenous panzers rumored to be coming from the south. Rumors had German saboteurs running around in American uniforms, turning signs and assassinating top commanders; Bradley was stopped three times by GIs who grilled him with questions only a true American would know, such as "What is the capital of Illinois?" (Correct answer, insisted one MP: Chicago.[17])

Brad's staffers, themselves showing signs of panic, began shoving thermite grenades between piles of top secret documents, to burn them if the place was overrun, and they relocated their headquarters aircraft back to Étain, George's old headquarters. Brad, however, refused to move Eagle TAC to the rear at this delicate time, telling his aide, "I will never move backwards with a headquarters. There is too much prestige at stake."[18]

He knew there was more than just prestige at stake now.

* * *

In Versailles, Ike was at it again, a cigarette permanently affixed between his index and middle fingers, a thread of smoke wafting from his left hand like a wizard's parlor trick.

Fourteen . . . sixteen . . . seventeen German divisions?

The war in the west would not end with an attack on that scale, he knew, but he would have to be a wizard to escape without a huge loss of time, of territory, of human life. The German offensive, he believed, *had* to be stopped before the Germans crossed the Meuse River, the last great barrier to Brussels and Antwerp. If they weren't, the present setback would unravel into a strategic disaster.[19]

Bradley wasn't taking the offensive seriously, Ike thought, and he decided he had best figure out what he could to do when Brad came calling. That was a knotty problem, since SHAEF had only two light divisions as its "strategic reserve," the 82nd and 101st Airborne, both refitting near Reims after the MARKET-GARDEN fiasco. He had his staff sketch out a rapid response in case Twelfth Army Group called for help, and Ike, Beetle, and SHAEF's assistant G-3, Major General John "Jock" Whiteley, mulled over where to put the theater's scant reserves.[20]

Sure enough, thirty-six hours after the panzers first hit Middleton's men, Brad came, helmet in hand, to ask for those two precious airborne divisions. Ike listened to Brad's plea, and while he didn't relish committing SHAEF's only reserves, he knew the risk was too great to keep any fighting men in the rear. He gave the word, and before long the All-Americans and Screaming Eagles were packed in deuce-and-a-half trucks and driven over the slippery roads to the Ardennes.[21]

General Patton had kept a heavily lidded eye to the north in early December. His astute G-2, Oscar Koch, smelled trouble in front of Hodges, and after a short discussion with Koch, Patton ordered his staff to make contingency plans for a move toward Luxembourg to help First Army.[22]

But that was as far as it went. George, self-centered as always, was more concerned with what he was going to do to the Germans in the east than with threats that were *mostly theoretical* and *mostly Hodges's problem*. He had a nice big surprise in store for Herr Hitler: a massive assault along the Saar River that strategic and tactical air assured him would be preceded by one hell of a bombing wave. Patton and Hap Gay, who had returned to the chief of staff role on December 3, had been working on this show since early December, when Bradley finally told George that Third Army would get the weight of attack on the next round. Patton had great faith in the Mustangs and "Flying Jugs" of Brigadier General Otto P. "Opie" Weyland's XIX Tactical Air Force, and he planned to hurl his javelin on the nineteenth. With any luck, George figured to put the first Americans over the Rhine.[23]

To Patton, the stakes in the south were enormous. Success would put him through the vaunted Siegfried Line and up against, perhaps over, the Rhine River. It would make him the hero he was in August, when his tankers had dashed to the Seine with dizzying speed. Failure would relegate him to the secondary theater again. It would mean more of the same bitter frustrations he had endured since September, and it would mean the loss of more divisions to other, less capable generals. The solitary fencer, the lonely runner, the man who competed for himself and not others, summed up his position in mid-December:

> My attack will still go through with my present short means, but if it fails to break through after the Blitz I will have to go on the defensive till more troops arrive. And in the meantime I may loose some troops. It is up to me to make a break through. I feel that I will God helping.[24]

George had more than general piety in mind when he wrote "God helping," for the uncontrollable weather was, as always, the wild card. It had nearly shut down his Moselle drive in November, and on December 14 he wrote Beatrice, "I have never seen or imagined such a hell hole of a country there is about four inches of liquid mud over every thing and it rains all the time." Lately, the weather had given him as many problems as the Germans had. Perhaps more.[25]

Not wishing to fight two enemies at once, in early December George decided to call in some supernatural help. The Lord had, after all, halted the sun long enough to let Joshua finish off those Amorites in good, killing daylight, so it would be a small matter for a kind and merciful God to blow that storm someplace else so Opie's bombers could bomb the hell out of the German bastards hiding along his front. Patton wanted a prayer, a damned good one, and he ordered his head chaplain, Colonel James O'Neill, to compose something appropriate to the occasion.[26]

An hour later, Father O'Neill came back with an Old Testament–style prayer that walked the fine line between beseeching divine assistance and requesting dispensation to kill. The prayer read:

Almighty and most merciful Father, we humbly beseech Thee, of Thy great goodness, to restrain these immoderate rains with which we have had to contend. Grant us fair weather for Battle. Graciously harken to us as soldiers who call upon Thee that armed with Thy power, we may advance from victory to victory, and crush the oppression and wickedness of our enemies, and establish Thy justice among men and nations. Amen.[27]

Beautifully put, thought George. If any prayer could get those clouds off his front, this one would do it. He had 250,000 copies printed up, one for each man in Third Army, on the back of a small Christmas greeting card. Then he turned back to temporal matters.[28]

On the fourteenth Patton had another talk with Bradley about the results of the Maastricht conference. *"Apparently Monty (SOB) with the help of the PM will get the Ninth Army,"* George growled. *"Monty is bitterly opposed to the operations of both Patch and myself. He wants all available forces massed on the north and wants to command them. He told Ike and Brad that when he commanded the war it was a success, but since he has been relieved of the Supreme Command it was stymied. What a fool!"*[29]

On Saturday the sixteenth, three days before his planned offensive, Lev Allen of Twelfth Army Group called General Gay. Middleton was under attack, Allen said, and he needed help. He told Gay that Third Army's 10th Armored Division would be transferred to Middleton's VIII Corps and moved north at once.[30]

This would not do, thought George when he learned of the call. The 10th Armored was a key part of his exploiting force, part of Third Army's last big chance to shift the war's focus to the south. Besides, the noise on Middleton's front might be a feint, a secondary attack; after all, the enemy was piling more divisions in front of Walker's XX Corps, a sign that the real attack could be on Third Army's front, not First Army's. He called Bradley to straighten the matter out, only to be disappointed.[31]

"George," Brad said, a hint of apology in his voice, "get the 10th Armored on the road to Luxembourg."

"But that's no major threat up there," said George. "Hell, it's probably nothing more than a spoiling attack to throw us off balance down here and make us stop this offensive."

"I hate like hell to do it, George, but I've got to have that division. Even if it's only a spoiling attack as you say, Middleton must have help."[32]

George wrote in his diary that night, *Bradley admitted my logic but took counsel of his fears and ordered the 10th to move. I wish he were less timid.*[33]

Patton resigned himself to the loss of the 10th Armored, but he was determined to launch his Big Blitz on schedule, and to ensure that nothing would happen to his favorite legion, the 4th Armored Division, he ordered General Manton Eddy to commit it to combat, local advances only, so none of the higher-ups could steal the division. With any luck, come December 19, his men would lunge over the Saar as scheduled.[34]

Midmorning on Monday, December 18, Bradley called again; he wanted Patton to bring his intel, operations, and logistics heads to Luxembourg right away to discuss the next steps. Ten minutes later, Patton's convoy was roaring over the mud-caked roads toward Luxembourg City. Patton and his senior staff arrived at Eagle TAC at one in the afternoon to find a grim-faced General Bradley, outwardly calm but clearly distressed, having emerged from a closed briefing with his staff. Brad ushered George into a conference room, and guards closed the doors behind them.[35]

"I feel you won't like what we are going to do but I fear it is necessary," Brad began, somewhat defensively for a commanding general. Then he showed the situation map to George, who was surprised to see the depth of the German penetration. The whole VIII Corps front, and a big part of Gerow's V Corps front, had been smashed in. Panzers were driving toward Hodges's headquarters at Spa. Paratroops had been dropped in small groups behind American lines, and the roster of identified German divisions was growing ominously long.[36]

Brad asked George what he could do, and the cavalryman snapped to the call. Sensing an opportunity, a chance to save the day, he told Brad he would halt Gaffey's 4th Armored Division and move Major General John Millikin's III Corps toward the southern border of the "bulge." He reassigned Major General Horace McBride's 80th Division to Millikin's corps, and arranged to set up a temporary field headquarters in Luxembourg, next to Eagle TAC. He called Lucky Main at Nancy and scheduled an 8:00 a.m. staff meeting for the next morning, then phoned General Gay with orders that underscored the urgency of the moment: "Stop Hugh and McBride from whatever they are doing. They should make no retrograde movement at this time, but this is the real thing and they will undoubtedly move tomorrow."[37]

So much for Patton's Big Blitz. But a fight to the north, George felt, was almost as good as one to the east.

"What the hell," he told Brad with a shrug, "we'll still be killing Krauts."[38]

That evening, George called Bradley from Nancy to check in. "The situation up there is much worse than it was when I talked to you," Brad confessed. He told George that Ike had called a meeting in Verdun the next day, and Brad expected him there. "I understand from General Eisenhower," he said in his Missouri twang, "that you are to take over the VIII Corps as well as the offensive to be launched by the new troops coming in the area."[39]

George's ears perked up. He was focused, he was in his element, and he promised to be ready. Hanging up the receiver, he placed calls to Lucky Forward and transferred two other divisions into III Corps, and he sent Millikin's headquarters and a combat command from Gaffey's division up the road to Luxembourg. He spent the rest of the night doping out the threat to the north.[40]

Patton told his staff the next morning that the solution was obvious: the Nazis, who had run their armor west, would have no way of stopping an assault from the south, especially if the attack had heavy air support, the kind Opie Weyland's fighter-bombers were best at. He directed his staff to plan an attack with the assumption that he would lead III and VIII Corps into the belly of the snake, and he outlined three possible targets: the bulge's tip, near the Meuse; the bulge's waist, near Bastogne; and the bulge's base, toward Bitburg. He concocted a simple code that he would use to phone in the final decision to General Gay after he spoke with Eisenhower and Bradley at Verdun. That meant moving a lot of everything ninety degrees, and it was a tall order.[41]

Taking Paul Harkins, his deputy operations officer, and aide Charlie Codman, Patton hopped into his command jeep and bounced down the road to Verdun, the old French city around which so many young men were blown to pieces during the first Great War. The icy wind on that harsh, dark morning ripped at the car's flimsy windows while inside George reviewed his mental calculations: *If Ike wants us at St. Vith, then Millikin moves here, Eddy here, Gaffey's division along this road, 35th up this road. . . . If he wants Bastogne, Millikin goes to Arlon, 4th Armored takes this road, McBride goes here. . . . If he wants St. Hubert, then . . .*[42]

By ten forty-five, his car rolled up the slush-encrusted entrance to Eagle Main.[43]

The meeting with Eisenhower, Bradley, Devers, and the rest shot a bolt of lightning through the American High Command. No longer merely reacting to the unexpected, Ike, George, and Brad settled on a plan that would, if successful, erase the bulge, destroy Hitler's best men, and leave the German border open to a final, sledgehammer blow. They agreed that Third Army would swing III Corps north in a combined attack with Middleton's corps. Patton would keep Walker's XX Corps at Saarlautern to the south, and everyone in Devers's group would stretch left to cover Third Army's former territory while Patton stabbed north. After gutting the south side of the bulge, the Allied armies would turn east—*together*, Ike emphasized—and a new race would begin.[44]

After the meeting, an electrified George Patton sent Harkins and Codman flying back to Nancy, to report to Gay and to retrieve George's trailer, personal effects, and field gear. Motoring around the front and taking calls from his new command post, Patton reorganized his Third Army, shuffling divisions like a blackjack dealer, and aligning corps commanders and supply routes with his new axis of attack.[45]

While he focused on his operation to the north, Patton kept one eye turned to the east, where he had unfinished business with the Germans along the Saar River. The coming battle, he predicted, would be followed by bigger campaigns and more river crossings. This "battle of the bulge" wasn't big enough to suit George, and his orders on the twenty-first warned his commanders to "be prepared to change direction to the northeast and seize crossings of the Rhine River." It took some wrangling with Brad and Devers to keep Walker's XX Corps—and its large stockpile of scarce bridging supplies—within Third Army's shifting boundaries, but as the man charging into the dragon's mouth, George got what he wanted.[46]

The Verdun conference had gone well for the Supreme Commander. He had Patton set on the path of righteousness—a path that led north rather than east—and he was reasonably certain that First and Third Armies could hold the shoulders of the salient, which would turn Hitler's offensive into another Mortain. Devers was doing his part in the south, stretching left and keeping his complaints about SHAEF to himself. Best of all, Ike knew, Tedder would eventually get some good flying weather; after a few days of clear skies, Ike would be touring more corpse-choked roads like at Falaise.[47]

Ike was especially pleased with the way his Third Army commander was coming through for everyone in this latest crisis. With a fluid battle looming and little time to prepare his attack, Patton was in his element, and Ike was about to collect his payoff for protecting the horse soldier these last few years. Everything Ike had done for George Patton, every time he had protected him from the slings and arrows of Marshall and Congress and Drew Pearson and the Navy, that was all being repaid handsomely, with an impossible ninety-degree turn and a blistering attack on three days' notice.[48]

He, of course, had to keep an eye on George, to ensure he didn't talk Bradley into letting him go off half-cocked toward Berlin. But a good, solid hand from Brad, he felt, would keep George subordinated to the larger picture.[49]

Ike's biggest concern at the moment was his other American generals. First Army's staff had skedaddled when the 1st SS Panzer Division threatened Spa, and Ike could only imagine what top secret materials they had inadvertently left behind. Hodges and his staff didn't seem to be coordinating their corps any better from Chaudfontaine, their new command post, and Bradley was still trying to run things from Luxembourg, south of the bulge and out of direct contact with Hodges. If the enemy reached the Meuse, Ike feared Hodges would be cut off almost entirely.[50]

Brad, for his part, hadn't visited Hodges since late on the seventeenth, when he had motored back from Ike's headquarters. To get to Chaudfontaine from Luxembourg's capital without crossing German lines, Bradley would have to drive west, cross the Meuse, move north into Belgium, then turn east. Twelfth Army Group's commo wires had been cut at the little town of Jemelle, and as the Germans advanced, Signal Corps radio stations had to leapfrog backward, interrupting the slender thread of communications among Bradley, Hodges, and Simpson.[51]

It was against this backdrop of worries that Ike walked into his morning staff meeting the day after the Verdun conference. There, Bedell Smith brought up something that had been weighing on his mind for the last twenty-four hours: command of the Twelfth Army Group.[52]

Bradley was troubled by the perception that Hodges was falling apart. To Brad, the Ardennes pounding was a calculated risk that everyone had agreed to long ago, one that SHAEF had to keep in its proper context. It was not a disaster, and it was not a strategic reverse. Hodges, Brad figured, could contain the enemy, and the Allies easily had enough weight on both sides to crush the bulge, which would inflict irreplaceable losses on the *Heer* and pave the road to Berlin.[53]

Trouble was, Brad couldn't tell Ike where the Germans would be stopped.

When Brad last spoke to Hodges on the telephone, the Georgian seemed tired and depressed. But he was holding on to the north shoulder of the bulge at Malmédy and the critical road juncture at St. Vith. Middleton's infantry divisions, while pulped, had delayed the enemy long enough for their neighbors to come to their rescue. Although the retreating front meant the Twelfth Army Group commander would have a hard time driving to First Army's command post, he still had his phone lines, and he spoke with Hodges a half dozen times on Monday the eighteenth. When phone lines were cut, he used VHF radio signals, though they needed two relay stations to convey the messages across the weak transmissions. The system didn't look pretty, but it worked.[54]

The problem, Brad soon learned, was one of perception far behind the lines. Eisenhower seemed outwardly calm, satisfied, and supportive of the American leadership—he said nothing negative to Brad during the meeting in Verdun—but that afternoon he sent Brad and Lee a cable suggesting that Lee's support troops be organized to defend and, if necessary, destroy the Meuse bridges. The message indicated low-level panic at SHAEF. And that evening, Brad got a call from General Bedell Smith.[55]

Beetle characteristically came straight to the point. "Ike thinks it may be a good idea to turn over to Monty your two armies on the north and let him run that side of the bulge from 21st Group. It may save us a great deal of trouble, especially if your communications with Hodges and Simpson go out."[56]

Brad would have been less shocked if Beetle had said he was being court-martialed for drunkenness. *Take away two armies?* It was an openhanded slap in the face, one that bore the hallmarks of another British writing campaign that was obviously getting to a jittery General Eisenhower.[57]

However Brad might burn inside, he didn't want to push himself, Montgomery-style, on Ike, not at this moment. Surely Ike would come around, understand the nonsense of such talk. So he mumbled to Beetle, "I'd question whether such a change is necessary."[58]

"It seems the logical thing to do," Beetle pressed, his voice never betraying the slightest trace of uncertainty. "Monty can take care of everything north of the bulge and you'll have everything south."[59]

Beetle, smelling blood, pushed harder. The change would be only a temporary transfer, he emphasized. Since Patton's attack was the mandible of the Allied bite, it made sense for Brad to stay in close touch with George down south until the line got fixed. Once the bulge was restored, the First and Ninth would of course go back to Brad. Besides, Beetle pointed out, with Monty in charge of the northern side, he might be more willing to commit British troops to the battle, and that might turn things around faster.

Brad thought it over quickly. It might be a way to get Monty's troops into the fight, but his instincts told him this was still a bad move—though he could not articulate precisely why. It was certainly a bad move for Omar Bradley, but that wasn't enough. He wasn't sure what to do.[60]

"Bedell," Brad said at last, "it's hard for me to object. Certainly if Monty's were an American command, I would agree with you entirely. It would be the logical thing to do."[61]

The call ended with Brad hoping that Beetle was just sounding out options. Surely Ike's chief of staff wouldn't be stupid enough to recommend something that drastic to Eisenhower. Not at a delicate time like this.

"It's an open-and-shut case," Beetle assured Ike the next morning. Sitting in Eisenhower's office with Ken Strong and Jock Whiteley on the morning of December 20, Beetle urged the Supreme Commander to transfer First and Ninth Armies to Montgomery's Army Group for the duration of the battle, and he laid out his case in blunt, logical terms.[62]

Ike was not the kind of man to change horses in midstream. For all his pontificating about the need to get rid of the unworthy, he had hesitated even to remove Fredendall at Kasserine. Ten months earlier, he had told General Marshall, "It is absolutely impossible in an Allied force to switch command of any unit from one nationality to another during a period of crisis." But in the midst of this crisis, Ike was more concerned with immediate strategy, the here and now, than with larger command issues, and his personal reluctance to drive change would give way to the needs of the battlefront.[63]

To be sure in his own mind, though, Ike needed to know how far back the Germans would go before they hit the inevitable wall. He had Kay get

General Bradley on the line. When Brad picked up, Ike asked him, "Where is the line you can hold the best and cheapest? I don't care how far back it is."

Brad didn't have a solid answer. He said he'd have to get back with Ike after talking to Hodges.[64]

Ike hung up the phone, his bare brow furrowing again. He needed to know how far von Rundstedt could advance, so he could figure out where to squeeze the bulge from above and below, like some big, bloody pimple. But Ike didn't get the feeling that Brad knew anything more than he did, which seemed to confirm Beetle's diagnosis of paralysis among First Army.

Beetle could be a Captain Bligh to his staff, and when Strong and Whiteley, both British, woke him in the wee hours of the twentieth with the idea of giving Montgomery the two northern U.S. armies, Beetle cursed them out and fired them. But turning it over in his head, Beetle knew they were right. The nose of the bulge split Bradley's army group into two separate wings: a northern wing, containing First and Ninth Armies, and a southern one, Patton's Third Army. Bradley, at Luxembourg, was able to coordinate with Patton, but he was more or less out of communication with First and Ninth. Strong's deputy had visited Chaudfontaine and found First Army headquarters a terrible mess, with confusion reigning and no apparent plans for what to do next.[65]

Later that morning, Beetle rehired Strong and Whiteley, who hadn't had time to pack their bags yet, and took them to see Eisenhower. Beetle told Ike he believed Montgomery should take over the battle north of the bulge, commanding the First and Ninth Armies, and Bradley should run the show to the south. What's more, Beetle said, he had already talked it over with Bradley, who agreed it was the "logical thing to do."[66]

If Brad wasn't going to kick, at least not too much, that made Ike's decision a little easier. And even if Brad did kick, Ike knew it had to be done. At noon the armies would execute the changeover.[67]

Ike called Brad back and explained his decision, Strong and others listening in. The two Midwestern voices grew loud and heated. Bradley, his worst fears confirmed, argued with all his might that a split in command was the worst possible decision in the middle of a battle. He bucked and he yelled, but Ike would have none of it. Eventually, Brad's even temperament reached its limit.[68]

"By God, Ike," he sputtered, "I cannot be responsible to the American people if you do this. I resign!"[69]

"Brad, I—not you—am responsible to the American people," Ike said coldly. "Your resignation therefore means absolutely nothing."[70]

Brad put down the receiver, dumbfounded. He had just lost two armies to the man he despised.

He was also furious over the insinuation, born of ignorance, that the Allies had cause for real alarm. The panic was not on the front lines, either from the fighting man or the headquarters echelons, so far as he could tell. It came from SHAEF, that acronym for the rear-echelon desk drivers the fighting men said stood for "Should Have Army Experience First."[71]

But to the casual visitor, Eagle TAC looked like a command post under siege. Rings of concertina wire surrounded its buildings and trailers, and road checkpoints were manned by stern-faced military policemen armed with submachine guns and an apparently endless litany of questions, the answers to which only genuine Americans would know. Walls were lined with sandbags, and the sandbags were topped with .30-caliber machine guns. Sentries guarded every doorway and demanded daily passwords, while officers inside demanded identification cards from everyone. Brad was driven to work along a different route every morning, a loaded pistol in his lap, its safety off; he was once detained by a zealous MP when he proved unable to identify Betty Grable's current husband—though the guard waved him through when the Army's former baseball star correctly answered the backup question, "Who is the starting shortstop for the Cleveland Indians?"[72]

Inside his bunker, Brad stormed and cursed as Patton and Chet Hansen joined him. He had been betrayed and humiliated, and he vilified Montgomery to visitors from both sides of the Atlantic. He knew that bastard Monty had gotten hold of Ike—probably through Brooke and Churchill—and Ike, no longer American in his outlook, was caving in to British pressure. To Brad, Monty was the incarnation of everything wrong with the British, everything wrong with SHAEF. Everything wrong with Ike.[73]

Before long, Brad's fury gave way to resignation. The time to kick with both feet had come and gone when Beetle phoned him on the night of the nineteenth. Brad hadn't reacted quickly enough, hadn't recognized the threat as it was unfolding. For a second time in four days, he had been caught blindsided, first by von Rundstedt, now by Beetle and Ike.

For the next five days, Brad's job would be to oversee Patton's drive north. Phone lines had to be rerouted, maps had to be printed, supplies had to be stockpiled, and his front along the Saar had to be protected. George had to move one hundred thousand men and tens of thousands of vehicles from the Saarland through Luxembourg City to Arlon. The Third Army staff, the outfit Brad's staff had sneered at in Sicily, was coming through in a big way, and it needed any assistance Bradley's men could provide.[74]

Bradley soldiered on, but he was running out of steam. When he got to sleep, he found himself waking up again, thinking, turning the battle over in his mind, and he went back to taking sleeping pills at night. Some anonymous staffer left four bottles of vitamin pills on his desk one morning. "To pep me up," Brad guessed with a hangdog smile.[75]

His heavy coat buttoned against the frigid December gusts, George Patton darted from point to point like a mountain lion ready to pounce. Physically imposing in his parka and helmet—he had strapped on the ivory pistols for the occasion, too—he set up a makeshift command post in an old-folks' home in Luxembourg, near Eagle TAC. Each morning he and Sergeant Mims drove to division and corps posts in his Dodge command jeep, its Plexiglas windows and .30-caliber machine gun protecting him against both the Germans and the cruel Belgian wind.[76]

As with anything involving Patton, some of it was pure showmanship. One frigid morning, for instance, George noisily rode up to Eagle TAC in an open jeep, with only his uniform, field jacket, and helmet to protect him against the icy December wind. Brad greeted him cordially, not mentioning a report phoned in from security that Patton's still-warm limousine had been spotted parked on the outskirts of town.[77]

His theatrics notwithstanding, George and Brad pulled together magnificently under adversity, for they were at their best when planning an attack. They worked well and joked often to keep up their own spirits and those of their staffs. They even called each other "Brad" and "George" in front of junior officers, instead of the usual "General Bradley" and "General Patton" they used in mixed company. Brad needed George to eradicate the bulge and return him to the offensive, and he had given Patton an extemporaneous mission that was the kind the cavalryman dreamed of: riding to the rescue, hitting the enemy in the flank and rear. Chet Hansen, who had been so bitter toward Patton back in Sicily and England, remarked in his diary earlier in the month: *"I have revised an early attitude. With Bradley to control and guide him, and with Gaffey to hold down his administration, Patton provides the leadership and aggressiveness needed to make an army an aggressive and going concern. Patton has daring, he has a great personal ambition to do spectacular things. . . ."*[78]

Always attuned to his place in the war, George, when he had time to reflect, was delighted to watch his star shooting over that of Hodges, Bradley's favorite. He wrote Beatrice, *"Even the tent maker admits that Courtney is dumb. He is also very jealous of me."*[79]

A natural focus of Third Army's attack was the city of Bastogne, a place vital to both sides because it fused a large road network that von Rundstedt desperately needed to keep his offensive alive. Thinly held by the 101st Airborne and elements of the 9th and 10th Armored Divisions, by December 20 the situation looked hopeless. Bastogne's defenders were being encircled; cut off from the rest of the Allies, supplies would soon run out, and as George aptly pointed out, "They can't live on love."[80]

Although Bastogne commanded a critical road network, even a bullish general like Patton could see that it was a lost cause, and he decided to order a fighting withdrawal. Still thinking of sucking the German armies into a trap, he blew his stack when he learned that Middleton instead ordered the Screaming Eagles to hold Bastogne at all costs. At a December 20 meeting in Luxembourg with division and corps commanders, he barked at Middleton, "Troy, of all the goddamn crazy things I ever heard of, leaving the 101st Airborne to be surrounded in Bastogne is the worst!" He ordered Middleton to pull out, retreating slowly. Blow bridges, play for time until help arrived from the south.[81]

Troy shook his head. The town, he argued, could be held, at least a little while longer. With Bastogne in Allied hands, the Fifth Panzer Army would have a terrible time moving ammunition, supplies, and reinforcements along the bulge's southern sector. Better to tell the defenders to hold their positions and fight it out until reinforcements arrived.[82]

Listening carefully to Middleton's arguments, George's own intelligence man, Oscar Koch, concurred. So did Bradley.

George backed down, and the course was fixed. The defenders would hold Bastogne, and Third Army would relieve the city from the south.[83]

To steel himself for the attack, Patton called in all the corps staffs he could locate and gave them his pre-battle pep talk. *"As usual on the verge of an attack,"* he wrote, *"they were full of doubt. I seemed always to be the ray of sunshine, and by God, I always am. We can and will win, God helping."* When asked by a British liaison from Twenty-First Army Group if he had any message to send to Field Marshal Montgomery, Patton grew conspicuously silent. He stared at the man for a thoughtful moment, flicking his cigar ash to the side.[84]

Then he nodded. "You tell Montgomery that the Third Army is attacking north and for him to get out of the way, because I'm going to run the German Army up his ass."[85]

It was the same old George Patton again. The thespian whose hammy speeches shouldn't motivate his men. The same horseman whose pious prayers shouldn't change the weather. The man whose scurrying around in jeeps and pistols, commanding a hopelessly substandard staff, shouldn't bring order out of chaos.

Yet somehow George's Old Black Magic had worked at Casablanca, and it worked at Gela. For the same inexplicable reason, it was working now.

By the morning of December 22, as promised, Patton had Millikin's three divisions knifing toward Bastogne. The weather was wretched, and the Germans, who had intercepted American radio messages, were ready for the attack. Millikin's men advanced only seven miles on the first day.[86]

Given the rotten road conditions and stiff resistance, it was a reasonable pace, George thought. But, nervous about the impression his rescue effort was making on General Eisenhower, Patton telephoned Ike each day with a progress report. It was a ritual, meant to keep George's spirits aloft as much as to inform the Supreme Commander. George would begin by saying, "General, I apologize for this slowness. This snow is God-awful. I'm sorry."

Ike would then ask, "George, are you still fighting?"

"Yes, sir."

"All right, then, that's all I've asked you to do. Just keep at it."[87]

On December 23, one day into the counterattack, the sun broke through. From his command post, George could hear the hum of Opie Weyland's fighter-bombers echoing over Luxembourg. Patton was delighted to know that Opie's pilots were airborne, for he knew those Mustangs and Jugs would leave plenty of charred carcasses and burned-out vehicles clogging roads Fifth and Sixth Panzer Armies needed to move toward the Meuse— the very same roads the few, dazed survivors would take back into Germany once their main armies were licked.[88]

But even with air support, it was slow going. His men spent Christmas Eve fending off counterattacks by panzers and infantry units. Part of the 4th Armored was pushed back with the loss of ten Shermans, due, Patton thought, to his own insistence on continuous day and night attacks, which worked well in pursuit but proved ineffective against fixed positions. *"It takes a long time to learn war,"* he confessed.[89]

That evening, George and Brad attended services at Luxembourg's Episcopal church. There they prayed for the souls penned up in Bastogne, those still fighting as well as those sleeping in the arms of their creator. The city was beautiful, and the silvery moon shone softly on white snow as the stars illuminated the winter skies.

Unfortunately the sky, so lovely to the inhabitants of Luxembourg, looked just as beautiful to the *Luftwaffe,* which launched two dozen air raids against Luxembourg that night. The raids marred what little peace the city might have embraced, and carols and hymns were interrupted by staccato bursts of flak and smoking antiaircraft shell fragments, which fell to earth, burying themselves in drifts of snow.[90]

The only Christmas present for Bradley the next day was a stomach-churning, miserable experience at Montgomery's headquarters in Zonhoven. On Christmas Eve, the Hero of El Alamein called Brad to request a conference the next day, at Zonhoven, of course. Bradley, bundled in helmet and parka, hopped a plane and flew there the next day to coordinate their attacks.[91]

It didn't take long for Brad to realize he had made a terrible mistake coming to see Montgomery. When he and Chet stepped off the plane at the airfield, they found no one there to meet them. No car, no aide, no directions, no nothing. A calculated insult, Brad supposed, and he suggested they turn around and go home. But Chet quickly managed to track down a First Army staffer, who loaned Brad and Chet his car, and the two men drove around looking for signposts until they managed to locate Montgomery's headquarters. Though Montgomery's men were obviously observing Christmas, neither the field marshal nor his lackeys offered Bradley anything to eat or drink. Another calculated insult, in Brad's mind.[92]

Montgomery came right to the point. In a short, biting interview that snuffed out any dying embers of civility between the two men, Montgomery scolded Bradley as if he were a floundering schoolboy. He told Bradley that they had been defeated, right and proper, and it was time everyone admitted it. There was no point in deluding themselves that the reverses could be turned into a victory of any kind, and the whole thing, he contended, was the fault of the Americans for insisting on a two-pronged assault against the Germans. Patton, he assured Bradley, was manifestly too weak to launch a successful attack against the bulge, and Bradley's remaining elements, he opined, should fall back to the Saar-Vosges line, perhaps even the Moselle.[93]

Bradley was shocked, hurt, and infuriated. But for a second time, the cat got his tongue. Instead of jumping down Montgomery's throat—instead of asking where this military genius was at Catania, at Caen, at Falaise, at the Scheldt, at Arnhem; instead of pushing Monty for an attack that would remedy the *failure* he so loved to babble about—Brad just nodded along. He was hardly in a position to dictate northern strategy, and he had labored under Monty so long, had been so outmaneuvered in high command politics so often, that his instincts told him to take refuge in the cloak of the good soldier: to nod and follow orders.

So when Montgomery spoke of shifting First Army into neutral for three months, told Bradley to pull Patton back along to the Moselle, and to hand Patton's extra divisions to Hodges, which Montgomery would appropriate for a decisive thrust in the north, Brad sat passively. Disturbed, angry, but unable to put into words his fury.[94]

After thirty long, miserable minutes, a red-faced Omar Bradley, his dentures grinding, climbed back into his plane and departed for Luxembourg. He left Lion speechless, enraged, and humiliated, convinced that what he wanted to have told Montgomery was incompatible with his duty to the greater alliance. But he was furious with the arrogant Briton.

In Luxembourg, Brad blew off some steam with George in a private after-dinner meeting. He told George that Monty wanted to halt First Army, pull Third Army back to the Moselle, and move the surplus divisions north, where they would obviously be used to protect Montgomery's delicate flanks as he made his legendary march into Berlin. George sympathized with Brad. *"I feel that this is disgusting and might remove the valor of our army and the confidence of our people,"* he wrote. *"If ordered to fall back, I think I will ask to be relieved."*[95]

The drama in the Ardennes reached its climax on December 26. To the west, the 2nd Panzer Division rumbled to within seventeen miles of the Meuse River, only to be cut to pieces by Patton's old division, the 2nd Armored. To the north, Montgomery was straightening out his lines and establishing a proper reserve as a bulwark against another German attack. To the south, George finally shot his way into Bastogne. A giant salient still remained in the Allied line like an undulating tumor, but the real danger had passed, and every day the bloody lesion drained a little more.[96]

Sensing the time was ripe for an "America first" push, Bradley called SHAEF the next day to argue for an immediate counterattack, a subject on which he and Patton were in perfect agreement. Learning that Ike was out of the office, Brad asked for Beetle. The "other fellow," he told Beetle, had hit his high-water mark. The only course of action left to the panzer armies was to pull back in a bloody retreat. Brad could pound the Germans, and the time for action was ripe. *Give my armies back to me now*, Brad pleaded, *and I'll move my headquarters, coordinate the U.S. forces, and slice the bulge off at the waist.* At the very least, he told Beetle, get Montgomery moving Hodges east.[97]

Nothing doing, the Hoosier said flatly. It was too late to cut that deal. Ike had given Montgomery the northern armies, and Montgomery was running the show there. Besides, he said, the enemy was almost to the Meuse, and it would be a close call whether the Boche would be over the river.[98]

"Nuts!" said Brad. The Germans wouldn't cross the Meuse, and they wouldn't counterattack, because they had nothing left to counterattack with. But Beetle wouldn't listen, and Bradley didn't know what to do next. Monty wouldn't budge, and Ike was letting the Englishman sit along the Meuse with two of Brad's armies.[99]

As Bradley turned in for the night on Tuesday the twenty-sixth, he wondered what Ike would do. If he could get through to Eisenhower, make him see the light, he might be able to convince him to give back the two armies. Bradley's armies. After all, they were old friends, and he was Ike's most senior and most trusted American lieutenant. That ought to count for something.

He turned off the light.

TWENTY-THREE

TO THE RHINE (AGAIN)

E. is afraid that Bradley will not like this arrangement, but after all it is not always possible in war to give way to personal feelings and ambitions.

—Kay Summersby, January 11, 1945

IKE WAS RECOVERING FROM THE HAMMERING of the last ten days. The Bulge had stabilized, his planes were flying, Montgomery had kept the panzers off the Meuse, and George had relieved Bastogne to the south.

Since December 20, Ike had hardly been able to move himself. Word spread through the American lines that a cold-blooded SS colonel, the same jackboot who sprang Mussolini from captivity in '43, had landed soldiers dressed in American uniforms with orders to assassinate General Eisenhower and his high-ranking subordinates. The SHAEF security boys, thoroughly alarmed, surrounded the Trianon with barbed wire, a cordon of tanks and sentries, while Beetle and the staff, armed with carbines and pistols and holed up inside like the Dillinger gang. To foil would-be assassins, they quietly moved Ike into Tex Lee's apartment, and they even shuttled around an unfortunate Eisenhower look-alike, to see if anyone would take a shot at him.[1]

It was briefly exciting, this cloak-and-dagger stuff, but after a few days Ike, who downplayed the reports, caught cabin fever. Against the abject pleas of his security detail, he left his office one afternoon for some fresh air. "Hell's fire, I'm going out for a walk," he said. "If anyone wants to shoot me, he can go right ahead."[2]

When he wasn't trying to bull past his bodyguards, Eisenhower stifled in the volatile mix that was Bradley, Montgomery, Marshall, and

Beetle. Bedell Smith grew testy as his stomach ulcers worsened, Marshall was unhappy with Ike's command shift, and Bradley was screaming for his armies back. SHAEF, buttoned down at Versailles, was a long way from the front, and even with Patton's frequent telephone briefings and a battalion of staffers, Ike didn't have much current information about the battle. Montgomery, always seeing failure in American efforts, had predicted Patton's counterattack would fail, and on the twenty-sixth, the day 4th Armored first broke into Bastogne, Ike complained to his staff, "I have just been set back thoroughly on my heels by this failure of the attack from the south to join up with the 101st."[3]

Something about the crisis had jarred Ike, shaken him the same way that Kasserine had shaken him. His generals had let him down. Bradley had been caught flat-footed, while Montgomery, who had things well in hand in the north, was content to merely have things well in hand in the north.[4]

But the Ardennes episode seemed to bring out the steel in Dwight Eisenhower. His days dealing with soft people in soft quarters had mellowed him in some ways, and it took a violent crisis to bring out the son-of-a-bitch in Ike. The Battle of the Bulge was just such a crisis, and in the heat of battle, he had pulled rank on his classmate and friend. The transfer of two American armies to Montgomery had hurt Brad deeply, of course, and Brad was howling to Bedell Smith about it. But militarily, Ike knew he had made the right move, and to Ike, an officer's personal feelings were worth little or nothing. It was what you signed up for when you took the oath.

Still, Brad was one of Ike's oldest, closest Army friends, and Ike respected his judgment. Montgomery had rubbed Brad's nose in the command shift over Christmas, and Brad understandably wanted that bulge erased so he could get back to *status quo ante Montgomery.*

Eisenhower didn't want the transfer to become a "no confidence" vote against Brad, and on the twenty-first he dictated an "eyes only" cable to General Marshall in which he suggested that "this would be a most opportune time to promote Bradley" to four-star general. He explained to Marshall,

while there was undoubtedly a failure, in the current operation, to evaluate correctly the power that the enemy could thrust through the Ardennes . . . Bradley has kept his head magnificently and has proceeded methodically and energetically to meet the situation. In no quarter is there any tendency to place any blame upon Bradley. I retain all my former confidence in him and believe that his promotion now would be interpreted by all American forces that their calm determination and courage in the face of trials and difficulties is thoroughly appreciated here and at home. It would have a fine effect generally.[5]

That was all Ike could do for Bradley at the moment. Eventually, he could make a stronger case for Brad's fourth star, but for now the cold logic of battle dictated that Bradley would have to wait patiently in the shadows, while Montgomery closed the bulge with two of Brad's three American armies.[6]

By nightfall on the twenty-sixth, as the 4th Armored took up positions in Bastogne, Bradley's clamor for an offensive in the north seemed less wishful than the day Ike had taken First and Ninth Armies from him. Ike wanted to see some return from all that force invested in Montgomery's group, and he began calling Lion to urge Montgomery to punch southeast toward Houffalize, at the base of the German salient. To satisfy himself that Montgomery was truly pushing, he made arrangements to meet the field marshal on the twenty-eighth. At Montgomery's headquarters, of course.[7]

The traveling weather was atrocious, and Montgomery had to content himself with meeting the Supreme Commander at the Hasselt, Belgium, railway station, the closest junction Eisenhower could reach. It was a true summit meeting—just the two commanders, no aides and no note takers, exactly as Monty had demanded. "What makes me so Goddamn mad," fumed Beetle afterward to Tedder, "is that Monty won't talk in the presence of anyone else. He gets Ike into a corner alone."[8]

As their retainers sat in frozen railcars parked alongside the station, Ike received a rude shock. In a thickly condescending accent, Montgomery told Ike that the broad-front approach had been a disaster from the start; that things had gone much better when he was running the ground war; that a single strike from the north was called for, not a broad front; and that he should be given permanent command of Bradley's armies for the death blow through the Ruhr. As for an immediate offensive, Montgomery assured Eisenhower that von Rundstedt would launch one last attack, which the Allied armies would wait to receive, and only then would Twenty-First Army Group would begin its counterattack.[9]

Ike demurred politely but firmly. He suggested that a counterattack was unlikely, and said he wanted an offensive launched by no later than the third of January. To this Montgomery eventually agreed, though he hedged on an ironclad date. "Praise God from whom all blessings flow!" Ike muttered to Tedder afterward in bitter sarcasm.[10]

After two hours of wrangling, Eisenhower shook Montgomery's hand, the locomotive got up steam, and Ike's train clattered over the frozen tracks back to Versailles. Ike said little to his entourage. He sat there, rubbing his cold, bald forehead, muttering to himself with an air of resignation more than bitterness, "Monty, as usual."[11]

Back in the warmth of the Trianon, Eisenhower made a beeline to Bedell Smith's office. There the two generals talked of how Montgomery had changed since those breezy, blissful Mediterranean days, days when everything wasn't a negotiation. Or at least, days when it was Alexander who had to deal with Monty, not Ike. Easier times.[12]

Well, no matter, said Ike. Montgomery understood that his orders were to launch an attack without waiting for von Rundstedt's hypothetical second assault, and orders were orders. Monty was a good soldier, and in the end he would do what he was told. After that, the Allies would go back to the game plan. The broad-front plan. Ike's plan.[13]

But the day after their meeting at Hasselt, another telex from Montgomery landed on Ike's desk, one that drove him into the Trianon's plastered ceiling. "We have had one very definite failure when we tried to produce a formula that would meet this case," the message began. The broad-front strategy, Monty said, was wrong. Control over the battlefield required a firmer grip on the Allied armies, and he, Field Marshal Montgomery, was the man to do it. Montgomery stressed, "I am so anxious not to have another failure," and he warned Ike that if SHAEF did not comply with his recommendations, "we will fail again." To make it easy on Eisenhower, Montgomery included with his letter a draft SHAEF directive to Eisenhower's other army group commanders, which he suggested Ike sign at once. Monty's helpful suggestion decreed,

FROM NOW ONWARDS, FULL OPERATIONAL DIRECTION, CONTROL, AND COORDINATION OF THESE OPERATIONS IS VESTED IN THE C-IN-C 21 ARMY GROUP, SUBJECT TO SUCH INSTRUCTIONS AS MAY BE RECEIVED FROM THE SUPREME COMMANDER FROM TIME TO TIME.[14]

Ike read the letter, his face reddening.

Monty sure as hell loved that word, "failure," didn't he? When Ike didn't follow his advice, it guaranteed *failure*. If other generals suffered a setback, it was a *failure*. Leaving Bradley in charge of the center would result in *failure*. For a man thwarted at Caen, at Argentan, at Nijmegen, and at Antwerp, Montgomery sure loved to throw around the word "*failure*" when speaking of others.

"I can work with anyone except that son-of-a-bitch," Ike once told reporter Hanson Baldwin. Now, he decided, he didn't have to.

He prepared a memorandum to the Combined Chiefs that would settle matters once and for all. It would be Eisenhower or Montgomery, but one of them would have to go. He knew he had Marshall's backing, and therefore the backing of the American chiefs, and he was reasonably sure the British chiefs would eventually give way.[15]

He discussed the draft memorandum with his staff, as usual, and he prepared to send it to the signal room. But as he was putting the finishing touches on it with Tedder, Jimmy Gault, and Bedell Smith, he received word that Montgomery's chief of staff, Freddie de Guingand, was asking Ike for an audience.

It was a bad time for Freddie to be flying back and forth between SHAEF and Twenty-First. The weather was dangerous, a mix of pea-soup fog and winter snowstorm. But no sense in keeping him waiting, Ike figured. He might as well see what Monty's emissary had to say.

Kay ushered Freddie into Ike's office, where Ike was conferring with Beetle and his pipe-smoking deputy, Air Chief Marshal Tedder. The tall, mustachioed de Guingand, normally a smooth diplomat, looked like a nervous royal courier whose neck was feeling long and fragile. Smith had told Freddie what was in the offing, and Freddie was on a one-man mission to rescue his chief.

As Tedder silently puffed clouds of white smoke from his pipe into the air, Eisenhower came straight to the point. He was tired of Monty's antics, tired of having to fight the same battles with him. The broad front, ground command, supplies, failure. Ike's plans or Monty's plans. It was too much of a distraction when Ike and his men should be running the war. Ike decided it was him or Monty, and the time had come for the Combined Chiefs to decide the question once and for all. One voice of Allied strategy, and the loser leaves town.[16]

He handed the draft cable to Freddie, who read it silently. The color that flushed Freddie's cheeks when he stepped into Ike's office ran back out.

But after a stunned moment, de Guingand rallied. He called up his Old

Guard reserves of charm and sincerity, and he waged a brilliant rearguard action. He said he understood Ike's concern. He promised to fix things with Monty. He could smooth it over with the field marshal, make him see the light, if only Ike would reconsider his decision.

Eisenhower was dubious, as they were long past the point where he believed he could bend Monty to his orders. But he agreed to a short stay of execution: twenty-four hours. A thankful de Guingand hustled back to his headquarters, desperate to mend fences before the momentum became irreversible.[17]

On the last day of the year, another "Dear Ike" letter from Montgomery landed on Eisenhower's desk. In stark contrast to his past missives, the obviously chastened Monty pledged his wholehearted support for Ike's broad-front approach, and he ended his letter with a personal message of reassurance:

> *Whatever your decision may be you can rely on me one*
> *hundred per cent to make it work, and I know Brad will do the*
> *same. Very distressed that my letter may have upset you and*
> *I would ask you to tear it up.*
>
> > *Your very devoted subordinate,*
> > *Monty*[18]

Ike, squinting through his reading spectacles, took in the letter's message.

Did Monty really have a change of heart? Or was it the same old pattern of demand, insult, and apology?

Maybe. Ike sure didn't know.

Down in Luxembourg, George Patton was enjoying a hell of a year end. Since the fall of 1943 he had gone from the doghouse to the top of the heap. His army stood at 344,935 men, seventeen divisions in all, and Bradley had just decorated him with a second Oak Leaf Cluster to his Distinguished Service Medal. He had captured Brittany and Lorraine, bridged the Seine, the Moselle, the Saar, and dozens of other smaller rivers, and had liberated hundreds of towns and cities. It had been a long wait in that dark, stinky Sicilian doghouse, but at the moment, George Patton's horse was the one to back.[19]

To be sure, there were still a few minor annoyances. Lack of appreciation from his superiors. Bradley's caution. Medal recommendations for

Third Army staffers, which he asked Brad to forward to Ike—they always seemed to come back disapproved.[20]

Then there was his old buddy Eisenhower. The man had gotten awfully big for his brushed-wool trousers. He was swimming in politics and forgetting his friends. As much water as George had carried for him, as hard as he had worked to bring honor to the United States Army—and therefore to its supreme commander—Ike never seemed interested in thanking George. Patton had long preached that a pat on the back is worth ten kicks in the ass, and he spent much of his days back-patting, despite what bastards like Drew Pearson wrote about him in the papers. Would it be too much to ask for a pat on the back from Ike every now and then?

George was morally certain that more aggressive leadership at the top would have put the Allies against the Rhine long ago. After Third Army relieved Bastogne, George, Beetle, Lightning Joe, and even Horrocks, Montgomery's XXX Corps commander, advocated cutting the Bulge at its base, rather than at Bastogne, which resembled a frontal attack now. But Ike wanted the safe bet, a coordinated "big picture" attack. George fumed, *"If Ike will put Bradley back in command of the 1st and 9th Armies, we can bag the whole German army. I wish Ike were more of a gambler. Monty is a tired little fart. War requires the taking of risks and he won't take them."*[21]

But for all the deficiencies in Ike's command, George feared that Eisenhower, or someone above him, would knuckle under and place Monty in command of the ground war. Ike was his friend, Ike had been there for him, and George could only imagine how intolerable life would be if Montgomery directed the war.

As he had on several occasions before, George steeled himself to quit in protest if Eisenhower gave in. He told his diary on January 3: *"Monty wants to be deputy ground commander of all troops in Europe. If this occurs, I will ask to be relieved."*[22]

Eisenhower rang in the year 1945 with outward smiles and inward frowns. On the credit side of the ledger, the war against Hitler was an undeniable success. He had driven the Nazis from France and, more or less, cleared the Low Countries. His G-2 bean counters reported that Allied forces had captured 860,000 prisoners since D-Day, and the *Wehrmacht* probably lost another 400,000 men killed and disabled. Even the Battle of the Bulge was turning into a victory, at least at the attritional level, as the battle had cost Germany some 85,000 casualties that she could no longer replace.[23]

But the weight of the New Year also bore down hard on Ike, much harder than when 1944 was young and Eisenhower's war was a matter of planning, not bloodshed. De Gaulle was threatening to pull the French out of SHAEF. Churchill urged Ike to dump Tedder and replace him with Alexander, and Ike could see Brooke moving behind the scenes to widen Montgomery's authority—or make Alexander the Allied ground commander, which was much the same thing. Montgomery continued to lobby for a massive thrust north of the Ruhr, this time with Churchill and Brooke joining the chorus, while Marshall just as loudly insisted that Ike's two-pronged attack to close upon the Rhine was the right approach. As Churchill, Roosevelt, and the Combined Chiefs prepared for their next big conference, on the island of Malta, Ike knew that as in Casablanca, the meeting would be a no-holds-barred referendum on his leadership.[24]

Bradley also concerned him, not just because of Brad's personal rancor over First and Ninth Armies, but because Ike had to make sure his top U.S. lieutenant didn't emerge from the Ardennes looking like a Fredendall. *The Washington Post* was clamoring for an explanation of what went wrong in December, and *Time*'s cover for the week of December 4 had featured a caricature of Brad's wrinkled, frowning face set against a muddy, rain-swept Belgian landscape. Brad often looked unhappy, and Eisenhower knew that senior generals could not afford to look unhappy for long. Ike had once counseled him, "You've got to be confident and cheerful all the time. Otherwise someone will report that you look discouraged. Soon someone whispers it to the Prime Minister and he tells Roosevelt. The President calls in the Combined Chiefs of Staff, and they listen and pretty soon they'll ask, 'What's wrong?'" With the tide of battle swinging against Germany, the last thing Ike needed was a fresh crop of Doubting Thomases back home.[25]

On January 14, Ike dictated a thoughtful cable to Marshall in which, for a third time, he recommended that the War Department nominate his friend to the rank of four-star general. He pointed out that Bradley was a three-star group commander with three-star subordinates, while his British counterpart, Field Marshal Montgomery, was the equivalent of a five-star general. General Bradley had led the American invasion of France, and he had masterminded the breakout from Normandy, which had changed the course of the war. He had certainly earned his star.[26]

Of course, the Ardennes was a problem, Ike acknowledged. But it had to be kept in perspective. The Bulge, he said, was "one of those incidents that is to be anticipated along a great line where contending forces are locked up in battle with varying fortunes in particular sections on the front." Going out on a limb, he argued, "The real answer is the leadership exhibited by the commander in meeting his problems. I consider that throughout this affair Bradley has handled himself admirably." The unspoken message was that, in Ike's estimation, Bradley was one of those critical ingredients in Ike's victory plan, and Eisenhower would do everything possible to keep Brad's position secure.[27]

Patton, at least, had been behaving himself, as he always did when there was fighting to keep his mind occupied. He badgered Ike for a longer supply leash, just like everyone else, and he pressed Ike for decorations for his staff—which Bradley forwarded with a private recommendation of disapproval, absent similar awards for First Army. But all things considered, George was doing a swell job. In a private memorandum, Ike rated Patton as his number four general, behind Spaatz, Bradley, and Beetle, and he characterized George as a "dashing fighter, shrewd, courageous." Ike would have been happy to recommend General Patton for his fourth star, and he told Marshall he would do so when the time was right.[28]

For all they had been through, for all the rough spots in their relationship, Ike still admired George. In a fluid battle or a hot pursuit, George Patton was a single-minded genius. He had proved that on battlefields in Sicily, Brittany, Normandy, Lorraine, and now the Ardennes.

But George's obsession with battle made him an awkward figure outside the surprisingly small universe of active combat. George had also proved that, many times, in Sicily, England, and France, and who could know where he would prove the point next. So Ike did not want the man whose indiscretions held up the promotions of senior officers to become another target of frustrated Senate Republicans, especially after the reverses in the Bulge. So he cautioned Marshall, "His promotion now would simply involve you in argument and I do not believe it necessary." His time would come, but like other mere mortals, George Smith Patton Jr. would have to wait his turn.[29]

Omar Bradley could not have been more relieved to rip the last page of his 1944 calendar off the wall. He had been mad as a wet tomcat when Ike had given First and Ninth Armies to Montgomery, and he was madder still when Ike told him that once the Bulge was erased and First Army came back to Bradley's group, the Ninth would stay with Monty until the Allies captured the Ruhr. Brad wanted both armies back, immediately, and he wanted Ike to kick Monty in the butt to get him moving again. He had argued the point with Beetle, he had argued it with Bull and Whiteley, and he had argued it with Ike.

On the twenty-seventh he had flown to Versailles to pitch a renewed offensive, but instead of concessions, Ike greeted him with a lunch of exquisitely prepared Chesapeake oysters in cream soup, a delicacy intended as a kind of welcoming present. Neither the food nor the discussion did the Missourian any good; the game plan remained unchanged, and to add insult to injury, Ike asked Bradley to move his forward headquarters from Luxembourg to Namur, where he would be closer to Hodges—and Montgomery. Bradley agreed reluctantly and politely choked down his soup, silently reminding himself that oysters gave him hives.[30]

The year 1945, Brad hoped, would offer him a fresh start. Von Rundstedt's Ardennes offensive had been halted, Patton had smashed the Bulge from the south, and sooner or later Montgomery would have to attack the salient from the north. Monty had overplayed his hand at Hasselt, and both Ike and Marshall had personally assured Brad he would never again serve under the detested Englishman.[31]

Perhaps the best news was that once First Army reverted to Bradley's control, Twelfth Army Group would stop playing second fiddle to the British. Sitting in the back of Bradley's Cadillac during a short visit to Eagle Main, Ike and Brad spread a crinkled map over their laps, chewed caramel candy from a box of K-rations, and discussed their strategy—*Ike's strategy*—for the final defeat of Germany. Everyone, Ike assured his friend, would get a shot at crossing the Rhine. After the armies were against the big river, the main effort would temporarily swing north of the Ruhr, as military logic dictated, but the Ninth Army would thereafter come back to Bradley. The route the Allies would take to Berlin was yet to be decided, but Brad figured his central position between Aachen and Saarlautern put his horse in a pretty good slot at the starting gate.[32]

But Bradley's Conestoga wagon rolled into a ditch on January 5, when SHAEF released a press statement disclosing to the public that two of Bradley's armies had been given to Montgomery during the Ardennes crisis. The reaction was instantaneous. The British press—the *Evening Standard,* the *Sunday Dispatch*, the *Daily Express* and the like—began howling about the American bumblers whom Saint Bernard had rescued at their moment of defeat. The American press jumped on the Monty bandwagon; *The New*

York Times told its readers that "The high tide of German reconquest began to recede the day after Marshal Montgomery took charge on the north," and *Stars and Stripes* dryly commented, "It is now presumed that Bradley continues to command 12th Army Group, which now consists of only Third Army." Even President Roosevelt felt compelled to enter the fray, explaining the awkward shift as a matter of momentary military necessity and not one of waning confidence. Hardly a ringing endorsement from the commander in chief.[33]

As the furor reached its crescendo, a wave of indignation washed over Twelfth Army Group. Bradley fumed, "[I am] goddamn sick and tired of this business. I won't listen to the BBC anymore; it makes me mad." Chet Hansen spoke for Bradley and his colleagues when he told his diary,

> *Many of us who were avowed Anglophiles in Great Britain have now been irritated, hurt and infuriated at the British radio and press. All this good feeling has vanished under these circumstances until today we regarded the people we once looked upon as warm and sympathetic friends, as people whom we must instead distrust for fear of being hoodwinked. . . . Their press is building a well of resentment among our American troops that can never be emptied, a distrust that cannot be erased.[34]*

At a time when Brad saw the British press advancing against him on all fronts, an unlikely ally came to his aid. George Patton, in his own press statement, gave General Bradley full credit for the decision to hold Bastogne, a pivotal struggle Patton likened to the Battle of Gettysburg. Although Patton's statement was soon contradicted by another from the 101st Airborne's commander, who claimed the decision was his, it was clear that George, one of the Bulge's heroes, was marching in step with his boss. To Brad, George's statement—one that went against George's instincts to hoard publicity—was a public signal about whom he stood by.[35]

But Patton's statement made little difference in the public perception of Bradley's handling of the attack, and worse was to come. On January 7, Montgomery held a press conference that, as Brad saw it, rubbed American noses into the ashes of the Ardennes. A confident Montgomery, standing before his adoring press in a flaming red beret and matching shirt, recounted his contribution to the battle,

[T]he situation began to deteriorate. But the whole allied team rallied to meet the danger; national considerations were thrown overboard; General Eisenhower placed me in command of the whole Northern front. I employed the whole available power of the British Group of Armies. . . .

[VII Corps] took a knock. I said, "Dear me, this can't go on. It's being swallowed up in the battle." I set to work and managed to form the corps again. Once more pressure was such that it began to disappear in a defensive battle. I said, "Come, come," and formed it again and it was put in offensively by General Hodges.

Finally it was brought into battle with a bang and today British divisions are fighting hard on the right flank of First U.S. Army. You thus have the picture of British troops fighting on both sides of American forces who have suffered a hard blow. This is a fine allied picture.

The battle has been most interesting; I think possibly one of the most interesting and tricky battles I have ever handled, with great issues at stake. . . . The battle has some similarity to the battle that began on 31 August 1942 when Rommel made his last bid to capture Egypt and was "seen off" by the Eighth Army.[36]

As soon as the statement reached Luxembourg by way of the BBC, Chet Hansen and two staffers burst into Brad's office with a transcript "Gentle Omar," one staffer recalled, "got all-out right-down-to-his-toes mad" when he heard the news. Brad began to rant about Montgomery's self-promotion campaign—a campaign unwarranted by the facts. As he put it in a personal memorandum a few weeks later,

> In my opinion, this whole campaign has led to an unsound command setup. In an endeavor to satisfy the British propaganda for putting Monty in command of the whole thing, we have arrived at a command setup which adversely affects our tactical operations. . . . I see no reason why it should be necessary to accede so much to British demands. While we are fighting our own war, we are certainly helping the British very materially, and our own interests should come first. In my opinion, the campaign to set up Monty and, in general, to increase British prestige in

this campaign, out of all proportion to the effort they have in it, is definitely harmful to the relations between the British and ourselves; and, more particularly, the campaign carried on recently by those papers backing Monty has caused great resentment among those American officers and men who have seen them.[37]

In a fury Brad rang up Versailles and gave his commander an ultimatum: "After what has happened," he told Ike, "I cannot serve under Montgomery. If he is to be put in command of all ground forces, you must send me home, for if Montgomery goes in over me, I will have lost the confidence of my command. . . . This is the one thing I cannot take."

He added that Patton would resign with him.

Ike was used to this sort of nonsense, but coming from a close friend, Brad's words stung. "I thought you were the one person I could count on for doing anything I asked you," he said.[38]

"You can, Ike," Brad said. "I've enjoyed every bit of my service with you. But this is one thing I cannot take."[39]

Bradley's ultimatum did not really address the press conference so much as the nebulous possibility of Montgomery's promotion to ground commander, a matter Ike knew in his heart had been settled. But he tried to assuage Brad's wounded pride. He promised Bradley that he would reverse the damage where it counted most, in Washington. He also promised to call Winston Churchill and explain the damage Fleet Street's campaign was doing within the Allied high command.[40]

Ike was trying re-stitch the torn fabric of his friendship, but the Ardennes episode had permanently scarred the implicit trust between the Supreme Allied Commander and his Twelfth Army Group leader. They might still be old friends, dear friends even. But trusting friends . . . well, Brad wasn't so sure. As one of his G-3 men saw it:

Until the Ardennes, Bradley and his officers had made an honest attempt to deal fairly and frankly with the British, to work together in open covenants openly arrived at. After the Ardennes, no one was ever frank with anyone. . . . Bradley—and Patton, Hodges and Simpson under Bradley's direction—proceeded to make and carry out their plans without the assistance of official command channels, on a new basis openly discussed only among themselves. This basis squarely faced the facts that in order to defeat the enemy, by direct attack and in the shortest possible time, they had (1) to conceal their plans from the British, and (2) almost literally to outwit Eisenhower's Supreme Headquarters, half of which was British and the other half of which was beyond their power to influence by argument.[41]

For all his bluster, Brad thought he understood Ike's predicament. The Supreme *Allied* Commander could not wave the Stars and Stripes too openly in the presence of his British, French, Canadian, and Polish allies. Eisenhower was an American, but he could not act too American if he wished to hold an effective team together.

But, Brad asked his confidants, who would speak for the American GI in the Allied councils of war? Who would speak for the man from Cleveland or Bloomington or Trenton who would one day tell his grandchildren that he had sat out the war on a quiet sector while the British captured Berlin? Montgomery was unabashedly British, and Devers was too far from the real action to take an effective role as the GI's advocate. That left only one senior commander.

Brad thought about that question, then decided that if Montgomery could slap him in the face—and by extension, the American leadership—he could slap back.

On January 9, two days after Monty's press conference, Brad issued his own press release, one he refused to clear with Ike. He recounted the four days in December when he ran the defense of the Ardennes, and he tried to place what was perceived as a disaster into its proper perspective. His dispositions had been a calculated risk, he contended. The risk was taken to facilitate advances in other sectors, and he pointed out that, had the American command been unwilling to take risks, "we would still be fighting west of Paris."[42]

Brad took a second calculated risk by announcing that SHAEF would be returning both First and Ninth Armies to his command shortly. This was only half true, as Ike had made clear to him that Simpson's Ninth would remain under Montgomery's command until everyone had crossed the Rhine. But Brad hoped the announcement would pressure SHAEF to return Simpson to his command. Even if Simpson remained with him for only a day, symbolically, Brad argued, giving Ninth Army back to Bradley would blunt any impression that Brad was being permanently stripped of an army due to the Bulge setback.[43]

The gambit failed. Ike was tired of the infighting between Bradley and Montgomery, and he was far too seasoned a politician to react to a bush-league play like Bradley's press announcement. Simpson would stay where he was. As Kay wrote in her desk diary on January 11, *"E. is afraid that Bradley will not like this arrangement, but after all it is not always possible in war to give way to personal feelings and ambitions."*[44]

The press war had been an awful time for Omar Bradley, but it had taught him one valuable lesson: pay attention to the press. That was how Eisenhower, Montgomery, and Patton were building their reputations, and correspondents, he was learning, could be as partisan as headquarters staffs. He had been naive to think he could leave his mark without allies among the news media.

The problem here was Brad's background and priorities. His religion had been the power of intellect and massed firepower, not public relations; the media was a game entirely foreign to him. Among political creatures, therefore, Bradley was frightfully, almost uncomprehendingly vulnerable, like a great auk on some isolated island who had never grown up around danger—and thus never evolved the instincts to perceive that an approaching man with a wooden club might not have benevolent intentions. If Brad didn't want to go the way of the great auk, he needed a cadre of reliable journalists who would see things from his point of view.[45]

Painfully aware of his mistakes, Bradley began having photographers accompany him on official trips into the field, and began courting major journalists who came to visit. But his real problem was the lack of a press corps accredited to Twelfth Army Group headquarters. Armies had them, and SHAEF had one, but as an army group, Brad's headquarters had only visiting journalists and long-distance relationships with the scribblers and warblers covering the war. He therefore requested from SHAEF authority to establish a press box at Namur, Twelfth Army Group's new command post.[46]

Soon afterward, during a late-night rubber of bridge with Eisenhower—which, uncharacteristically, Ike and Kay lost—Eisenhower casually asked Brad why he thought he needed a press camp.[47]

Brad knew exactly where Ike's question was heading. Montgomery had been using his pressmen for a ground command campaign against his American rivals, and a whispering campaign had run through SHAEF about the motives behind Twelfth's request. The last thing Ike wanted was Twelfth Army Group mobilizing its own troops for a war over headlines.[48]

Not to worry, Brad assured him. The problem, brought out by misleading reports of the Bulge, was that the press assigned to Bradley's armies didn't have any real conception of where those armies fit into the Army Group's strategy. A press corps at Eagle Main, he said, would help the public understand the bigger picture, or at least the picture between the Saar and the Roer. He promised his briefings would be short, factual, and certainly not used as a weapon. In other words, not Montgomery-like.

Mulling it over momentarily, Ike nodded. He trusted Bradley. Twelfth Army Group would get its own press corps.[49]

Bradley's flash of anger over the army transfer simmered, but did not entirely burn out that winter, and Eisenhower made a special point of mollifying him. He awarded the Missourian the Bronze Star, and after a word from Eisenhower, Churchill (who had privately called Bradley a "sour-faced blighter") made a gracious speech to the House of Commons in which he praised the skill of Bradley in handling his forces, and painted the Bulge as a great American victory.

And most important, at one minute after midnight on the morning of Churchill's speech, SHAEF returned the First United States Army to Bradley's command.[50]

Ike's efforts fell short, in Brad's mind. Like Patton two months earlier, a suspicious Bradley saw new threats converging from north and south. Above the Ardennes, Eisenhower planned to let Montgomery take the lead against the Ruhr with two operations, code-named VERITABLE and GRENADE. The first, Operation VERITABLE, was a rush to the Rhine's west bank by Second British Army, while the second, Operation GRENADE, was a Ninth Army crossing of the Roer River, with a follow-up push to the Rhine. If successful, these moves would put Montgomery's group up against the Rhine opposite the coveted Ruhr.

First Army's role would be rather minimal; it's job was to capture the Roer's "damn dams," as Bradley called them, to ensure the safety of the flood zone for Ninth Army's crossing. Third Army would, once again, sit on its hands. With Montgomery calling the plays against the Ruhr, Twelfth Army Group would be the campaign's tired, overworked bridesmaid.[51]

To the south, Bradley sniffed out another threat. Jacob Devers, he learned, had left some fifty thousand Germans holding a pocket around Colmar, a city near the Swiss border. When Ike ordered the pocket reduced, it became painfully clear that the force Devers had assigned to the task,

General Lattre de Tassigny's First French Army, was not up to the job. Ike wanted that pocket cleared before sending his men over the Rhine, and he decided to give Devers a five-division corps to reduce the pocket.[52]

The question that troubled Bradley was, "Whose troops would be drafted?" Brad certainly did not want to lose another corps. He was about to launch a counteroffensive in the Schnee Eifel, to unhinge the German line near Montgomery, and he could ill afford to lose five more divisions. But on January 22, less than a week after Ike gave back First Army, SHAEF directed Bradley to send Devers one of George's infantry divisions, and a SHAEF staffer called to ask Bradley how many additional divisions his army group could send south to Colmar. Brad blew up over the request, furious that SHAEF would ask for divisions whose absence would cripple his new offensive—the only offensive that was moving the Allies east at the moment. He placed a call to Ike the next morning, where he talked the Supreme Commander out of doing something so tactically insane.[53]

Or so he thought. The next day, while Brad was conferring with Hodges, Patton, Gay, and several staffers, his aide called him to the phone: General Smith was on the line.

Beetle bluntly told Bradley to transfer enough divisions to Devers to form a U.S. corps in the Colmar area. Whatever Ike may have said before, he evidently had changed his mind, or perhaps Bradley had misunderstood him.

Brad gripped the phone and gritted his artificial teeth. Then he roared back into the receiver:

> The reputation and the good will of the American soldiers and the American Army and its Commanders are at stake. If you feel that way about it, then as far as I am concerned, you can take any goddam divisions and/or corps in the Twelfth Army Group, do with them as you see fit, and those of us that you leave back will sit on our ass until hell freezes over. I trust you do not think I am angry, but I want to impress upon you that I am goddam well incensed![54]

Brad's office suite, always a buzz of bureaucratic activity, froze in silence. His officers stared at him for a second, stunned. Then someone began clapping, and the whole room burst into applause. Men in khaki, sick of the favoritism SHAEF had shown others, cheered the general who was giving it to the chumps who had dished out misery to them for the past six weeks.

And over the applause flew a squeaky, faintly Southern voice: "Tell them to go to hell and the three of us will resign. I will lead the procession!"[55]

George Patton spent the first half of January locked in a tough, set-piece struggle, the kind he hated and the kind he wasn't better at winning than anyone else. The Germans were fighting savagely, and to push them back Patton had no choice but to attack in the sort of cadenced, methodical fashion he belittled when made by others. But on the sixteenth, George's 11th Armored Division shook hands with First Army's 2nd Armored Division at Houffalize. They had cut the Bulge off at the waist, and in accordance with Eisenhower's stipulation, George had bought Omar Bradley a second army.[56]

Patton paid a quick visit to the town his men had fought so hard to capture, and even he was shocked by the unsparing destruction. In his diary that evening, he jotted down a few lines from a rude parody of "O Little Town of Bethlehem," couplets he apparently picked up from GIs he passed along the way:

> O little town of Houffalize, how still we see thee lie
> Above thy steep and battered streets the aeroplanes sail by.
> Yet in thy dark street shineth not any Goddamned light
> The hopes and fears of all thy years were blown to hell last night.[57]

Two days after First and Third Armies reunited, a friendly face turned up in the theater. Everett Hughes, George's old confidant, dropped in on Third Army headquarters and reported, unofficially, that he might be taking over Beetle's job as chief of staff. George, who counted Ev as one of his best friends in the Army, welcomed the news, for he despised Beetle, whom he knew to be an unscrupulous, cowardly Iago around whom a man needed a sentry to watch his back.

What also piqued George's interest was a comment from Eisenhower. "Do you know, Everett," the Supreme Commander had told him, "George is really a very great soldier and I must get Marshall do to something for him before the war is over?"[58]

Not long afterward, Ike spoke candidly with George about the subject of promotions. Bradley's promotion to full general was beginning its salmon-like journey across Marshall's desk, to Stimson's desk, to Roosevelt's desk, and eventually to the Senate. George accepted that the Army's policy of merit-based promotions had its limits, and regardless of his qualities as a combat leader, George knew he could not be promoted until Bradley, and probably Devers, too, had been bumped to full generals. So when the subject later came up, Ike, George wrote, *"was quite apologetic about the 4-star business, but has, however, good reasons—that is, you must maintain the hierarchy of command or else relieve them, and he had no reason for relieving them."* He promised George that he would be the first army commander promoted on the next list, and George feigned disinterest. *"I am having so much fun fighting that I don't care what the rank is."*[59]

Whatever Ike's future intentions may have been, George Patton had a more immediate concern than tactical matters. At the end of January, he received orders directing him to send more troops to Montgomery, which meant canceling another big attack, this one by Manton Eddy's XII Corps. A sympathetic Bradley told George that Ike, in conformance with a plan approved by the Combined Chiefs, had ordered him to transfer the 95th Division and five or six artillery battalions to Ninth Army for Montgomery's great Ruhr offensive. *"Hell and Damn,"* George smoked when he heard the news. *"This is another case of giving up a going attack in order to start one that has no promise of success except to exalt Monty, who has never won a battle since he left Africa and only El Alemeine there."*[60]

Since the dawn of organized warfare, fighting men have been expected to follow orders without necessarily knowing why. Patton and Hodges were no different. But one of Brad's duties as army group commander was, from time to time, to make his army commanders understand where they fit into the grand scheme, to act as a kind of conciliator between SHAEF and the armies. So after a lunch meeting at Spa with Hodges, Simpson, and Patton on February 2, Brad took Patton and Hodges aside and gave them the inside story of the transfers that had depleted their armies. The Combined Chiefs, he explained, had ordered Ike to make the main thrust to the Rhine with the Twenty-First Army Group. Devers and his Sixth Army Group, he reported, would remain on the defensive. In the meantime, Patton would be permitted to launch his planned attack against Bitburg and Prüm in the south, "provided the casualties and the ammunition expenditures are not excessive."[61]

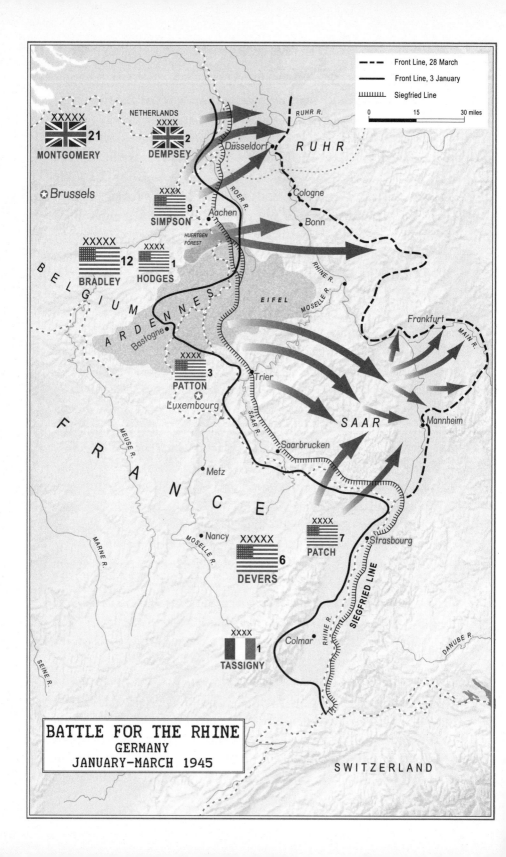

BATTLE FOR THE RHINE
GERMANY
JANUARY–MARCH 1945

＊　＊　＊

". . . Provided casualties and ammunition expenditure are not excessive. . . ."

Patton had long ago mastered the art of interpreting orders, and the more he thought about it, the more he realized Bradley's limits on casualties and ammunition were, in fact, no limits at all. Patton expected to move so quickly that casualties would be minimal, and he reasoned that if the attack worked, he'd be in a fine position to turn his armored divisions loose on the enemy rear, perhaps unhinging the entire Siegfried Line. If not, he'd still be advancing the overall goal of putting Monty to the Rhine, since the Germans he would be fighting in the south would be unable to move north to fight Montgomery. Either way, Ike should be happy.[62]

George's reasoning certainly convinced George, and he decided to push through Bitburg with Eddy's corps. But while he was personally convinced of his logic, he was circumspect enough to know Ike and Brad might not see it the same way. Recognizing that his attack might violate the spirit of the Combined Chiefs' order, and probably the letter, too, he concluded, *"If Bradley knew I was starting a new attack with the XII Corps he might stop it, so I shall not tell him."*[63]

Since his plan was, more or less, a movement of a hundred thousand men on the sly, Patton's warning bells clanged when Brad called him on February 5, two days before the attack, to ask if George could meet him and Ike in Bastogne that afternoon. *"I am going to Bastogne to meet with Destiny and the tent maker,"* he told Bea, and he fretted to himself, *"I am trying to keep the impending Bitburg offensive secret so that the powers that be will not order it stopped."*[64]

A few hours later George, clad in battle helmet, tall boots, and a thick GI parka cinched with his gun belt, rolled into Bastogne to meet Ike and Bradley. The place, they noticed, looked a damned sight different than the last time Ike, Brad, and George had been there, back in early November, back before the disaster of the Ardennes, back before George had been the man of the hour.[65]

It turned out to be a simple Signal Corps photo session staged amid a carefully selected pile of rubble. Ike and Bradley wore their pressed general's uniforms and neckties, while Patton, in his heavy, rain-spotted parka, looked like he had just stepped off the front lines. Photographers snapped away as George shook hands warmly with Ike as Omar Bradley hovered in the background, beaming at Ike as if to gauge the Supreme Commander's approval.

To George, the photograph captured perfectly the way the Bastogne operation really went over.[66]

While George was happy to paste another historic photograph into his scrapbook, one he'd tell his grandchildren about before they went to West Point someday, he was mostly grateful that Ike and Brad didn't press him for details about his upcoming plans for XII Corps. When Bradley asked about the "probing attacks" he had been told Eddy's corps would make, Patton vaguely replied that Eddy would make a "determined probe" to see what was in front of him. He didn't tell Bradley, much less Eisenhower, that the "determined probe" would be a full-scale attack, and the next day he told General Eddy that he didn't want to be anywhere near a telephone when SHAEF found out about the advance. His operating principle, he told his brother-in-law, was, "if I win, no one will say anything, and I am sure I will win."[67]

Unfortunately for Patton and his men, unseasonably warm temperatures sent snowmelt rushing into the Moselle and Saar rivers, stalling Eddy's advance. Patton, worried that another Metz would prompt Ike to freeze him in his tracks, decided to ram Eddy's attack home with reinforcements, and he called Bradley to ask if he could hang on to the 17th Airborne Division, which he had been ordered to ship north to Simpson's Ninth Army.[68]

Nothing doing, Bradley said. The orders came straight from SHAEF; Simpson was to get the 17th, and Third Army would have to make do without the division.

What bothered George about Bradley was that, now that they were out of the Ardennes, now that Bradley had First Army back, the Missourian didn't seem willing to stand up to SHAEF. If anything, Brad seemed more determined than Ike to keep the Third Army from advancing. *"He was no help,"* George complained to his diary on February 8. *"His success is due to his lack of back bone and servile deference to those above him. I will manage without him. In fact, I always have; even in Sicily he had to be carried."*[69]

Patton's anger toward Brad flared into the open the next day, when Brad told him that in keeping with SHAEF's plans, Third Army would have to return to the defensive. *"I said I was the oldest leader both in age and in days of combat in the Army and that if I had to go on the defensive, I would ask to be relieved,"* he wrote. Bradley tried to calm his oldest leader, in age and days of combat, reminding Patton of his duty as a soldier; George, he counseled, owed it to his Third Army troops to protect their interests by staying in the fight.

"I said that there was a lot owing to me too," George wrote. *"I was very mad."*[70]

Well, what the hell, George figured, after calming down. He had done what he could, and there would be other offensives soon. He canceled his plans, and that night a frustrated Third Army headquarters threw a late-night party, where the hostess, Patton's "niece" Jean Gordon, plied staff and generals with bourbon until they all got roaring drunk. "Everybody was pretty high when I got there," a confused General Eddy wrote in his diary. "Frankly I didn't know what was going on."[71]

As Ninth Army was about to kick off Operation GRENADE, its lunge over the Roer River, George had reason to think his time in the shadows would soon be over. Bradley hinted that First and Third Armies might be back in business if Simpson's Ninth Army stalled, and that looked quite likely due to a fiasco on the Roer. First Army's February 2 attack against the Roer River dams had floundered, and seven days later German engineers jammed the gates of one of the dams, effusing a moderate but steady stream of water that turned river bends into lakes and stopped Ninth Army in its tracks.

Brad had snorted at the VERITABLE-GRENADE operation as "the biggest mistake SHAEF had yet made," to which George privately remarked, *"It is, or at least it is one of the biggest. The biggest was when Ike decided to turn the First Army north to help Monty at the end of August, cut off my gas. But for that we would have beat the Russians to Berlin."*[73]

With Big Simp's men stuck behind the Roer, Bradley thought he might get orders to send his armies toward Koblenz and Cologne. This would allow Patton to move on Trier, Germany's oldest city and a key point on the juncture of the Moselle and Saar rivers.[72]

To Patton, Brad sure didn't seem happy about Ike's orders forcing Third Army to give up, for a second time, the 10th Armored Division, which SHAEF wanted to hold as a strategic reserve. He blamed Bradley for not standing up to Ike, and he wrote Beatrice, *"There is much envy, hatred, and malice, and all unchareatableness. To hell with them."*[74]

On February 20, frustrated with inactivity, he penned a "My dear General Bradley" letter, pointing out places along Third Army's front where offensive operations could take place. George's letter was clearly for the historical record, as he concluded, *"We must squarely face the fact that all of us in high position will surely be held accountable for this failure to take offensive action when offensive action is possible.*"

Bradley, tired of George's histrionics, sat down at his desk and drafted a return letter. *"As you know,*" he told George, *"the decision has already been made by higher authority that the main effort be made elsewhere. Regardless of what you and I think of this decision, we are good enough soldiers to carry out those orders."*[75]

He may have been stuck along the Saar, but George Patton had enough ammunition for at least a couple of moves, and while he could not take the offensive, he had enough elasticity in his orders to use the same "aggressive defense" that had kept his army moving in September. "Can't you, Walton," he asked at a meeting of his corps commanders, "sort of *sidle* ahead about ten kilometers and capture Trier? And Manton, what's to keep you from *edging* forward and capturing Bitburg?" He turned to Middleton. "Troy, don't you think you could *maneuver* about eight kilometers and take Gerolstein?"

Middleton, one of the Army's more intellectual generals, was dubious. This was, after all, the same George Patton who had sworn there weren't more than five hundred Germans in St.-Malo, the same General Patton whose nose had been pulped at Metz. And Bradley had seemed pretty emphatic about no attacks. If Third Army got into a jam while going beyond Army Group orders, Bradley might have George's head.

"If you should fail in this endeavor," Middleton warned, "there might be serious consequences as far as you're concerned."

"I'll take that risk," George snapped.[76]

But to hedge that risk, Patton staged a group sales pitch during an impromptu meeting with his commander. On February 25, as George was meeting with his corps commanders and Opie Weyland, commander of the reliable XIX Tactical Air Force, Twelfth Army Group aides called to ask if Generals Bradley and Allen could stop by Lucky Forward for lunch. Patton was happy to oblige, and as Brad and Lev were making their way toward Luxembourg, George began rehearsing themes his lieutenants would push on their leader and his chief of staff.[77]

When Brad arrived for lunch, the table talk gravitated to the need for Walker to keep the 10th Armored Division with his XX Corps until he had taken Trier. The officers also seemed to agree, with odd unanimity, that VIII and XII Corps should be allowed to move as far northeast as the Kyll

River, which would straighten out Third Army's lines. Even Opie joined in, pointing out that with the Trier airfields in Allied hands, his wing commanders could shorten the distance of their bases to targets, effectively giving Weyland the equivalent of two more air groups.[78]

Patton's pitch won the day, and Bradley gave his tentative assent to the proposed maneuver. The men passed the rest of the lunch with friendly banter and shop talk, and George, anxious as a Fuller brush salesman to close the deal, summarized their agreement by telling Bradley, "It is my understanding that I have the authority to push the attack of the Third Army east to secure the line of the Kyll River . . . and furthermore, if opportunity presents itself for a quick breakthrough by armor supported by motorized infantry to the Rhine River, that I have the authority to take advantage of the situation."

Brad nodded. "You have that authority."[79]

George could almost smell the Rhine's dark waters.

To Bradley, the late winter of 1945 was a time of Army politics, a subject that made him uncomfortable. He swallowed orders from SHAEF, played counselor to Patton and Hodges, and cajoled Ike into letting the American armies close up to the Rhine before Montgomery swept in, possibly for the dramatic last act.[80]

Staring at maps in the baroque château that was now home to Eagle TAC, Brad saw a military picture no brighter than the political one. First Army's failure to take the Roer dams before they were blown was an "American boner," as one of his staffers admitted, and that boner had dramatically stalled Ninth Army's Operation GRENADE.[81]

About the only silver lining in Brad's world was that with things slow and sticky along the Roer, Ike gave Bradley permission to let Patton push toward the Kyll River, so long as he could do it quietly enough not to raise Montgomery's ire. An "aggressive defense," they called it.

"Aggressive defense" was not a precisely defined term in any officers' manual or West Point schoolbook; the term—comprised of two contradictory terms—invited a lot of subjectivity, which was just what Brad and George intended. They agreed that an aggressive defense authorized them to send out patrols—battalion-size patrols, it turned out—beyond Third Army's frontline positions. Of course, it was only natural that when these battalions patrolled forward, they had to ensure their own safety by consolidating their positions. Those positions were, in turn, inevitably threatened by enemy positions flanking them to the north and east, so those flanks had to be aggressively defended by other battalions in a similar manner. Before long, hills, rivers, and forests also had to be cleared of enemy forces, creating a new front line that was ripe for more aggressive defense.

Whatever the spirit of Eisenhower's orders, to the outsider, an aggressive defense looked a lot like a subdued offensive, but Brad told George to push ahead until SHAEF called to stop them. And, Brad promised, he would not hang around the phone waiting for Versailles to call.[82]

By late February, the skies began to brighten for Bradley as Montgomery's Ninth Army paddled its way over the flooded Roer. When Montgomery went back to the drawing table to plot his big-budget, all-star Rhine crossing, Operation PLUNDER, Brad had a few days of maneuvering room with Ike. By the end of February, Patton's men had crossed the Saar-Moselle juncture, captured Trier, and had bitten off a portion of the Siegfried Line. Then, on the first of March, Eisenhower approved Operation LUMBERJACK, an offensive to put Hodges against the Rhine at Cologne. LUMBERJACK came off beautifully, and by March 10, Bradley had his soldiers covering the meandering stretch of river that lay north of the Moselle.[83]

But the real leverage fell into Bradley's lap when his men, almost by accident, captured the most valuable piece of iron in the world: an intact bridge over the Rhine.

The Rhine River had stood as a forbidding barrier to invasion since long before the days of Caesar. In modern times, the German heartland belonged to the one who controlled the river's bridges, and Hitler was careful not to let any of those bridges fall into Allied hands. One by one the great arches over the Rhine crashed into the river as German engineers turned their detonators on stone and steel supports.

All except one. As First Army closed on the Rhine, the imposing Ludendorff railroad bridge at Remagen, square in the middle of Bradley's sector, became caught in a bureaucratic tug-of-war between the German army, the *Waffen-SS*, the local military commandant, and the *Luftwaffe*, all of whom laid claims to jurisdiction over the bridge. When the 9th Armored Division approached the city, engineers assigned to blow the bridge were frustrated by faulty explosives and a dispute over authority to order the bridge's destruction. Taking the bridge at a rush, the Americans fanned out onto the Rhine's east bank and fought off the few locals who resisted. The prize every Allied commander prayed for had fallen into Bradley's hands.[84]

That evening, Bradley found himself at his command post, red-faced and furious with Pink Bull, Ike's G-3 chief. Bull had just communicated orders from SHAEF putting most of First Army's divisions into "reserve," and transferring the balance to Jake Devers for use in the far south. Bull, whose stern face resembled that of an officious high school principal, was one of those stereotypical staff officers who thought in terms of settled plans rather than fluid events. Thinking outside the parameters of an approved playbook was not part of Bull's job description, and that didn't trouble him in the slightest.[85]

Brad was in the midst of his row with Bull when the door opened and a sheepish aide asked him to take a telephone call. It was General Hodges with some important news, the aide said.

Brad listened a moment, thunderstruck at the report.

"We've got a bridge."

His face lit up.

"Hot dog, Courtney! This will bust him wide open," he bellowed into the phone. "Shove everything you can across it, Courtney, and button the bridgehead up tightly."[86]

Brad hung up the phone. A wide grin spreading over his lined face, he turned back to General Bull.

"There goes your ball game, Pink," he said. "Courtney's got across the Rhine on a bridge."[87]

It was one of the most exhilarating moments of Bradley's life. The prize since D-Day, the mythical Rhine River, had been the holy grail of the Allied effort ever since they reached the Seine. After the capture of Paris, the taming of the Rhine was the most coveted objective in the west, for it was the last major physical barrier to Berlin.

The capture of the Remagen bridge was all the sweeter because it had come two weeks before Montgomery was to make his leap over the Rhine, an operation Monty was planning with airborne, naval, and artillery forces, the kind of massive orchestration that smacked of the last war. So Ludendorff Bridge was not just a victory for the Americans. It was a factory for Bradley, a thrilling personal triumph, one earned by pluck and quickness.[88]

"You're not going anywhere down there at Remagen," Bull said. "You've got a bridge, but it's in the wrong place. It just doesn't fit the plan."[89]

Brad's elation turned to shock. The gods had dropped a golden apple into the Allied lap, and the SHAEF operations chief was acting like he didn't want it![90]

"Plan—hell," Brad sputtered. "A bridge is a bridge and mighty damned good anywhere across the Rhine. What the hell do you want us to do, pull back and blow it up??"[91]

To this Pink had no answer, but neither would he budge. It was time to call Eisenhower.[92]

"Brad, that's wonderful!" Ike beamed when he heard the news. "Get right on across with everything you've got. It's the best break we've had!" Warmly congratulating Bradley, he authorized First Army to rush four divisions onto the Rhine's east bank.[93]

But Bradley wasn't about to let it go with that. Looking Pink in the eye, he quietly told Ike he understood the move conflicted with SHAEF's big plans, that the terrain wasn't what SHAEF wanted.[94]

"What if it does upset the planners?" Ike said. "It will upset the Germans worse. Sure. Go on, Brad, and I'll give you everything we've got to hold that bridgehead. We'll make good use of it even if the terrain isn't too good."[95]

Twenty-four hours later, Bradley had 8,000 men encamped on the German side of the Rhine.[96]

Although he was elated by the news of the Remagen bridge capture, the early weeks of 1945 had been hard on the Supreme Commander. Aside from the weather, the French, and the recurring question of ground commander, the campaign to promote Montgomery stood out as his biggest recurring problem. As Ike told Field Marshal Brooke the following month, "No single incident that I have ever encountered throughout my experience as an Allied commander has been so difficult to combat as this particular outburst in the papers."[97]

Ike could see both sides of the emotionally charged dynamic. On one hand, Bradley was still bitter over British press comments, and Ike and his inner circle privately didn't blame him. American officers, as junior partners in the war, long groused over boasts that the British Eighth Army had won the war in Tunisia, that Bradley's GIs "ate grapes" in Sicily while Monty's army did the heavy fighting, and that American bumbling in the Ardennes had cost the Allies an early end to the war. Back home, papers were running headlines that read, "Monty Gets the Glory, Yanks Get the Brushoff," and Ike knew Marshall read every one of those articles. Montgomery had done little to tamp down British criticism of Bradley, and this naturally led many Americans—and many Britons—to assume the worst possible motives on

Montgomery's part. Beetle, himself a backroom deal broker, later said he "did not see how it would be possible to give a correct portrayal of Montgomery without showing him to be a SOB," and Brad's animosity, stoked by Patton, was so deeply ingrained by 1945 that there was little Montgomery could say, honestly and sincerely, that would satisfy the American camp.[98]

On the other hand, while Montgomery may have been the most egotistical showman this side of MacArthur, Ike saw that Monty sincerely believed he knew how to win the war. The Briton was often right, was deferential to a point, and while he argued until unequivocally told to shut up, he never refused a peremptory order on those occasions when a firm, clear decision was made. He was a decent man and an undeniably good soldier whose great failing was his inability to consider the human element. His press conference, however unfortunate its interpretation by the American camp, was sincerely intended as a tribute to the American soldier. In his remarks, Monty had devoted much of his emphasis to a call for Allied unity, and Monty's statements, in Ike's opinion, were "eminently correct."[99]

Monty's problem, then, was not so much that he overstepped his boundaries; he simply couldn't see them. In this regard, he was like another of Ike's generals—though George, an American, and a subordinate one at that, could be reined in much more easily when his mouth caused trouble.

The camaraderie of early June had faded, and Bradley's frustration with Monty reached another fever pitch as they drove into Germany. Brad sought no personal or national aggrandizement, and that made it difficult for him to identify what made Monty tick. As Montgomery told a postwar interviewer, "I've often thought that things might have been different [in Europe] if Patton had been on my right flank. Then they might have understood me better."[100]

Ike knew there was no general order capable of changing the attitudes of middle-aged men with old-age prejudices. He could lead by example, he could preach, and he could eliminate a few—a *very* few—troublemakers in his own house. But the lingering problem of nationalism, like the lingering problems of supply, the weather, the French, and the Germans, was one Ike had to content himself with minimizing, but not eliminating.

Other problems, Ike found, could be just as intractable as the rivalries. Ike's health, a chronic source of misery, was giving him nearly as many fits as his subordinates did. A doctor was flown in from London to tend to Ike's bad knee, he spent an unhappy thirty-six hours confined to his bed in February, and he had a growth removed from his back that, he lamely joked, left him "in stitches." He smoked more than ever, the barracks bags under his eyes grew thick and dark, and he weakly complained there was not a single part of his body that didn't ache. To make matters worse, he sorely missed the stabilizing presence of his naval aide, Harry Butcher, who had moved into SHAEF's Public Relations Division and was spending less time with Ike.[101]

The fatigue of dealing with the political leaders, his poor diet, lack of sleep, and the carbon monoxide in his lungs left Ike in a habitually foul mood that he took out, with growing frequency, on his subordinates. The peaks and valleys he had hiked for so long had caught up with him once again, and curses and threats began spewing from his mouth at a rate that alarmed his old friends. "Ike shouts and rants," Everett Hughes scribbled in his diary after one particularly vicious outburst. "He acted like a crazy man."[102]

Strung like an Appalachian fiddle, Ike's obvious decline became even too much for his gaunt, health-plagued chief of staff, who, in typical Beetle Smith fashion, took on Ike directly.[103]

"Look at you," Beetle scolded. "You've got bags under your eyes. Your blood pressure is higher than it's ever been, and you can hardly walk across the room." He needed to get out of Paris, he needed a rest, and he needed it soon.

Ike said nothing. What could he say? Beetle was right. But there was a war going on, if none of his staff had noticed, and he didn't have the luxury of a vacation. Not yet.[104]

As he considered the interests of his commanding generals, Eisenhower believed that Patton had earned some kind of reward. In a private memorandum evaluating his American lieutenants, Ike's cavalryman ranked fourth, after Brad, Tooey Spaatz, and Bedell Smith, but ahead of Clark, Truscott, Doolittle, and Gerow. In February Ike cashed in some of his chits with Marshall to promote four staffers in Third Army—compared to one for Twelfth Army Group and none for First Army—and he sent a memo to Bradley and Devers praising the work of George's 4th Armored and 35th Divisions in breaking the siege of Bastogne. Before long, Eisenhower would be telling Marshall, "Patton is a particularly warm friend of mine and has been so over a period of 25 years. Moreover, I think I can claim almost a proprietary interest in him because of the stand I took in several instances, well known to you, in this war. In certain situations he has no equal."[105]

Of course, Ike's number four general was not exactly worry-free. A correspondent told Butcher that the War Department had instructed General Patton to tone down his official reports, which were too colorful to make good military prose, a claim that, for George, seemed plausible. Ike was also embarrassed to learn that George had threatened to jail Bill Mauldin, the popular *Stars and Stripes* cartoonist of the "Willie & Joe" series, for encouraging unkempt appearance and poor discipline through his depictions of the two slouching, unshaven foxhole neighbors.

But as Ike saw it, the running back from California had been on top of his game since August. He had been looking to reward him with a fourth star for his accomplishments. When the time was right, that is.[106]

That time would not be right for a while, not so long as Bradley and Devers were three-star generals, and Ike kept a firm grip on George's promotion prospects, to prevent his fans in Washington from disrupting the logical pattern of advancement. "I trust the Secretary of War will wait for my recommendation before putting in Patton's name for promotion," he told Marshall. "There is no one better acquainted than I with Patton's good qualities and likewise with his limitations. In the past I have demonstrated my high opinion of him when it was not easy to do. In certain situations Bradley and I would select Patton to command above any other general we have, but in other situations we would prefer Hodges. . . . I think he should wait to be considered by the War Department with his own appropriate group." Ike felt strongly enough about the subject that he followed his letter to Marshall with another one that same day, adding,

> *I can see why Patton's color and publicity appeal so mightily to the Secretary of War, but as long as I have absorbed Devers and he is doing his job satisfactorily, the appointments should be made in the order I have already given. Both Bradley and I believe that our successful Army commanders should eventually be promoted to four star rank, but I would consider it unwise at this time to imply a comparison to the discredit of Hodges, Patch and Simpson by making Patton on a separate list ahead of them.*[107]

Bradley and Devers, the two Army Group commanders, were the key to future promotions, now that the December round of five-star promotions had justified a number of four-star bumps. Ike continued to press Marshall for Bradley's promotion to full general, even though he and Marshall recognized that promoting Bradley would create a thornbush of problems with more senior generals like McNarney, Devers, Clark, and eventually, George Patton.[108]

The Remagen bridgehead made it easier for Ike to move Bradley up another rung, however, and in mid-March, President Roosevelt sent Bradley's name, along with Devers and Clark, to the Senate. Ike, relieved that Secretary Stimson did not push Patton at this time, was glad he could do something concrete for his faithful friend. He wrote Brad on March 14, *"As you know, I have long felt that such action was overdue, and it is almost needless for me to say, 'Congratulations.' I am truly happy, the more so because I believe that this action on the part of the President and the War Department will do much to reestablish a proper understanding at home of the effectiveness of American leadership in this Theater."*[109]

By mid-March, fortune had begun to smile again on Ike. Bradley had redeemed the American reputation by throwing his men over the Rhine at Remagen, the U.S. chiefs had driven a stake through the heart of Brooke's "ground commander" schemes, and the Allies were now focused on the campaigns for the Ruhr and Berlin. With Montgomery's huge Rhine crossing, Operation PLUNDER, set to launch on March 24, it was only a matter of time before Hitler's Thousand-Year Reich crumpled into history's ash can.[110]

With the end of his mission in sight, Ike tried to relax a bit. *He* didn't want to become the war's last casualty, and he recognized that high blood pressure could kill him as dead as an eighty-eight shell. Occasionally, General Spaatz would bring his guitar over to Eisenhower's quarters, and the two West Pointers—sometimes accompanied by aides, WACs, Red Cross girls, or correspondents—would belt out off-key renditions of Old Army favorites like "The Artillery Song" or "Beer-Barrel Polka." Ike welcomed Brad's visits to Versailles, and while the first order with Bradley was always business, after hours Ike enjoyed sitting around with Brad swapping off-color jokes, talking about the hunting dogs they would buy when the war was over, and sipping drinks. Ike sat in on bridge games a little more often, and he even planned to take a few days off, a long-overdue vacation arranged for him at an opulent villa on the French Riviera.[111]

The Riviera of 1945 bore only a vague resemblance to the prewar playground of Europe's nobility. It had been the target of Operation DRAGOON the previous August, and the slug trails of bulldozers, DUKWs, and cargo craft still scarred its fabled beaches. But Sous le Vent, an overpowering Cannes mansion reputed to have cost three million dollars, lay just outside the DRAGOON landing zone, and it seemed the perfect place to find solace from the strains of Versailles. On March 19 a mentally and physically drained Dwight Eisenhower left for Cannes with Kay, Beetle, Beetle's secretary, Mickey, Brad, and a few others in tow.[112]

If the idea of the Supreme Commander, his close friends, and an attractive secretary retreating to a villa on the Riviera seems like a recipe for a licentious junket, it was anything but that for Ike. With the iron levers of war safely in the hands of others for a few days, his depleted mind permitted his body to lapse into the unconsciousness it had been begging for; when he reached his bedroom, he slept for nearly two solid days. As Kay recalled, he stared vacantly, barely ate, and for some time he could muster the mental energy to do very little. When Kay suggested a round of bridge, he refused. "I can't keep my mind on cards," he told her, the monosyllables slurring their way past his lips. "All I want to do is sit here and not think."[113]

By the third day on the Riviera, Ike seemed "somewhat human" to Kay, and when he left Cannes on March 23, the day before Monty was to launch PLUNDER, he was something of his old self—smiling, smoking, joking, playing bridge, itching to get back to the eye of the hurricane. The return of his energy brought renewed confidence, confidence that had eroded during the fights with Brooke and Monty in January, during the aftermath of the Ardennes. His spirits were high enough that he even felt able to congratulate himself—and Bradley—on his insistence on a broad-front strategy. As he wrote Marshall shortly afterward:

> Naturally I am pleased that the campaign west of the Rhine that Bradley and I planned last summer and insisted upon as a necessary preliminary to a deep penetration east of the Rhine, has been carried out so closely in accordance with conception. You possibly know that at one time the C.I.G.S. [Brooke] thought I was wrong in what I was trying to do and argued heatedly upon the matter. Yesterday I saw him on the banks of the Rhine and he was gracious enough to say that I was right, and that my current plans and operations are well calculated to meet the current situation. . . . I hope this does not sound boastful, but I must

admit to a great satisfaction that the things that Bradley and I have believed in from the beginning and have been carried out in the face of some opposition within and without, have matured so splendidly.[114]

Eisenhower was now ready to return to the war, where he would see a final, satisfying act of his life's great drama.[115]

TWENTY-FOUR

THE THOUSAND-YEAR REICH

Whenever [Bradley and Eisenhower] get together, they get timid.

—George, March 31, 1945

WHEN HE LOOKED AT BRADLEY, Patton saw a good, workmanlike soldier, but no inspired commander. Since Tunisia, Brad's method almost never varied: Push, but not too hard. Take risks, but not audacious ones. If your flank is exposed, start worrying. *"A good officer but utterly lacks 'it,'"* George commented in late January. *"He just fails to see war as a struggle, not as an educational course."*[1]

But with the captures of Trier and the Remagen bridge, the Tent Maker seemed a little more willing take risks, to give George's army a longer leash. One afternoon in March, as Patton was getting a shave and a haircut at his command post, Bradley entered the makeshift barbershop and told George he wanted to discuss a sweep south to flank the Siegfried Line at the juncture of Third and Seventh Armies. George, his interest piqued, sat up, bellowed for another barber, and minutes later the two generals sat side by side, their heads buried under steaming towels while they jawed strategy.[2]

Patton, they decided, would send Bulldog's XX Corps in and behind the Siegfried Line and across Patch's Seventh Army front, cracking Seventh Army's opponents from behind. If successful, the move would roll up the Siegfried Line and encircle the Saar Palatinate, western Germany's second-largest industrial region. It would also open several good crossing points along the Rhine and Main rivers, opening the side door to central Germany. "[I]t'll save us from sitting on our asses while SHAEF makes up its mind as to whether we're going to cross the Rhine," George said, in words that, for him, approximated a compliment to Twelfth Army Group's foresight.[3]

Perhaps Bradley was finally getting "it."

Two days later, in Namur on March 9, George showed Bradley a telegram he received from General Eddy informing him that XII Corps had captured an intact bridge over the Moselle not far from its confluence with the Rhine. His mind exploding with possibilities, Patton convinced Bradley to ask Devers to pull Seventh Army's boundary to the south temporarily, so Third Army could close up the Rhine at Mainz. (When he found out afterward that the bridge had been blown during its capture, he decided to keep that information to himself, throw up three pontoon bridges, and forge ahead.)

To give himself a little more room to maneuver, politically and militarily, George also made a secret deal with his friend Sandy Patch, Seventh Army's commanding general. Patch and Patton agreed that the borders of the Seventh and Third Armies would be adjusted between themselves, and each promised the other not to go to his superior if the army boundaries needed adjusting for "complications." With any luck, George figured he would have the Saar Palatinate, and a fat bag of enemy prisoners, behind his front lines before month's end.[4]

Patton liked the way things were working out, but with the sands of the present war running low, he felt an acute need to gain both ground and headlines. When Bradley called on March 11, George told him, "I apologize for not being on the front page." To this an unconcerned Brad replied, "Well, even you have to regroup once in a while." But "regroup" was one of the few dirty words in George's vocabulary, and two days later Patton was relieved to see his offensive against the Palatinate step off as scheduled.[5]

Third Army's attack went splendidly. Walker's infantry and artillery opened the show with a noisy demonstration, drawing German reserves to the south; then Eddy's XII Corps leaped over the Moselle. His tankers gunned their Shermans, blasted the thin crust of resistance, and sped toward the Rhine. Before long, George's lead elements, four armored divisions, charged behind the vaunted Siegfried Line, scattering defenders as they went, and cut across Patch's front to the south as they secured a new line along the Rhine River. Using the reliable combination of fast armor, close air support, and rapid infantry advance, the German First and Seventh

Armies were encircled, then crushed between Patton and Patch. By March 21, the Saar industries were in Allied hands, and Patton was finally against the Rhine.[6]

As the Palatinate campaign moved into high gear, Eisenhower and Bedell Smith paid Third Army an unplanned visit. They had to land in Luxembourg when their original destination, Brad's headquarters, was off-limits due to bad flying weather, and George rolled out an impromptu honor guard for Smith, who, he figured, had never been given one before. Bidding the dignitaries welcome, George took Ike and Beetle on a jeep tour of the 10th Armored Division's sector—the same 10th Armored that SHAEF had previously ordered Patton to send back to SHAEF's reserve pool. The goodwill tour worked. Eisenhower, delighted with the results, predicted that George's swift move would save thousands of lives down the line. As a measure of Third Army's success, a beaming Eisenhower granted Patton's request for one of Patch's armored divisions, the 12th Armored, so Third Army could strike even harder to the east. For once, George noted, Third Army was receiving reinforcements, not shipping them off to someone else.[7]

Ike spent the night at Third Army headquarters, and the next morning he paid what George uncharitably claimed to be *"the first compliment he has ever vouchsafed."* At a staff briefing, George later wrote, *"He stated that we of the Third Army were such veterans that we did not appreciate our own greatness and should be more cocky and boastful, because otherwise people would not realize how good the American soldiers are. . . . He was also extremely complimentary and stated that not only was I a good general but also a lucky general, and that Napoleon preferred luck to greatness."* George then *"told him that this was the first time he had ever complimented me in the 2-1/2 years we have served together."*[8]

Ike didn't flinch. It was just George.

Afterward, Patton escorted Ike and Beetle to Patch's headquarters in George's personal C-47, a leather-upholstered gift from General Spaatz that came with its own air crew and a Red Cross stewardess. The meeting was a happy one, everyone fell over themselves to be cooperative, and upon Patton's return his Army family had a relaxing dinner in which they recapped Eisenhower's visit.[9]

"I think Ike had a good time," George said to Hap Gay. "They ought to let him out oftener."

"What I can't get over," replied Gay, "was his statement to the effect that Third Army isn't cocky enough. How do you explain it?"

"That's easy," George said, stirring his soup with a spoon. "Before long Ike will be running for president. Third Army represents a lot of votes."

The group broke into bemused smiles. George glanced up from his soup. "You think I'm joking? I'm not. Just wait and see."[10]

The Palatinate Campaign was Patton's last great offensive of the war. His army had bagged much of Kesselring's First Army and had shattered the Siegfried Line, all while sweeping around Patch's Seventh U.S. Army. George and Hap considered the campaign Third Army's finest hour, Hodges watched Patton's advance with admiration, and the good-natured Gee Gerow, now commanding Fifteenth Army, cabled Patton to congratulate him on his "masterpiece" of surrounding several armies, "including one of our own." Twelfth Army Group's chief engineer called a Seventh Army staffer in mock alarm to warn, "For God's sake, start running for Paris or you'll end up in one of Patton's prison cages!"[11]

Everything was going George's way. As word spread of another successful Patton dash, senior journalists began filtering south like carpetbaggers with notepads. *Time* dispatched Sid Olson to prepare a cover story on Patton, and George's third *Time* cover featured a watercolor of the scowling lieutenant general next to a tank crowned with a giant brass-knuckled fist.[12]

The cream of the *Wehrmacht*, or what was left of it, was demoralized, shorthanded, and low on everything from shells to sauerkraut. *Now*, not later, was the time to seize a river crossing and ram a steel spear through Germany's dying heart. Bradley, with one eye on the calendar, agreed George needed to move, and quickly, and on March 19 he gave Patton permission to cross the Rhine as soon as he was able.[13]

With the smashing success at the Palatinate, pressure mounted on Patton to get his army across the Rhine. To the north, Montgomery was scheduled to cross the great river on the twenty-third, and if Patton didn't get to the Rhine's east bank soon, rumor had it, he and Patch would lose up to ten divisions to Montgomery's army group. The stakes, therefore, were more than just the prestige of beating Monty across the river, and after taking the Rhine on the run, the conqueror of Messina planned to launch a drive so furious that SHAEF couldn't pull his divisions away and give them to Monty. That honor, he hoped, would fall to Patch.[14]

So desperate was he to beat Montgomery over the Rhine that he toyed with the idea of using tiny artillery spotter planes to ferry a battalion of riflemen men over the river, one at a time. But Third Army's crossing was more conventional than an improvised paratroop lift. On the morning of March 22, Patton got his break near the winemaking town of Oppenheim. Receiving word that the crossing point was virtually undefended, he ordered Eddy to carve a bridgehead over the Rhine by nightfall. The first wave, from Eddy's 5th Infantry Division, crossed without opposition at ten that night. By eight the next morning the obedient 5th, moving steadily in motorboats and rafts, had put six battalions of boots on the east bank of the Rhine.[15]

"God be praised," exclaimed George.[16]

On the morning of March 23, the day Monty was scheduled to begin his great Rhine crossing, Brad took his usual breakfast in the elegant dining hall of Château de Namur. As he was sipping his second cup, an aide passed through a telephone call from Third Army. Patton.

Over the receiver Brad heard the low voice of a conspirator, the squeaky voice that meant George was excited.

"Brad, don't tell anyone but I'm across."

"Well, I'll be damned—you mean across the Rhine?"

"Sure am. I sneaked a division over last night," George said. "But there are so few Krauts around there they don't know it yet. So don't make any announcement—we'll keep it a secret until we see how it goes."[17]

Before hanging up, Bradley instructed George to push ten divisions over the Rhine.[18]

The short March day had passed into twilight when another call came from the same squeaky voice.

"Brad, for God's sake tell the world we're across! We knocked down 33 Krauts today when they came after our pontoon bridges. I want the world to know Third Army made it before Monty starts across!"[19]

Bradley was quick to oblige, and he gathered his press pool to detail the crossings at Oppenheim. Montgomery, he knew, was on the verge of his long-planned, million-man crossing to the north, a mass migration preceded by a month-long aerial bombardment, heavy naval, air, smoke, and artillery support, even studies of soil samples of the Rhine's banks. Bradley emphasized that Third Army had crossed the famous river without firing so much as a mortar round, knowing the unfavorable comparisons the press would draw to Montgomery's loud, expensive crossing. With a second Rhine bridgehead to crow about, Brad took great pleasure in stealing Montgomery's thunder.[20]

It was not a great bridgehead, however. In his haste to grab the limelight, Patton had pushed the 5th Division into a thrown-together crossing that kept the division's commander on pins and needles. Worse, to get across the Rhine with minimal resistance, Patton had directed the crossing to take place south of the intersecting Main River, which meant he would have to make a second river crossing, over the Main, to reach his immediate objective, Frankfurt.

But George, now safely ahead of Montgomery, didn't care. He had accomplished what he had set out to do over the last three weeks: wage a brilliant campaign in hostile country, encircle an enemy army, and cross the Rhine ahead of his British rival. And to ensure no one would forget his arrival, on the twenty-fourth he had Sergeant Mims drive him halfway across a pontoon bridge, where he could stand over the middle of the Rhine. With the preamble, "I have been looking forward to this for a long time," he unbuttoned his fly and pissed into Germany's mighty river.[21]

George's excretory message to Berlin gave Ike's spirits another lift, for it was a graphic indication of how close the war's end must be. It was also further validation of the faith he had kept with his eccentric friend. A few days later, Ike wrote George,

> *The purpose of this little note is to express to you personally my deep appreciation of the splendid way in which you have conducted Third Army operations from the moment it entered battle last August 1. . . . I am very proud of the fact that you, as one of the fighting commanders who has been with me from the beginning of the African campaign, have performed so brilliantly throughout. . . .*
>
> *With warm personal regard,*
> *as ever,*
> *Dwight D. Eisenhower*[22]

As his army sawed through the eastern Rhineland, one piece of real estate caught George's attention. In February, Beetle's secretary had informed Hap Gay that Colonel John Waters, George's son-in-law, had been moved from a prisoner-of-war camp in central Poland to somewhere in western Germany. The Allies had known that Oflag XIII-B, a prison camp near Hammelburg, was housing American officers, and George figured there was a good chance that Waters was being held there. The camp lay well outside Third Army's boundaries, in Seventh Army territory, but as he sat at his desk, George found it hard to take his eyes off that spot on the map. For all he knew, the prisoners might be moved or even massacred before the camp was liberated. Moreover, across the globe General MacArthur had garnered headlines by sending a Ranger force to liberate a prison camp in the Philippines, where they freed some five hundred Americans who would have been slaughtered by their Japanese captors. Perhaps it was time, he thought, for a similar raid in Germany. No—a better one.[23]

On March 26 Patton flew to Manton Eddy's headquarters to propose a regiment-size raid on the camp. It was hardly an unworthy cause—Eddy had liberated one camp just before the Bulge attack—but Eddy and the 4th Armored Division's commander, Brigadier General William Hoge, expressed grave doubts about the mission. Pointing out the obvious risks of going so deep behind enemy lines, Eddy warned George that if the mission failed, he would be censured for risking an entire regiment, some three thousand men, to save a *relative* few.[24]

Patton, as usual, was unmoved. He had broken through the Siegfried Line, captured the Saar, and crossed the Rhine River. Like Lee before Gettysburg, nothing seemed impossible for his Third Army. He ordered Eddy and Hoge to launch the raid, though at Eddy's insistence, he allowed Hoge to pare down the expedition to two motorized companies, about 300 men, to allow greater mobility and surprise. With some badgering from his long, tall Texas aide, Major Alex Stiller, George attached Stiller to the expedition. "Because I'll recognize Johnny Waters," Stiller said.[25]

The raid was a disaster. The task force, which had counted on stealth, was forced to shoot its way to the camp and then surround it. As Waters and another U.S. officer walked out the camp's gates under a flag of truce, a German sentry fired a Mauser round through the colonel's lower back, dropping him to the ground, and Waters was dragged back into the compound. Local troops, armed with *Panzerfaust* bazookas and small arms, converged on the American raiders and destroyed all fifty-three vehicles. Of the 293 men sent out, only fifteen made it back to the American lines.[26]

George knew he would catch hell for ordering such a reckless mission, and he grew frantic as he thought about Johnny Waters and what may have happened to his gun-toting aide. Middleton recalled a visibly worried Patton showing up at VIII Corps headquarters one afternoon.

"Troy," he said, "I'm in trouble again. This time I've really done it. I've sent Alex Stiller off to his death."

A look of pain washed over him. "I loved that boy like a son," he continued. "Why did I let him talk me into letting him go along?"

"What sort of outfit did you send?" Middleton asked, his eyes narrowing.

"Oh, something like a reinforced company."

"A reinforced company!" Middleton gasped. "You surely have played it. You needed at least a combat command for a mission like that."

George wasn't listening. He was thinking only of poor Alex and John. He lamely muttered that Stiller had "looked so sick" when George told him he couldn't go along, he gave in and told Stiller to go ahead.[27]

Back at Lucky Forward, George knew he would have to limit the damage to his reputation, and to keep the press from making a stink over it, he censored the story. He eventually would lift the news ban, of course, but he would do that later, when he had good news to overshadow the story of the raid. For now, his eyes were fixed on central Germany.[28]

In late March, Omar Bradley assumed the mantle of his hero, General Sherman, as he pursued the ragged remnants of the *Wehrmacht*. The sting of the Bulge had abated, and the logistical problems plaguing the "Great Mediocrity," as Brad called the vast supply zone between Paris and Cherbourg, were less constricting than they had been the previous September. He was running his part of the war, as a fellow Missourian once put it, with the serene confidence of a Christian holding four aces. Ike had given Bradley the starring role in the last campaign, and with his men pouring onto German soil, Brad took comfort in the knowledge that, within reason, he could disregard the British, just as Montgomery had disregarded him for most of the war. While Versailles would occasionally order Bradley to surrender troops to Sixth Army Group, SHAEF's larceny was less pronounced now that Brad had a Rhine bridgehead and had conquered the Saar Palatinate.[29]

The commander of the largest force in U.S. history was now at the peak of his career, one that was the envy of every man in uniform. His personal life was also pleasant; he enjoyed a luxurious command post and the enticing company of Marlene Dietrich, with whom he had sharing private dinners since the previous December. Over cocktails, Bradley would listen to Dietrich's ramblings, such as how she could have been Hitler's mistress once upon a time, and she seemed to enjoy provoking Brad's staff; once,

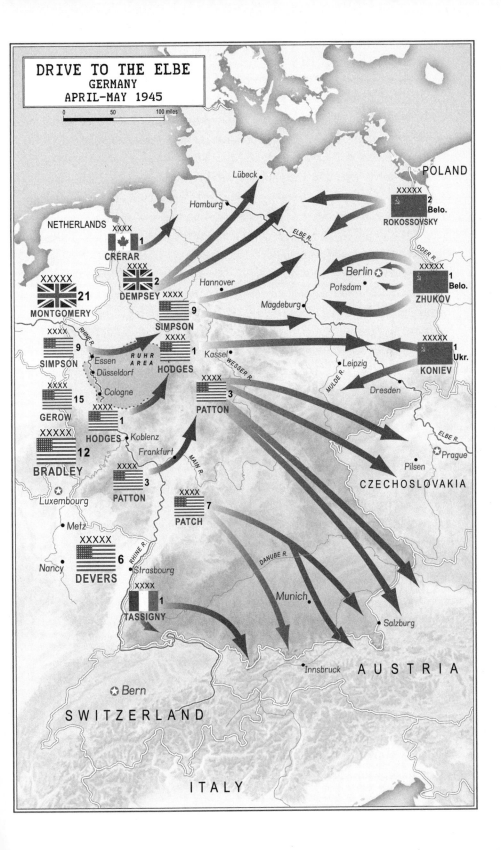

DRIVE TO THE ELBE
GERMANY
APRIL–MAY 1945

0   50   100 miles

after a few martinis, she blithely told Brad's aides how she had been using a jacket Brad had given her as a dressing gown.

Her complaints of less-than-stellar quarters at Master and Eagle Main, as well as her gripes about boorish colonels and one-stars, rankled Brad's staffers, who didn't need any more crosses to bear—leastwise, any crosses marked "Hollywood." But they put up with her, because Brad, a little star-struck, delighted in her company, which for Dietrich was motivated by more than just her desire to keep up troop morale; as American armies occupied western Germany, access to the Twelfth Army Group commander helped the German actress in her desperate search for relatives lost amid the fog and destruction of the war.[30]

Omar Bradley had also come to terms with the man who had once been the biggest thorn in his side. The battles with SHAEF and Montgomery had cemented a solid relationship between Brad and George, and Brad had, he hoped, finally come to understand the man who was George Smith Patton. As George's father, and Katherine Marshall, and Ike Eisenhower had realized years earlier, many of Patton's more irritating traits were only as potent as the reactions they elicited. They were, in some ways, like a child's outburst, something that if ignored lost its effect. In mid-February, Brad's aide Chet Hansen, one of George's long-running critics, summarized his revised opinion of Patton:

> General Patton, who has been described as a swaggering, noisy general, is actually a shrewd and brilliant one, highly regarded as an Army commander. His eccentric habits are obviously affectations designed to attract his troops. It is amusing to listen to him at dinner when he makes a startling statement without fact and draws his head back to await the explosive reaction of others that always follows.[31]

But the transmission that drove Third Army couldn't remain trouble-free for long, and around March 27 a newspaper reporter asked Bradley about a mission General Patton had ordered to liberate a POW camp behind enemy lines. Bradley, frowning, gave no information about the raid, because he had none to give. But he promised to find out.

He rang up George's headquarters at Idar-Oberstein and got the commanding general on the line. After a few polite but direct questions, Patton apologetically told Bradley that he had ordered the Hammelburg raid.

George swore he didn't know his son-in-law was interned at the camp, but whether he knew it or not was beside the point. The fiasco put Patton, and by extension, Bradley and Eisenhower, in a bad way with the press. The raid had turned into a public relations nightmare as well as an unnecessary disaster. "[George] knew damn well if he asked me for permission I would have vetoed it," Brad said later. "He lost his whole force. . . . And it was just a spectacular stunt. [H]e could have rescued his son-in-law and gotten a lot of headlines about this raid and so forth. But I think it was doomed from the start and it was a foolhardy operation to do."[32]

If the Hammelburg raid was foolhardy, Brad recognized that it was one of George's few such lapses—lately. As Patton spurred his divisions through bombed-out little towns and across the Rhine's foothills, Bradley's confidence in his horseman of the German apocalypse grew. Patton played to the hilt the role of the reckless adventurer, and those blue lines of grease pencil creeping across his maps appeared perilously thin. But he trusted George's intuition; the man wasted nothing on flank and counterattack protection, but somehow he always had the right ingredients standing by when an enemy attack came. Even as vestiges of George's old showboating ways resurfaced—the ivory-handled pistols were turning up a lot these days—as long as Third Army was advancing, Brad didn't mind all that much.[33]

While Bradley didn't bristle at George's theatrics, he couldn't help but notice the headlines the Third Army commander was garnering. He didn't mind his generals making the papers, but the inequity of the ink spilled over George bothered him. As Harry Butcher commented, "It takes a lot of color in any man to balance Patton," and Hodges, Brad thought, was getting shortchanged. In the papers, other generals had to be introduced; Patton was simply "Patton." Third Army was "Patton's army," the hard-charging janissaries who captured over three thousand towns and 140,000 soldiers, while Hodges, a mere mortal, was simply the commanding general of "First Army." In describing the battle for the Siegfried Line, *Time* magazine had recently gushed:

Patton was playing his favorite role. He was the swift, slashing halfback of Coach Eisenhower's team. His quarterback, General Omar N. Bradley, had set up a climax play and had called Patton's signal. Halfback Patton had had superb blocking from Lieut. General Courtney Hicks Hodges' First Army. Now the star open-field runner was ripping into the secondary defense. . . . Now, as he had after

Saint-Lô, it was Halfback Patton who captured the headlines. He was definitely in nomination for Public Hero No. 1 of the war in Europe. . . . In slim, big-chested Patton, hero-worshiping Americans had a candidate to fit the mass idea of what a Hero General should be—the colorful swashbuckler, the wild-riding charger, the hell-for-leather Man of Action, above all the Winner.[34]

That sort of Madison Avenue rot was the farthest thing from the truth, Brad thought. Yes, Hodges was, in some ways, a coach who ran his plays up the middle. But as the inside army commander, it was his job to slug against the center. He wasn't sitting still, and at the Ruhr, Hodges had formed the southern arm of the great pincer that swallowed up nearly 325,000 Germans—a bag larger than the Red Army had captured at Stalingrad. Hodges had crossed the Rhine first and captured the first German city, and Hodges would be the first to reach the Russians. *Patton,* not Hodges, was the bridesmaid.[35]

Publicity was a problem Bradley claimed not to think about, and most of the time he didn't. Naturally modest, Brad couldn't see why the press should make such a fuss over one of the million-plus Americans fighting in Europe, shiny pistols or no. But as Montgomery, Patton, and Eisenhower grew larger than life in the public eye, Omar Bradley would have been less than human if he didn't feel a little slighted by the press, as he often was. Three days after the Normandy landings, he had borrowed a newspaper from Montgomery and eagerly scanned it for news of the invasion; what he found instead was the press gushing about Patton at Dover, about Monty at Normandy. When a journalist asked Bradley in early April when Patton would link up with the Russians, Bradley was quick to remind the man that "any of the armies might reach the Russians." In January, as Patton and Montgomery were erasing the Bulge, Brad's aide griped:

> *Brad is the strategist, Patton the executer. Though all the credit in the newspapers continues to go to Patton. It is evidence enough of Brad's anonymity that his great control of the planning of the American assault was not sufficiently recognized to get him a vote as the TIME Magazine man of the year—in the AP poll, Patton ran second to Ike—a totally unreal situation if there ever was one.*[36]

* * *

Eisenhower limped the last hundred feet of his tightrope, praying he would not slip as he reached the end. By late March, the utter defeat of Germany had become a certainty, and Ike, immodestly yet understandably, wasn't shy about reminding certain colleagues that over the objections of others— he was too savvy to point out *whom*, but everyone knew who the "others" were—he had insisted on confronting the German army west of the Rhine, rather than run around the enemy to the north. Now the Germans had nothing left to fight with, and Ike could practically walk to Berlin. His confidence, which had been hammered so many times since Pearl Harbor, was cresting, and he decided the time had come to move Montgomery into the backseat and put Omar behind the wheel.[37]

Ike spent the next few weeks watching his G-3 maps sprout forests of blue arrows as Patton cut loose in the south and Hodges broke away from his Remagen bridgehead. On both sides of the Ruhr, Montgomery passed beyond Essen to Lippstadt, and Hodges moved on Paderborn to trap the Ruhr Valley's defenders. News of the Ruhr's encirclement reached SHAEF on March 28, and with it, Ike knew the snake's head had been sliced from its body. To Eisenhower the war was as good as over.[38]

But the war wasn't over, of course. A snake's head, lopped from its body, can still deliver a lethal bite. With the Ruhr's capture, the head had to die, but the question on everyone's lips was, Will the Allies take Berlin?

It was an old question that had been academic. But now that the Allies were beyond the Ruhr, Ike had to face the conundrum squarely. As with Paris, he considered an attack against Berlin a military matter rather than a political one. He did his best to ignore the obvious political implications of Hitler's capital and focus on the situation maps, not what politicians might say. And, as with most military matters, he solicited the opinion of his most trusted lieutenant.

Bradley had long believed some cadre of fanatical Nazis would continue to fight even if Berlin fell. The G-2 sections at Twelfth and SHAEF had been picking up rumors of a "National Redoubt," a rural base in southern Germany from which hard-core Nazis would fight a guerrilla war until the resurrection of the Reich. Moreover, he estimated that a campaign for the German capital would cost about a hundred thousand casualties. "A pretty stiff price to pay for a prestige objective," Brad cautioned. Directing Ike's attention to the south, Brad suggested that a major effort against Bavaria, Austria, maybe Czechoslovakia, was the right approach. Not a battle for Berlin.[39]

Ike listened. He had never liked prestige objectives, and he couldn't formulate a solid military rationale for taking Berlin. The Red Army, a juggernaut boasting 1.2 million men, was a scant thirty-five miles from the city, while the closest Allied army was some 150 miles away. Ike's orders were to "undertake operations aimed at the heart of Germany and the destruction of her armed forces," and until the Combined Chiefs gave him specific instructions to capture Berlin, he felt no obligation to sacrifice the lives of American, British, French, or Polish soldiers.

He also placed great faith in Brad's military judgment about Berlin, and while evidence of a national redoubt was not conclusive, he couldn't afford to make a mistake at this late point in the war. Like Grant at Appomattox, Ike was horrified at the prospect of an incomplete victory that would give way to a protracted, bloody hunt in the hills of Bavaria for Hitler's twisted disciples. Despite the enormous political value of Berlin, he would consider only military strategy, and that strategy dictated an American drive to the center and south, and a British drive to Germany's north coast. The Russians would have Berlin.[40]

With the question of Berlin answered, Eisenhower approved a two-pronged approach to the dying Third Reich. In the main effort, Bradley would advance beyond Frankfurt through central and southern Germany. SHAEF would return Simpson's Ninth Army to Bradley, and Brad would launch Simpson and Hodges on the last big drive of the war, meeting the Russians somewhere around the line of Erfurt-Leipzig-Dresden. To prevent a last stand by Nazi diehards in the south, Patton and Devers would sweep through Bavaria and into northwestern Austria. To the far north, Montgomery would scoop up the German port cities and cut off Denmark. It was another version of his "broad-front" approach, but with a new twist: This time, the usual Montgomery-Bradley role would be reversed. Monty would guard Bradley's left flank, and Bradley would bag the remaining prizes.[41]

As the curtain rose for the Reich's final, tragic act, the thought of blood needlessly shed bore down upon Ike with each passing day. It was a gift of Ike's that he never stopped thinking of the man at the front: what he ate, where he slept, whether he had dry socks and working weapons—and more recently, whether he would be one of those unlucky pawns who would meet death in the war's last days. Added to this general burden was the specter of friendly fire as Russian and Western soldiers first met, for if dying at war's end from a Mauser bullet was a senseless tragedy, dying from a Tokarev round was even more senseless.[42]

Well, thought Ike, he could at least take steps to minimize the second hazard. On March 28, he composed a short letter to Marshal Stalin outlining his plans for the final weeks of the war. He told the generalissimo that before he firmed up his decisions on final drives, he wanted to coordinate movements with the Red Army to ensure the rapid destruction of the German forces, and he asked Stalin for his intended course of action.

A few days later, Stalin's reply made its way back through U.S. representatives in Moscow. Stalin agreed with Ike's suggestion of a linkup between the Allies and the Red Army on the Erfurt-Leipzig-Dresden line. The dictator ominously made no suggestion that he needed any help reducing Berlin. He knew what he would do with that city.[43]

The day his letter to Stalin went out, Eisenhower informed Montgomery of his decision to return Ninth Army to Bradley, explaining that Twelfth Army Group would make the main drive to meet the Soviets along the Elbe. "The mission of your army group," he told Monty, "will be to protect Bradley's northern flank."[44]

Churchill and Brooke were naturally inflamed over Eisenhower's shunting the Commonwealth's armies off to a secondary theater. In his seductive prose, Churchill argued that the fate of the postwar world depended on the Allies taking the German capital. If the dreaded hammer and sickle flew over the Reichstag, the Reds would drive an intolerable bargain at the peace table, where Europe's fate would be decided.[45]

Ike flew into another outburst when he read Churchill's cable, for it asked him to send men to their deaths for a militarily insignificant city. This he would not do without a clear order from the Combined Chiefs, and he sent Marshall a letter explaining his rationale for driving into Germany's periphery. Marshall's reply indicated that he would never order the Allies to throw soldiers against Berlin without the Supreme Commander's stamp of approval, so Eisenhower knew his position was secure. With Stalin and Marshall of one mind on Berlin, Churchill and Brooke would have to content themselves with mutterings among themselves and pro forma objections. Whatever His Majesty's ministers might think, Ike's strategy would be the Allied course of action. There was no one left to challenge Eisenhower's power in Western Europe.[46]

* * *

George knew he'd be in Dutch with Ike and Brad over the Hammelburg raid, but he didn't dwell on it. The best way to get a bad headline behind him, he knew from experience, was to replace it with a good headline, and Third Army was well-placed to make good headlines. His army—not Third Army, but *Patton's* Third Army—had a reputation as a fast-charging, hard-hitting bunch. A *Time* cover article opened with a quip from the Supreme Commander that would capture the public image of George during that heady spring. When asked where the fast-moving Patton was, Ike replied, "Hell, I don't know. I haven't heard from him in three hours."[47]

So George didn't worry much about Hammelburg; pay Ike in victories, in mileage, in prisoners, villages, and bridgeheads, and Ike would back his old pal George seven days a week.

But Bradley, as Patton saw it, was still too timid to cut the kite strings and let him soar. At the end of March, Brad told George his army couldn't head east toward the Elbe River, which George protested as a dangerous lapse when the enemy was on the run. The next evening Brad and Ike got on the phone and cautioned Patton not to push too hard against a big German communications center near Weimar, Ohrdruf, and Erfurt, and George had to promise big gains to continue his attack. After the call he quipped, *"Whenever those two get together, they get timid. I am sure that had a bold policy throughout been used in this war, it would have long since been over."* As George told Second Lieutenant John Eisenhower, whose unit was briefly in George's sector, "I've been told to hold up and let the rest of them catch up with me. But I'm advancing fifteen miles a day anyhow." With a wry smile, he pointed a long index finger at John and said, "Don't tell your Daddy!"[48]

George kept advancing, and by the sixth of April he had bagged the Erfurt-Ohrdruf region, which, Eddy reported, included a potassium mine near Merkers where a large Reichsbank gold reserve was hidden, probably Germany's entire remaining gold stock. George's first reaction, upon confirmation of the news, was that SHAEF should announce the capture to the world; that, he thought, would devalue the hell out of Germany's currency system, and it might do more to end the war than putting another army in the field. But because ownership of the gold might become a political issue, he called Bradley and urged him to get someone from SHAEF to take custody of the money right away. He also clamped down a news embargo on the capture until the story was confirmed; when he learned that a SHAEF censor attached to Third Army had passed the story, he had the man relieved.[49]

Acting on Patton's suggestion, SHAEF dispatched Colonel Bernard Bernstein, Ike's financial adviser, to arrange for the loot's safekeeping. Bernstein tentatively selected the Reichsbank at Frankfurt am Main, far to the west, as the storage facility. When Bernstein informed General Patton of the move to Frankfurt, George, in high spirits, replied that Bernstein could leave the gold at Merkers as long as he liked, since the Germans weren't about to push Third Army out of the region.[50]

That wasn't what he meant, Bernstein said. The Big Three had decided that the portion of Germany they were standing on would be handed over to the Soviets when the fighting ended. Patton's conquests would become part of the Red Army's zone.

A cloud fell over George's face. He hadn't heard that, he said quietly.[51]

Two days later, at Bradley's headquarters, Brad and Ike quashed any lingering hopes of campaigns to the Oder River or beyond. They told George he would have to shut down Walker's XX Corps on the Elbe's west bank. The Reds were getting everything to the east, and Patton's plans for a bridgehead farther were to be canceled. George's war would end with a handshake somewhere along the Elbe River.[52]

On April 12, a few days after the discovery of the Merkers treasure hoard, Generals Eisenhower and Bradley flew to Patton's headquarters at Hersfeld for a tour of Third Army's domains, which included the potassium mine and a local "labor" camp near Ohrdruf. George had previously told Bradley about a concentration camp in his territory and thought Brad ought to check it out. "You'll never believe how bastardly these Krauts can be," he said. Ike joined Bradley for the inspection, to document evidence of Nazi looting and atrocities, and Ike wanted a blue-ribbon parade of generals, reporters, photographers, and eventually, politicians, to bear witness to the conduct of the "master race."[53]

The three men piled into jeeps for the short trip to Merkers, and made the brief drive through a series of heavily guarded roadblocks to the mine entrance. Walking into the cavern's gaping mouth, the generals and a small entourage squeezed onto a rickety wooden elevator car operated by a German national. The sound of the elevator's motor reverberated through the dark shaft as Ike, Brad, and George nervously descended two thousand feet into the abyss. Nodding to the elevator's spindly cable silhouetted against a shrinking dot of daylight, George quietly remarked, "If that clothesline should part, promotions in the United States Army would be considerably stimulated."

From the blackness, a flat Kansas voice replied, "O.K., George, that's enough. No more cracks until we are above ground again."[54]

The three men pulled their overcoats tight as they combed the cool, unventilated tunnels beneath bare lightbulbs. Grim-faced, they inspected wooden pallets of gold bullion, paper currency tightly baled, Reichsbank currency printing plates, and several tons of coins packed in crates, suitcases, and steamer trunks. As their footsteps echoed in the dungeon-like shafts, the men poked among a portion of the mine filled with a different sort of loot: long, neat rows of suitcases filled with false teeth, watches, cigarette cases, jewelry, silverware, and other personal possessions left behind when their owners were systematically murdered. Stacked in another cavern were tall wooden crates containing art treasures pillaged from museums across Europe. Ike flipped through some of the artworks as Brad and George, wide-eyed, stared over his shoulder. *"The three that I looked at, were, in my opinion, worth about $2.00 each and are of the type formerly found in barrooms,"* sneered George, though many of the works, by Manet, Titian, Raphael, and other masters, had been formerly housed at the Kaiser Friedrich Museum in Berlin and other private and public art galleries throughout the Continent.[55]

The Merkers mine was a sinister introduction to the underbelly of the Nazi empire; the three men were glad to take the creaking wooden platform back to the surface. Blinking in the harsh daylight, they climbed back into their jeeps and lunched at Eddy's headquarters before boarding a flock of L-5 planes for the prison camp at Ohrdruf.[56]

After passing through the gates of the eerily quiet camp, the visitors dismounted from their jeeps. As the Allied commanders walked through the camp, MPs, cameramen, interpreters, and aides trailing behind them, from the wooden barracks emerged former prisoners in striped rags, who gazed at the generals with large, sunken eyes.

The Ohrdruf camp was officially designated a "labor camp." It was, in actuality, a death camp where the standard method of execution was exhaustion and malnutrition—though the piles of bullet-ridden corpses and camp gallows implied that hunger was not the exclusive means of dispatch. The party's first stop was the gallows, a crude execution post strung with piano wire and wide enough for three humans to dangle. It was also low enough to ensure that a victim would not die from a broken neck, but would suffer a slow, terrifying strangulation that would take many agonizing minutes, giving inmates and guards the opportunity to witness death up close.

The next stop was a large wooden whipping table on which prisoners would be strapped and beaten with thick wooden poles. Just beyond, in a ragged circle of dried blood, lay the first of many piles of semi-clothed, shriveled bodies. About forty, George estimated, each shot through the head. Another pile just beyond, about the same size, held more skeletal remains, clothed with only a thin layer of quicklime to squelch the smell of rotting flesh.[57]

The gothic horror was too much for George, who had always been prone to gyrations of emotion. His robust body proved unable to absorb the camp's many obscenities, and the warrior who had gleefully photographed dead German soldiers in the Ardennes gaped at the scene, speechless. Without warning he bolted from the group, wheeled around the corner of a building, and vomited. Controlling his gag reflex, if not his composure, George refused to accompany Ike and Brad into a large holding shed through which some three thousand corpses had passed since the previous January. In one part of the camp, they saw a giant makeshift pyre, hastily built to destroy evidence of the atrocities, an irregular pyramid of skulls, bones, and charred torsos that had been badly cooked but not destroyed.[58]

Following the slug trail of Lucifer, Ike walked, eyes glowering, lips twisted into a tight scowl. Emerging from one filthy bunkhouse, Dwight Eisenhower, once a fresh-faced lad from Abilene, Kansas, just stood there among the dead, his words failing him. He had no stirring oratory about the justness of the Allied cause, no eloquent condemnation of the Nazi menace the United Nations were battling. "The things I saw beggar description," he told Marshall afterward. "The visual evidence and the verbal testimony of starvation, cruelty and bestiality were so overpowering as to leave me a bit sick." Bradley recalled, "I was too revolted to speak. For here death had been so fouled by degradation that it both stunned and numbed us." "Blood and Guts" called it "one of the most appalling sights I have ever seen."[59]

The three generals returned to Patton's headquarters that night for dinner, where they slowly absorbed the sights of the day with drinks and conversation. George had invited some Red Cross girls to lighten the atmosphere, and the officers sipped champagne confiscated from the German commandant as they talked. Patton joked that they ought to keep the loot in the mine a secret, so when Congress cut the Army's funding after the war, they could bring it out and buy weapons for Third Army.[60]

Ike, still steaming from the visit to the camp, was in a bitter mood. Over dinner he vented his spleen at George for firing that SHAEF censor who passed the story of a treasure mine in Russian territory. George, unwilling to back down this time, defended his judgment call. Defiantly stabbing his meat with a fork, he threw back his head and said, "I knew I was right on that one."

Ike shot back, "For Christ's sake, George, until you said that, maybe you were. But if you're that positive, I know you're wrong."[61]

It had been a hell of a day for everyone.

As the clock stretched toward midnight, the three men sat together in a sparse room on the second floor of Lucky Forward. As the rumble of army traffic came and went outside, Ike led a discussion about the line where George and Brad would halt their forces for good. First and Ninth Armies, he said, would be finished when they reached the other side of the Saale River west of Leipzig, a line that George's army had already reached. Third Army, Ike said, would halt its drive east and turn south, toward Bavaria. That was Ike's thinking, at least for now.[62]

What about Berlin? George asked.

Berlin, said Ike, was just a city on a map, another Paris filled with hungry mouths, one that would cost plenty of American lives before they charged up the Reichstag steps. Better to let the Russians crack that nut.[63]

George shook his head. "Ike, I don't see how you figure that one. We had better take Berlin and quick and move on to the Oder," he said. Patton, like Churchill, saw the lion's share of postwar Europe, to say nothing of military glory, entwined with the capture of the German capital. He didn't want to see the Red Army take both just because Ike wanted to avoid another battle.[64]

But the decision was not George's to make, and about midnight, the group broke up for the night, Ike and Brad retiring to a nearby house, Patton to his trailer.

As he turned in for bed, George noticed his watch had stopped; he had forgotten to wind it. He flipped on the radio to get the correct time and heard news that was shaking the nation from New York to Okinawa: President Franklin Delano Roosevelt was dead.[65]

Patton's long day was not over. Pulling on his boots, George marched over to his guesthouse and gave Brad the news. Then he and Brad gathered in Ike's room and the three soldiers grieved the loss of their Commander in Chief, the great man who had pulled their nation through some of its worst crises.[66]

They also mulled over what the future would hold. None of them, including fellow Missourian Omar Bradley, knew much about the incoming chief magistrate, Vice President Harry S Truman. Everyone knew he had served in the Great War, and had risen through the ranks of a corrupt political machine. Truman had chaired several powerful Senate committees, but he was new to international diplomacy; Ike wondered whether Truman lacked the Machiavellian cunning needed to handle Stalin. Patton, as apolitical as any soldier, had little good to say of the new man. *"It seems very unfortunate that in order to secure political preference, people are made Vice Presidents who were never intended neither by the Party nor by the Lord to be Presidents,"* he wrote. Their only consolation was that a man whom they all trusted, General George C. Marshall, remained near the helm of power.[67]

Biting the bullet, Patton lifted the news blackout of the Hammelburg raid on April 13. Privately, he knew the adventure had been a screwup, and until Roosevelt died he worried that the papers would try to make another slapping incident of it. But with the passing of the Commander in Chief, he figured the Hammelburg news wouldn't be news at all. He smirked to staffers, "With the president's death you could execute buggery in the streets and get no farther than the fourth page."[68]

Patton's theory, while left untested in its specifics, seemed generally correct. In a war with bloody battles, raids, and skirmishes reported each day, the Hammelburg raid, a much more serious incident than any of George's past indiscretions, lacked the thunderous reverberation of his outbursts in Sicily. The story passed with virtually no comment, and he turned a corner on April 18 when, sitting down to breakfast with Ev Hughes, he read in *Stars and Stripes* that he had been nominated to full, four-star general.

"Well, I'll be . . ." he said, the news sinking in.[69]

But he soon checked himself. For achieving one of his life's great goals, George claimed to be nonplussed, as Bradley and other lesser men had made full general the previous month. Moreover, Hodges had been "made" on the same list, though his date of promotion was one day after Patton's. *"While I am glad to be a full General,"* George told his diary, *"I would have appreciated it more had I been in the initial group, as I have never had an ambition to be an also-ran."* In fact, a brevet four-star rank posed some long-term problems for Patton, for the promotion would make it harder to sign him up for the Pacific after he had beaten those Nazi sons of bitches into the ground. In MacArthur's theater, there weren't a lot of job openings for someone at that rank.[70]

Still, it was a nice gesture by Stimson, Marshall, and Eisenhower, even if George considered it something of an afterthought. Charlie Codman, his aide, managed to track down two four-star pins and a four-star flag, and George's inner circle celebrated his exalted status with a bottle of Four-Star Hennessy. The aides set to work repainting the large placards that adorned the general's convoy transports, and the next time Patton arrived at his staff briefing room, he found his lieutenants broken into squads of four men apiece. George was genuinely flattered.[71]

Before long, those four-starred vehicles were roaring through southeastern Germany, straining against the twin leashes of SHAEF and Twelfth Army Group. In early May, Third Army got the green light to go into Czecho-slovakia; pleased with his new assignment, though a little nonplussed with German opposition, Patton drove his men toward Prague virtually without incident.[72]

Hardly had he set his men in motion when Bradley called to say Third Army could go no farther than Karlsbad-Pilsen, about fifty-five miles west of Prague. Unfortunately for the citizens of German-occupied Prague, the word reached the city of the American advance—no one there knowing, of course, of the restraining line. They burst into revolt, provoking the SS stormtroopers occupying Prague into an orgy of violence that left some fif-teen thousand Czech civilians dead. Patton called Bradley for permission to move forward, but was told to stay where he was; the Red Army would be there shortly and Eisenhower didn't want any "international complica-tions" with the Soviets.[73]

"It seems to me that as great a nation as America should let the other people worry about the complications," George complained. But he obeyed orders, even though he knew he would regret it later. *"I felt, and still feel, that we should have gone on to the Moldau River, and if the Russians didn't like it, let them go to hell."*[74]

But George knew the stop line at Pilsen was merely the last move in a polo match that had been won months ago, and like everyone else in the theater, he was waiting for the crazies in Berlin to give up and die. On the first of May he remarked, "Not even SHAEF can keep this goddamned war going another week." As the fighting died down, he wrote from his headquarters at Erlangen, "Things like this are what is going to make peace so terrible, because nothing exciting will ever happen." [75]

Like Bradley, one monster Ike worked to tame was the Patton publicity machine. George, he felt, had garnered far more than his fair share of laurels back home, and it seemed to Ike that Hodges and Bradley were being unfairly cut out of the limelight. He decided to set things right, and used his considerable clout with the press to do it. In an interview with *Time,* he touted Bradley as "the greatest field commander of World War II," and he sent General Marshall a lengthy cable explaining how First Army, Hodges, and Bradley had been shortchanged on the publicity side. Perhaps, he suggested, the War Department's Public Relations Office could put together a piece on the First Army's story, to give Hodges some of the newsprint he richly deserved. As Ike told Harry Butcher, who was handling public relations for SHAEF, "Not only Hodges' but Bradley's magnificent contribution in this campaign should be painted in more brilliant colors." In mid-April, he rendered his final verdict on his classmate to the Chief: "Bradley, of course, remains the one whose tactical and strategic judgment I consider almost unimpeachable."[76]

George, by contrast, was a scratch on an otherwise melodic performance. He had, without doubt, been the one army commander in whose tactical judgment Ike trusted more than any other. He had also been, without a doubt, the one army commander who kept Ike awake the most, worrying about the next bombshell indiscretion. In mid-April Ike caught wind of the Hammelburg raid, as well as the firing of the SHAEF press censor who passed the story of the capture of the German gold. Bradley privately agreed with Patton that the censor had erred, but Ike took George behind closed doors and read him the riot act over both incidents. *"Ike had taken Patton's hide off,"* Butcher wrote. But he added, *"I think Patton must have as many hides as a cat has lives, for this is at least the fourth time that General Ike has skinned his champion end runner."*[77]

Ike would have liked to have kept the Hammelburg and censor stories within the theater, but he knew the papers back home would make a fuss, and he wanted to stay aboveboard with Marshall. So the day after sending Patton a written rebuke, he dictated to the Chief what had now become a standard form letter, the verbiage was changed to fit George's most recent indiscretion:

> *Patton's latest crackpot actions may possibly get some publicity. One involved the arbitrary relief of a censor (over whom he had no authority whatsoever) for what Patton considered to be an error in judgment. All the censor did was to allow the printing of a story saying we had captured some of the German monetary reserves. Three or four newspapers have written very bitter articles about Patton, on this incident, and to my disgust they call it another example of "Army Blundering." I took Patton's hide off, but there is nothing else to do about it. Then again, he sent off a little expedition on a wild goose chase in an effort to liberate some American prisoners. The upshot was that he got 25 prisoners back and lost a full company of medium tanks and a platoon of light tanks. Foolishly, he then imposed censorship on the movement, meaning to lift it later, which he forgot to do. . . .*

"Patton," Ike concluded, *"is a problem child, but he is a great fighting leader in pursuit and exploitation."*[78]

Problem child or not, Ike knew George was a necessary burden while there was fighting to be done, and there was still fighting to be done. Now that he'd chewed George out—Step One in his standard jacking-up process—then put General Marshall on notice without giving too many details (Step Two), Step Three would be to give George something to occupy his mind and mouth. The drive into Austrian and Czech territory would serve nicely, even though it meant shifting Patton's army into what was presently Jake Devers's territory. He wrote George on the eighteenth, "You are getting set for the drive in a slightly new direction, but I cannot be quite certain yet when I can pull the trigger for that one. I have another task that I must make sure is performed before I can let you go."[79]

Omar Bradley knew the end of George's rail line would come somewhere in Czechoslovakia. He and Ike had discussed it as far back as March 26, when they pegged the Elbe as the American stop line. A rough line through the center of Germany seemed to be the logical way to split the remaining German forces, and making the main thrust into central and southern

Germany—not toward Berlin—would keep Bradley's army group on center stage and relegate Montgomery and Devers to flank roles.[80]

If there was any doubt in Montgomery's mind who was running the show, it was erased when Ike sent Brad to meet Montgomery to urge him to push faster along the northern coast. The Hero of El Alamein, Brad thought, looked defeated, almost indifferent. Brad took pleasure in assuring Montgomery that Ike was not going to let Twenty-First swoop down on Berlin, and he patronizingly asked whether Twelfth Army Group could help Montgomery accomplish his primary mission—once Bradley's main objectives to the south had been captured, of course. A sullen Monty told Brad that he lacked the strength to cover Twelfth Army Group's flanks, and a self-satisfied Bradley reported to Ike that Twelfth Army Group would provide its own flank protection.[81]

Back at Eagle TAC, now located in Wiesbaden, Bradley reported Montgomery's state of numbed refusal to Eisenhower, and opined to Ike that Monty probably couldn't even take his final objective, to cut off Denmark and seize the port of Lübeck, the northernmost meeting point with the Red Army. Ike frowned when he heard this—Montgomery was slow enough when his heart *was* in the fight—but he took the news with equanimity. The war was as good as over, and U.S. forces could, more or less, end the war on SHAEF's terms.[82]

Which was all just too damned bad for Monty, Brad thought.

Bradley stopped Hodges and Simpson along the Elbe-Mulde line, near Leipzig, which would end the war for those fellows. He sent Patton down to meet the Russians deep in the Danube Valley. He made a few changes to Patton's southern lineup, sending home Troy Middleton and Manton Eddy, each for compelling health reasons, but in general he let George do what George did best: move rapidly through light resistance.[83]

On April 19, Ike flew in for a short visit to Wiesbaden, and George came up from Lucky Forward for their last conference of the war. The men gathered at the large trailer from which Bradley had run the American side of the campaign. As George tacked up a large map of his planned movements, aides flipped on the long fluorescent lamps. The men conferred for an hour, and Ike and Brad gave Patton his marching orders.[84]

As the war's curtain descended, Brad had every reason to feel pleased. It had been a long, frustrating road, but the end was at hand, and he could watch George's fifteen-division army sweep forward to the Danube, as First

Army joined hands with the Russians on the Elbe. His armies had captured 842,000 German soldiers since crossing the Rhine—they would bag 1.86 million enemy troops from Normandy to the Elbe—and they had put plenty in the ground. His duties kept him pleasantly busy, but they were less stressful, and they mainly consisted of sitting in his command trailer, taking calls and fielding logistical questions. For a man commanding one and a third million men, there was remarkably little for Omar to do as he waited for the call from Eisenhower.[85]

The fighting in the south proved strangely anticlimactic. As the noose tightened around Berlin, word reached the Allies that Hitler had committed suicide on April 30. Allied tanks, trucks, and half-tracks roared through a broken Germany, playing out the tragedy's last act as every man in a helmet, German and Allied, tried to survive the next few unpredictable days.

Through thick reading glasses, Ike Eisenhower watched the sweep of armies from his forward command post, a brick schoolhouse in Reims where wall-size maps were updated regularly as Patton's divisions crossed the Danube, swept into northern Austria, and drove east to the outskirts of Prague.[86]

In the early evening of May 4, Ike found himself sitting in his office at Reims, watching the green-handled telephone as if a hard stare could make it ring. Joined by Butcher and Kay, he awaited a call from Marshal Montgomery, who had been contacted by General Admiral Hans-Georg von Friedeburg, an emissary of the late Adolf Hitler's successor, Grossadmiral Karl Dönitz. Montgomery was supposed to call Ike at six thirty with a report on Germany's willingness to surrender. But twenty minutes after the appointed time, the blasted phone remained silent.[87]

By six fifty-five, Ike, tired of waiting, told Kay he was heading back to his quarters. Kay urged him to wait another five minutes, suggesting, "The call may come." Sure enough, in five minutes, the phone exploded with a clang. Ike snatched up the receiver as Butch and Kay craned to listen.

"Fine . . . Fine . . . That's fine, Monty."

He hung up. The Germans, he said, were coming to see him the next day. Ike went to dinner.[88]

At five the next afternoon, Admiral von Friedeburg arrived at SHAEF and was ushered into the cluttered office of Beetle Smith, the man who would negotiate the armistice for the Allies. The admiral played for time, arguing every point, pleading for license to continue the struggle against the communists in the east while surrendering to the West. But Smith would have none of it, and discussions quickly broke down. Beetle sent Friedeburg back to his lines with an unyielding message for Dönitz: Unconditional surrender to *all* allies, or the fighting continues, and men will die.[89]

The fighting did continue, and men did die, but the next day Dönitz dispatched General Alfred Jodl, chief of staff for the western armies, to see if Jodl could do any better. While Ike smoked and fidgeted in his office down the hall, Jodl presented a renewed case to Smith for a "West-only" surrender. But Jodl was negotiating against Ike's son-of-a-bitch at his son-of-a-bitchiest. If Beetle had played tough with the Italians in '43, it was nothing to what he was prepared to do with the real enemy. He showed Jodl a map revealing the next Allied-Soviet offensive—a complete fabrication, actually—and promised the Bavarian that if Germany did not surrender on both fronts by midnight, he would break off negotiations, seal the western border, and continue to slaughter Jodl's people.[90]

Jodl stalled, but Beetle's ultimatum deprived him of any maneuvering room. Jodl called his superiors, and at one thirty on the morning of Monday, May 7, he returned to Reims with authority to accept the demand of unconditional surrender.

SHAEF's war room. Wall-size maps with slashing red and blue arrows. Klieg lights and cameras lined against the cluttered walls, cables snaking over the floor. Generals, aides, WACs, guards, journalists. All of them cramming into the classroom to witness one of history's turning points.

Into this surreal scene Jodl and von Friedeburg arrived, their gray uniforms sharply pressed under long, black leather coats. As they sat down, the squad of cameramen opened fire, bulbs flashing and shutters snapping at the impassive faces of the Thousand-Year Reich's surviving ministers. At 2:41 a.m. Jodl put his gold pen to the Act of Military Surrender as every man and woman in the room stared in silence.

But among the bevy of generals watching the dreaded Reich give up its ghost, one face was missing.[91]

Eisenhower's.

Ike had despised the men who had overrun his ancestral homeland and forced his nation into 1,244 days of bloodshed. He did not consider the war against Nazism a romantic, gentlemanly affair among professional soldiers, and he was not a man to shake hands with a vanquished field marshal, congratulate him on a jolly good show, and offer him his sword back with a toast to peace and friendship. When von Arnim had surrendered Tunisia in 1943, Ike refused to meet with him, declaring, "I won't shake hands with a Nazi." Since that first victory, Ike's bile toward Hitler's minions had only grown thicker and blacker. The horrors of the camps, the blitz bombings, the vengeance weapons, prisoner massacres, looted treasures, ravaged villages, and an immense dossier of other crimes had hardened his heart against the German people. On that Monday in May, the man in the jet-black coat was, to Eisenhower, an ambassador of evil.[92]

As a matter of principle, Ike refused to see Jodl or any other German before the instruments of surrender were signed. In his office down the hall, he squirmed and paced as his subalterns concluded the transaction without him. He slumped, he fretted, he inhaled long drags on smokes, and to Kay, General of the Army Dwight David Eisenhower, victor of Africa, Sicily, and Western Europe, did not look like a man at the moment of supreme triumph. Studying him with a woman's eye, she thought his long, drooping face was the window to a lonely, pathetic soul.[93]

When word reached Eisenhower that the surrender documents had been signed, Ike summoned Jodl to his office for a single interview, which he hoped to make brief. He stood stiffly behind his desk, Tedder at his side, Telek growling under his desk, as jackboots marched into his office. Dispensing with pleasantries and formalities, Ike asked Jodl whether he understood the terms of surrender. The sour-faced Jodl answered in the affirmative. Eisenhower, ice piercing his words, curtly told Jodl he would be held personally responsible for any violation of its terms.

"That is all," he said, and the interview ended.[94]

After Jodl left, Ike's body and mind relaxed. His breath came easy now, and he gathered Beetle, Strong, Tedder, Mickey, Kay, and others in the war room for a photograph the world would never forget: a beaming Eisenhower holding two gold surrender pens, which he formed into a Churchillian "V" for "Victory."[95]

After several minutes of smiles, laughter, and more photos, Ike turned on his heel and went back to his office. Completing a round of calls to announce the cease-fire deadline—the first one was to Omar Bradley—a tired Ike Eisenhower slumped into a chair at his quarters. Munching on a fried-egg sandwich, courtesy of Mickey, he pondered what to tell the Combined Chiefs in his next cable. Aides suggested a number of heroic-sounding phrases, lines that rang magnificently within the confines of Ike's office.

But Ike sensed those bromides would sound corny or fall flat when read to the folks of Kansas, the folks of Middle America. So Eisenhower nodded along, politely thanked their authors, and dismissed them graciously.[96]

Then he dictated a single sentence:

THE MISSION OF THE ALLIED FORCE WAS FULFILLED AT 0241, LOCAL TIME, MAY 7TH, 1945.

—EISENHOWER.[97]

TWENTY-FIVE

CLOSING THE SHOP

The more I see of people, the more I regret that I survived the war.

—George, September 22, 1945

RINGING.

George blinked as he shook off the morning fog. He lifted his head off the pillow. He was lying in the darkness of his trailer, and the ringing in his ears was the Green Phone, the long, thin wire that connected him to Twelfth Army Group headquarters.

With a heavy effort, he craned his arm to the receiver and picked it up.[1]

"It's all over, George," came the melodic voice on the end of the line. Bradley. George listened.

"Ike has just telephoned from Reims. The German has surrendered, effective midnight tomorrow, May 8. As of now, everyone is to stay put in line."[2]

So that was it. His war was over.

George grasped the implications at once, for he had been anticipating this call for a long time. He had begged Marshall for anything from a division up in China or one of the frontline islands, when the war in Europe ended. But the War Department, he had learned, wouldn't consider it. The problem, a friend in Washington told him, was that Patton's bypass and flank methods were well suited to fighting Germans, but not the Japanese. These tactics wouldn't work on the small islands of the Pacific, since most positions on small islands could not be bypassed; if the island couldn't be

★ 518 ★

"hopped," the defenders had to be rooted out with grenade, flamethrower, and shell.[3]

That was the reason they gave him. But inside, Patton knew the real reason: The Pacific was MacArthur's show, and Mac didn't want another big shot in his ballpark any more than Monty wanted one in his. When no further encouraging news came from General Marshall or his emissaries about a posting in China, Wedemeyer's theater, George sank into the reality that he would never see battle again. His place in history was now fixed. He had reached the end of his life as a warrior.[4]

"There is a species of whale," Patton told his staff on May 9, "which is said to spend much of its time lying on the bottom of the deepest part of the ocean. I don't mind saying at the present moment I feel lower than that whale's arse." Content with this metaphor, he repeated it to Beatrice, adding, *I love war and responsibility and excitement. Peace is going to be hell on me. I will probably be a great nuisance.*[5]

Four days after Jodl's surrender, Patton and Opie Weyland flew to Bad Wildungen for an "all-American" luncheon hosted by Bradley in honor of the Supreme Commander, the American army commanders, and their air officers. It was an elegant feast among the victors, the first of many to be held in a land stripped of its food, people, and industry. After the last course was finished and the valets had cleared the plates, the wineglasses were refilled and Eisenhower excused everyone except his senior commanders. The MPs shut the doors and took their places outside.[6]

A cigarette in his left hand, Ike's blue eyes flashed around the table. A congressional investigation was coming, he told them. It was inevitable, always had been. Politicians would review the war's conduct, comb through reports, question officers, and judge whether there were mistakes made—or scapegoats to be slaughtered.

It had been a long, tough struggle, Ike said, and every man had done his duty. But it was important that every general in the American command maintain a united front when called before Congress or interviewed by congressional gumshoes. They needed to keep the record clear and consistent, to avoid their stewardship of blood and treasure becoming the target of politically motivated attacks. Ike also stressed the need for America's generals to cooperate with America's allies—the Soviets, the French, the Chinese, and, especially, the British.

George, watching his old friend carefully, was dubious. He saw political motives behind Ike's words, and he told his diary, *"It is my opinion that this talking cooperation is for the purpose of covering up probable criticism of strategic blunders which he unquestionably committed during the campaign. Whether or not these were his own or due to too much cooperation with the British, I don't know. I am inclined to think that he over-cooperated."*[7]

The War Department put General Patton's reputation as a fighter to one last use when Marshall and Ike ordered Bradley to line Patton's tanks up along the Enns River, to back down Marshal Tito, who was raising hell in northern Yugoslavia. Tito backed down, and that was the end of George's wartime career.[8]

As in Casablanca, Patton's next assignment was an administrative function. The Third Army straddled Bavaria, and as its commanding general, Eisenhower installed Patton as the military governor of the Eastern District of Bavaria. There from his headquarters—a former SS officer training school—Patton would oversee the denazification of the birthplace of Nazism.[9]

But before he could get to work in Bavaria, the War Department summoned George back to the United States, where he would make a round of war bond and victory tours, paired with fellow Californian General Jimmy Doolittle. For good publicity, of course. Because George made for good publicity.

Although he spent most of his post-VE days celebrating with General Eisenhower, attending banquets with the Soviets, and pinch-hitting as Supreme Commander during Ike's brief victory tour of the United States, Bradley's dark eyes, like George's, were fixed on the Pacific. He had told an aide back in August, "I want only one more amphibious invasion, [and] that's the invasion of Japan," and with the fighting over in Europe, General MacArthur could take the cream of Ike's crop for his Pacific war. And who better to take than the commander of Twelfth Army Group, the leader of four armies and 1.3 million men? MacArthur had gladly accepted Hodges and his First Army headquarters staff, and Bradley figured there was an even chance that Mac would take him on as an army group commander. After all, Brad wasn't a showboater, like Patton, and he didn't have a history with MacArthur, like Eisenhower.[10]

Problem was, Bradley was a four-star army group commander. While the Pacific was a vast theater, it had little real estate, and what fighting ground there was had to be divided between the Army and the Marines. With Mac's entire force totaling only 800,000 men, a half million fewer than Brad's own group, it would be a hard sell to wedge in a second group leader.

In fact, it was an impossible sell. Hodges was acceptable to MacArthur because he was quiet, capable, and an *army* commander. Bradley met only two of those three entrance requirements. On April 25, General Marshall cabled Eisenhower: "MACARTHUR DOES NOT ANTICIPATE ANY ARMY GROUP COMMANDERS IN JAPANESE HOMELAND OPERATION OTHER THAN HIMSELF. WOULD BRADLEY CARE TO GO OUT AS AN ARMY COMMANDER WITH THE PRESENT GROUP STAFF?"[11]

In Bradley's office at Wiesbaden, an aide called him to the phone; telephone call from General Eisenhower. Taking the call, Brad listened carefully as Ike asked him whether he'd be willing to transfer to the Pacific as an army commander. Brad voiced his concern that the American Army in Europe would look like small potatoes if Bradley, an army group commander, begged for a mere army command under MacArthur. It was not about himself, he assured Ike; he was no prima donna. But it would reflect badly on the men serving under his command if their leader took a demotion of sorts just to get onto the Pacific team. With little enthusiasm in his voice, he managed to intone the words basic to his duty: "I will serve anywhere in any position that General Marshall assigns me."[12]

Whether Brad's objections were driven by pride, career, or the interests of his men, Ike was reluctant to put Bradley in that position. He passed his thoughts on Bradley's reassignment to the Chief: *"To give him an army assignment in the Pacific would make it appear to all soldiers in this theater and to the public that this war was a rather minor league or easy affair . . . such an assignment would have the further effect of diminishing Bradley's stature in the post-war army and public opinion and it is my conviction that we should prevent any such possibility at all costs."* Ike added, "in the remote eventuality that anything should happen to me, Bradley is the logical person to succeed my position." While the Missourian told Ike he would go wherever Marshall sent him, Ike wrote, *"I distinctly got the impression that he feels that to go to the Pacific as an army commander would be belittling in the American mind the magnitude of American accomplishments here, and the services of more than 3,000,000 U.S. soldiers."*[13]

Next day, Marshall wrote back to tell Eisenhower that Bradley was no longer in the running for the Pacific. Ike passed along word, and with that, Omar Bradley's thoughts of moving to the war's final battlefield died.[14]

Ike shared none of Brad's illusions about the Pacific. He and MacArthur had parted on bad terms back in '39, and the Pacific was simply not big enough for two five-star Army generals. Ike knew his job of waging war was over; his next task would be to establish the occupation force in Germany, begin the demobilization process, ensure against rebellion, and get home for that long fishing trip he had been planning since 1942. He even toyed with the idea of resigning his commission when he got home—not merely retiring—so he would be free to speak his mind in support of the nation's military preparedness.[15]

But on May 17, when an aide handed him a cable from Washington, his stomach churned anew. The cable told Ike that Marshall, the Army's Rock of Gibraltar, the most trusted man in government, was going to ask President Truman to release him from active duty. Marshall was going to retire.

Then it came to him.

If Marshall leaves they'll probably make me Chief of Staff.

Ike had said before that he didn't want the job. Before the German surrender, he had a war to run, and he liked being in the middle of the war. He held real command, accepted real responsibility, made real strategy. The wellspring of Ike's prodigious energies was the mission, and victory over Hitler was the goal his eyes had fixed upon that far-off day in 1942, when he became "the Guy."[16]

But the guns were silent, and Ike wanted a Telegraph Cottage, maybe somewhere in rural Pennsylvania, where his job would be to grow the biggest vegetables and fry the freshest fish. The Army Chief of Staff position was a desk function, a *political* function, nestled in the deepest part of that great marble cesspool of intrigue. Worse yet, the next Chief of Staff would preside over the dismemberment of an army Ike had devoted so much of his life to building. He remembered the wind falling from his sails as he dismantled Camp Colt after the last war. He remembered the demotions and the pay cuts that accompanied the 1920 Demobilization Act. Would he want to do that to men who trusted him on a far larger scale? The prospect of haggling with Congress over how deeply the Army would be cut was repugnant to any soldier, and the last thing an exhausted Eisenhower wanted to preside over was an army in decline.

The cable told Ike something else, something of concern to his closest friend: President Truman was having trouble with the Veterans Administration. The press was howling about how bureaucratic, politicized, and dysfunctional the bureau had become. Acknowledging that the news would be a "great disappointment" to Bradley, Truman wanted to know if General Bradley was available to take it over.[17]

He might just as well have asked if Brad would be willing to join the Navy. If Brad didn't cotton to an army command in the Pacific, what would he say to a desk job with an overwhelmed, embarrassed War Department bureau? But Ike dutifully picked up the phone and called Brad, who was entertaining Soviet Marshal Ivan Koniev at his headquarters in Kassel. "[A]s soon as he leaves," Ike said, "come on back to Reims and spend the night with me. I've got something to take up with you."[18]

Omar Nelson Bradley, Commanding General, Twelfth Army Group, was looking forward to a well-deserved leave. There were the expected formalities, of course—banquets, toasts, exchanges of medals, photo sessions, and, he hoped, the victory parades that would soon bring him home to Mary and Lee. Like his brother officers, he had grown used to the frantic pace, the high station, the publicity, the raw power, and the importance of military command during wartime. Having commanded 1.3 million men in combat, he didn't relish the prospect of lengthy occupation duty, an administrative post that men like Lucius Clay or Beetle Smith were better equipped to handle. If he couldn't fight, he looked forward to a return to life as a simple soldier, and he had joked that after the war he would go back to Fort Benning, because the fishing and hunting there were great.[19]

Looking ahead, however, Bradley did have his eye on one administrative post, the Chief of Staff job, one in which he hoped to become a worthy successor to General Marshall. So when Eisenhower called from Reims on March 17, he was not surprised when Ike's voice carried a tone of gravity seeping over the scrambler lines. Scurrying to Reims, Brad was shown to the Supreme Commander's quarters. The Kansan was seated in a comfortable chair, sipping a bourbon with his British aide, Jimmy Gault. Ike waved Brad in and pointed to a cable he was holding.

"Brad, before I show you this, you had better pour yourself a good stiff drink," he said.[20]

Bradley nodded. The ice cracked as the amber fluid flowed into the glass. He sat down and Ike handed him the telegram.

Brad's heart skipped a beat as he saw the reference to Marshall's relief. But when he got to the second paragraph, his heart nearly stopped.

The Veterans Administration?

The idea floored him. He had been living in trailers, tents, and captured palaces for over two years. He was king of nearly everything he surveyed. He had become a god of the battlefield—at least, if gods worked with committees and had unwieldy staffs—and he had never remotely considered asking for, or even accepting, a post so demeaning, so bureaucratic, so inconsequential.[21]

Calm down, Ike said in a reassuring tone. The backstory, he explained, was that Ike was going to take the chief of staff post for only two years, rather than the usual four, and once he had completed his two years, he would do everything in his power to have Bradley appointed his successor. Hell, if he could get Brad the job *now*, he would. Marshall's cable had suggested only that Truman wanted Bradley for "probably a year or two," so it wasn't a long sentence. Taking the job would also show Truman that Bradley was a true team player. And as Bradley knew better than most, team play was rewarded.[22]

Brad slowed down and reflected. The war was over—his war, at least—and balking at the president's request was not the way to get his postwar career off the ground. He would take the job if that was what Ike and the Chief wanted.[23]

In early July, Brad began wrapping up his affairs in Europe. As a member of the board to decide the fate of the Army's bloated general ranks, one of Brad's jobs was to prepare an efficiency report on his senior men. Though he would evaluate many officers, the ones he would begin with, his lieutenants at the highest echelon, included Generals Simpson, Gerow, Hodges, and Patton.

Patton. Having spent virtually his entire wartime career with George—under, alongside, and above him—he, more than any other man except Ike, should have been able to give the War Department a succinct, neat summary of the man of so many contradictions. Setting aside the hurt feelings of Mostaganem, the bitterness of Sicily, and his doubts in England, Brad came to terms with the man who had been his mentor, his tormentor, his confidant, and, in a strange way, his friend. Of General George Patton, he wrote: "Courageous, colorful, a great showman, sometimes shows anger too readily but really is very kind-hearted, possesses high degree of leadership, bold in operations. . . . One of our great combat leaders."[24]

* * *

Shortly before he left for the States, Brad sat down at his desk and wrote several farewell letters to his closest associates. The men who had helped him through twenty-six months of the fiercest combat the world had ever known. To the men who had made Omar Nelson Bradley, that obscure officer from southern Missouri, a hero to millions. One of these letters read:

Dear George:

I expect to leave this Theater on July 21. This will officially end our close relationship, which has existed with only short interruptions since March 7, 1942. We have seen a lot of fighting during that time and have had the satisfaction of being in at the victorious conclusion of three campaigns.

It has been a pleasure to serve with you, and I know of no one whom I would rather have on the team on which I was fighting. In particular, I want to thank you and congratulate you on the magnificent accomplishments of you and your Army during the invasion of the Continent. I also want to thank you for your loyal personal support at all times.

I will be looking forward to shooting skeet with you after the war, and again here I want to be on the same team. . . .

So long, good luck, and may our paths cross often in the future.

Sincerely,
Brad[25]

That same day, Ike, sitting at his desk, dictated a letter that read:

Dear Brad:

I have already sent to my former principal subordinates, including yourself, in the Allied organization, a rather formal letter of appreciation of their services. In your own case I cannot resist the urge, upon your departure to the United States, to attempt once more to give some expression of the personal sense of gratitude and admiration I feel towards you.

Since you first joined me in North Africa in early 1942 I have consistently depended, with perfect confidence, upon your counsel and advice. . . . In my opinion you are pre-eminent among the Commanders of major battle units in this war. Your leadership, forcefulness, professional capacity, selflessness, high sense of duty and sympathetic understanding of human beings, combine to stamp you as one of America's great leaders and soldiers. . . .

From your old friend,
Ike[26]

Before he took the reins of OVERLORD, Ike had wondered aloud to Mamie,

whether anyone who has carried heavy responsibilities and has had to jump constantly from hither to thither to yon can really settle down and live a serene life. The eternal pound, pound, pound seems a burden, but when it once ceases it is possible that many of us will be will nigh unto nervous wrecks, and wholly unfit for normal life.[27]

But in 1945 Ike Eisenhower was making the transition to peacetime magnificently, returning at a higher plane than when he left it that abrupt day in December 1941. In late May, his bloated entourage—it now included a train, two cows, three Scottish terriers, Shaef the cat, jeeps, billiard and Ping-Pong tables, a movie projector, and a portable generator, in addition to the general's baggage and a household staff—moved into a country home in Bad Homburg, twelve miles from Frankfurt. His office staff set up shop in the IG Farben Industries building in Frankfurt, practically the only large building in the city that hadn't been flattened by five-hundred-pound bombs during the last three years. He went home in mid-June for a victory parade, with the usual round of speeches, war bond drives, photo opportunities, and more speeches, and Ike was briefly reunited with Mamie, then with West Point, then with Abilene. The visits, so long overdue, brought new warmth into that all-too-often-forced smile, and the America of 1945 reminded Ike why he had fought so hard, for so long.[28]

* * *

In July, as the curtain dropped on Eisenhower's combat command, the War Department approached him about a movie of his life, to be written by dramatist Robert Sherwood and produced by MGM's Samuel Goldwyn. It was to be an ambitious picture with a budget of $3 million to $4 million. The profits of the film, the producers agreed, would fund exchange scholarships for British and American university students, as well as a foundation for education against racial discrimination. Ike wrote to Brad and George, telling them the producers wanted actors to portray key players in the story of Eisenhower's war and asking for their opinion.[29]

George was wary of this kind of publicity. He had long known how fickle the press could be, and he had no wish to toss up a goofball caricature of himself now that he was a genuine war hero. A movie portrayal of himself was hardly the best way of ensuring his own legacy.

On the other hand, Ike was one of his oldest friends, a man to whom he owed much. Ike most likely saw the motion picture as a springboard to the White House, and it was not much to ask. So the on-again, off-again loyal soldier sent a letter back to Ike: *"I would have no objection . . . provided he does not have me impersonated by a bandit and also provided it does not give other movie people the right to make movies about me."* He added, *"I am sure, too, that it is going to be quite difficult to find two bald headed old men to impersonate you and myself."*[30]

The team's last bugle call blew at the Potsdam Conference between Truman, Churchill, who would be recalled to England when the voters of his home district turned him out, and Stalin, whose twenty million dead citizens entitled him, as he saw it, to set the agenda for Eastern Europe. For Ike, Brad, and George, the gathering was purely ceremonial, reminiscent of Patton's "Palace Guard" days at Fort Myer. None of them had any responsibilities, other than to stand with Truman, stiff at attention, for salutes to the Stars and Stripes while the national anthem played.

But for that last team review, they indeed looked like the core of a brotherhood that had overthrown an empire. General Patton, resplendent in his shining battle helmet and polished boots, stood alongside a sharply creased Ike and Brad. Pressed together with the rest of the American high command, the three men saluted as the colors waved and the Big Three ushered in the uncertain era of *pax Americana.*

* * *

In June the War Department double-billed George Patton and Jimmy Doolittle on a victory tour, complete with whistle stops, speeches, and ticker-tape parades in Boston and Los Angeles. It was the return George had envisioned, an Americanized Roman *triumph*, the ancient procession down the Via Sacra accorded to the old republic's greatest generals.

But it gave Patton none of the thrill he savored in Germany, and he kept his handlers on edge every time he opened his mouth. His Press Relations Officer, Major James Quirk, told his wife he was "scared to death" over what Patton might say when the general stepped before an uncensored microphone, and Doolittle recalled that when Patton spoke to a crowd of 100,000 cheering fans at the Los Angeles Coliseum, the Army had "a little guy sitting under the podium with a switch to turn Georgie off if Georgie said anything he shouldn't."[31]

The little guy under the podium wasn't quick enough. Patton's speech, as recounted in the paper, was classic Blood and Guts, full of chest-thumping bombast and thoughtless quotes like "men were frequently fools when they got killed in battle"—the kinds of things that shocked the families of the 135,000 men who died in the European Theater of Operations, to say nothing of the War Department's political echelons.[32]

As in 1919, peacetime America was a world George simply could not penetrate. After so much destruction in Europe, he still saw war as a burnishing fire in which to temper the greatest attributes of the human spirit. He refused to believe, as one German general had remarked, that war is the worst possible way to distill the best in a nation's blood, because there the bravest soldiers tend to die first. In 1945, too many families of brave soldiers lived with this truth every moment of their lives.[33]

Echoing Eisenhower's words to Mamie, George wrote,

> *the whole attitude of the people in America is quite inimical to that which exists in Europe. None of them realizes that one cannot fight for two and a half years and be the same. Yet you are expected to get back into the identical groove from which you departed and from which your non-warlike compatriots have never moved.*[34]

On the day the rest of the world celebrated the victory over Japan, George saw the end of his life looming near. "Another war has ended, and with it my usefulness to the world," he wrote in his diary. "It is for me personally a very sad thought. Now all that is left to do is to sit around and await the arrival of the undertaker and posthumous immortality." With no definite job in the peacetime world, George had become the lucky card player who, after the game breaks up, sits alone, looking into the faces of passersby for anyone interested in a new game. But after four years of blood and mourning, there were no takers.[35]

That summer George returned to Germany a melancholy, tired man. He scrounged for something productive to do, and he lobbied for a new assignment when Eisenhower visited him in mid-September. The two men had another of their late-night talks that stretched until three in the morning, where they discussed George's future in light of Ike's move to Washington and General McNarney's transfer to head the ETO, which would make him Patton's new boss. George told him, "I did not care to serve under General McNarney, not because I had anything personal against him but because I thought it unseemly for a man with my combat record to serve under a man who had never heard a gun go off."[36]

All right, asked Ike, what job would you accept?

"There were only two jobs in the United States which I felt I could take," said George. "One was President of the Army War College, which I believed was taken, and the other was Commanding General of the Army Ground Forces."

Ike nodded. Either would be appropriate. The problem was, those jobs were changing, as the services were being reorganized into one great Department of Defense. The War College would soon expand to include the Navy and Air Force, and it would probably get a naval officer for its next president. As for the AGF, well, Ike would not mind replacing the current incumbent, General Devers, with George. But with the establishment of the Air Force as its own branch in the new organization, there would be no reason for having an Army "Ground" Force, and that job would likely be phased out.

The fact apparent to Ike, more than to George, was that times were changing. The world was changing, and the Regular Army, the army of Black Jack and the horse soldier, the army George and Ike had grown up with, was becoming a thing of the past.

"Therefore, at the present writing it would seem the only thing I can do is go home and retire," wrote George. *"However, General Eisenhower asked me*

to remain at least three months after he left so as to get things running quietly. I tentatively agreed to do this."[37]

"Ike, when we finish licking these bastards, I want you to make me the Heinrich Himmler of the occupation. I'll show them a reign of terror like they have never imagined."

That was a gleeful Patton in 1944, sitting in the teak-paneled living room of Bayonet as he, Eisenhower, and a small retinue of brass clicked their way up England's railroad tracks to visit the 35th Division. At the time, Ike looked upon his bellicose friend with annoyance, perhaps a little embarrassment.[38]

Since the invasion, Ike's attitude toward his former enemies had changed, and so had Patton's. The prisoner massacres, SS child soldiers, death camps, blitz bombings, and the misery of millions had lit an unquenchable coal that burned within his breast as the German empire crumbled. Patton, by contrast, had fallen behind the postwar attitudes Eisenhower embodied, and Ike must have begun to feel that his decision to have George installed as military governor of Bavaria was an ill-conceived one. George's latent anti-Semitism bubbled to the surface whenever he visited a camp for "displaced persons"—the Allied designation for a quarter million Jews, Slavs, and other groups who allowed themselves to be conquered—and his disgust for "DPs" ran particularly high with groups that failed to keep their compounds in good order. After a visit to one camp, he told his diary, he and Eisenhower "returned home and went for a fishing trip on the lake which, while not successful, at least removed from our minds the nauseous odors and aspects of the camps we had inspected. We then took as long and as hot a bath as we could stand, to remove from our persons the germs which must have accumulated during the day."[39]

In fact, with the exception of the French, a people he would always hold dear, George didn't give a damn for any people weak enough to be overrun, be they Arab, Sicilian, Jew, Pole, or, though momentarily on top, Russian. He was the product of a secure, proud family in a part of the world that had never seen the ravages of war, and chauvinism was part and parcel of Patton's mentality, a Bushido code he would not have cared to admit he shared with the Japanese warriors on the far side of the world. As governor of a quarter million displaced persons living in former concentration camps, he rendered the following verdict on his wards: *"I have seen them from the beginning and marveled that beings alleged to be made in the form of God can look the way they do, or act the way they act.*"[40]

The biggest problem confronting the military governor of the Eastern District of Bavaria—and the commanding general of Third U.S. Army—was the care and feeding of Bavaria's civilian population without employing any former National Socialists. The Nazis had held a monopoly on administrative jobs for the last twelve years, and George was having a hell of a time keeping the sewers running and getting food to the locals. From his headquarters in Bad Tölz, south of Munich, he wrote, "It is very evident that anybody who was in business, irrespective of his real sentiments, had to say he was a Nazi and pay dues. The only young people who were not Nazis came out of the internment camps and are therefore either Jews or Communists. We are certainly in a hard position as far as procuring civil servants is concerned." In a letter to Eisenhower, he complained, "It is no more possible for a man to be a civil servant in Germany and not have paid lip service to Nazism than it is possible for a man to be a postmaster in America and not have paid at least lip service to the Democratic Party, or the Republican Party when it is in power."[41]

But Ike was a true believer. To rid the world of the scourge of Nazism was his vow, and he meant to keep that vow with the determination of a holy abbot—in Ike's case, an abbot who didn't mind executing or exiling a few thousand German officers. Ike had issued stringent orders on the subject of removal of former Nazis, and he was confident within his element when laying down the law of occupied territory, a fact George should have learned when he suggested that Ike distribute penicillin to French whorehouses the previous fall.

But when he replied to George, Ike didn't so much disagree with his position on the Nazis as reaffirm basic Allied policy that "all members of the Nazi Party who have been more than nominal participants in its activities . . . be removed and excluded from public office and from positions of responsibility in private enterprise." He assured George, "I believe our directive will permit the continued operation of necessary services such as railroads, telephone and other utilities. . . . I therefore think we should continue our earnest effort to carry out the denazification directives given to us by the Joint Chiefs of Staff. . . ."

Whether because of inadvertence, or uncharacteristically poor wording, or merely not realizing the depth of his friend's disagreement with Allied policies, Ike's rabid anti-Nazi feelings did not come through clearly enough for George to understand how hot this issue had become with his friend.[42]

As the weeks passed, George's impatience with Allied policy grew from quiet discontent into barely concealed hostility. "What the Military Government is trying to do is undemocratic and follows practically Gestapo methods," he complained privately in late August. When ordered to hand German prisoners over to the French to be used as forced labor, he jibed, "It is amusing to recall that we fought the Revolution in defense of the rights of man, and the Civil War to abolish slavery, and we have now gone back on both principles." He grew bitter at the press, which no longer had to curry favor with a general who couldn't censor their stories, and after ranting to his diary about the arrogance of the newspapers and the shortsightedness of American policies, he wrote, "The more I see of people, the more I regret that I survived the war."[43]

When he fought the Germans, George fought them with heart and soul. He had once cussed out a group of soldiers during bayonet practice in North Africa, screaming, "That's a German! You don't hate him enough. You're all too gentlemanly. Just because you've been brought up not to kick your grandmother in the ass, don't think he hasn't, because he has—they all have. They are the lowest sons of bitches that crawl the earth, except perhaps the Japs. . . ."[44]

But with the war's end, the German was just another ex-competitor, and Patton saw National Socialists as, more or less, just another defrocked political party—albeit one that needed to get the boot because it had the temerity to challenge the United States. Because political parties were of little concern to Patton, he began dipping his toe into the dangerous tides of political opinion. A year before, when asked about rank-and-file Nazis living among the German people, he replied, "How many million Democrats are there now? How many will there be if the Republicans come in. The Nazis are a political party really and not a fraternity, and when they find their people are out they will join the other side. I have a relative who has been Postmaster of Glendale, California under every form of government. He votes with both hands." On the day the Germans surrendered, he had told the press,

SS means no more in Germany than being a Democrat in America—that is not to be quoted. I mean by that that initially the SS people were sons-of-bitches, but as the war progressed, they ran out of sons-of-bitches and then they put anybody in there. Some of the top SS men will be treated as criminals, but there is no reason for trying someone who was drafted into this outfit.[45]

George knew quotes like that, if publicized, could get him sent home. He had once remarked in passing, "It is funny that I have never had any doubts about licking the Germans any place I meet them. The only question in my mind is being able to survive the lapses between campaigns when I always seem to get myself into trouble." During his first week of combat with Third Army, he had told reporters of another general who, Patton said, "was quoted as saying nothing stopped him but orders from higher authority. That is the way they ruin a man like that. You get canned on stuff like that. That is what gets him sent home; I am not fooling."[46]

But Patton's antipathy toward displaced persons, his distrust of the Reds, his admiration for the German war record, his frustration with a broken Bavarian government, and the discharge or reassignment of moderating influences like Charlie Codman and Major Quirk meant he could not avoid saying something that would land him in the doghouse. True to form, the moment came when he was speaking off the cuff to reporters he had invited to sit in on a staff meeting at his headquarters in Bad Tölz.

The staff briefing on the twenty-second of September was a small affair, posted on the headquarters bulletin board only three days earlier. Only eleven reporters showed up, and no stenographer was present. After the briefing was over, while maps were being removed and staffers shuffled out of the room, journalists Edward P. Morgan of the *Chicago Daily News*, Carl Levin of the *New York Herald Tribune*, and Raymond Daniell of *The New York Times* asked General Patton if he would answer a few questions.[47]

George later insisted that he had been sandbagged. He hadn't intended to answer any questions, and had tried to leave when the newsmen persisted. He grudgingly gave them only four and a half minutes of his time, and the reporters used those four and a half minutes to box him into another headline-grabbing gaffe. They began asking him very pointed, almost combative questions about his handling of Nazis in Bavaria, the numbers of Nazis still employed, and why he hadn't gotten rid of more; they argued with him over his denazification orders, and, Hap Gay claimed, put words in his mouth. Patton defended himself, arguing that if he threw out accused managers indiscriminately with winter coming, the resulting leadership vacuum would cause the deaths of many elderly, children, and women through sickness and lack of adequate necessities. With the reporters hounding him for more answers, he took his leave and rejoined his staff.[48]

George did not take the implied criticism seriously, but he grumbled in his diary that night, "There is a very apparent Semitic influence in the press. They are trying to do two things: first, implement Communism and second, see that all businessmen of German ancestry and non-Jewish antecedents are thrown out of their jobs. They have utterly lost the Anglo-Saxon conception of justice and feel that a man can be kicked out because somebody else says he was a Nazi."

But the more George reflected on his responses to their questions, the more his uneasiness grew. "If people have time to read anything besides the number of points which will get a soldier home," he wrote, "I will probably make the front page, but, frankly, do not give a damn."[49]

He was essentially right on both counts. On September 23 the *Times* ran a headline that screamed, "PATTON BELITTLES DENAZIFICATION." The article found Patton's views to conflict with Eisenhower's directives and the ideals laid down at the Potsdam Conference, and it declared, "The most surprising statement of many that the general—who declared himself much given to 'hyperbole'—made in the course of the remarkable discussion was that the Nazi thing is just like a Democrat and Republican election fight." The next day, the *Times* opined, "When, therefore, General Patton belittles the very purpose for which the war in Europe was fought—namely, the denazification of Germany—we do not believe his remarks should go unchallenged by his commanding officer, General Eisenhower, or by his superiors in Washington."[50]

Two days after the article ran, Beetle Smith placed a phone call to Bad Tölz. He chided Patton in a friendly sort of way, remarking that because George was one of his best friends, he had caused Beetle more trouble than any other man in the theater. His voice cooling, he began to read aloud clippings from headlines in the States. This was serious business, he said.[51]

George's bile rose from his craw. The war was over, he snapped, and if the press didn't like the way he ran things in Bavaria, he would resign his commission so he could fight back in public.[52]

Don't go overboard, Beetle told him. There were going to be a lot of changes in the European Theater, now that the Army was demobilizing, and both he and George might be out of jobs soon anyway. But for now, to control the damage, Beetle told him to hold a follow-up press conference and give the reporters a written statement to clarify what he really meant. To set the record straight. This George agreed to do.[53]

If George thought a written statement would suffice, he soon learned otherwise. After suppertime, a telegram arrived at Bad Tölz from Eisenhower's headquarters. "Press reports make it appear that you and I are of opposite conviction concerning methods to be pursued in denazification of Germany, and that in spite of repeated orders, you have given public expression to your own views on the matter," it said. As Patton claimed he had been misquoted, he was instructed to hold a press conference to clarify his remarks. "I hope you are completely successful because this question is a very serious one," Ike warned. After his press conference, George was to send General Eisenhower a complete report detailing the numbers of former Nazis still in official positions, then fly up to Ike's headquarters as soon as the weather would allow for a personal interview.[54]

George knew what that meant. He had been to Ike's woodshed so many times before, he could draw the damned shed from memory. He admitted to himself, "It may well be that the Philistines have at last got me." He also told Bea, "If Ike etc. don't like what I do they can relieve me then I will resign not retire and can tell the world a few truths which will be worth hearing."[55]

Unfortunately, George's second press conference only dug his six-by-three hole deeper. He declared himself wholly committed to the Allied policy of denazification, but Daniell and the *Times* editorial board declared that his clarification did not go far enough to repair the "damage done by his remarks." Beetle Smith told the press, in an extraordinarily public rebuke, "[Patton's] mouth does not always carry out the functions of his brain. George acts on the theory that it is better to be damned than say nothing."[56]

Ike erupted into a fury, a real, Midwestern-swearing, red-faced fury as he stared at the news reports. Election year or not, this kind of thing was something no administration, no two-party system, could tolerate. The public and Congress would work itself into a frenzy again, and editorialists from the *Times* and the *Daily News* were stoking the fires with fresh columns each weekday. As he told Mamie, after calming down a bit, "George Patton has broken into print again in a big way. That man is going to drive me to drink. He misses more good opportunities to keep his mouth shut than almost anyone I ever knew."[57]

Of course, it was not like Ike couldn't have foreseen George saying something stupid. George was no politician, and he had given him the post of military governor because it was the only place he could put an old friend who was a four-star general. But he wasn't cleaning house. Ike had been hearing unsettling reports about former Nazis holding high office in Bavaria. His civil government staff chief, Brigadier General Clarence L. Adcock, was telling him that Walter Dorn, a former history professor from Ohio State University, told him that Patton was allowing right-wingers under the banner of the Christian Social Union party to run the government in a kind of neo-Nazi fashion. Eleven days before Patton's press remarks, Ike had felt the need to remind George that the denazification issue "had long been decided. We will not compromise with Naziism in any way." Patton, he said, would have to keep the water running and the houses heated without using former Nazi party members, no matter what his field officers and local administrators might say.[58]

George had run up whopping bills with Ike before. The Navy. Sitrep. The Sicily paratroopers. The hospitals. Knutsford, Hammelburg, and who the hell knew how many more stories Ike didn't catch wind of during their three-year partnership. And, like a merchant in a bull market, George had always been able to pay his bills, since the coin of Ike's realm was not rank, nor bootlicking, nor even politics, but military victory. Enemy dead, enemy captured, towns liberated, ground gained—the Third Army's account alone had paid Ike back for most of George's screwups. As Ike once told Marshall, "He does the kind of fighting I like. . . . I'll take care of Georgie and I'll catch hell once in a while. You will, too, but you better let me have him."[59]

But the guns were silent now, and the market for what George was selling had dried up. His account balance was at zero, and George, being George, was a future liability. Ike could not afford to extend him any more credit, so with this last indiscretion, George would probably have to go. Probably.

* * *

Clad in plain trousers and an Eisenhower jacket, on September 28 Patton drove the three hundred miles to Frankfurt, where Eisenhower had set up his headquarters in the massive Farben Industries building. Once again, he didn't know what destiny had in store for him. As George saw it, he had been to Golgotha before and walked back down on his own power, but as he approached the outskirts of Frankfurt, he pondered what his old friend—the friend who had so often saved him from himself—would say this time. And what he would say back.[60]

He was shown into the Farben boardroom. George shuffled across the long, intimidating boardroom that formed part of Eisenhower's office suite, his shoes echoing on the immaculate floor until he reached the thick carpet where Eisenhower waited. As he stood there, the five-star general launched into a diatribe about George's inability to keep his mouth shut. How he had shown such bad judgment at the worst possible times. How his audacity was a virtue but also a deadly vice. Ike's voice grew in tempo and volume until the crescendo became a five-star bawling out. As Kay put it afterward, it was "one of the stormiest sessions ever staged in our headquarters. It was the first time I ever heard General Eisenhower really raise his voice."[61]

Ike then called in Adcock and Professor Dorn and quizzed them about whether the Ministry of Food could function with its senior Nazis thrown out. After cross-examining the two men for several minutes, Ike reached the conclusion that ex-Nazis in Patton's sector were not indispensible to the safety of Bavaria's citizens. As Dorn later recalled, General Eisenhower "was seized by a holy rage of anger and he asked in vigorous and colorful language 'what the hell' the American army was doing in Germany if not to purify the German government and the administration of notorious and conspicuous Nazis. He said the Russians were killing off the leading Nazis and we were keeping them in office. Then he launched out on a discussion that lasted for some 10 to 15 minutes of the thousands of soldiers he had sent to their certain death in order to destroy this foul and inhuman thing called National Socialism." The Nazis, and any like-minded successors, had to go.[62]

But did Patton also have to go?

George's only defense, as it had been with the Knutsford incident, was that he had been deliberately misquoted, probably by pinks and their liberal friends at the *Times*. Ike knew he might be right. But who could know how many more times Patton would be misquoted? Ike sure didn't.

Ike made up his mind that George, for all his genius at battlefield pursuit, was not the right tool for a world at peace. After rambling about the need to sweep away the vestiges of the Nazi regime for a few minutes, he claimed to be struck by the idea—"probably acting on his part," thought George—that General Patton should take over General Gerow's Fifteenth Army, a rear-echelon outfit tasked with writing the history of the war in Europe. Gee was being transferred home, and for a man with Patton's historical bent, Ike said, Fifteenth Army would be a perfect posting.[63]

George was horrified at the prospect of losing his beloved Third Army, and he saw himself sinking fast. He scrambled to change Ike's perception of the problem. He had fired nearly fifty thousand former Nazis out of a quarter million government employees his army had screened. Statistically, they were cleaning out Nazis better than any other army, and most of the people the press were complaining of, such as the local minister of finance, had been inherited from Patch's Seventh Army when Ike had shifted the army boundaries. He pleaded to remain with his fighting army, not with a desk outfit. He was a four-star general, and it would tarnish his reputation to take over a three-star general's job. No, he said, if he had to leave the Third Army, it would be better for Ike to relieve him and be done with him.[64]

Ike shook his head. He was under no pressure from the States to relieve George, he said, and he would not fire him. But George obviously did not believe in the policies the Allies were pursuing, and it was clear that Patton's staff was taking cues from its commander's privately expressed opinions. The public wanted Germany scoured of Nazi influence, and now that the war was over, conformity with political policy was the most important thing. No, he decided, it was in everyone's best interest to move Patton out of Bavaria. George could have another ten days to wrap up his affairs with Third Army; then he would assume command of the Fifteenth. At half past six Ike put an end to the emotional interview by telling his friend that he was welcome to stay with him overnight if he felt it necessary, "but since I feel you should get back to Bad Tölz as rapidly as possible, I have my train set up to take you and it leaves at seven o'clock."[65]

Ike accompanied George down the long hallway to the exit. The corridor was dotted with reporters who asked what General Eisenhower had said to General Patton. Ike brushed off their questions, muttering, "I have conferences with army commanders whenever I feel like it, period." He assured the reporters that "General Patton and myself remain the best of friends," and he walked George to the door. They shook hands, and then they parted.

Ike aged ten years as he thought about the order he would sign firing his friend.[66]

There was little George could have said to Ike in that large boardroom to change his mind. Like Bradley during the Bulge crisis, Ike's impression had been formed before George could plead his case, and from that impression, there could be but one conclusion. So a forlorn-looking George Patton sat in a train car that clicked and chugged through the beautiful foothills of western Bavaria, pondering his last years in military service.

"If I am kicked upstairs to the Fifteenth Army should I accept or should I ask for relief and put in my resignation?" he asked himself.

> By adopting the latter course I would save my self-respect at the expense of my reputation but on the other hand, would become a martyr too soon. It is my belief that when the catchword "denazification" has worn itself out and when people see it is merely a form of stimulating Bolshevism, there will be a flop of the pendulum in the opposite direction. When that occurs I can state that I accepted the job with the Fifteenth Army because I was reluctant, in fact unwilling, to be a party to the destruction of Germany under the pretense of de-Nazification.[67]

Ike's decision to relieve him, George thought, was a symptom of an ego run amok, a man who had sniffed the aroma of the presidency and was now more concerned with his political future than with soldiering. After the meeting in the Farben boardroom, George wrote in his diary, *"Apparently Ike has to a high degree got the Messiah complex for which he can't be blamed, as everybody bootlicks him except myself."* Ike's anxiety during their meeting, George felt, *"can be traced to the fact that he is very much worried about the delay in getting appointed as Chief of Staff at home and fears that if he stays here, he will lose some of his prestige. I think this fear is well grounded, but I do not believe that a fear psychosis should make him so utterly regardless of his own better nature as to make him practically unmoral in his treatment of the Germans."* When George received official word of his relief, he muttered to Robert Murphy, the State Department liaison from the TORCH days, *"Ike wants to be President so much you can taste it."*[68]

The ax fell when Beetle Smith called to read a letter Ike had just signed. George would be transferred to Fifteenth Army around October 7; General

Truscott, who served under him during TORCH, and whom Ike had considered as Patton's replacement during the Knutsford incident, would take Patton's place at Third Army's helm. No public announcement would be made in advance. The move was not a reflection on Ike's feelings for George, the letter assured him. *"It results merely from my belief that your particular talents will be better employed in the new job and that the planned arrangement visualizes the best possible utilization of available personnel."*[69]

This last paragraph, George remarked, *"was full of soap which meant a little less, probably, than the paper used to receive it."*[70]

Ike was blue. As he rode down the quiet autobahn toward Bad Nauheim, command post for Fifteenth Army, he told his son, John, who was riding with him, "I had to relieve George Patton from Third Army today." He recounted to John the press conference, the newspaper uproar, the blowup at the War Department. It was in George's nature to cause a stink, he said. "We could survive this tempest," he said, but added ruefully, "Actually, I'm not moving George for what he's done—just for what he's going to do next."[71]

Ike had intended to make no public announcement until just before the change, hoping to spare George another press circus, but word leaked out prematurely, and on October 2 Ike called George to tell him he would make the announcement the following day, October 3. George went along with Ike's explanation for the change in plans, though he later concluded, *"Eisenhower is scared to death, which I already knew, and believes that a more prompt announcement of my relief than the one he had originally planned will be beneficial to him. The alleged leak is nothing but a figment of the imagination, which is a euphemism for a damned lie."*[72]

"Civil life will be mighty dull—no cheering crowds, no flowers, no private airplanes. I am convinced that the best end for an officer is the last bullet of the war." That was how George saw the war's end back when the war's end was far over the horizon. But George still stood on two feet, five months after the war's conclusion, and the end of his career, like so many aspects of peacetime life, would not live up to his expectations.[73]

He bade his beloved Third Army a final farewell on October 7, handing it over to Lucian Truscott in a short but emotional ceremony. He spent his final months as an army commander writing the history of the European Theater—*"a lot of stuff which no one will ever read,"* he grumbled, and he nursed a grudge against the newsmen, Beetle Smith, and Eisenhower. As he told one journalist, off the record, "I had not had quite a square deal because I believe it will be proven that Bavaria is more de-Nazified and more reorganized than any other section of Germany. . . . I have the unfortunate habit of making statements which sound spectacular and then explaining them. In this case the explanation was not reported—just the statements."[74]

Regardless of what Ike had told the press, the bond had been snapped; he and George were no longer the best of friends. Ike kept his visits to Patton's new headquarters at a lower profile now, as he didn't want to associate with his old friend too openly, for it had become, as Kay observed, "not politic for the Supreme Commander to spend time with him"—a fate she would share once Ike left Europe for the War Department, Mamie, and politics. In George's mind, Ike's transformation from an army officer to a presidential hopeful was complete: He was placing politics over friendship, votes over victory. Ike, George concluded, *has no moral courage.* Where George once saw a trusted comrade in arms, he now saw the dorsal fin of a political shark skimming the choppy seas.[75]

Ike visited Patton at Fifteenth Army headquarters at Bad Nauheim on October 12, and did what he could to reassure George of his continuing friendship, but to George, it was far too little and much too late. Patton, not wanting to believe the very worst about Ike, laid most of the blame for his relief on Beetle Smith, and he told Ike he would never eat at the same table as Smith again. Eisenhower told George that Beetle wanted to apologize, but Beetle was, once and for all, dead to Patton. Strangely, George wrote that Ike claimed to be interested in Patton running for Congress—*"I presume in the belief that I might help him."* But while George had tentatively decided to retire around the end of the year, he was determined to avoid anything that smacked of politics.[76]

The last time George and Ike saw each other was in Frankfurt at a football game between headquarters staff and members of the 508th Parachute Infantry Regiment. MPs placed George next to General Eisenhower. The two men sat side by side as they watched the game, a cordial picture of exactly what they wanted the world to see: a unanimity among two of America's best-known, most respected commanders, cheering together as brothers in arms.[77]

But inside, George's distrust of Ike deepened, for as he looked at Ike he saw a good soldier who had been seduced by politics and forsaken his old friends. *"[Eisenhower's] continuous and futile attempts to ride the super-heated winds of public opinion are amusing and, I believe, destructive,"* he scribbled in his diary. As he told Beatrice, *"Perhaps the best approach to DD['s] down fall would be a note of sorry. How can we expect any back bone in a man running for President?"*

His bitterness growing, a week later he wrote an old friend, *"while I think General Eisenhower is most pusillanimous in yielding to the outcry of three very low correspondents, I feel that as an American it will ill become me to discredit him—that is, until I shall prove even more conclusively that he lacks moral fortitude. This lack has been evident to us since the first landing in Africa but now that he has been bitten with the presidential bee, it is becoming even more pronounced."* He foresaw disappointment to his onetime friend in another letter to Beatrice, dated October 15: *"Ike is bitten with the Presidential bee and is also yellow. He has convinced him self that he did me a favor by getting me out of the realy grave risks entailed by being a governor. He will never be president!"* Loading for his last salvo, he edited his handwritten diary—which he intended to have published in expurgated form as his war memoirs—to cast his old comrade in a bad light and elevate his own tactical mastery.[78]

In early November, Eisenhower left his ETO staff—including a distraught Kay Summersby—and prepared to resume his place in a peaceful world of postwar America.[79] Shortly before his departure from Frankfurt, he rang up Patton. "I am going to go to the United States for a little while," Ike said. "Now, you will be the senior man in the theater on my departure and you just issue the regular little thing that on, or by virtue of such and such Army Regulation, I assume command of the United States Theater." Patton would command all American forces in Europe.[80]

"Some joke," he told Beatrice. But he would enjoy being nominal commander of the Army's expansive if gutted shell, and he didn't see that his additional duties would require much of him. He and Beetle, whom he still despised, made plans for Ike's final farewell to the troops, scheduled for sometime between December 20 and 30, and he marked time until Ike's replacement, General McNarney, arrived to assume command. He spent his days hunting, overseeing the Army's official history, and pressing for improvements in the former POW camps that still housed displaced persons.[81]

When McNarney arrived to supersede Patton at the beginning of

December, George attended his welcome reception. *"I have rarely seen assembled a greater bunch of sons-of-bitches,"* he wrote. *"The whole luncheon party reminded me of a meeting of the Rotary Club in Hawaii where everyone slaps everyone else's back while looking for an appropriate place to thrust the knife. I admit I was guilty of this practice, although at the moment I have no appropriate weapon."*[82]

On Sunday morning, December 9, George bent his six-foot, one-inch frame into the back door of a Cadillac that would take him, Hap Gay, and a short-haired pointer to a field outside Mannheim for a morning pheasant hunt. He leaned into the backseat of the touring car in fine spirits; he had recently been ordered home, and he was glad to shake the dust of postwar Europe off his boots as he left what had become a snake pit of reporters, glad-handers, and politicians in uniform.[83]

The party had not gone far when a heavy Signal Corps truck made a sharp left into the path of Patton's car and ran into the Caddy at low speed. The car rebounded from the impact, and George lay sprawled awkwardly across the rear seat, his forehead peeled back, his skull exposed to the frigid December air.[84]

Regaining his senses, he weakly asked if Hap and his driver, Private Horace Woodring, were injured. Pulling himself out from under Patton's 180-pound body, Gay assured him they were safe. Then George said, "Hap, I can't seem to move." Gay took Patton's arms and began rubbing them vigorously, but the cavalryman felt nothing.[85] Medics rushed General Patton to the Army hospital in Heidelberg, twenty miles away. Conscious, he arrived with a weak pulse, cold extremities, and complaints of neck pain. A round of X-rays revealed a fracture of his third cervical vertebrae and a dislocation of his fourth and fifth vertebrae. It was a paralyzing, perhaps life-threatening injury.[86]

It is hard for anyone to look dignified in a hospital, but George, the warrior lionized by his family and friends, looked so pitiable he drove hardened generals like Hugh Gaffey to tears. He was paralyzed from the neck down, and his head was fixed in place by horrendous-looking implements. His breath came normally, but he lacked command of his bladder and bowels, and his face bore the fresh scabs of the painful traction devices. He was a grotesque picture of misery when Beatrice arrived on December 11, courtesy of a military transport plane provided by Ike.

George knew he resembled a tortured man near death, but he put on his best face for Bea, and she put on her bravest front for him. He was a model patient, took orders from his caregivers, and passed his long hours of paralysis dictating to Beatrice memoirs and letters to well-wishers. He even joked with the doctors and orderlies who encased his body in plaster for his voyage home, to be made at the insistence of the War Department, which did not want to see an American icon die in a far-off land.[87]

George's bitterness toward Ike seemed to ebb as his strutting, martial spirit gave way to resignation that his recovery would be long, slow, and painful. He took comfort from a letter from his old friend, which he had Bea read to him. The Army's new chief of staff, a man whom Patton predicted would run for higher office, had written:

Dear George:

You can imagine what a shock it was to me to hear of your serious accident. At first I heard it on the basis of rumor and simply did not believe it. . . . I immediately wired Frankfurt and learned to my great distress that it was true. . . .

I gave orders that everything possible was to be done, including the very fastest transportation for Big Bee in the event that she was in a position to go to Germany. Last evening, just before she took off, she called me but there was nothing I could think of to send on that I have not already said to you in my telegram. Actually, I awoke out of a sound nap and probably was not functioning too well. . . .

By coincidence, only the day before, on Saturday, I had directed that you be contacted to determine whether you wanted a particular job that appeared to be opening up here in the States. The real purpose of this note is to assure you that you will always have a job and not to worry about this accident closing out any of them in your selection.

As you know, it is always difficult for me to express my true sentiments when I am deeply moved. I can only assure you again that you are never out of my thoughts and that my hopes and prayers are tied up in your speedy recovery. If anything at all occurs to you where I might be of some real help, don't hesitate a second to let an aide forward the message to me.

The whole Country shares my sentiments. The President, the Secretary of War and the whole public have been notified of your accident and without exception all are praying for your complete and speedy recovery.

With my affectionate and warm regard,

As ever,
Dwight D. Eisenhower[88]

Looking for hope, George asked Beatrice to read the part about a stateside job for him twice. It was a small but welcome gift, a faint ray of hope weaving into his antiseptic dungeon. Perhaps Ike did value him, despite all that had happened. Despite the times Ike had cast him into the wilderness, to wander far from the fighting that beckoned him in Africa. In Sicily. In England. In Germany.[89]

In his waking moments, he asked Beatrice to send Ike his regards, though some embers of bitterness simply wouldn't be extinguished. He channeled his ebbing fury into his old nemesis, Beetle Smith, and on the fourteenth he issued one of his last commands to be obeyed: He had Bea keep Beetle away from his hospital room.[90]

Two days later, another message arrived from Washington among the hundreds pouring into the hospital. This one, from the Veterans Administration's head office, read:

Dear George:

A truck can't do what the German tried so long to do and failed. Your friends everywhere pray for your recovery. I am sure that if they could the thousands of your troops now veterans would join me in these good wishes. My best to you as always.

Bradley[91]

The next day, Brad stopped by Ike's Pentagon office. Sitting in the room once occupied by their mentor, the two soldiers talked about George and his hopeless condition. They talked of the war, and they talked of not-so-old times together. Afterward, Ike dictated another "chin up" letter, just as he had done so many times before, when George's spirits were low and he needed an old friend's encouragement:

> *Just a year ago this month we became engaged in one of our critical battles. It resulted in a splendid victory and one of the decisive factors was your indomitable will and flaming fighting spirit. Bradley has just come to my office to remind me that when we three met in Verdun to consider plans you and your Army were given vital missions. From that moment on our worries with respect to the battle began to disappear. Nothing could stop you, including storms, cold, snow-blocked roads, and a savagely fighting enemy. We want you to know that in your present battle we are supremely confident that your spirit will again bring victory. We send you our prayers and hopes and our assurances that we are looking forward to an early reunion when the three of us can review your winning fight of this December and the one a year ago.*

> *Best of luck to you*
> *and love to Bee.*
> *Ike.*[92]

The end, for the man who had lived a dozen full lives, was never far off. At George's age, massive neurological damage compromised many physical systems. His lungs were failing, his blood was clotting, and he knew his sands were running out. On the morning of Friday the twenty-first, he turned his head slightly to Beatrice, his blue-gray eyes closed. He whispered, "It's too dark. . . . I mean, too late."[93]

For George, it was.

EPILOGUE

IN HIS LATER YEARS, former President Eisenhower loved to sit by the fireside at his home near Gettysburg and tell colorful stories of George Patton, the fighting court jester whom he described as "one of my oldest and dearest friends—lovable, colorful, generous, a splendid fellow." For all of Patton's flaws, idiosyncrasies, and public gaffes, Ike reserved a special place in his heart for the brash horseman who strutted onto the fields at Camp Meade in that lifeless autumn of 1919.[1]

Though he treasured his friendship with George, Ike also recognized the long shadow cast by the flashy cavalier, whose larger-than-life statue now gazed over the grounds of their alma mater, West Point. Vaguely bothered by the growing legend of "Blood and Guts," a man he knew to have flaws to rival his strengths, Eisenhower vigorously defended the fighting records of other, less showy men whose place in history was in danger of eclipse from the Third Army commander. Shortly after the war, Ike read magazine articles and books that claimed George Patton was Ike's favorite commander. Nonsense, he told an interviewer: While he had enjoyed a close friendship with "Georgie" for three and a half decades, Omar Bradley was, in Ike's opinion, the greatest American ground commander in recent memory. As he wrote in one of his personal memoirs, *At Ease: Stories I Tell to My Friends,*

Brad was outstanding. I have yet to meet his equal as an offensive leader and a defensive bulwark, as a wielder of every army that can be practically employed against an enemy. In the aftermath of war, I'm surprised that he seems at times to be ignored or undervalued by those who write of the Mediterranean and European campaigns. Patton, for instance, was a master of fast and overwhelming pursuit. Headstrong by nature, and fearlessly aggressive, Patton was the more colorful figure of the two. . . . Bradley, however, was the master of every military maneuver, lacking only in the capacity—possibly the willingness—to dramatize himself. This, I think, is to his credit.[2]

Toward the end of his life, Ike heard about an obscure project to make a movie depicting the life of George Patton. In response to an inquiry, he wrote to one of its producers:

> *[George's] temperament made him a headliner in the press but he was not the kind of all-around, balanced, competent and effective commander that Bradley was—or Simpson or Hodges. But he was a genius in pursuit. Recognizing this I was determined to keep him in my war organization no matter how often the public might scream for his scalp because of some publicized and foolish episode. He disliked, intensively, the heavy fighting necessary to break through, and because of this I did not use him in the slugging match that finally brought about the break-out from the beach head, in late July, 1944. Once, however, we had broken through, he was a natural to put in for exploiting the weaknesses of the Nazi forces on our right flank. The same was true in Sicily, where he overran the entire western side of the island, racing through that area at high speed. He later did the same thing after we had crossed the Rhine in March of 1945.*
>
> *On the other hand, when we got into dirty ding dong fighting in Moselle and later when he was trying to fight his way into Bastogne, he was apt to become pessimistic and discouraged. In such instances he liked a great deal of moral "patting on the back."[3]*

While he always kept a special place in his heart for George, until the end of his public life Ike continued to nurture the career of the Missourian whose loyalty he never doubted. As Ike had promised, Bradley became Army Chief of Staff. Later, partly through Ike's influence, he was named the first Chairman of the new Joint Chiefs of Staff. In 1950, Bradley's reputation as a team player for the Truman Administration bore fruit when he became the last of the permanent five-star generals, a rank that carried the handsome salary of $17,000 per year. His promotion spurred a telegram of congratulations from his "devoted and admiring friend" from Kansas.[4]

Ever the faithful soldier, Omar Bradley weathered the storms of the Berlin Airlift, Korea, MacArthur, NATO, and the early Cold War as Eisenhower ascended the ladder to the presidency. During Ike's 1952 campaign, Brad's admiration of Ike hit a pothole as the Republican candidate stumped against the "mess" left by the Truman Administration—of which Brad and Marshall were two senior policymakers. Brad's tenure with the Joint Chiefs during the Eisenhower Administration made for a colder, more formal relationship than those early days when the two classmates were simply "Ike" and "Brad" to one another. In 1953, after a ceremony marking Bradley's retirement from active duty, President Eisenhower presented the general with the last of his Distinguished Service Medals. He also sent Brad a valedictory letter, one that Brad treasured to the end of his days:

Dear Brad:

> *You are probably so worn out with dinners and ceremonies to salute you as you leave your post of active duty that you are glad you have to go through the thing only once in a lifetime. Nevertheless, I hope you will never forget that each of those occasions is merely an effort on the part of others to express to you something of their appreciation of a long, useful and brilliant career in the service of our common country.*

> *The purpose of this note is simply to assure you once again— as I have so many times in the past—that I have always counted on your approval to be almost the certification of the value of any proposal or project; your disapproval to be equally conclusive that the matter had better be discarded without further to-do.*

> *You well know that my admiration and continued affection go with you to your new occupation. . . .*

With love to Mary and your family, and, as always, with the very best to yourself.

As ever,
Ike.[5]

Ike and Brad aged gracefully. As civilians who, by law, never "retired" from the Army's muster rolls, they could be seen together at West Point reunions and D-Day festivities, smiling for cameras and chatting together about fishing trips, golf, skeet shooting, old times, and family news. As the shadow of the Vietnam War lengthened, they appeared together in interviews discussing the military challenges facing the country they loved. The friendship that began on the banks of the Hudson in 1911—a dormant partnership that flourished under the pressure of war—remained a source of pride and nostalgia for both men until 1969, when President Dwight D. Eisenhower, known universally to his countrymen as "Ike," passed into history.[6]

The soft-spoken "GI's General" was the last of the great World War II commanders. He soldiered on for another dozen years as a living legend. Like Eisenhower, his feelings about Patton, at least in the years following George's death, were warm. In 1951, Bradley wrote in his memoirs, "To this day I am chagrined to recall how hesitatingly I first responded to Patton's assignment, for when George joined my command in August, 1944, he came eagerly and as a friend without pique, rancor, or grievance. My year's association with him in Europe remains one of the brightest remembrances of my military career." He told Chet Hansen, "As far as I know he was one of the most loyal people that ever served under me. I have had several people—different people—tell me that George was obviously loyal to me. They had heard him cuss out every single officer in the Army, both above and below him, frankly, except me. The had never heard him say one word against me."[7]

But the legend of Omar Bradley was perceptibly dimmed by the aura of his two more famous brothers in arms, and this gnawed at him when he pictured his place in history.

Brad felt he understood Eisenhower's appeal to the American public; Ike was, after all, the Supreme Commander, a man with razor-sharp political instincts, and a manifestly popular figure—though Brad did not vote for him during his two presidential campaigns. George, however, was a different matter. Brad could never grasp why one of his *four* army commanders—a man leading secondary forces in a secondary front—should garner so much celluloid, so much ink, so much public acclaim. In a campaign comprised of millions of men, many of whom did their jobs with far fewer complaints and complications, why, he wondered, did the American public choose to canonize George Patton?[8]

The more Brad thought of George, the more his feelings toward his former superior, former subordinate breathed new life into resentment he had once felt in Sicily. Brad and his aide Chet Hansen edited their postwar writings to paint George in mixed colors and elevate other generals in his stead. Bradley was rediscovered by the public when he served as technical adviser to the Academy Award–winning film *Patton*, but the film merely served to confirm Patton's apotheosis in the public mind. The thought that Brad's wartime legacy had become an appendage to the greater legends of Patton and Eisenhower whetted his feelings into a sharp resentment toward George, and a muted contempt for Ike.[9]

The 1974 publication of George's diaries and letters disabused Bradley of any notion of Patton's loyalty. In the last full decade of his life, he decided to set the record straight, as he saw it. Bradley's second autobiography—a work completed by his collaborator after his death in 1981—portrayed Eisenhower as a political wizard but a tactical bumbler who was better at directing a conference than an army. Referring to George as "the most fiercely ambitious man and the strangest duck I have ever known," Brad's postscript depicted George Patton as a deeply flawed, insecure man whose brief explosions of genius were bookends to long pauses filled with depression, egotism, and ineptitude. Physically and mentally robust until the day he died, Bradley claimed the last word in a story written over three decades of idealism, frustration, resentment, and mutual respect.[10]

Omar Bradley, Dwight Eisenhower and George Patton, were but three notes in a larger symphony played by scores of talented musicians. But what a masterful chord these three notes struck. Many of Eisenhower's crucial decisions, such as his counterattack in the Bulge and his drive on central Germany, were, in great measure, reflections of the advice of his brilliant classmate and the inspiration of his polo-playing mentor. Bradley and Patton, in turn, were beholden to Eisenhower for the positions they occupied in war and history; neither would have realized their full potential, or left such a deep imprint on the American consciousness had Ike wavered for a moment in his support. At the highest level, Ike, Brad, and George were, as the Army had trained them to be, members of a team whose value to the Allied cause was exponentially greater than the sum of its parts. In the end, it was not the blare of the cavalryman's bugle, the bark of the infantryman's command, or the echo of a general's oratory that shaped the course of the war. It was, rather, a blend of the three, an evolving partnership, animated by friendship, that shaped the contours of victory.

SELECT BIBLIOGRAPHY

PRIMARY SOURCES

ARCHIVAL COLLECTIONS

Dwight D. Eisenhower Presidential Library, Abilene, Kansas

Henry Aurand Papers

Ruth M. Briggs Papers

Harold R. Bull Papers

Harry C. Butcher Papers

Craig Cannon Papers

Joseph L. Collins Papers

Gilbert Cook Papers

Norman D. Cota Papers

Thomas Jefferson Davis Papers

Dwight D. Eisenhower, Pre-Presidential Papers

Dwight D. Eisenhower, Presidential Papers

Dwight D. Eisenhower, Post-Presidential Papers

Alfred Gruenther Papers

Courtney Hicks Hodges Papers

C. D. Jackson Papers

Ernest R. Lee Papers

Floyd L. Parks Papers

William E. Robinson Papers

Charles B. Ryder Papers

Henry B. Salyer Papers

Thor M. Smith Papers

Walter Bedell Smith, Personal Papers

Walter Bedell Smith, World War II

Barbara Wyden Papers

George C. Marshall Foundation Library, Lexington, Virginia

George C. Marshall Papers

Frank M. McCarthy Patton Movie Collection

Library of Congress, Washington, D.C.

Omar N. Bradley Papers

Everett S. Hughes Papers

George S. Patton Jr. Papers

National Archives and Records Administration, College Park, Maryland

Ohio University, Athens, Ohio

Cornelius Ryan Papers

Patton Museum, Fort Knox, Kentucky

Albert Collections I and II

Grow, Robert W. Collection

Patton, George S. Jr. Collection

United States Military Academy, West Point, New York

Omar N. Bradley Papers

United States Army Military History Institute, Carlisle Barracks, Pennsylvania

Clay and Joan Blair

Omar N. Bradley

Robert E. Coffin

Richard Collins

Donald E. Currier

Garrison H. Davidson

James Gavin

Hobart R. Gay

Peter C. Hains III

Elton F. Hammond

Chester B. Hansen

Courtney Hicks Hodges

William T. Hornaday

Kenyon A. Joyce

Albert W. Kenner

John P. Lucas

Raymond G. Moses

Sidney H. Negrotto

Office of the Center of Military History

George S. Patton Jr.

D. Kenneth Reimers

BOOKS

Allen, Robert S., *Lucky Forward* (New York: Manor Books, 1947, 1977 ed.).

Ayer Jr., Frederick, *Before the Colors Fade* (Boston: Houghlin Mifflin, 1964).

Bland, Larry I., ed., *George C. Marshall Interviews and Reminiscences with Forrest C. Pogue* (Lexington, Virginia: George C. Marshall Foundation, 1986, 1996 ed.).

Bradley, Omar N., *A Soldier's Story* (New York: Henry Holt & Co., 1951, New York: Modern Library ed., 1999).

——, and Clay Blair, *A General's Life* (New York: Simon and Schuster ,1983).

Alanbrooke, Field Marshal Lord, *War Diaries: 1939-1945,* Alex Danchev and Daniel Todman, eds. (London: Widenfield & Nicolson, 1957; Los Angeles: University of California Press, 2001 ed.).

Butcher, Harold C., *My Three Years with Eisenhower: The Personal Diary of Captain Harry C. Butcher, USNR, Naval Aide to General Eisenhower, 1942 to 1945* (New York: Simon & Schuster, 1946).

Chase, Margaret, *Never Too Late* (San Francisco: Ausonia Press, 1983).

Churchill, Winston S., *The Grand Alliance* (Boston: Houghton Mifflin, 1950).

——, *The Hinge of Fate* (Boston: Houghton Mifflin, 1950).

——, *Closing the Ring* (Boston: Houghton Mifflin, 1951).

——, *Triumph and Tragedy* (Boston: Houghton Mifflin, 1953).

Clark, Mark W., *Calculated Risk* (New York: Harper Bros., 1950).

Codman, Charles R., *Drive* (Boston: Little, Brown, 1957).

Davidson, Garrison, H., *Grandpa Gar* (Self-published, 1974).

de Guingand, Francis, *Operation Victory* (New York: Charles Scribner's Sons, 1947).

——, *Generals at War* (London: Hodder & Stoughton, 1964).

Eisenhower, Dwight D., *Crusade in Europe* (New York: Doubleday & Co., 1949).

——, *At Ease: Stories I Tell My Friends* (New York: Doubleday & Co., 1967).

——, *The Papers of Dwight David Eisenhower: The War Years*, Alfred D. Chandler, Jr., ed. (5 vols., Baltimore: Johns Hopkins Press, 1970).

——, *The Eisenhower Diaries*, Robert H. Ferrell, ed. (New York: W. W. Norton & Co., 1978).

——, *Letters to Mamie*, John S. D. Eisenhower, ed. (New York: Doubleday & Co., 1978).

——, *Eisenhower: The Prewar Diaries and Selected Papers, 1905–1941*, Daniel D. Holt and James W. Leyerzapf, eds. (Baltimore: Johns Hopkins Press, 1998).

——, *Dear General: Eisenhower's Wartime Letters to Marshall*, Joseph P. Hobbs, ed. (Baltimore: Johns Hopkins University Press, 1999).

Eisenhower, John S. D., *Strictly Personal: A Memoir* (New York: Doubleday & Co., Inc., 1974).

——, *General Ike: A Personal Reminiscence* (New York: Free Press, 2003).

Harkins, Paul D., *When the Third Cracked Europe: The Story of Patton's Incredible Army* (Harrisburg, PA: Stackpole Books, 1969).

Harmon, Ernest N., *Combat Commander: Autobiography of a Soldier* (New York: Prentice-Hall, 1970).

Ingersoll, Ralph, *Report on England, November 1940* (New York: Simon & Schuster, 1940).

——, *The Battle Is the Payoff* (New York: Harcourt, Brace & Co., 1943).

——, *Top Secret* (New York: Harcourt, Brace, 1946).

Koch, Oscar W., *G-2: Intelligence for Patton* (Atglen, PA: Schiffer Military History, 1999 ed.).

McKeogh, Michael J., and Richard Lockridge, *Sgt. Mickey and General Ike* (New York: G. P. Putnam's Sons, 1946).

Montgomery, Bernard Law, *Normandy to the Baltic* (Boston: Houghton Mifflin, 1948).

——, *Despatch Submitted by Field Marshal the Viscount Montgomery of Alamein . . . to the Secretary of State for War, Describing the Part Played by 21st Army Group, and the Armies Under His Command, From D-Day to VE Day* (New York: British Information Services, 1946).

——, *The Memoirs of Field-Marshal Montgomery* (London: World Publishing Co., 1958; New York: Signet Books, 1959 ed.).

Moorehead, Alan, *Mediterranean Front* (New York: Whittlesey House, 1942).

Morgan, Frederick, *Overture to Overlord* (London: Hodder & Stoughton Ltd., 1950).

Murphy, Robert, *Diplomat Among Warriors* (New York: Doubleday & Co., 1964).

Odom, Charles B., *General George S. Patton and Eisenhower* (New Orleans: World Picture Productions, 1985).

Patton, George S. Jr., *War as I Knew It* (Boston: Houghton Mifflin, 1947; Boston: Houghton Mifflin, 1995 ed.).

——, *The Patton Papers, vol. I: 1885–1940*, Martin Blumenson, ed. (Boston: Houghlin Mifflin, 1972).

——, *The Patton Papers, vol. II: 1940–1945*, Martin Blumenson, ed. (Boston: Houghton Mifflin, 1974; Da Capo Press, 1996 ed.).

Pogue, Forrest C., ed., *George C. Marshall Interviews and Reminiscences* (Lexington, VA: George C. Marshall Foundation, 1996).

Pyle, Ernie, *Here Is Your War* (New York: Henry Holt & Co., 1943).

——, *Brave Men* (New York: H. Holt, 1944, Lincoln: University of Nebraska Press, 2003 ed.).

Reynolds, Quentin, *The Curtain Rises* (New York: Random House, 1944).

——, *By Quentin Reynolds* (New York: McGraw-Hill, 1963).

Semmes, Harry H., *Portrait of Patton* (New York: Appleton-Century Crofts, 1955).

Smith, Walter Bedell, *Eisenhower's Six Great Decisions* (New York: Longmans, Green, 1956).

Snyder, Marty, *My Friend Ike* (New York: Frederick Fell, 1956).

Strong, Kenneth, *Intelligence at the Top* (New York: Doubleday, 1969).

Summersby, Kay, *Eisenhower Was My Boss* (New York: Prentice Hall, Inc., 1948; reprint, New York: Dell Publishing, n.d.).

Summersby Morgan, Kay, *Past Forgetting: My Love Affair with Dwight D. Eisenhower* (New York: Simon and Schuster, 1975).

Tedder, Lord Arthur, *With Prejudice* (Boston: Little, Brown & Co., 1966).

Totten, Ruth Ellen Patton, *The Button Box: A Daughter's Loving Memoir of Beatrice Ayer Patton* (Columbia, Missouri: University of Missouri Press, 2005 ed.).

Truscott, Lucian, *Command Missions* (New York: Dutton ,1954; New York: Arno Press, 1979 ed.).

Wallace, Brenton G., *Patton and His Third Army* (Harrisburg, PA: Military Service Publishing, 1946).

ORAL HISTORIES AND TRANSCRIBED INTERVIEWS

Alexander, Harold (USAMHI)

Aurand, Henry S. (COHP)

Barker, Ray W. (EL)

Bernstein, Bernard (Truman Library)

Berg, Harold (EL)

Betts, Thomas J. (EL)

Bolte, Charles (EL)

Bonesteel, Charles H. III (USAMHI)

Boyle, Andrew J. (USAMHI)

Bradley, Omar N. (USAMHI)

Brooke, Alan (USAMHI)

Broushous, Charles R. (EL)

Cannon, Craig (EL)

Cheever, Charles E. (USAMHI)

Clark, Mark W. (EL)

Clay, Lucius D. (EL)

Coffin, Robert E. (USAMHI)

Collins, J. Lawton (USAMHI)

Coningham, Arthur (USAMHI)

Decker, George H. (USAMHI)

Dempsey, Miles (USAMHI)

Devers, Jacob L. (EL)

Dickson, Benjamin A. (USAMHI)

Eisenhower, Dwight D. (EL)

Eisenhower, Dwight D. (Ohio University)

Eisenhower, John S. D. (EL)

Eisenhower, John S. D. (COHP)

Eisenhower, Milton (EL)

Gault, James (USAMHI)

Gay, Hobart R. (USAMHI)

Gruenther, Alfred (EL)

Hains, Peter C. III (USAMHI)

Hamlett, Barksdale (USAMHI)

Harkins, Paul D. (USAMHI)

Harrell, Ben (USAMHI)

Hart, Charles E. (USAMHI)

Hechler, Ken (Truman Library)

Heilbronn, Kurt (EL)

Howze, Hamilton H. (USAMHI)

Huebner, Clarence L. (USAMHI)

Hull, John E. (USAMHI)

Ismay, Hastings L. (USAMHI)

Jehl, Sue Sarafian (EL)

Kenner, Albert W. (USAMHI)

Lee, Fred L. (Truman Library)

Lee, John C. H. (USAMHI)

Lucas, John P. (USAMHI)

Marshall, George C. (GCML)

Morgan, Frederick E. (USAMHI)

Murphy, Robert D. (EL)

Richards, George J. (USAMHI)

Robb, James M. (USAMHI)

Rooks, Lowell K. (USAMHI)

Rosengartern, Adolph (USAMHI)

Scarman, Leslie (USAMHI)

Scott, Inez G. (EL)

Simpson, William H. (COHP)

Smith, Walter Bedell (USAMHI)

Strong, Kenneth W. D. (USAMHI)

Tedder, Arthur (USAMHI)

Train, William F. (USAMHI)

Truscott, Lucian K. (USAMHI)

Waters, John K. (USAMHI)

Whiteley, John F. M. (USAMHI)

PHOTOGRAPHIC COLLECTIONS

Eisenhower Library, Abilene, Kansas

Ruth M. Briggs

Harold R. Bull

Harry C. Butcher

Craig Cannon

Courtney Hicks Hodges

Floyd L. Parks

Elwood R. Quesada

George C. Marshall Foundation, Lexington, Virginia

George S. Patton Jr. Museum, Fort Knox, Kentucky

Oakes, John J.

George S. Patton Jr.

Library of Congress, Washington, D.C.

Everett Hughes Papers

George S. Patton Jr. Papers

National Archives and Records Administration, College Park, Maryland

Sound and Motion Picture Recordings

Still Photograph Records

USAMHI, Carlisle Barracks, Pennsylvania

Clay Blair   *Samuel L. Myers*

Chester B. Hansen   *George S. Patton Jr.*

Hamilton H. Howze   *Small Photograph Collection*

Geoffrey Keyes   *William V. Soloman*

John P. Lucas   *Henry L. Stimson*

Halley G. Maddox   *Robert W. Wilson*

H. U. Milne   *World War II Miscellaneous*

OTHER PRIMARY SOURCES

O'Neill, James H., "The True Story of the Patton Prayer," *Review of the News* (Oct. 6, 1971), reproduced at www.pattonhq.com/prayer.html.

SECONDARY SOURCES

BOOKS

Abrams, Joe I., *A History of the 90th Division in World War II* (Baton Rouge: Army & Navy Publishing, 1946).

Ambrose, Stephen E., *Eisenhower and Berlin, 1945* (New York: W. W. Norton & Co., 1967; New York: W. W. Norton, 2000 ed.).

——, *The Supreme Commander* (New York: Doubleday, 1970; Jackson: University of Mississippi Press, 1999 ed.).

——, *Eisenhower: Soldier and President* (New York: Simon & Schuster, 1990; New York: Simon & Schuster, Paperbacks, 2003 ed.).

——, *The Victors: Eisenhower and His Boys: The Men of World War II* (New York: Simon & Schuster, 1998).

Astor, George, *Terrible Terry Allen: The Soldier's General* (Novato, CA: Presidio Press, 2003).

Atkinson, Rick, *An Army at Dawn* (New York: Henry Holt, 2002; New York: Owl Books, 2003 ed.).

——, *Day of Battle* (New York: Henry Holt, 2007).

Axelrod, Alan, *Bradley* (New York: Palgrave-Macmillan, 2008).

Beevor, Anthony, *D-Day: The Battle for Normandy* (New York: Viking, 2009).

Blumenson, Martin, *The United States Army in World War II: Breakout and Pursuit* (Washington, D.C.: Center of Military History, 1961, 1993 ed.).

——, *Kasserine Pass: An Epic Saga of Desert War* (Jove Books: 1983 ed.).

——, *Mark Clark* (New York: Congdon & Weed, 1985).

——, *Patton: The Man Behind the Legend, 1885–1945* (New York: William Morrow, 1985).

——, *Battle of the Generals: The Untold Story of the Falaise Pocket—The Campaign That Should Have Won World War II* (New York: William and Morrow, 1993).

Brandon, Dorothy, *Mamie Doud Eisenhower: A Portrait of a First Lady* (New York: Charles Scribner's Sons, 1954).

Breuer, William B., *Hoodwinking Hitler: The Normandy Deception* (Westport, Conn.: Praeger, 1993).

Brighton, Terry, *Patton, Montgomery, Rommel: Masters of War* (New York: Crown Publishers, 2008).

Charles, Roland W., *Troopships of World War II* (Washington, D.C.: Army Transportation Association, 1947).

Clark, Jeffrey J., and Robert Ross Smith, *The United States Army in World War II: Riviera to the Rhine* (Washington, D.C.: Center of Military History, 1991, 1993 ed.).

Cline, Ray S., *Washington Command Post: The Operations Division* (Washington, D.C.: U.S. Government, 1951; Center of Military History, 1990 ed.).

Coffman, Edward M., *The Regulars: The American Army, 1898–1941* (Cambridge: Belknap Press, 2007).

Cole, Hugh M., *The United States Army in World War II: The Lorraine Campaign* (Washington, D.C.: Center of Military History, 1950, 1993 ed.).

——, *The United States Army in World War II: The Ardennes: Battle of the Bulge* (Washington, D.C.: Center of Military History, 1965, 1993 ed.).

Colley, David P., *Decision at Strasbourg: Ike's Strategic Mistake to Halt the Sixth Army Group at the Rhine in 1944* (Annapolis: Naval Institute Press, 2008).

Cray, Ed, *General of the Army: George C. Marshall, Soldier and Statesman* (New York: Cooper Square Press, 1990; New York: Cooper Square Press, 2000 ed.).

Crosswell, D.K.R., *The Chief of Staff: The Military Career of General Walter Bedell Smith* (New York: Greenwood Press, 1991).

——, *Beetle: The Life of General Walter Bedell Smith* (Lexington: University Press of Kentucky, 2010).

D'Este, Carlo, *Patton: A Genius for War* (New York: HarperCollins, 1986; New York: HarperPerennial, 1996).

——, *World War II in the Mediterranean, 1942–1945* (New York: Workman Publishing Co., 1990).

——, *Eisenhower: A Soldier's Life* (New York: Henry Holt, 2002; New York: Owl Books, 2003 ed.).

Eisenhower, David, *Eisenhower at War 1943–1945* (New York: Random House, 1986; New York: Wings Books, 1991 ed.).

Eisenhower, John S. D., *The Bitter Woods: The Battle of the Bulge* (New York: G. P. Putnam's Sons, 1969; Cambridge: Da Capo Press, 1995 ed.).

——, *Allies: Pearl Harbor to D-Day* (New York: Doubleday & Co., 1982; Cambridge: Da Capo Books, 1990 ed.).

Erickson, John, *The Road to Berlin* (Boulder, Colorado: Westview Press, 1983; London: Cassell Military Paperbacks, 2003 ed.).

Farago, Ladaslas, *Patton: Ordeal and Triumph* (New York: Dell Paperbacks, 1970 ed.).

——, *The Last Days of Patton* (New York: McGraw-Hill, 1981; New York: Berkeley Books, 1986 ed.).

Follain, John, *Mussolini's Island* (London: Hodder & Stoughton, 2005).

Funk, Arthur Layton, *The Politics of TORCH: The Allied Landings and the Algiers Putsch 1942* (Lawrence, KS: University of Kansas Press, 1974).

Gabel, Christopher R., *The U.S. Army GHQ Maneuvers of 1941* (Washington, D.C.: U.S. Government, 1991).

Garland, Albert N., and Howard M. Smythe, *The United States Army in World War II: Sicily and the Surrender of Italy* (Washington, D.C.: Center of Military History, 1963, 1993 ed.).

Gelb, Norman, *Ike & Monty: Generals at War* (New York: William Morrow & Co., 1994).

Gilbert, Martin, *The Second World War* (New York: Henry Holt, 1989).

Greenfield, Kent R., and Robert R. Palmer, *Origins of the Army Ground Forces: General Headquarters U.S. Army, 1940–1942* (Washington, D.C.: Historical Section: U.S. Army, 1946).

Harrison, Gordon A., *The United States Army in World War II: Cross-Channel Attack* (Washington, D.C.: U.S. Government, 1951; Washington, D.C.: Center of Military History, 1993 ed.).

Hart, Stephen Ashley, *Montgomery and "Colossal Cracks"* (Westport, Conn.: Praeger, 2000).

Hastings, Max, *Overlord: D-Day and the Battle for Normandy* (New York: Simon & Schuster, 1984).

Hirshson, Stanley P., *General Patton: A Soldier's Life* (New York: HarperCollins, 2002; HarperPerennial, 2003 ed.).

Hogan, David W., *Command Post at War: First Army Headquarters in Europe, 1944–1945* (Washington, D.C.: Center of Military History, 2000).

Howe, George F., *The United States Army in World War II: Northwest Africa: Seizing the Initiative in the West* (Washington, D.C.: U.S. Government, 1957; Washington, D.C.: Center of Military History, 1993 ed.).

Korda, Michael, *Ike: An American Hero* (New York: HarperCollins, 2007; New York: HarperPerennial, 2008 ed.).

Lande, D. A., *I Was with Patton* (St. Paul: MBI Publishing, 2002).

MacDonald, Charles B., *The United States Army in World War II: The Siegfried Line Campaign* (Washington, D.C.: Center of Military History 1963, 1993 ed.).

——, *The United States Army in World War II: The Last Offensive* (Washington, D.C.: Center of Military History, 1973, 1993 ed.).

——, *A Time for Trumpets: The Untold Story of the Battle of the Bulge* (New York: HarperCollins, 1985).

Manchester, William, *The Arms of Krupp* (New York: Little, Brown & Co., 1968, 2003 ed.).

Marshall, S.L.A., *Bastogne: The First Eight Days* (Washington, D.C.: Infantry Journal Press 1946, Washington D.C.: Center of Military History 1988 ed.).

Maycock, Thomas J., "The North African Campaigns," in Wesley Frank Craven and James Lea Cate, *Army Air Forces in World War II: TORCH to POINT-BLANK, August 1942 to December 1943* (Washington, D.C.: U.S. Government, 1948).

Mayo, Lida, *The United States Army in World War II: The Technical Services: The Ordnance Department: On Beachhead and Battlefront* (Washington, D.C.: Center of Military History, 1968, 1991 ed.).

Miller, Edward G., *A Dark and Bloody Ground: The Hürtgen Forest and the Roer River Dams, 1944–1945* (College Station: Texas A&M University Press, 1995).

Miller, Merle, *Ike the Soldier: By Those Who Knew Him* (New York: G. P. Putnam's Sons, 1987).

Moorehead, Alan, *African Trilogy: The North African Campaign 1940–43* (London: Hamish Hamilton, 1944; London: Cassell, 1998 ed.).

Morelock, J. D., *Generals of the Ardennes: American Leadership in the Battle of the Bulge* (Honolulu: University Press of the Pacific, 2002).

Morgan, Ted, *FDR: A Biography* (New York: Simon & Schuster, 1985, 1986 ed.).

Murray, G. E. Patrick, *Eisenhower Versus Montgomery: The Continuing Debate* (Westport, Conn: Praeger, 1996).

Neillands, Robin, *Battle for the Rhine: Arnhem and the Ardennes—The Campaign in Europe, 1944–45* (London: Weidenfield & Nicholson, 2005).

Patton, Robert H., *The Pattons: A Personal History of an American Family* (New York: Crown Publishers, 1994; Dulles, Virginia: Potomac Books, Inc., 2004 ed.).

Perret, Geoffrey, *Eisenhower* (Holbrook, MA: Adams Media, 1999).

Perry, Mark, *Partners in Command: George Marshall and Dwight Eisenhower in War and Peace* (New York: Penguin Press, 2007).

Pitt, Barrie, *Churchill and the Generals* (London: Sidgwick & Jackson Ltd., 1981; Yorkshire: Pen & Sword Books Ltd., 2004).

Pogue, Forrest C., *The United States Army in World War II: The Supreme Command* (Washington, D.C.: Center of Military History, 1954, 1989 ed.).

——, *George C. Marshall: Ordeal and Hope 1939–1942* (New York: Viking Press, 1965).

——, *George C. Marshall: Organizer of Victory 1943–1945* (New York: Viking Press, 1973).

Prefer, Nathan H., *Patton's Ghost Corps: Cracking the Siegfried Line* (Novato, CA: Presidio Press, 1998).

Price, Frank James, *Troy H. Middleton: A Biography* (Baton Rouge: LSU Press, 1974).

Reynolds, Michael, *Monty and Patton: Two Paths to Victory* (Staplehurst, Kent: Spellmouth Ltd., 2005).

Roberts, Andrew, *Masters and Commanders: How Four Titans Won the War in the West, 1941–1945* (New York: Harper, 2009).

Rogers, Russ, *Historic Photos of General George Patton* (Nashville: Turner Publishing Co., 2007).

Ruppenthal, Roland G., *The United States Army in World War II: Logistical Support of the Armies* (2 vols.) (Washington, D.C.: Center of Military History, 1953, 1995 ed.).

Ryan, Cornelius, *The Longest Day* (New York: Simon & Schuster, 1959; New York: Simon & Schuster Paperbacks, 1994 ed.).

——, *A Bridge Too Far* (New York: Simon & Schuster, 1974; New York: Simon & Schuster Paperbacks, 1995 ed.).

Shirer, William L., *The Rise and Fall of the Third Reich* (New York: Fawcett Crest, 1962, 1992 ed.).

Spires, David N., *Air Power for Patton's Army: The XIX Tactical Air Command in the Second World War* (Washington, D.C.: Air Force History and Museums Program, 2002).

Toland, John, *The Last 100 Days* (New York: Random House, 1965).

Weigley, Russell F., *Eisenhower's Lieutenants* (Bloomington: Indiana University Press, 1981).

Weintraub, Stanley, *11 Days in December: Christmas at the Bulge, 1944* (New York: Free Press, 2006).

——, *15 Stars: Eisenhower, MacArthur, Marshall* (New York: Free Press, 2007).

OTHER SECONDARY SOURCES

Anderson, Charles R., "Algeria-French Morocco 1942," CMH Pub. 72-11 (Washington, D.C.: Center of Military History, 1990).

——, "Tunisia," CMH Pub. 72-12 (Washington, D.C.: Center of Military History, n.d.).

Barnhart, Barton V., "The Great Escape: An Analysis of Allied Actions Leading to the Axis Evacuation in Sicily in World War II," unpublished MA Thesis, Command and General Staff College (Fort Leavenworth, 2003).

Becker, Marshall O., "The Amphibious Training Center: Study No. 22" (Washington, D.C.: Army Ground Forces, Historical Section, 1946).

Bilgé, Kerem, "Admiral Leahy: U.S. Ambassador to Vichy," *World War II Magazine* (November 2006).

Birtle, Andrew J., "Sicily 1943," CMH Pub. 72-16 (Washington, D.C.: Center of Military History, n.d.).

Bodner, Diana L., "The Relationship Between Fox Conner and Dwight Eisenhower," Army War College Study (April 2002).

Bradsher, Greg, "Nazi Gold: The Merkers Mine Treasure," *Prologue: Quarterly of the National Archives and Records Administration* (Spring 1999).

Carpenter, Douglas C., "A Failure of Coalition Leadership: The Falaise-Argentan Gap," Army War College Study (April 2002).

Condit, Howard, "General George C. Marshall, Strategic Leadership and Coalition Warfare," Army War College Study (April 1996).

Dale, Matthew B., "The Professional Military Development of Major General Ernest N. Harmon" (Leavenworth, Kansas: U.S. Army Command and General Staff College, 2008).

D'Este, Carlo, "Monty's Armored Smokescreen," *World War II* (July 2009).

——, "The Storm Before the Storm," *World War II* (May/June 2010).

Doubler, Michael D., "Busting the Bocage: American Combined Arms Operations in France, June–July 31, 1944" (Leavenworth, Kansas: Combat Studies Institute, 1988).

Gabel, Christopher R., "The Lorraine Campaign: An Overview, September–December, 1944" (Leavenworth: Combat Studies Institute, 1985).

——, "The 4th Armored Division in the Encirclement of Nancy" (Leavenworth, Kansas: Combat Studies Institute, 1986).

Gabel, D. L., "Leadership or Management: The Cadet Chain of Command and the West Point Class of 1915" (December 4, 1989), (accessed at http://digital-library. usma.edu/libmedia/archives/toep/cadet_chain_command_wp_class_1915.pdf).

Gavin, James M., "Bloody Huertgen: The Battle That Never Should Have Been Fought," *American Heritage* (December 1979).

Hall, John L., "Eisenhower, Strategic Operator and Leader," Army War College Study (February 1996).

Johnson, Richard H., "An Investigation into the Reliefs of Generals Orland Ward and Terry Allen," unpublished monograph, Command and General Staff College (Fort Leavenworth, 2009).

Kiefer, Todd A., "The Most Reasonable of Unreasonable Men: Eisenhower as Strategic General," unpublished MA Thesis, Command and General Staff College (Fort Leavenworth, 1999).

King, Michael J., "Rangers: Selected Combat Operations in World War II," No. 11 (Leavenworth, Kansas: Combat Studies Institute, U.S. Army Command and General Staff College, June 1985).

Kirkpatrick, Charles E., "Joint Planning for Torch," *Parameters* (Summer 1991).

Laurie, Clayton D., "Rome-Arno," CMH Pub. 72-20 (Washington, D.C.: Center of Military History, 1990).

Lowder, Joseph B., "The Falaise-Argentan Gap: Dysfunctional Unity of Effort," Army War College Study (April 2001).

Morelock, Jerry D., "Darkest of Times: A Critical Analysis of Bradley's Leadership in the Battle of the Bulge" (unpublished monograph).

——, "General Omar Bradley's Battle of the Bulge," *Armchair General* (January 2007).

——, "Ike's Warriors," *Armchair General* (April/May 2009).

——, "Terrible Terry Allen," *Armchair General* (April/May 2010).

Niederost, Eric, "A Fool's Errand," *World War II* (July/August 2006).

Renstrom, Danielle Stout, "Roosevelt's Olive Branch: The Diplomacy of Unconditional Surrender," unpublished MA thesis (North Carolina State University, 2006).

Reynolds, Michael, "The Final Days of General George S. Patton Jr.," *World War II History* (November 2007).

——, "Patton's End Run," *World War II History* (September 2009).

Ruppenthal, Roland G., "Utah Beach to Cherbourg," CMH Pub. 100-12 (Washington, D.C.: U.S. War Department, Historical Division, 1948; Washington, D.C.: Center for Military History, n.d.).

Smith, Kenneth V., "Naples-Foggia 1943–1944," CMH Pub. 72-17 (Washington, D.C.: Center for Military History, n.d.).

Sullivan, John J., "The Botched Air Support of Operation Cobra," *Parameters* (March 1998).

Tozer, Eliot, "How Eisenhower Gambled on History's Most Fateful Weather Forecast," *Popular Science* (June 1957).

U.S. War Department, Historical Division, "To Bizerte with the II Corps," CMH Pub. 100-6 (Washington, D.C.: U.S. War Department, Historical Division, 1943; Washington, D.C.: Center of Military History, 1990).

Vannoy, Allyn, "American Drive to the Moselle," *Military Heritage* (August 2009).

Weintraub, Stanley, "Patton's Last Christmas," *MHQ: The Quarterly Journal of Military History* (April 2007). "The Winning of World War II: Top Command: Field Commanders: Omar N. Bradley and George S. Patton Jr." (Viewmark Production, 1996).

GLOSSARY OF SELECTED ALLIED CODE NAMES

ARCADIA: Anglo-American conferences in Washington, D.C., December 1941–January 1942

AVALANCHE: Invasion of Italy at Salerno by Fifth U.S. Army, September 1943

BAYTOWN: Invasion of Italy at Calabria by Eighth British Army, September 1943

BOLERO: Buildup of U.S. forces in England, 1942–1944

CADET: Patch's Seventh U.S. Army headquarters

COBRA: U.S. breakout from the Normandy beachhead around St.-Lô, July 1944

CONQUER: Simpson's Ninth U.S. Army headquarters

CORKSCREW: Allied air campaign against Pantelleria, June 1943

DRAGOON/ANVIL: Invasion of Southern France, August 1944

EAGLE: Bradley's Twelfth Army Group headquarters, July 1944–June 1945

EUREKA: Roosevelt-Churchill-Stalin conference, Tehran, Iran, November–December 1943

FORTITUDE: Deception plan to pin German forces north of Normandy, April–August 1944

GARDEN: Armored thrust into Holland to secure bridgehead (connected with **MARKET**)

GOODWOOD: British breakout attempt at Caen, July 1944

GRENADE: Ninth U.S. Army attack in support of **VERITABLE**

GYMNAST: Allied invasion of French North Africa, November 1942 (later **TORCH**)

HOBGOBLIN: Pantelleria Island, between Tunisia and Sicily

LION: Montgomery's Twenty-First Army Group headquarters

LUCKY: Patton's Third U.S. Army headquarters

LUMBERJACK: First U.S. Army's operation to close upon the Rhine at Cologne, March 1945

MARKET: Allied air drop into Holland to secure bridgehead (connected with **GARDEN**)

MASTER: Hodges's First U.S. Army headquarters

NEPTUNE: Allied landings on Normandy beaches, June 1944

OVERLORD: Development of an Allied lodgement in Normandy, 1944

PLUNDER: Crossing of the Rhine by Twenty-First Army Group, March 1945

POINTBLANK: Allied strategic bombing campaign against Germany

QUICKSILVER: Allied plan to focus German attention on Calais as the main **OVERLORD** landing site

ROUNDUP: Invasion of France ahead of projected collapse of Nazi government (later **OVERLORD**)

SEXTANT: Roosevelt-Churchill-Chiang conferences in Cairo, Egypt, November–December 1943

SHARPENER: SHAEF forward headquarters near Portsmouth, May–July 1944

SHELLBURST: SHAEF forward headquarters in France

SHINGLE: Invasion of Italy near Anzio, January 1944

SLEDGEHAMMER: Invasion of France to secure beachhead for later operations, fall 1942

SYMBOL: Roosevelt-Churchill conference in Casablanca, Morocco, January 1943

TORCH: Invasion of French North Africa, November 1942 (formerly **GYMNAST**)

TRIDENT: Roosevelt-Churchill conference in Washington, D.C., May 1943

ULTRA: Decryption program for German radio intercepts, 1941–1944

UNDERTONE: Sixth Army Group operation to close up to the Rhine, March 1945

VARSITY: Airborne operation in support of **PLUNDER**, March 1945

VERITABLE: Offensive into the Lower Rhineland by Twenty-First Army Group, February 1945

WIDEWING: SHAEF headquarters at Bushy Park, England, 1944

ENDNOTE ABBREVIATIONS

12AG	Twelfth Army Group
21AG	Twenty-First Army Group
AAR	After Action Report
BAP	Beatrice Ayer Patton
BLM	Bernard Law Montgomery
CARL	Combined Arms Research Library
CCOS	Combined Chiefs of Staff
COHP	Columbia Oral History Project, Columbia University
DDE	Dwight D. Eisenhower
EL	Dwight D. Eisenhower Library
EP	*The Papers of Dwight David Eisenhower: The War Years*
EP:P	*Eisenhower: The Prewar Diaries and Selected Papers*
FDR	Franklin D. Roosevelt
FUSA	First U.S. Army
GCM	George C. Marshall

GCML	George C. Marshall Library
GSP	George S. Patton Jr.
GSP II	George S. Patton II (General Patton's father)
JSDE	John S. D. Eisenhower
MDE	Mamie Doud Eisenhower
MP	George C. Marshall Papers, GCML
ONB	Omar N. Bradley
ONB, GL	ONB, *A General's Life*
ONB, SS	ONB, *A Soldier's Story*
PP	*The Patton Papers*
PP-LC	Patton Papers, Library of Congress
TUSA	Third U.S. Army
USAMHI	United States Army Military History Institute
USMA	United States Military Academy
VMI	Virginia Military Institute
WBS	Walter Bedell Smith
WSC	Winston Spencer Churchill

Dates without corresponding titles represent diary entries.

ENDNOTES

Prologue

1 WBS 92.

2 12AG, AAR, 3:25 (NARA RG 331, entry 200A, box 266); JSDE, *Bitter Woods*, 160–61; Charles C. Wertenbaker, "Americans Battle the German Big Push," *Life*, 1/8/45; "Explosion," *Time*, 12/25/44.

3 ONB, GL, 358; Weintraub, "Patton's Last Christmas," 8–9.

4 JSDE, *Bitter Woods*, 34; 12AG, AAR, vol. 1 (photo), (NARA RG 331, entry 200A, box 266); Hansen, 12/19/44, USAMHI (Hansen Papers, box 5).

5 ONB, GL, 356 ("flat-footed"); Morelock, "General Omar Bradley's Battle of the Bulge," 79.

6 Tedder 625.

7 Harold R. Bull, "Record of Meeting," 12/19/44, EL (Bull Papers); GSP, 12/19/44, PP-LC (box 3); Codman 232; Paul D. Harkins, interview, 4/28/74, USAMHI, 29 (three days meeting engagement, six days with six divisions); ONB, "Memoirs Rejects," n.d., USAMHI (Blair Collection, box 49); Cole, *Ardennes*, 487. But see GSP, "Notes on the Bastogne Operation," 1/16/45 (NARA RG 407, entry 427, box 1572), (attack with III Corps on December 23).

8 GSP, "Notes on the Bastogne Operation," 1/16/45 (NARA RG 407, entry 427, box 1572) (120 miles).

9 Strong 163; Codman 231–33.

10 Gay, 12/19/44, USAMHI (Gay Papers); GSP, "Notes on the Bastogne Operation," 1/16/45 (NARA RG 407, entry 427, box 1572); Codman 232–33.

11 FUSA, War Diary, 12/26/44, EL (Collins Papers); Hansen, 12/26/44, USAMHI (Hansen Papers, box 5).

12 GSP, 12/19/44, PP-LC (box 3); Codman 232.

One: A Hangover of War

1 DDE, *At Ease*, 155. See also DDE to Mary Louise Doud, 7/15/44, EP 3:2012; Gruenther, interview, 9/7/67, EL, 92.

2 DDE, draft notes on GSP, 4/6/65, EL (Post-Pres Papers, Secretary's Series, box 3), 7; Robert E. Coffin, USAMHI interview, 7/25/80, 63.

3 Jehl, interview, 2/13/91, EL, 39; Gruenther, interview, 4/20/67, EL, 27; McKeogh 51; JSDE, interview, 3/10/72, EL, 224; D'Este, *Patton*, 291–92.

4 D'Este, *Patton.*, 281, 290–91.

5 Totten 122.

6 DDE, *At Ease*, 169.

7 Ibid., 172–73.

8 D'Este, *Eisenhower*, 153 (citing DDE, "Unpublished Assessments of World War II Personalities," EL (Post-Pres Papers, box 7).

9 DDE, draft notes on GSP, 4/6/65, EL (Post-Pres Papers, Secretary's Series, box 3).

10 JSDE, *General Ike*, 2.

11 DDE, *At Ease*, 172.

12 Ibid., 171.

13 D'Este, *Eisenhower*, 147 ("coaxed"); DDE, *At Ease*, 150 ("Icky"); D'Este, *Patton*, 291, 865 n.19.

14 DDE, *At Ease* 17-79; D'Este, *Eisenhower*, 147.

15 DDE, *Crusade*, 41.

16 JSDE, *General Ike*, 4; Coffman 230; GSP, "Tanks in Future Wars," *Infantry Journal* (May 1920) ("third leg to a duck"); DDE, "A Tank Discussion," *Infantry Journal* (November 1920), EL (Pre-Pres Papers, Misc. File, box 22); DDE, *At Ease*, 172–73 ("zealots").

17 DDE, *At Ease*, 173; DDE, draft notes on GSP, 4/6/65, EL (Post-Pres Papers, Secretary's Series, box 3); JSDE, *General Ike*, 4; D'Este, *Eisenhower*, 152; Coffman 230.

18 DDE, "Tanks with Infantry," unpublished MS (approximately May 1921), EL (Pre-Pres Papers, Misc. File, box 22).

19 Hirshson 144–45; D'Este, *Patton*, 285–96.

20 DDE, *At Ease*, 173; D'Este, *Eisenhower*, 154.

21 DDE, *At Ease*, 174.

22 D'Este, *Eisenhower*, 153 (citing DDE, "Unpublished Assessments of World War II Personalities," EL (Post-Pres Papers, box 7).

23 Ibid.

24 ONB, GL, 36; Blair, ONB interview notes, n.d., USAMHI (Blair Collection, box 44).

25 Ibid.

26 ONB, GL, 45; Blair, ONB interview notes, n.d., USAMHI (Blair Collection, box 44).

27 ONB, GL, 44–45; Blair, ONB interview notes, n.d., USAMHI (Blair Collection, box 44).

28 Blair, ONB interview notes, n.d., USAMHI (Blair Collection, box 44).

29 ONB, GL, 46.

30 Blair, ONB interview notes, n.d., USAMHI (Blair Collection, box 44); ONB, GL, 46 ("professionally ruined").

Two: Different Paths

1 D'Este, *Patton*, 221, 245, 304–18, 329–31, 334; Hirshson 162–63, 168–69, 173, 193.

2 D'Este, *Patton*, 341.

3 Hirshson 38–39 (quoting Patton notebook, at 15); PP 1:195; GSP to GSP II, 1/6/06, PP 1:138 ("I am not").

4 Hirshson 39; Semmes 75.

5 Paul D. Harkins, interview, 4/28/74, USAMHI, 19.

6 William F. Train, interview, 1/3/83, USAMHI, 81.

Endnotes ★ 573

7   GSP, "Federal Troops in Domestic Disturbances," 11/32, PP-LC (box 12) ("distasteful").

8   Hirshson 217; D'Este, *Patton*, 360–61.

9   PP 1:154 ("hit the booze"); Totten. 258–60; Robert Patton 233–34.

10   Totten 245 ("for every Napoleon"); GSP to GSP II, 11/12/04, PP 1:115.

11   JSDE, interview, 2/28/67, EL, 1; JSDE, *General Ike*, 7; D'Este, *Eisenhower*, 156 (quoting DDE to Louis Marx, 1/27/48, Pre-Pres Papers, EL).

12   DDE, *At Ease*, 178, 181; JSDE, *General Ike*, 6; D'Este, *Eisenhower*, 163 (quoting Michael E. Bigelow, "Brigadier General Fox Conner and the American Expeditionary Forces," unpublished master's thesis, Temple University, 1984, copy in GCML).

13   DDE, *At Ease*, 178; JSDE, *General Ike*, 7.

14   JSDE, *General Ike*, 8–11.

15   DDE, *At Ease*, 187; DDE, 6/14/32–8/10/32, EP:P 226–27; D'Este, *Eisenhower*, 168.

16   Milton Eisenhower, interview, 10/15/71, EL, 16–17, 21–23.

17   GSP to DDE, 7/9/26, EL (Pre-Pres Papers, box 91) ("HE man"); DDE, "On the Command and General Staff School," 8/26, EP:P 43–58; DDE, *At Ease,* 199–200; D'Este, *Eisenhower*, 178, 180 (citing GSP, "Notes on the Command and General Staff School Course," Box 59, PP-LC).

18   Hirshson 182 (citing Chynoweth to GSP, 7/16/26, 3/8/72 USMA (Chynoweth Papers, box 1), and Chynoweth, *Bellamy Park* (Hicksville, NY: Exposition Press, 1975), 121–25).

19   GSP to DDE, 7/9/26, EL (Pre-Pres Papers, box 91).

20   D'Este, *Eisenhower*, 187 (citing interview with Milton Eisenhower).

21   GSP to BAP, 9/3/28, PP-LC (box 10); D'Este, *Patton*, 341; JSDE, *Strictly Personal*, 8–9.

22   DDE, 4/10/30, 3/28/31, 6/15/32, in EP:P 115, n.1., 170, 228; Gruenther, interview, 9/7/67, EL, 79; D'Este, *Eisenhower*, 209–13.

23   DDE, 8/10/32, EL (Pre-Pres. Papers, Misc. File, box 22); EP:P 233–46; JSDE, interview, 2/28/67, EL, 11.

24   JSDE, interview 2/28/67, EL, 6–7; DDE, "Diary of the American Military Mission in the Philippine Islands," EL (DDE Diaries); DDE, 2/16/26, EP:P 306–7; DDE, *At Ease*, 219–20; D'Este, *Eisenhower*, 232, 247–49.

25   Clark, interview, 1/4/70, EL, 2; Hansen, "Sicily," n.d., USAMHI (Hansen Papers, boxes 2, 9); Atkinson 43; D'Este, *Eisenhower*, 251–52.

26   D'Este, *Eisenhower*, 252 (citing Daniel D. Holt, "An Unlikely Partnership and Service: Dwight Eisenhower, Mark Clark, and the Philippines," *Kansas History* (Autumn 1990)); Blumenson, *Clark*, 44.

27   DDE, *At Ease*, 237; Clark, interview, 1/4/70, EL, 2; D'Este, *Eisenhower*, 252–53.

28   ONB, GL, 47–50.

29   D'Este, *Eisenhower*, 80.

30   ONB, GL, 50 ("quiet life"); Veterans Administration, "Biographical Sketch of General Omar Nelson Bradley," 4/1/46, USAMHI (Hansen Papers, box 9); Blair, ONB interview notes, n.d., USAMHI (Blair Collection, box 44).

31   ONB, GL, 25 (skating); ONB, interview, n.d., USMA (Bradley Papers, box 30) (Kitty Buhler–Chet Hansen interview), 132; Blair, ONB interview notes, n.d., USAMHI (Blair Collection, box 44).

32   Hansen, notes on ONB, n.d., USAMHI (Hansen Papers, box 9); "Biographical Sketch," 8/7/43, USAMHI (Hansen Papers, box 9).

33   Hansen, notes on ONB, n.d., USAMHI (Hansen Papers, box 9); ONB, GL, 52–56.

34   ONB, GL, 56 ("weekends"), 58 ("rotgut"). *But see* ONB, interview, n.d., USMA (Bradley Papers, box 30), (Kitty Buhler–Chet Hansen interview, 132 (allergic to corn).

35   ONB, GL, 58 ("extraordinary"), 59 ("In Hawaii").

36   Ibid.

37 Hansen, notes on ONB, n.d., USAMHI (Hansen Papers, box 9); ONB, GL, 59-60, 681 n. 12.

38 ONB, interview, n.d., USMA (Bradley Papers, box 30), (Kitty Buhler interview), 48–49.

39 ONB, GL, 63.

40 Cray 19-28, 34-37, 51-56, 67-69, 178-82; Coffman 209, 212-13; D'Este, *Patton*, 248.

41 Cray 84-85, 95–102 (July 1924 to May 1927), 104–6; Coffman 264–65.

42 Herbert B. Powell, interview, 11/2/73, USAMHI, 16; ONB, GL, 67; ONB, GL, 682 n.14 (citing ONB Efficiency Reports).

43 Blair, ONB interview notes, 2/6/80, USAMHI (Blair Collection, box 44); ONB, GL, 77-79, 82, 83.

44 "George C. Marshall," *Time*, 1/3/44; Pogue, *Ordeal and Hope*, 2; Cray 143–45; Coffman 373–74.

Three: Marshall's Men

1 Cray 175.

2 GSP to BAP, 7/27/39, PP-LC (box 10, folder 8) ("pretty snappy move"); GSP to BAP, 7/29/39, PP 1:1025 (boat); Hirshson 223 (citing GSP to GCM, 7/20/39, and GCM to GSP, 7/24/39); GCM to GSP, 9/23/39, PP 1:1030 (silver stars).

3 Pogue, *Ordeal and Hope*, 163; D'Este, *Patton*, 376–77; GCM to Gerow, quoted in Farago 29 ("Patton is").

4 D'Este, *Patton*, 377 (quoting GCM, Pogue interviews 510).

5 DDE, *At Ease*, 269.

6 GSP II to GSP, 2/20/19, PP 1:745.

7 PP 2:20.

8 John K. Waters, interview, 4/9/80, USAMHI, 132–33 ("Nobody was"); Hirshson 236 (quoting Albert N. Garland, "From the Papers of Lt. Gen. Raymond S. McLain: They Had Charisma," *Army* (May 1971), 30); Coffman 390; PP 2:20; D'Este, *Patton*, 386.

9 DDE to ONB, 7/1/40, EL (Pre-Pres Papers, box 13); DDE, *Crusade*, 9.

10 DDE to MacArthur, 12/11/40, EP:P 513; DDE, *Crusade*, 11.

11 DDE to GSP, 9/17/40, EL (Pre-Pres Papers, box 91). *See also* DDE, *At Ease*, 237

12 GSP to DDE, 10/1/40, EL (Pre-Pres Papers, box 91).

13 GSP to DDE, 11/1/40, EL (Pre-Pres Papers, box 91); PP 2:15.

14 DDE to GSP, 11/16/40, EL (Pre-Pres Papers, box 91).

15 DDE to Clark, 10/31/40, EP:P 497. D'Este, *Eisenhower*, 275.

16 DDE, 12/27/35, EP:P 293; DDE to Davis, 10/31/40, EP:P 491–92, 499.

17 DDE to GSP, 11/16/40, EP:P 503.

18 PP 2:863; Coffman 388–89; Gabel 24–27.

19 Devers, interview, 11/18/74, EL, 91–93; PP 2:863; Coffman 389.

20 GSP to Mrs. William L. Wills, 5/15/41, PP 2:27 ("great drag").

21 ONB, GL, 87.

22 Maxwell D. Taylor, interview, 11/10/72, p. 25, USAMHI; ONB, GL, 90.

23 ONB, GL, 93.

24 Ibid., 93–94. See also Hansen, 2/17/45, USAMHI (Hansen Papers, box 5), (less embellished version).

25 ONB, GL, 94; ONB, SS, 21; ONB, interview, n.d., USMA (Bradley Papers, box 30), (Kitty Buhler interview), 45; ONB, GL, 94–95.

26 ONB, GL, 97, 100.

27 Coffman 393-94.

28 Gabel 53–54, 64–65; Coffman 394; D'Este, *Eisenhower*, 277.

29 "Big Maneuvers Test U.S. Army," *Life*, 10/6/41, 33–43; Gabel 69–87; Coffman 395–96; Hirshson 247 (quoting Henry Cabot Lodge, *The Storm Has Many Eyes* (New York: W. W. Norton, 1973), 76) ("s.o.b."), 249 (quoting *New York Times*, 9/17/41); D'Este, *Eisenhower*, 277; D'Este, *Patton*, 396.

30 Gabel 104-5; D'Este, *Eisenhower*, 279.

31 Gabel 109–11; Coffman 392; Hirshson 250.

32 Ibid., 99 ("extraordinary generals").

33 ONB, GL, 89, 99 ("Patton broke"); Hirshson 5 (citing McNair, "Memorandum for General Marshall," 10/7/41, PP-USMA); PP 2:47, 863; D'Este, *Patton*, 403.

34 Henry J. Aurand, interview, 1/23/68, EL, 4; JSDE, interview, 2/28/68, EL, 23; D'Este, *Eisenhower*, 278–81 (citing Robert Eichelberger, in Eichelberger papers, USAMHI).

35 Clark 16–17; Blumenson, *Mark Clark*, 53–54; D'Este, *Eisenhower*, 281.

36 Ambrose, *Supreme Commander*, 3.

37 DDE, interview, 6/28/62, EL, 3; Gruenther, interview, 4/20/67, EL, 8.

38 DDE, interview, 6/28/62, EL, 5.

39 DDE, *Crusade*, 17–22.

40 EP 1:5–6.

41 Ibid., and n.1; D'Este, *Eisenhower*, 283–84 (quoting DDE, "Churchill and Marshall" EL (Post-Pres Papers, Series A-WR, box 8)); DDE to Marshall, 12/14/41, EP 1:5–6

42 Ambrose, *Supreme Commander*, 6; Pogue, *Ordeal and Hope*, 337 ("Eisenhower,"). See also DDE, interview, 6/28/62, EL, 8.

43 GSP to DDE, 1/22/42, PP 2:49.

44 Blumenson, *Patton*, 176; GSP to Edward K. Thompson, 2/10/42, PP 2:53–54.

45 GSP to A. D. Surles, 2/10/42, PP 2:54; GSP to Jacob L. Devers, 2/11/42, PP 2:54; Devers, interview, 11/18/74, EL, 100–1.

46 GSP to DDE, 2/20/42, PP 2:55–56.

47 DDE to GSP, 2/25/42, EP 1:142; PP 2:56.

48 DDE to GSP, 4/4/42, EP 1:227.

49 GSP to DDE, 4/13/42, PP 2:62 and EP 1:263 n.2.

50 DDE to GSP, 4/21/42, EP 1:262.

51 GSP to DDE, 5/1/42, EL (Pre-Pres Papers, Principal File, box 91) and PP 2:65–66.

52 Ben Harrell, interview, 12/17/71, USAMHI, 68–69.

53 ONB, SS, 13; ONB, GL, 102.

54 Pyle, *Brave Men*, 328; Blair, ONB interview notes, 2/6/80, USAMHI (Blair Collection, box 44); ONB, SS, 13; ONB, GL, 104-5.

55 Hansen, notes on ONB, n.d., USAMHI (Hansen Papers, box 9); ONB, GL, 105.

56 McNair to ONB, 6/18/42, USAMHI (Bradley Papers); ONB, SS, 14; ONB, GL, 108.

Four: Striking the Match

1 Jonathan W. Jordan, "George C. Marshall," *World War II Magazine* (October 2006); Harrison 2–4; D'Este, *Eisenhower*, 288; Ambrose, *Supreme Commander*, 26–27.

2 Harrison 11–18.

3 Ibid. 10–11; Atkinson 13; Maycock 42; DDE, *Crusade*, 77–78; Ambrose, *Supreme Commander*, 24–25.

4 DDE, 1/4/42, EL (Pre-Pres Papers, Misc. File); DDE to LeRoy Lutes, 12/31/41, EP 1:33; Atkinson 60.

5 DDE, 3/10/42–3/11/42, EL (Pre-Pres Papers).

6 DDE, 1/19/42 and 3/10/42, EL (DDE Diaries, box 1) ("shoot King"); DDE to Gerow, 7/16/42, EP 1:386; McKeogh 51 (profanity); D'Este, *Eisenhower*, 292 (quoting DDE, 3/21/42, et seq., EL (Pre-Pres Papers), 293.

7 DDE, *At Ease*, 249.

8 Ibid.

9 D'Este, *Eisenhower*, 302–3 (citing DDE, Pogue interview and JSDE Oral history, EL).

10 JDSE, interview, 2/28/68, EL, 24; DDE, 3/30/42, EP 1:220; D'Este, *Eisenhower*, 303 and 752, n.17 (quoting DDE, 3/21/42, et seq., EL (Pre-Pres Papers)).

11 DDE, 5/21/42, EP 1:315; DDE to MDE, 6/26/42, *Letters to Mamie*, 23; Clark 17–18; DDE, *At Ease*, 49.

12 DDE, 5/23/42–5/30/42, EP 1:319–22; Summersby 78; D'Este, *Eisenhower*, 305.

13 D'Este, *Eisenhower*, 338–39; Strong 205 (voice).

14 Alanbrooke, 365, 632; Roberts 140-42; D'Este, *Eisenhower*, 338 (quoting DDE, "Reflections on the ARCADIA Conference," Post-Pres Papers, Box 8, A-WR series, EL).

15 DDE, 5/27/42, EP 1:319; Clark 18–19.

16 D'Este, *Eisenhower*, 304–5 (citing Clark interview); Blumenson, *Mark Clark*, 58.

17 Summersby, *Past Forgetting*, 24–25.

18 DDE 6/4/42, EL (Pre-Pres Papers); DDE to GCM, 6/3/42, EP 1:327; DDE, *Crusade*, 50.

19 D'Este, *Eisenhower*, 306–7 (quoting Hatch, *General Ike*, 113).

20 DDE, 6/11/42, EP 1:337.

21 Codman 102 ("hickory"); PP 2:56–57.

22 PP 2:70.

23 D'Este, *Eisenhower*, 300.

24 DDE, *Crusade*, 41.

25 D'Este, *Eisenhower*, 301. See also DDE, *Crusade*, 41.

26 D'Este, *Eisenhower*, 301 (quoting DDE, unpublished assessments of WWII personalities, Box 7, Post-Pres Papers, Series A-WR, EL).

27 Pogue, *Ordeal and Hope*, 404; PP 2:70.

28 Ibid.; D'Este, *Patton*, 415.

29 PP 2:70–71; D'Este, *Patton*, 415–16.

30 Pogue, *Ordeal and Hope,* 333 (tanks and guns); DDE, *Crusade*, 40-41; D'Este, *Patton*, 416; Atkinson 16.

31 Pogue, *Ordeal and Hope*, 405 ("way to handle Patton"), 406.

32 GSP to Floyd Parks, 7/42, PP 2:71.

33 Jake L. Devers to GSP, 6/11/42, PP 2:71; GSP to Jake L. Devers, 7/14/42, PP 2:71.

34 DDE, *Crusade*, 52–53.

35 DDE, 2/23/42, EL (DDE Diaries, box 1).

36 DDE to MDE, 10/31/42, *Letters to Mamie*, 52–53; Butcher 4; Summersby 21; DDE to Milton S. Eisenhower, 6/24/42, EP 1:414 ("lonely life"); Summersby, *Past Forgetting*, 39 ("sick dog"), 52-55; McKeogh 40.

37 DDE to Davis, 12/6/39, EL (Thomas J. Davis Papers); Butch 5 ("roly-poly"); Summersby 31–32; DDE to Nina Davis, 1/11/43, EL (Davis Papers).

38 Summersby 22; Summersby, *Past Forgetting*, 40, 104.

39 Clark 24; McKeogh 2; D'Este, *Eisenhower*, 311 (quoting Clark, *Captain's Bride*, 97) ("Don't worry").

40 Pogue, *Supreme Command,* 39; Harrison 3–4; DDE to GCM, 3/12/45, EP 4:2521 ("arrange the blankets").

41 D'Este, *Eisenhower*, 326 (citing Mattingly, "A Compilation of the General Health Status of Dwight D. Eisenhower," EL) (bursitis); Butcher 18 (diet); McKeogh 39–49 (cigarettes); Summersby 29 (stress).

42 Summersby 29 ("wrinkles deepened"); D'Este, *Eisenhower*, 327.

43 Hirshson 265 (quoting GSP to DDE, 7/8/42, Box 91, Pre-Pres Papers, EL); Butcher, 7/10/42, EL (Pre-Pres Papers) (lieutenant general).

44 DDE to GSP, 7/20/42, EP 1:399–400.

45 Summersby 10–12; Chase 47–48 ("heavily lidded").

46 Summersby 11, 18-19; EP 1:659, n.1 ("Skib"); DDE to WBS, 11/16/42, EP 2:718 ("Skib").

47 D'Este, *Eisenhower*, 324–25; Truscott 170.

48 DDE, 7/11/42, 7/17/42, EP 1:370, 389 ("strategically unsound"); EP 1:381, n.1.

49 Ambrose, *Supreme Commander*, 50–51; DDE, *Crusade*, 69 (citing FDR to Hopkins, King, and GCM, 6/16/42); Ray W. Barker, interview, EL, 7/16/72, 44; Clark 34; Pogue 2:326–27; Maycock 45–46.

50 Harrison 31.

51 DDE, *Letters to Mamie*, 22; DDE, *Crusade*, 71–72, 156; Pogue, *Ordeal and Hope*, 348; Ambrose, *Supreme Commander*, 78 (citing DDE, interview, 12/7/65); Cray 334; Butcher 32; D'Este, *Eisenhower*, 335.

52 D'Este, *Eisenhower*, 337 ("bulldog and cat"); Bolte, interview, 1/29/75, EL 143; D'Este, *Patton*, 417.

53 Ambrose, *Supreme Commander*, 80–81.

54 D'Este, *Eisenhower*, 315 (citing Clark oral history, Clark Papers, USAMHI).

55 Clark 39–40; DDE, *Crusade*, 76; Butcher 36, 48–49; DDE, *Crusade*, 55; D'Este, *Eisenhower*, 336.

56 D'Este, *Eisenhower*, 336.

57 Butcher 40, 43; Clark 42; Summersby, *Past Forgetting*, 47.

58 Atkinson 27.

59 DDE to GCM, 8/9/42, Hobbs 32; DDE, *Crusade*, 78–79; D'Este, *Eisenhower*, 343, 360.

60 DDE to GCM, 7/29/42, Hobbs 31; DDE to Vernon E. Pritchard, 8/27/42, EP 1:505 ("I have developed"); DDE, *At Ease*, 253.

61 GSP to BAP, 7/30/42, PP 2:73; Floyd Parks to GSP, 7/29/42, PP 2:73.

62 Gay, interview, 10/4/80–10/5/80, USAMHI (Gay Papers), 1–13, 15; TUSA, "Biographical Sketch—Hobart R. Gay" (NARA RG 407, entry 427, box 1588); Lucas, 6/8/43, USAMHI (Lucas Papers); PP 2:757; D'Este, *Patton*, 418.

63 GSP, *War*, 30 (tech sgt.); Semmes 75–76 (10th Cavalry Regiment).

64 GSP, 8/5/42–8/6/42, PP-LC (box 2).

65 Butcher, 8/9/42, EL (Pre-Pres Papers, box 165).

66 Ibid., 8/12/42 ("Ike said"); GSP, 8/7/42–8/9/42, PP-LC (box 2); GSP, 8/9/42, PP-LC (box 2) ("had supper"); GSP to BAP, 8/11/42, PP-LC (box 10); DDE to Thomas P. Handy, 8/13/42, EP 1:461–62.

67 GSP, 8/11/42 ("not Pro-British"), 8/12/42 ("not as rugged mentally"), PP-LC (box 2).

68 Butcher, 8/9/42, EL (Pre-Pres Papers, box 165) ("Although friendship").

69 Clark 40; D'Este, *Patton*, 420; GSP, 8/17/42 ("megalomania"), 9/28/42 ("Clark seems"), 8/14/42, PP-LC (box 2).

70 DDE to GCM, 8/17/42, Hobbs 37.

71 Butcher, 8/17/42, EL (Pre-Pres Papers, box 165); DDE, *Crusade*, 485, n.13; Hirshson 268–69.

72 Atkinson, 118 (citing Charles W. Ryder, interview, March 1949, Sydney T. Matthews Papers, USAMHI) Howe 25–26; Anderson, "Algeria-French Morocco," 25; D'Este, *Eisenhower*, 350.

73 DDE to GSP, 9/5/42, EP 1:542.

74 GSP to DDE, 8/25/42, EL (Pre-Pres Papers, box 91).

75 DDE to GSP, 8/31/42, EP 1:517–18.

76 Koch 21; GSP, *War*, 393 (Appendix A); Anderson, "Algeria-French Morocco," 6 (34,871 officers and men); Robert E. Coffin, interview, 7/25/80, USAMHI (3rd ID at Fedala); Hirshson 271 (250 tanks); Atkinson 22 (33,843 soldiers).

77 GSP, *War*, 393; Anderson 9; Atkinson 141 (citing Lucian K. Truscott, Jr., *Twilight of the Cavalry*, xiii–xv; John K. Waters, USAMHI interview, 1980); D'Este, *Patton*, 422.

78 GSP, *War*, 393.

79 Hansen, "Memorandum for the Record," 10/21/46, USAMHI (Blair Collection, box 47) ("Poor man's Patton"); GSP, *War*, 394; Dale 3; Atkinson 111.

80 Koch 87; Hirshson 269; Anderson, "Algeria-French Morocco," 6–7; GSP, 9/28/42, PP 2:87 ("very pessimistic"); D'Este, *Patton*, 419; Kirkpatrick 30.

81 Atkinson 22 (citing John Clagett, "Admiral H. Kent Hewitt, U.S. Navy," *Naval War College Review* (Summer/Fall 1975)).

82 DDE, *Crusade*, 82; PP 2:88; D'Este, *Patton*, 421, quoting Pogue, *Ordeal and Hope*, 405; Farago 96–97.

83 D'Este, *Patton*, 422 (citing BAP, personal notes, 12/7/49, PP-LC [box 36]). *See also* GSP 10/21/42, PP 2:92–93 (slightly different quote); Hirshson 275.

84 DDE to GCM, 8/15/42, EP 1:469; DDE, *Crusade*, 91; Ambrose, *Supreme Commander*, 100.

85 Butcher, 8/19/42, EL (Pre-Pres Papers, box 165); Summersby 34; DDE to GCM, 10/20/42, Hobbs 51.

86 Summersby 29–30; McKeogh 40–41; Summersby, *Past Forgetting*, 48; DDE to MDE, 10/27/42, *Letters to Mamie*, 49; D'Este, *Eisenhower*, 322.

87 Summersby 32-33 (clothes, highball); McKeogh 13, 15, 34–35, 41 (food, golf balls); Ambrose, *Supreme Commander*, 58; D'Este, *Eisenhower*, 323.

88 DDE to MDE, 10/13/42, *Letters to Mamie*, 46 ("can't talk war"); Butcher 137, 143; Summersby 36; Summersby, *Past Forgetting*, 66; McKeogh 41.

89 McKeogh 41–42; 67–68; D'Este, *Eisenhower*, 322–23.

90 Butcher 90; DDE, *Crusade*, 54–55; Smith 2; Summersby 52 ("S.S. general"); Ray W. Barker, interview, 7/15/72, EL, 19 ("chopper-off").

91 ONB, SS, 206.

92 Ray W. Barker, interview, 7/15/72, EL, 19; Strong 116 ("we hired you"); Inez G. Scott, interview, 1/79, EL, 23; Robert D. Murphy, interview, 10/12/72, EL, 9, 26; D'Este, *Eisenhower*, 318–19 (quoting William P. Snyder, "Walter Bedell Smith," *Military Affairs* (Jan. 1984)) ("He was terrifying"); Ambrose, *Supreme Commander*, 82 (quoting Pogue, interview, 9/11/67) ("She's an idiot"); Summersby 52; Crosswell 198.

93 DDE to MDE, 10/13/42, *Letters to Mamie*, 46; Pogue, *Ordeal and Hope*, 408; Charles H. Bonesteel III, interview, 11/9/72, USAMHI, 136–37; Summersby 52–53; Butcher 90; DDE to Charles Gailey, 9/19/42, EP 1:568 ("fishing-rod"); D'Este, *Eisenhower*, 317, 446 (quoting Arthur Nevins, interview, EL) ("no such thing"); DDE, "Associates," 7/5/67, Post-Pres Papers, A-WR Series, box 7, EL.

94 Butcher 90; DDE, *Crusade*, 76.

95 Murphy 103–5; Robert D. Murphy, interview, 10/12/72, EL, 2–4; Butcher 103; DDE, *Crusade*, 88; Summersby 37–38; D'Este, *Eisenhower*, 344–45.

96 Murphy 103–5; "Combat Estimate: French Morocco Army, May 1, 1942," USAMHI, 1; Atkinson 26–27; Bilgé 17; Butcher 178a ("kiss Darlan's stern"); D'Este, *Eisenhower*, 344, 354 (quoting DDE to MDE, 10/8/42).

97 DDE to GSP, 10/13/42, EP 1:618.

98 Farago 23.

99   DDE to OPD and GSP, 10/13/42, EP 1:614; Farago 23.

100 DDE to GCM, 10/12/42, Hobbs 49; D'Este, *Eisenhower*, 345.

101 DDE to Charles Gailey, 9/19/42, EP 1:568.

102 McKeogh 85–86; Butcher, 11/7/42, EL (Pre-Pres Papers, box 165); Summersby 42.

103 GSP, 10/18/42, PP-LC (box 2).

104 GSP, 10/21/42, PP 2:94; Atkinson 30–31.

105 GSP, 10/21/42, PP-LC (box 2); Atkinson 32.

106 Butcher, 11/6/42, EL (Pre-Pres Papers, box 165); DDE to WBS, 11/6/42, EP 1: 658;
     DDE to WSC, 11/6/42, EP 1:653; Butcher 162; Clark 93; DDE, *Crusade*, 94.

107 DDE to MDE, 11/15/42, *Letters to Mamie*, 62.

108 Butcher, 11/6/42, EL (Pre-Pres Papers, box 165) ("damned well"); Clark 94; McKeogh
     46; DDE, *Crusade*, 95 ("dismal"); Atkinson 58 (30 miles); D'Este, *Eisenhower*, 350.

109 Atkinson 58 (quoting AFHQ message, 11/5/42, NARA RG 407, E 427, "Pre-Invasion
     Planning," box 24350).

110 DDE to GCM, 11/7/42, EP 2:667 ("brickbats"); DDE, *Crusade*, 106; D'Este, *Eisen-
     hower*, 348.

111 Butcher, 11/7/42, EL (Pre-Pres Papers, box 165).

112 Ibid.

Five: Tracks in the Desert

1   Butcher, 11/8/42, EL (Pre-Pres Papers, box 165).

2   Ibid.

3   Clark 101, 103; Butcher 176.

4   Butcher 175-79; Atkinson 127. Initial reports of Darlan's capture turned out to be false.

5   Butcher, 11/8/42, EL (Pre-Pres Papers, box 165); DDE to GCM, 11/8/42, EP 2: 673;
     Butcher 173.

6   Butcher, 11/8/42, EP 2:675.

7   DDE to AGWAR and ABFOR, 11/8/42, EL (Pre-Pres Papers, box 165); Butcher 176-77;
     Clark 103–4.

8   DDE to GCM, 11/9/42, EP 2:680; Butcher xviii (navy signal regarding Darlan's
     capitulation).

9   DDE to Clark, 12/25/42, EP 2:860 ("yellow-bellied"); Butcher 178a ("Darlan's stern").

10   Butcher, 11/8/42, EL (Pre-Pres Papers, box 165) ("assassin"); DDE to WBS, 11/9/42, EP
     2:677 ("conceited worms"); DDE to GCM, 11/9/42, EP 1:680 ("stupid Frogs").

11   DDE to GCM, 11/7/42, PP 2:103; Atkinson 61.

12   DDE to WBS, 11/9/42, EP 2:678; D'Este, *Eisenhower*, 355.

13   Butcher 175; Atkinson 114.

14   Atkinson 114.

15   Butcher 176.

16   GSP, 11/7/42–11/8/42, PP-LC (box 2).

17   GSP, "Description of the Visit of the Commanding General and Staff to General Nogues
     and the Sultan of Morocco," 11/16/42, PP-LC (box 10).

18   Atkinson 103-5 (quoting Reminiscences of Rear Admiral Elliott B. Strauss, 1989, USNI
     OHD).

19   Ibid. 104.

20   GSP, *War*, 8.

21   GSP, 11/8/42, PP 2:105; Howe, *Northwest Africa*, 123–25; USS *Augusta*, ship's log,
     11/8/42; D'Este, *Patton*, 434–35.

22 Farago 39.

23 GSP to BAP, 11/8/42, PP 2:103; GSP, 11/8/42, PP-LC (box 2); Farago 40 ("toothbrush").

24 D'Este, *Patton*, 435; Farago 198–99 (citing George Raynor Thompson, et al., *The Signal Corps: The Test (December 1941 to July 1943)*, (part of the *U.S. Army in World War II* series, Washington, D.C., 1957)); Butcher 182.

25 GSP, 11/8/42, PP 2:105; GSP, *War*, 9; Anderson, *Algeria*, 9; Hirschon 281; D'Este, *Patton*, 435; Farago 39, 42.

26 GSP, 11/8/42, PP-LC (box 2); GSP to DDE, 11/19/42, EL (Pre-Pres Papers, box 91); Semmes 135; Anderson, *Algeria*, 9–14.

27 GSP, *War*, 373–74; DDE, "Report of the Commander-in-Chief of Allied Forces to the Combined Chiefs of Staff on Operations in North Africa," n.d., 13 (at http://www.ibiblio.org/hyperwar/USA/rep/TORCH/DDE-Torch.html#plans) (hereinafter, "DDE, North Africa Report"); Anderson, *Algeria*, 16–17; Atkinson 138 (citing Arthur R. Wilson to GCM, 12/12/42, NARA RG 165 E13, Ofc. Chief of Staff, box 106); Farago 194–95.

28 Atkinson 148; D'Este, *Patton*, 436–37.

29 Butcher, 11/9/42, EL (Pre-Pres Papers, box 165); DDE, *Crusade*, 98 ("prayer of Thanksgiving"); DDE to GSP, 10/10/42, PP-LC (box 10) ("Georgie").

30 DDE to GSP, 11/9/42, EP 2:684–85, n.2.

31 DDE to GSP, 10/10/42, PP-LC (box 10).

32 DDE to Hewitt, 11/12/42, EL (Pre-Pres Papers, Principal File, box 91); Butcher, 11/12/42, EL (Pre-Pres Papers, box 165); Butcher 189; DDE, *Crusade*, 104; Butcher, 11/12/42, EL (Pre-Pres Papers, box 165).

33 D'Este, *Patton*, 242 (quoting Samuel Rockenbach, "V.M.I. Smoker on the Anniversary of the Battle of New Market," Washington, D.C., 5/14/22, PP-USMA); GSP to DDE, 11/15/42, PP-LC (box 24) ("I regret").

34 GSP to BAP, 11/11/42, PP 2:110; Atkinson 149.

35 GSP to BAP, 11/11/42, PP 2:110; Farago 200.

36 GSP, 11/11/42, PP 2:110; Clark 113; Farago 203; Atkinson 149.

37 Hirshson 288 (11 million); Butcher, 12/6/42, EL (Pre-Pres Papers, box 166), (17 million Arabs in French North Africa, 1.5 million Europeans, 300,000 Jews); Atkinson 151.

38 GSP, *War*, 375.

39 Codman 46 ("Rising to his full height"); GSP, *War*, 375–76; GSP, 11/11/42, PP 2:110.

40 DDE to GCM, 11/17/42, Hobbs 89.

41 Howe, *Northwest Africa*, 173 (losses).

42 GSP, 11/12/42, PP-LC (box 2) ("I assumed");.GSP to DDE, 11/14/42, PP 2:114–16; DDE to GSP, 11/15/42, EP 2:714–15 ("As reports"); GSP to DDE, 11/15/42, EL (Pre-Pres Papers, Principal File, box 91).

43 GSP to DDE, 11/15/42, EL (Pre-Pres Papers, Principal File, box 91) ("When I had").

44 DDE to GCM, 11/17/42 EP 2:731.

45 Howe 262–63; Butcher 185 ("De Gaulle").

46 Clark 105–11; Ambrose, *Supreme Commander*, 121; Atkinson 163, 171.

47 "Minutes of a Meeting Held in the St. Georges Hotel, Algiers, on the 13th of November," in Butcher, 11/15/42, 11/25/42, EL (Pre-Pres Papers, box 165); Clark 121–22.

48 Butcher 184; DDE, *Crusade*, 106.

49 Atkinson 159.

50 JSDE, interview, 2/28/68, EL, 29.

51 Renstrom 61; Milton Eisenhower, in Butcher, 12/15/42, EL (Pre-Pres Papers, box 166).

52 Clark 125.

53 DDE to CCOS, 11/14/42, EP 2:701–10; WSC to DDE, 11/14/42, in WSC, *Hinge of Fate*, 631; GSP to DDE, 11/19/42, EL (Pre-Pres Papers, Principal File, box 91); Ambrose,

Supreme Commander, 129–30; WBS to DDE, 11/16/43, EL (WBS World War II Collection, box 15); EP 2:739, n.4; Renstrom 60 (quoting FDR, *Complete Presidential Press Conferences of Franklin D. Roosevelt*, Jonathan Daniels, ed., vols. 19–20 (New York: Da Capo Press, 1972, 246–47) ("walk with the Devil"); WSC, *Hinge of Fate*, 633.

54 Butcher, 11/25/42, EL (Pre-Pres Papers, box 165); Robert D. Murphy, interview, 10/12/72, EL, 26–27; A. M. Gruenther to MWC, 11/19/42, EL (Pre-Pres Papers, Principal File, box 23); DDE to WBS, 11/14/42, EP 1:712 ("The authorities in London"); DDE to MDE, 11/27/42, *Letters to Mamie*, 66 ("boiling kettle").

55 GSP to DDE, 11/19/42, PP-LC (box 2); Farago 222–23.

56 Butcher 224; AFHQ to Fifth Army, 2/8/43, EL (Pre-Pres Papers, Principal File, box 14); Farago 223–24; GSP to DDE, 11/19/42, EL (Pre-Pres Papers, box 91).

57 GSP to BAP, 11/17/42, PP 2:122, PP-LC (box 10).

58 GSP, 11/17/42, PP-LC (box 2).

59 GSP to BAP, 11/19/42, PP-LC (box 10). See also PP 2:123.

60 Ernest Hemingway, *Death in the Afternoon* (NY: Scribner, 1932, 2003 ed.), 100.

61 Pyle 328; Blair, ONB interview notes, 2/6/80, USAMHI (Blair Collection, box 44); ONB, GL, 108–9 (quoting McNair to ONB, 6/23/42, BP-USMA) ("need of help").

62 ONB, SS, 15–16; ONB, GL, 110–11 ("The media").

63 ONB, GL, 110-10.

64 GCM to ONB, 12/23/42, Marshall Papers, GCML; GCM, Pogue Interview, 10/5/56, 596.

65 GCM, interview, 7/25/49, GCML; GCM to ONB, 12/23/42, folder 9, GCML, quoted in ONB, GL, 111 ("I think they have asked").

66 DDE to GSP, 11/26/42, EP 2:775; GSP to DDE, 11/19/42, PP-LC (box 2); GSP, *War*, 10–41; D'Este, *Patton*, 436, 440–43, 887, n.18; Hirshson 286.

67 GSP, 11/24/42, PP-LC (box 2) ("Top Dog"); GSP to BAP, 11/27/42, PP-LC (box 10) ("awful blues").

68 GSP to BAP, 12/2/42, PP-LC (box 10).

69 Clark, interview, 1/4/70, EL, 24.

70 GSP, 12/1/42, PP-LC (box 2) ("I had expected this"); GSP to BAP, 12/5/42, PP-LC (box 10) ("Ike and Wayne").

71 GSP, 2/18/43, PP-LC (box 2).

72 D'Este, *Eisenhower*, 361–62; Hirshson 293 (quoting Hanson W. Baldwin, "Notes on General Eisenhower," 4/26/46, Hanson W. Baldwin Papers, Sterling Memorial Library, Yale University, 3) ("The battle line").

73 Anderson 3.

74 DDE to Clark, 11/21/42, EP 2:750.

75 Clark 127.

76 D'Este, *Eisenhower*, 377 ("elderly spinsters"); Atkinson, DOB, 30.

77 Butcher, 11/27/42, EL (Pre-Pres Papers, box 165); Butcher, 199, 205-6; Chase 44.

78 DDE to MDE, 12/9/42, 1/1/43, *Letters to Mamie*, 69, 80; Chase 44 ("whorehouse French"); Butcher 205–6, 221; McKeogh 50, 61; Summersby 51; Summersby, *Past Forgetting*, 105.

79 Butcher, 1/5/43, EL (Pre-Pres Papers, box 166); DDE to MDE, 11/18/42, *Letters to Mamie*, 64; Butcher 230 (francs).

80 DDE to MDE, 2/15/43, *Letters to Mamie*, 94.

81 Betts, interview, 11/20/74, EL, 98.

82 Atkinson 199 (quoting Guy Ramsey, *One Continent Redeemed* (Garden City, NY: Doubleday, Doran, 1943)) ("talk politics"); DDE to GCM, 11/30/42, EP 1:781 ("ten years"); McKeogh, 74; Butcher 189; Atkinson 248 (quoting GCM to Elmer Davis, 12/13/42, NARA RG 165, E13, OCS Corresp., box 106).

83 McKeogh 84.

84 Butcher 203–5, 208; DDE to GCM, 11/30/42, EP 2:780; D'Este, *Eisenhower*, 364–65; Atkinson 217–18.

85 Butcher, 11/30/42, EL (Pre-Pres Papers, box 166); Butcher 210–11.

86 Anderson to DDE, 12/5/42, in Butcher, 12/4/42, EL (Pre-Pres Papers, box 166) ("nasty setback"); Butcher, 12/3/42, EL (Pre-Pres Papers, box 166); Butcher 222; Clark 139; Atkinson 218–24.

87 Butcher, 12/4/42, EL (Pre-Pres Papers, box 166); Atkinson 235.

88 Butcher, 12/9/42, EL (Pre-Pres Papers, box 166); GSP, "Account of General Patton's Visit to the Tunisian Front," PP-LC (box 2).

89 DDE to Butcher, 12/10/42, EP 2:824.

90 GSP, 12/13/42, PP-LC (box 2) ("lack of decision"); GSP to BAP, 12/26/42, PP 2:143 ("fed up").

91 GSP to BAP, 12/30/42, PP-LC (box 10).

92 Butcher, 12/17/42, 12/20/42, EL (Pre-Pres Papers, box 166); Butcher 218; Atkinson 248.

93 DDE to P. A. Hodgson, 12/4/42, EP 2:795.

94 Anderson, *Tunisia*, 11–13.

95 DDE to JSDE, 12/20/42, EP 2:855.

96 Atkinson 246 (quoting GCM to DDE, 12/22/42).

97 Butcher 227; Ernest R. Lee to Hansen, 1/30/51, USAMHI (Hansen Papers, box 2); McKeogh 63; Atkinson 246.

98 Ibid.

99 DDE, *At Ease*, 258 (36 hours); Butcher 227; DDE, *Crusade*, 124; Atkinson 249.

100 Butcher 227–28 ("bitter disappointment"); DDE, *Crusade*, 124; DDE to GCM, 11/30/42, EP 2:780 ("despair"); Atkinson 249 ("continual rain").

101 DDE to MDE, 12/16/42, 12/30/42, *Letters to Mamie*, 72–75; Summersby, *Past Forgetting*, 97, 102; Truscott 125; McKeogh 51.

102 Butcher 229. See also Clark 130.

103 DDE to GSP, 12/29/42, EL (Pre-Pres Papers, box 91); Butcher, 12/22/42, EL (Pre-Pres Papers, box 166; Summersby 52; Summersby, *Past Forgetting*, 98.

104 Butcher 234 ("Carpetbags"), 235 ("Ike went to bed"); Summersby, *Past Forgetting*, 104.

105 Butcher 236; Truscott 135–39.

106 DDE to JSDE, 6/27/42, EP 1:365–66; DDE, *Crusade*, 127; Truscott 124; Butcher 236; Clark 136–37, 140–41, 143; Chase 89; DDE, 12/10/42, *Eisenhower Diaries*, 84; Atkinson 272.

107 PP 2:145, 148–49.

108 GSP, 11/12/42, PP-LC (box 2); GSP to BAP, 11/14/42 PP-LC (box 10); GSP to Frederick Ayer, 12/16/42, PP-LC (box 14); Semmes 142–43.

109 GSP to BAP, 1/9/43, PP 2:149.

110 GSP, 1/10/43, PP-LC (box 2).

111 GSP to BAP, 1/11/43, PP-LC (box 10).

112 GSP, 1/10/43, PP-LC (box 2).

113 Butcher 444 ("VGDIPs"); Hirshson 297.

114 GSP, 1/16/43, PP-LC (box 2); GSP, 1/17/43, PP 2:155–56.

115 GSP, 1/15/43 (King), 1/16/43 ("I am better"), 1/18/43 (Hopkins), 1/19/43, PP-LC (box 2) (Roosevelt).

116 Butcher, 1/19/43, EL (Pre-Pres Papers, box 166); DDE, *At Ease*, 259.

117 DDE, *Crusade*, 137; Atkinson 286.

118 GSP, 1/16/43, PP 2:154; Butcher, 1/19/43, EL (Pre-Pres Papers, box 166).

119 Butcher, 1/19/43, EL (Pre-Pres Papers, box 166) (Clark); GSP, 1/15/43, PP-LC (box 2) ("old self"); DDE to GCM, 1/17/43, Hobbs 96.

120 Butcher, 1/20/43, EL (Pre-Pres Papers, box 166).

121 GCM to GSP, 1/23/43, PP-LC (box 10); WSC to GSP, 1/25/43, PP-LC (box 10); Cunningham to GSP, 1/20/43, PP-LC (box 10); GSP, 1/16/43, PP-LC (box 2).

122 Jacob L. Devers to BAP, 2/12/43, PP-LC (box 13); GSP to Helen Sprigg, n.d., PP 2:163 ("Personally,").

123 DDE, North Africa Report, 40; Clark 152; DDE, *Crusade*, 138; ONB, SS, 35; Atkinson 328.

124 GSP, 1/26/43, PP-LC (box 2).

125 DDE, 1/19/43, in Butcher, 1/19/43, EL (Pre-Pres Papers, box 166); Cline 374.

126 DDE to GCM, 2/11/43, USAMHI (Hansen papers, box 1); DDE, *At Ease*, 260-61; D'Este, *Eisenhower*, 386–87.

127 Jehl, interview, 2/13/91, EL, 44; DDE to MDE, 2/26/43, 2/28/43, 5/14/43, 6/11/43, 7/3/43, 5/12/44, *Letters to Mamie*, 98–99, 123, 127, 132, 179; Summersby 46–47; Chase 41; DDE to MDE, 3/2/43, *Letters to Mamie*, 104–5 ("banal and foolish"); Butcher xvii.

128 Jehl, interview, 2/13/91, EL, 19–20, 37; Hansen, 9/22/44, USAMHI (Hansen Papers, box 4); "WAC Captain to Marry Elliott Roosevelt," Pittsburgh *Post-Gazette*, 7/6/44 (Roosevelt).

129 Hughes, 12/30/42, LC (Hughes Papers, box 2) ("Discussed Kay"); Inez G. Scott, interview, 1/79, EL, 12 ("didn't like Kay"); ONB, GL, 133 fn. ("Their close relationship is quite accurately portrayed, as far as my personal knowledge extends, in Kay's second book, *Past Forgetting*."); Summersby *Past Forgetting*, 124 (Bradley referred to Kay as "Ike's shadow"); GSP, 6/10/43, PP-LC (box 1) (after dinner with Ike, Kay, Butcher, and "a girl of Butcher's," "Kay also came to breakfast?").

130 Margaret Chase, 2/4/43, EL (Chase Papers); Summersby 61-63; Summersby, *Past Forgetting*, 107; D'Este, *Eisenhower*, 388–89; Hughes, 2/12/43, LC (Hughes Papers, box 2) ("Maybe Kay").

131 GSP to DDE, 2/12/43, EL (Pre-Pres Papers, box 91); DDE to GSP, 2/18/43, EL (Pre-Pres Papers, box 91); DDE, *Crusade*, 141; D'Este, *Eisenhower*, 388–90; Atkinson 329; Butcher, 2/15/43, EL (Pre-Pres Papers, box 166); Summersby 58; McKeogh 73; Summersby, *Past Forgetting*, 82.

Six: A Long-Lost Brother

1 D'Este, *Eisenhower*, 391.

2 GSP, 1/28/43, PP-LC (box 2).

3 Butcher, 2/20/43, EL (Pre-Pres Papers, box 166); DDE, *Crusade*, 140; Atkinson 322.

4 "G-2 Estimate No. 6," 1/30/43, USAMHI (Hansen Papers, box 1); "G-2 Estimate No. 7," 2/3/43, USAMHI (Hansen Papers, box 1); "G-2 Estimate No. 9," 2/15/43, USAMHI (Hansen Papers, box 1); Dickson to Hansen, 5/9/49, USAMHI (Hansen Papers, box 1); Butcher, 2/18/43, 2/20/43, EL (Pre-Pres Papers, box 166); Truscott 152–53; Clark 153; DDE, *Crusade*, 141; Atkinson 332.

5 Butcher, 2/2/43–2/4/43, EL (Pre-Pres Papers, box 166); Truscott 150; DDE, *Crusade*, 140–42; D'Este, *Eisenhower*, 391–92; Atkinson 276, 325.

6 Butcher, 2/15/43, EL (Pre-Pres Papers, box 166); Truscott 146; Atkinson 275.

7 Butcher 259; Truscott 151; DDE, *Crusade*, 14.

8 Butcher, 3/4/43, EL (Pre-Pres Papers, box 166) ("high-schoolish"); D'Este, *Eisenhower*, 392–93; Atkinson 333.

9 DDE to GCM, 2/15/43, EP 1:955; D'Este, *Patton*, 860, n.15.

10 DDE, North Africa Report, 34; II Corps, "Report of Operations, 15 Jan–15 May 43," n.d., USAMHI (Hansen Papers, box 10); D'Este, *Eisenhower*, 393; Atkinson 223–24, 357.

11 DDE to GCM, 2/21/43, Hobbs 103 (112 medium tanks); Truscott 155–56; Butcher, 2/17/43, EL (Pre-Pres Papers, box 166); DDE, *Crusade*, 143; Atkinson 362–63; Anderson, *Tunisia*, 16.

12 Atkinson 389-90; Butcher 263; Summersby 61; Hirschon 308; D'Este, *Eisenhower*, 394.

13 Butcher, 2/23/43, EL (Pre-Pres Papers, box 166) ("one of the greatest defeats"); McKeogh 73.

14 GCM to DDE, 2/17/43, EP 2:958; Atkinson 391.

15 DDE to JSDE, 2/19/43, EP 2:965.

16 Fredendall to DDE, 2/19/43, EL (Pre-Pres Papers, box 43); D'Este, *Eisenhower*, 394; Atkinson 364.

17 D'Este, *Eisenhower*, 396 (quoting "Personal Memoirs of Major General E. N. Harmon"); Harmon, interview, 9/15/52, USAMHI.

18 DDE to Fredendall, 2/23/43, EP 2:980.

19 DDE, "On the Command and General Staff School," ca. August 1926, EP:P 57 ("Trust not"); DDE to GCM, 2/21/43, Hobbs 102–3; DDE, *Crusade*, 143; D'Este, *Eisenhower*, 395; Atkinson 399.

20 Atkinson, DOB, 8; DDE to Gerow, 2/24/43, VMI Archives.

21 Harmon 120 ("No damned good"); Alexander, interview, 1/10/49–1/15/49, USAMHI (OCMH Collection, Sydney Matthews Papers, box 2) ("better man").

22 Butcher, 2/23/43, EL (Pre-Pres Papers, box 166).

23 "Biographical Sketch," 8/7/43, USAMHI (Hansen Papers, box 9).

24 ONB, SS, 15–16.

25 GCM to ONB, 2/12/43, USAMHI (Hansen Papers, box 1); ONB, SS, 16.

26 GCM to ONB, 2/15/43, USAMHI (Hansen papers, box 1); Adjutant General to ONB, 2/16/43, USAMHI (Bradley Papers); ONB, GL, 113; ONB, SS, 16–17 (slightly different chronology).

27 Adjutant General to ONB, 2/16/43, USAMHI (Bradley Papers).

28 GCM to DDE, 2/15/43, USAMHI (Hansen Papers, box 1); EP 2:952 n.4; DDE, *Crusade*, 215.

29 ONB, GL, 113.

30 Hansen, 2/20/43, USAMHI (Hansen Papers, box 4); ONB, GL, 131.

31 ONB, GL, 132.

32 Ibid.

33 DDE, *Howitzer*, 1915, in ONB, GL, 192–93 (photo); ONB, GL, 132.

34 ONB, SS, 31.

35 ONB, GL, 132.

36 Ibid.

37 ONB, GL, 135.

38 Butcher, 2/23/43, EL (Pre-Pres Papers, box 166); ONB, GL, 135 (citing Hansen-ONB interview); Howze, interview, 10/14/72, USAMHI, 110–11; D'Este, *Eisenhower*, 765, n. 27.

39 ONB, GL, 137; ONB, SS, 42.

40 MWC to DDE, 1/30/43, EL (Pre-Pres Papers, box 23).

41 GSP to BAP, 5/1/43, 5/10/43, PP-LC (box 11); DDE, "Memorandum for Personal File," in Butcher, 6/11/43, EL (Pre-Pres Papers, Principal File).

42 D'Este, *Eisenhower*, 396–97; DDE, "Memorandum for Personal File," in Butcher, 6/11/43, EL (Pre-Pres Papers, Principal File); Clark 39–40.

43 Atkinson 272 (quoting Butcher) ("manure pile").

44 GSP, 1/28/43, PP-LC (box 2) & PP 2:164.

45 Ibid.

46 DDE to GSP, 2/4/42, EP 2:938–39.

47 GSP, 2/5/43, in D'Este, *Patton*, 445; PP 2:168–69.

48 GSP to DDE, n.d., EL (Pre-Pres Papers, box 91).

49 GSP, 2/6/43, PP 2:169.

50 EP 2:939 n.1; GSP to BAP, 2/19/43, PP-LC (box 10) ("great man").

51 GSP to BAP, 2/28/43, PP-LC (box 10); Codman 89; GSP, 2/19/43, PP-LC (box 2) ("damned poor bet").

52 GSP to BAP, 2/23/43, PP-LC (box 10) ("very quiet," "Stone Wall Jackson type," "wonderfully conceited"); GSP, 2/14/43, PP-LC (box 2) ("clerical types"); Maycock (dating this meeting February 16).

53 GSP to BAP, 3/4/43, PP-LC (box 10); Davidson, *Grandpa Gar*, 79; GSP, 3/4/43, PP-LC (box 2) ("Victory").

Seven: Forging the Partnership

1 GSP, *War*, 395; ONB, SS, 37; PP 2:183.

2 Butcher 272–73 (3/7 entry); GSP to BAP, 3/6/43, PP-LC (box 10).

3 Butcher 273.

4 Butcher 273; DDE to GSP, 3/6/43, EP 2:1010; ONB, SS, 45; Farago 237.

5 Butcher 273; DDE to GSP, 3/6/43, PP 2:182.

6 GSP 3/5/43, PP-LC (box 2); Farago 236–37.

7 GSP 3/6/43, PP-LC (box 2); ONB, SS, 43 ("charioteer").

8 GSP to BAP, 3/6/43, PP 2:181; GSP, 3/6/43, 3/13/43, PP-LC (box 2); GSP to BAP, 3/15/43, PP-LC (box 10).

9 ONB, interview, n.d., USMA (Kitty Buhler interview), 53; ONB, SS, 45 ("spies").

10 ONB, SS, 45.

11 GSP 3/7/43, PP-LC (box 2).

12 GSP, 3/6/43, PP 2:181; GSP to Hansen, 3/6/43, 3/26/43 USAMHI (Hansen Papers, boxes 3 & 4); Bruce Medaris to Hansen, 2/7/51, USAMHI (Hansen Papers, box 2); ONB, interview, n.d., USMA (Kitty Buhler interview), 137

13 Koch 148 ("buttons"); GSP 3/11/43, PP-LC (box 2).

14 ONB, interview, n.d., USMA (Kitty Buhler interview), 52; GSP to DDE, 3/13/43, EL (Pre-Pres Papers, box 91); ONB, SS, 44–45; Lande 45–46.

15 ONB, SS, 44 ("pocketbooks"); GSP to DDE, 3/13/43, EL (Pre-Pres Papers, box 91) ("Just soaked").

16 McKeogh 77.

17 ONB, SS, 52.

18 D'Este, *Patton*, 465 (quoting Bradley Commentaries, USAMHI).

19 Blair, ONB interview notes, 2/8/80, USAMHI (Blair Collection, box 44) (El Paso); "Terry de la Mesa Allen," *Time*, 8/9/43; D'Este, *Patton*, 465–66; Atkinson 82–83.

20 ONB, interview, n.d., USMA (Bradley Papers, box 30) (Kitty Buhler–Chet Hansen interview), 162–63. ONB, GL, 140 ("try to use it").

21 ONB, GL, 140; D'Este, *Patton*, 465, 891, n. 43; Atkinson 402 (citing Mason, "Reminiscences and Anecdotes of World War II," 1988, McCormick Research Museum, First Division Museum, Cantigny, IL). Bradley's biographer's claim that Roosevelt's bodyguards flipped the safeties off their Thompson submachine gun with "an audible click" is probably poetic license, as Thompson gun safeties rotate and, based on the author's experience, they make virtually no sound when disengaged.

22 ONB, interview, n.d., USMA (Kitty Buhler–ONB interview), 138; Blair, ONB interview notes, 2/1/80, USAMHI (Blair Collection, box 44); ONB, SS, 52 ("command himself");

ONB, GL, 140 ("boss"); Blair, notes on GSP, n.d., USAMHI (Blair Collection, box 27) ("Prussians").

23 Hansen, 6/2/44, USAMHI (Hansen Papers, box 4) ("wrestling belt"); U.S. Army Heritage and Education Center (Bradley pistol display); George S. Patton Cavalry Museum (Patton pistols).

24 Ingersoll 311 ("shy"); Price 390–91 (quoting Middleton); Alex Stoute, interview, 11/8/80, USAMHI (Blair Collection, box 47); Veterans Administration, "Biographical Sketch of Omar Nelson Bradley," 4/1/46, USAMHI (Hansen Papers, box 9); JSDE, *Strictly Personal*, 81–82; Pyle 326-28 ("His voice").

25 Hansen, notes for *A Soldier's Story*, n.d., USAMHI (Hansen Papers, box 22) (Coca-Cola, language); ONB, interview, n.d., USMA (Bradley Papers, box 30) (Kitty Buhler–Chet Hansen interview), 132, 145; ONB, interview, n.d., USAMHI (Blair Collection, box 44) (ice cream); Ingersoll 311–12; Pyle 326–28 (Southernisms). One of his very few perquisites, acquired later in Europe, was a private outhouse, which his aides had emblazoned with the appropriate number of stars. ONB, interview, n.d., USMA (Kitty Buhler–ONB interview), 139.

26 Butcher, 11/27/42, EL (Pre-Pres Papers, box 165) (Clark publicity); ONB, interview, n.d., USMA (Bradley Papers, box 30) (Kitty Buhler interview), 56; ONB, interview, n.d., USAMHI (Blair Collection, box 27), 56; JSDE, *Strictly Personal*, 82 ("day to the good").

27 JSDE, e-mail to author, 1/14/07; JSDE, *Strictly Personal*, 82; Pyle 327 ("Despite his mildness"); Blair, ONB interview notes, 2/6/80, USAMHI (Blair Collection, box 44) (bifocals).

28 D'Este, *Patton*, 466–67; W. Moxley Sorrell, *At the Right Hand of Longstreet: Reflections of a Staff Officer* (New York: Neal Publishing Co., 1905; Lincoln, NE: University of Nebraska Press, 1999 ed.), 242 (Longstreet).

29 Drew Middleton, "Bradley's Stature Remains Undiminished," *Lexington* (KY) *Dispatch*, 4/11/81.

30 ONB, SS, 39 ("I explained"); Hansen, notes on ONB, n.d., USAMHI (Hansen Papers, box 9); Hansen, "A Discussion on Tactics," n.d., USAMHI (Hansen Papers, box 22).

31 Paul D. Harkins, interview, 4/28/74, USAMHI, 36.

32 Strong 124; Charles E. Hart, interview, 1973, USAMHI, 8; Hobart R. Gay, interview, 10/4/80–10/5/80, USAMHI (Gay Papers), 18–19; Lucas, 6/7/43, 10/28/48 USAMHI (Lucas Papers) ("spur of the moment").

33 ONB, interview, n.d., USMA (Bradley Papers, box 30) (Kitty Buhler interview), 53 ("very fine association"); GSP, 3/15/43, PP 2:191 ("swell fellow"); GSP to ONB, 4/23/43, PP-LC (box 27) ("I want to repeat").

34 GSP 3/12/43, PP-LC (box 2); CG NATOUSA to GSP and Spaatz, 3/13/43, PP-LC (box 10).

35 ONB, "The War America Fought," *Life*, 4/9/51; ONB, SS, 46.

36 GSP 3/12/43, PP-LC (box 2).

37 ONB, SS, 38 (map).

38 Atkinson 420; Alfred Toppe, *Desert Warfare: German Experiences in World War II* (2 vols., 1952; U.S. Army Command and General Staff College, 1991 ed.), Combined Arms Research Library, Leavenworth, Kansas.

39 ONB, GL, 141 ("up against the champ"); Butcher 274; GSP, 3/19/43 PP 2:194 ("Desert Fox"); Atkinson 410–11, 441; D'Este, *Eisenhower*, 404.

40 ONB, GL, 141.

41 ONB, SS, 50–51; ONB, GL, 141–42, D'Este, *Patton*, 471; Hirshson 313.

42 ONB, GL, 142.

43 Alexander to DDE and GSP, 4/11/43, in Butcher, 4/12/43, EL (Pre-Pres Papers, box 166); Michael J. King, "Rangers: Selected Combat Operations in World War II," Leavenworth Papers, No. 11 (June 1985) ("WOP"); D'Este, *Patton*, 472.

44 ONB, SS, 52.

45 ONB, GL, 141; McKeogh 77; DDE to Handy, 3/20/43, EL (Pre-Pres Papers, box 54) ("What a godsend"); GSP 3/16/43, 3/18/43, PP-LC (box 2).

46 Butcher 286; Atkinson 435, 438; Farago 244 (quoting Alexander to GSP, 3/19/43).

47 PP 2:195.

48 D'Este, *Patton*, 474; Farago 244–45 (10th Panzer arrived there by May 22).

49 Hansen, 3/26/43, USAMHI (Hansen Papers, box 4); ONB, interview, n.d., USMA (Bradley Papers, box 30) (Kitty Buhler–Chet Hansen interview), 170–71; PP 2:196; Hirshson 323.

50 Atkinson 279; ONB, GL, 143-44.

51 ONB, SS, 55; Koch 36–37; Howe, *Northwest Africa*, 407; Farago 245; Atkinson 442.

52 GSP to BAP, 3/18/43, PP-LC (box 10).

53 Atkinson 443 (twenty-six tanks remained in the 10th Panzer Division after El Guettar).

54 ONB, SS, 54–55; D'Este, *Patton*, 474; Anderson, *Tunisia*, 21.

55 ONB, interview, n.d., USMA (Kitty Buhler interview), 55.

56 ONB, GL, 144 ("solid, indisputable"); GSP to BAP, 3/18/43, PP-LC (box 10).

57 Atkinson 443 (citing II Corps G-3 Journal, 3/43, NARA RG 407, E 427, box 3175), 445.

58 R. F. Akers Jr. to Hansen, 1/12/51, Hansen Papers, USAMHI (Atkinson 449); D'Este, *Patton*, 476 (quoting Bradley Commentaries).

59 GSP 3/24/43, PP-LC (box 2).

60 GSP 3/27/43, PP-LC (box 2).

61 Alexander to DDE, 4/1/43, EL (Pre-Pres Papers, box 91); DDE to GSP, 4/2/43, EP 2:1066; GSP 4/4/43, PP-LC (box 2).

62 ONB, SS, 65; Hansen, 4/4/43, USAMHI (Hansen Papers, box 4).

63 Atkinson 450.

64 ONB, interview, n.d., USMA (Bradley Papers, box 30) (Kitty Buhler–Chet Hansen interview); ONB, GL, 149 ("he asked if I"); D'Este, *Patton*, 477.

65 DDE, *Crusade*, 82.

66 Orlando Ward, 4/4/43, Orlando Ward Papers, USAMHI, in Atkinson 452.

67 Harold R. Bull, 4/1/43, EL (Bull Papers); GSP 4/1/43, PP-LC (box 2); GSP to Frederick Ayer, 4/1/43, PP-LC (box 14).

68 Hansen, 4/1/43, USAMHI (Hansen Papers, box 4); GSP to BAP, 4/1/43, PP-LC (box 10).

69 Hansen, 4/1/43, USAMHI (Hansen Papers, box 4); GSP to BAP, 4/1/43, PP-LC (box 10); GSP to Echo Jensen, 4/1/43, USAMHI (Patton Papers, box 4); GSP 4/1/43, PP-LC (box 2); ONB, SS, 62.

70 GSP 4/1/43, PP-LC (box 2).

71 GSP to BAP, 3/25/43, PP-LC (box 10); GSP to DDE, 3/29/43, EL (Pre-Pres Papers, box 91); Hansen, 3/26/43–3/29/43, USAMHI (Hansen Papers, box 4).

72 Hirshson 316 ("You can't get the Air Force"); GSP 4/2/43, PP-LC (box 2) ("Our air").

73 NATAF to II Corps, et al., 4/2/43, EL (Pre-Pres Papers, box 91).

74 Ibid; ONB, SS, 63; Tedder 410; D'Este, *Eisenhower*, 400–1; PP 2:206–7.

75 Spaatz to DDE, 4/3/43, EL (Pre-Pres Papers, box 115).

76 Harold R. Bull, 4/4/43, EL (Bull Papers); Tedder 411; DDE to Tedder, 4/1/43, EL (Pre-Pres Papers, box 115).

77 Harold R. Bull, 4/4/43, EL (Bull Papers).

78 Tedder 411; Crosswell 163.

79 Tedder to DDE, 4/4/43, EL (Pre-Pres Papers, box 115); Hansen, 4/1/43-4/3/43, USAMHI (Hansen Papers, box 4).

80 GSP, 4/3/43, PP-LC (box 2); Tedder 410–11; Hansen, 4/3/43, USAMHI (Hansen Papers, box 4); Harold R. Bull, 4/3/43, EL (Bull Papers).

81 Tedder to DDE, 4/3/43, EL (Pre-Pres Papers, box 115); GSP, 4/3/43, PP-LC (box 2).

82 NATAF to AFHQ, 4/3/43, EL (Pre-Pres Papers, box 91); ONB, SS, 63 ("inadequate apology").

83 DDE to GSP, 4/5/43, EL (Pre-Pres Papers, box 91).

84 GSP to Coningham, 4/5/43, EL (Pre-Pres Papers, box 91); GSP to Alexander, 4/5/43, EL (Pre-Pres Papers, box 91).

85 GSP, 4/12/43, PP-LC (box 2).

86 Ibid., 4/4/43.

87 Ibid., 4/5/43.

88 Ibid., 4/7/43.

89 Farago 249.

90 GSP, 4/11/43, PP-LC (box 2).

91 DDE to GCM, 3/11/43, EP 2:1024. See also DDE to GCM, 5/3/43, EP 2:1110 (recommending Bradley for promotion).

92 ONB, SS, 53. See also DDE to GCM, 3/11/43, EP 2:1016–17.

93 GSP to BAP, 3/13/43, PP-LC (box 10); Butcher 86.

94 Butcher 283 (FDR thought Patton should be able to shell the Tunisian coast); GSP to BAP, 4/8/43, PP-LC (box 10) ("Swell fellow"); GSP, 4/13/43, PP-LC (box 2) ("I would like").

95 Ibid., 4/14/43.

96 ONB, GL, 144.

97 DDE to MDE, 3/23/43, *Letters to Mamie*, 112; ONB, GL, 145; ONB, SS, 59.

98 GSP, 4/14/43, PP-LC (box 2); Butcher, 4/17/43, EL (Pre-Pres Papers, box 166).

99 Ibid.

100 GSP, 4/14/43, 4/16/43, PP-LC (box 2).

101 Butcher, 4/14/43, EL (Pre-Pres Papers, box 166).

102 Ibid., 4/17/43.

103 Ibid.

104 GSP, 4/17/43, PP-LC (box 2).

105 DDE to GSP, 4/14/43, PP-LC (box 10); Butcher, 4/14/43, EL (Pre-Pres Papers, box 166); GSP to ONB, 4/13/43, USAMHI (Bradley Papers); GSP to ONB, 4/23/43, PP-LC (box 27).

Eight: "Mission Accomplished"

1 ONB, SS, 81.

2 Pyle 328–29; DDE to AGWAR, 3/20/43, EL (Pre-Pres Papers, box 13); ONB, GL, 154–55; Harold R. Bull, 4/21/43, EL (Bull Papers).

3 ONB, SS, 80.

4 DDE to ONB, 4/16/43, EL (Pre-Pres Papers, box 13); ONB, GL, 154; ONB, SS, 77; War Department, pamphlet, "To Bizerte with the II Corps" (Washington, D.C.: U.S. Government 1943), 12; Harold R. Bull, 4/21/43, EL (Bull Papers); Hansen to Fletcher Pratt, 3/4/47, USAMHI (Hansen Papers, box 2); ONB, GL, 155 ("another Kasserine").

5 ONB, SS, 75.

6 Pyle 326 ("no more panache"); Atkinson 486.

7 Atkinson 483 (map), 486.

8 Hansen, 4/22/43, USAMHI (Hansen Papers, box 2).

9 Butcher, 4/25/43, EL (Pre-Pres Papers, box 166); Butcher, 288; ONB, GL, 156; Atkinson 501.

10 Hansen, 4/22/43, USAMHI (Hansen Papers, box 2); ONB, GL, 156; DDE to GCM, 3/30/43, EP 2:1104; Butcher 288.

11 Howe, *Northwest Africa*, 614; Hansen, 4/22/43, USAMHI (Hansen Papers, box 2).

12 Hansen, "Memorandum for the Record," 10/21/46, USAMHI (Blair Collection, box 47).

13 ONB, SS, 84.

14 DDE, North Africa Report, 46; Hansen, "Memorandum for the Record," 10/21/46, USAMHI (Blair Collection, box 47); War Department, pamphlet, "To Bizerte with the II Corps" (Washington, D.C.: U.S. Government, 1943), 20; Hansen, 5/1/43, USAMHI (Hansen Papers, box 2); ONB, GL, 157; ONB, SS, 87.

15 ONB, "Memoir Rejects," USAMHI (Blair Collection, box 49) (squirrel hunt); Hansen, 5/1/43, USAMHI (Hansen Papers, box 2).

16 ONB, SS, 89.

17 Ibid., 89–90.

18 Ibid., 89; ONB, GL, 157.

19 ONB, GL, 158.

20 DDE to ONB, 5/5/43, EP 2:1117 ("You must know"); Butcher 298; Butcher, 5/10/43, 5/14/43, EL (Pre-Pres Papers, box 166).

21 ONB, GL, 158.

22 Truscott 191–92; ONB, interview, n.d., USAMHI (Blair Collection, Box 27), 123–24.

23 ONB, interview, n.d., USMA (Bradley Papers, box 30) (Kitty Buhler–Chet Hansen interview), 123–24; Blair, ONB interview notes, 2/8/80, USAMHI (Blair Collection, box 44); ONB, SS, 98 ("No other single incident").

24 ONB to DDE, 5/9/43, EL (Pre-Pres Papers, box 13).

25 Butcher, 5/12/43, EL (Pre-Pres Papers, box 166).

26 GSP, 5/8/43, PP-LC (box 2). Ike did congratulate George while passing along President Roosevelt's thanks. DDE to GSP, 5/10/43, PP-LC (box 11); GSP, 5/14/43, PP-LC (box 2)

27 Butcher, 5/10/43, EL (Pre-Pres Papers, box 166); DDE to ONB, 5/10/43, EL (Pre-Pres Papers, box 13) ("bursting with pride"); DDE to GCM, 5/8/43, EP 2:1117; DDE to Benjamin G. Ferris, 5/21/43, EP 2:1149 ("Omar Tunisus"); "Second Corps Led by Gen. Bradley," *New York Times*, 5/9/43; Butcher 298 ("discover Bradley").

28 GSP, 5/8/43, PP-LC (box 2); Butcher, 5/10/43, EL (Pre-Pres Papers, box 166).

Nine: Looking North

1 "Report of the Adjutant General, Allied Force Headquarters," n.d., EL (Thomas J. Davis Papers), 1, GSP, 5/22/43, PP-LC (box 2); Vice Adm. H. K. Hewitt, "Action Report, Western Task Force," n.d., www.ibiblio.org/hyperwar/USN/Admin-Hist/148.3-Sicily/index. html ("Hewitt Husky Report"), 17; Farago 231; ONB, SS, 105; Clark, interview, 1/4/70, EL, 24; GSP to BAP, 5/5/43, PP 2:233.

2 GSP, 5/18/43, PP 2:253.

3 GSP, 5/20/43, PP-LC (box 2); Summersby 68 (heat); GSP to BAP, 5/21/43, PP-LC (box 11) ("middle class Frogs"); Butcher, 5/25/43, EL (Pre-Pres Papers, box 166).

4 ONB, SS, 109; D'Este, *Eisenhower*, 425 (quoting GSP, "Description of Victory Parade," PP-LC (box 13)); GSP to BAP, 5/21/43, PP-LC (box 11).

5 GSP, 5/8/43, PP-LC (box 2).

6 Blair, ONB interview notes, 2/1/80, USAMHI (Blair Collection, box 44); ONB, GL, 170.

7 Butcher 299, 315; Butcher, 5/5/43, EL (Pre-Pres Papers, box 166); ONB, GL, 161.

8 DDE to GCM, 3/29/43, EP 2:1060.

9 DDE to MDE, 5/27/43, *Letters to Mamie*, 125.

10 Butcher 307–8 ("impatient and irritated"); Butcher, 5/5/43, EL (Pre-Pres Papers, box 166).

11 Butcher, 4/17/43, EL (Pre-Pres Papers, box 166); D'Este, *Eisenhower*, 420.

12 Butcher, 6/11/43, EL (Pre-Pres Papers, box 166) (Col. Arnold's death); Hirshson 346; D'Este, *Eisenhower*, 420.

13 DDE, "Commander-in-Chief's Dispatch, Sicilian Campaign, 1943," 2–5 (NARA RG 331, entry 1, box 26); "Report of the Adjutant General, Allied Force Headquarters," n.d., EL (Thomas J. Davis Papers), 1.

14 Atkinson 418.

15 Butcher, 5/27/43, EL (Pre-Pres Papers, box 166).

16 Summersby, *Beyond Forgetting*, 25 ("the relationship"); DDE to GCM, 4/5/43, EP 2:1071 (editing out commentary on Montgomery) ("so proud").

17 Weintraub 159; Atkinson 466; Coningham, interview, 2/14/47, USAMHI (OCMH, "WWII—Supreme Command—1A2(b)—Forrest Pogue").

18 D'Este, *Eisenhower*, 410 (quoting Montgomery to Brooke, 4/4/43, Montgomery Papers, IWM).

19 Charles H. Bonesteel III, interview, 11/9/72, USAMHI, 138–40; Ingersoll 85 ("syndicates"), 161 ("petrol").

20 GSP, 5/7/43, PP-LC (box 2) ("forceful"); ONB, SS, 138 ("George"); Ambrose, *Supreme Commander*, 222.

21 GSP, 4/28/43, PP-LC (box 2) ("Allies"); AFHQ, "Commander-in-Chief's Dispatch, Sicilian Campaign, 1943," 6 (NARA RG 331, entry 1, box 26); Garland and Smythe, *Sicily*, 58–59.

22 BLM, *Memoirs*, 162; D'Este, *Eisenhower*, 422; D'Este, *Mediterranean*, 46.

23 Hirshson 408 (citing John P. Marquand, "The General," Draft A, folder 676, John P. Marquand Papers, Beinicke Library, Yale) (Stiller); GSP, 5/3/43, PP-LC (box 2) ("that's alright").

24 BLM, "Remarks Made at Conference at Algiers on 2 May 32 by General Montgomery, Eighth Army," in Butcher, 5/2/43, EL (Pre-Pres Papers, box 166); Tedder 435.

25 Atkinson, DOB, 54.

26 GSP, 5/3/43, PP-LC (box 2) ("quite frank"); GSP to BAP, 5/5/43, PP-LC (box 11) ("fears for his head").

27 GSP, 5/5/43, PP-LC (box 2).

28 GSP to BAP, 5/17/43, PP-LC (box 11).

29 GCM to DDE, 5/24/43, GCML (GCM Papers, #3-666); GSP, 6/10/43, PP-LC (box 1).

30 GSP, 6/10/43, PP-LC (box 1); DDE, interview, 6/28/62, EL 26.

31 GSP, 6/7/43, PP-LC (box 1).

32 Ibid.

33 GSP, 6/2/43, PP-LC (box 2).

34 Ibid; GSP, 4/15/43 PP-LC (box 2); GSP, *War*, 354.

35 ONB, GL, 171, 179.

36 Price 119–24, 134–35.

37 D'Este, *Patton*, 312 ("Wars aren't won").

38 82nd Airborne Division, "82nd Airborne in Sicily and Italy," n.d., USAMHI; GSP to Frederick Ayer, 5/5/43, PP 2:243.

39 GSP to BAP, 5/10/43, PP-LC (box 11).

40 GCM, interview, 7/25/49, GCML; Clark 175.

41 ONB, SS, 69.

42 ONB to GSP, 5/13/43, PP-LC (box 11).

43 GSP, 5/16/43, PP-LC (box 2); GSP to BAP, 5/17/43, PP-LC (box 11).

44 Lucas, 6/24/43, USAMHI (Lucas Papers).

45 ONB, GL, 170 ("petty, demeaning"); ONB, SS, 108–11.

46 Hansen, notes for *A Soldier's Story*, n.d., USAMHI (Hansen Papers, box 22); ONB, SS, 106, 111, 114 ("hot mustard").

47 Hewitt Husky Report, 39; ONB, SS, 106, 112; Truscott 197; Garland and Smythe, *Sicily*, 97–98; ONB, GL, 171; Birtle 6.

48 ONB, SS, 113.

49 GSP, 5/17/43, PP-LC (box 2).

50 Ibid., 5/22/43; Bonesteel, interview, 11/9/72, USAMHI, 89.

51 GSP, 5/22/43, PP-LC (box 2).

52 Ibid., 6/20/43.

53 Ibid., 5/28/43.

54 Lucas, "From Algiers to Anzio," 10/28/48, USAMHI (Lucas Papers); GSP, 6/7/43-6/8/43, PP-LC (box 2) ("Lucas too").

55 Summersby 74–75; Garland and Smith 60–61; Butcher, 7/16/43, EL (Pre-Pres Papers, box 167); DDE to GCM, 3/12/43, EP 2:1033 ("Every indication").

56 DDE to CCOS, 5/11/43, EP 2:1122.

57 DDE to GCM, 5/13/43, EP 2:1130.

58 Ibid., 6/12/43, EP 2:1186; Butcher 319–20; DDE, interview, 6/28/62, EL, 28; D'Este, *Eisenhower*, 429.

59 Strong 133.

60 Butcher, 6/11/43, EL (Pre-Pres Papers, box 166).

61 Butcher, 6/11/43, EL (Pre-Pres Papers, box 166); Edith C. Rogers, "Army Air Forces Historical Study No. 52, The Reduction of Pantelleria and Adjacent Islands: 8 May–14 June 1943," (Washington, D.C.: Air Historical Office, 1947); Ambrose, *Supreme Commander*, 215; Butcher 343 (wager); EP 2:1186, n.5 (11,000 prisoners).

62 AFHQ, "Commander-in-Chief's Dispatch, Sicilian Campaign, 1943," 5, 10 (NARA RG 331, entry 1, box 26); Garland and Smythe, *Sicily*, 80–81; ONB, GL, 175.

63 Atkinson, DOB, 33; Birtle 5; D'Este, *Eisenhower*, 421–23.

64 DDE, "Memorandum for Personal File," 6/11/43, in Butcher, 6/11/43, EL (Pre-Pres Papers, box 166).

65 Ibid.

66 GSP, 6/24/43, 6/30/43, 7/1/43, PP-LC (box 2); Lucas, 6/27/43, USAMHI (Lucas Papers); ONB, GL, 171; Blair, ONB interview notes, 2/1/80, USAMHI (Blair Collection, box 44); GSP, 7/5/43, PP-LC (box 3) ("no one whips").

67 Gay, notes to GSP, 7/26/43, PP-LC (box 3).

68 GSP, 7/5/43, PP-LC (box 3).

69 Butcher 340, 345; Butcher, 7/6/43-7/8/43, EL (Pre-Pres Papers, box 167); DDE to MDE, 7/9/43, *Letters to Mamie*, 134–35.

70 "Report of the Adjutant General, Allied Force Headquarters," n.d., EL (Thomas J. Davis Papers), 3; Butcher, 7/8/43-7/9/43, EL (Pre-Pres Papers, box 167); McKeogh 87; Atkinson, DOB, 51; Miller 520 (quoting DDE to MDE, 7/9/43); D'Este, *Eisenhower*, 431.

71 Butcher 348; Hewitt Husky Report 36.

72 McKeogh 87; Butcher 349; DDE, *Crusade*, 172–73; Atkinson, DOB, 67–68.

73 ONB, SS, 116–18; "North Africa Honor Won by 7 Generals," *New York Times*, 6/12/43; Hansen, notes for *A Soldier's Story*, n.d., USAMHI (Hansen Papers, box 22); ONB, GL 170–74; Hewitt Husky Report 31.

74 ONB, SS, 117.

75 Harold R. Bull, 6/2/43, EL (Bull Papers).

76 Harold R. Bull, autobiographical sketch, n.d., EL (Bull Papers); ONB, SS, 119; ONB, GL, 174.

77 ONB, GL, 176; ONB, SS, 120 (six days); Charles 8; ONB, 7/4/43, USAMHI (Bradley Papers); Hansen, "Sicily," n.d., USAMHI (Hansen Papers, box 4).

78 GSP, 6/30/43, PP-LC (box 2); GSP to BAP, 7/2/43, PP-LC (box 11); Odom 8.

79 Atkinson, DOB, 60 (quoting "Reminiscences of Walter C. W. Ansel," 149, and Hewitt, AAR, "The Sicilian Campaign," 44); GSP, 7/6/43, PP-LC (box 3).

80 GSP, 7/6/43, PP-LC (box 3).

81 GSP, 7/9/43–7/10/43, PP-LC (box 3) (dream).

Ten: Under Fire

1 "March from the Beaches," *Time*, 7/26/43; James A. Burchard, "Sicily Invasion Diary," *Stars and Stripes*, 7/17/43.

2 Lucas, 7/10/43, USAMHI (Lucas Papers); Atkinson, DOB, 54, 69; Lande 66 (quoting Truscott).

3 Hewitt Husky Report 38, 40.

4 "March from the Beaches," *Time*, 7/26/43.

5 Gay, 7/10/43, USAMHI (Gay Papers); Hewitt Husky Report 4–6 (reports from Allen and Truscott); Atkinson, DOB, 80-83.

6 Hewitt Husky Report 6 (Patton ordered KOOL reserve ashore at Gela at 1430); GSP, 7/10/43, PP-LC (box 1) ("cur").

7 J. M. Swing, "Comments on Night Operation, 82nd Airborne Division Night D-plus-1/D-plus-2," 7/16/43, USAMHI (Gay Papers) (appended, Gay diary 7/13/43); GSP to Commanders, 7/6/43, PP 2:281; Gay, 7/11/43, USAMHI (Gay Papers).

8 Matthew Ridgway, "Reported Loss of Transport Planes and Personnel Due to Friendly Fire," 8/2/43, USAMHI (Hansen Papers, box 2); Garland and Smythe, *Sicily*, 175–76.

9 Hewitt Husky Report 106–7 (*Ancon* commanding at CENT landings).

10 Hansen, 7/10/43, USAMHI (Hansen Papers, box 2).

11 Hansen, 7/10/43, USAMHI (Hansen Papers, box 2); Hewitt Husky Report 4-6, 40-41, 109; ONB, SS, 128; "45th Infantry Division in the Sicilian Campaign as Compiled from G-3 Journal for period July 10, 1943–Aug. 22, 1943," n.d., CMH, 26–27.

12 ONB, GL 182; Gay, 7/10/43, USAMHI (Gay Papers) (counterattack at 1030).

13 ONB, GL, 181.

14 ONB, SS, 129.

15 ONB, SS, 132; PP 2:282; Atkinson, DOB, 107 (citing AAR, Seventh Army G-3, n.d., NARA); Garland and Smythe, *Sicily*, 176; PP 2:277.

16 Rogers 95–98 (photos); PP 2:277.

17 GSP, 7/5/43, PP-LC (box 3), PP 2:277–78; Atkinson, DOB, 102; Hirshson 368 (citing ONB, memorandum, n.d., USMA (ONB Papers, ONB *General's Life* files, box 3); Garland and Smythe, *Sicily*, 174.

18 Gay, 7/11/43, USAMHI (Gay Papers); Atkinson, DOB, 103; Lucas, 7/12/43, USAMHI (Lucas Papers).

19 Lucas, 7/12/43, USAMHI (Lucas Papers); GSP, 7/11/43, PP-LC (box 3).

20 GSP, 7/11/43, PP-LC (box 3).

21 Gay, 7/11/43, USAMHI (Gay Papers).

22 Matthew Ridgway, "Reported Loss of Transport Planes and Personnel Due to Friendly Fire," 8/2/43, USAMHI (Hansen Papers, box 2); AFHQ, "Commander-in-Chief's Dispatch, Sicilian Campaign, 1943," 22 (NARA RG 331, entry 1, box 26); ONB, SS, 133; D'Este, *Eisenhower*, 433.

23 Truscott to WBS, 7/31/43, in Butcher, 8/3/43, EL (Pre-Pres Papers, box 167); ONB, SS, 139; Hewitt Husky Report 11; PP 2:280; Birtle 11–12.

24 Butcher, 7/9/43, EL (Pre-Pres Papers, box 167).

25 Butcher, 7/10/43, EL (Pre-Pres Papers, box 167); Atkinson, DOB, 52.

26 Ibid.

27 Butcher, 7/10/43, EL (Pre-Pres Papers, box 167).

28 Ibid.

29 Butcher, 7/13/43, EL (Pre-Pres Papers, box 167); GSP, 7/12/43, PP 2:283; Hewitt Husky Report 11 (0630 report); Butcher 358.

30 Gay, 7/12/43, USAMHI (Gay Papers); GSP, 7/12/43, PP-LC (box 3).

31 Hewitt Husky Report 10 (Ike left at 0715 and the report came in at 0747); Butcher, 7/13/43, EL (Pre-Pres Papers, box 167); Reynolds 293.

32 Butcher, 7/13/43, EL (Pre-Pres Papers, box 167); Reynolds 293.

33 GSP, 7/12/43, PP-LC (box 3).

34 Butcher, 7/13/43, EL (Pre-Pres Papers, box 167).

35 Ibid.

36 Ibid.; Garland, *Sicily*, 206 (quoting Lucas diary).

37 Lucas, 7/21/43, USAMHI (Lucas Papers).

38 GSP, 7/12/43, PP-LC (box 3); Hewitt Husky Report 11.

39 Butcher, 7/13/43, EL (Pre-Pres Papers, box 167); DDE to GSP, 7/12/43, in Butcher, 7/13/43, EL (Pre-Pres. Papers, box 167).

40 GSP, 7/13/43, PP-LC (box 3) ("cussing me out); Gay, 7/13/43, USAMHI (Gay Papers); DDE to GSP, 7/12/43, EL (Pre-Pres Papers, box 3) ("I want a statement").

41 J. M. Swing, "Comments on Night Operation, 82nd Airborne Division Night D-plus-1/D-plus-2," 7/16/43, USAMHI (Gay Papers) (appended to Gay diary entry, 7/13/43); GSP, 7/5/43, PP-LC (box 3).

42 Hansen, 7/11/43, USAMHI (Hansen Papers, box 2); ONB, GL, 183; Blair, ONB interview notes, 2/1/80, USAMHI (Blair Collection, box 44).

43 ONB, 7/11/43, USAMHI (Bradley Papers); ONB, SS, 129.

44 ONB, GL, 183.

45 Ibid.; Astor 199.

46 ONB, SS, 130. See also GSP, 10/14/43, PP-LC (box 3).

47 Hansen, "Sicily," n.d., USAMHI (Hansen Papers, boxes 2, 9).

48 Hansen, "Sicily," n.d., USAMHI (Hansen Papers, boxes 2, 9); ONB, GL, 183.

49 Pyle 330.

50 GSP, 7/15/43, PP-LC (box 3); Atkinson, DOB, 118–20. However, Hansen's undated notes indicate that at some point, George's response was, "Try the bastards." Hansen Papers, "Sicily," n.d., USAMHI (Hansen Papers, box 9).

51 Atkinson, DOB, 116 (citing Raymond S. McLain, "Account Written by Brig. Gen. McLain," 1943, NARA); ONB, SS, 139–40.

52 Hewitt Husky AAR at 54 (531st Engineer Shore Regiment and 40th Combat Engineer Regiment); Mayo 166–67.

53 ONB, SS, 145–46 ("Have your people"); Lucas, 8/14/43, USAMHI (Lucas Papers) ("never bothers").

54 Alexander, interview, 1/10/49–1/15/49, USAMHI (OCMH Collection, Sydney Matthews Papers, box 2); ONB, GL, 187.

55 Butcher 362; Brighton 195 (quoting Alexander, AAR, 15th Army Group) ("tougher and less spectacular"); Farago 272.

56 Garland, *Sicily*, 207.

57 GSP, 7/13/43, PP-LC (box 3); 15th Army Group to 7th Army, 7/14/43, USAMHI (appended, Gay diary, 7/14/43); Garland and Smythe, *Sicily*, 209.

58 BLM, *Memoirs*, 171; Atkinson, DOB, 69; ONB, GL, 186–87.

59 Lucas, 7/13/43, USAMHI (Lucas Papers); ONB, GL, 188–89.

60 GSP to BAP, 7/16/43, PP-LC (box 11).

Eleven: Cracks in the Wall

1 Hansen, "Sicily," n.d., USAMHI (Hansen Papers, boxes 2, 9); ONB, SS, 135.

2 Ibid.

3 Ibid., 136.

4 Garland, *Sicily*, 210 (called Brad to his headquarters).

5 ONB, GL, 188.

6 Ibid.

7 Ibid., 189; Hirshson 372 (citing Benjamin A. Dickson, "G-2 Journey: Algiers to the Elbe," 84, and Benjamin A. Dickson Papers, USMA).

8 Lucas, 7/20/43, USAMHI (Lucas Papers). See also Butcher, 2/23/43, EL (Pre-Pres Papers, box 166).

9 Lucas, 7/20/43, 7/23/43, USAMHI (Lucas Papers).

10 GSP, 7/13/43, PP-LC (box 3); Garland and Smythe, *Sicily*, 224–26.

11 Gay, 7/13/43, USAMHI (Gay Papers); GSP, 7/13/43, PP-LC (box 3); Truscott to WBS, 7/31/43, in Butcher, 8/2/43, EL (Pre-Pres Papers, box 167); Garland, *Sicily*, 209, 224.

12 GSP, 7/13/43-7/14/43, PP-LC (box 3); GSP to Wedemeyer, 8/1/43, PP-LC (box 11); Truscott, interview, 4/19/51, USAMHI (OCMH Collection, Smythe Papers, box 3).

13 Will Lang, "Lucian King Truscott, Jr.," *Life*, 10/2/44, 106; B. C. Price, "Report of Operations, July 10–18, 1943," 3rd Division, G-3 Dept., 9/10/43, USAMHI; GSP, 7/16/43, PP-LC (box 3); Garland, *Sicily*, 230; Birtle 16.

14 Garland and Smythe, *Sicily*, 234–35.

15 15th Army Group to 7th Army, 7/16/43, in GSP, 7/5/43, PP-LC (box 3) and Gay, 7/16/43, USAMHI (Gay Papers) ("will protect rear"); Garland, *Sicily*, 235–36; GSP, 7/17/43, PP-LC (box 3) ("General Alexander").

16 Ibid.

17 Butcher, 7/18/43, EL (Pre-Pres Papers, box 167).

18 GSP, 7/17/43, Appendix 29 ("Proposed Change in Directive of July 16, 1943"), PP-LC (box 3); Garland and Smythe, *Sicily*, 236.

19 GSP, 10/1/42, PP-LC, box 2; Gay, 7/17/43, USAMHI (Gay Papers).

20 GSP, 7/17/43, PP-LC (box 3); 15th Army Group to 7th Army, 7/18/43, in Gay, 7/18/43, USAMHI (Gay Papers); Butcher, 7/18/43, EL (Pre-Pres Papers, box 167); Atkinson, DOB, 130; Birtle 16.

21 ONB, SS, 144.

22 Hansen, "Sicily," n.d., USAMHI (Hansen Papers, box 2), 3; ONB, SS, 141 (Middleton); Lande 82 (dust); Atkinson, DOB, 133 (citing Edmund F. Ball, *Staff Officer with the Fifth Army* (Exposition Press 1958), 176–78).

23 Butcher 370, 374, 384, 388-89; Hughes, 8/6/43, LC (Hughes Papers, box 2).

24 Gay, 7/18/43, 7/20/43, USAMHI (Gay Papers); ONB, SS, 145; Garland and Smythe, *Sicily*, 244–45, 300; GSP, 7/19/43, PP 2:293–94 ("Alex has").

25 15th Army Group to 7th Army, 7/18/43, in Gay, 7/17/43, USAMHI (Gay Papers); Garland and Smythe, *Sicily*, 246; Hirshson 381.

26 Gay, 7/19/43, USAMHI (Gay Papers).

27 GSP, 7/20/43, PP 2:294; GSP to BAP, 7/20/43, PP-LC (box 11) ("Atilla"); Gay, 7/21/43, USAMHI (Gay Papers) ("You have the ball").

28 "The Surrender of Palermo," *Life*, 8/23/43; "Historical Record, Operations, Second Armored Division, Apr 22–July 25, 1943," 8/5/43, CARL; "Last Stand," *Time*, 8/2/43; Garland and Smythe, *Sicily*, 255; GSP to BAP, 7/22/43, PP 2:296 ("By the time"); Codman 110.

29 Atkinson, DOB, 134 (citing After Action Report, HQ, Provisional Corps, July 15–Aug. 20, 1943, CMH); Truscott 226–27.

30 GSP, 7/22/43–7/23/43, PP-LC (box 3); Garland and Smythe, *Sicily*, 226, n. 18 (quoting Truscott commentaries).

31 GSP, 7/25/43, PP-LC (box 3); GSP to BAP, 7/27/43, PP-LC (box 11); Butcher 376.

32 Butcher 369–71; Gay, 7/21/43, USAMHI (Gay Papers); ONB, SS, 145; Garland and Smythe, *Sicily*, 303–4.

33 Gay, 7/24/43, USAMHI (Gay Papers).

34 GSP, 7/24/43, PP-LC (box 3) ("I fear the worst"); Garland and Smythe, *Sicily*, 319; GSP to BAP, 7/24/43, PP-LC (box 11) ("little lamb").

35 Hansen, 7/20/44, USAMHI (Hansen Papers, box 2) ("bohemian painter"); Gay, 7/25/43, USAMHI (Gay Papers).

36 GSP, 7/25/43, PP-LC (box 3).

37 Ibid.

38 Ibid.

39 Gay, 7/25/43, USAMHI (Gay Papers).

40 Hansen, 7/21/43, USAMHI (Hansen Papers, box 2); "The Fall of Troina," *Time*, 8/23/43; Gay, 8/4/43–8/6/43, USAMHI (Gay Papers); Garland and Smythe, *Sicily*, 305, 325; ONB, GL, 193-94.

41 "The Fall of Troina," *Time*, 8/23/43; ONB, SS, 151–52; Atkinson, DOB, 155–59.

42 ONB, interview, n.d., USMA (Bradley Papers, box 30) (Kitty Buhler–Chet Hansen interview), 159–60; Margaret Chase, 6/26/43, EL (Chase Papers); Astor 177 ("let me remind you"), 223; Johnson 25; ONB, SS, 333 ("men worship Ted").

43 DDE to ONB, 4/16/43, EL (Pre-Pres Papers, box 13); ONB to DDE, 11/2/44, EL (Pre-Pres. Papers, box 13).

44 ONB to DDE, 7/25/43, EL (Pre-Pres. Papers, box 13).

45 GSP, 7/26/43, 7/31/43, PP-LC (box 3); GSP to DDE, 7/26/43, EL (Pre-Pres Papers, box 91); Butcher, 8/2/43, EL (Pre-Pres Papers, box 167); GSP to Leslie J. McNair, 8/10/43, PP-LC (box 11); DDE to ONB, 6/30/43, EP 2:1304; ONB, interview, n.d., USMA (Bradley Papers, box 30) (Kitty Buhler–Chet Hansen interview), 159–60; ONB, SS, 155; Astor 228–29.

46 GSP, 8/3/43, PP 2:311; Terry Allen to Mary Fran Allen, 8/14/43, in Astor 219; GSP to McNair, 8/10/43, PP-LC (box 11); ONB, interview, n.d., USMA (Bradley Papers, box 30) (Kitty Buhler–Chet Hansen interview), 159–60; ONB, GL, 171; Astor 224; GSP, 7/29/43 ("While I think General Roosevelt"), 7/30/43, 8/3/43, PP-LC (box 3).

47 Butcher, 8/14/43, EL (Pre-Pres Papers, box 167) ("warm glow"); DDE to GCM, 7/17/43, EP 2:1258 ("doing well"); DDE to GCM, 8/4/43, EP 2:1317 ("Seventh Army"); *Time*, 7/26/43; Atkinson, DOB, 143; Hirshson 385 ("doing right well").

48 Lucas, 7/23/43, 8/7/43, USAMHI (Lucas Papers).

49 Butcher 371.

50 D'Este, *Eisenhower*, 770, n. 24.

51 Butcher 370; Summersby, *Past Forgetting*, 156 ("bellyful").

52 Truscott 228 ("like to beat Montgomery"); Atkinson, DOB, 142–43 ("We hope").

53 GSP to BAP, 7/27/43, PP-LC (box 11). See also GSP to BAP, 7/24/43, PP-LC (box 11).

54 GSP, 7/31/43, PP-LC (box 3); Butcher, 8/2/43, EL (Pre-Pres Papers, box 167).

55 Butcher, 8/2/43, EL (Pre-Pres Papers, box 167) (Spam); Butcher 377.

56 GSP, 7/30/43, PP-LC (box 3).

57 DDE to GSP, 8/2/43, PP 2:310.

58 Follain 268.

59 GSP, 7/28/43, PP-LC (box 3); Gay, 8/5/43, USAMHI (Gay Papers); GSP to Middleton, 7/28/43, PP 2:306 ("horse race").

60 Ibid., 8/5/43–8/6/43; GSP to BAP, 8/10/43, PP-LC (box 11); Farago 323.

61 Gay, 7/30/43, USAMHI (Gay Papers); GSP, 7/27/43, 7/28/43, PP 2:306–7; Garland and Smythe, *Sicily*, 305, 319, 349–53; Butcher, 8/6/43, EL (Pre-Pres Papers, box 167); Butcher 388; ONB, GL, 193 fn.

62 GSP, 8/8/43, PP-LC (box 3); Truscott 230–34; Garland and Smythe, *Sicily*, 362–67.

63 Truscott 234; Eighth Army to Seventh Army, 8/6/45; in Gay, 8/6/43, USAMHI (Gay Papers); GSP, 8/9/43, PP-LC (box 3) ("We are trying").

64 Gay, 8/8/43, USAMHI (Gay Papers).

65 Gay, 8/5/43-8/6/43, USAMHI (Gay Papers); GSP, 8/10/43, PP-LC (box 3); ONB, interview, n.d., GCML (McCarthy Papers, box 17); Garland and Smythe, *Sicily*, 389, n. 3.

66 Truscott 234–35; Gay, 8/10/43, USAMHI (Gay Papers).

67 GSP, 8/10/43, PP-LC (box 3); Truscott 235; Garland and Smythe, *Sicily*, 389.

68 Gay, 8/10/43, USAMHI (Gay Papers); Truscott 235 ("what's the matter with you?"); GSP, 8/10/43, PP-LC (box 3); Atkinson, DOB, 163 (quoting Hansen, "Research Draft," USAMHI, Hansen Papers, 10/24–25); Hirshson 390–91; D'Este, *Patton*, 527; GSP to BAP, 8/11/43, PP-LC (box 11).

69 ONB, SS, 158 ("more exasperated"); ONB, GL, 197.

70 ONB, SS, 158–59; Truscott 240; GSP, 8/11/43, PP-LC (box 3); Garland and Smythe, *Sicily*, 404.

71 D'Este, *Patton*, 525, 899, n. 16; Reynolds 142 (citing Bradley Commentaries, USAMHI); ONB, interview, n.d., GCML (McCarthy Papers, box 17).

72 Farago 329 (quoting Bradley) ("Canny a showman"); D'Este, *Patton*, 525, 899, n. 16 (citing Bradley Commentaries, USAMHI).

73 ONB, interview, n.d., GCML (McCarthy Papers, box 17); Hirshson 392 (citing ONB, "Confidential and Personal Memoir of Omar N. Bradley," 1947, USMA (Bradley Papers, box 38)).

74 Lucas, 8/14/43, USAMHI (Lucas Papers); ONB, GL, 199.

75 Garland and Smythe, *Sicily*, 412.

76 Odom 11–12; GSP, 8/14/43, PP-LC (box 3); ONB, GL, 199; Garland and Smythe, *Sicily*, 323.

77 Garland and Smythe, *Sicily*, 414.

78 "45th Infantry Division in the Sicilian Campaign as Compiled from G-3 Journal for period July 10, 1943–Aug. 22, 1943," n.d., USAMHI, 26–27.

79 ONB, SS, 162; Blair, ONB interview notes, 2/1/80, USAMHI (Blair Collection, box 44).

80 GSP, 8/15/43, PP-LC (box 3).

81 Truscott 243; Hirshson 392 (citing ONB, "Amphibious Landings on North Coast of Sicily," USMA (Bradley Papers, box 66)).

82 Gay, 8/17/43, USAMHI (Gay Papers); GSP, 8/16/43, PP-LC (box 3).

83 GSP, 8/17/43, PP-LC (box 3).

84 Ibid., PP 2:322; GSP to BAP, 8/18/43, PP-LC (box 11).

85 Truscott 243.

86 Atkinson, DOB, 169 (quoting Hansen, "Research Draft for SS," Hansen Papers, USAMHI, box 1, 16-A, S-27) ("I'll be damned"); D'Este, *Patton*, 529–30 and 900, n. 34 (citing Bradley Commentaries, USAMHI). See also ONB, GL, 211.

87 D'Este, *Patton*, 529–30 and 900, n. 34 (citing Bradley Commentaries, USAMHI).

88 Butcher 397.

89 Truscott 243.

90 Rodgers 118 (photo dated 8/17/43); Gay, 8/17/43, USAMHI (Gay Papers); George Murnane to Hansen, 1/30/51, USAMHI (Hansen Papers, box 2); Lucas, 8/17/43, USAMHI (Lucas Papers).

91 GSP, 8/17/43, PP-LC (box 3).

92 PP 2:326.

93 Ibid.

94 Ibid.

95 Alexander to GSP, 8/17/43, in Gay, 8/17/43, USAMHI (Gay Papers).

96 Katherine Marshall to GSP, 8/2/43, PP-LC (box 11); Lande 86–87.

Twelve: Avalanche

1 GSP to BAP, 3/25/43, PP-LC (box 10); Coffin, interview, 7/25/80, USAMHI, 66.

2 GSP to BAP, 4/13/43, PP-LC (box 10); GSP, 8/3/43, PP 2:311 ("All were brave"); GSP, 8/6/43, PP 2:315 ("That would be fatal"); Atkinson, DOB, 143.

3 F. Y. Leaver to Richard T. Arnest, 8/4/43, EL (Pre-Pres Papers, box 91); Lucas, 8/3/43, USAMHI (Lucas Papers).

4 F. Y. Leaver to Richard T. Arnest, 8/4/43, EL (Pre-Pres Papers, box 91); Perrin H. Long, "Mistreatment of Patients in Receiving Tents of the 15th and 93rd Evacuation Hospitals," NATOUSA, 8/16/43, PP-LC (box 3); Lucas, 8/3/43, USAMHI (Lucas Papers).

5 GSP, 8/1/43, PP-LC (box 3).

6 Donald E. Courier to Surgeon, II Corps, 8/12/43, EL (Pre-Pres Papers, box 91); Milton Bracker, "Patton Struck Ailing Soldier; Apologized to Him and Army," *New York Times*, 11/24/43; D'Este, *Patton*, 544–45.

7 Donald E. Courier to Surgeon, II Corps, 8/12/43, EL (Pre-Pres Papers, box 91); Perrin H. Long, "Mistreatment of Patients in Receiving Tents of the 15th and 93rd Evacuation Hospitals," NATOUSA, 8/16/43, PP-LC (box 3); GSP to Henry L. Stimson, 11/27/43, PP-LC (box 11); Harkins, interview, n.d., in Lande 91–92; Hirshson 395.

8 Demaree Bess, "Report of an Investigation," 8/19/43, EL (Pre-Pres Papers, box 91).

9 GSP, 8/10/43, PP-LC (box 3).

10 ONB, interview, n.d., GCML (McCarthy Papers, box 17); Blair, ONB interview notes, 2/1/80, USAMHI (Blair Collection, box 44).

11 ONB, interview, n.d., GCML (McCarthy Papers, box 17); Blair, ONB interview notes, 2/1/80, USAMHI (Blair Collection, box 44).

12 DDE to MDE, 8/12/43, *Letters to Mamie*, 139; GCM, interview, 7/25/49, GCML; DDE to GSP, 8/18/43, PP-LC (box 11); GCM, *Pogue Interviews*, 2/4/57, 388; Butcher 372-73, 390–91 (saying "this forenoon" on August 17).

13 D'Este, *Eisenhower*, 439.

14 Farago 332–33.

15 Butcher, 8/21/43, EL (Pre-Pres Papers, box 167).

16 DDE, *At Ease*, 172.

17 DDE to Vernon Prichard, 8/27/41, EP 1:505.

18 Butcher, 8/21/43, EL (Pre-Pres Papers, box 167) ("deplorable"); Ambrose, *Supreme Commander*, 229 ("indispensable").

19 Butcher, 8/21/43, EL (Pre-Pres Papers, box 167).

20 GSP to BAP, 4/17/43, PP-LC (box 10); Butcher, 8/19/43, EL (Pre-Pres Papers, box 167).

21 Reynolds 296–97.

22 Butcher, 8/20/43, EL (Pre-Pres Papers, box 167) ("50,000"); Demaree Bess, "Report of an Investigation," 8/19/43, EL (Pre-Pres Papers, box 91).

23 Reynolds 296.

24 Ibid.

25 Butcher, 8/21/43, EL (Pre-Pres Papers, box 167).

26 DDE to GCM, 8/24/43, in Butcher, 8/24/43, EL (Pre-Pres Papers, box 167).

27 DDE to GSP, 8/17/43, PP-LC (box 11).

28 Follain 298.

29 GSP, 8/20/43, PP-LC (box 3).

30 DDE to GSP, 8/20/43, PP 2:328.

31 Lucas, 8/21/43, USAMHI (Lucas Papers).

32 Ibid.; GSP, 8/20/43, PP-LC (box 3).

33 Ibid., 8/21/43.

34 Statements of Captain Henry A. Carr and Lieutenant Colonel Robert Watson, 9/14/43, EL (Pre-Pres Papers, box 91); GSP, 8/21/43, 8/23/43, PP-LC (box 3); Hirshson 401, 409 (citing Currier to DDE, 9/15/64, USAMHI (Donald Currier Papers) and John P. Marquand, "The General," Draft A, folder 676, John P. Marquand Papers); Currier, memorandum, 8/12/43, USAMHI (Donald Currier Papers); Currier to Inspector General, 9/7/43, USAMHI (Donald Currier Papers); PP 2:336.

35 D'Este, *Patton*, 111–12.

36 Codman 114; GSP, 8/21/43, PP-LC (box 3); Hirshson 400 (quoting Pete Martin, *The Last Christmas Show* (Garden City, NY: Doubleday, 1974), 14, 17).

37 Gay, 8/23/43–8/26/43, USAMHI (Gay Papers); PP 2:338–39; Butcher 417; Theodore J. Conway, interview, 9/29/77, USAMHI, 2–4.

38 GSP to DDE, 8/29/43, USAMHI (Donald Currier Papers); Hughes, 8/27/43, LC (Hughes Papers, box 2).

39 Butcher, 9/2/43, EL (Pre-Pres Papers, box 167); GSP to BAP, 8/30/43, PP 2:341; Gay, 8/29/43, USAMHI (Gay Papers); DDE to MDE, 9/1/43, *Letters to Mamie*, 142; GSP, 8/29/43, PP-LC (box 3) (that was a near thing").

40 GSP, 8/29/43, PP-LC (box 3).

41 Butcher, 8/21/43, EL (Pre-Pres Papers, box 167); Butcher 396.

42 DDE to GCM, 8/24/43, EP 2:1353.

43 Butcher 403.

44 Lucas, 9/2/43, USAMHI (Lucas Papers).

45 GSP, 9/2/43, PP-LC (box 3); Gay, 9/2/43, USAMHI (Gay Papers); Lucas, 9/3/43, USAMHI (Lucas Papers); Hughes, 9/2/43, LC (Hughes Papers, box 2).

46 Butcher, 9/2/43, EL (Pre-Pres Papers, box 167); H. S. Clarkson to DDE, 9/18/43, EL (Pre-Pres Papers, box 91); Hirshson 417; Lucas, 9/5/43, USAMHI (Lucas Papers) ("sit tight").

47 DDE to GCM, 9/6/43, EP 2:1388.

48 Ibid., 9/20/43, EP 3:1439–40.

49 Ibid., EP 3:1440.

50 GSP to ONB, 8/19/43, USAMHI (Hansen Papers, box 3).

51 DDE to GCM, 8/24/43, EP 2:1353 ("little I need tell you"); Ibid., 9/6/43, EP 2:1388 ("already designated").

52 *Time*, 12/6/43 ("tall, tough"); "King Gives a Party for Yank Veterans," *New York Times*, 11/25/43; "General's Daughter Shares His Fame," *New York Times*, 5/10/43.

53 GCM to DDE, 12/21/43, GCML; GCM to DDE, 8/25/43, USAMHI (Hansen Papers, box 8) ("My choice").

54 DDE to GCM, 8/27/43, EP 2:1358; Alexander, interview, 1/10/49–1/15/49, USAMHI (OCMH Collection, Sydney Matthews Papers, box 2).

55 DDE to GCM, 8/27/43, EP 2:1357–58.

56 Ibid., 8/28/43, EP 2:1364.

57 GSP, 9/2/43, PP 2:345; Mayo 153–54, 166–67 (logistics); DDE to GCM, 8/27/43, EP 2:1358 ("[Patton] has planned").

58 ONB, 9/2/43, USAMHI (Bradley Papers); Hansen, notes on ONB, n.d., USAMHI (Hansen Papers, box 9).

59 Hansen, notes on ONB, n.d., USAMHI (Hansen Papers, box 9).

60 ONB, 9/2/43, USAMHI (Bradley Papers); Hansen, 9/3/43, USAMHI (Hansen Papers, box 4).

61 Hansen, 9/3/43, USAMHI (Hansen Papers, box 4); Hansen, "Sicily," n.d., USAMHI (Hansen Papers, boxes 2, 9).

62 Hansen, 9/3/43, USAMHI (Hansen Papers, box 4) ("luckiest man"); GCM to DDE, 9/1/43, USAMHI (Hansen Papers, box 8); F. W. Zeis to ONB, William B. Kean, Chester Hansen, orders dated 9/8/43, USAMHI (Hansen Papers, box 8).

63 Hansen 9/4/43, USAMHI (Hansen Papers, box 4).

64 ONB, GL, 209 ("dither"); M. V. Roberts to ONB, Bridges, and Hansen, orders dated 9/9/43, USAMHI (Hansen Papers, box 8); S. H. Gamble to ONB, Bridges, and Hansen, orders dated 10/18/43, USAMHI (Hansen Papers, box 8); Hansen, 9/8/43–9/9/43, USAMHI (Hansen Papers, box 4).

65 ONB, GL, 209 (citing interviews with Averill Harriman and ONB); Hansen, 9/10/43, USAMHI (Hansen Papers, box 4); "Memorandum, General Bradley: European War," 10/21/46, USAMHI (Hansen Papers, box 8); ONB, SS, 172–73.

66 Photograph, West Point baseball team, 1915, USAMHI (Blair Photograph Collection, box 1); ONB, SS, 171–72; Devers, interview, 8/19/74, EL, 4; Summersby, 10/31/44 and 1/22/45, EL (Pre-Pres Papers, box 140); Butcher, 5/5/43, EL (Pre-Pres Papers, box 166); ONB, GL, 210 ("overly garrulous"); Albert Norman, *The History of Twelfth Army Group*, 15 (NARA RG 331, entry 199, box 25).

67 Memorandum, "Interview of Mr. Pogue with General Bradley," 11/6/46, USAMHI (Hansen Papers, box 8); "Memorandum, General Bradley: European War," 10/21/46, USAMHI (Hansen Papers, box 8); ONB, SS, 173; Charles H. Bonesteel III, interview, 6/8/47, USAMHI (OCMH, "WWII—Supreme Command—IA2(b)—Forrest Pogue"); ONB, SS, 174; Ingersoll 85–87; Hansen, 9/12/43, USAMHI (Hansen Papers, box 4).

68 John Eisenhower 91; Cray 396–97.

69 DDE to CCOS, 7/18/43, EP 2:1261–62; CCOS to DDE, 7/26/43, EP 2:1262, n. 3.

70 Smith, *Naples-Foggia*, 5; D'Este, *Eisenhower*, 448.

71 Butcher, 8/3/43, EL (Pre-Pres Papers, box 167); Devers to DDE, 7/29/43, EL (Pre-Pres Papers, Principal File, box 23) ("overall war effort"); DDE to Butcher, 9/14/43, EP 3:1418; Butcher 416; Tedder 457–60.

72 Butcher 392; Garland and Smythe, *Sicily*, 442.

73 DDE to Marshal Badoglio, 9/8/43, EL (Lee Papers, microfilm roll 1); WBS, interview, 5/13/47, USAMHI (OCMH Collection, Smythe Papers, box 3); Smith, *Naples-Foggia*, 5.

74 DDE to CCOS, 9/8/43–9/9/43, EP 3:1401, 1405; Smith, *Naples-Foggia*, 5, 12; D'Este, *Eisenhower*, 451.

75 DDE to Butcher, 9/14/43, EP 3:1418; DDE to CCOS, 9/9/43, EP 3:1406; Butcher 416, 420.

76 Smith, *Naples-Foggia*, 14 (3,500 American and 5,500 British); GSP, 11/30/43, PP 2:383 (21,000 losses under George's command); Hirshson 417 (citing Butcher, 9/16/43, EL (Pre-Pres Papers, box 167)) ("In case of evacuation"); DDE to GCM, 9/19/43-9/20/43, EP 3:1440, 1436 ("carrying his full weight").

77 Butcher 423–24; EP 3:1454, n. 1; D'Este, *Eisenhower*, 453–54.

78 Butcher 424; D'Este, *Eisenhower*, 454.

79 Butcher 437; DDE to CCOS, 10/9/43, EP 3:1497 ("hard and bitter fighting"); D'Este, *Eisenhower*, 459.

80 GSP to BAP, 11/7/43, PP-LC (box 11).

81 GSP, 9/2/43, PP 2:345; Lucas, 9/7/43, USAMHI (Lucas Papers); Butcher, 9/2/43, EL (Pre-Pres Papers, box 167).

82 GSP to BAP, 9/4/43, PP-LC (box 11).

83 CINC to CG Seventh Army, 9/5-6/43, PP-LC (box 11).

84 GSP, 9/6/43, PP-LC (box 3).

85 DDE to GSP, 9/7/43, in Gay, 9/7/43, USAMHI (Gay Papers); GSP, 9/6/43, PP-LC (box 3) ("[Ike] said"); Hirshson 410 (quoting John P. Marquand, "The General," Yale University (John P. Marquand Papers, folder 676)) ("didn't know what a latrine was").

86 GSP, 9/6/43, PP-LC (box 3).

87 GSP, 9/2/43–9/6/43, 9/7/43, PP-LC (box 3) ("Bradley has a chance"); ONB, GL, 208.

88 GSP, 9/7/43, PP-LC (box 3) ("poor old destiny").

89 Lucas, 9/7/43, USAMHI (Lucas Papers); Odom 15, 17; GSP to Frederick Ayer, 7/28/43, PP-LC (box 14) ("Sicily is the dirtiest"); GSP to BAP, 9/19/43, PP-LC (box 11) ("Alone alone").

90 GSP to WBS, 11/26/43, PP-LC (box 33); Summersby 82–83.

91 GSP, 9/17/43, PP-LC (box 3).

92 DDE to GSP, 10/4/43, PP-LC (box 11).

93 GSP to DDE, 10/6/43, EL (Pre-Pres Papers, box 91).

94 GSP, 10/16/43, PP-LC (box 1).

95 WBS to GSP, 10/25/43, PP-LC (box 11).

96 GSP, 10/27/43, PP-LC (box 3).

97 Ibid ("I have been told"); GCM to DDE, 11/21/43, EL (WBS, World War II Papers, box 15); Davidson, *Grandpa Gar*, 84.

98 GSP, 10/27/43, PP-LC (box 3).

Thirteen: Knight, Bishop, Rook

1 Butcher, 11/23/43, EL (Pre-Pres Papers, box 167); "Patton and Truth," *Time*, 12/6/43 ("severely reprimanded"); Office of War Information, telegram, n.d., EL (Pre-Pres Papers, box 91) ("high-ranking officers").

2 "Headquarters Denies Reprimanding Patton," *New York Times*, 11/23/43; Butcher, 11/23/43, EL (Pre-Pres Papers, box 167); WBS to GSP, 11/23/43, EL (WBS World War II Collection, box 15); Butcher 450; Hirshson 423–24; PP 2:374–75; Transcript, Reuters broadcast, n.d., EL (Pre-Pres Papers, box 91) ("mercilessly berated").

3 "Army Releases Patton Story after Denial," *Boston Traveler*, 11/23/43; "Patton and Truth," *Time*, 12/6/43; "Command: Conduct Unbecoming," *Time*, 12/6/43; Office of War Information, telegram, n.d., EL (Pre-Pres Papers, box 91); WBS to GSP, 11/23/43, EL (Pre-Pres Papers, box 91); Milton Bracker, "Patton Struck Ailing Soldier, Apologized to Him and Army," *New York Times*, 11/24/43; Donald Coe, broadcast transcript, 11/23/43, EL (Pre-Pres Papers, box 91); Atkinson, DOB, 296.

4 GCM, interview, 7/25/49, GCML; GSP, 11/28/43, PP 2:382 ("I seem to be").

5 DDE to Stimson, 11/25/43, PP-LC (box 12); Stimson to Senator Robert B. Reynolds, 11/25/43, PP-LC (box 12); DDE to GCM, 11/24/43, EP 3:1571–72.

6 McKeogh 91; DDE to GSP, 10/4/43, PP 2:360 ("You have lived").

7 DDE to GSP, 11/24/43, PP 2:378.

8 GSP, 11/23/43, PP-LC (box 3); GSP to DDE, 11/25/43, PP 2:378.

9 GSP to BAP, 12/23/43, PP-LC (box 11). See also DDE to GSP, 11/19/43, EP 3:1569.

10 Hirshson 416; Atkinson, DOB, 294 (quoting Garrison H. Davidson, interview, 11/80, Army Corps of Engineers, Office of History, 231).

11 GSP to BAP, 10/22/43, 11/11/43, PP-LC (box 11).

12 GSP, 11/25/43, PP-LC (box 1).

13 Crosswell 196; DDE to Sweeney, 12/23/43, EL (Pre-Pres Papers, box 91); GSP to DDE, 11/28/43, EP 3:1576, n. 1; DDE to GSP, 12/1/43, PP-LC (box 11).

14 *Time*, "Patton and Truth," 12/6/43; Hirshson 427 (quoting Hughes 12/11/43); DDE to Walter C. Sweeney, 12/28/43, EP 3:1629.

15 "Memorandum for the Record," n.d., USAMHI (Hansen Papers, box 1); "Memorandum, General Bradley: European War," 10/21/46, USAMHI (Hansen Papers, box 8); Blair, ONB interview notes, 2/6/80, USAMHI (Blair Collection, box 44); Hansen, notes on ONB, n.d., USAMHI (Hansen Papers, box 9); ONB, SS, 178; ONB, GL, 211.

16 ONB, SS, 179–80; Albert Norman, *The History of Twelfth Army Group*, NARA RG 331, entry 199, box 25, 15-17, 19; Harrison 114, 116; Hansen, 9/5/43, USAMHI (Hansen Papers, box 4); EP 4:2360, n. 2. Because the acronyms for the two headquarters were confusingly similar, for a time the Signal Corps and War Department abbreviated the group organization as "USFAG." Norman 21.

17 ONB, SS, 180–81, 222; Ingersoll 88; Hansen, notes on ONB, n.d., USAMHI (Hansen Papers, box 9); ONB, GL, 212.

18 Harrison 88.

19 Pogue, *Organizer of Victory*, 3:312; Cray 8.

20 Jehl, interview, 2/13/91, EL, 5; D'Este, *Eisenhower*, 461.

21 Ibid., 462.

22 Butcher, 11/23/43, EL (Pre-Pres Papers, box 167); EP 4:2210, n. 1; "Personal Contact Close in Tehran," *New York Times,* 12/7/43.

23 Butcher, 12/5/43, EL (Pre-Pres Papers, box 167); Summersby 94; Pogue, *Organizer of Victory*, 303.

24 Ibid.

25 Butcher, 11/23/43, EL (Pre-Pres Papers, box 167).

26 D'Este, *Eisenhower*, 464 (citing DDE, "Churchill and Marshall," EL (Post-Pres Papers, A-WR Series, box 8) ("President has to make"); Cray 11 ("I don't see why").

27 DDE to GCM, 8/24/43, 9/20/43, EP 2:1354, 3:1439.

28 Butcher, 12/5/43, EL (Pre-Pres Papers, box 167) ("Arlington Cemetery"); Butcher 427–28.

29 Butcher, 12/5/43, EL (Pre-Pres Papers, box 167); T. J. Davis to H. P. Lewis, 11/17/43, EL (Thomas J. Davis Papers); GCM to DDE, 12/6/43, in Butcher, 12/10/43, EL (Pre-Pres Papers, box 167).

30 Ray W. Barker, interview, 9/16/72, EL, 92–94; Butcher, 12/4/43, EL (Pre-Pres Papers, box 167); Ernest Lee to "My Dear Ones," 12/16/43, EL (Lee Papers, microfilm roll 1); Butcher 452–53; Summersby 101–4, 106; D'Este, *Eisenhower*, 465.

31 DDE, *Crusade*, 207; Hastings 28.

Fourteen: England

1 Butcher, 12/29/43, EL (Pre-Pres Papers, box 167); "Wielders of the Weapon," *Time*, 1/3/45; Laurie, "Rome-Arno 1944," 3; Butcher 465; D'Este, *Eisenhower*, 470, 473.

2 Laurie, "Rome-Arno 1944," 4–13; Hastings 25 ("We hoped").

3 D'Este, *Eisenhower*, 473.

4 David Eisenhower 56; DDE to MDE, 1/20/44, *Letters to Mamie*, 164.

5 Butcher, 1/16/44, EL (Pre-Pres Papers, box 168); Jehl, interview, 2/13/91, EL, 5; Craig Cannon, interview, 10/69, EL, 6; Summersby, *Past Forgetting*, 79; Butcher 477 (moved from 20 to 47 Grosvenor Square); McKie 100 (20 Grosvenor Square).

6 Summersby 85; Butcher 473; Blumenson, *Breakout and Pursuit*, 8.

7 Alanbrooke 418 (bomber).

8 DDE to GCM, 12/17/43, USAMHI (Hansen Papers, box 3); ONB, SS, 207 ("Had Alexander").

9 D'Este, *Eisenhower*, 472.

10 Butcher, 12/29/43, 1/20/44, EL (Pre-Pres Papers, boxes 167, 168); GSP, 1/25/44, PP-LC (box 3); Devers to DDE, 12/27, 43, in Butcher, 12/12/43, 12/28/43, EL (Pre-Pres Papers, box 167); Thomas J. Betts, interview, 11/20/74, EL, 122; Butcher 458; D'Este, *Eisenhower*, 482-85.

11 ONB, 12/30/43, USAMHI (Hansen Papers, box 1); ONB, SS, 210; Hansen, 5/4/44, USAMHI (Hansen Papers, box 4); Butcher 463; DDE to Gerow, 7/16/42, EP 1:385; DDE to GCM, 1/29/44, EL, in Butcher, 1/29/44, EL (Pre-Pres Papers, box 168); Butcher, 1/27/44, EL (Pre-Pres Papers, box 168); J. Lawton Collins, interview, 1/25/72, USAMHI, 122.

12 Butcher, 12/12/43, EL (Pre-Pres Papers, box 167); Butcher 463, 481; DDE to Stimson, 12/26/43, EL (Pre-Pres Papers, box 111) ("my conviction").

13 D'Este, *Eisenhower*, 471 (quoting DDE, interview, 6/3/46, USAMHI).

14 Dan Gilmer, "Minutes of Supreme Commanders Conference, Room 126, Norfolk House, 1030 Hrs.," 1/21/44, in Butcher, 2/2/44, EL (Pre-Pres Papers, box 168); Harrison 160; Ray W. Barker, interview, 7/16/72, EL, 91–92; Pogue, *Supreme Command*, 108–9; D'Este, *Eisenhower*, 471-73, 493 (quoting DDE, interview, 6/3/46, USAMHI and citing WBS, interview, 5/9/47, OCMH file, USAMHI); Montgomery, *Memoirs*, 190-93, 199-201; Tedder 505; Blumenson, *Battle of the Generals*, 75.

15 Summersby, *Eisenhower*, 123–24.

16 Butcher, 6/8/44, EL (Pre-Pres Papers, box 168); Tedder 505–7.

17 "Order of Battle as of 6 April, 44" (map), USAMHI (Richard Collins Papers, box 1); Thomas J. Betts, interview, 6/25/75, EL, 173–74; ONB, SS, 245–46 (overall numbers); ONB, GL, 253 (21st SS Panzer).

18 Butcher, 2/7/43, EL (Pre-Pres Papers, box 166); SHAEF to Ramsay, Montgomery, and Leigh-Mallory, 3/10/44, Appendix "F," EL (Pre-Pres Papers) ("coordinate"); Butcher 472, 487 ("my contributions"); D'Este, *Eisenhower*, 499.

19 Ibid.

20 Butcher, 1/20/44, 1/23/44, EL (Pre-Pres Papers, box 168); WBS 36; Butcher 477, 499 ("snowballs"); McKeogh 106 ("army family").

21 Summersby 130-31; Butcher 499; Summersby, *Past Forgetting*, 180; Butcher 8/7/44, EL (Pre-Pres Papers, box 169).

22 DDE to MDE, 5/30/44, *Letters to Mamie*, 184; McKeogh 105, 111; Summersby 124–25.

23 D'Este, *Eisenhower*, 494; Butcher 502, 519.

24 Ibid., 525.

25 Summersby 91; SHAEF G-2, memorandum re: OVERLORD security, 5/10/44, EL (Butcher Papers, box 3); D'Este, *Eisenhower*, 489 ("no secrets").

26 GSP, 3/1/44, PP-LC (box 3); Miller 639; Miller 638–40; D'Este, *Eisenhower*, 489.

27 ONB, SS, 180 ("mild"); Ingersoll 310–11.

28 ONB, interview, n.d., USMA (ONB Papers, Kitty Buhler interview), 45–47; ONB, SS, 226 ("implicit faith").

29 Atkinson, DOB, 295, 363 ("I didn't think"); GSP to BAP, 12/10/43, PP-LC (box 11) ("pink medecin").

30 Summersby, *Past Forgetting*, 144 ("I always"); Hirshson 409–10; Atkinson, DOB, 496 (quoting GSP to D. S. Miller Sr., 12/27/43, PP-LC, box 44) ("Very few of us").

31 GSP, 12/7/43, PP-LC (box 3); Atkinson, DOB, 297 (citing Clark, "General Patton," t.s., n.d., subject file, MWC, Citadel, biography folder, box 3).

32 Clark, interview, 1/4/70, EL, 17; GSP, 12/8/43, PP-LC (box 3); Atkinson, DOB, 297.

33 GSP to BAP, 12/9/43, 12/23/43, PP-LC (box 11) ("Destiny has"); GSP, 12/27/43, PP-LC (box 3) ("I wish").

34 GSP, 1/18/44, PP-LC (box 3).

35 ONB to GSP, 1/17/44, PP-LC (box 33).

36 CG, NATOUSA to CG Seventh Army, 1/22/44, in GSP, 1/22/44, PP-LC (box 3); GSP, 1/25/44, PP-LC (box 3); Clark 256–57; Hughes 1/24/44–1/25/44, in Hirshson 433.

37 GSP, 1/25/44, 2/27/44, 3/28/44, PP-LC (box 3); Price 139–40.

38 Codman 138; GSP, 3/28/44, 8/7/44, PP-LC (box 3) ("one of the starry-eyed boys and pro-British," "pompous").

39 Butcher, 1/27/44, EL (Pre-Pres Papers, box 168).

40 GSP, 1/26/44, PP-LC (box 3) ("very nasty"); Butcher 480–81.

41 Butcher, 1/27/44, EL (Pre-Pres Papers, box 168).

42 Butcher 490 ("greatest general"); Summersby, *Past Forgetting*, 141–42; GSP, 1/31/44, 2/18/44, 3/2/44, PP-LC (box 3) ("Washed mouth," "ass kissing").

43 ONB, interview, n.d., GCML (McCarthy Papers, box 17); see also ONB, SS, 229–30; Blair, notes on GSP, n.d., USAMHI (Blair Collection, box 27).

44 ONB, SS, 230 ("I did not dispute"), 473; ONB, GL, 218–19.

45 ONB, SS, 229–30 ("All he wants"), 355 ("I feared"); Blair, notes on GSP, n.d., USAMHI (Blair Collection, box 27); ONB, interview, n.d., GCML (McCarthy Papers, box 17) ("Ike and George").

46 ONB, SS, 232.

47 ONB, SS, 222, 226, 240; Harrison 187-88.

48 ONB, SS, 221–24.

49 Ibid., 223-24.

50 ONB, SS, 242; GSP, 3/28/44, PP-LC (box 3); Blumenson, *War Between the Generals*, 107 (citing Montgomery to Leese, 6/23/44); ONB, GL, 226-32.

51 Montgomery, *Memoirs*, 193, 214; GSP, 4/7/44, PP-LC (box 3); Pogue, "Memorandum, General Bradley: European War," 10/21/46, USAMHI (Hansen Papers, box 8); ONB, SS, 239, 241; Blumenson, *War Between the Generals*, 80-81.

52 ONB, GL, 233; Hastings 38.

53 ONB, SS, 247.

54 Ibid., 248.

55 Butcher, 4/28/44, EL (Pre-Pres Papers, box 168).

56 Butcher, 4/28/44, EL (Pre-Pres Papers, box 168); ONB, SS, 248.

57 ONB, SS, 239.

58 Odom 34; Lande 105 (quoting Major Frank Pajerski); GSP to BAP, 3/16/44, PP-LC (box 11) ("Piss-Over"); GSP, 1/27/44, 2/5/44, 2/10/44, PP-LC (box 3).

59 Hobart R. Gay, interview, 10/4/80–10/5/80, USAMHI (Gay Papers), 28.

60 GSP, 1/27/44, 2/11/14-2/12/44 ("fundamentally honest"), PP-LC (box 3).

61 Ibid., 3/1/44.

62 GSP to BAP, 3/16/44, PP-LC (box 11); GSP, 2/12/44, 3/1/44, 3/6/44 ("self-respect"), PP-LC (box 3); Butcher 490.

63 DDE to AGWAR, 3/8/44, PP-LC (box 11).

Fifteen: Fix Bayonets

1 GSP to BAP, 12/3/44, PP-LC (box 11); GSP, 3/14/44, PP-LC (box 3) ("not very clever").

2 GSP, 3/1/44 ("drinking too much"), 3/8/44 ("listen, Arthur"), PP-LC (box 3).

3 GSP, 3/5/44, PP-LC (box 3); Pedigree, Mrs. Lesmoir-Gordon's Dog Bureau, PP-LC (box 11); Hirshson 451; GSP, 12/9/44, PP 2:588; Hansen, 2/20/45–4/21/45, USAMHI (Hansen Papers, box 5); Hansen, "Memorandum for the Record," 10/21/46, USAMHI (Blair Collection, box 47); Lande 271 (quoting Horace Woodring); Codman 155.

4 Lande 98 (quoting interview with Fred Hose); D'Este, *Patton*, 576-77, 581–82.

5 GSP, 4/7/44, PP-LC (box 3).

6 Ibid. See also GSP to BAP, 4/9/44, PP-LC (box 11).

7 GSP to BAP, 4/11/44, PP-LC (box 11) ("one year ago"); GSP, 4/13/44, PP-LC (box 3) ("I have a feeling").

8 Hirshson 458–59 (citing Reminiscences of John J. McCloy, 1:15, 11–14, 1973, Eisenhower Administration Project, Oral History Research Office, Columbia University).

9 D'Este, *Eisenhower*, 517 (citing McCloy interview, EL).

10 GSP, 4/7/44, PP 2:434 ("I shall certainly attempt to say nothing which can be quoted").

11 GSP, 4/26/44, PP 2:442; D'Este, *Patton*, 585.

12 Hirshson 460 (quoting GSP to Everett Hughes, 4/26/44, Appendix 141, PP-LC).

13 PP 2:440–41.

14 GSP, 4/26/44, PP 2:442; ONB, SS, 230.

15 D'Este, *Patton*, 586.

16 GCM to DDE, 4/26/44, EL (Pre-Pres Papers, box 91).

17 D'Este, *Eisenhower*, 507.

18 Summersby, 4/30/44, EL (Wyden Papers, box 1).

19 ONB, SS, 231; ONB, interview, n.d., GCML (McCarthy Papers, box 17).

20 ONB, GL, 222.

21 DDE to GCM, 4/29/44, EL (Pre-Pres Papers, box 91).

22 DDE to GCM, 4/29/44, EP 3:1838.

23 GCM to DDE, 4/26/44, EL (Pre-Pres Papers, box 91) ("only available Army Commander"); GCM to DDE, 5/2/44, EP 3:1841, n. 2; GSP, 5/1/44, PP-LC (box 1); Atkinson, DOB, 21.

24 GSP, 4/26/44, PP-LC (box 3); Crosswell 236.

25 Ibid., 4/27/44.

26 Statements of P. A. Bowers, 4/27/44, N. W. Campanole, 4/27/44, T. Blatherwick, 4/26/44, and Constantine Smith, 4/26/44, PP-LC (box 12).

27 DDE to GSP, 4/29/44, EP 3:1839–40; D'Este, *Patton*, 588.

28 GSP to Hughes, 4/30/44, PP 2:448 ("damn fed up with me"); D'Este, *Patton*, 907, n. 2.

29 GSP, 4/30/44, PP-LC (box 3).

30 GSP, 4/30/44, PP-LC (box 3).

31 Ruth Ellen Totten to Nita Patton, PP 2:445.

32 GSP, 4/30/44, PP-LC (box 3); DDE to GCM, 4/30/44, EP 3:1840.

33 Butcher, 5/9/44, EL (Pre-Pres Papers, box 168).

34 DDE to GCM, 4/30/44, EL (Pre-Pres Papers, box 91).

35 DDE to GCM, 4/30/44, EL (Pre-Pres Papers, box 91); DDE to ONB, 9/25/44, USAMHI (Bradley Papers).

36 Summersby, 5/1/44, EL (Wyden Papers, box 1).

37 GSP, 5/1/44, PP-LC (box 1).

38 DDE, *At Ease*, 270–71.

39 Hirshson 463–65 (citing "Some Personal Memoirs of Justus 'Jock' Lawrence, Chief Public Relations Officer, European Theater of Operations," 4, 145–47, PP-LC (miscellaneous box)).

40 DDE, *At Ease*, 270.

41 GSP, 5/1/44, PP-LC (box 3).

42 GSP, 5/1/44, PP-LC (box 3); GSP to BAP, 5/1/44, 6/8/44, PP-LC (box 18).

43 GSP, 5/2/44, PP-LC (box 3); GSP to BAP, 5/2/44, PP-LC (box 18) ("ain't dead yet").

44 DDE, memo, 12/10/42, EP 1:824.

45 DDE to GSP, 5/3/44, PP-LC (box 12) ("I am once more"); Hirshson 463–65 (citing "Some Personal Memoirs of Justus 'Jock' Lawrence, Chief Public Relations Officer, European Theater of Operations," 4, 145–47, PP-LC [miscellaneous box]).

46 Hirshson 465 (quoting Butcher, 5/11/44, EL).

47 GSP, 5/3/44, PP-LC (box 3) ("Sometimes I am very fond"); GSP to BAP, 5/4/44, PP-LC (box 18) ("badly frightened").

48 GSP to Frederick Ayer, 5/4/44, PP-LC (box 14).

49 D'Este, Patton, 591 (quoting Stimson to GSP, 5/5/44 USAMHI (Irving Microfilm)).

50 D'Este, *Patton*, 907, n. 12 (citing Justus Lawrence, USMA-Special Collections).

51 Butcher, 7/17/44, EL (Pre-Pres Papers, box 169); Thomas J. Betts, interview, 8/16/76, EL, 242.

52 SHAEF G-2, *Weekly Intelligence Summary*, 4/1/44 (55 divisions total), USAMHI; Harrison 175 & Map V ONB, GL, 253.

53 David Eisenhower, *Eisenhower at War*, 108; Blumenson, *Breakout and Pursuit*, 32; D'Este, *Eisenhower*, 504–5.

54 Hirshson 472.

55 WBS 43; Norman 114.

56 Butcher 546; WBS 41; Harold R. Bull, "Behind the Scenes with the 'Overlord' Weathermen," n.d., EL (Bull Papers); DDE, interview, n.d., Ohio University Library (Ryan Papers).

57 Butcher 546.

58 Ibid., 539, 550.

59 D'Este, *Eisenhower*, 780, n. 66.

60 Harrison 176-77 (citing CCS 454/6, "Review of Conditions in Europe (10 May 44)," 5/17/44); ONB, GL, 239-40.

61 Hansen, 5/4/44, USAMHI (Hansen Papers, box 4).

62 Hansen, 6/2/44-6/4/44, USAMHI (Hansen Papers, box 4).

63 Tedder 543; Butcher 551; Harrison 186.

64 ONB, SS, 234.

65 Leigh-Mallory to DDE, 5/29/44, EP 3:1895, n. 1.

66 ONB, SS, 235–36.

67 DDE to Leigh-Mallory, 5/30/44, EP 3:1894–95; D'Este, *Eisenhower*, 516–17.

68 ONB, GL, 242.

69 Thomas Hoge, "A Tremendous Invasion Toll? 'Tommyrot!' Says Gen. Bradley," *Stars and Stripes*, 4/8/44, USAMHI (Bradley Papers); "Casualty Forecasts," *Time*, 4/17/44; "Commander Doubts Big 2nd Front Toll," n.d., USAMHI (Bradley Papers); Hansen, notes on ONB, n.d., USAMHI (Hansen Papers, box 9); ONB to Robert A. McClure, 4/14/44, USAMHI (Bradley Papers); ONB to J. C. H. Lee, 4/21/44, USAMHI (Bradley Papers); ONB, SS, 238.

70 Gay, 6/1/44, USAMHI (Gay Papers); Hansen to ONB, n.d., USAMHI (Bradley Papers), (6/1/44 entry).

71 GSP, 6/1/44, PP-LC (box 3).

72 Ibid.

73 Hansen, 6/2/44, USAMHI (Hansen Papers, box 4).

74 Ibid., 6/3/44; ONB, SS, 250 ("If we run into trouble").

75 ONB, 6/3/44, USAMHI (Bradley Papers); Hansen, 6/3/44, USAMHI (Hansen Papers, box 4); ONB, SS, 251-52 ("For the first time").

76 ONB, SS, 252; ONB, GL, 243.

Sixteen: Password: "Mickey Mouse"

1 Snyder 57.

2 DDE to GCM, 6/1/44, EP 3:1902, 6/3/44, EP 3:1903; D'Este, *Eisenhower*, 519; Montgomery, *Memoirs*, 225.

3 Summersby, 6/2/44, EL (Pre-Pres Papers, box 140); McKeogh 106–7; Tedder 544; Thomas J. Betts, interview, 6/25/75, EL, 184.

4 Thomas J. Betts, interview, 6/25/75, EL, 187.

5 Ibid., 178–79; Eliot Tozer, "How Eisenhower Gambled on History's Most Fateful Weather Forecast," *Popular Science* (June 1957), 76.

6 Harold R. Bull, "Memorandum of Record," 6/4/44, EL (Bull Papers); Summersby, 6/3/44, EL (Pre-Pres Papers, box 140); Thomas J. Betts, interview, 6/25/75, EL, 178, 190.

7 Tedder 544–45; Montgomery, *Memoirs*, 226; D'Este, *Eisenhower*, 519.

8 DDE, 6/3/44, EP 3:1904.

9 Butcher 559; Tedder 544–45; Montgomery, *Memoirs*, 226.

10 Butcher, 6/4/44, EL (Pre-Pres Papers, box 168).

11 Summersby, 6/3/44, EL (Pre-Pres Papers, box 140); Summersby, 6/3/44, EL (Wyden Papers, box 1); Ryan, *Longest Day*,

12 D'Este, *Eisenhower*, 527 (citing Mattingly, "A Compilation of the General Health Status of Dwight D. Eisenhower," EL); Summersby 137 ("anxiety ridden"); Summersby, *Past Forgetting*, 189 ("hope to God").

13 Harold R. Bull, "Memorandum of Record," 6/5/44, EL (Bull Papers); WBS 53–54; Strong 184–85; Harold R. Bull, "Behind the Scenes with the 'Overlord' Weathermen," n.d., EL (Bull Papers).

14 Strong 186.

15 WBS 55; Tedder 545.

16 WBS 55. See also WBS, memorandum, 2/22/45, EL (WBS World War II Collection, box 36).

17 Summersby, 6/4/44, EL (Pre-Pres Papers, box 140); Harrison, *Cross Channel Attack*, 274 (quoting Vice Air Marshal J. M. Robb).

18 Harold R. Bull, "Memorandum of Record," 6/5/44, EL (Bull Papers); D'Este, *Eisenhower*, 524.

19 Montgomery, *Memoirs*, 226.

20 Hansen, 6/2/44, 6/4/44-6/5/44, USAMHI (Hansen Papers, box 4); ONB, SS, 252, 256.

21 ONB, interview, n.d., USMA (Bradley Papers, box 30) (Kitty Buhler–Chet Hansen interview), 140; Hansen, 6/5/44, USAMHI (Hansen Papers, box 4); ONB, interview, n.d., USAMHI (Blair Collection, Box 27), 141.

22 Hansen, 6/6/44, USAMHI (Hansen Papers, box 4).

23 Hansen, 6/3/44, 6/5/44, USAMHI (Hansen Papers, box 4); ONB, SS, 253.

24 ONB, SS, 253.

25 ONB, SS, 261, 264, 267.

26 Hansen, 6/6/44, USAMHI (Hansen Papers, box 4).

27 Ibid.; ONB, SS, 267.

28 ONB, SS, 267; ONB, GL, 244 (citing Dickson, diary p. 117); DDE to CCOS, 6/8/44, in Butcher, 6/8/44, EL (Pre-Pres Papers, box 168); WBS 8.

29 Hansen 6/7/44.

30 ONB, SS, 267–68.

31 Jeanne Manning, *A Time to Speak* (Nashville: Turner Publishing Co. 2000), 405 ("Mickey Mouse"); ONB, SS, 267–68.

32 Ibid., 268.

33 Hansen, 6/6/44, USAMHI (Hansen Papers, box 4); ONB, SS, 271-72; Butcher 571; Ruppenthal, *Logistical Support*, 1:298.

34 Hansen, 6/8/44–6/10/44, USAMHI (Hansen Papers, box 4) ("Someday I'll tell"); ONB, SS, 269; ONB, GL, 251.

35 ONB, SS, 272–73.

36 ONB, GL, 248.

37 Summersby 145.

38 Butcher, 6/5/44–6/6/44, EL (Pre-Pres Papers, box 168); Summersby, *Past Forgetting*, 190.

39 Pogue, *Supreme Command*, 275; Butcher, 6/6/44, EL (Pre-Pres Papers, box 168).

40 McKeogh 116–17; Butcher, 6/6/44, EL (Pre-Pres Papers, box 168).

41 McKeogh 117 ("Not too bad"); Butcher, 6/6/44, EL (Pre-Pres Papers, box 168).

42 Summersby, 6/6/44, EL (Pre-Pres Papers, box 140); Butcher, 6/6/44, EL (Pre-Pres Papers, box 168) ("this must be bad").

43 McKeogh 117 ("We just waited"); Butcher 574.

44 McKeogh 117.

45 Butcher, 6/8/44, EL (Pre-Pres Papers, box 168); Hansen, 6/7/44, USAMHI (Hansen Papers, box 4).

46 ONB, SS, 280–81.

47 Hansen, 6/7/44, USAMHI (Hansen Papers, box 4); Butcher, 6/8/44, EL (Pre-Pres Papers, box 168); ONB, SS, 280–81.

48 Butcher 575.

49 ONB, GL, 257.

50 ONB, GL, 254.

51 ONB, interview, n.d., USAMHI (Blair Collection, box 27), 142; Hansen, 6/9/44, USAMHI (Hansen Papers, box 4).

52 Hansen to ONB, 6/17/44, USAMHI (Bradley Papers).

53 ONB, SS, 285.

54 GSP, 6/6/44, PP-LC (box 3).

55 GSP to BAP, 6/6/44, PP-LC (box 18) ("It is Hell"); GSP, 6/6/44, PP-LC (box 3) ("started to pack up").

56 Ibid., 6/10/44.

57 Hansen, 6/14/44, 7/13/44, USAMHI (Hansen Papers, box 4); ONB, interview, n.d., USAMHI (Blair Collection, box 27), 153–54; ONB, SS, 297-98; ONB, GL, 262, 269; Price 202–6.

58 ONB, SS, 65.

59 Butcher, 2/17/44, EL (Pre-Pres Papers, box 168).

60 Hansen, 6/14/44, USAMHI (Hansen Papers, box 4) ("want to go like hell"); ONB, SS, 295.

61 Hansen, 6/14/44, USAMHI (Hansen Papers, box 4).

62 Casualties totaled 28,346 as of June 22, per FUSA's war diary. FUSA, War Diary, 3/24/44, EL (Collins Papers).

63 ONB, SS, 299.

64 Butcher 581; Tedder 550–52; Blumenson, *Breakout and Pursuit*, 14.

65 Butcher 591; Strong 189–90; Tedder 553–54.

66 Blumenson, *Breakout and Pursuit*, 14 (citing Montgomery to DDE, 6/25/44) ("pull the enemy").

67 Butcher 587, 588; EP 3:1948, n. 1; WBS 70–73.

68 Butcher 579-80; JSDE, *Strictly Personal*, 56.

69 Summersby, *Past Forgetting*, 196–97 (bridge); JSDE, *Strictly Personal*, 63 ("there isn't an officer").

70 Ibid., 71.

71 Hansen, 7/1/44, USAMHI (Hansen Papers, box 4).

72 ONB, SS, 323–24.

Seventeen: Slow March

1 ETOUSA, "Outline of Operation Overlord," www.history.army.mil/documents/WWII/ g4-OL/g4-ol.htm; Blumenson, *Battle of the Generals*, 109; Blumenson, *Breakout*, 4 (citing FUSA G-3 Journal; and WBS and Harold R. Bull, interview, 9/14/45–9/15/45, OCHM Files); Ingersoll 170.

2 DDE, *Crusade*, 266–67.

3 DDE to GCM, 6/19/44, EP 3:1936; DDE to GCM and Ernest J. King, 6/20/44, EP 3:1937.

4 Blumenson, *Breakout*, 30 (fewer tanks facing Bradley); Ingersoll 162; Chester Wilmot to J. Lawton Collins, 6/13/47, USAMHI (Hansen Papers, box 2); ONB to Collins, 7/22/47, USAMHI (Hansen Papers, box 2).

5 Blumenson, *Breakout*, 11, 13.

6 Ibid., 44.

7 ONB, GL, 266–67 (citing Hansen 6/28/44 and 7/3/44); Blumenson, *Breakout*, 37.

8 Blumenson, *Breakout*, 37 (citing 21st AG Directive, 6/19/44); DDE to ONB, 6/25/44, EP 3:1948 ("all possible speed"), 46 (citing 21st Army Group memorandum, 6/30/44; FUSA, G-2 "Special Estimate 7," 6/29/44, and "Special Estimate 4," 6/30/44) ("full blooded"); DDE to ONB, 6/27/44, USAMHI (Bradley Papers) ("I feel very sure").

9 ONB to DDE, 6/29/44, EL (Pre-Pres Papers, box 13); Blumenson, *Breakout*, 37 (citing FUSA, *Report of Operations*, I, 82).

10 ONB to DDE, 6/25/44, EL (Pre-Pres Papers, box 13); DDE to ONB, 6/27/44, EL (Pre-Pres Papers, box 13); Butcher 595 (6/27/44); Hansen, 6/26/44, USAMHI (Hansen Papers, box 4); ONB, SS, 305; ONB to DDE, 6/29/44, EL (Pre-Pres Papers, box 13); ONB, "Summary of Conference Held at 21 Army Group at 1600 Hours 30 June 1944," USAMHI (Bradley Papers); ONB to BLM, 6/29/44, USAMHI (Bradley Papers). See also ONB to DDE, 6/29/44, EL (Pre-Pres Papers, box 13).

11 Butcher 601; Summersby 164; BLM to ONB and Miles Dempsey, 6/30/44, in DDE to ONB, 7/1/44, EL (Pre-Pres Papers, box 13); Summersby, 6/30/44, EL (Pre-Pres Papers, box 140); DDE, 6/20/44, EL (Wyden Papers, box 1).

12 DDE to ONB, 7/1/44, EL (Pre-Pres Papers, box 13).

13 Ibid.; Hansen, 7/1/44, USAMHI (Hansen Papers, box 4); Crosswell 247.

14 Hansen, 7/1/44–7/2/44, USAMHI (Hansen Papers, box 4); ONB, GL, 267.

15 McKeogh 79; Hansen, 11/8/44, USAMHI (Hansen Papers, box 5) ("something about that guy").

16 Drew Middleton, "Bradley's Stature Not Diminished," *Lexington* (KY) *Dispatch*, 4/11/81 ("plain as an old shoe"); Alex Stoute, interview, 11/8/80, USAMHI (Blair Collection, box 47); Hansen, 2/4/45, 7/20/44, USAMHI (Hansen Papers, box 5).

17 Summersby, 6/18/44 and 8/1/44, EL (Pre-Pres Papers, box 140); Summersby 166.

18 Tedder, 556–57; Butcher 605; Collins, interview, 5/17/83, USAMHI; GSP, 7/5/44, PP 2:472; ONB, GL, 267; EP 3:1983, n. 1.

19 Hansen, 7/4/44, USAMHI (Hansen Papers, box 4); James Gault, "Gen. Eisenhower's Visit to France, 1st to 5th July, 1944," in Butcher, 7/1/44, EL (Pre-Pres Papers, box 168) ("not flying to Berlin").

20 Butcher, 7/7/44, EL (Pre-Pres Papers, box 168); "Eisenhower Flies over Nazi Lines," *New York Times*, 7/6/44; McKeogh 123; ONB, SS, 325 ("watermelon patch"); DDE to MDE, 7/11/44, *Letters to Mamie*, 194.

21 Hansen, 7/2/44, USAMHI (Hansen Papers, box 4).

22 Ibid.

23 ONB, SS, 320–21; ONB, GL, 269; Blumenson, *Breakout*, 37.

24 VIII Corps G-3 Journal, 7/2/44, in Blumenson, *Breakout*, 55; DDE to GCM, 7/5/44, EP 3:1971; Blumenson, *Breakout*, 76; ONB, SS, 321.

25 Blumenson, *Breakout*, 127, 174-75; James Gault, "Gen. Eisenhower's Visit to France, 1st to 5th July, 1944," in Butcher, 7/1/44, EL (Pre-Pres Papers, box 168); Hansen, 7/4/44, USAMHI (Hansen Papers, box 4); Butcher, 7/7/44, EL (Pre-Pres Papers, box 168); ONB, SS, 321; ONB, GL, 269–70.

26 ONB, interview, n.d., USAMHI (Blair Collection, box 27), 151–52; DDE to GCM, 7/5/44, EP 3:1973; Blumenson, *Breakout*, 178.

27 DDE to GCM, 7/5/44, EP 3:1971; GCM to ONB, 7/12/44, USAMHI (Hansen Papers, box 1) ("The weather"); ONB, SS, 350; Blumenson, *Breakout*, 134 (citing Miles Dempsey to Liddell Hart, "Operation Goodwood," 1952, File 1/230/22A, Liddell Hart Papers).

28 Gay, 7/6/44, USAMHI (Gay Papers); ONB to DDE, 7/6/44, EL (Pre-Pres Papers, box 13); Codman 151-52; GSP, 7/6/44, PP-LC (box 3) ("hatched"); ONB, GL, 271.

29 Hansen, 7/6/44, USAMHI (Hansen Papers, box 4).

30 GSP, 7/6/44, PP-LC (box 3); GSP, 7/2/44, PP 2:470.

31 Ibid.

32 Collins, interview, 1/25/72, USAMHI, 198–202; GSP, 7/7/44, PP-LC (box 3) ("too prone"); GSP to ONB, 10/31/44, USAMHI (Bradley Papers) (John Millikin); Basil H. Liddell Hart, "Notes for History," p. 1, Doc. 11/1944/39, Basil H. Liddell Hart Papers, Liddell Hart Centre for Military Archives, King's College, London, in Hirshson 482–83 ("One should never").

33 GSP, 7/14/44, ("such nothings"), 7/12/44 ("result of lack"), PP-LC (box 3).

34 GSP, 7/12/44, PP 2:481 ("any backbone"); GSP, 7/7/44, PP-LC (box 3); Codman 153.

35 DDE to BLM, 7/7/44, EP 3:1982–83.

36 BLM to DDE, 7/8/44, EP 3:1990, n. 1 ("quite happy"); Blumenson, *Breakout*, 120.

37 BLM to DDE, 7/12/44–7/13/44, in Blumenson, *Breakout*, 190; Butcher 611; Miles Dempsey, interview, 3/12/47–3/13/47, USAMHI (OCMH, "WWII—Supreme Command—1A2(b)—Forrest Pogue"), D'Este, "Monty's Armored Smokescreen," 51–52; Hirshson 493.

38 DDE to BLM, 7/14/44, EP 3:2004 ("old classics"); Butcher, 7/3/44, EL (Pre-Pres Papers, box 168); Butcher 612.

39 BLM to DDE, 7/18/44, in Blumenson, *Breakout*, 194 ("threatening Falaise"); Summersby, 7/20/44, EL (Pre-Pres Papers, box 140); Blumenson, *Breakout*, 191; Blumenson, *Battle of the Generals*, 122.

40 Blumenson, *Breakout*, 191, 193-94 (five hundred tanks); Blumenson, *Battle of the Generals*, 122; Ingersoll 163; Terry Copp, *Fields of Fire: The Canadians in Normandy* (Toronto: University of Toronto Press, 2004), 153–54; D'Este, *Eisenhower*, 557–58.

41 Butcher, 7/20/44, EL (Pre-Pres Papers, box 169); Strong 191; Hirshson 493.

42 Butcher, 7/20/44, 7/25/44, EL (Pre-Pres Papers, box 169); EP 3:2020, n. 2; Blumenson, *Breakout*, 194; EP 2019, n. 1; Blumenson, *Battle of the Generals*, 110, 115; Summersby, 7/23/44, EL (Pre-Pres Papers, box 140); Butcher 617–18, 624; Strong 192; Tedder to DDE, 7/23/44, EL (Pre-Pres Papers, box 115).

43 Butcher, 7/20/44 ("blue as indigo"), 7/22/44, EL (Pre-Pres. Papers, box 169).

44 Tedder 371, 569-70; D'Este, *Eisenhower*, 553–54; ONB, "Memorandum to Accompany Operations Report, Twelfth Army Group, For Period August 1 Through August 31, 1944," USAMHI (Bradley Papers); Butcher, 8/2/44, EL (Pre-Pres Papers, box 169) ("Monty has issued").

45 Summersby 169.

46 Hansen, 7/14/44, USAMHI (Hansen Papers, box 4); Butcher, 7/19/44, EL (Pre-Pres Papers, box 169) ("[Ike's] troubles").

47 D'Este, *Eisenhower*, 553.

48 David Eisenhower 383 (quoting Brooke, 7/27/44); Butcher, 7/20/44, EL (Pre-Pres Papers, box 169).

49 DDE to BLM, 7/21/44, EP 3:2018–19.

50 Ibid.

Eighteen: Open for Business

1 Ingersoll 195; Blumenson, *Battle of the Generals*, 120.

2 ONB, interview, n.d., USMA (Bradley Papers, box 30) (Kitty Buhler–Chet Hansen interview), 117–19; ONB, interview, n.d., GCML (McCarthy Papers, box 17); ONB, SS, 329.

3 "Conference Held in War Tent—12 July 1944—General Bradley and Staff" (NARA RG 407, entry 27, box 1387); ONB, interview, n.d., USAMHI (Blair Collection, box 27), 7, 118; ONB, SS, 329; Blumenson, *Battle of the Generals*, 143.

4 Blumenson, *Breakout*, 197 (citing FUSA Outline, Plan Operation COBRA, 7/13/44), 198 (citing Joseph Collins, interview, 3/30/56), 215; ONB, SS, 330; Blumenson, *Battle of the Generals*, 131.

5 "Conference Held in War Tent—12 July 1944—General Bradley and Staff" (NARA RG 407, entry 27, box 1387) ("Of course," "The whole thing"); FUSA, War Diary, 7/17/44, EL (Collins Papers); Ingersoll 168; Hansen, 7/23/44, USAMHI (Hansen Papers, box 4); Tedder 563.

6 Leigh-Mallory to ONB, 7/19/44, and ONB to Leigh-Mallory, 7/25/44, OCMH, in Blumenson, *Breakout*, 220; ONB, SS, 341; Blumenson, *Breakout*, 215 (citing FUSA Outline, Plan Operation COBRA, 7/13/44); David Eisenhower, 379.

7 William C. Sylvan, 7/20/44, USAMHI (Blair Collection, box 47); ONB, "Combined Air and Ground Operations West of St.-Lo on Tuesday, 25 July 1944," USAMHI (Hansen Papers, box 4).

8 Hansen, 7/23/44, USAMHI (Hansen Papers, box 4).

9 J. Lawton Collins, interview, 1/25/72, USAMHI, 157, 192–94, 268; Blumenson, *Breakout*, 213.

10 Norman 64; Gay, 7/6/44–7/18/44, USAMHI (Gay Papers); Blumenson, *Breakout*, 207–10; ONB, "Memorandum to Accompany Operations Report, Twelfth Army Group, For Period August 1 Through August 31, 1944," USAMHI (Bradley Papers); ONB, SS, 350; DDE to ONB, 7/25/44, EP 3:2027–28 ("My high hopes").

11 FUSA, War Diary, 7/19/44, EL (Collins Papers); Blumenson, *Breakout*, 220 (citing Leigh-Mallory to ONB, 7/19/44, and ONB to Leigh-Mallory, 7/25/44, OCMH); ONB, SS, 340–41.

12 Sullivan 101; Blumenson, *Breakout*, 221 (citing Eighth Air Force Draft, "Summary of Planning and Execution of Missions 24 and 25 July 1944," n.d.).

13 "Conference Held in War Tent—12 July 1944—General Bradley and Staff" (NARA RG 407, entry 27, box 1387).

14 Blumenson, *Breakout*, 221; Blumenson, *Battle of the Generals*, 135–36.

15 Blumenson, *Breakout*, 222–23; ONB, SS, 347 ("helluva chance").

16 Codman 153.

17 Gay, 7/17/44–7/19/44, USAMHI (Gay Papers); ONB, interview, n.d., GCML (McCarthy Papers, box 17).

18 ONB, SS, 356-57. See also Hansen, 7/18/44, 7/20/44, USAMHI (Hansen Papers, box 4); ONB, interview, n.d., GCML (McCarthy Papers, box 17).

19 "Notes on Meeting Between General Patton and Correspondents," 7/17/44, PP-LC (box 53); TUSA, "Report Incident to Briefing of Newspaper Correspondents," 7/18/44, PP-LC (box 53); Gay, 7/18/44, USAMHI (Gay Papers); GSP, 7/17/44, PP-LC (box 3).

20 William Sylvan, 7/24/44, EL (Hodges Papers).

21 ONB, "Combined Air and Ground Operations West of St.-Lo on Tuesday, 25 July 1944," USAMHI (Hansen Papers, box 4); William C. Sylvan, 7/24/44, USAMHI (Blair Collection, box 47).

22 William C. Sylvan, 7/24/44, USAMHI (Blair Collection, box 47); Hansen, 7/24/44, USAMHI (Hansen Papers, box 4); ONB, "Combined Air and Ground Operations West of St.-Lo on Tuesday, 25 July 1944," USAMHI (Hansen Papers, box 4); Blumenson, *Breakout*, 229 (23 dead, 131 wounded); Blumenson, *Battle of the Generals*, 137.

23 Blumenson, *Breakout*, 232 (citing Quesada to Brereton, 7/24/44); ONB, "Combined Air and Ground Operations West of St.-Lo on Tuesday, 25 July 1944," USAMHI (Hansen Papers, box 4); ONB, SS, 347.

24 Blumenson, *Breakout*, 233.

25 William C. Sylvan, 7/25/44, USAMHI (Blair Collection, box 47); EP 3:2029, n. 1; ONB, "Combined Air and Ground Operations West of St.-Lo on Tuesday, 25 July 1944," USAMHI (Hansen Papers, box 4); ONB, SS, 347–48.

26 ONB, SS, 348.

27 Butcher 593 ("bombs short") William C. Sylvan, 7/25/44, USAMHI (Blair Collection, box 47); Hansen, 7/25/44, USAMHI (Hansen Papers, box 4); ONB, SS, 349 ("lost all faith").

28 Blumenson, *Breakout*, 236.

29 Ernest R. Lee, 7/25/44, EL (Lee Papers, microfilm roll 1); FUSA, War Diary, 7/25/44, EL (Collins Papers); ONB to DDE, 7/28/44, USAMHI (Bradley Papers); William C. Sylvan, 7/25/44–7/26/44, USAMHI (Blair Collection, box 47); Hansen, 7/25/44, USAMHI (Hansen Papers, box 4); DDE to GCM, 8/2/44, EP 4:2051; GSP, 7/25/44, PP-LC (box 3); Butcher, 7/25/44, EL (Pre-Pres Papers, box 169); Blumenson, *Breakout*, 236; David Eisenhower, 381.

30 EP 5:161; Summersby, 7/25/44, EL (Wyden Papers, box 1); FUSA, War Diary, 7/25/44, EL (Collins Papers); Hansen, 4/23/43, USAMHI (Hansen Papers, box 2); DDE to ONB, 7/26/44, EP 3:2030; Butcher, 7/25/44, EL (Pre-Pres Papers, box 169); DDE to GCM, 7/26/44, in Butcher, 7/31/44, EL (Pre-Pres Papers, box 169).

31 William C. Sylvan, 7/25/44, USAMHI (Blair Collection, box 47); Hansen, 7/25/44, USAMHI (Hansen Papers, box 4).

32 David Eisenhower, 381; Summersby, 7/25/44, EL (Wyden Papers, box 1); DDE to ONB, 7/26/44, EP 3:2029 ("perfectly certain").

33 ONB to DDE, 7/28/44, ER (Pre-Pres Papers, box 13); Summersby, 7/25/44, EL (Pre-Pres Papers, box 140); Butcher 626; Collins, interview, 1/25/72, USAMHI, 200; Blumenson, *Breakout*, 244.

34 Blumenson, *Breakout*, 246; Telephone conference, Leland S. Hobbs and Hammond D. Birks, 7/27/44, in Blumenson, *Breakout*, 252.

35 Blumenson, *Breakout*, 263, 267-80; David Eisenhower, 382.

36 Blumenson, *Battle of the Generals*, 150; Hansen, 7/28/44, USAMHI (Hansen Papers, box 4); ONB to DDE, 7/28/44, EL (Pre-Pres Papers, box 13) ("riding high").

37 12th Army Group, "General Order No. 3," 8/1/44, USAMHI (Hansen Papers, box 4).

38 Butcher 545.

39 Butcher, 12/28/43, EL (Pre-Pres Papers, box 167); Butcher, 8/2/44, 8/4/44, EL (Pre-Pres Papers, box 169); BLM to DDE, 7/28/44, in WBS, memorandum, 2/22/45, EL (WBS World War II Collection, box 36) ("step on the gas").

40 Butcher, 7/25/44, 8/2/44, EL (Pre-Pres Papers, box 169) ("hell and gone"); Hansen, 8/6/44, USAMHI (Hansen Papers, box 4); GSP to DDE, 7/28/44, PP 2:489 ("wonderful job"); Transcript, GSP and correspondents, 9/7/44, PP-LC (box 12) ("hasn't gotten the praise").

41 J. F. M. Whiteley, interview, 12/18/46, USAMHI (OCMH, "WWII—Supreme Command—1A2(b)—Forrest Pogue"); Blair, ONB interview notes, 2/6/80, USAMHI (Blair Collection, box 44); James Gault, 10/16/44, in Butcher, 10/13/44, EL (Pre-Pres Papers, box 169); Summersby 171 ("like brothers"); Summersby, *Past Forgetting*, 211, 232; DDE to GCM, 8/2/44, EP 4:2053; GCM to DDE, 8/16/44, GCML.

42 Summersby, 8/7/44, EL (Pre-Pres Papers, box 140); Butcher 8/7/44, EL (Pre-Pres Papers, box 169); Summersby, *Past Forgetting*, 208; Pogue, *Supreme Command*, 276.

43 Butcher 634, 639; DDE to GCM, 8/5/44, EP 4:2055; DDE, memorandum, 8/6/44, EP 4:2057.

44 DDE to GCM, 8/19/44, EP 4:2074–76; EP 4:2077, n. 1; ONB, SS, 352–54; Gelb 346 (quoting London *Daily Mirror*, 8/17/44); GCM to DDE, 8/17/44, GCML.

45 ONB, SS, 352–54; Butcher 648–49 (8/19); Ryan, *Bridge Too Far*, 82n ("British have never").

46 Butcher, 9/1/44, EL (Pre-Pres Papers, box 169).

47 BLM to DDE, 10/7/44 and 10/14/44, in Butcher, 10/7/44, 10/14/44, EL (Pre-Pres Papers, box 169); Montgomery, *Memoirs*, 260; DDE to GCM, 8/19/44, EP 4:2075; ONB, SS, 353 ("unfortunate August split").

48 12AG, "Letter of Instructions No. 1," 7/29/44; TUSA, AAR, 1:16; GSP, 7/23/44, 7/27/44, PP-LC (box 3) ("I can sympathize").

49 TUSA, AAR, 1:16; "The Star Halfback," *Time*, 4/9/45 (headquarters van and desk); GSP, 7/31/44, PP-LC (box 3).

Nineteen: "We May End This in Ten Days"

1 Hansen, 8/2/44, USAMHI (Hansen Papers, box 4).

2 ONB, SS, 358 ("Whereas Patton"); Hansen, 8/6/44, USAMHI (Hansen Papers, box 4) ("difficulty keeping").

3 Ibid., 8/14/44.

4 Blumenson, *Breakout*, 348–49.

5 Price 187 ("aren't 500"); Blumenson, *Breakout*, 350, 376–77, 394–95.

6 Price 287.

7 Hansen, 8/2/44, USAMHI (Hansen Papers, box 4).

8 TUSA, AAR, 1:18; Hansen, 8/2/44, USAMHI (Hansen Papers, box 4) ("Germans could hit us").

9 Hansen, 8/2/44, USAMHI (Hansen Papers, box 4).

10 Gay, 8/3/44–8/6/44, USAMHI (Gay Papers); TUSA, AAR, 1:18; Blumenson, *Breakout*, 428; Hansen, 8/2/44, USAMHI (Hansen Papers, box 4); ONB, SS, 363 ("Fine").

11 Hansen, 8/2/44, USAMHI (Hansen Papers, box 4).

12 GSP, 8/2/44, PP-LC (box 3).

13 Hirshson 502 (quoting William Randolph Hearst Jr. and Jack Casserly, *The Hearsts: Father and Son* (Niwot, Colorado: Roberts, Rinehart, 1991), 148).

14 GSP, 8/1/44, 8/9/44–8/10/44, PP-LC (box 3); Blumenson, *Breakout*, 379, n. 32; ONB, interview, n.d., GCML (McCarthy Papers, box 17).

15 TUSA, AAR, 1:22; GSP, 8/7/44, PP-LC (box 3) ("slightly risky").

16 Blumenson, *Breakout*, 431; GSP, 9/9/44, PP-LC (box 1) ("More emotion").

17 12AG, "Directive for Current Operations," 8/2/44; 12AG, "Letter of Instructions No. 2," 8/3/44; Butcher, 8/8/44, EL (Pre-Pres Papers, box 169); WBS, memorandum, 2/22/45, EL (WBS World War II Collection, box 36); Blumenson, *Breakout*, 326, 347, 424–25, 431-32.

18 Blumenson, *Battle of the Generals*, 165–68; Blumenson, *Breakout*, 425.

19 GSP to Gaffey, 8/8/44, in Gay, 8/8/44, USAMHI (Gay Papers); TUSA, AAR 1:24; Blumenson, *Breakout*, 439; Blumenson, *Battle of the Generals*, 167.

20 DDE to GCM, 8/2/44, EP 4:2049–50; Butcher 631; Hansen, 7/29/44, USAMHI (Hansen Papers, box 4) ("biggest hotel").

21 Butcher 8/7/44, 8/14/44, EL (Pre-Pres Papers, box 169) ("communications"); TUSA, AAR 1:32.

22 DDE to GCM, 7/30/44, EP 4:2043; Butcher 8/7/44, EL (Pre-Pres Papers, box 169) ("Why should I tell"); ONB, SS, 393 ("gray hairs")

23 Hansen, 7/28/44, USAMHI (Hansen Papers, box 4).

24 Hansen, 4/26/44, 7/28/44, 8/27/44, USAMHI (Hansen Papers, box 4); ONB, interview, n.d., USMA (Bradley Papers, box 30) (Kitty Buhler–Chet Hansen interview), 134–35; ONB, interview, 12/31/79, USAMHI (Blair Collection, box 27), 12.

25 Blumenson, *Breakout*, 452; Ingersoll 180; Blumenson, *Battle of the Generals*, 148.

26 Blumenson, *Breakout*, 465, 498 (map).

27 Ibid., 491.

28 Blumenson, *Battle of the Generals*, 177; Hansen, 8/7/44, USAMHI, Hansen Papers (box 4).

29 Blumenson, *Breakout*, 434–37; Strong 193.

30 Hansen, 8/7/44, USAMHI, Hansen Papers (box 4); Raymond G. Moses, 8/13/44–8/14/44, USAMHI (Raymond G. Moses Collection); WBS, memorandum, 2/22/45, EL (WBS World War II Collection, box 36); Tedder 575; Pogue, *Supreme Command*, 208–9 (citing DDE, diary memorandum, 8/8/44); Blumenson, *Breakout*, 491.

31 Butcher 8/9/44, EL (Pre-Pres. Papers, box 169); Blumenson, *Battle of the Generals*, 188–90.

32 Hansen, 8/12/44, USAMHI, Hansen Papers (box 4); Blumenson, *Battle of the Generals*, 190.

33 ONB, SS, 372, 374–75; Blumenson, *Breakout*, 492.

34 JSDE, *General Ike*, 118–19.

35 ONB, SS, 375–76.

36 12AG, "Letter of Instructions No. 4," 8/8/44; GSP to Haislip, 8/8/44, in Blumenson, *Breakout*, 494; TUSA, AAR 1:26; Blumenson, *Breakout*, 497 (French 2nd Armored).

37 GSP to BAP, 8/9/44, PP 2:504–5; Butcher 8/9/44, EL (Pre-Pres Papers, box 169); Blumenson, *Battle of the Generals*, 190.

38 Blumenson, *Breakout*, 479, 494–95 (citing 21AG Operational Situation and Directions, 8/11/44).

39 Hansen, 8/13/44, USAMHI, Hansen Papers (box 4); TUSA, AAR 1:28; Blumenson, *Breakout*, 506.

40 Hansen, 8/13/44, USAMHI, Hansen Papers (box 4); Miles C. Dempsey, 8/13/44, in Hirshson 516; Hirshson 519–20 (citing ONB, "Memorandum for the Record: Argentan Falaise Gap Operation," 1–2, ONB Papers, box 66, USMA).

41 Gaffey, "Daily Log," 8/10/44, in Gay, 8/10/44, USAMHI (Gay Papers).

42 Hansen, 8/10/44, USAMHI, Hansen Papers (box 4).

43 Blumenson, *Breakout*, 497.

44 Ibid., 501, 504 (citing Haislip to GSP, 8/12/44, 2130, XV Corps COS Journal); Gaffey to Haislip, 8/12/44, in Gay, 8/12/44, USAMHI (Gay Papers).

45 Blumenson, *Breakout*, 497; Blumenson, *Battle of the Generals*, 504 (citing Gaffey to Haislip, 8/13/44, 0040, XV Corps COS Journal); Blumenson, *Battle of the Generals*, 208.

46 Hirshson 515.

47 GSP, 8/16/44, PP 2:508; Butcher 8/14/44, EL (Pre-Pres Papers, box 169); Gaffey, "Daily Log," 8/13/44, in Gay, 8/13/44, USAMHI (Gay Papers); TUSA, "Directive (Confirmation of verbal orders issued 13 August 44)," 8/13/44; GSP to CG XV Corps, 8/13/44, in Gay, 8/13/44, USAMHI (Gay Papers); Hansen, 8/21/44, USAMHI (Hansen Papers, box 4); Blumenson, *Battle of the Generals*, 208–9.

48 Hansen, 8/12/44, USAMHI, Hansen Papers (box 4).

49 Blumenson, *Breakout*, 504–6.

50 Hansen, 8/21/44, USAMHI (Hansen Papers, box 4).

51 Hirshson 516 (citing ONB, "Memorandum for the Record: Argentan Falaise Gap Operation," 1–2, ONB Papers, box 66, USMA); ONB, SS, 376 ("button up"; reference to Brigadier General Edwin L. Sibert, 12th AG's G-2).

52 ONB, SS, 377 ("solid shoulder"), 378 ("let him ask"); Hansen, "Memorandum for the Record," 10/21/46, USAMHI (Blair Collection, box 47).

53 GSP, 8/13/44, 8/16/44, PP-LC (box 3) ("great mistake," "jealousy"); Codman 163; Blumenson, *Battle of the Generals*, 210.

54 Blumenson, *Breakout*, 556–58; EP 4:2072, n. 1.

55 ONB, SS, 377; Hirshson 519–20 (citing ONB, "Memorandum for the Record: Argentan Falaise Gap Operation," 1–2, ONB Papers, box 66, USMA).

56 Hansen, 3/28/45, USAMHI (Hansen Papers, box 5); ONB, SS, 379.

57 12AG, "Directive for Current Operations," 8/15/44; TUSA, AAR 1:29; Hansen, 8/21/44, USAMHI (Hansen Papers, box 4).

58 GSP, 8/14/44, PP 2:510; GSP to CG XV Corps, 8/14/44, in Gay, 8/14/44, USAMHI (Gay Papers).

59 GSP, 8/14/44, PP 2:510.

60 GSP, 8/13/44, PP-LC (box 3).

61 Butcher 645 (8/15).

62 Allen to GSP, 8/16/43, PP-LC (box 12); Summersby, 8/15/44, EL (Pre-Pres Papers, box 140).

63 Butcher, 8/21/44, EL (Pre-Pres Papers, box 169); Hansen, 8/24/44, USAMHI (Hansen Papers, box 4).

64 DDE, *Crusade*, 279; Gault, 8/26/44, in Butcher, 8/26/44, EL (Pre-Pres Papers, box 169); 12AG War Department Visitors Board letter, 8/31/44, in Blumenson, *Breakout*, 558.

65 DDE to GCM, 8/2/44, EP 4:2053.

66 D'Este, *Eisenhower*, 571 ("Dear Ike"); *New York Herald-Tribune*, 8/24/44, EL (Pre-Pres Papers, box 91) ("Old Blood-and-Guts").

67 WSC, *Tide of Victory*, 34.

68 DDE to CCOS, 8/22/44, in Butcher, 8/22/44, EL (Pre-Pres Papers, box 169); Summersby, 8/22/44, EL (Pre-Pres Papers, box 140); ONB, SS, 386. But see Hansen, 8/21/44, USAMHI (Hansen Papers, box 4) (six thousand tons).

69 Summersby, 8/22/44, EL (Pre-Pres Papers, box 140); DDE to WBS, 8/22/44, in EP 4:2089–90.

70 ONB, SS, 386.

71 ONB, SS, 392; Blumenson, *Breakout*, 615. Contrary to Bradley's recollection, Leclerc did not dawdle when driving on Paris. Beevor 501.

72 Gault, 8/26/44, in Butcher, 8/26/44, EL (Pre-Pres Papers, box 169); Hansen, 8/26/44, USAMHI (Hansen Papers, box 4); David Eisenhower 425.

73 Hansen, 8/26/44, USAMHI (Hansen Papers, box 4); ONB, SS, 394 ("without any fuss"). But see ONB to DDE, 8/27/44, USAMHI (Bradley Papers).

74 Hansen, 8/26/44-8/27/44, USAMHI (Hansen Papers, box 4); Summersby, 8/27/44, EL (Pre-Pres Papers, box 140).

75 Gault, 8/26/44, in Butcher, 8/26/44, EL (Pre-Pres Papers, box 169); Hansen, 8/27/44, USAMHI (Hansen Papers, box 4); Summersby, 8/27/44, EL (Pre-Pres Papers, box 140); Summersby 176–77.

76 Hansen, 8/27/44, USAMHI (Hansen Papers, box 4); Hansen, incidental comments, 8/24/44, USAMHI (Hansen Papers, box 4); ONB, SS, 395; Summersby, *Past Forgetting*, 212.

77 D'Este, *Eisenhower*, 581.

78 Butcher, 9/13/44, EL (Butcher Papers, box 6); Butcher 660; Summersby 181–82; Charles Bolte, interview, 8/14/74, EL, 126; Memorandum, "Interview of Mr. Pogue with General Bradley," 11/6/46, USAMHI (Hansen Papers, box 8).

79 Ruppenthal 2:31-32; WBS, interview, 5/13/47, USAMHI (OCMH Collection, Pogue Interviews); Ingersoll 207; DDE to John C. H. Lee, 9/16/44, in Butcher, 9/16/44, EL (Pre-Pres Papers, box 169); Summersby, 9/18/45, EL (Pre-Pres Papers, box 140); J. C. H. Lee, interview, 3/21/47, USAMHI (OCMH Collection, Pogue Interviews); EP 4:2154, n. 2.

80 Summersby, 9/28/45, EL (Pre-Pres Papers, box 140); Hughes, 7/21/44, LC (Hughes Papers, box 2); Summersby, 9/30/45, EL (Pre-Pres Papers, box 140); WBS, interview, 5/13/47, USAMHI (OCMH Collection, Pogue Interviews).

Twenty: P.O.L.

1 D'Este, *Eisenhower*, 588.

2 Pogue, *Supreme Command*, 244, 250; Ruppenthal 1:488.

3 Pogue, *Supreme Command*, 244–45 (quoting SHAEF Weekly Intel Summaries 23, 24, 26 August and 2 Sep 44, SHAEF G-2 Rpts) ("almost within reach"); Butcher 657 ("Militarily"); Butcher 8/9/44, EL (Pre-Pres Papers, box 169); Hansen, 8/22/44, 9/1/44, 9/5/44, USAMHI (Hansen Papers, box 4) ("now qualified"); Raymond G. Moses, 9/19/44–9/20/44, USAMHI (Raymond G. Moses Collection); Crosswell 258.

4 Butcher 8/15/44, EL (Pre-Pres Papers, box 169); Pogue, *Supreme Command*, 245; "$100,000,000,000 Guess," *Time*, 1/29/44; "The Fate of the World," *Time*, 1/1/45; D'Este, *Eisenhower*, 587.

5 EP 4:2117, n. 3. Most Americans referred to it as the "Siegfried Line."

6 Thomas J. Betts, interview, 6/25/75, EL, 122; Pogue, *Supreme Command*, 249 (citing SHAEF G-3, "Post-Neptune Courses of Action after Capture of Lodgement Area," 5/3/44, SHAEF SGS 38,1 Post-OVERLORD Planning, I); Manchester 477–78.

7 DDE to BLM, 9/5/44, EP 4:2120–21; Pogue, *Supreme Command*, 254; Cole, *Lorraine*, 2; D'Este, *Eisenhower*, 594–96. Eisenhower's and Grant's names evidently changed during their respective youths. Hiram Ulysses Grant's name changed permanently to Ulysses Simpson Grant when he matriculated to West Point under a name erroneously submitted by his congressman. Eisenhower's name in the family Bible was "David Dwight," but he was commonly called Dwight, the name he bore when he entered West Point.

8 BLM, *Memoirs*, 243-45; D'Este, *Eisenhower*, 594; WSC, *Tide of Victory*, 404 (not just Montgomery); Pogue, *Supreme Command*, 250–51.

9 Ibid.

10 BLM, *Memoirs*, 245–46.

11 Ibid., 246–47.

12 Ingersoll 233, 235; Crosswell 257 (citing Pogue interview, 5/7/47) ("balderdash").

13 DDE to CCOS, 8/22/44, EP 4:2087; Guingand, *Generals at War*, 104–5.

14 DDE to GCM, 8/24/44, EP 2:2092–93.

15 Ibid; Norman 66. SHAEF redesignated 21st Army Group as the "Northern Group of Armies" and 12th Army Group as the "Central Group of Armies." Neither name caught on outside SHAEF, and they are referred to here by their numerical designations.

16 EP 4:2092, n. 1; David Eisenhower 422; Hirshson 532–33 (quoting Chester Wilmont, "Notes on Conversations with Montgomery," Public Record Office, London); BLM, *Memoirs*, 247 ("operational coordination"); DDE to Ramsay, et al., 8/29/44, EP 4:2100–1; ONB, GL, 314–15.

17 Strong 200; EP 4:2092, n. 1; Crosswell 256-57.

18 DDE to GCM, 8/19/44, EP 4:2074 ("great pity"); Butcher, 8/19/44, EL (Pre-Pres Papers, box 169).

19 D'Este, *Eisenhower*, 602 (citing WBS, Pogue interview, 5/8/47); Crosswell 259-60.

20 Charles H. Bonesteel III, interview, 6/8/47, USAMHI (OCMH, "WWII—Supreme Command—IA2(b)—Forrest Pogue"); ONB to DDE, 9/21/44, USAMHI (Hansen Papers, box 8); ONB to DDE, 9/10/44, EL (Pre-Pres Papers, box 13).

21 BLM to DDE, 9/5/44, EP 4:2121, n. 1 ("full-blooded thrust"); D'Este, *Eisenhower*, 596 (quoting BLM to Brooke, 8/14/44, Montgomery Papers, IWM) ("Ike is apt").

22 DDE, *Eisenhower*, 607 (quoting Colin F. Baxter, *Field Marshal Bernard Law Montgomery, 1887–1976: A Selected Biography* (Westport, Conn: Greenwood Press, 1999), 91); Gelb 352.

23 DDE to P. A. Hodgson, 9/15/44, EP 4:2151; Butcher, 9/3/44, EL (Pre-Pres Papers, box 169); Summersby 179–80; Summersby, *Past Forgetting*, 212–13; McKeogh 136–37; D'Este, *Eisenhower*, 604–5 (citing Laurence J. Hansen, *What Was It Like Flying for "Ike"* (W. Largo, FL: Aero-Medical Consultants, Inc., 1983)); DDE to MDE, 9/13/44, *Letters to Mamie*, 209; BLM to DDE, 9/7/44, in Butcher, 9/6/44, EL (Pre-Pres Papers, box 169); Summersby, 9/9/45, EL (Pre-Pres Papers, box 140).

24 DDE to BLM, 9/5/44, EP 4:2120 ("exploit our success"); DDE to Ramsay, et al., 9/4/44, EP 4:2115; DDE, memorandum, 9/5/44, EP 4:2121 ("no reason to change"); Miller 712 (quoting Lauris Norstad).

25 See also EP 4:2166, n. 6.

26 D'Este, *Eisenhower*, 606 (quoting Miles A. P. Graham, interview, 1/19/49, Liddell Hart Papers, King's College, London).

27 DDE, 9/12/44, EL (Wyden Papers, box 1); D'Este, *Eisenhower*, 606 (quoting Bertram Ramsay, 9/11/44) ("behaving badly"); Kenneth W. D. Strong, interview, 5/14/63, Ohio University Library (Ryan Collection).

28 Blumenson, *Battle of the Generals*, 241-43; Summersby, 9/11/44, EL (Pre-Pres Papers, box 140); Cole, *Lorraine Campaign*, 13; Ingersoll 211–12.

29 ONB, interview, n.d., USAMHI (Blair Collection, box 44); ONB, SS, 399; Hansen, 9/25/44, USAMHI (Hansen Papers, box 4) ("make it clear").

30 DDE to ONB, 9/15/44, EP 4:2146–47; Tedder 592.

31 ONB to DDE, 9/21/44, USAMHI (Hansen Papers, box 8); Hansen, 9/1/44, USAMHI (Hansen Papers, box 4); Ingersoll 210–11; ONB, SS, 411.

32 Hansen, 9/5/44, USAMHI (Hansen Papers, box 4); ONB to DDE, n.d., in Butcher, 9/13/44, EL (Pre-Pres Papers, box 169) ("very hopeful").

33 DDE to ONB, et al., 9/13/44, EP 4:2136; ONB to DDE, 9/12/44, EL (Pre-Pres Papers, box 13); ONB, SS, 399–400; Ingersoll 222; Pogue, *Supreme Command*, 253.

34 Pogue, *Supreme Command*, 254; EP 4:2135; ONB, SS, 401.

35 Ruppenthal, *Logistical Support*, 1:306–7, n. 77; GSP to ONB, 10/22/44, in Gay, 10/22/44, USAMHI (Gay Papers); ONB, SS, 401 ("To make up").

36 ONB to DDE, 9/12/44, in Butcher, 9/14/44, EL (Pre-Pres Papers, box 169) ("You cannot cut"); DDE, 9/11/44, EL (Wyden Papers, box 1); Gay, 8/30/44, USAMHI (Gay Papers).

37 ONB and Hugh Gaffey, telephone conversation, 11/4/44, in Gay, 11/4/44, USAMHI (Gay Papers).

38 Hansen, 9/12/44, USAMHI (Hansen Papers, box 4); ONB, interview, 11/6/46, USAMHI (OCMH Collection, Pogue Interviews); Memorandum, "Interview of Mr. Pogue with General Bradley," 11/6/46, USAMHI (Hansen Papers, box 8).

39 Memorandum, "Interview of Mr. Pogue with General Bradley," 11/6/46, USAMHI (Hansen Papers, box 8); ONB to DDE, 9/10/44, EL (Pre-Pres Papers, box 13) ("I consider").

40 GSP, 8/31/44, PP-LC (box 3).

41 GSP to BAP, 8/18/44, in Blumenson, *Battle of the Generals*, 241; GSP, 8/23/44, PP-LC (box 1).

42 Ibid.

43 Ibid., 8/25/44.

44 Ibid., 8/28/44.

45 Gay, 8/29/44–8/30/44, 9/2/44, USAMHI (Gay Papers); Ruppenthal, *Logistical Support*, 1:503 (table); Cole, *Lorraine*, 24–25, 52; Charles Broushous, interview, 3/17/76, EL, 68, 73; "Telephone Conversation," Generals Gaffey and Eddy, 8/30/44, in Gay, 8/30/44, USAMHI (Gay Papers); Manton Eddy, 8/25/44, USAMHI (OCMH Collection); ONB, SS, 402 ("Dammit, Brad"). But see Hansen, 9/1/44, USAMHI (Hansen Papers, box 4) (not including "Dammit, Brad" and "two days"); Gay, 8/30/44, USAMHI (Gay Papers).

46 Manton Eddy, 8/25/44, USAMHI (OCMH Collection); Gay, 8/30/44, USAMHI (Gay Papers); Arthur Tedder, interview, 2/13/47, USAMHI (OCMH, "WWII—Supreme Command—IA2(b)—Forrest Pogue"); Arthur Coningham, interview, 2/14/47, USAMHI (OCMH, "WWII—Supreme Command—IA2(b)—Forrest Pogue"); Butcher, 9/1/44, EL (Pre-Pres Papers, box 169); Cole, *Lorraine*, 2; ONB, SS, 402.

47 Hansen, 9/14/44, USAMHI (Hansen Papers, box 4); Memorandum, "Interview of Mr. Pogue with General Bradley," 11/6/46, USAMHI (Hansen Papers, box 8); Pogue, *Supreme Command*, 253.

48 Pogue, *Supreme Command,* 253 (citing "Notes of Meeting of Supreme Commander and Commanders," 9/2/44).

49 GSP, 9/2/44, PP-LC (box 3).

50 Ibid ("all for caution"); Ibid., 9/12/44.

51 Transcript, GSP and correspondents, 9/23/44, PP-LC (box 12) ("can't piss"); GSP, 9/3/44, PP-LC (box 3).

52 ONB, 9/13/44, USAMHI (Bradley Papers); Ingersoll 209; ONB, SS, 412; Hansen, 9/15/44, USAMHI (Hansen Papers, box 4); DDE to BLM, 9/16/44, EP 4:2152; GSP, 9/15/44, PP-LC (box 1).

53 Hansen, 9/15/44, 9/21/44, USAMHI (Hansen Papers, box 4).

54 Ibid., 9/15/44 ("kept the flag"); GSP, 9/15/44, PP-LC (box 1); GSP, 9/17/44, PP 2:550.

55 Hansen, 9/15/44, USAMHI (Hansen Papers, box 4).

56 GSP, 9/17/44, PP-LC (box 1).

57 GSP, 9/21/44, PP 2:552; TUSA, AAR, 89.

58 GSP, 9/21/44, PP-LC (box 1) ("spike [Devers'] guns," "clever son-of-a-bitch"); DDE to ONB, 9/15/44, EL (Pre-Pres Papers, box 13).

59 GSP, 9/21/44, PP-LC (box 1) ("good omen," "One has to fight"); 12AG, "Letter of Instruction Number 8," 9/10/44 (Chalons).

60 DDE to GCM, 7/12/44, EP 3:2000; ONB to GSP, 9/23/44, USAMHI (Hansen Papers, box 1); DDE to GCM, 9/18/44, EP 4:2158-59; Cole, *Lorraine*, 258, 263.

61 GSP, 9/23/44, 9/27/44 PP-LC (box 1).

62 DDE to GCM, 9/14/44, EP 4:2144 ("sacrificed").

63 ONB, SS, 415.

64 Summersby, 9/20/45, EL (Pre-Pres Papers, box 140); EP 4:2153, n. 4; Pogue, *Supreme Command*, 276–77; Jehl, interview, 2/13/91, EL, 17; Hansen, 9/22/44, USAMHI (Hansen Papers, box 4) (plywood); Summersby, *Past Forgetting*, 214–15; Summersby 182–83; Kurt Heilbronn, interview, 3/9/93, EL.

65 McKeogh 135, 138, 143; Snyder 66; Butcher, 9/13/44, EL (Butcher Papers, box 6); Butcher 660–61; Snyder 65; Summersby 178, 220; Hansen, 3/5/45, USAMHI (Hansen Papers, box 5).

Twenty-one: To the Rhine

1 ONB, SS, 428; ONB to DDE, 9/12/44, USAMHI (Bradley Papers); Hansen, 9/3/44, USAMHI (Hansen Papers, box 4); ONB, SS, 357–58 ("If you don't cut us back").

2 DDE to ONB, 9/28/44, EL (Pre-Pres Papers, box 13); ONB to DDE, 9/25/44, EL (Pre-Pres Papers, box 13); GSP to ONB, 9/30/44, USAMHI (Hansen Papers, box 1).

3 Hansen, 9/21/44, 9/27/44, USAMHI (Hansen Papers, box 4); ONB to DDE, in Butcher, 9/23/44, EL (Pre-Pres Papers, box 169); Gay, 9/23/44, USAMHI (Gay Papers); ONB to GSP, 9/23/44, PP-LC (boxes 12, 33); Summersby, 9/20/45, EL (Pre-Pres Papers, box 140); MacDonald, *Siegfried Line*, 384; EP 4:2183, n. 3.

4 ONB to DDE, 9/25/44, EL (Pre-Pres Papers, box 13); GSP, 9/23/44, PP-LC (box 3); DDE to CCOS, 9/29/44, EP 4:2200–1; ONB to DDE, 9/12/44, USAMHI (Bradley Papers); Cole, *Lorraine*, 257–58 (citing ONB to GSP, 9/23/44).

5 GSP, 9/23/44, PP-LC (box 1) ("feeling low").

6 TUSA, "Letter of Instruction No. 4," 9/25/44; Cole, *Lorraine*, 259–60; Cole, *Lorraine*, 259 (quoting ONB to DDE, 9/25/44) ("In accordance").

7 EP 4:2201; Gay, 9/29/44,USAMHI (Gay Papers).

8 Hansen, 9/16/44, USAMHI (Hansen Papers, box 4).

9 GSP, 9/23/44, PP-LC (box 3); ONB to DDE, 9/25/44, EL (Pre-Pres Papers, box 13); ONB, SS, 355–56 ("repent").

10 Hansen, 9/12/44, 9/14/44, USAMHI (Hansen Papers, box 4); GSP, transcript, 9/7/44, PP 2:542.

11 Hansen, 11/5/44, USAMHI (Hansen Papers, box 5).

12 JSDE, *General Ike*, 73. ONB, SS, 433, has a different version (a dozen Arabs).

13 MacDonald, *Siegfried Line*, 380; GSP, 9/25/44, PP-LC (box 3); ONB to DDE, 9/25/44, EL (Pre-Pres Papers, box 13); ONB, SS, 405.

14 Hansen, 9/27/44, USAMHI (Hansen Papers, box 4; Ruppenthal, *Logistical Support*, 1:562–66.

15 GSP, 10/29/44, PP-LC (box 3); Codman 203 ("We roll").

16 ONB, SS, 414; Cole, *Lorraine*, 56–183; Transcript, GSP and correspondents, 9/23/44, PP-LC (box 12).

17 Gay, 9/29/44,USAMHI (Gay Papers); Blumenson, *Lorraine*, 122; Transcript, GSP and correspondents, 9/23/44, PP-LC (box 12) ("not going to get").

18 Cole, *Lorraine*, 126–27, 163, 261-62; Hansen, 9/27/44, 10/7/44, USAMHI (Hansen Papers, box 4); Gay, 9/29/44, USAMHI (Gay Papers).

19 GSP, 10/4/44–10/7/44, PP 2:562–63; Cole, *Lorraine*, 275; Hirshson 552 (quoting GSP to Doolittle, 10/19/44) ("low bastards"). See also Codman 194.

20 ONB, SS, 427.

21 GSP, 10/17/44, PP-LC (box 3).

22 GSP to DDE, 10/19/44, PP-LC (box 12); DDE to GSP, 10/21/44, PP-LC (box 12) ("most emphatically").

23 GSP to ONB, 10/19/44, USAMHI, in Gay, 10/19/44, USAMHI (Gay Papers); Cole, *Lorraine*, 299–300.

24 GSP, 10/7/44, PP 2:563; GSP, 10/17/44, 10/19/44, PP-LC (box 3); GSP to ONB, 10/19/44, in Gay, 10/19/44, USAMHI (Gay Papers); GSP to DDE, 10/19/44, PP-LC (box 12); Cole, *Lorraine*, 300, 302.

25 Cole, *Lorraine*, 296; DDE to ONB, 10/8/44, EP 4:2212 (SHAEF); Gay, 10/22/44, USAMHI (Gay Papers).

26 GSP, 10/22/44, PP-LC (box 3).

27 ONB to DDE, 9/21/44, EL (Pre-Pres Papers, box 13); William C. Sylvan, 10/21/44, USAMHI (Blair Collection, box 47).

28 Hansen, 10/18/44, USAMHI (Hansen Papers, box 4; ONB, SS, 434; MacDonald, *Siegfried Line*, 390; Cole, *Lorraine*, 298.

29 ONB, "Memorandum for the Record," 11/19/44, USAMHI (Bradley Papers); ONB, SS, 438–39; 12AG, memorandum, "Change of Plan," 11/1/44, A. Franklin Kibler Papers, VMI; MacDonald, *Siegfried Line*, 391; DDE to Ramsay, et al., 11/2/44, EP 4:2276; 12AG, "Amendment No. 3 to Letter of Instructions No. 10," 11/4/44; MacDonald, *Siegfried Line*, 391.

30 Gay, 10/22/44, USAMHI (Gay Papers); Hansen, 10/27/44, USAMHI (Hansen Papers, box 4).

31 Pogue, *Supreme Command*, 310; BLM to DDE, 10/7/44, EP 4:2213, n. 2.

32 DDE to ONB, 10/8/44, EP 4:2212; MacDonald, *Siegfried Line*, 319, 378, 399; Gay, 9/5/44, USAMHI (Gay Papers); B. A. Dickson, interview, 12/22/47, USAMHI (OCMH Collection, Pogue Interviews); ONB, SS, 436–37.

33 Gay, 11/2/44, USAMHI (Gay Papers); Gay, 11/7/44, USAMHI (Gay Papers); Cole, *Lorraine*, 302, 311.

34 Cole, *Lorraine*, 299.

35 Ibid., 201.

36 GSP, 11/2/44, PP 2:567; GSP to BAP, 11/6/44, PP 2:569.

37 GSP, 11/5/44, 11/7/44–11/8/44, PP-LC (box 1); GSP to BAP, 11/6/44, PP 2:569.

38 Cole, *Lorraine*, 303; TUSA, AAR, 1:123–27; William C. Sylvan, 11/12/44, USAMHI (Blair Collection, box 47); ONB, SS, 438.

39 GSP, 11/7/44, PP 2:570.

40 GSP, transcript, press conference, 11/6/44, PP-LC (box 53); GSP, 11/2/44, PP-LC (box 3); Codman 211; Cole, *Lorraine*, 318.

41 TUSA, AAR 1:126.

42 Codman 213.

43 GSP, 11/8/44, PP-LC (box 1).

44 ONB, "Directive for Current Operations," 10/30/44; TUSA, AAR, 1:123, 1:136; Cole, *Lorraine*, 374, 488, n. 3; GSP, transcript, press conference, 11/6/44, PP-LC (box 53); GSP, 11/11/44, PP-LC (box 1) ("If you are").

45 Allen, "Amendment Number Four to Letter of Instructions Number 10," 11/12/44 (USAMHI); Gay, 11/4/44, USAMHI (Gay Papers); Gay to Walker, 11/1/44, in Gay, 11/11/44, USAMHI (Gay Papers); GSP, 11/11/44, PP-LC (box 1) ("I suppose").

46 Ibid., 1/22/45 (box 3).

47 TUSA, AAR, 1:131; Codman 213.

48 GSP, 11/11/44, PP-LC (box 3); GSP to DDE, 11/11/44, EL (Pre-Pres Papers, box 91); Hansen, 11/11/44, USAMHI (Hansen Papers, box 5) ("November 11").

49 Butcher, 11/15/44, EL (Pre-Pres Papers, box 169); Codman 217; DDE to ONB, et al., 11/6/44, EP 4:2290; Butcher 702; Butcher, 11/20/44, EL (Butcher Papers, box 6); Gay, 11/12/44, USAMHI (Gay Papers); Summersby, 11/12/45, EL (Pre-Pres Papers, box 140); GSP, 11/15/44, PP 2:574 ("well pleased").

50 Summersby 195–96.

51 McKeogh 143–45; Summersby 195-96; GSP to DDE, 3/29/45, PP-LC (box 13); GSP to DDE, 3/15/45, EL (Pre-Pres Papers, box 91); GSP, 11/15/44, PP-LC (box 3).

52 Gault, 11/24/44, in Butcher, 11/27/44, EL (Pre-Pres Papers, box 169); Hansen, 11/24/44, USAMHI (Hansen Papers, box 5) ("I seem").

53 TUSA, AAR, 1:136–38; GSP, 11/19/44–14/20/44, PP-LC (box 3); Gay, 12/8/44, USAMHI (Gay Papers); ONB to G-3, 12AG, 11/26/44, USAMHI (Bradley Papers).

54 GSP, 11/24/45, PP-LC (box 1).

55 Hansen, 11/24/44, USAMHI (Hansen Papers, box 5) ("I'll ask"); ONB to G-3, 12AG, 11/26/44, USAMHI (Bradley Papers); GSP, 11/25/44, PP-LC (box 1).

56 TUSA, AAR, 1:157; GSP, 12/7/44, PP-LC (box 1) ("promised complete cooperation").

57 Hansen, 11/14/44, USAMHI (Hansen Papers, box 5); MacDonald, *Siegfried Line*, 400; ONB, SS, 438–39.

58 William C. Sylvan, 11/14/44, USAMHI (Blair Collection, box 47); Jacob M. Williams to ONB, 1/5/79, USAMHI (Blair Collection, box 49); Hansen, 11/14/44, USAMHI (Hansen Papers, box 5) ("This is").

59 MacDonald, *Siegfried Line*, 404, n. 39; EP 4:2297, n. 2; ONB, SS, 441, 444–45; Summersby 184.

60 Strong 211; Pogue, *Supreme Command*, 364.

61 Strong 209.

62 WBS, interview, 5/8/47, USAMHI (OCMH, "WWII—Supreme Command—IA2(b)—Forrest Pogue"); Hansen, 12/1/44, USAMHI (Hansen Papers, box 5); ONB, SS, 442; MacDonald, *Siegfried Line*, 324–27, 406.

63 Gavin, "Bloody Huertgen," 40.

64 William C. Sylvan, 6/30/44, USAMHI (Blair Collection, box 47); MacDonald, *Siegfried Line*, 493, quoting Thorson, interview, 9/12/56 ("had the bear").

65 Ibid.

66 ONB, 11/29/44–12/3/44, USAMHI (Bradley Papers); Hansen, 11/28/44–12/6/44, USAMHI (Hansen Papers, box 5).

67 Hansen, 12/5/44–12/6/44, USAMHI (Hansen Papers, box 5) (Twelfth faced the equivalent of eighteen divisions, Twenty-First, ten); D'Este, *Eisenhower*, 634 (quoting ONB, "Memorandum for the Record," 12/13/44) ("would be an indication"); ONB to BLM, 12/3/44, in BLM, *Memoirs*, 275; ONB, 12/7/44.

68 EP 5:174 (Luxembourg); Hirshson 560–61 (citing Reminiscences of General Otto P. Weyland, 6/60, 22, Aviation Project, COHP).

69 Hansen, 12/6/44, USAMHI (Hansen Papers, box 5).

70 DDE to GCM, 10/26/44, EP 4:2252–53; D'Este, *Eisenhower*, 630, 662.

71 Summersby 192–95; Hansen, 11/7/44, USAMHI (Hansen Papers, box 5); D'Este, *Eisenhower*, 631 (quoting Alanbrooke, "Notes on My Life," 11/14/44) ("I was interested").

72 DDE to MDE, 11/12/44, *Letters to Mamie*, 219–20.

73 BLM to DDE, 11/30/44, in Butcher, 11/27/44, EL (Pre-Pres Papers, box 169); Tedder 617; EP 4:2325, n. 4 ("not so good").

74 DDE, interview, n.d., Ohio University Library (Ryan Papers).

75 DDE to BLM, 12/1/44, EP 4:2323–25.

76 BLM to DDE, 12/2/44, in Butcher, 12/1/44, EL (Pre-Pres Papers, box 169); Summersby, 12/2/45, EL (Pre-Pres Papers, box 140) ("most anxious").

77 DDE to BLM, 12/2/44, EP 4:2326.

78 Cole, *Ardennes*, 43 (photo); BLM, *Memoirs*, 276-78; Harold R. Bull, "Notes of Meeting at Maastricht on 7.12.44," EL (Bull Papers); Harold R. Bull to Chief of Staff, 12/10/45, EL (Bull Papers); DDE to CCOS, 12/3/44, EP 4:2330; Tedder 620–21; Pogue, *Supreme Command*, 316.

79 BLM, *Memoirs*, 280.

80 Harold R. Bull, "Notes of Meeting at Maastricht on 7.12.44," EL (Bull Papers); ONB, "Memorandum for the Record," 12/13/44, USAMHI (Bradley Papers); Tedder 620–21.

81 D'Este, *Eisenhower*, 635-36 (quoting BLM to Brooke, 12/7/44, Montgomery Papers, IWM); Tedder, 622–23; D'Este 635–36 (quoting Brooke, 12/12/44–12/13/44); EP 4:2342, n. 1; DDE to GCM, 12/13/44, EP 4:2341–42.

82 Summersby, 12/5/45, EL (Pre-Pres Papers, box 140); DDE to BLM, 12/2/44, EP 4:2326; ONB, SS, 424; BLM to DDE, 12/15/44, in Butcher, 12/15/44, EL (Pre-Pres Papers, box 169); "Extract of Report of Major-General K. W. D. Strong, dated 29th November, 1944," in Butcher, 12/3/44, EL (Pre-Pres Papers, box 169); DDE to BLM, 12/16/44, EP 4:2350 (Montgomery); Pogue, *Supreme Command*, 369, n. 30 (de Guingand).

83 Tedder 625; EP 4:2361, n. 2; ONB to DDE, 12/1/44, USAMHI (Hansen Papers, box 8).

84 Butcher, 12/16/44, EL (Pre-Pres Papers, box 169); Hansen, 12/16/44, USAMHI (Hansen Papers, box 5) ("just want to see").

85 *Letters to Mamie*, 228, n. 1; Butcher, 12/16/44, EL (Butcher Papers, box 6); Butcher 722; McKeogh 151–52; Summersby 196–97.

86 Snyder 76; Summersby 196–97.

87 Summersby 196-97.

Twenty-two: A Forest, a Crossroads, and a River

1 Gay, 12/6/44, 12/14/44, USAMHI (Gay Papers); Hansen, 12/16/44, USAMHI (Hansen Papers, box 5).

2 FUSA, War Diary, 12/9/44, EL (Collins Papers) (First Army); Kenneth W. D. Strong, interview, 12/12/46, USAMHI (OCMH, "WWII—Supreme Command—1A2(b)—Forrest Pogue") (SHAEF); ONB to GSP, 12/13/44, USAMHI (Bradley Papers).

3 Hansen, 12/16/44, USAMHI (Hansen Papers, box 5); James Gault, 12/2/44, in Butcher, 11/27/44, EL (Pre-Pres Papers, box 169).

4 Strong 212-16; DDE to WBS, 11/13/44, EP 4:2302; DDE to Thomas T. Handy, 11/17/44, EP 4:2305, 12/15/44, EP 4:2347 and n.1; ONB, SS, 448–49; D'Este, *Eisenhower*, 640.

5 Strong 216; 21 Army Group, "General Situation," 12/16/44, USAMHI (Hansen Papers, box 2); Weigley 462 (quoting 12AG G-2 estimates dated 12/12/44 and 12/15/44); Ingersoll 247; ONB, interview, 11/6/46, USAMHI (OCMH Collection, Pogue Interviews); Memorandum, "Interview of Mr. Pogue with General Bradley," 11/6/46, USAMHI (Hansen Papers, box 8); Edwin I. Sibert to Hanson W. Baldwin, 1/2/47, USAMHI (Hansen Papers, box 1); Hanson W. Baldwin to Edwin I. Sibert, 12/12/46, USAMHI (Hansen Papers, box 1); Kenneth W. D. Strong, interview, 12/12/46, USAMHI (OCMH, "WWII—Supreme Command—1A2(b)—Forrest Pogue"); Charles E. Hart, interview, 1973, USAMHI, 46–56; Weigley 465.

6 Hansen, 12/17/44, USAMHI (Hansen Papers, box 5); Strong 217; Miller 723.

7 Strong 217–18; Hansen, 12/17/44, USAMHI (Hansen Papers, box 5); ONB, SS, 455; Pogue, *Supreme Command*, 376; JSDE, *Bitter Woods*, 179–80; Crosswell, *Chief of Staff*, 283 (quoting Hughes, 12/17/44).

8 Hansen, memorandum, 7/29/46, USAMHI (Hansen Papers, box 8); EP 4:2361, n. 2.

9 ONB, SS, 455-65; Hansen, 12/17/44, USAMHI (Hansen Papers, box 5); Hughes, 12/16/44, LC (Hughes Papers, box 2); 12AG, AAR, 3:25 (NARA RG 331, entry 200A, box 266).

10 Pogue, *Supreme Command*, 365, n. 20 (quoting Pogue interviews with Strong and Smith); Hansen, memorandum, 7/29/46, USAMHI (Hansen Papers, box 8) ("Well, Brad").

11 ONB, SS, 450.

12 Hansen, memorandum, 7/29/46, USAMHI (Hansen Papers, box 8); Butcher, 12/23/44, EL (Pre-Pres Papers, box 169); Hansen, memorandum of conversation with ONB dated

9/11/46, USAMHI (Hansen Papers, box 8); WBS 93; Cole, *Ardennes*, 332; DDE, 12/23/44, EP 4:2373.

13 JSDE, *Bitter Woods*, 215; DDE, 12/23/44, *Eisenhower Diaries*, 130; Gay, 12/16/44, USAMHI (Gay Papers).

14 ONB, 12/18/44, USAMHI (Bradley Papers).

15 Hansen, 12/17/44, USAMHI (Hansen Papers, box 5); ONB, SS, 466.

16 Ingersoll 248; Hansen, 12/18/44, USAMHI (Hansen Papers, box 5); Butcher 723.

17 Butcher 723; FUSA, War Diary, 12/18/44, EL (Collins Papers); William C. Sylvan, 12/18/44, USAMHI (Blair Collection, box 47); Thomas J. Betts, interview, 8/16/76, EL, 262–63; Summersby, 12/20/45, EL (Pre-Pres Papers, box 140); Butcher, 12/20/44, EL (Pre-Pres Papers, box 169); ONB, SS, 469.

18 Ingersoll 261; Hansen, 12/17/44, USAMHI (Hansen Papers, box 5).

19 WBS 95; Thomas J. Betts, interview, 8/16/76, EL, 254–55.

20 WBS 95; Cole, *Ardennes*, 305; D'Este, *Eisenhower*, 643.

21 Cole, *Ardennes*, 305.

22 GSP, 12/12/44, PP-LC (box 1); TUSA, AAR, 1:160; Lande 205 (quoting Fred Hose of TUSA's G-2 section); Weigley 498–99; Koch 93; Paul D. Harkins, interview, 4/28/74, USAMHI, 28–29.

If you have been diligent enough to read the source notes this far, I would like to thank you for your patience by including a nugget about Patton you may find interesting: For many years historians have credited Patton's intuition with forecasting the attack against VIII Corps in the Ardennes in late November of 1944. See, e.g., Blumenson, *Patton Papers*, 2:582; Weigley, *Eisenhower's Lieutenants*, 498; MacDonald, *Time for Trumpets*, 68; Hirshson 568. The genesis of this oft-repeated claim is the typescript edition of Patton's diary entry for November 25, 1944, now housed at the Library of Congress, which includes the notation: "Furthermore, the First Army is making a terrible mistake in leaving the VIII Corps static, as it is highly probable that the Germans are building up east of them." GSP, 11/25/44, PP-LC (box 3, folder 8). However, Patton's original handwritten entry for November 25, 1944, also housed at the Library of Congress, mentions nothing of VIII Corps or a German buildup east of the Ardennes on that day, or any other day in the late 1944 time frame. GSP, 11/25/44, PP-LC (box 1, folder 11). The warning about a German attack in the VIII Corps area was evidently added to his diary sometime after the fact.

This is not to take away from Patton's tactical acumen as a general matter, and it should be noted that on December 12, four days before the Ardennes Offensive—and after Patton had spoken with his astute G-2 chief, Oscar Koch—Patton did note in his diary that Third Army's III Corps would be able to assist VIII Corps in the event of an enemy attack. GSP, 12/12/44, PP-LC (box 1, folder 11).

23 TUSA, Operational Directives, 12/11/44; TUSA, AAR, 1:154-55; Paul D. Harkins, interview, 4/28/74, USAMHI, 28–29; Lande 205 (quoting Fred Hose of TUSA G-2 section); Codman 226; GSP, 12/9/44, PP-LC (box 1); Hirshson 566 (citing Gay, 12/10/44, 12/13/44).

24 GSP, 12/14/44, PP-LC (box 1).

25 GSP to BAP, 12/14/44, PP-LC (box 18).

26 Joshua 10:12–14.

27 TUSA, AAR, 1:177.

28 James O'Neill, "The True Story of the Patton Prayer"; Christmas Greeting, n.d., PP-LC (box 18).

29 GSP, 12/14/44, PP-LC (box 1).

30 Gay, 12/16/44, USAMHI (Gay Papers); TUSA, AAR, 1:166–67; Cole, *Ardennes*, 331-33.

31 GSP, 12/16/44, PP-LC (box 3).

32 Cole, *Ardennes*, 465.

33 GSP, 12/16/44, PP-LC (box 1). Later versions of Patton's diary include the caveat, "He probably knows more than he can say over the telephone." GSP, 12/16/44, PP-LC (box 3); Weigley, *Eisenhower's Lieutenants*, 498. Patton's handwritten version lacks this sentence.

34 TUSA, AAR, 1:167; GSP, 12/17/44, PP-LC (box 1); GSP, "Notes on the Bastogne Operation," 1/16/45 (NARA RG 407, entry 427, box 1572).

35 GSP, 12/18/44, PP-LC (box 1); TUSA, AAR, Command Section Report, 2:6; Weigley 499; Codman 230; Hansen, 12/18/44, USAMHI (Hansen Papers, box 5); Raymond G. Moses, 12/18/44, USAMHI (Raymond G. Moses Collection).

36 GSP, 12/18/44, PP 2:596.

37 Hansen, 12/26/44, USAMHI (Hansen Papers, box 5); Gay, 12/18/44, USAMHI (Gay Papers) ("Stop Hugh and McBride").

38 ONB, SS, 469.

39 Gay, 12/18/44, USAMHI (Gay Papers); GSP, "Notes on the Bastogne Operation," 1/16/45 (NARA RG 407, entry 427, box 1572); Cole, *Ardennes*, 512.

40 TUSA, Operational Directives, 12/18/44; TUSA, AAR, 1:168; Cole, *Ardennes*, 486–87; EP 4:2359, n. 2; Codman 231.

41 GSP, "Notes on the Bastogne Operation," 1/16/45 (NARA RG 407, entry 427, box 1572); GSP, 12/19/44, PP-LC (box 1); TUSA, AAR, Command Section Report, 2:6.

42 Codman 231.

43 GSP, 12/19/44, PP-LC (box 1).

44 Cole, *Ardennes*, 487–88; DDE to CCOS, 12/19/44, EP 4:2358.

45 GSP, 12/19/44, PP-LC; Codman 233; TUSA, AAR, 1:168–72 (18 December).

46 TUSA, Operational Directives, 12/21/44 ("be prepared"); ONB, SS, 469–70; Hirshson 577.

47 Thomas J. Betts, interview, 8/16/76, EL, 264; DDE to CCOS, 12/19/44, EP 4:2358.

48 Summersby 199.

49 DDE, 12/23/44, EP 4:2374–75; Cole, *Ardennes*, 509; Pogue, *Supreme Command*, 382 (citing Robb, "Notes of Meetings in Supreme Commander's Office," 12/21/44).

50 Hansen, 12/19/44, USAMHI (Hansen Papers, box 5); Thomas J. Betts, interview, 8/16/76, EL, 265–66; Cole, *Ardennes*, 259, 424.

51 Ibid., 424–25; Ingersoll 265.

52 Strong 224–25.

53 DDE, memorandum, 12/23/44, EP 4:2373; DDE, press statement, 2/24/45, EL (Thor Smith Papers, box 6); Hansen to Fletcher Pratt, 3/4/47, USAMHI (Hansen Papers, box 2); Cole, *Ardennes*, 56.

54 ONB, GL, 363 (citing Hansen, 12/11/44); ONB, SS, 474; Cole, *Ardennes*, 274, 424–25.

55 DDE to ONB, J. C. H. Lee, 12/19/44, EL (Pre-Pres Papers, box 13); Pogue, *Supreme Command*, 380; Hansen, memorandum, 7/29/46, USAMHI (Hansen Papers, box 8); Cole, *Ardennes*, 423–24; Crosswell 285.

56 ONB, SS, 476.

57 ONB, "Memoirs Rejects," n.d., USAMHI (Blair Collection, box 49), 217.

58 Ibid., 218; ONB, SS, 476 ("I'd question").

59 ONB, SS, 476.

60 Memorandum, "Interview of Mr. Pogue with General Bradley," 11/6/46, USAMHI (Hansen Papers, box 8); ONB, "Memoirs Rejects," n.d., USAMHI (Blair Collection, box 49), 217; ONB, "Memorandum for the Record," 1/23/45, USAMHI (Bradley Papers).

61 ONB, GL, 364; ONB, "Memoirs Rejects," n.d., USAMHI (Blair Collection, box 49), 217.

62 WBS, interview, 5/8/47, USAMHI (OCMH, "WWII—Supreme Command—IA2(b)— Forrest Pogue"); D'Este, *Eisenhower*, 646 (citing James M. Robb, "Notes of Meeting Held

in Supreme Commander's Office, Dec. 20, 1944"); Harold R. Bull to Hanson Baldwin, 9/12/46, EL (Bull Papers); Bull to DDE, 9/12/46, EL (Bull Papers); Cole, *Ardennes*, 423.

63 DDE to GCM, 2/16/44, EP 3:1731 ("absolutely impossible"); Harold R. Bull to Hanson Baldwin, 9/12/46, EL (Bull Papers); Bull to DDE, 9/12/46, EL (Bull Papers).

64 D'Este, *Eisenhower*, 646 (quoting James M. Robb, "Notes of Meeting Held in Supreme Commander's Office, Dec. 20, 1944"); Tedder 627.

65 Thomas J. Betts, interview, 8/16/76, EL, 264–65.

66 ONB, SS, 476.

67 DDE to CCOS, 12/20/44, EP 4:2363; DDE to Devers, ONB, BLM, 12/20/44, EP 4:2363–65.

68 Strong 226.

69 Ambrose, *Eisenhower*, 174 (quoting Strong interview).

70 Ibid.

71 Adolf Rosengartern, 12/33/46, USAMHI (OCMH Collection, Pogue Interviews).

72 Lande 206 (quoting Fred Hose of TUSA's G-2 section); ONB, "Memoirs Rejects," n.d., USAMHI (Blair Collection, box 49), 215.

73 Arthur Coningham, interview, 2/14/47, USAMHI (OCMH, "WWII—Supreme Command—1A2(b)—Forrest Pogue"); Ingersoll 269.

74 12AG to NUSA, et al., 12/22/44; TUSA, AAR, 1:169; Hirshson 580.

75 Hansen, 12/20/44, USAMHI (Hansen Papers, box 5).

76 Ibid., 12/21/44 (pistols); Lande 206 (quoting Fred Hose of TUSA's G-2 section); TUSA, AAR, 1:172; Hansen, 12/20/44, USAMHI (Hansen Papers, box 5).

77 George W. Shine, "Seeing Stars," n.d., and Shine to ONB, 1/16/79, USAMHI (Blair Collection, box 49).

78 Hansen, 12/8/44, 12/22/44, USAMHI (Hansen Papers, box 5).

79 GSP to BAP, 1/16/45, PP 2:625.

80 GSP, 12/20/44, PP-LC (box 3); TUSA, AAR, 1:175; Hansen, 12/25/44, USAMHI (Hansen Papers, box 5).

81 General Gay also believed VIII Corps should fall back some fifteen miles or so. Gay, 12/21/44, USAMHI (Gay Papers); TUSA, AAR, Command Section Report, 2:7; Price 262 ("Troy"); GSP, 12/20/44, PP 2:602.

82 W. B. Ragsdale, "General Who Made Decision to Hold Bastogne Says Desire Factor Important in War, Peace," *Ocala* (FL) *Star-Banner*, 12/18/58.

83 Hansen, 12/26/44, USAMHI (Hansen Papers, box 5); GSP, 12/20/44, PP-LC (box 3); Koch 110; Price 262.

84 GSP, 12/21/44, PP-LC (box 1).

85 Lande 207–8.

86 Gay, 12/22/44, USAMHI (Gay Papers); TUSA, AAR, 1:174, 176–77; EP 4:2359, n. 5.

87 GSP, 12/22/44, PP-LC (box 3); D'Este, *Eisenhower*, 654 (quoting DDE, "Patton," EL (Post-Pres Papers, box 7)) ("General").

88 TUSA, AAR, 1:177; Hansen, 12/23/44, USAMHI (Hansen Papers, box 5).

89 TUSA, AAR, 1:179–81; GSP, 12/25/44, PP-LC (box 3); GSP, 12/24/44, PP-LC (box 1).

90 Hansen, 12/24/44, USAMHI (Hansen Papers, box 5); GSP, 12/25/44, PP-LC (box 1).

91 Miller 731; ONB, 12/25/44, USAMHI (Bradley Papers); Hansen, 12/25/44, USAMHI (Hansen Papers, box 5); ONB, SS, 480–81.

92 Hansen, 12/25/44, USAMHI (Hansen Papers, box 5); ONB, SS, 481.

93 BLM to Brooke, 12/25/44, in ONB, GL, 369–70; GSP, 12/25/44, PP 2:606.

94 Hansen, 12/25/44, USAMHI (Hansen Papers, box 5); GSP, 12/25/44, PP-LC (box 3) ONB, GL, 370.

95 GSP, 12/25/44, PP-LC (box 1); ONB, GL, 370.

96 ONB, SS, 481–82; Gay, 12/26/44, USAMHI (Gay Papers); TUSA, AAR, 1:181; TUSA, AAR, Command Section Report, 2:7.

97 ONB, SS, 482; GSP, 12/26/44, PP 2:607; Leland Stowe, "Old Blood-and-Guts Off the Record," *Esquire* (10/49), EL (Pre-Pres Papers, Principal File, box 76); Tedder 629; ONB, GL, 371; Blair, ONB interview notes, 2/1/80, USAMHI (Blair Collection, box 44).

98 ONB, SS, 482. But see Cole, *Ardennes*, 509 (Strong's report on 12/20/44 that Hitler had committed all his resources to the initial attack).

99 ONB, "Memoirs Rejects," n.d., USAMHI (Blair Collection, box 49), 219–20; Blair, ONB interview notes, 2/1/80, USAMHI (Blair Collection, box 44).

Twenty-three: To the Rhine (Again)

1 Butcher 728; Hansen, 12/21/44, USAMHI (Hansen Papers, box 5); GSP to BAP, 12/21/44, PP 2:603; Strong 235–36; WBS 114–15; McKeogh 154–55; Summersby 200–1; Murphy 239; "It's Nice Getting Back," *Time*, 5/28/45; McKeogh 155; Summersby, 12/21/45, EL (Pre-Pres Papers, box 140).

2 Summersby 203.

3 Clay Blair, notes on Smith, n.d., USAMHI (Blair Collection, box 27); BLM to DDE, 12/23/44, in Butcher, 12/23/44, EL (Pre-Pres Papers, box 169); D'Este, *Eisenhower*, 651, 654 (citing Robb, 12/26/44, Robb Papers, EL) ("set back").

4 Pogue, *Supreme Command*, 374–75.

5 DDE to GCM, 9/21/44, EP 4:2168; DDE to GCM, 12/21/44, EP 4:2367–68.

6 "Appomattox, 1944," *Time*, 9/11/44.

7 Butcher, 12/27/44, EL (Pre-Pres Papers, box 169); Summersby, 12/28/45, EL (Pre-Pres Papers, box 140).

8 Butcher, 12/27/44, EL (Pre-Pres Papers, box 169); BLM, *Memoirs*, 246; Tedder 631 ("What gets me").

9 Summersby, 12/28/45, EL (Pre-Pres Papers, box 140); D'Este, *Eisenhower*, 655 (citing Brooke, 12/30/44).

10 DDE, *Crusade*, 361; Pogue, *Supreme Command*, 385 (citing DDE to BLM, draft letter dated 12/29/44); Tedder 629 ("Praise God").

11 D'Este, *Eisenhower*, 655 (citing E. T. Williams, 5/30/47–5/31/47, USAMHI).

12 McKeogh 154–57; Summersby, *Eisenhower*, 202–8; Summersby, 12/31/45, EL (Pre-Pres Papers, box 140).

13 DDE to Montgomery, 12/29/44, EP 4:2384.

14 BLM to DDE, 12/29/44, in Butcher, 12/29/44, EL (Pre-Pres Papers, box 169) ("one definite failure"), EP 4:2387, n. 2.

15 Atkinson 466 (quoting Hanson W. Baldwin, interview, 1976, USNI).

16 DDE, interview, n.d., Ohio University Library (Ryan Papers).

17 Ibid.; de Guingand, *Generals at War*, 108–10; D'Este, *Eisenhower*, 657 (quoting de Guingand, interview, "The World at War, 1939–1945," Thames Television series, IWM film archives).

18 BLM to DDE, 12/31/44, in Butcher, 12/31/44, EL (Pre-Pres Papers, box 169).

19 TUSA, AAR, 1:196; TUSA, AAR, Command Section Report, 2:8; GSP, 12/28/44, PP-LC (box 3); Hansen, 12/28/44, USAMHI (Hansen Papers, box 5). But see GSP to BAP, 12/29/44, PP 2:602 (sixteen divisions).

20 ONB to DDE, 12/8/44, EL (Pre-Pres Papers, box 13); DDE to GSP, 12/11/44, EP 4:2340.

21 GSP, 12/27/44-12/28/44, 1/3/45, PP-LC (boxes 1, 3) ("If Ike will"); Tedder 629.

22 GSP, 1/3/45, PP-LC (box 3).

23 Butcher 755–56; WBS 119–20; "Note for General Eisenhower on the Destruction Inflicted on German Armies West of the Rhine," n.d., in Butcher, 4/4/45, EL (Pre-Pres Papers, box 169).

24 Butcher 737–38; Summersby, 1/3/45, EL (Pre-Pres Papers, box 140); Pogue, *Supreme Command*, 398–401; D'Este, *Eisenhower*, 667 (citing Smith, Pogue interview, 5/8/47); DDE to GCM, 1/10/45, EP 4:2420; DDE to GCM, 1/15/45, EP 4:2430–31; Pogue, *Supreme Command*, 411–12; ONB, GL, 379.

25 *Time*, 12/4/44; *Washington Post*, 12/28/44; Hansen, 7/29/44, USAMHI (Hansen Papers, box 4) ("What's wrong?").

26 DDE to GCM, 12/21/44, EP 4:2367-68, 1/12/45, EP 4:2425, 1/14/45, EP 4:2426; Butcher 752.

27 DDE to GCM, 1/14/45, EP 4:2426 ("one of those incidents").

28 ONB to DDE, 12/8/44, EP 4:2341, n. 1; DDE, memorandum, 2/1/45, EL (Cannon Papers) ("dashing fighter"); DDE to GCM, 1/14/45, EP 4:2426.

29 DDE to GCM, 1/14/45, EP 4:2426.

30 Hansen, 12/27/44, 1/2/45, USAMHI (Hansen Papers, box 5); ONB, SS, 483, 497-98.

31 Hansen, 1/8/45, USAMHI (Hansen Papers, box 5); ONB, GL, 373–75.

32 Hansen, 1/2/45, USAMHI (Hansen Papers, box 5); ONB, GL, 379.

33 "Montgomery Has Command of U.S. 1st and 9th Armies," *New York Times*, 1/6/45 ("high tide"); Hansen, 1/6/45-1/8/45, USAMHI (Hansen Papers, box 5) ("now presumed").

34 Hansen, 1/6/45, USAMHI (Hansen Papers, box 5).

35 GSP, transcript, press conference, 1/1/45, 4, PP-LC (box 53); Hansen, 1/3/45, USAMHI (Hansen Papers, box 5).

36 Drew Pearson, "Ike Deals Strictly with Press," *Washington Post*, 4/22/52; BLM, *Memoirs*, 285–86 (not including the "[VIII Corps] took a hard knock" paragraph). See also JSDE, *General Ike*, 132; Pogue, *Supreme Command*, 388 (quoting *New York Times*, 1/8/45).

37 Hansen, 1/8/45, USAMHI (Hansen Papers, box 5); ONB, SS, 485; Ingersoll 279; ONB, "Memorandum for the Record," 1/23/45, USAMHI (Bradley Papers).

38 JSDE to author, 1/14/07; Summersby 209.

39 Hansen, 1/8/45, USAMHI (Hansen Papers, box 5); Summersby, 1/8/45–1/9/45, EL (Pre-Pres Papers, box 140); Strong 232–33; ONB, SS, 488; ONB, "Memoirs Rejects," n.d., USAMHI (Blair Collection, box 49), 220.

40 Ingersoll 283; Hansen, 1/8/45, USAMHI (Hansen Papers, box 5).

41 Ingersoll 284.

42 12AG Press Release, 1/9/45, USAMHI (Hansen Papers, box 1) ("still be fighting"); "Our 'Risk' May Win, Bradley Declares," *New York Times*, 1/10/45; Hansen, 1/8/45, USAMHI (Hansen Papers, box 5); Hansen, 1/10/45, USAMHI (Hansen Papers, box 5).

43 Hansen, 1/9/45, USAMHI (Hansen Papers, box 5).

44 ONB, GL, 384 (citing ONB, "Memorandum for the Record," 1/23/45); ONB, SS, 492; Ingersoll 281; Summersby, 1/11/45, EL (Pre-Pres Papers, box 140) ("E. is afraid").

45 Butcher 694; Blair, ONB interview notes, 2/1/80, USAMHI (Blair Collection, box 44).

46 Hansen, 1/10/45, 1/23/44–1/26/44, USAMHI (Hansen Papers, box 5); ONB, interview, n.d., USAMHI (Blair Collection, Box 27), 83.

47 Summersby 216–17; Summersby, 1/6/45, EL (Pre-Pres Papers, box 140).

48 Butcher, 10/29/44, EL (Butcher Papers, box 6); Hansen, 2/22/45, USAMHI (Hansen Papers, box 5).

49 Ibid.; ONB, SS, 498–99.

50 Brooke, 12/4/44 ("sour-faced blighter"); WSC, *Tide of Victory*, 281–82; ONB, SS, 488–89; Hansen, 1/17/45–5/21/45, USAMHI (Hansen Papers, box 5).

51 JSDE, *Strictly Personal*, 81.

52 ONB, "Memorandum for the Record," 1/23/45, USAMHI (Bradley Papers); DDE to GCM, 1/12/45, EP 4:2425; Pogue, *Supreme Command*, 402.

53 WBS 135, 137; MacDonald, *Last Offensive*, 57; ONB, GL, 388; ONB, "Memorandum for the Record," 1/23/45, USAMHI (Bradley Papers); Tedder 657.

54 Gay, 1/24/45, USAMHI (Gay Papers) (quote); GSP, 1/24/45, PP-LC (box 3).

55 Gay, 1/24/45, USAMHI (Gay Papers).

56 GSP, 1/8/45, PP 2:619; GSP, 1/16/45, PP-LC (box 3); MacDonald, *Last Offensive*, 43.

57 GSP, 2/2/45, PP-LC (box 3).

58 Ibid., 1/18/45.

59 GSP to BAP, 2/25/45, PP 2:647–48; GSP, 2/26/45, PP 2:648; GSP to BAP, 3/16/45, PP 2:656.

60 GSP, 2/1/45, PP-LC (box 1); Summersby, 1/31/45, EL (Pre-Pres Papers, box 140).

61 Gay, 2/2/45–4/3/45, USAMHI (Gay Papers).

62 Ibid., 2/3/45.

63 GSP, 2/3/45, PP-LC (box 3) ("If Bradley").

64 Gay, 2/5/45, USAMHI (Gay Papers); GSP to BAP, 2/5/44, PP 2:635 ("meet with Destiny"); GSP, 2/5/45, PP-LC (box 1) ("am trying").

65 Butcher, 11/4/44, EL (Pre-Pres Papers, box 169).

66 GSP, 2/5/45, PP-LC (box 1).

67 GSP, 2/5/45, PP-LC (box 1); Gay, 2/5/45, USAMHI (Gay Papers); Manton Eddy, 2/6/45, USAMHI (OCMH Collection); GSP to Frederick Ayer, 2/6/45, PP-LC (box 14) ("if I win").

68 Manton Eddy, 2/6/45, USAMHI (OCMH Collection); MacDonald, *Last Offensive*, 100.

69 GSP, 2/8/45, PP-LC (box 1).

70 Ibid., 2/10/45.

71 Manton Eddy, 2/10/45, USAMHI (OCMH Collection).

72 DDE to GCM, 2/20/45, EP 4:2491; ONB, GL, 395–96; GSP to BAP, 2/6/45, PP 2:636 ("Big Simp"); Hansen, 2/23/45, USAMHI (Hansen Papers, box 5).

73 GSP, 2/10/45, PP-LC (box 1).

74 Hansen, 2/23/45, USAMHI (Hansen Papers, box 5); GSP, 2/19/45, PP 2:644; GSP to BAP, 2/21/45, PP 2:645.

75 GSP to ONB, 2/20/45, USAMHI (Bradley Papers) ("We must squarely"); ONB to GSP, 2/21/45, PP-LC (box 12) ("As you know").

76 DDE to ONB, 2/20/45, EL (Pre-Pres Papers, box 13); Hansen, 3/1/45, USAMHI (Hansen Papers, box 5); ONB, SS, 501; Price 278.

77 Gay, 2/25/45, USAMHI (Gay Papers); Hansen, 2/25/45, USAMHI (Hansen Papers, box 5); GSP, 2/25/45, PP 2:643.

78 Gay, 2/25/45, USAMHI (Gay Papers).

79 GSP to BAP, 2/25/45, PP-LC (box 12); Gay, 2/25/45, USAMHI (Gay Papers); GSP, 2/25/45, PP-LC (box 3).

80 ONB, SS, 502.

81 "Memorandum for the Record," n.d. (based on interview with Colonel Russell Akers), USAMHI (Hansen Papers, box 1); Hansen to Monique Munson, 1/26/51, USAMHI (Hansen Papers, box 2); ONB, SS, 502; Ingersoll 306 ("American boner"); MacDonald, *Last Offensive*, 70, 81.

82 Ingersoll 290–91; GSP, 2/27/45, PP 2:648.

83 MacDonald, *Last Offensive*, 134, 183–84, 186, 205–6.

84 Ibid., 217.

85 Hansen, 3/7/45, USAMHI (Hansen Papers, box 5); GCM, interview, 7/25/49, GCML.

86 ONB, SS, 510–15. See also Memorandum, "Interview of Mr. Pogue with General Bradley," 11/6/46, USAMHI (Hansen Papers, box 8).

87 ONB, SS, 511; Toland, *Last 100 Days*, 214–16; MacDonald, *Last Offensive*, 217.

88 Pogue, *Supreme Command*, 429–31.

89 Bull to DDE, 5/31/51, EL (Pre-Pres Papers, Principal File, box 14); "Memorandum for the Record," n.d. (based on interview with Colonel Russell Akers), USAMHI (Hansen Papers, box 1).

90 Bull, biographical sketch, n.d., EL (Harold R. Bull Papers).

91 Hansen, 3/7/45, USAMHI (Hansen Papers, box 5) (toned-down version); ONB, SS, 510–13, 526; ONB, GL, 407.

92 Bull to DDE, 5/31/51, EL (Pre-Pres Papers, Principal File, box 14).

93 Butcher, 3/11/45, EL (Butcher Papers, box 6) ("that's wonderful"); WBS 140; Bull, "Memorandum for the Record," 3/9/45, EL (Harold R. Bull Papers); MacDonald, *Last Offensive*, 219.

94 Bull, "Memorandum for the Record," 3/9/45, EL (Harold R. Bull Papers).

95 Butcher, 3/11/45, EL (Butcher Papers, box 6).

96 MacDonald, *Last Offensive*, 221.

97 DDE to Brooke, 2/16/45, EP 4:2481.

98 DDE to GCM, 2/9/45, EP 4:2473; "Phony," *Time*, 1/22/45 (quoting New York *Daily Mirror*); WBS, interview, 5/8/47, USAMHI (OCMH, "WWII—Supreme Command—IA2(b)—Forrest Pogue") ("SOB").

99 BLM, *Memoirs*, 286–88; DDE to CGM, 2/9/45, EP 4:2473 ("eminently correct"); Brooke, 6/3/43.

100 BLM, interview, 6/24/63, Ohio University Library (Ryan Papers) ("if Patton").

101 Summersby, 2/9/45, EL (Pre-Pres Papers, box 140); EP 5:182; Summersby 218-19 ("stitches"); Summersby, *Past Forgetting*, 216.

102 Summersby, *Past Forgetting*, 217; Summersby 225–26; Hughes, 3/4/45, LC (Hughes Papers, box 2) ("crazy man").

103 Summersby 223.

104 Summersby, *Past Forgetting*, 217 ("Look at you").

105 DDE, memorandum, 2/1/45, EP 4:2466; DDE to Thomas T. Handy, 2/2/45, EP 4:2470; Butcher 770 (3/14/45); DDE to GCM, 3/26/45, EP 4:2544 ("Patton is").

106 Butcher 762, 774, 796; DDE to GCM, 2/2/45, EP 4:2503.

107 DDE to GCM, 3/12/45, EP 4:2522.

108 DDE, "Notes on Conference with General G. C. Marshall," 1/28/45, EP 4:2460–61.

109 DDE to ONB, 3/14/45, EL (Pre-Pres Papers, box 13).

110 Butcher 768.

111 Butcher 769 (3/13/45).

112 Summersby, 3/19/45, EL (Pre-Pres Papers, box 140); Summersby 224.

113 Summersby, *Past Forgetting*, 218.

114 Summersby, *Past Forgetting*, 218 ("somewhat human"); DDE to GCM, 3/26/45, EP 4:2544.

115 "Eisenhower Meets Aides over Rhine," *New York Times*, 3/27/45; McKeogh 164; EP 5:186.

Twenty-four: The Thousand-Year Reich

1 Ibid., 1/26/45 ("lacks it"), 3/6/45 ("he just fails").

2 GSP, 3/1/45, PP 2:649; GSP to BAP, 3/1/45, PP-LC (box 13); Hansen, 3/7/45, USAMHI (Hansen Papers, box 5).

3 Gay, 3/18/45, USAMHI (Gay Papers); McDonald, *Last Offensive*, 236; ONB, SS, 516 ("It'll save us").

4 Gay, 3/9/45, 3/11/45, USAMHI (Gay Papers); GSP, 3/9/45, 3/11/45, 3/20/45, PP-LC (box 3); Codman 261.

5 GSP, 3/11/45, PP-LC (box 3) ("I apologize"); Hirshson 611 (quoting Henry J. Taylor, *Men and Power* (New York: Dodd, Mead, 1946), 15).

6 Codman 264; MacDonald, *Last Offensive*, 245–47; Ingersoll 304.

7 GSP, *War*, 259; Gay, 3/16/45, USAMHI (Gay Papers); GSP, 3/16/45, PP-LC (box 3).

8 GSP, 3/17/45, PP-LC (box 1) ("first compliment"); Gay, 3/17/45, USAMHI (Gay Papers).

9 Codman 183; Lande 174.

10 Codman 265.

11 GSP, 3/16/45, 3/20/45–3/21/45, PP-LC (box 3); Gay, 3/20/45–3/21/45, USAMHI (Gay Papers) ("masterpiece"); William C. Sylvan, 3/14/45–3/17/45, USAMHI (Blair Collection, box 47); Hansen, "Memorandum for the Record," 10/21/46, USAMHI (Blair Collection, box 47) ("start running").

12 "The Star Halfback," *Time*, 4/9/45.

13 MacDonald, *Last Offensive*, 267.

14 GSP, 3/19/45, PP-LC (box 3) (ten divisions); MacDonald, *Last Offensive*, 266.

15 GSP, 3/21/45, PP-LC (Piper Cubs) (box 3); Gay, 3/21/45–3/22/45, USAMHI (Gay Papers); MacDonald, *Last Offensive*, 268; Codman 268; TUSA, "Crossing of the Rhine River by Third U.S. Army."

16 GSP, 3/22/45, PP-LC (box 3).

17 ONB, SS, 521.

18 Gay, 3/23/45, USAMHI (Gay Papers).

19 ONB, SS, 522; ONB, 3/22/45, USAMHI (Bradley Papers); Butcher 776 (3/24/45).

20 ONB, SS, 523; Summersby 225; Gay, 3/23/45, USAMHI (Gay Papers); ONB, GL, 412 (quoting GCM to ONB, 3/23/45, ONB Papers, USMA).

21 Manton Eddy, 3/24/45, USAMHI (OCMH Collection); GSP, 3/24/45, PP 2:661; Codman 269 ("looking forward").

22 DDE to GSP, 3/26/45, PP-LC (box 13).

23 Manton Eddy, 3/26/45, USAMHI (OCMH Collection).

24 TUSA, AAR, 1:165 (15 December).

25 Manton Eddy, 3/26/45, USAMHI (OCMH Collection); MacDonald, *Last Offensive*, 280–82; Hirshson 621 ("Johnny Waters").

26 GSP to Ruth Ellen Totten, 4/7/45, PP-LC (box 19); MacDonald, *Last Offensive*, 284.

27 GSP, 3/31/45, 4/4/45, PP-LC (box 3); Price 285–86.

28 DDE to GCM, 4/15/45, EP 4:2617.

29 Hansen, 12/20/44, 3/7/45, 3/29/45, USAMHI (Hansen Papers, box 5); Ingersoll 289.

30 Hansen, 11/20/44, 12/8/44–12/9/44, 5/8/14–5/9/45, 5/12/45, USAMHI (Hansen Papers, box 5); ONB, "Ifs of History," n.d., USAMHI (Blair Collection, box 49) ("mistress"); Blair, ONB interview notes, 2/6/80, USAMHI (Blair Collection, box 44); Toby Helm, "Film Star Felt Ashamed of Belsen Link," *Daily Telegraph*, 6/24/00.

31 Hansen, 2/20/45–2/21/45, USAMHI (Hansen Papers, box 5).

32 Hirshson 623 (citing Bradley, interview, 2/28/75, ONB Papers, USMA). See also ONB, interview, n.d., GCML (McCarthy Papers, box 17).

33 ONB, SS, 519.

34 Butcher 657 (9/7/44) ("a lot of color"); Gene Currivan, "Path to Berlin Is Now Open, German Officer Tells Third," *New York Times*, 3/31/45; "The Star Halfback," *Time*, 4/9/45.

35 ONB, interview, n.d., USMA (Kitty Buhler interview), 46–47; DDE to the Allied Expeditionary Forces, 4/20/45, EP 4:2628; WBS 173, 186; Strong 254; ONB, SS, 528–29.

36 Hansen, "A Discussion on Tactics," n.d., USAMHI (Hansen Papers, box 22); Hansen, 4/7/45 ("any"), 5/1/45, 6/9/45, USAMHI (Hansen Papers, boxes 4, 5).

37 DDE to GCM, 3/26/45, EP 4:2543, 3/30/45, EP 4:2560–61; Miller 735–36.

38 MacDonald, *Last Offensive*, Map XII; ONB, SS, 525; WBS 170.

39 Hansen, 1/29/45, 4/7/45, USAMHI (Hansen Papers, box 5); ONB, SS, 535; ONB, "Ifs of History," n.d., USAMHI (Blair Collection, box 49) ("pretty stiff"); Kenneth W. D. Strong, interview, 5/14/63, Ohio University Library (Ryan Papers).

40 Ambrose, *Berlin*, 64–65.

41 DDE to ONB and Devers, 3/29/45, EL (Pre-Pres Papers, box 13); DDE to John Deane and Ernest Archer, 3/28/45, EP 4:2551; ONB to DDE, 4/10/45, EL (Pre-Pres Papers, box 13).

42 DDE, interview, n.d., Ohio University Library (Ryan Papers).

43 DDE to John Deane and Ernest Archer, 3/28/45, EP 4:2551, 3/29/45, EP 4:2557–58; Stalin to DDE, 4/1/45, EP 4:2584, n. 1; Tedder 675–76.

44 DDE to BLM, 3/28/45, EP 4:2552.

45 DDE to GCM, 3/30/45, EP 4:2559, 2560; DDE to WSC, 3/30/45, EP 4:2562, 2563, n. 2; WSC to DDE, 3/31/45, EP 4:2563, n. 2.

46 Summersby, 3/31/45, EP 4:2563, n. 2; DDE to GCM, 2/28/45, EP 4:2552–53, 4/7/45, EP 4:2592; DDE to GCM, 4/15/45, EL (Pre-Pres Papers, box 80).

47 "The Star Halfback," *Time*, 4/9/45.

48 GSP, 3/30/45–3/31/45, PP-LC (box 3) ("timid"); JSDE, *Strictly Personal*, 84 ("Don't tell").

49 Bradsher, n.p. ("potassium"); Summersby, 4/12/45, EL (Pre-Pres Papers, box 140); GSP, 4/6/45, PP 2:681; Gay, 4/6/45–4/7/45, 4/13/45, USAMHI (Gay Papers).

50 Gay, 4/9/45, USAMHI (Gay Papers).

51 Bernstein, interview, 7/23/75, 116–17, Truman Library.

52 Gay, 4/11/45, USAMHI (Gay Papers).

53 Gay, 4/11/45, USAMHI (Gay Papers); Codman 280 (Hersfeld); Hansen, 4/12/45, USAMHI (Hansen Papers, box 5) (photographers); Toland 370.

54 Codman 281; Odom 72.

55 GSP, 4/12/45, PP-LC (box 3).

56 Gay, 4/12/45, USAMHI (Gay Papers, box 1).

57 GSP, 4/12/45, PP-LC (box 3).

58 Codman 282; SHAEF, "Press Censors' Guidance No. 937," 4/17/45, EL (Thor Smith Papers, box 6; GSP, 4/12/45, PP-LC (box 3); Gay, 4/12/45, USAMHI (Gay Papers, box 1).

59 DDE to GCM, 4/15/45, EL (Pre-Pres Papers, box 80) ("beggar description"); ONB, GL, 428 ("revolted"); GSP, 4/12/45, PP-LC (box 3) ("appalling").

60 GSP, 4/12/45, PP-LC (box 3); Hansen, 4/12/45–4/13/45, USAMHI (Hansen Papers, box 5); Toland 370.

61 McKeogh 165; Hughes, 4/17/44, LC (Hughes Papers, box 2); GSP to DDE, 4/14/45, PP-LC (box 3); Hansen, 4/12/45, USAMHI (Hansen Papers, box 5) ("I know you're wrong").

62 Hansen, 4/12/45, USAMHI (Hansen Papers, box 5); GSP, 4/12/45, PP-LC (box 3); Gay, 4/12/45, USAMHI (Gay Papers); DDE to GSP, 4/18/45, EL.

63 Gay, 4/12/45–4/13/45, USAMHI (Gay Papers).

64 Ibid ("I don't see").

65 GSP, 4/12/45, PP-LC (box 3); Hansen, 4/12/45, USAMHI (Hansen Papers, box 5).

66 Hansen, 4/12/45, USAMHI (Hansen Papers, box 5).

67 ONB, SS, 541; DDE, *Crusade*, 409–10; ONB, GL, 429; GSP, 4/12/45, PP-LC (box 3) ("very unfortunate").

68 GSP, transcript, 4/13/45, PP-LC (box 53); Gay, 4/13/45, USAMHI (Gay Papers); Hansen, 4/13/45, USAMHI (Hansen Papers, box 5) ("buggery").

69 Hughes to BAP, 4/18/45, PP-LC (box 13).

70 Ibid.; PP 2:690; Hirshson 630 (citing GSP to GCM, 3/1/45, GCM Papers, GCML); GSP, 4/18/45, PP-LC (box 3) ("While I am glad").

71 GSP, 4/18/45, PP-LC (box 3); Codman 291.

72 Gay, 4/19/45, USAMHI (Gay Papers); PP 2:687–88; GSP, 5/4/45, PP 2:696; Codman 295.

73 GSP, 5/5/45, PP-LC (box 3); GSP, 5/6/45, PP 2:696; Hirshson 633.

74 GSP, 5/6/45, PP-LC (box 3) ("It seems"); Hirshson 633 ("I felt").

75 Note, undated, referring to GSP, 5/1/45, EL (C. D. Jackson Papers, box 17) ("Not even SHAEF"); Gay, 4/22/45, USAMHI (Gay Papers); Codman 293; GSP, 5/4/45, PP-LC (box 3) ("Things like this").

76 Butcher 793 ("Not only Hodges'"); Hansen, 4/6/45, USAMHI (Hansen Papers, box 5) ("greatest field commander"); DDE to GCM, 3/30/45, EP 4:2564; DDE to GCM, 4/15/45, EP 4:2616 ("Bradley, of course").

77 Hansen, 4/21/45, USAMHI (Hansen Papers, box 5); DDE to GSP, 4/14/45, PP-LC (box 13); Summersby, 4/12/45, EL (Pre-Pres Papers, box 140); Butcher 803 ("I think Patton").

78 DDE to GCM, 4/15/45, EL (Pre-Pres Papers, box 80).

79 DDE to GSP, 4/16/45, PP-LC (box 13).

80 ONB, SS, 528; ONB, GL, 417–20.

81 ONB, 4/10/45, USAMHI (Bradley Papers); ONB, GL, 427 (ONB to DDE, 4/10/45, EL).

82 12AG, AAR, 1:1 (map) (Wiesbaden); ONB, GL, 427.

83 ONB, GL, 430–31; MacDonald, *Last Offensive*, 422.

84 EP 5:188; Hansen, 4/19/45, USAMHI (Hansen Papers, box 5).

85 Hansen, 4/19/45, 4/24/45–4/26/45, 4/29/45, USAMHI (Hansen Papers, box 5); Hansen, "Union with the Russians," n.d., USAMHI (Hansen Papers, box 5); ONB, GL, 433; DDE to GCM, 4/26/45, EP 4:2647 (1.2 million).

86 Summersby, 2/21/45–4/22/45, EL (Pre-Pres Papers, box 140); WBS 87 (move effective March 1); Summersby 220. Ike's personal quarters were in a large clubhouse. Jehl, interview, 2/13/91, EL, 17.

87 Butcher, 5/4/45, EL (Butcher Papers, box 6); MacDonald, *Last Offensive*, 474.

88 Butcher, 5/4/45, EL (Butcher Papers, box 6); Butcher 821; Summersby 236.

89 Summersby 237–38; MacDonald, *Last Offensive*, 474.

90 WBS 204–6; Strong 273.

91 Butcher 824–25; WBS, 210–11.

92 Murphy 255 ("won't shake hands").

93 Butcher 822; Summersby 235–36, 239.

94 WBS 211; Strong 207; Butcher, 5/7/45; D'Este, *Eisenhower*, 703.

95 Butcher 830.

96 DDE, *At Ease*, 293; Summersby 241; McKeogh 172; WBS 229.

97 Butcher 834.

Twenty-five: Closing the Shop

1 Hansen, 5/7/45, USAMHI (Hansen Papers, box 5) (awakened each army commander).

2 Codman 297.

3 GSP to GCM, 3/13/45, PP 2:654; Gilbert R. Cook to GSP, 5/3/45, EL (Gilbert Cook Papers).

4 PP 2:693; GSP to A. C. Wedemeyer, 7/6/45, PP 2:726.

5 Codman 301 ("species of whale"); GSP to BAP, n.d., PP-LC (box 13); PP 2:695 ("I love war").

6 Hansen, 5/11/45, USAMHI (Hansen Papers, box 5).

7 GSP, 5/10/45, PP-LC (box 3) ("my opinion").

8 Ibid., 5/17/45–5/18/45.

9 PP 2:718.

10 Hansen, 5/5/45, 5/8/45, 9/1/45, USAMHI (Hansen Papers, box 5); Summersby 254, 261.

11 GCM to DDE, 4/25/45, EP 4:2648, n. 3; Summersby, 4/26/45, EL (Pre-Pres Papers, box 140).

12 DDE to GCM, 4/26/45, EP 4:2647–48; Summersby, 4/26/45, EL (Pre-Pres Papers, box 140).

13 DDE to GCM, 4/26/45, EP 4:2647–48.

14 GCM to DDE, 4/27/45, EP 4:2684, n. 4; Hansen, 4/21/45, USAMHI (Hansen Papers, box 5).

15 Butcher 817-20.

16 JSDE, interview, 2/28/68, EL, 48.

17 GCM to DDE, 5/16/45, EL (Pre-Pres Papers, box 80).

18 Ibid.; ONB, GL, 439 (citing ONB, notes, 12/31/64, Hanson-ONB interview, and ONB, interview with Clay Blair).

19 Hansen, 8/12/44, USAMHI, Hansen Papers (box 4); ONB, SS, 528.

20 ONB, GL, 439 (citing ONB, notes, 12/31/64, Hanson-ONB interview, and ONB, interview with Clay Blair).

21 Blair, ONB interview notes, 2/6/80, USAMHI (Blair Collection, box 44).

22 DDE, 11/28/59, *Eisenhower Diaries*, 370.

23 DDE to GCM, 5/18/45, EL (Pre-Pres Papers, box 80).

24 ONB, Memorandum, 6/1/45, EL (Pre-Pres Papers, box 91), USAMHI (Hansen Papers, box 8).

25 ONB to GSP, 7/19/45, PP-LC (box 13).

26 DDE to ONB, 7/19/45, EL (Pre-Pres Papers, box 13).

27 DDE to MDE, 12/2/43, *Letters to Mamie*, 157.

28 McKeogh 174–75, 177–81; Summersby 256.

29 DDE to GSP, 7/13/45, PP-LC (box 13); DDE to ONB, 7/16/45, USAMHI (Bradley Papers); DDE to GSP, 7/16/45, PP-LC (box 13).

30 GSP to DDE, 7/23/45, PP-LC (box 13).

31 Hirshson 641–42 (citing Quirk to wife, 6/5/45, and Doolittle, interview, 9/26/71, USAF Academy Library, copy in Oral History Research Office, Columbia University Library).

32 PP 2:721; Office of the Adjutant General, "Army Battle Casualties and Nonbattle Deaths in World War II," Final Report, USAMHI, 5 (casualties); Hirshson 642 (citing Frank McCarthy to GCM, 6/12/45, GCML (Marshall Papers, box 79)); Reynolds, "Final Days," 56.

33 Beevor 474 ("bravest").

34 GSP, 7/4/45, PP-LC (box 3).

35 Ibid., 8/10/45.

36 Ibid., 9/16/45.

37 Ibid.

38 JSDE, *General Ike*, 60.

39 DDE to GSP, 9/11/45, PP 2:749; SHAEF G-5, Displaced Person Branch, "Situation Report No. 16," 6/7/45, EL (WBS Papers, box 37) ("quarter million"); GSP, 9/17/45, PP-LC (box 3) ("returned home").

40 GSP, 9/17/45, PP-LC (box 3) ("I have seen").

41 GSP, 8/8/45, PP-LC (box 3) ("very evident"); Hirshson 653 (citing GSP to DDE, 8/11/45) ("no more possible").

42 Butcher, 7/10/44, EL (Pre-Pres Papers, box 168); USFET to CGs, TUSA and Seventh U.S. Army, 8/15/45, PP-LC (box 51); Memorandum, 3/26/45, EL (WBS Papers, box 38) ("all members"); DDE to GSP, 8/11/45, 8/25/45, EL (Pre-Pres Papers, box 91) ("I believe").

43 GSP, 8/27/45 ("Gestapo methods," "It is amusing"), 9/22/56 ("more I regret"), PP-LC (box 3) .

44 Codman 94.

45 Transcript, GSP and correspondents, 9/23/44, PP-LC (box 12) ("How many million"); GSP, transcript, press conference, 5/8/45, PP-LC (box 53).

46 GSP, 7/3/44, PP 2:472 ("It is funny"); Transcript, GSP and correspondents, 9/7/44, PP-LC (box 12) ("not fooling").

47 TUSA, "War Correspondents at Headquarters Third Army Briefing on 22 September," PP-LC (box 51); TUSA, "Memorandum on General Patton Interview," 9/25/45, PP-LC (box 12); TUSA, "Memorandum," 9/27/45, PP-LC (box 51); PP 2:770.

48 Ibid.

49 GSP, 9/22/45, PP-LC (box 3).

50 "General Patton on Policy," *New York Times*, 9/24/45.

51 Gay, 9/25/45, USAMHI (Gay Papers).

52 Croswell 235-37 (longstanding hatred).

53 GSP, 9/25/45, PP-LC (box 12); Gay, 9/25/45, USAMHI (Gay Papers); "Patton Statement to Press," *New York Times*, 9/26/45; Raymond Daniell, "Patton Alters Stand on Nazis," *New York Times*, 9/26/45.

54 Gay, 9/26/45, USAMHI (Gay Papers); DDE to GSP, 9/25/45, PP-LC (box 3, 51).

55 GSP, 9/25/45, PP-LC (box 12); GSP to BAP, 9/26/45, PP-LC (box 19).

56 Transcript, GSP and reporters, 9/25/45, PP 2:770; "General Patton Reconsiders," *New York Times*, 9/27/45 ("damage"); "You Don't Know What You Want," *Time*, 10/8/45.

57 Summersby 275 ("granddaddy of all tempers"); DDE to MDE, 9/24/45, *Letters to Mamie*, 272 ("drive me to drink").

58 GSP, 9/29/45, PP-LC (box 3); DDE to GSP, 9/11/45, EL (Pre-Pres Papers, box 91) ("long been decided"); Hirshson 652.

59 DDE, interview, 6/28/62, EL, 26.

60 Gay, 9/28/45, USAMHI (Gay Papers); Raymond Daniell, "Eisenhower Silent after Patton Talk," *New York Times*, 9/29/45; Butcher 856 (6/2/45); Hirshson 666.

61 Lande 278–88, quoting Coy Elkund (Patton shuffled); Summersby 257, 276 (office description).

62 Hirshson 667 (citing Walter L. Dorn, interview, 5/19/49–5/20/49, Columbia University (Dorn Papers, box 16)); Raymond Daniell, "Eisenhower Silent After Patton Talk," *New York Times*, 9/29/45.

63 GSP, 9/29/45, PP-LC (box 3).

64 Ibid.

65 GSP, 9/29/45, PP-LC (box 3); Gay, 10/2/45, USAMHI (Gay Papers).

66 GSP, 9/29/45, PP-LC (box 3); Hirshson 667 (citing Walter L. Dorn, interview, 5/19/49–7/20/49, Columbia University (Dorn Papers, box 16)) ("best of friends"); Summersby 276.

67 GSP, 9/29/45, PP-LC (box 3).

68 Ibid. ("Messiah complex"); Hirshson 670 (quoting C. L. Sulzberger, *Last of the Giants* (New York: Macmillan, 1970), 323).

69 DDE to WBS, 9/29/45, EL (Pre-Pres Papers, box 91); DDE to GSP, 9/29/45, EL (Pre-Pres Papers, box 91) and PP-LC (box 12).

70 GSP, 9/30/45, PP-LC (box 3).

71 JSDE, *Strictly Personal*, 114.

72 Gay, 10/2/45, USAMHI (Gay Papers); TUSA, press statement, 10/3/45, PP-LC (box 51); GSP, 10/2/45, PP-LC (box 3) ("scared").

73 GSP, 8/19/44, PP-LC (box 3).

74 Gay, 10/7/45, USAMHI (Gay Papers); "Auld Lang Syne," *Time*, 10/25/45; GSP to BAP, 10/10/45, PP-LC (box 19) ("a lot of stuff"); GSP, interview, 10/8/45, PP-LC (box 51) ("square deal").

75 GSP to BAP, 10/31/45, PP-LC (box 14) ("moral courage"); GSP, 10/13/45, PP-LC (box 3).

76 GSP to BAP, 10/11/45, PP 2:796; GSP, 10/13/45, PP-LC (box 3) ("I presume"); GSP to BAP, 10/15/45, PP-LC (box 14).

77 GSP, 10/14/45, PP-LC (box 3); GSP to BAP, 10/15/45, PP-LC (box 19); "People," *Time*, 10/22/45; JSDE, *General Ike*, 72.

78 GSP, 11/2/45, PP-LC (box 3) ("super-heated"); GSP to BAP, 10/22/44 ("best approach"), 10/15/45 ("never be president!"), PP-LC (box 19) ("best approach"); GSP to James Harbord, 10/22/45, PP 2:799 ("while I think").

79 GSP, 11/23/45, PP-LC (box 3).

80 DDE and GSP, transcript, 11/9/45, PP-LC (box 14).

81 GSP to BAP, 11/9/45, PP-LC (box 14) ("some joke"); GSP, 11/23/45, PP-LC (box 3).

82 GSP, 12/3/45, PP-LC (box 3).

83 Joseph Driscoll to *New York Herald Tribune*, 11/11/44, PP-LC (box 12) (height); Statement, Horace Woodring, n.d., PP 2:817–18; PP 2:813.

84 Statement, Horace Woodring, n.d., PP 2:817–18.

85 Lande 272–74 (quoting Gay and Woodring); Gay, interview, 10/4/80–10/5/80, USAMHI (Gay Papers), 41–43.

86 Hirshson 677.

87 Ibid., 678.

88 DDE to GSP, 12/10/45, EL (Pre-Pres Papers, box 91).

89 BAP to DDE, 12/14/45, EL (Pre-Pres Papers, box 91).

90 Ibid.; BAP to WBS, 12/14/45, EL (WBS Papers, box 10).

91 ONB to GSP, 12/12/45, EL (Pre-Pres Papers, box 91).

92 DDE to GSP, 12/13/45, EL (Pre-Pres Papers, box 91).

93 "Death & the General," *Time*, 12/31/45; Farago, *Last Days of Patton*, 271; Hirshson 678 (quoting Frederick Ayer, 12/21/45, PP-LC (Miscellaneous Box)) ("too late"). There are various versions of Patton's last words, none authored by direct witnesses.

Epilogue

1 DDE to Earl of Halifax, 12/24/45, EL (Pre-Pres Papers, box 54).

2 DDE, interview, 8/29/67, EL, 7; W. E. Robinson, confidential notes on interview with DDE, 10/17/47, EL (W. E. Robinson Papers, Eisenhower (Personal), box 1); DDE, *At Ease*, 261.

3 DDE to Frank McCarthy, 1/6/66, EL (Post-Pres Papers, Secretary's Series, box 14).

4 DDE to Alden Hatch, 11/1/47, EL (Pre-Pres Papers, box 23); JSDE to author, 1/14/07; ONB, GL, 504–5, 553.

5 Ibid., 655-56, 660–63 (quoting DDE to ONB, 8/13/53).

6 ONB to DDE, 4/17/61, EL (Pre-Pres Papers, box 3); James Hagerty to DDE, 11/29/67, EL (Hagerty Papers, box 110).

7 ONB, SS, 230 ("To this day"); ONB, interview, n.d., GCML (McCarthy Papers, box 17) ("obviously loyal").

8 Blair, ONB interview notes, 2/6/80, USAMHI (Blair Collection, box 44); ONB, interview, n.d., USAMHI (Blair Collection, box 27), 42.

9 ONB, interview, n.d., GCML (McCarthy Papers, box 17); ONB to Hansen, 3/31/51, USAMHI (Hansen Papers, box 1); Blair, "First Army—Tired Physically and Hard to Do Business With," "Hodges Vis-à-Vis Kean," "Kean Finds Himself Making Decisions for Hodges," n.d., USAMHI (Blair Collection, box 27).

10 ONB, GL, 99.

PHOTO INSERT CREDITS

Page One
Background photograph of Generals Bradley, Patton and Eisenhower (USAMHI)
Inset photograph of Cadet Patton (Patton Museum)
Inset photograph of Cadet Bradley (Eisenhower Library)
Inset photograph of Cadet Eisenhower (Eisenhower Library)

Pages Two and Three
Background photograph of U.S. Tank Corps, Camp Meade, Maryland, 1920 (USAMHI)
Inset photograph of Patton and a Renault tank (Patton Museum)
Inset photograph of Eisenhower and a light tank (Eisenhower Library)
Inset photograph of Patton in his "Green Hornet" uniform (Patton Museum)
Inset photograph of Fort Benning faculty (USAMHI)

Page Four
Photograph of Eisenhower during Louisiana war games (Eisenhower Library)
Photograph of Eisenhower and his London staff (Eisenhower Library)

Page Five
Background photograph of American tank destroyer group in Tunisia (National Archives)
Inset photograph of Walter Bedell Smith (National Archives)
Inset photograph of Eisenhower and Kay Summersby (Eisenhower Library)
Inset photograph of Admiral François Darlan (National Archives)

Page Six
Photograph of Eisenhower, Alexander and Patton (Patton Museum)
Photograph of Eisenhower pinning a third star on Patton (Patton Museum)

Page Seven
Photograph of Bradley and Maj. General Terry Allen (National Archives)
Photograph of Patton and Montgomery (Eisenhower Library)
Photograph of Eisenhower and Patton in Sicily (Eisenhower Library)

Pages Eight and Nine
Background photograph of American infantrymen (National Archives)
Inset photograph of President Roosevelt and Eisenhower (Eisenhower Library)
Inset photograph of Lt. General Mark W. Clark (National Archives)
Inset photograph of Lt. General William Simpson (National Archives)
Inset photograph of Brig. General Manton Eddy (National Archives)
Inset photograph of Brig. General Hobart "Hap" Gay (National Archives)
Inset photograph of Eisenhower, Churchill and Bradley (USAMHI)
Inset photograph of Patton and Henry Stimson (Patton Museum)
Inset photograph of Admiral Ernest King (National Archives)
Inset photograph of Maj. Gen. John P. Lucas (National Archives)
Inset photograph of Lt. Gen. Lucian Truscott (National Archives)

Page Ten
Photograph of Normandy beach, D-Day (National Archives)
Photograph of Bradley, Eisenhower, Maj. General "Gee" Gerow, and Maj. General J. Lawton
    Collins (National Archives)
Photograph of Eisenhower visiting troops in Normandy (National Archives)
Inset photograph of Bradley aboard the USS *Augusta* (National Archives)

Page Eleven
Background photograph of Collins and Bradley (National Archives)
Inset photograph of Theodore Roosevelt, Jr.'s funeral (USAMHI)
Inset photograph of Bradley at his desk (National Archives)
Inset photograph of Patton, Bradley and Montgomery (USAMHI)

Page Twelve
Background photograph of American soldiers in Saint-Lô, France (National Archives)
Inset photograph of crowds in liberated Paris (National Archives)
Inset photograph of Eisenhower in Paris (National Archives)
Inset photograph of Montgomery and Eisenhower (National Archives)

Page Thirteen
Photograph of Bradley, Smith, and Maj. General Francis de Guingand (USAMHI)
Photograph of Maj. General Courtney Hodges, Bradley, Patton, and Maj. General Hugh Gaffey
    (USAMHI)
Photograph of Patton and Bradley (Patton Museum)

Page Fourteen
Photograph of Eisenhower and Patton (Patton Museum)
Photograph of Bradley, Hodges, Eisenhower and Millikin (USAMHI)
Photograph of Eisenhower and Patton laughing (Patton Museum)

Page Fifteen
Background photograph of Eisenhower and Patton (Patton Museum)
Inset photograph of Eisenhower, Field Marshal Alan Brooke, and Churchill (National Archives)
Inset photograph of American soldiers at the Siegfried Line (National Archives)

Page Sixteen
Background photograph of Patton and Truscott (National Archives)
Inset photograph of Eisenhower, Patton and Bradley at Nazi camp (Patton Museum)
Inset photograph of Eisenhower, Patton, President Truman, Stimson and Bradley at the Potsdam
    Conference (Patton Museum)

INDEX

Fredendall, Lloyd, 70, 85, 89, 101, 103, 110, 111, 115, 119, 121–25, 128–30, 134, 136, 137, 154, 164, 277, 446
Free French movement, 79, 95
French Committee of National Liberation, 214
French First Army, 364, 471
French Foreign Legion, 90
French XIX Corps, 115, 145, 164
French Riviera, 486–88
French 2nd Armored Division, 385
Friedeburg, Hans-Georg von, 514–15
FUSA (First U.S. 1st Army headquarters), 256, 270, 291
FUSAG (First U.S. Army Group), 256, 270, 283, 296, 311, 342, 360

Gabès, Tunisia, 110, 145–48
Gaffey, Hugh J., 73, 135, 195, 295, 309, 344, 379, 380, 441, 442, 449, 543
Gafsa, Tunisia, 119, 121, 122, 136, 146, 147, 152, 155, 157, 158
Gault, James, 276, 283, 287, 326, 338, 385, 459, 523
Gay, Hobart R. "Hap," 16, 67, 93, 179, 180, 185, 194, 195, 197, 200, 201, 294–95, 303, 309, 439, 440, 442, 443, 471, 491, 492, 494, 534, 543
Gela, Sicily, 176–78, 180, 183, 194, 196–99, 203, 204, 206, 210, 211, 220, 451
George VI, King of England, 251, 291, 413
Gerhardt, Charles H., 329
German Afrika Corps, 145
German Army Group Center, 389
German First Army, 490–92
German I SS Panzerkorps, 311
German 1st SS Panzer Division, 346, 444
German 2nd Panzer Division, 453
German Fifth Panzer Army, 96, 102, 110, 119, 121, 145, 168–69, 377, 383, 435, 450, 451
German 10th Panzer Division, 106, 121, 122, 148–49, 157, 311
German 12th SS Division, 325
German XIV Panzerkorps, 214
German Fifteenth Army, 311, 336, 340, 342, 352
German 15th Panzergrenadier Division, 187, 197
German Hermann Göring Panzer Division, 187, 196–98, 200, 220
German Panzer Lehr, 311, 325, 359, 361, 374
German Sixth Panzer Army, 435, 451
German Seventh Panzer Army, 372, 377, 382, 383, 490–91
German 21st Panzer Division, 121, 122, 157, 346
German 29th Panzergrenadier Division, 224, 225
German 352nd Division, 323

German LXXXIV Corps, 362
German LXXXVI Corps, 258
Gerolstein, Germany, 478
Gerow, Leonard T. "Gee," 25, 33, 42, 125, 278, 289, 293, 323–24, 328–30, 341, 362, 385, 441, 484, 492, 524, 538
Gettysburg, Battle of, 9, 39, 465, 495
Gibraltar, 75, 79, 81, 82–83, 85–87, 190
Giraud, Henri Honoré, 79, 80, 86–87, 95, 96, 113, 172, 215, 238, 398
GOLD beach, 280, 326, 327
Goldwyn, Samuel, 527
Gordon, Jean, 21, 477
Gothic Line, 347
Grand Council of Fascism, 222
Grant, Ulysses S., 22, 117, 272, 387, 392, 502
Great White Fleet, 74
Green Hornet Suit, 34
Grenoble, France, 364
Grow, Robert, 420
Gruenther, Al, 61
Guadalcanal, 278
Guam, 278, 347
Gulf of Gabès, 158
Gulf of Hammamet, 102
Guzzoni, Alfredo, 187, 213

Haïdra, Tunisia, 159
Haislip, Wade, 371, 375, 377–81, 423
Hamburg, Germany, 392
Hammelburg prison raid, 494–96, 498, 504, 509, 511, 512
Handy, Tom, 129
Hannibal, 13, 272
Hansen, Chester "Chet," 48, 99, 127–28, 163, 182, 196, 217, 252–55, 271, 288, 313–14, 316, 322, 324, 327, 328, 341, 343, 367, 373, 389, 412, 422, 431, 433, 448–50, 452, 465, 466, 498, 550, 551
Hargrave, Pearlie, 432
Harkins, Paul, 67, 416, 442, 443
Harmon, Ernest J., 73, 90, 93, 124, 125, 163, 165–67
Harris, Sir Arthur "Bomber," 276, 345–46
Hasselt, Belgium, 457, 464
Hellcat fighters, 75
Hemingway, Ernest, 99
Hewitt, H. Kent, 74, 80, 82, 86, 88–90, 92, 93, 94, 178, 188, 193, 194, 198, 200, 201
Highway 113, Sicily, 218
Highway 120, Sicily, 218
Highway 124, Sicily, 207, 209, 210, 214
Hill 609, Tunisia, 165, 166
Hitler, Adolf, 1, 2, 43, 66, 95, 102, 170, 187, 271, 280, 310, 311, 345, 362, 374, 375, 382, 391, 392, 431, 434, 480, 496, 514
H.M.S. Apollo, 326